Victorian Will

VICTORIAN WILL

BY

JOHN R. REED

OHIO UNIVERSITY PRESS

ATHENS

Ohio University Press books are printed on acid-free paper. ∞

Library of Congress Cataloging-in-Publication Data

Reed, John Robert, 1938–
    Victorian will / by John R. Reed.
      p.   cm.
    Bibliography: p.
    Includes index.
    ISBN 0-8214-0928-X
    1. English fiction—19th century—History and criticism. 2. Free will and
determinism in literature. 3. Philosophy, English—19th century. 4. Fate and
fatalism in literature. 5. Philosophy in literature. 6. Will in literature. I. Title.
PR878.F67R4   1989
823'.8'09384—dc19   88-33695
                                                CIP

For George and Pat Ford

Contents

Preface

ICTORIAN *Will* is not intended as an exhaustive study of the will in nineteenth-century England. No such study is really required, since it would be so murderously repetitive. Instead I offer here a core sample of attitudes toward the will understood in its different senses as free will (as opposed to determinism), volition (as the power to initiate action), and strength of will (as a character trait revealed in assertion and self-control). I have tried to direct this core sample in such a way that it discloses a chronological order while also traversing various intellectual strata from philosophy, through moral injunction, historical interpretation, scientific theorizing, medicine, and law, to literature, which here chiefly means fiction.

This book could have been much shorter if I had confined my investigations to literature, but I believe that the literature of a period is so bound up with intellectual, social, political, and other influences and events that context is essential for proper understanding. Context is especially important when the subject under study is one broadly discussed and constantly before the minds of all intelligent and interested members of society. The subject of the will surfaced almost everywhere, not only in specialized scholarly books. It was the theme of sermons in church and chapel, appeared in popular journals, and was an important issue in courts of law. In many different guises, the will constantly manifested itself as a topic in both serious and superficial literature. Although I have chosen to examine attitudes about the will in the nineteenth century, other major topics would have served as well to illuminate the relationship of literary works to their time. Mine is only one of many approaches possible to achieve the same effect.

In discussing the literature of the Victorian period, I have tried to be representative, in the process eliminating some interesting and worthwhile figures like Charles Reade and Emily Brontë, and seriously abbreviating others like Charlotte Brontë and Anthony Trollope, while giving extended consideration to minor figures like Bulwer-Lytton and George MacDonald. However, my purpose was to provide a sufficiently broad sampling from the great to the less-than-mediocre.

Beyond recounting and interpreting Victorian perceptions about the will, an important aim of this study is to demonstrate how attitudes about the will influence or manifest themselves in style, narration, and characterization. To achieve this aim, I have frequently quoted passages, sometimes at length, because I believe that their actual language indicates how well or ill writers understood the implications of the volatile terms that they were using and the philosophical and theological tradition out of which these terms emerged. Of course there is a great deal of weak and false argument along with much special pleading and simple error or bald assertion without proof in much of the writing that I examine here, but these deviations are as illuminating as the logically rigorous samples, perhaps more so. Even the best intentioned writers could not avoid some distortions. In two essays entitled "Aristotle on Free Will" that appeared in *The Spectator* for 24 July and 31 July 1880, their presumed author, W. G. Ward, outlines Aristotle's qualification of disinterestedness for discussing the free will and necessity issue, a subject, Ward says, that is generally obscured by prejudice. He goes on to explain Aristotle's defense of free will, but it soon becomes apparent that Ward himself does not enjoy the disinterestedness he admired in Aristotle, for much of the argument in these two essays aims to prove that men are responsible and therefore both redeemable and subject to punishment. Ward's articles suffer from the common rhetorical fault of equivocation; he confuses "free will" and "freedom." This is all the more troubling in that modern research concludes that the ancient Greeks had no word for free will, nor, in fact, for will itself. Ward used the terms that made sense in his own cultural context, and Tennyson is said to have praised him for his effort. These men, and other writers equally sincere, understood not only their own time but the past as well in the light of their own preoccupations. Such culturally shaped interpretations are by no means extraordinary, but it is nonetheless worthwhile to examine the process by which they operate.

This study covers so broad an area that is so well served by excellent scholarship that citing all the works that I have found helpful would produce notes as ample as the text itself. Therefore, I have tried to hold my references to a minimum, mentioning scholarly works of which I have made obvious use. This restraint was especially difficult for me in the areas of literary and historical scholarship, but practicality asserted itself over professional courtesy and many critical essays and books that I consulted profitably remain unmentioned here.

Parts of this text have appeared elsewhere in somewhat different form. Chapter 9 is based upon "Inherited Characteristics: Romantic to Victorian Will," *Studies in Romanticism,* 17, no. 3 (Summer 1978); chapter 10 is based upon "Will and Fate in *Frankenstein,*" *Bulletin of Research in the Humanities,* 83, no. 3 (Autumn 1980); and chapter 13 is based upon "Freedom, Fate and the Future in *Bleak House,*" *Clio,* 8, no. 2 (Winter 1979).

A good portion of this work was completed through the assistance of a Simon Guggenheim Fellowship.

I wish to thank Dwight Culler and the anonymous reviewers of the original version of this text who provided me with many useful suggestions for its improvement, and also Holly Panich, who saw the manuscript through the press and Hilah Anne Selleck, who did a splendid job of copy-editing the text.

Introduction

IN a study as long and widely referential as this, the reader deserves some cartographical assistance in recognizing the main routes and distinguishing them from byways of discussion, so I offer here a brief map of what follows. This study consists of two main parts with several subdivisions. Part 1 (chapters 1 through 8), establishes representative attitudes toward the will in selected fields of interpretation (philosophy, history, science, medicine, law, etc.) where the issue of free will became controversial. The purpose of part 1 is to demonstrate how widespread, public, and informed discussion of the free will versus determinism debate was. Part 2 (chapters 9 through 19) explores the degree to which creative writers, mainly fiction writers, were aware of this philosophical issue and examines the ways in which philosophical assumptions manifested themselves in literary method.

Because a theory of the self is intimately bound up with belief or disbelief in free will, chapter 1 presents some concepts of the self current in the nineteenth century. This chapter shows that during the nineteenth century there were at least two main competing concepts of the self with differing consequences as far as theories of behavior were concerned. Chapters 2 through 4 deal with interpretations of the moral being. Chapter 2 provides a very brief survey of major problems addressed by British philosophers in dealing with the free will controversy, problems that resurface throughout the nineteenth century in various guises. Chapter 3 describes the ways in which different Christian denominations treated free will, most of them insisting upon its central function of submission to the will of God. Chapter 4 turns to secular commentators on the will from theists to agnostics writing in professional or popular forms. Chapters 3 and 4 point to shared fundamental assumptions about the nature of the self and its place in a moral economy. Interestingly, despite widely opposed creeds and programs, most Victorian writers assume the necessity for the submission of the self to some higher principle, whether God, law, or the State. And believers in free will and necessity alike urge the need for human improvement, chiefly through some form of education.

Chapters 5 through 8 are concerned with immediate social implications involving theories of free will and necessity. It has become a commonplace of Victorian studies to consider the nineteenth century a particularly time-conscious era. I have, therefore, begun in chapter 5 with one of the great developmental "myths" that shaped a good deal of modern thought—the concept of progress, indicating at the same time the fundamental importance of the free will versus determinism debate for that concept in the Christian context of nineteenth-century England. The popularity of the idea of progress cannot easily be separated from a second developmental preoccupation of the age—the rethinking of history, discussed in chapter 6. Here again the terms we have been considering in their abstract or personal significance—such as "free will," "necessity," "providence," "determinism"—take on a larger social meaning and affect the way historians and their readers viewed individuals, races, and nations. Closely related to the developmental concepts of progress and history was the new developmental theory of biological evolution, which quickly extended itself to fields as widely separated as moral growth and political economy. Chapter 7 surveys evolutionary views, from serious scientists to facile popularizers, noting how powerfully a teleological impulse, usually assuming a human capacity to shape destiny, is implied. Finally, in chapter 8, I return to the relationship of the individual to society in the most compelling of spheres—those of medicine and law—which I try to deal with succinctly by confining discussion mainly to the issue of insanity and responsibility. Thus I return through a wide circuit to the central problem of defining the self and the limits of the self's authority over itself and hence its responsibility to the larger society of which it is a part.

The introduction to part 2 considers the ways in which the several approaches to the question of free will and necessity manifest themselves as themes and methods in the literature, chiefly fiction, of the nineteenth century. The overwhelmingly narrative character of the nineteenth-century world view, as demonstrated in its teleological emphases in history, evolution, and other areas, coincides with the massive demand for a literature that could satisfy that appetite for story. If the Romantics fastened on the heroic individual at the center of dramatic events, the Victorians favored a hero more concerned with finding his place in a larger structure of experience, a structure often seen as prescripted by providence. Chapter 9 demonstrates how widespread discussion of the central issues of free will and necessity was among the great literary figures of the nineteenth century. By way of a few central images, such as the circle, it indicates ways in which attitudes toward the individual and freedom changed from Romantic to Victorian.

The chapters that follow treat a range of "major" and "minor" authors, who were well known in their own day or who have subsequently become significant to students of English literature, in an attempt to illuminate attitudes toward the will in their fiction and to analyze the manner in which those attitudes relate to narrative strategies. Because I believe there was some change over time both in the attitudes toward free will and necessity and in the narrative strategies employed by fiction writers in expressing those attitudes, I have arranged these chapters in a roughly chronological order.

Chapter 10 touches briefly on the philosophical, domestic, and adventure fiction of the early part of the century. Chapter 11 scrutinizes Mary Shelley's *Frankenstein* in depth because it is a major work of art incorporating elements of all three of these popular forms. Chapter 12 examines the work of Edward Bulwer-Lytton, one of the most popular novelists of the early Victorian period who was also highly articulate about his art, his philosophical beliefs, and the relationship between the two. Chapter 13 is devoted to Charles Dickens, a firm believer in the Christian scheme who said relatively little about his philosophical views, but whose narrative experiments reveal an acute awareness of the dilemmas addressed in this study. Chapter 14 begins an examination of midcentury writers, grouped together not only because they begin to manifest doubts and reservations about the traditional Christian interpretation of man's freedom and God's providence but also because they exhibit different modes of narrative presentation that seem to agree with this skepticism. These doubters are contrasted with writers like Charles Kingsley who tried stoutly to adapt traditional beliefs to new times. Chapters 15 and 16 examine in depth the methods of such nontheological but variously hopeful writers as Eliot, Meredith, Butler, and Hardy in dealing with the many new ideas—from philosophy to biology—touching the problem of freedom and necessity.

Chapter 17 deals with a diverse group of writers who tried by various fictional approaches to revive a sense of morality while opposing what they considered a threatening materialist view of human existence. Chapters 19 and 20 consider two very different, but curiously related late-century responses to the free will question: the subjective retreat into a complex self whose main creative effort is aesthetic appreciation and the more objective attempt to impress the will upon a mysterious existence through action. The opposition of subjectivity and action recalls the tension in Romantic litera-ture but reveals as well how that tension was transformed during the century and how it anticipated literary developments in the twentieth century.

I conclude with a basic summary before going on to an afterword that reviews the subject of this study from a slightly different perspective and relates it to fiction and philosophy beyond the nineteenth century.

PART ONE

Preparatory

Introduction to Part 1

I F man is free, he is responsible. Start there. Even if gods or fates deal unjustly with him, he has his chance to respond in some way and to assert his identifying humanity, perhaps only in the form of rebellious resistance, but in some measurable action. The history of western culture (to go no further) is complicated by a desire to explain man's individual existence as part of some grander, or at least more extensive, order. But if there is such a larger order, it must have a form; and to have a form it requires the subordination of parts to the whole. Without such order, man confronts an inexplicable and unpredictable world of chaotic random happenings or the capricious intervention in natural processes by sportive, mischievous, or worse, unknowable beings. Religious and philosophical explanations of the universe proposed an organization interpretable along time coordinates. Ontology, teleology, and eschatology described origins and ends. Assume a beginning and an end, and the rules for going from one to the other become conceivable. But if man was part of an ordered plan, he could not be entirely free. The questions then became, how free was he, and then, what was freedom? Though it had long existed in religious and philosophical controversies (especially those involving predestination), the issue of freedom became acute when science replaced religion and philosophy in the nineteenth century as the principle means of conceiving order in the universe because it now appeared that some hypotheses were becoming susceptible of proof.

Much of the free will versus determinism debate concerns definitions and redefinitions of key terms such as "free," "will," "volition," "necessity," "law," and so forth. But certain important concepts lie behind the muddle of linguistic details. Some of the key terms, for example "will" itself, were fairly recent additions to the western vocabulary of moral interrogation. As Albrecht Dilhe explains, the ancient Greeks did not have a theory of the human will. They did not even have a word denoting will or intention.[1] Greek philosophy presumed that the universe was rational and that the human intellect was the only means of perceiving order in it.

> According to them moral freedom is guaranteed by the free intellectual activity of the human mind, which leads, however, to a proper insight into the immutable laws that determine the whole of reality. On the other hand, awareness of one's own intellectual deficiency as well as of one's inescapable duty towards human affairs seems to be essential in free and responsible human activities. (Dilhe, 47)

Some fundamentally opposed world views may emerge from this basic outlook. Epicureans believed that everything owes its existence to chance; hence no moral order governs the world. Platonic philosophy asserted that the world perceived by the senses constituted a small part of reality because it was perishable and irrational. Reality was that which was structured by reason and therefore lasting and unchanging and discoverable through knowledge. The Stoics' position was an early statement of materialism. For them, everything is predetermined by nature or fate, and freedom of choice, responsibility, and morality exist only with reference to human consciousness. But reason permits man to understand this determinism and adapt his own intention freely to what is ordained, this free assent itself causing moral perfection and happiness (Dilhe, 41).

Though these philosophies differed in their concepts of reality, they all located human freedom, morality, and happiness in the soul, or consciousness, of the individual. This attitude differed considerably from the biblical view that God's law was set down clearly to be obeyed, but that mankind had the power to refuse obedience and take the consequences. Unlike the Greeks, the Jews did not consider the human intellect capable of discovering God's purpose. What man knows of the universal order he learns from God. The Christian tradition growing out of Scripture developed many variations upon this scheme, but despite numerous heresies and disputes, one thing remained clear: the correct application of man's free will was to make it accord with God's. For this, Christianity required a coherent concept of the will, which Augustine provided by using the Latin term *voluntas* to describe that part of human spiritual being (the others were *memoria* and *intelligen-*

tia) that exists prior to and independent of cognition, of which it partakes (Dilhe, 123ff).

I am not going to produce yet another history of the will but offer this summary to show that throughout modern western history some significant attitude toward freedom or nonfreedom of the human will has underlain ways of perceiving man's relationship to a universal order, a religion, a political system, and so forth. In this book, I want to show how pervasive concern with the will was during a limited period of time in a specific culture, and then to demonstrate how attitudes toward the will manifested themselves in literature. But to get to that matter, I must summarize a little more.

Augustine may have originated the concept of the will, but his view of the self was rather different from what we know by that term today. As we shall see in chapter 1, at some time in the eighteenth century, Europeans began to reconceive the self, making it both more assertive and more vulnerable, more bound to the world of matter (through Locke's philosophy, for example) and more determined to assert its superiority over mere matter.

Some of the most confident statements in this latter mode come from the German Romantic philosophers. Schleiermacher declared that the purpose of the will was to fashion a human individuality.[2] Goethe's *The Apprenticeship of Wilhelm Meister* also suggested that the individual could form his or her nature through the exertion of will. Like other German Romantics, Goethe was interested in the relationship between creativity and spirituality, especially as it was manifested in the power of imagination and expressed in language. Friedrich von Schlegel drew a detailed map of language's spiritual dimensions.

> The *roots* are the positive divine in language, the original source of the natural revelation deposited and expressed in words, as the understanding of the *first Man* perceived them at first in the yet *pure light*. The grammatical forms of language and their whole artificial structure are the work of Reason: Images and Tropes on the other hand are the element of the Imagination, and the undulations of rhyme and of metrical movement, the ebb and flow of the desire and of the *Will* are expressed.[3]

In "On the Sublime," Schiller announced that achieving the sublime in art required exceptional strength of will.[4] This identification of language and will went through various transformations during the nineteenth century, emerging now and then in curious forms, as in the developing field of folklore and anthropology. At the end of the century, Andrew Lang set his theory about the origin of mythology against Max Müller's, whose approach was philological. For Müller, the root words for rivers, winds, and so on reflected human animation because language necessitated that connection. Lang endorsed instead an anthropomorphic theory. "From the beginning, man was eager *causas cognoscere rerum*. The only cause about which self-consciousness gave him any knowledge was his own personal will. He therefore supposed all things to be animated with a like will and personality. His mythology is a philosophy of things, stated in stories based on the belief in universal personality."[5]

Will, both as free will and as power of volition, was associated not merely with the tools of language and myth making but with the tool user. The genius figured as the highest representative of this capacity. Through such exponents as Edward Young, in *Conjectures on Original Composition* (1759), and Alexander Gerard, in *An Essay on Genius* (1774), a theory about the nature of artistic genius as associated with the capacity for original composition through an enhanced confidence in the self and immediacy of perception developed. Romantic writers refined the details of this emerging theory. Thus in explaining "gusto" and its relationship to genius, William Hazlitt used the example of Michelangelo's powerful "will."[6] This view remained current through the nineteenth century. Jacob Burckhardt commented in "The Great Men of History" (1870) that the artist creates and expresses ideals beyond the contingent, and T. H. Greene, in "The Influence of Genius," also assumed the exceptional individual's ability to transcend the limitations of ordinary circumstantiality.[7]

As attitudes toward genius and artistic creation changed, so did the nature of artistic products. Karl Kroeber contrasts the doom-laden characters in Augustan compositions with the potentially free characters of the Romantics.[8] As others have shown, the Romantics were fascinated by the definition and operation of the will in itself or when contrasted with necessity or fate—as in the works of Wordsworth and Byron, for example.[9] Kant had proposed a spiritual self but felt that that deepest self was unavailable. The Romantic theorist Friedrich Schelling believed that artistic intuition could reveal that fundamental being because it transcended distinctions between determinism and choice. David B. Greene, in *The Temporal Processes in Beethoven's Music* (1982), demonstrates how Schelling's theories might apply to musical composition. "The theme for the set of variations in the third movement of Beethoven's 'Archduke' Trio (Op. 97, 1811), for example, can be said to project an atemporality that is analogous to the deepest self's way of being."[10] Greene argues that music reveals the temporal assumptions of its time; thus "Bach's music is an aural image of Newtonian time," exhibiting an unfolding necessity (Greene, 7). By contrast, the sonata-allegro form so favored by Classical and Romantic composers calls a future into being. Greene's description does not mention free will, but assumes free choice: "the process of a phrase or a section forming a pair with the phrase or section from which it is separated yet forward to which it presses is an image of the process in which the self makes a decision and actualizes itself through the event which that decision shapes" (Greene, 24). The Romantic composers differed from their Classical predecessors in the use of this revealing musical form. "Unlike Classical sonata movements . . . Romantic music does not exemplify a process that resembles a free self creating an empirically visible future which adequately fufills both the past and the self. It is as though the Romantics were disillusioned with the confidence and hope that preceded the French Revolution and sensed that the late eighteenth century's preoccupation with publicly manifest events suppressed the irreducibly private depths of human experience" (Greene, 28). The self imaged in the temporal movement of Beethoven's music falls between optimistic Classicism and disillusioned late Romanticism. "It may have limits and may know that it cannot fully actualize itself; yet because, perhaps, it cannot know where those limits lie, it continues to behave as though total self-actualization were possible" (Greene, 178–79).

Greene's detailed analyses may not be entirely supportable, but his general assumptions seem credible and were voiced years ago by Morse Peckham when he explored the connection between Schopenhauer's philosophy and Romantic music's assertion of the self in *Beyond the Tragic Vision* (1962).[11] Others have noted different patterns in Romantic to Modern music that may be said to reflect changing views about the will. Martin Meisel calls attention to Wagner's preoccupation with cause and effect.[12] Stefan Jarocinski seriously examines the operation of will in Debussy's music.[13] Composers themselves have testified to the importance of the will in their work. A notable example is the poem that Skryabin wrote to accompany his *Poem of Ecstasy* (1905–8), which expresses a fervent belief in the exertion of the will.[14]

The movement from Romantic to Victorian years is a movement also from aggressive heroism, or what might be called the imperial will, to controlled heroism, or the reflective will. Napoleon and Wellington give way to Disraeli and Gladstone, Beethoven and Paganini to Brahms and Wagner. Carlyle's way of encouraging this movement from external command to self-control was to advise his contemporaries to close their Byron and open their Goethe.[15] When Gladstone praised Wellington, he thought less of the great soldier's military conquests than of his command over himself.[16] A central image of the right application of the will for mid-Victorians was Florence Nightingale, to them a model of self-renunciation in the service of a great cause.[17] But the English had always admired the person of independent spirit, no matter what his or her walk of life. William Cobbett is a good example. His *London Times* obituary singled out his will as a central feature of his character.[18] He himself emphasized his power of will in creating his own character and he was proud of his role as a self-made man.[19] His biography

9

says it is in "*will*, this determination not to be borne down, this love of living in an element of opposition, this finding in every new misfortune a spring of fresh and flowing energy, we solve the secret that preserved to Cobbett a certain share of greatness, in spite of changes and tergiversations of principle, and in the face of the inconsistencies and whimsicalities of his human nature."[20] The mid-Victorian embodiment of this respect for self-command at a practical and daily level was Samuel Smiles with his creed of self-help.

As subsequent chapters will show, Victorians had various interpretations of human character, some of them rather remote from those popular in our own day. They generally emphasized conscious over unconscious motivation and were eager to credit overt manifestations of character type. Two "sciences" claiming to assist character analysis were physiognomy and phrenology. Johann Caspar Lavater was the chief proponent of physiognomy—the analysis of character traits especially by facial features. Physiognomy's great vogue lasted from 1775 to 1810, but interest in it continued almost to the end of the nineteenth century; some important novelists, for example Charlotte Brontë and Stendhal, made use of Lavaterian detailed portraiture.[21] Not all promoters of this technique were scientific or even rational. Lavater himself stereotyped women, claiming that they were made for religion and were incapable of careful reasoning.[22] But James W. Redfield went well beyond this conventional stereotype in *Comparative Physiognomy or Resemblances between Men and Animals* (1866). One example suffices: Redfield likened Jews to goats. To begin with, they look alike, he said, and they share the same character traits. The goat's "combination of combativeness, subterfuge, love of climbing, love of eminence, and balance and sure-footedness . . . must be something very nearly allied to *diplomacy*" in which Jews excel. Both are supposedly acquisitive as well. "Boldness and impudence are cheap in those places where the 'old-clo' men congregate; and what we have already said of the love of antiquity, and of old smells, and of bodily excretions, explains the partiality manifested by these people for trading in cast-off garments, old furniture, and the like."[23] Much of the literature of this time depends on stereotyped descriptions—usually not so far-fetched as Redfield's—to indicate traits of character. Thus a dark-featured man with straight nose and piercing eyes is likely to have an imperious will.[24] A dark-haired, dark-eyed woman of impressive stature and posture will exhibit similar power.

Phrenology, a more reputable pursuit, assumed that the shape of the human head, corresponding to the configuration of the brain, whose parts could be associated with various character traits such as will, amativeness, reason, and so forth, revealed character when examined by a trained specialist. As we shall see later, phrenology remained a quasi-reputable theory for much of the century and defended itself with capable arguments.

After all, however, the most characteristic attitude toward the will during

Victorian years was supernatural, that is, human will was seen primarily in relation not merely to the necessary choices of daily life but to the great design of providence. Texts for demonstrating this equation of human and divine will are numberless, and I shall examine some in later chapters, but here I want to provide a brief general picture.

Providence was mainly the property of theology, but popular moralists appropriated it readily. John Abercrombie's *The Philosophy of Moral Feelings* (1833) was a well-known example. Abercrombie divided man's moral being into four parts: (1) desires, affections, self-love; (2) the will; (3) the moral principle or conscience; and (4) the moral relationship of man to deity. Will, for him, was the state of mind preceding action. Moral causes operate upon the will before it acts, constituting motives by which men act according to their differing moral constitutions.[25] Will is central but vaguely defined. Establishing good habits strengthens the will, whereas bad habits atrophy the power of moral decisions. Ultimately, man's chief moral decision is oneness with Providence, the will of God. Free will permits this submission of the will to God.

> Such a submission of the soul to the appointments of God does not preclude the use of all legitimate means for bettering our condition, or for preventing or removing sources of distress. But when, under the proper use of such means, these are not removed, it leads us habitually to that higher power, to whose will all such attempts must be subservient; and, while it elevates our thoughts above present events and second causes, it reminds us of that great scheme of discipline through which we are passing, and the purposes which these events are calculated to promote in our own moral improvement. Viewed under such feelings, the ills of life lose that aspect in which we are too apt to contemplate them; and will be considered with new and peculiar interest, as essential to that system, the great object of which is to prepare and purify us for a higher state of being.[26]

Less responsible popularizing moralists not entirely in control of their own natures mixed up occultism with traditional Christianity but still ended by asserting, as Catherine Crowe did in *The Night Side of Nature* (1848), the importance of exerting the will to achieve spiritual experience and arguing for a world of design in which no chance existed.[27] These professional moral views were echoed in daily opinions. The precocious Arthur Henry Hallam as a very young man declared, "I can conceive nothing more awful than the mystery of Will, nothing more beautiful than its manifestation."[28] He charged himself with having set his will against God's before discovering how to appreciate "that Providential chain, which binds all in this world, save that will in man which it was created to help in freedom (Hallam, 309). He instructed Emily Tennyson that the "fatality" of the Tennyson family would not cease until "a Tennyson discovers and proves that there is no fatality, which undaunted Will & patient Piety, may not resist & overcome" (Hallam, 695).

The providential view found its most vulgar expression in tracts like *Remarkable Escapes from Peril* distributed by the Religious Tract Society, wherein such remarkable deliverances are said to be reminders of "our constant dependence on the providence of God." [29] Here, too, chance is denied. An outstanding example of God's providence is his preservation of Luther so that he could deal the strongest blows against the Jesuits (*Escapes*, 17). This is, of course, a Protestant Providence. The chapters of this booklet include "Signal Deliverances from Imminent Perils of Men Who Eventually Became Eminent for Piety or for Usefulness," "Faith and Prayer Rewarded by Signal Deliverances from Imminent Peril," and "Providential Deliverances from Danger by Instrumentalities of a Remarkable Character." Few of the instances given would convince a nonbeliever, and, indeed, the author is indignant with two of his subjects, Captain James Wilson and Thomas Paine, who, though marvelously preserved from peril, failed to credit providence, and remained hard-hearted, Paine dying, "as is well known, with his mouth filled with alternate blasphemies and supplications for mercy."[30]

Literature of this kind simple-mindedly assumed a connection between narrative and moral purpose. Many more serious narratives of the nineteenth century had the same purpose, from Robert Plumer Ward's *Tremaine* (1825) to George Eliot's *Daniel Deronda* (1876). The author of an article entitled "The Vanity and Glory of Literature" in the April 1849 issue of the *Edinburgh Review* raised the subject to a higher plane, discussing literature as a whole. Though prompted by a desire for fame, the article declares, most authors are doomed to oblivion. Great literature survives, though individual careers are lost. "Individuals and nations perish, but the progress of humanity is continued; and in this persuasion, the author who has in any tolerable measure endeavored conscientiously 'to serve his generation,' awaking from his ideal dream of immortality,—must find, like every other man who has done the same in other ways, his grounds of resignation and consolation."[31] But even if writers pass out of memory, they will have had the nearest thing to spiritual communion with their readers, not only influencing the mood of the moment "but in their measure cooperat[ing] to the formation of those *habits* which issue in character and conduct," and thus guiding moral character ("Vanity," 324). Great authors have a responsibility to encourage virtue and avoid anything in their writing tending to vice. This author's position, though presented in an unusual mode, was a familiar one, for England had, by the nineteenth century, a solid tradition of moral seriousness about literature.[32] But, of course, the morality that writers inculcated depended largely upon the fabric of their beliefs. Thus, as Leo Braudy explains, "The Tory view of history concentrated upon personalities, while the Whig emphasized the teleological growth of abstract principles like liberty."[33] Braudy examines the connection between Fielding and other writers' philosophical and political views and the themes and methods of their publication. These beliefs may be discovered even at the level of style.

> Gibbon's style reflects his belief that any interpretation of the past is at best tentative. Hume attempted to express his balanced and measured view through the order of his periodic sentences. Fielding's typical sentence moves from certainty to contingency through a haze of qualifying clauses. Gibbon's method often seems similar to Fielding's. But his most typical device is a kind of epistemological doublet—'through sincerity or duplicity'—held in unresolved balance by the comprehension of his narrative voice.[34]

Beyond this, as Paul Ricoeur avers, "The world unfolded by every narrative work is always a temporal world. . . . time becomes human time to the extent that it is organized after the manner of a narrative."[35] Sequential temporal worlds are generally causal worlds as well, so the natural impulse is to construct a story showing a causal pattern; that causal pattern is likely to reflect the beliefs and opinions of the author of the narrative. Ricoeur's way of saying this is that the reader takes up a traversal from what he calls mimesis$_1$ to mimesis$_2$. "*We are following therefore the destiny of a prefigured time that becomes a refigured time through the mediation of a configured time.*"[36] For the purposes of the present study, this means that stories yearn toward, and reinforce a belief in, causal relations; the process of telling stories introduces a necessary choice between pretold stories retold by a narrator who resembles fate, destiny, or providence, and untold stories shaped by a narrator who has the power equivalent to free will. An author's preconceptions heavily incline him or her toward one or another narrative mode.

The introduction of a writer's character and philosophy into the very style of his or her lyric or narrative methods of writing will be anathema to many adherents of certain recent critical theories, but it is really a reintroduction of what was understood and appreciated by many of the nineteenth-century writers whose works I shall discuss in the chapters that follow. Edward Dowden, a skilled appreciator of his contemporaries, often referred to the influence of their philosophies upon their texts, and will was a theme he touched upon frequently because it was as important to him as it was to the writers he evaluated and explained. Moreover, he took for granted the influence of such interests on literary composition. "But in life as in art, is not style the true rendering of soul into form, and related to the mind of the man, as it is to that of the artist, in other and far closer ways than is the brute matter which he fashions with his hands? Style is definable as the outcome of the habitual formative tendencies, and these in a great creative nature are always very numerous."[37]

W. L. Burn wrote in *The Age of Equipoise*, "One of the cardinal differences between the mid-Victorians and ourselves lies not in their optimism and our pessimism but in the much greater faith they had in the power of the human will."[38] The following pages demonstrate how complicated and conflicted Victorian ideas about the will were, how they found application in various areas of thought and life, and especially how they may be traced in the creative literature of the time.[39]

CHAPTER ONE

The Self

To appreciate the moral significance of attitudes toward the will in the nineteenth century, it is helpful to understand new perceptions of and new emphases upon the self at that time. Two basic approaches are distinguishable: one identifiable with the Rousseauistic assertion of the subjective self, the other equatable with the German attention to control of the self through association with some social or philosophical ideal, an approach attributable to Goethe and Hegel but manifest widely elsewhere in secular and religious writings. The self is described as a prison restraining the spirit but also as the agent struggling to overcome barriers of the not-self.

During the nineteenth century in England, relatively simple concepts of the self give way to images of fragmentation and atomization. The Wordsworthian call for wholeness yields to a Paterian acknowledgment of dispersal. Schiller was an early promoter of the idea that the harmonious integration of the classical Greek represented a natural totality lost in the fragmentation of modern man. He recognized that increased human knowledge occasioned this fragmentation and called for a restoration of harmony in a higher knowledge.[1] Hegel asserted the difference between classical and modern worlds in terms of human self-consciousness and freedom, declaring that only after Christ had man become a fully independent and infinitely free personality.[2] Victorians faced apparently contradictory recommendations of asserting and suppressing the self, contradictions that they embodied in fictional characterizations and narrative strategies, as we shall see in part 2 of this study.

~ ~ ~

"What is SELF? What is that many-sided Unity which is centered in the single Ego of a man's being?" Bulwer-Lytton asked in an essay on self-control, then offered his own definition. To him the self was the representation of an integral individual human being, a fabric of flesh and blood with its unique predispositions and properties determined by heredity that can be moved from its original bias "by circumstance, by culture, by reflection, by will, by conscience, through means of the unseen inhabitant of the fabric."[3] For a great many people in the nineteenth century, this definition, assuming a human soul working through the will to govern the body, would have seemed very apt. For Bulwer, self-control was the first essential to integrity of the self, requiring generalship and method. It is a calm science based on self-knowledge. This need to renounce selfishness in favor of a larger purpose was to become characteristic of much Victorian writing. Arthur Henry Hallam agreed with Gladstone "that it is a painful thing not to be able to think, feel, live in the happiness of others, rather than the gratification of self—self, that poor mathematical point, having position not magnitude in the abyss of infinite being!"[4] Employing the model of Newtonian physics, Hallam pictured men as particles in a greater whole. Variously stated, this was a common opinion of the time.

Self, so important an issue for Victorians, was a relatively recent concern. Wylie Sypher considers it a Romantic discovery. Romanticism, he says, "created the self and destroyed the self."[5] He describes Romanticism as "a form of irresponsible freedom," and asserts that "at its extreme, the romantic ideal of freedom is a form of *dis*-relationship of the self from other selves" (Sypher, 20–21). It is a means of preserving individual integrity and authenticity against external demands, a necessity arising from the growing awareness that the individual was being threatened by social forces. This concern becomes more acute in modern times as we try to determine "in what sense we have an existence that is really 'ours' " (Sypher, 28).

Wayne Shumaker, investigating the development of English autobiography, observes that it requires the assumption that lives of individual persons were important in themselves. He calculates that after 1660 a change of thought occurred; truth was no longer seen as established, but as discoverable in the slow accumulation of particulars.[6] John Lyons places the 'invention' of the self a century later in the 1760s, arguing that an increasing sense that no eternal and external truth existed prompted men of faith to generate religious enthusiasm from within. This focus upon man's inward nature bred greater anatomization of the self, a preoccupation that ultimately affected the way men viewed time and history.[7] As long as Truth remained eternal and immutable, there could be no real change or progress, but when Truth became a product of the slowly maturing self, time, and especially past time, began to serve as a model of virtue or a warning against error. Hence the remarkable growth of interest in history during the nineteenth century. "For the nineteenth-century thinker," wrote William H. Marshall, "the acceptance of time as the substratum of continuity gradually appeared as the key to the understanding of the Self. The orderly description of time, at once dynamic and heterogeneous, became one of the central problems of the century."[8] One of the major literary forms to emerge during the century was the memoir in justification of the self, a form that had considerable influence in fiction as well as in autobiography.

In the second half of the eighteenth century, according to Lyons, the self was at first treated as a "whole organic complex of the perceiving being in sympathetic relation to the world around it," and was described in terms of passions, motives, and the reality of nature. A second concept of the self, however, hypothesized an "ineffable something in a human being that was an abstract of the pure and intuited natural laws without." In one view, the mind looked outward to find a reflection of itself; in the other, it looked inward, dissolving and appropriating the world of things to its subjective reality (Lyons, 16–17).

Despite Hume's dismissal of the self, belief in it increased, sometimes retaining the traditional dualism manifest in Bulwer's definition, sometimes attempting to reduce the self to a single entity. Much of the credit for European fascination with the self after 1760 goes to Rousseau. In reaction against a rationalist perception of human nature, Rousseau conceived the self as manifest essentially in the feelings, which, untainted, he considered morally good. Accordingly, he associated the soul not with wisdom and intellect, but with the refinement of the feelings and passions. In focusing on private sources of knowledge through personal feeling, Rousseau emphasized autonomy of the self, a quality that would become central for many nineteenth-century writers. In *Confessions, Reveries*, and elsewhere, Rousseau's model of self-sufficiency involved what Frederick Garber calls "limited desires in a small space."[9] He establishes clear boundaries within which the self was free, the outer world representing a lack of freedom (Garber, 10). This contrast implies a rebellious self wishing to extend its range of freedom. As source of its own development through right feelings, the self cannot afford to submit to the deadening or distorting influences beyond itself. Never content with things as they are, it assumes a revolutionary character (Lyons, 197–98).

Friedrich von Schlegel expressed the sentiment of an entire generation of Romantic writers by asserting that the very essence of Romantic poetry was its state of becoming. "It alone is infinite just as it alone is free, and it acknowledges as its primary law that the will of the poet can tolerate no law over itself" (quoted in Garber, 79). This attitude leads toward the Byronic hero. However, developing alongside this assertive mood was the apposite recommendation promoted by Novalis, Coleridge, and Shelley that the self merge with nature.

As we shall see in chapter 9, a rough progression may be charted from the Romantic to the Victorian picture of the self. Wordsworth and Carlyle are pivotal figures in that progression, for Wordsworth moved from a youthful assertion of the self that included active revolutionary sentiments to an affirmation of the self as part of a communal existence. He wanted an Edenic enclosure somehow linked to the contours of immediacy. The self of *The Prelude* is capable of expanding outward in all directions, not through domination but by absorbing more and more of the non-self. Wordsworth always remained conscious of the boundary between the two. Carlyle, on the other hand, like many Victorians to follow, reacted against the cult of the self, seeking instead to render life meaningful by submerging the self in a higher purpose made manifest in God's abiding natural law of justice. Carlyle reflected the Goethean perception of individualism as a negative and thus destructive concept of freedom.[10] For Carlyle, as for Wordsworth, Emerson, James Hinton, Henry Drummond, George Eliot, and many others, man was part of the web of existence. Carlyle believed it was man's duty to help reweave that web. To do so, each man must accept his personal isolation, discipline his will, and find the work fit for him to do. Though related, the Wordsworthian and Carlylean are clearly two very different attitudes toward the self.

It may also be argued that, at least in England, the fascination with the self that culminated in Romantic subjectivity was a natural inheritance of Puritan and Protestant self-analysis for purposes of religious redemption. Leopold Damrosch, Jr.'s, excellent study *God's Plot and Man's Stories* shows the affinity of Puritan individualism and the novel. Self was all-important for the Puritans, who tried to locate it in a universe controlled by a mysterious and inexorable Providence. Fiction's inheritance from the Puritan view of life was the perception of life as a narrative invented by God but interpreted by human beings.[11] A central question arose from this concentrated subjectivity. Was the self—whether multiple and fractured, or single and integrated—free? A full range of opinions existed among the Romantics. Coleridge asserted freedom of the will as essential; Wordsworth assumed some degree of freedom; Shelley was a declared necessarian. More ambiguous views appear in other writers such as Byron, Keats, and Mary Shelley.

But even if the individual possessed free will, what was the relation of that will to the non-self? Godwin declared that man was essentially a communal not a solitary being, yet much of the literature of his time emphasized the theme of isolation even in the midst of society. Byron's *The Corsair* is an interesting variation. Conrad is the leader of a private community. Though he lives among the pirates with his beloved companion, he is a misanthrope essentially invulnerable to the forces of society.[12]

Genius generally appeared at odds with conventional society, not only when it rebelled against, but also when it dominated, that society. Romantic writers, and the population in general, were fascinated by titanic figures who transcended the rules and who seemed embodiments of self. David Morse lists Casanova, Napoleon, and Paganini as figures characteristic of their time in their "drive to transcend all boundaries and limits, to impose the individual will upon others and to compel recognition from the world through a mixture of skill, resourcefulness and daring."[13]

To some degree, the social conflicts of the Victorian period are grounded in contending images of the self. Carlyle voiced one paradoxical attitude that contributed to these conflicts by calling for a renunciation of self while exalting the heroic man of superior will. He assumed, of course, that the exceptional will was itself in the service of a higher purpose. Mill, by contrast, defended individual liberty and the integrity of the self, yet argued that only communal man could achieve moral or material progress, since the isolated individual was the product of necessity. With less confidence than Hegel in the mediating power of the free individual within a State that is the embodiment of the substantial will, Matthew Arnold, though he located moral good in man's "best self," considered that best self so deeply buried that it was unavailable for daily commerce, and therefore recommended a well-organized State to guide a populace too much given to doing as it pleased.[14] James Fitzjames Stephen advised strong external moral and political authority to govern the independent and capricious self.

Developmental theories, evolutionary or not, played an important part in nineteenth-century thought. Many opponents of Darwin's theories nonetheless believed that the individual self, the race, and civilization developed from primitive to sophisticated forms. The providential view of history pictured mankind as slowly maturing toward the fulfillment of Christian doctrine. At the same time, nontheists like Godwin, Bentham, and Mill, imagined mankind progressing through its own patient and laborious efforts. Sometimes progress was moral, as seen by F. D. Maurice or James Martineau; sometimes it was scientific, as seen by W. K. Clifford or Winwood Reade. Lying behind these developmental theories were, once more, differing conceptions of the self and its ability to direct its own course. Wayne Shumaker writes: "So long as the will maintained a princely rank in the hierarchy of the 'faculties,' life inevitably appeared self-directed, unpredictable, arbitrary. People willed honesty, perseverance, industry, or other qualities of character, and throve or suffered in accordance with their deserts." But later autobiographers such as Darwin, Galton, Bray, Mill, Spencer, and Wallace emphasized the influence of necessity. An acknowledgment of the importance of heredity and environmental influence caused a marked change in autobiography and hence, we may assume, in the way people viewed their selves.[15]

Although there was no single entirely acceptable notion of the self in the nineteenth century, most intelligent persons assumed that it was the central focus of identity and was related to the continuity of memory and mental perceptions dependent upon physical sensation. After Hume, one set of beliefs reduced the self to a mechanism governed by material laws, an assembler of data that transformed impressions into actions. Another set of beliefs assumed a spiritual or inexplicable quality in the self testifying to the existence of a higher organizing being. In "On the Scientific Basis of Morals" (1875), W. K. Clifford offered an interesting Victorian version of the positivist conception of the self.

> In the metaphysical sense, the word "self" is taken to mean the conscious subject *das Ich*, the whole stream of feelings which make up a consciousness regarded as bound together by association and memory. But, in the more common and restricted ethical sense, what we call *self* is a selected aggregate of feelings and of objects related to them which hangs together as a conception by virtue of long and repeated association. My self does not include all my feelings, because I habitually separate off some of them, say they do not properly belong to me, and treat them as my enemies. On the other hand, it does in general include my body regarded as an object, because of the feelings which occur simultaneously with events which affect it.[16]

For Clifford, whose views derive from Hegel, the self is an abstract of feelings, a *Gestalt* somehow fashioned by the individual being according to the laws of causation. But man also has a "tribal self" that is the true determinant of his behavior because it is based on the rules and conventions of the social group.[17] But the most intriguing self is "that inner and deeper motive-choosing self which is called Reason, and the Will, and the Ego," which makes choices through the power of directing attention. This habit of directing attention over time creates the responsible character or self that is recognized as *me*.[18]

Clifford retained a picture of a self contained ("deeper," "inner") within a protective identity, governing its material part through discipline of the will. Though convinced of determinist causation, he still sees that disciplining force, or will, as a free agent. Man's self remains answerable for its deeds and educable toward perfection though bound within the wider ring of necessity. An analogy for Clifford's model of the self might be a small but powerful oligarchy directing the affairs of a nation from within a well-defended palace through the military and political arms of government. It is an embarrassing analogy for a declared republican.

Some Victorians rejected any but a monarchical model, with the monarch residing outside the self. Christ, wrote Frederick Denison Maurice in his *Theological Essays*, is the righteous king of your heart and God has been trying to teach you this. "He has taught you that you have been in chains, but that you have been a willing wearer of the chains. To break them He must set you free. Self is your great prison-house. The strong man armed, who keeps that prison in safety, must be bound. The rod of the enchanter, who holds your will in bondage, must be broken by some diviner spell before the arms can be loosed, and the captive rise and move again."[19]

If Clifford saw the self as a directive power from within, Maurice saw it as a barrier to directive power from without. William Boyd Carpenter, like Clifford and Maurice aiming at a final objective of the self in service to others, offered a compromise. Nature, he explained, taught man first the need for self-preservation and through effort educated him in the consciousness of self, urging him to be and express himself, but once this maturation of the self is achieved and this discipline and self-mastery are learned, nature teaches the final, highest lesson of self-sacrifice.[20]

For Carpenter, self-consciousness was a great ally in preparing for self-sacrifice, but for James Hinton, man's consciousness of self was "the feeling of his want of being."[21] Like Bulwer, Hinton thought that the perennial question for man was: "What is that 'I' that has consciousness?" In a passage that sounds remarkably modern, he explained that "persons are states of humanity, they are forms or states from the actual, by a 'not.' "[22] Like Maurice, Hinton saw the self as a hindrance to absorption in God. Without his material nature, man is one with humankind. Consciousness is a symptom of disease, and self its manifestation. Hinton declared that the entire point of his philosophy was "that *self is negation*." God's purpose is to destroy the self, and establish man's true trust in Him against the self.[23] God is boundless, man bound. Hinton's proof of man's defective self echoes Carlyle. Self's limitation is evident because it accepts the phenomenal world as real; "Real to the SELF, unreal to the MAN," Hinton adds. "The inert and transient world, which does but seem, is the reality to the self. Hereby we know the self: it is that to which the unreal is the real. When we are freed from that, the phenomenal shall be reality to us no more."[24] Yet the material world as a manifestation of law is beautiful and what gives matter beauty is form. All life is "*growth under limits*."[25] Nature itself is self-control without restraint. "It is perfect liberty; absolute, self-enjoying freedom."[26] And this is the model of human life as well. The essential form of all living things is spiral, revealing growth under resistance.[27]

Hinton's design seems to move in the direction of the evolutionary schemes that we shall examine in a later chapter, but there is a crucial difference. Endorsing Coleridge's assertion that "life is not a thing, but an act and process," Hinton describes physical life not as an organism composed of living cells but as an organic structure composed of inorganic atoms, a living relation of unliving parts.[28] Ultimately the self is a mathematical point, as Hallam so cleverly noted, that possesses life only insofar as the Universal Idea unites it to other mathematical points. The idea of the self is bondage but a bondage necessary in the phenomenal world.

Samuel Butler shared Hinton's vision of an aggregate universe but inverted the paradigm, locating life within the units of the larger organism. Each atom, he speculated, may have its own free will.[29] Similarly, each individual person is a compound of an infinite number of centers of sensation and will, each having a soul and individual existence, reproductive system, intelligence and memory of its own.[30] Men, as part of a larger organism, are made up of divisible parts: "this 'we,' which looks so simple and definite, is a nebulous and indefinable aggregation of many component parts which war not a little among themselves," and which are themselves not stable but constantly undergoing change. Our personality is a fleeting entity in any case, but made even less tangible "because the parts that compose it blend some of them so imperceptibly into, and are so inextricably linked on to, outside things which clearly form no part of our personality, that when we try to bring ourselves to book, and to determine wherein we consist, or draw a line where we begin or end, we find ourselves baffled. There is nothing but fusion and confusion."[31] Butler likens the self to an island, perhaps with conscious echoes of Donne, if not of Matthew Arnold, but immediately qualifies the metaphor, suggesting that the island gradually blues into its surrounding. Men, too, Butler says, are infinite in duration and extension, and adds, "If those who so frequently declare that man is a finite creature would point out his boundaries, it might lead to a better understanding."[32]

Carlyle saw the self as a nodule of will ringed round by necessity yet also described existence as a web of filaments endlessly extending. This contradiction epitomizes a central conflict in the nineteenth-century perception of the self as both an independent, willing, even embattled entity and an elusive, yielding, self-less medium for transmitting the energy of some divine or natural power. Butler resolved this dilemma by atomizing all of Being and announcing that the boundaries we assign to personality are merely arbitrary. In this he echoes another common view of the time, represented by Maurice and Hinton, that the arbitrary boundary of the self applies only in the prison-house of phenomenal existence. Past that, all blend into the Unity of God.[33]

One of the most acute perceptions of the nature of the self was offered by James Ferrier in his *Institutes of Metaphysic* (1854). Although Ferrier's language seems to sustain the traditional metaphysical discourse, there are important new implications in his position. He begins by assuming, in what today sounds like a variation of Heisenberg's principle, that "Matter *per se*, the whole material universe by itself, is of necessity absolutely unknowable"; in fact, "matter *per se*" is a contradictory locution because all things are known only as a synthesis of subject and object.[34] Matter is known as the element peculiar to some cognition, that is, to some action of an ego. However, the self, too, is unknowable *per se*. "It can know itself only in some particular state, or in union with some non-ego; that is, with some element contra-distinguished from itself" (Ferrier, 235). To know is to combine the agent of perception with the object of perception. All being, then, is in *relation*. Nothing exists in and of itself. "Absolute Existence is the synthesis of the subject and object—the union of the universal and the particular—the concretion of the ego and non-ego; in other words, the only true, and real, and independent Existences are minds-together-with-that-which-they-apprehend" (Ferrier, 300). Ferrier finds in this conclusion the basis for a theistic faith because, at the cosmic level, the existence of the universe is impossible without the existence of mind, and that mind, antedating man, is God, who encompasses the Universal whole (Ferrier, 512).[35]

Mandell Creighton, a particularly keen and level-headed clergyman, offered a simpler, and more moving version of the same basic attitude in a summary of his belief that manages to be both practical and transcendental. "What is life?" he asks in a letter to a friend, and then explores the answer himself.

> The only answer is, Life is a sum of relationships. There is no independent or self-centred existence. I am what I am in relation to others. . . . The Christian claim is that my life, my capacities, my relationships are part of an eternal order running through the universe, beginning and ending in God. Nothing short of this conception gives happiness of strength or reality. It is a conception which entirely corresponds to the needs of human nature, and its great proof must always be this correspondency.[36]

On the eve of the Freudian revolution, which was to transfer psychological conflict into the labyrinth of the self and divorce it from any power beyond the dynamism of biology, James Ward made an effort to bridge the gap dividing contemporary images of the self. Self is only one grade of consciousness—the focus of consciousness within; other grades of consciousness include wider fields with varying focuses and the subconscious. Self is thus one differentiation of a continuum of experience. It begins as object and becomes the subject that knows itself. It is unique as a presentation of consciousness that persists, is active, and knows itself. But all grades of self blend into one another gradually from the lowest level of sentience to the highest of volition.[37]

Ward later elaborated this view. The reasoning, self-regulating self is not localized, he said. We never think or will without also feeling. But there is a subject of experience he called the pure Ego or Self which is related to the thinking and willing self by two zones or aspects, one connecting man more with society, the other more with the self. We all play many parts in life, have many social roles, and, from time to time, must make decisions to sustain one role or another. It is in moments such as these that the pure Ego comes into play and the individual is "autonomous and creates or enacts." This self "is the thinker of all our inmost thoughts, the doer of all our very deeds—no longer any presentation of self, but the self that has these and all other presentations."[38] But this self within the self cannot in itself be known.

Ward saw the self as evolutionary, its growth dependent upon attention as is all differentiation. Dismissing the notion of free will as uncaused cause, he considered freedom that state when a person's whole being approves his or her actions. Ward believed that, though man was bound to some degree by heredity, he had the capacity to shape himself. "In other words, man in becoming spirit, i.e. self-conscious and reflective, acquires being for himself over against the world and sets to work mediately making himself by his conduct in it" (Ward, "Principles," 463). Stability is the basis for personality's evolution and originality its shaping force. A man with character is a man with a will of his own, and the more single and resolute his purpose, "the more 'inward' the self that he seeks to realise," the greater his progress may be for good or ill (Ward, "Principles," 468).[39]

And here we return to a pattern that is becoming familiar and which will recur in later chapters. Both Thomas Carlyle and Samuel Smiles praised the man who could direct his will to a single purpose, thereby shaping events to his desire. Both men assumed that man was free, despite certain reservations. Both assumed that men operated in a field of energy that extended beyond the material limitations of humankind. Ward, aware like many of his late-century fellows of the multiplicity of the self, nonetheless attempted to preserve the focus of *character* through the unknowable abstraction he called the pure Ego. But this fiction amounts to little more than the traditional picture of the soul, and Ward's "personality" and "character" are premised upon the traditional assumption that men truly choose the direction in which their natures will develop.

After all, during the nineteenth century, though men had many models of the self from which to choose, in the end they were forced to make only a few central decisions. Either the self was coherent and directed from within, or it lacked integrity and depended upon external energy. If the self moved itself as a part of natural law, as Clifford believed, it escaped the prison of necessity and of providence and could shape the world. But this perception fudged the dilemma of determinism. If the self moved itself as a function of providential design, man could shape himself only through God's will, or else he was capable of rebelling against the will of God and hence denying the divine omnipotence that Christian doctrine demanded. If man was moved by the external laws of causation, he was not free in any but legal and political terms. If he was moved by the external power of divinity, he did not initiate his own deeds and always implicated God in his conduct. In both cases, man could be perceived as a puppet of some higher power, conscious or unconscious. Few persons act on rigorously logical decisions; most behave according to slightly examined beliefs. But underlying all attitudes, now as in the nineteenth century, is one crucial commitment—a belief that man at his center, in whatever passes for his essential self, is either free or not. All else follows from this central belief, all notions of good and evil, responsibility, progress, and man's relationship to a seen or unseen world. The chapters that follow take up a few of these concerns.

Will and the Moral Being

CHAPTER TWO

The Free Will Controversy

T HE free will versus determinism controversy was not new to the nineteenth century. Its central problems were an established part of the
English philosophical tradition, not to mention its continental leg-
acy. This chapter highlights some of the central conflicts in this ongoing
debate that remained important in the nineteenth century.

To begin with, language was slippery. Much depended on the way key
terms were defined. "Will" might be defined as the potential for choice or as
action. It might be seen as a mere abstraction or as an entity. Also the question of the will's relationship to natural law was crucial. One approach presented the will as the medium of external natural laws; another saw the will as
an independent motivating agency. A major dilemma for those who championed the necessarian theory was explaining how a character, personality,
or self, governed by laws of causation, could initiate actions to improve itself.
By contrast, the dilemma for libertarians was offering a convincing explanation of how the subjective sense of freedom could be defended. Ultimately,
nineteenth-century commentators on the will were forced to deal with the
moral consequences of a will that was free or unfree. Affecting their attitudes
was the powerful tradition of Calvinist predeterminist thought.

~ ~ ~

In his inaugural address opening Manchester New College in October of

1840, James Martineau concisely noted certain issues that characterize the intellectual ferment of nineteenth-century England. In his first meditations on existence, man seems to have had a consciousness that he was a meeting point of Free Will and Necessity, Martineau said, that his nature was environed by a greater, and that his animal nature was united with a higher. Analogically, in "the youthful mind of individuals, as of nations, the same origin of the philosophical tendency may be traced. A deep curiosity respecting the great problem of Free-will is usually, I believe, the first symptom of speculative activity of intellect; a confident solution of it, the first triumphant enterprise; a relapse into the consciousness of its mystery, the first sign of a more comprehensive wisdom."[1] Seeking to comprehend free will, man achieves self-knowledge, itself essential in tracing the boundary separating internal from external nature, which is, Martineau argued, the one office of mental philosophy (Martineau, 7). Distinguishing right from wrong is the most important concern of mental philosophy, and the conflict between free will and necessity leads directly to the problem of responsibility—the arena for making that distinction (Martineau, 11). Thus, to define himself and his duties, man must first determine that he is free. If he is not free, he is not morally responsible, and hence all notions of blame and punishment are redundant.

We shall return to Martineau later in this study, for he was an acute spokesman for a particular view on the human will, but here his remarks serve to exhibit how persistent the dispute about will was from ancient to modern times. It seems that men have always *acted* as though free while for a good part of their history questioning that freedom. I cannot canvass the whole history of the debate between free will and necessity here.[2] Nor do I intend a full review of that philosophical debate in England. In the past as now the controversy was largely semantic. The free will debate was lively in the seventeenth century in England, and from then to the nineteenth century most of its basic arguments were aired. For Thomas Hobbes (1588–1679), liberty and necessity were consistent with one another because liberty did not mean freedom of will, desire, or inclination, but that man finds "no stop, in doing what he has the will, desire, or inclination to do."[3] Men's voluntary actions proceed from liberty because they proceed from the will and yet are necessary because every act of man's will proceeds from some cause, itself a part of a chain of causation leading back to God.[4] Ralph Cudworth (1617–88) argued for free will in a larger sense, emphasizing the intuitive impulses of praise and blame in men. He recognized the semantic danger of accepting abstractions as realities when he challenged the received psychology of his day that divided the rational soul into understanding and will.[5] Man's soul is "hegemonical over itself," Cudworth explained, for not only is it the means of understanding, it is also the subjective source of will and action.[6] John Locke also cautioned against reifying understanding and will as agents acting in the soul but then himself divided all actions into either thought or motion. The power of doing or refraining from doing constituted man's freedom, which Locke called liberty, thus begetting a new confusion of terms.[7] Locke agreed that mind determines will but substituted for a deity or higher good an "uneasiness" in man that prompts him to choose what we call good (apt to give pleasure) over evil (apt to give pain). Man's ability to suspend the prosecution of desires and to deliberate on them is the source of his liberty and this ability is what we call free will.[8] In short, will is the power to choose. At this point, metaphysics and politics become entwined and adumbrations of Benthamism are already evident. Samuel Clarke (1675–1729), asserting a Kantian idealism, ventured little by way of redefinition, simply claiming that to all whose understandings are not depraved reason shows us the natural order of things and that we should accommodate our wills to that divinely inspired order.[9] Misunderstandings and passions prevent men from making this accommodation.

The arguments for and against free will could be couched in many ways, but the usual emphasis was on the composition of man's nature. *A Treatise of Human Nature*, by David Hume (1711–76), is an outstanding instance of this approach, and his arguments remained so formidable that Thomas Henry Huxley was able to review them favorably at the end of the nineteenth century. Basically, Hume assigned all of the causal conditions admitted in the world of external nature to the internal workings of man's nature as well. Necessity governs all phenomena, material and mental. Although we may feel the power of volition over the body, we cannot prove that will is an agent on its own. The apparent irregularity and uncertainty in human behavior is an illusion resulting from our ignorance about operative causes.

Hume was acutely aware of the semantic dangers besetting this subject. At the outset of his prickly argument, he flagged one key term: "I desire it may be observ'd, that by the *will*, I mean nothing but *the internal impression we feel and are conscious of, when we knowingly give rise to any new motion of our body, or new perception of our mind.*"[10] And at the end of his argument, he once more very pointedly acknowledged the slipperiness of language and attempted to nail down his usage.

> According to my definitions, necessity makes an essential part of causation; and consequently liberty, by removing necessity, removes also causes, and is the very same thing with chance. As chance is commonly thought to imply a contradiction, and is at least directly contrary to experience, there are always the same arguments against liberty or free-will. If any one alters the definitions, I cannot pretend to argue with him, 'till I know the meaning he assigns to these terms.[11]

Hume assigned reason to the realm of ideas and will to that of realities; he denied that reason could move the will and granted that power to the passions, acknowledging the great variety of those passions both calm and violent. With reason quarantined from the will, Hume's acceptance of the concept of responsibility may be surprising, but Huxley was particularly taken by this phase of his argument. The doctrine of necessity is essential to moral responsibility, not destructive of it, for if men did not believe that actions necessarily followed from will, itself prompted by motives, they could not assign blame, since all actions would be random and unrelated.[12] Hume thus linked necessarianism to the argument for cause and effect relationships.[13]

James Beattie (1735-1803) opposed Hume's conclusions, offering conscience and man's natural conviction of his freedom as evidences of free will. To these Thomas Reid (1710-96) added the human ability to carry out a preconceived system of conduct. Bishop Joseph Butler's (1692-1752) *The Analogy of Religion* (1736) was slier in responding to Hume's necessarianism. Butler's argument, incorporating the concept of causality, has preserved its vigor to our own day. He declared that "Necessity, alone and of itself, is in no sort an account of the constitution of nature, and how things came *to be* and *to continue* as they are; but only an account of this *circumstance* relating to their origin and continuance, that they could not have been otherwise than they are and have been."[14] Furthermore, Necessity, like Freedom, requires and supposes a Necessary Agent to be the former of the world (Butler, 114). Thus Butler turned Hume's defense of causation into a proof of divine existence. He then reversed the process by observing that since men are rewarded and punished in this life, and since they discover a deliberating will in themselves, it is only reasonable to assume a similar will in the Governor and Designer (or Necessary Agent) who shaped them and this world (Butler, 119). Ergo, "if it be incredible, that Necessary Agents [man operating under necessity] should be thus rewarded and punished; then, men are not necessary but free; since it is a matter of fact, that they are thus rewarded and punished" (Butler, 128). There are some obvious problems with Butler's reasoning, especially the assumption that the good and evil coming to men are equatable with divine reward and punishment. Such an argument assumes that reward and punishment are certain entities, though as we shall see in our discussion of providence, they can rarely be so clearly perceived. Still, Butler based his argument for human freedom and the existence of God on the same faith in cause and effect relationships that formed the ground for Hume's "atheistical" case.

Another prominent atheistical writer based a good deal of his thinking about free will and necessity upon Hume. William Godwin (1756-1836) posed the paradoxical notion that because man is subject to necessity, he is perfectible. He dismissed the existence of will as a separate entity and argued that free will as a distinct and separate faculty capable of resisting arguments, education, and instruction would actually be a handicap. Man is better off, he claimed, being subject to fixed and invariable principles.[15] Free will would be detrimental to morality, since it abandons the concept of discernible motive. The necessarian acknowledges an unbroken chain of cause and effect in human behavior with no point of absolute freedom. Hence responsibility is rationally assignable. The necessarian feels no indignation or anger at those who commit vice, for crime and vice are like infectious diseases and must be treated, not avenged. A necessarian view of existence is like a happy stoic's in "its tendency to make us survey all events with a tranquil, placid temper, and approve and disapprove without impeachment to our self-possession" (Godwin, *Enquiry*, 395).

But though Godwin authoritatively dismissed free will with one hand, he quietly beckoned it back with the other. Denouncing all forms of deceit and hypocrisy, he nonetheless endorsed a belief in what he called the "delusion" of liberty of human action. In *Thoughts on Man* (1831), Godwin reasserted his necessarian faith that the absolute laws of external nature apply as well to "the universe of mind," but acknowledged that neither libertarian nor necessarian can for a moment "when he enters the scenes of real life, divest himself of this persuasion" of liberty of action.[16] Indeed, all that is noble in man—the ability to praise and blame, to recognize virtue and duty—arise from adherence to this belief. Duty, which was to become such a totem of the Victorian years, is an important instance, for it requires "the conception of the empire of will, the notion that mind is an arbiter, that it sits on its throne, and decides, as an absolute prince, this way or that (Godwin, *Thoughts*, 237).

Free will, Godwin concluded, may be said to constitute "the most important chapter" in the science of man (Godwin, *Thoughts*, 239). So, despite his belief that man is a machine governed by external impulses, he argued that men should not discard this "delusive sense of the liberty of human actions" because the sentiments that arise from that sense "form the highest distinction between men and other animals, and are the genuine basis of self-reverence, and the conceptions of true nobility and greatness, and the reverse of these attributes, in the men with whom we live, and the men whose deeds are recorded in the never-dying page of history" (Godwin, *Thoughts*, 240-41).

Godwin singled out phrenology as a depressingly fatalistic hypothesis in which the predetermined character of the individual based on the structure of the brain cancels all hope in the power of education and the ability to improve intellect and to regulate and modify moral qualities. Craniology, he complained, "exhibits us for the most part as the helpless victims of a blind and remorseless destiny" (Godwin, *Thoughts*, 372-73).[17] He saw no parallel between his own necessarianism—assuming that man is a machine powerlessly transmitting cause to effect—and the fatalism of phrenology. In the peculiar compromise that Godwin achieved there is a splendid, almost willful, ignorance. He recognized man's discomfort in the flesh, his sense of exile generating dreams of a life beyond the sublunary world, and respected that restlessness but nevertheless believed that, like all impatience and power hunger of youth, it must be tamed. The fundamental purpose of education was to subdue this wildness in us. To Godwin, man was fundamentally innocent, with an inborn trait of benevolence to be fostered through an education based on love. But all of this admirable shaping of a strong character manifesting love, duty, and virtue depends on some initiating act. Nowhere does Godwin explain how man, bound to the wheel of necessity, can ever begin the process of altering his own nature. For this most crucial aspect of human existence, he falls back upon the "delusion" of human liberty.

Godwin's is an instructive case, prefiguring issues that we shall be taking up later. Many nineteenth-century thinkers shared his dilemma: how to preserve and even strengthen traditional morality while abandoning the unsuitable structures that had sustained it. The dilemma was old, but the nineteenth century marked it with distinctive shades. In a sense, David Hartley (1705-1757) had begun this tinting with his *Observations on Man* (1749), where his theory of association supported a firm necessarianism excluding all possibility of uncertainty in the world.[18] While it accepted free will in the "popular and practical sense" of the power of initiating motion or the power of doing an action or its contrary, it rejected free will in the philosophical sense (Hartley, 1:500-501). This rejection followed from Hartley's belief in the Doctrine of Mechanism and the omnipotence of God. He argued that philosophical free will amounted to the denial of cause and was tantamount to chance. But chance is impossible in a world governed by God: "as Freewill is inconsistent with the infinite Power of God, so it is with his infinite Knowledge also" (Hartley, 2:67).

What distinguished Hartley's necessarianism was its physical grounding in mental operations. Like Hume, Hartley revised the internal cosmos of man. Hume had applied physical law to operations of mind, but Hartley made that application of laws physically determining. Hume assumed that laws operated; Hartley demonstrated how. Hume's philosophy was viewed by many as a challenge to theism, whereas Hartley openly claimed that his hypotheses, in removing philosophical free will, actually reconciled the practical or popular doctrine of free will with the prescience of God. Contemporary objections to Hartley's scheme were practical, since it was seen to eliminate human responsibility.[19] Later exponents of Hartley's philosophy, like James Mill, eliminated divine responsibility instead, and by extending human effort from personal initiative to the onward progress of the race generally, approached Godwin's position, creating a secular power inherent in man though not freely guided by him.[20]

William Drummond (1770-1828) and Joseph Priestley (1733-1804) both adopted a Hartleyian materialism. Underlying Drummond's materialism was a conviction that if matter exists, it owes that existence to a supreme intelligence whose laws regulate and whose beauty adorns it.[21] Priestley unequivocally declared his belief in materialism and necessity: "Whether man be wholly material or not, I apprehend that proof enough is advanced that every human volition is subject to certain fixed laws, and that the pretended self-determining power is altogether imaginary and impossible.[22] Priestley contrasted his concept of necessity with Calvinist predestination in which man is damned unless predestined for salvation, leaving the elect to behave in any way and yet be saved. The necessarian believes "that in the most proper sense of the words, it depends entirely upon himself whether he be virtuous or vicious, happy or miserable."[23] Man must therefore exert himself, Priestley urged, for the harder he works at his moral nature, the better he will be. But there Priestley tumbled into that tiger trap of necessarian moralists. If man is absolutely governed by physical laws of the universe and has no free will, in what way and from what source does he derive the power to initiate the necessary actions that will permit him to improve? How can the will-less exert themselves to reshape themselves? And what becomes of such notions as virtue and vice if man cannot guide his own destiny? Godwin engagingly concluded, as Priestley could not, that we must conduct ourselves according to the fiction of freedom and responsibility while believing at heart that we are mere mechanisms.

In 1799, William Belsham (1752-1827) attempted to mediate the developing controversy in his *Essays, Philosophical, Historical, and Literary.* The necessarians (Hume, Hobbes, Collins, Leibnitz, Hutcheson, Edwards, Hartley, Priestley, and possibly Locke), he said, assumed that what exists must have an adequate cause and that similar causes in similar circumstances produce similar effect. A man in any given situation must form volitions and determinations and these will follow such a law, every volition resulting from a motive, while the stronger, hence necessary, motive prevailing. Every event comes to pass from causes previously existing, and therefore the whole series is one absolute and uncontrollable scheme of necessity. Belsham also included the argument from the prescience of God.

The advocates of philosophical liberty (Clarke, Beattie, Butler, Price, Law, Bryant, Wollaston, Horsley, and others), Belsham explained, claimed that God endowed man with a self-determining power which is the cause of each volition. They argued that all motives are not traceable, hence not provably necessitated. Moreover, they asserted that men are moved not only by passions, but also by reason. Unless this were true, neither praise nor blame could be justified. Finally, they said, because humans cannot understand God's understanding, His foreknowledge does not deny their freedom.

After these clear and evenhanded summaries, Belsham enlisted himself in the necessarian camp. His arguments repeat what has already become familiar to us and need not be restated here. However, his conclusion retains the nettle already evident in Priestley's. The necessarian philosophy, Belsham declared, does not lead to vice, but to virtue through the cultivation of proper habits and associations in men's minds. "To incite us to the practice of [virtue], and to deter us from the commission of vice, motives, must, agreeably to the frame and constitution of the human mind, be held out to our view: peace and happiness be annexed to the one, shame and misery to the other. These associations once implanted in the mind must produce the most beneficial effects."[24] Once more the question is begged. How does society in the aggregate arrive at a condition where it can *decide* to improve its individual members if all previous events have been ineluctably determined? At what point does the capacity to plan emerge?

These issues aside, Belsham concluded sanely that necessarians were under no greater obligation than libertarians to answer the question of why there is evil in the world. Belsham was undoubtedly correct, and yet it was precisely the question of evil in the world that fueled the free will debate in the nineteenth century, as conduct rather than theory became the determining basis of judgment.

We have thus far examined the opinions of various churchmen and nonbelievers, but we cannot conclude this chapter without mentioning one group very deeply concerned about evil in the world; I refer to the Calvinist sects to whom the question of the will was central because they believed that God had predestined a chosen elect to salvation, consigning the remainder of the race to perdition. The doctrine of predestination, thus interpreted, was a bleak intensification of Augustine's original reading of St. Paul, especially of Romans 8:28–30.[25] Article XVII of the Thirty-Nine Articles of the Church of England, composed in 1553 when predestination was a burning issue, thanks largely to Calvin himself, echoes Pauline language. "Of Predestination and Election" opens with this sentence: "Predestination to Life is the everlasting purpose of God, whereby (before the foundations of the world were laid) he hath constantly decreed by his counsel secret to us, to deliver from curse and damnation those whom he hath chosen in Christ out of mankind, and to bring them by Christ to everlasting salvation, as vessels made to honour."[26]

St. Paul is credited with establishing the Christian theory of the will based largely upon the assumption of original sin and human depravity (Alexander, 79). Man's will is in slavery to sin; hence, he is not free. God's grace liberates him. Archibald Alexander summarized Paul's position. "In a state of sin, the will is determined towards the bad; in a state of grace, the will is determined toward righteousness; but not wholly so, for the flesh is not at once subdued, and there is a war between the good and the bad principles of action in the soul of him who has been pardoned" (Alexander, 85). Thus, for the first time in the history of thought, Paul offers a subjective view of man in conflict between two moral alternatives. Hannah Arendt puts the case succinctly. "The Will, split and automatically producing its own counter-will, is in need of being healed, of becoming one again." The will is impotent "not because of something outside that prevents willing from succeeding, but because the will hinders itself." It is a simple question of obedience, "Thou-shalt" against "I-will."[27] But, because man is both carnal and spiritual, he must disobey unless aided by God's grace. By himself, he is helpless.

This is a hard doctrine but a durable one, and among its chief proponents was the redoubtable Jonathan Edwards (1703–58), whose *Freedom of the Will* (1754) was perhaps the most significant late exposition of it. Edwards's philosophy was close to that of Spinoza, Hobbes, and Hume and insisted upon the centrality of causation. For Edwards, causation leads back inevitably to God's original design. Only God's will can operate in existence, since all events following his initial act of creation are causally dependent upon it. No other being, including man, can have a self-determining will without infringing God's omnipotence. As Paul Ramsey puts it, "For Edwards as a theologian the issue is a simple one: either contingency and the liberty of self-determination must be run out of this world, or God will be shut out."[28]

Milder influences prevailed in the Church of England, and its doctrines were gradually made more consoling to the laity, but the Calvinist strain was always near at hand, and Article XVII could not always be dismissed as merely inconvenient. Throughout the nineteenth century these issues remained important in narrow theological circles, but also circulated widely through pulpit, public lecture, and popular philosophical writings and can be discerned as important influences in the fiction of the age.

CHAPTER THREE

The Religious Moralists

C HRISTIANITY was, of course, the overwhelmingly influential religious view in nineteenth-century England. Despite a variety of doctrinal commitments, from Coleridge and his followers, to Spurgeon's
Calvinism, and the Catholicism of Newman and Ward, a certain uniformity
emerges regarding the nature of the Christian will and Christian character.
Even when free will is dismissed, as with Spurgeon, self-will remains the chief
source of human frailty. Christianity requires endeavor but endeavor
through self-sacrifice. The will must subject itself to a higher will to make it
free. Freedom is bondage to sin; submission to God's will is freedom. The
chief icon of this principle was the parent-son relationship; the universal
example of sonhood, obedience, and sacrifice was Jesus Christ.

This chapter surveys some representative Christian assertions about the
will beginning with Liberal Anglicans, then comparing and contrasting
those views with Calvinist and Roman Catholic positions before sampling
some moderate and popularized Church of England sentiments about the
will. It concludes with a look at the work of Christian apologists who sought to
use materialist arguments in favor of religious views. Most notable here is
James Martineau.

This chapter aims to demonstrate the insistence among religious thinkers
that man identify self-will as his chief enemy. The obligation placed on the
good Christian, generally phrased in masculine paternal and filial terms, was

at first glance paradoxical. To triumph, man must submit. He must yield his will to express it. His highest ideal is self-sacrifice, by which he achieves victory over evil. This was the most widely disseminated Christian message of the age, but its contradictions made acting upon it in daily life problematic. Fiction of the age incorporated this paradox with many strange consequences for characterization and narrative method to be explored in part 2 of this study.

~ ~ ~

One of the most potent influences upon religious thought in the nineteenth century was Coleridge, and he had a great deal to say about the will.[1] The introduction to part 1 emphasized the importance of the will for nineteenth-century thinkers, and Coleridge is a major example of this concern. He referred to free will as "our only absolute *self*," and based his entire scheme of thought upon the assumption that man's will brought him to faith and hence to salvation.[2] "In vain the informing Reason, in vain the inspiring Life, the fecundating Love—if there be not that germ in the *Will*, which is the Individual in his essential individuality, which is deeper than all understanding—and till it have been stirred and actualized by that ineffable *Will* [God], which is the mysterious Ground of all things visible and invisible."[3] Reason and religion can neither exist nor coexist, Coleridge asserted, unless they are actuated by Will, which is "the sustaining, coercive and ministerial power." He elaborated this function of the will and added a warning about it.

> In its state of immanence (or indwelling) in reason and religion, the WILL appears indifferently, as wisdom or as love: two names of the same power, the former more intelligential, the latter more spiritual, the former more frequent in the Old, the latter in the New Testament. But in its utmost abstraction and consequent state of reprobation, the Will becomes satanic pride and rebellious self-idolatry in the relations of the spirit to itself, and remorseless despotism relatively to others; the more hopeless as the more obdurate by its subjugation of sensual impulses, by its superiority to toil and pain and pleasure; in short, by the fearful resolve to find in itself alone the one absolute motive of action, under which all other motives from within and from without must be either subordinated or crushed.[4]

For Coleridge, a man is both mad and miserable if he does not seek "at-one-ment" with God, making his will concentric with that holy power.[5] Man's *spirit* is simply "reason in the process of its identification with the will."[6]

By reasserting the claims of free will against what he took to be necessarian reductionism, Coleridge established a current of thought that was to run strongly through the nineteenth century in England. He associated a belief in free will with an inward conviction of the existence of God and expressed in contemporary terms the traditional assertion that man's will, which underlies all his spiritual experience, is also the conduit for transmitting God's will.[7] In *Aids to Reflection* (1825), Coleridge acknowledged that other forces than his own will operate upon a man, for he is part of a vast and complex system. However, these are not blind forces, but expressions of divine purpose.[8] For Coleridge, the will was supernatural, above nature, and therefore he rejected the mechanical dynamics of necessarian cause and effect. He described man as a creature diseased in his will; since evil cannot derive from God's will, it must be a product of man's. When human will is at one with Divine Will, it constitutes the Law; when opposed, sin arises as deviation from the Law. A Christian must remain steadfast in faith, not in will (Coleridge, *Aids*, 281).

Coleridge's is the venerable Christian objective of redeeming the will from slavery, but he distinguishes between traditional Lutheran and Calvinist thought and the harsher, more necessarian doctrines of Jonathan Edwards and his followers. Both forms of Christian teaching assert that the will becomes free when it is at one with God's will, but "the difference between the Lutheranism of Calvin and the Calvinism of Jonathan Edwards" is the difference between "a captive and enslaved will, and no will at all" (Coleridge, *Aids*, 170).

For Coleridge, man is free to bring himself out of slavery partly because he recognizes the reality of the spiritual and the illusoriness of the material. He achieves this understanding through his reason, which, as with Kant, has a twofold nature. Speculative reason deals with formal or abstract truth, whereas practical reason operates through conscience. "Whenever by self-subjection to this universal light, the will of the individual, the particular will, has become a will of reason, the man is regenerate: and reason is then the spirit of the regenerated man, whereby the person is capable of a quickening intercommunion with the Divine Spirit" (Coleridge, *Aids*, 211).

Coleridge's influence was significant on generations of writers after him. Though an exponent of revolutionary ideas associated with the Romantic movement, Coleridge was also an early Cassandra regarding the danger of a self that defines itself in opposition to the social and natural world. If the self is primarily a will asserting its own individuality, it is doomed to misery or madness, for true freedom arises not from resistance to *what is*, but in humble acceptance of what *must be*.[9] As we shall see in later chapters, this dilemma of character is important in the imaginative literature of the nineteenth century, for it requires concepts of character and strategies of narrative that illustrate a "correct" pattern of redemption.

Coleridge's thought laid the groundwork for a Christianity based on intuition, faith, and active pursuit of the good and the true. He may not have been much given to action himself, but many of his admirers were, among them Thomas Arnold, F. D. Maurice, Charles Kingsley, and Julius C. Hare. The last of these did his good works mainly in his parish and his pulpit, translating ideas that he shared with Coleridge into a more accessible language. Like Coleridge, he saw man's greatest effort as manumission from the slavery of evil. He put it thus in his sermon entitled "The Great Prison, or All Concluded Under Sin":

For this is the craft and subtilty [sic] of the Evil One,—that he makes us fancy we are free, when we are in prison: he makes us fancy that we are at liberty, when we are in bondage: he makes us fancy that we are our own masters, when we are his slaves: he blinds and cheats and stupefies us, until we deem we are doing our own will, and pursuing our own pleasure, when in fact we are drudging in his toils, and rushing into the jaws of destruction before his lashing scourge.[10]

In his sermons, Hare urged his audience to recognize the goodness of God's design and the importance of man's dependence upon the Lord—either Christ as personal redeemer, or God as Father and protector. In "The Power of the Christian," Hare described the two main Christian heresies: Pelagianism, a typification of Pride because it asserts that man can live a sinless life through the power of his own will, and Antinomianism, a typification of Sloth because it states that man can do nothing toward the fulfillment of the law and therefore need attempt nothing. Paul's message is that a man can do all things, though not through his own strength. He must be reminded that "there is a heavy weight on his will, that the spring of it is broken, so that, when he attempts to wind it up, it flies off in an opposite direction" (Hare, 441). God gives us strength, and if we turn to Christ we can do all things. "But this we do not. We choose to go our own way, to do our own will, to walk after our own devices, to work in our own strength. Thus we are perpetually taught that our own strength is very weakness" (Hare, 457).

Hare's images are familiar ones. Sin is confinement and bondage, virtue is freedom and happiness. To those in error, the world seems disordered, but to the faithful, the goodness of the design is evident. The poor may learn a lesson hidden from the rich because wealth disguises the truth of man's condition—his dependence upon a higher power—while poverty reveals to man the redemptive truth that he must seek aid from God (Hare, 271–72). According to this view, man deceives himself through assertions of his will because such struggles only tighten the iron ring of Necessity around him.

Once he learns self-subjection to the Divine Will, he is set free to act effectively in the harmoniously designed world that God has provided.

This scheme was familiar to F. D. Maurice, who also felt that "there is in men a sense of bondage to some power which they feel that they should resist and cannot." It is in contending against this evil spirit that men confront the question of free will.[11] Traditional Christianity sees the evil spirit as the source of transgression, whereas Calvinism emphasizes man's fallen nature. Maurice urged self-conquest and the Coleridgean pursuit of at-one-ment with God. Like the Calvinists, he accepted the idea that the will of God underlies all things, but rejected the concept of a Despot God.[12] To him, the contest within man is between love and selfishness. The Holy Spirit whispers the ideals represented by Christ to the human heart and carries on the debate in man's inmost being against a reluctant will that seeks to become mere self-will (Maurice, *Essays*, 373).

Drawing upon one of the most powerful topoi of the century, Maurice defined the will in familial terms. Perfect rest comes from the conviction that the universe is not capricious but guided by God's will, and this conviction "is bound inseparably with a name which speaks of Relation, which tells him what he was sure must be; that his own Will has an author; that he is not merely a creature of the highest God, but a child" (Maurice, *Essays*, 419). This echo of Tennyson's *In Memoriam* is not inconsequential, since *Theological Essays* is dedicated to that poet. The same sense of infant abandonment colors both works. Maurice's remedy is more thorough than Tennyson's: obedience. "The child must confess its Father, and confess itself to Him; then it knows whose Will rules it, and with what Will it has been striving" (Maurice, *Essays*, 420). In "Lectures on the Religion of Rome," Maurice argued that when Christianity came to Rome it caught on because it found hospitable ground for the belief in a fatherly God in the Roman valuation of a fatherly god and fatherly government in the state and in the household that was the foundation of Rome's greatness.[13] He asserted that the concept of fatherly guidance remained the basis of civil and moral strength, especially among European nations.

Maurice rejected fate and necessity because they cannot give life or energy as God does. Unlike fate, divine will seeks to make other wills resemble its own (Maurice, *Essays*, 425). Human will is itself an earnest of a divine parental will. Maurice seconded the Coleridgean emphasis upon self-sacrifice, though, like Hare, conceiving of God in more personal terms. Like a child, man must learn to trust in God's purpose and achieve peace in freeing himself from bondage to evil and liberating himself by losing his own will in God's. Maurice's theology was not generally well received in his day. But his beliefs urged him to put in practice his notions of love and duty. The great Baptist preacher Charles Haddon Spurgeon described Maurice and his friend Charles Kingsley as members of "the cloudy schools" of religious thought.[14] Nonetheless, both men vigorously applied their convictions in the day-to-day world, and their influence was ultimately considerable.[15]

Kingsley also endorsed the parental image of God but emphasized the importance of human effort. Christ's withdrawal from the world left the Holy Spirit as the agent to whisper God's message to mankind. In a sermon entitled "Self-Help," Kingsley explained that Christ went away in order that the Comforter would come. To remain might have been harmful, but by leaving, Christ obliged men to learn self-government and to "love the right, and to do the right, not from fear of punishment but of their own heart and will."[16]

In direct opposition of Calvinist thought, Kingsley affirmed the essential nobleness of man and stressed the active ways in which men can seek the right. His sermons on heroes showed that trust in God may help men to perform acts normally beyond their powers.[17] Beyond obedience to divine will, men must shape their own natures to carry out that high purpose. In a sermon entitled "Discipline" that he preached at a Volunteer Camp in 1867, Kingsley took as his test: "He couched, he lay down as a lion; and as a great lion. Who dare rouse him up?" (Numbers 24:9) His subject was the transformation of the wandering Israelites from a chaotic band to a disciplined troop through adherence to Moses' moral law. Kingsley did not refer only to military discipline. "Whatever they may have gained by that—the younger generation at least—of hardihood, endurance, and self-help, was a small matter compared with the moral training which they had gained—a small matter, compared with the habits of obedience, self-restraint, self-sacrifice, mutual trust, and mutual help; the inspiration of a common patriotism, of a common national destiny" (Kingsley, 26:7).

In their parent paradigm, Maurice and Tennyson favored the image of man as dependent infant and God as trustworthy father. But Kingsley's offspring is more mature and forceful. To begin with, he is Christ. In answering the question: What was the Spirit of Christ? he replies: "A spirit of truth, honour, fearless love of what was right: a spirit of duty and willing obedience, which made Him rejoice in doing His Father's will. In all things the spirit of a perfect *Son*, in all things a lovely, noble, holy spirit" (Kingsley, 24:52). Later, when he refers to human sons, he still has Christ in mind as a model. Submission is as important for Kingsley as for Maurice, but he does not stop there: an obedient man will find that "the finest and noblest parts of his character come out . . . by copying his Father in everything; that going where his Father sends him; being jealous of his Father's honour; doing not his own will, but his Father's; that all this, I say, is its own reward; for instead of lowering a man, it raises him, and calls out in him all that is purest, tenderest, soberest, bravest. (Kingsley, 24:134)[18]

These ideas find a peculiar, more secular expression in Thomas Hughes's *The Manliness of Christ* (1879). Self-assertion is a basic form of courage, Hughes wrote, but self-sacrifice is the higher courage. And the object of self-sacrifice is the accomplishment of duty. Drawing upon Tennyson, Hughes concluded:

> Tenacity of will, or wilfulness, lies at the root of all courage, but courage can only rise into true manliness when the will is surrendered; and the more absolute the surrender of the will the more perfect will be the temper of our courage and the strength of our manliness.
>
> Strong Son of God, immortal Love,
>
> our laureate has pleaded, in the moment of his highest inspiration,
>
> Our wills are ours to make them thine.
>
> And that strong Son of God to whom this cry has gone up in our day, and in all days, has left us the secret of his strength in the words, "I am come to do the will of my Father and your Father."[19]

What emerges from this Coleridgean line of thought is a picture of the self as liberated from sin by submission to the will of God. At first this submission seems entirely subjective, but in time it becomes a form of assertion. With Kingsley it is missionary. Man's will must be disciplined like a soldier's. He must keep down the rebel self-will that would lead him into slavery and serve instead in the holy band dedicated to truth. True manliness, as Hughes claims, is restraint and self-sacrifice. The difficulty, of course, is in determining what the will of God is. Before submitting, one must recognize the truth. Maurice, Kingsley, and Hughes did not seriously doubt their possession of the truth; other writers struggled with the issue.

Conservative as they were in many ways (for example, their theology encouraged an acceptance of class hierarchy), in others religious thinkers like Coleridge, Maurice, and Kingsley were considered innovative and even radical. There was not much that was radical about Charles Haddon Spurgeon. Spurgeon also believed himself secure in the truth, but his truth did not include the free will so important to Coleridge. He was one of the most popular ministers to the Evangelical school of his time and may serve as a representative figure here. Spurgeon's biographer Ernest W. Bacon states that the great preacher did not deviate from the strict Calvinist program, though his sermons evinced a gradual moderation over the years. Bacon quotes from a doctrinal statement on predestination Spurgeon made in 1861:

> All the difficulties which are laid against the doctrine of predestination might, with equal force, be laid against that of Divine foreknowledge. God hath predestinated all things from the beginning, but there is a difference between the predestination of an intelligent, all-wise, all bounteous God, and that blind fatalism which

simply says, "It is because it is to be." Between the *predestination* of Scripture and the *fate* of the Koran every sensible man must perceive a difference of the most essential character. . . . I hold God's election, but I testify just as clearly that if any man be lost he is lost for sin. . . . If he be lost, damnation is all of man; but if he be saved, salvation is all of God.[20]

Spurgeon made clear that the faith called Calvinism sprang not from Calvin but from the Creator and was evident already in Augustine. He felt that he was preaching the word of God, not the doctrine of a sect. And examining his sermons, one is struck by how much they resemble those of other denominationalists. In "The Fatherhood of God," Spurgeon declared that Fatherhood implies love by God but also the responsibility of sonship's duty of love to God. Moreover, this relationship implies an important commitment. "*Sonship is a thing which all the infirmities of our flesh, and all the sins into which we are hurried by temptation, can never violate or weaken.*"[21] Spurgeon elaborated this familiar parental image with the equally familiar example of Christ as the perfect son and servant who comes into the world not to do his own will but the will of the Father who sent him.[22] Like other Christian apologists, Spurgeon emphasized the importance of submitting individual will to God's will. In "Samson Conquered," he explained that Samson was strong because he was a consecrated man and added that all consecrated men are strong. In fact, we are all potentially consecrated men (Spurgeon, *Sermons, Fifth Series*, 245). Such men are strong because God is with them; their great danger is to forget this and yield to pride, which is a razor to their strength, as is the illusion of self-sufficiency. Another danger is when a consecrated man "begins *to change his purpose in life and live for himself*—that razor shaves clean indeed" (Spurgeon, *Sermons, Fifth Series*, 246–48).

Spurgeon believed firmly in a detailed Divine Providence and defended it from charges of fatalism. "There is just this difference between fate and providence. Fate is blind; providence has eyes." Fate is what must be, whereas with providence, "the thing is, because it is right it should be" (Spurgeon, *Sermons, Fifth Series*, 378). He assures us "that the will of man, the thought of man, the desire of man, that every purpose of man, is immediately under the hand of God" (Spurgeon, *Sermons, Fifth Series*, 379). When man forgets that all he has is the gift of providence, he is liable to fall into pride, the inherent sin of man, and Spurgeon warns his listeners: "Oh be not rashly self-confident, Christian man. Be as confident as you can in your God, but be distrustful of yourself."[23]

Here Spurgeon and his kind differ from the Anglicans, Unitarians, and others in the great stress they place upon man's utter depravity. But will is still the offending agent. Man refuses to come to Christ, Spurgeon charges, because of the "*obstinacy of the human will. . . . Christ* himself declares it—'*Ye will not come unto me that ye might have life;*' and as long as that '*ye will not come*' stands on record in Holy Scripture, we shall not be brought to believe in any doctrine of the freedom of the human will." Human will is so depraved that without the influence of the Holy Spirit, "no human will will ever be constrained toward Christ."[24] Arminians admit that man is fallen but say that he has the power of will left to raise himself, and Antinomians say that man can do nothing to change his condition and is therefore not responsible for it. To Spurgeon all such diminishings of man's depravity are great theological errors. "But once get the correct view, that man is utterly fallen, powerless, guilty, defiled, lost, condemned, and you *must* be sound on all points of the great gospel of Jesus Christ. Once believe man to be what Scripture says he is—once believe his heart to be depraved, his affections perverted, his understanding darkened, his will perverse, and *you must* hold that if such a wretch as that be saved, it must be the work of the Spirit of God, and of the Spirit of God alone" (Spurgeon, *Sermons, Sixth Series*, 188–89).

In a sense at the opposite scale of religious belief was Roman Catholicism. By the time he joined its ranks, John Henry Newman was convinced of the truth of its creed and became a representative and distinctive spokesman for it. Newman stressed the importance of faith over reason, declaring reason's tendency "toward a simple unbelief in matters of religion."[25] Reason is appropriate for the arranging of sensory evidence but not dependable in other areas of human experience. Faith is not achieved by reason, but by an act of will.[26] Nonetheless, Newman sought a faith based upon more than hunger for belief and warned against anticipating providence instead of facing moral decisions day by day (Newman, *Apologia*, 130). He rejected the natural theology associated with Paley because it reduced God to a mere collection of his laws; still he argued for a careful examination of the nature of things. "First let us ascertain the fact—then theologize upon it. Depend upon it, when once the laws of human affairs are drawn out, and the philosophy into which they combine, it will be a movement worthy of the Lawgiver, but if we begin speaking of Him first of all, we shall never get at His laws."[27]

In *An Essay in Aid of A Grammar of Assent* (1870), Newman offered a theoretical plan for getting at those laws, assuming that they were sufficiently clear, especially as they operated in man himself, to be discoverable by the mind. Newman was sensitive to the untrustworthy subjective nature of much logical argumentation, while appreciating that "the mind itself is more versatile and vigorous than any of its works, of which language is one. . . . It determines what science cannot determine, the limit of converging probabilities and the reasons sufficient for a proof."[28] The laws governing the physical universe speak to man of God, similarly "the laws of the mind are the expression, not of mere constituted order, but of His will," and therefore "throw a reflex light upon themselves," which substitutes for resignation to destiny "a cheerful concurrence in an overruling Providence" (Newman, *Assent*, 226). Newman called the human power for judging and concluding the Illative Sense, a kind of superior intuition. It was both a manifestation of and a means for determining the laws of the mind. Another such means was conscience, which, through the influence of emotion upon the reason indicated a natural acceptance of a Divine Master (Newman, *Assent*, 76ff). The proof of true faith already exists, therefore, within the perceiving individual, and its manifestation is in the certitude of faith. It is here that Newman's concepts of the will as freedom of choice and as strength of purpose become important. As M. Jamie Ferreira points out, both certitude and conscience require freedom of the will. Certitude is achieved by an act of unconstrained will and adhered to by a deliberate act of intention. Free will is the starting place for assent because it must be an act for which the doer is responsible.[29] Religious faith itself thus requires an independent exertion of the will.

Like the Anglicans, Newman placed faith above reason, thus emphasizing the role of will and choice over calculation and logic. His chief example of willed sacrifice was the same—Jesus Christ. In his discourse "God's Will the End of Life," delivered not long after he established himself as a Catholic priest at the Oratory of St. Philip Neri near Birmingham, he repeated the familiar lesson that Christ came to earth to do God's will not his own but also observed that He "chose to take on Him man's nature, and the will of that nature; He chose to take on Him affections, feelings, and inclinations proper to man, a will innocent indeed and good, but still a man's will, distinct from God's will; a will, which had it acted simply according to what was pleasing to its nature, would, when pain and toil were to be endured, have held back from an active co-operation with the will of God."[30] Each man has his special vocation to fulfill, and to achieve it he, like Christ, must overcome selfishness and self-will. In a later sermon entitled "Omnipotence in Bonds," Newman repeated some of these points, noting that all-powerful God chose to imprison himself in human form. By contrast Lucifer's sin was "the resolve to be his own master," Adam's was "impatience of subjection, and a desire to be his own god," and all of ours is pride. "The very principle of sin is insubordination, hence the significance of God's model of the love of subjection" (Newman, *Discourses*, 371–72).

Newman had his own notable experience of submission to the will of God, of which the hymn "Lead, Kindly Light" was the testimony.[31] In the months and days just before Newman set out on the Mediterranean journey during which he was to compose that hymn, he was much occupied with the issue of the will and preached two major sermons on the subject, "Human Responsibility, as Independent of Circumstance" and "Wilfulness, the Sin of Saul." He remained faithful to the beliefs expressed in these sermons through his conversion to Catholicism.

Newman put his case in the most rudimentary terms. Beginning with the fall of man, Adam and Eve "committed sin that they might be independent of their Maker; they defended it on the ground that they were dependent upon Him. And this has been the course of lawless pride and lust ever since; to lead us, first, to exult in our uncontrollable liberty of will and conduct; then, when we have ruined ourselves, to plead that we are the slaves of necessity." But the truth is that, despite circumstances, "we are accountable for what we do and what we are."[32] This truth is supported not only by the operations of nature but by Scriptural evidence as well. Newman cited some instances, remarking that even Paul asserts the real independence of the will of man. Fatalism is merely a recourse for seeking to avoid the pain of remorse. The Calvinist doctrine, Newman said, is a forerunner of the neglect of the doctrine of responsibility. "Its practical error is that of supposing that certain motives and views, presented to the heart and conscience, produce certain effects as their necessary consequence, no room being left for the resistance of the will, or for self-discipline, as the medium by which faith; and holiness are connected together" (Newman, *Sermons*, 136).

Newman was unequivocal on the existence of true free will and consequent accountability in mankind. He was equally clear on the occasion of misusing that free will, as "Wilfulness, the Sin of Saul" suggests. Newman established Saul, along with Lot and Balaam, as an antitype of faith against Abraham, David, and Moses, who are its types. Saul appears to be a man of moral excellence whose first actions as a ruler are noble but are followed by "wilfulness, the unaccountable desire of acting short of simple obedience to God's will, a repugnance of unreserved self-surrender and submission to Him" (Newman, *Sermons*, 150). Saul is a type of the Jewish nation, elected by God, but failing in faith. The moral lesson of Saul and the Jewish nation applies, however, to all mankind; "whatever be the trial of those who have not revelation, the trial of those who have is one of Faith in opposition to self-will" (Newman, *Sermons*, 164). The consequence of wilfulness is bondage to a usurped authority, a lesson to keep in mind, Newman cautioned, in a time of open resistance to constituted power and irreverence toward antiquity.

This issue of self-will and submission obviously was personally important to Newman in 1832, but as he became more and more convinced of the direction his own faith would lead him, he strengthened his sense of man's freedom and accountability. Still, until 1843–44, he said that he believed in God "on a ground of probability," but God has so willed that we shall act upon the grounds of accumulated probabilities and helps us to faith "if our will does but co-operate with His to a certitude which rises higher than the logical force of our conclusions" (Newman, *Apologia*, 157). Newman believed that man was essentially a fallen, willful creature capable of exerting himself toward his own salvation through faith and an act of free will which culminated in the submission of that will to divine purpose. Despite Newman's distinctive expression of his views, they are fully in keeping with the general Christian pattern we have been examining.

Newman is perhaps the most famous Catholic apologist of nineteenth-century England, but there were many others. William George Ward, for example, was a fine English spokesman of Catholic views. Ward was a shrewd thinker, a leader of the Oxford movement, advocate of conservative Catholic loyalty, and a friendly antagonist of Mill and Huxley. His arguments are well reasoned and not merely doctrinal. On the will he had much to say, though it comes down to one fundamental position variously expressed.

Ward argued for intuitive knowledge against the "Experience" school, but recognized the merits of the determinist argument, even admitting that a large proportion of men's lives was passed in obedience to the "spontaneous impulse" of the will. But the doctrine of free will he considered one of the four essential doctrines of genuine theism.[33] Ward's defense of free will amounted to an assertion that man was capable of an anti-impulsive movement which restrained or redirected action that would have followed from the will's spontaneous impulse. In short, *free will* controls *impulsive will*. He restated his case in various ways, but here is a condensed version of it from a letter to J. S. Mill (who acknowledged its strength but considered it an admirable simplification and enlargement of the dispute rather than a solution of it):

> We maintain, then, that so far as regards, not the will's *actual movement*, but its *spontaneous impulse*, there is a theory of motives as strictly scientific, as abstractedly capable of scientific calculation, as any theory of mechanics or chemistry. But we further maintain that, in applying that theory to practice, allowance must always be made for the fact that in every instance the will has a real power of acting above the level of such spontaneous impulse. How far the will may *choose* to do so is a matter incapable of calculation, and external to science altogether. And this circumstance precisely, neither more nor less, constitutes that one particular in which the doctrine of Freewill interferes with the strictly scientific character of psychology. (Ward, 292)

Ward was willing to follow the physiological and utilitarian argument a long way but felt that at a certain point science was incapable of any conclusive analysis to prove or disprove free will. Man's experience testified that he *did* have the power to govern spontaneous impulse. Many arguments could be raised against Ward's position. For example, if the will has power to resist the will, is it the same entity or force? Usually the will, unlike the divisible reason, was pictured as necessarily integral. Was it logically possible to conceive of a force resisting itself? On a more practical level, Mill objected that Ward's distinction left the philosophical question open, concluding that "our foresight in this matter cannot be certain because we never can be really in possession of sufficient data" (Ward, 294). There is more to Ward's argument than I have presented here, but I merely wish to emphasize his attempt, like that of others we have been discussing here, to move the ground of the free will debate away from the abstract, theoretical level to that of moral action, specifically in individual conduct.

The figures we have considered thus far were rigorous in asserting their faith. But many believers were not so firmly fixed in their views and allowed more room for doubt. Frederick W. Robertson, the highly respected incumbent of fashionable Trinity Chapel, Brighton, was an outstanding representative of this group. Admiring Newman as well as Maurice and Kingsley, he was no adherent of the High Church and placed little confidence in the Evangelicals. He was a successful minister and preacher, appealing to educated parishioners and their unlearned servants alike. He sympathized with working-class causes and established a Working-Man's Institute, but here too he was ambivalent. He said of himself, "My tastes are with the aristocrat, my principles with the mob."[34]

Robertson believed in duty. Like Carlyle, Kingsley, and Maurice, he felt that each man had a role to play in life, a destiny, and it was his first task to discover that role. Like Kingsley, Robertson asserted that what God has created is not evil. "Sin resides in the will," he explained, "not in the natural appetites" (Brooke, 129). To him, the material world was imbued with the spirit of God; it was "but manifested Deity. . . . The sounds and the sights of this lovely world are but the drapery of the robe in which the Invisible has clothed himself," he said in his sermon "Worldliness."[35] This is a Carlylean attitude with a positive slant. Robertson believed that "it will some day be demonstrated that the Creator is much more closely united to His own works than our unspiritual conceptions represent him" (Brooke, 121–22).

Robertson placed a strong emphasis upon free will but also upon will as determined effort, with the usual contradictions. Man must be strong in will through discipline and restraint but always with the provision that human will is entirely submissive to God's will. In his own daily life he required a sense of triumphant will. Burdened by the sense of onrushing time, he composed a list every evening of the next day's engagements and duties. By this means, he explained to a friend, one feels great satisfaction in measuring what has been accomplished at the end of a day. "This is the secret of giving dignity to trifles. As units they are insignificant; they rise in importance when they become parts of a plan. Besides this—and I think the most important thing of all—there is gained a consciousness of will, the opposite of that which is the sense of impotency" (Brooke, 177). It was against just such a specter that figures like Robertson labored. In doing so, they valued intuition above intellect. Reason was a deceptive tool, largely suborned by the things of the world because it was able to express itself through them only, whereas intuition or feeling was allied with the spirit and transcended the errors of intellect.

In a letter of 1849, in which he tried to answer the question What makes a man turn to God in the first instance? Robertson gave a moving account of his own case that described the struggle between intellect and feeling in direct terms. The passage is worth quoting at length.

> Reasoning tells me I am a leaf, blown about by the breath of the spirit-wind as it listeth. I review the reasoning step by step, find no flaw in it. Nothing but a horrible predestination environs me. Every act of my past and future life, external and internal, was necessitated. The conclusion is irrefutable. I act upon this. Immediately I find that practically, I have got wrong. I can not act upon the idea of being fated, reft of will, without injuring my whole being. My affections are paralyzed, my actions disordered. I find, therefore, that the view which is theoretically truth, translated into conduct, becomes practically a lie. Now, on the other hand, conscience tells me I am free. I am to seek God. I am not to lie passive, waiting for the moving of the waters, but to obey a voice within me which I recognize as divine, and which says, "Arise, take up thy bed and walk." My intellect stands in contradiction to my conscience; but I am bound to obey my conscience rather than my intellect. I believe the voice which says, "You can seek God and find him," rather than the one which says, "Poor victim of fantasy, you can not stir; you can only wait!" There is the best concise reply I can give you to your question. (Brooke, 155–56)

Like so many religious men of his time, Robertson believed in discipline. To him, doing good was the best discipline, "for goodness is the habit of the will, not perceptions or aspirations" (Brooke, 122). He admired military effort and heroic death. Self-sacrifice was a watchword of his faith. Upon the death of the great Duke of Wellington, Robertson reflected that the Duke's love of England rested in those qualities symbolized by the Duke—goodness, sacrifice, and duty (Brooke, 312). In his sermon "The Sacrifice of Christ," he stressed the fact that self-denial, self-sacrifice, and self-surrender are no good in themselves, but must be irradiated by love.[36] Christ is Robertson's model for self-sacrifice. His life is striking because it is characterized by submission to another will. "I came not to do mine own will, but the will of Him who sent me," Christ said (Robertson, *Sermons . . . Trinity*, 55). It is this selflessness, Robertson argues in a self-helpish tone agreeable to his audience, that makes for leadership. "And this is the secret of all influence, and all command. Obedience to a law above you subjugates minds to you who never would have yielded to mere will. 'Rule thyself, thou rulest all' " (Robertson,

Sermons . . . Trinity, 56). Free will and strength of will again become associated with authority and domination by the devious route of submission.

Nonetheless, Robertson dwelt mainly on the necessity of overcoming self-will in order to learn the truth. He believed that truth was advancing, as evidenced in the increasing glory accorded to meekness, humbleness, and purity instead of strength and intellect. One discovers the truth by feeling, not intellect. God's law is equated with natural law. The universe is governed by laws, and by submission to them we make them our own.[37] Thus, in the physical as well as in the moral realm, to submit to laws external to the self is to conquer. Freedom comes in the acknowledgment of God's will. "And so he learns of his own free-will, and uses them as the sailor does the winds, which *as* he uses them become his enemies or his friends" (Robertson, *Sermons . . . St. Paul's*, 45).

Robertson sought to overcome the problem of predestination more diplomatically than had Kingsley, arguing that all high truth is the union of opposites. "Thus predestination and free will are opposites; and the truth does not lie between these two, but in a higher reconciling truth, which leaves both true" (Robertson, *Sermons . . . Trinity*, 75). But man must not believe in a "tyrannous destiny" or it will paralyze his will, a paralysis that is cured "the moment a man wills to do the Will of God" (Robertson, *Sermons . . . Trinity*, 134). Though providence guides us, we must nonetheless strive to fulfill its aims. Our strength of will and power to lead come from our submission of our free will to the greater will of God which we recognize not through imperious intellect but through the gentler sympathies of the heart. The message is by now markedly familiar.

Robertson died in 1853 at the age of 37. His life encapsulates much of the genuine inward struggle so little appreciated in some accounts of smug Victorianism. He was a sincere minister who believed each man had a destiny assigned by God. Dismayed at being viewed as a highly popular and therefore successful preacher, he never felt that he was truly fulfilling the duties he had undertaken and never considered himself a genuine success. Yet he typifies the constant self-examination and self-sacrifice that represented true piety to much of his generation.

W. Boyd Carpenter, bishop of Ripon, coming later in the century with more conservative views, asserted the same attitude toward will, except that, for him, the relation of individual to God was advanced from sonship to fellowship. In the introduction to *The Permanent Elements of Religion* (1889), he praised Professor John Caird's *An Introduction to the Philosophy of Religion* (1880) stressing submission to God's will and added "If religion be thus the surrender of our will to the will of God, the element of Dependence is included in the definition, but inasmuch as the surrender is a voluntary identification of our will with the will of God, the communion or fellowship of the Divine and the human will has taken place. The finite finds itself in the infinite and the infinite finds expression in the finite. The element of Fellowship is here."[38]

Bishop Carpenter wished to demonstrate the necessity of religion and how the individual might best live up to its moral requirements. He listed three elements necessary to perfect human nature—conscience, intelligence, and will. "In other words, a character is not perfect unless it is sensitive to right, clear in thought and firm in action" (Carpenter, 207–8). Accordingly, moral behavior involves the perception of a higher principle, the sense that we ought to be at one with it, and the choice of it. The means of uniting religion and morals is personality. Bishop Carpenter claimed that nature teaches man self-preservation, self-consciousness, self-expression, and ultimately self-sacrifice. "Here is a law which has been working up to the perfecting of the personality and the development of character in the conscious possession of our will, and in the obligation of sacrifice" (Carpenter, 255). Some, he admitted, may argue that all is determined beforehand. "But even were it so, and the freedom of man an illusion, the consciousness of that freedom would be enough for the education of a man's character" (Carpenter, 256). Like the atheistical Godwin before him, Bishop Carpenter wants the benefits of free will even if he cannot dismiss the possibility of a determined world. But here, as with Godwin, causation is an unforgiving ghost. If the illusion of freedom alters character, then it too is part of the determined design and is not illusory. In any case, it is a questionable defense of morality and begs the question of responsibility. Bishop Carpenter expressed his faith in authoritative tones, but it is no more sophisticated than Kingsley's after all, for it comes down to this conclusion: "Morality is the expression of God's will; religion is the expression of our trust in that will" (Carpenter, 268).

Bishop Carpenter and Robertson represented a moderate Anglican view regarding the will. But there were other voices, expressing a wide range of religious commitment and offering variations upon this central question of the will. William Ewart Gladstone, a strong defender of traditional religious views, declared in a letter to his wife: "The final state which we are to contemplate with hope, and to seek by discipline, is that in which our will shall be *one* with the will of God: not merely shall submit to it, not merely shall follow after it, but shall live and move with it even as the pulse of the blood in the extremities acts with the central movement of the heart."[39] We can achieve this end by repressing the will's impulse to act with reference to self as center and by cherishing the power of acting according to the will of God.

Gladstone was not troubled by challenges to the concept of free will and could easily reconcile it with God's foreknowledge. "*All* things are foreseen: both the acts of the free agents and of the unfree."[40] He did not fear that God's sovereignty compromised human responsibility. Others, however, were moved to argue this difficult point. John Cumming's effort in his popular *The Daily Life; or Precepts and Prescriptions for Christian Living*

(1855) was typical, if not very convincing. Cumming said that God's absolute sovereignty does not take away human responsibility because "no man
was ever admitted into heaven except with his own will, freely, fully, heartily
expressed. . . . God in his sovereignty does not drag man to heaven, or
force man to ruin," but works within man. "He changes the will, makes it
willing, and then he saves in our willingness, and not in spite of that willingness."[41] Cumming did not seem to notice that if God changes man's will, he
is exerting his absolute sovereignty and man's "will" is not free but a simple
expression of God's own power. Man is puppet or dupe but no free agent.

Another defender of Christian views sought to reconcile free will with the
image of a completely law-bound universe. W. R. Greg, in his widely read *The
Creed of Christendom* (1851), rejected the concept of divine foreknowledge, which amounted, he said, to divine foreordainment. This doctrine,
"however metaphysically true and probable, we *cannot* hold, so as to follow
it out fairly to its consequences. It negatives the free-will of man at least as
peremptorily as the efficacy of prayer:—yet in the free will of man we do
believe, and must believe, however strict logic may struggle against it."[42] All
that Greg could offer in defense of such a belief was an instinctive or intuitive
need to believe in man's freedom. God, he concluded, has placed man in a
world and surrounded him with fixed laws "on knowledge of which, and on
conformity to which, his well-being depends."[43]

If Cumming's and Greg's arguments resemble traditional defenses that we
met with in earlier defenders of free will, the high Anglican J. B. Mozley had
more up-to-date arguments to offer. Reviewing the philosophical tradition
on the subject of causation, Mozley said that men are required to think se-
quentially, that is, in time, and thus perceive operations as caused. Each
cause must have an agent, which is either necessary or free. We are all conscious of what we call free will despite the fact that all of visible nature is
moved from without. Not simply falling back upon intuition, as Greg did,
Mozley argues that man's self and will provide the very model for the arrangement of the universe and that all of nature is moved by a similar First Cause.
If you trace cause back to an origin, it must be God—an Eternal, Original,
Self-Existent Being, an uncaused Cause of the world.[44] Scientists, Mozley
said, claim that the universe was formed by law, but that expression is not
inconsistent with a Divine Creator who initiated the law. Again, though they
do not connect it with God, scientists incline to see mind in nature. Mozley
suggested that the existence of intelligence and moral nature in man argues
for an originating moral Personality. The Being that implanted the Ideal in
man's conscience must be the embodiment of that Ideal. For Mozley, then,
the human self, with its sense of free will, becomes the hinge upon which the
door to the truth of God's existence turns.

A similar pattern of thought underlies the more elaborate approach that
appears in the writings of the intensely learned and extremely shrewd Uni-

tarian James Martineau, who was able to balance nicely between philosophical theory and practical morality. Like Nonconformists and Anglicans, Martineau acknowledged that man's spiritual nature had always been a theater of conflicting impulses. Among pagans, however, self-conquest was *self-assertion*; among Christians *self-surrender*.[45] This pagan self-assertion he aligns with the scientific, or Darwinian, position, while insisting upon the Christian trust in compassion and self-forgetfulness. To be self-forgetful assumes the power of choice. Martineau's assertion of human free will differs little from others we have cited, though his phrasing has a novel tang. "Not left, like the mere animal, to be the passive resultant of forces without and instincts within, but invested with an alternative power, we are conscious partners in the architecture of our own character, and know ourselves to be the bearers of a *trust*; and this fiduciary life takes us at once across the boundary which separates nature from what transcends it" (Martineau, *Essays*, 4:182).

To achieve divine knowledge, man must have self-knowledge, which involves an understanding not merely of himself but of his place in nature.[46] The mind, however, is a slippery tool and Martineau adroitly demonstrates how the language of science is frequently no more dependable as a basis for truth than is that of metaphysics or theology. For example, he admitted that the combination of a *known* materialism and a *created* God, the product of modern materialist philosophy, is one that thought repudiates and reverence abhors, but he went on to observe "that the atomic hypothesis is a thing *not known but created*, while God is *not created but known*" (Martineau, *Essays* 4:194). By thus turning the tables on materialists, he showed that scientific theories are products of fallible human understanding (or imagination) and thus as subject to doubt as any fiction, whereas the evidence of God is spiritual, transcending the limits of reason and hence trustworthy.

An example of his treatment of scientific reasoning is his defense of the concept of will as the operating power in the universe. Materialists refer to a power in nature that facilitates action, he says, but this power is only mentally posited and not actually discoverable. In ourselves we call this power will. Our whole idea of Power is identical with Will, just as we recognize causality in nature as related to what we are conscious of within ourselves (Martineau, *Essays*, 4:242). By a simple effort of trust, men convey the qualities they perceive in themselves to the universe at large. "If the collective energies of the universe are identified with Divine Will, and the system is thus animate with an eternal consciousness as its moulding life, the conception we frame of its history will conform itself to our experience of intellectual volition" (Martineau, *Essays*, 4:249).[47] The materialist view is, in fact, merely a *reduction* of the religious position. "The scientific idea of force is nothing but Will *cut down*, by dropping from it some characters which are irrelevant for the purposes of classification and prediction."[48]

55

Ultimately the dispute between Force and Mind is as meaningless as a man's quarrel with his own image, for the two are expressions of the same nature. What scientists call the inexorable law of nature may equally be viewed as God's faithfulness. To affirm purpose in the universe is not to set up a rival principle outside the concept of force, but to establish an integrating thought within it.

In *The Seat of Authority in Religion* (1890), Martineau restated in simpler terms some of his basic principles. He explained that man discovers the power of Will in himself and attributes a similar power to life that sustains nature (Martineau, *Seat*, 2).[49] The concept of a Divine Will may appear redundant to some, Martineau said, but it is not less than we long for. He reassured his readers: "We are not lost, then, in our modern immensity of space; but may still rest, with the wise of every age, in the faith that a realm of intellectual order and purest purpose environs us, and that the unity of nature is but the unity of the all-perfect Will" (Martineau, *Seat*, 9). Science reveals that all forces behind the changes of the world are One. But this finding is consistent with a belief in a Divine Intellect and Will, "eternally transmuting itelf into the cosmical order, and assuming the phases of natural force as modes of manifestation and paths of progression to ends of beauty and good" (Martineau, *Seat*, 27).[50] A. W. Jackson says of this line of argument: "The inference is clear: Regarding Force as the expression of Will, and Will as a function of mind, the seemingly material universe is really crystallized Intelligence."[51]

Returning to the individual, Martineau explained that there are three orders of power in man: physical, spiritual, and personal. Personal will may concur or conflict with the others but is the source of human responsibility. "God's part is done, when, having made us free, he shows to us our best: ours now remains to pass on from illumination of the conscience to surrender of the will" (Martineau, *Seat*, 414–15). It all comes back to the same message. Man's true freedom is in the abandonment of his will to God's. Once relieved of the torment of choice, the integrated self, fueled by God's power, will be able to carry out its destiny or mission which the rebellious will might have prevented. Martineau clearly asserted that Christianity was founded on the principle of obedience, with self-will as nothing more than insurrection against authority. The moral law of God and the moral freedom of man were the theater of endeavor, and endeavor itself, seated in the will, was the heart of Christianity (Martineau, *Essays*, 4:448, 453).

Martineau was shrewd in dealing with numerous traditional gambits in the free will dispute. In the second volume of *A Study of Religion* (1888), he clearly and fairly described the conflicting philosophical positions of free will and determinism—or libertarianism and necessarianism—noting that the two schools have such different understandings of words "that language, pushed by them to its ultimate analysis, ceases to be common to the two"

(Martineau, *Study*, 187). Human experience tells us that "within a certain range of responsibility, [we] are the authors of our own characters" (Martineau, *Study*, 184). The associationist-necessarian line that declares pleasure as the motive force for willing, and action and developed habit as the basis for complex behavior, does not account for a major difficulty. "Who compares the conflicting impulses?" Martineau's question is characteristic of someone who had lived through the nineteenth century with its severe attention to the nature and integrity of the self. The question is telling, though not one that the eighteenth-century framers of the necessarian theory would have considered significant. By the end of the nineteenth century, however, the concept of the multiple self was becoming commonplace, and the belief in a focus of discipline or seignorial authority within to guide these potentially wayward selves all the more essential. The self cannot merely be defined as the sum total of feelings, impulses, and so forth, Martineau argued, because a sum total can deliberate no more than individual impulses can. Only mind can deliberate. Against the mechanism of the necessarians, he asserted: "A self constitutes a permanent, but a permanent order repeated does not constitute a self" (Martineau, *Study*, 222).

Martineau concluded that empirical psychology neither disposes of the consciousness of personal causation nor succeeds in reducing the self to "a theatre of felt antecedents and sequents." From this conclusion, he moved to an immensely interesting development to be exploited later by philosophers such as Henri Bergson. We are not the slaves of the past, Martineau declared.

> It is matter only that moves out of the past: all mind acts for the future: and though that future operates through the preconception of it which is earlier than the act, and so might seem to conform to the material order, yet, where two or more rival preconceptions enter the field together, they cannot compare themselves *inter se*: they need and meet a superior: it rests with the mind itself to decide. The decision will not be *unmotivated*, for it will have its reasons. It will not be uncomformable to the characteristics of the mind, for it will express its preferences. But none the less is it issued by a free Cause that elects among the conditions, and is not elected by them. (Martineau, *Study*, 266)

The mind's capacity to reach into the future frees it from the materialist notion of a mechanical entrapment in what *is*. The present becomes malleable to the future under the authority of the will. This complex issue was soon to be taken up by creative writers like H. G. Wells, but it had a traditional clog upon it. If God had already predetermined the entire universe, then future events were also already mechanically fixed and the mind's reach into the future was no freer than its footsteps in the past. But Martineau was prepared for this objection as well.

> An infinite Mind, with prevision thus extended beyond all that is to all that can be, is lifted above surprise or disappointment, and able to provide for all events and combinations; yet, instead of being shut up in a closed and mechanized universe, lives amid the free play of variable character and contingent history, into which there is room for approval, pity, and love to flow. Is this a *limitation* of God's foresight, that he cannot read all volitions that are to be? Yes: but it is a *self-limitation*, just like his abstinence from causing them: lending us a portion of his causation, he refrains from covering all with his omniscience. (Martineau, *Study*, 263)

Writing in the latter half of the century and freed from orthodox views, Martineau was able to support traditional Christian and libertarian views with surprising arguments. Alert to the limitations of the scientific method, he was capable of countering modern attacks against free will as deftly as he managed traditional logical ploys. At the same time, he offered a justification of fundamental Christian belief and endorsed the Victorian values of endurance, exertion, and self-sacrifice.

Among the various spokesmen for Theism or Christianity that we have examined here, there is a common assumption about the justness of authority—that God is a father who has the absolute rights of a father and exacts obedience from his children. The degree of filial attachment differs. Maurice cannot endure the thought of eternal punishment and banishes it from his scheme, whereas Spurgeon finds it essential as part of a just God's punitive armory. But both men believe that man's highest effort is to subdue his own impulses, which are innately selfish and misconceived, and to consecrate himself to God's purpose. Kingsley and Robertson concentrate more on the splendidness of human nature and the freedom man has to *elect* such submission—to choose not to be enslaved by selfish impulses and freely to enter God's service. Obedience and subordination are central to both men, but implicit in their arguments is the suggestion that by placing themselves in God's camp they regain the power, authority, and justification for action against error that was denied them when they were mere selfish individuals. Newman and Ward must believe in free will as intensely as Kingsley and in human depravity almost as much as Spurgeon because it is only by free will that man can prove himself by drawing himself out of depravity and yielding himself up to God. If God did this for him, man would not, in Newman's view, be responsible and therefore not open to reward and punishment. Mozley and Martineau are less concerned with reward and punishment than with establishing a firm ground of faith in the world open to discovery by men, not revealed to them by documents. They accept revelation and experience, doctrine and science, and winnow them for what is valuable to them. All but Martineau among these apologists for faith agree on the radical importance of that major step toward human salvation, the basis of human morality, the submission of the individual will to God's will, the losing of the self in the service of others, the imitation of the way of Christ.

CHAPTER FOUR

The Secular Moralists

I
F the religious moralists emphasized self-sacrifice and submission of the
will, secular moralists tended more toward affirmation of the human capacity for self-direction. Few, even of those who nominally rejected free
will, could profess the absolute skepticism of a Leslie Stephen. Most sought
some logical means of justifying moral behavior.

This chapter studies writers in nineteenth-century England who wished to
preserve behavioral morality without requiring a theological base for it. Hazlitt early in the century defended free will but placed its province in the
future, thereby arguing that human life is formable and improvable by the
self. Determinists such as Bray, Mill, Spencer, and others tried variously to
justify the human capacity to guide and improve individual and communal
character. Attempts to reconcile determinism and moral freedom grew
more internalized in the latter half of the century in the writings of men like
Clifford and Green. With Sidgwick, Stephen, and others, another current of
argument tended to divorce the concept of free will from issues of morality
altogether. With many thinkers, a growing ambivalence about the nature of
morality and philosophical concepts is evident near the end of the century,
an ambivalence that found expression in the works of Hardy, Eliot, Pater,
and other imaginative writers.

Through much of the century, secular moralists stressed the identification
of will with reason, whereas religious moralists more often connected it with
feeling and intuition. But by the end of the century, much writing on the

subject began to turn away from claims upon reason. Apologists for morality such as Balfour and Huxley tried to preserve a credible moral scheme through the balancing of reason and feeling. By the end of the century, however, a flood of simplified guide books for building character, following from if not patterned upon Smiles's schema for self-help, reduced the issue of free will to simple assertions about will as the freedom, even the duty, to act, a sentiment much in keeping with the adventure literature then coming into fashion.

~ ~ ~

In one of the most intriguing essays of the Victorian period, "An Agnostic's Apology," Leslie Stephen sought to explain why he preferred an intellectual stance of thoughtful skepticism to any form of orthodoxy. Near the end of this essay, he stated the agnostic's position wryly.

> Amidst all the endless and hopeless controversies which have left nothing but bare husks of meaningless words, we have been able to discover certain reliable truths. They don't take us very far, and the condition of discovering them has been distrust of *a priori* guesses, and the systematic interrogation of experience. Let us, say some of us, follow at least this clue. Here we shall find sufficient guidance for the needs of life, though we renounce for ever the attempt to get behind the veil which no one has succeeded in raising; if, indeed, there be anything behind.[1]

He concluded by asking his antagonists to refrain from attacking agnostics until they themselves could present a coherent system of belief. Stephen was only one of many skeptics and nonbelievers who sought a reasoned approach to moral problems. In this chapter, we shall examine a small sampling of them.

Stephen's essay is worthwhile reading in any case but is of particular interest here for the skeptical, balanced approach to the subject of determinism and free will. In a theist context, the problem appeared insoluble to him. Explaining that the ablest and most logical thinkers have declared the free will doctrine fallacious, Stephen defined it as "the device by which theologians try to relieve God of the responsibility for the sufferings of His creation" (Stephen, 18, 21). He equated free will with chance and closed the door on further argument by declaring that "if my free-will [an advocate] means anything else than a denial of causation, his statement is irrelevant" (Stephen, 19). For Stephen, the basic Christian position assumes that our conduct is the result of fate and free will, but since fate is merely a name for the will of God, God must share the responsibility for his creatures' behavior or be unjust. To avoid agnosticism, theists resort to some version of pantheism, identifying God with phenomenal nature, but cannot thereby avoid the problem of evil and responsibility. "We escape from Pantheism by the illogical device of free-will," which exempts God from responsibility for evil but deprives Him of omnipotence (Stephen, 28).[2]

For anyone not seriously engaged in the dispute, Stephen's account of the free will controversy can be amusing. But a true antagonist would quickly note that, in order to reach his conclusion, he had to ignore a good deal, including some subtle arguments on causation by figures like James Martineau and the central Christian paradox that the true exercise of free will is in submission. That he disregarded the notion that freedom is achieved through renunciation of self is a sign of what was important in Stephen's world view. He was not concerned with metaphysics and was relatively uninterested in man's place in nature, considering it another insoluble mystery. What interested him was ethics—human conduct. In 1865, he wrote to a friend, "I now believe in nothing, to put it shortly; but I do not the less believe in morality, &c. &c." (Maitland, 144). He considered himself neither an optimist nor a pessimist. "My view of the Universe—if you want to have it," he wrote to O. W. Holmes in 1877, "is that it is kind of mixed, but that, on the whole, the good has decidedly the best of it" (Maitland, 297). F. W. Maitland says that though he was influenced by such optimistic figures as Comte and Lewes, Stephen believed that a definite ring-fence could be drawn around the knowable at an assignable place and for assignable reasons (Maitland, 406). This image itself suggests how remote his posture toward experience was from that of the Romantics, who wished to extend personality into the unknown, to penetrate it with their own being. But, unlike many of his fellow Victorians, who wished to preserve moral conduct while rejecting dogma (George Eliot is a standard example), he did not substitute a scheme whereby the self achieves freedom through renunciation. Within his ring-fence of the known is the hard stone of ego.

Early in the century, William Hazlitt made an effort to dissolve the selfish nodule of ego and prove that man was essentially a benevolent being. In *An Essay on the Principles of Human Action and Some Remarks on the System of Hartley and Helvetius* (1805), he put forward an interesting theory. The proof of man's essential beneficence was in his capacity to imagine future conditions. If one can image a future self, he argued, one can identify with other persons. "For there is no reason to be shewn why the ideas of the imagination should not be efficient, operative, as well as those of memory, of which they are essentially compounded."[3] Imagination frees man from necessity by liberating him from what he has experienced and opens the doors of action through the ability to sympathize with others and to project the story of his existence into an as yet nonexistent state. By converting his existence into narrative, man becomes a moral agent (Hazlitt, *Essay*, 3). But merely to imagine the future is not enough. We also need the power to enact it, and that power resides in the will, which is inescapably linked with the future, because all voluntary action must relate to what is yet to be (one cannot, for example, will the past). Through will man may escape the limits of himself and empathize with the ideas and sensations of others. The two efforts are identical (Hazlitt, *Essay,* 21, 113).

Hazlitt had intended to discuss the will itself in this work but put the subject aside, returning to it a decade later in two essays. In "On Liberty and Necessity," he described man as a free and accountable agent and asserted his belief in liberty, which he defined as the power of an agent in given circumstances to operate in a certain manner if left to itself. This belief did not prevent him from accepting necessity, which he considered merely the regular succession of cause and effect in matter and mind. Hobbes and Spinoza could reconcile liberty with necessity, he said, and so could he. For him, true freedom of choice, will, and action were consistent with necessity.[4]

In "The Doctrine of Philosophical Necessity," Hazlitt quoted Wordsworth's poetry ("For I had learnt a sense sublime") as an excellent expression of the doctrine of philosophical necessity. He agreed that everything exists by necessity, that the fabric of the universe is held together by a chain of causation and that there is no chance or accident. But he also contended that man has unique qualities and contrasted him with animals, who can learn but are not free. "As far as they have understanding, they have free-will, for these two words mean one and the same thing. Man is the only religious animal, because he alone (from a greater power of imagination) extends his views of consequences to another state of being."[5] The human mind differs from a mechanism because it is actuated by sympathy as well as by necessity.

Spinoza, to whom Hazlitt referred approvingly, rejected the philosophical concept of free will because he perceived the will as determined by preceding events. It is backward-looking, a prisoner of inescapable preliminary consequences. Freedom is an illusion produced by man's capacity to act. This image of man's potential was consistent with a historical time when political regimes encouraged a rigorous maintenance of traditions and privileges. But Hazlitt wrote in a time when traditions were toppling or under siege. To him, man was not thrust forward from behind toward eternity, but strode boldly forward, attracted by an ideal. Spinoza might look back and understand the past through the exercise of intellect, but Hazlitt looked forward with the power of imagination. For Hazlitt, life becomes art. Men begin to conceive of a future malleable to their wills. A story of mankind begins to shape itself. Though life becomes secular, ironically it also becomes more intensely moral, because overcoming individual selfishness means salvation for mankind. The notion is scarcely new, but Hazlitt's secular version is indicative of a hopeful strain of thought nearly exhausted by the time Leslie Stephen wrote "An Agnostic's Apology." In the meantime, numerous variations of the secular preoccupation with will and conduct were promulgated.

One unusual version was Charles Bray's in *The Philosophy of Necessity* (1841). Bray credited Jonathan Edwards and Jeremy Bentham as strong influences upon his thinking, and cited Dr. John Elliotson and George Combe (both advocates of phrenology) as authorities for his physiological position that mind is dependent upon brain. Bray argued that heredity determines physical condition, which in turn determines behavior. He insisted that man, in a scientific way, confine himself to examining those truths which his senses make evident to him, at the same time indicating the danger of man's tendency to abstraction. For example, *power* is not an existing entity but simply an idea derived from the function of causality. Because we perceive causality operating in time, we construct the idea of succession, hence power, which we then attribute to a personality or god, before which we stand in awe, though we have merely lent that Great Cause qualities of our own intelligence.[6] By contrast, Bray believed that animal magnetism and mesmerism could be proven by practical experiments (Bray, 136).

Bray's commitment to materialism is consistent with his determinism. "The doctrine of necessity, in plain language, means that a man could in no case have acted differently from the manner in which he did act, supposing the state of his mind, and the circumstances in which he was placed, to be the same; which is merely saying, that the same causes would always produce the same effects" (Bray, 167–68). Motive is to volition in the moral world what cause is to effect in the physical; the one is as fixed as the other. Thus far, Bray's determinism, a little modernized by new "scientific" views, seems quite traditional. But Bray was a reformer, and his desire to alter human conduct and institutions inevitably conflicted with his acceptance of determinism, his claim that all men were in their right places, and that an inevitable progress guided human history. Bray endorsed Bentham's principle of the greatest good for the greatest number, saying that men must look always to final consequences. "The performance of duty, therefore, not the pursuit of happiness, may be considered as the safest road to happiness" (Bray, 292). Men must correct their outmoded image of the Deity, make benevolence His main attribute, and conceive the laws of nature as the presence of God. He quoted *Sartor Resartus* approvingly to end his chapter (Bray, 299).[7]

Bray's position is strange but far from unique. He believed in a deity of some kind but preferred to interpret the world in material and secular terms. As I have already suggested, this divided focus led him into contradictions. Volume 2 of Bray's treatise is given over to a description of the various ways in which the condition of the poor may be alleviated. In it, Bray recommended many changes, beginning with a cure for selfish capitalism through the establishment of workingmen's industrial associations or communities where they themselves would control production. But there is an obvious discontinuity between volumes 1 and 2 of Bray's book, for in a world where all act as they must act and every man is in his proper place, how can such revolutionary changes come about? How, indeed, does the whole process of improvement begin? Hazlitt also asserted the dominance of the benevolent spirit in man but provided an argument that made man's improvement through his own exertions possible. Bray, trusting to Bentham and Godwin, did not delineate the necessary logical connection.

Bray's philosophy of necessity was essentially derivative. John Stuart Mill's, also originating with Benthamism, had its own original contribution. Mill is, in fact, one of the clearest expositors of the free will controversy. Being an atheist, he was occupied primarily with the ethical consequences of philosophical positions, their application to conduct and character. John Tulloch wrote of him: "He never ceased to be the Apostle of Circumstance, as opposed alike to Free Will in human conduct and the freedom of Divine Action in Nature, although with a wider knowledge and a more candid perception of the difficulties of the doctrine than most of his school had."[8] Mill's views on free will and necessity appear throughout his writings, but most clearly in *A System of Logic* (1843, with subsequent revisions), *An Examination of Sir William Hamilton's Philosophy* (1865), and the *Autobiography* (1873). To begin with, Mill objected to the term "necessity" because it implied irresistibleness; he complained that many necessarians assumed a mysterious tie between cause and effect and therefore created an illusion as troubling as that which he felt vitiated arguments in support of free will.

> Correctly conceived, the doctrine called Philosophical Necessity is simply this: that, given the motives which are present to an individual's mind, and given likewise the character and disposition of the individual, the manner in which he will act might be unerringly inferred: that if we knew the person thoroughly, and knew all the inducements which are acting upon him, we could foretell his conduct with as much certainty as we can predict any physical event.[9]

In *An Examination*, he underlined the point. "If necessity means more than this abstract policy of being foreseen; if it means any mysterious compulsion, apart from simple invariability of sequence, I deny it as strenuously as any one."[10]

Mill placed himself among necessarians and rejected the free will doctrine, but his position is not so absolute as it may seem, for he declared that, just as others have the power to alter our character, so we have the same power to alter our own character. "Our character is formed by us as well as for us" by ourselves or others putting us under certain influencing circumstances (Mill, *Works*, 8:840). Men can learn to create themselves and will is the agent of this creation. Moreover, the belief that we have the power to modify our character is the source of the feeling of moral freedom, though consciousness of this freedom is the product of long practice. Choosing right must become habitual. "And hence it is said with truth, that none but a person of confirmed virtue is completely free" (Mill, *Works*, 8:841). The ideal of this habituated will is stability and unity of personality.[11] He admired hs father's and other men's characters for their strength and consistency. Charles Austin, for example, gave him the impression "of boundless strength, together with talent which, combined with such apparent force of will and character, seemed capable of dominating the world."[12]

This interest in strength of character did not stop with individual power but extended to the ideal of improving mankind in general. Mill shared his father's respect for reason. James Mill's "fundamental doctrine was the formation of all human character by circumstances, through the universal principle of association, and the consequent unlimited possibility of improving the moral and intellectual condition of mankind by education" (Mill, *Autobiography*, 109-11). In *An Examination*, John Stuart Mill spelled out in detail how moral education works. The difference between a bad and a good man, he explained, is that the latter's desire for doing right and aversion to doing wrong are strong enough to overcome any other desires or aversions that may conflict with them. The object of moral education is, therefore, to educate the will by exalting to the highest pitch desires and aversions that lead to good and extinguishing those that may lead to evil, while judiciously cultivating and moderating auxiliary desires and aversions. Moral education also requires a clear intellectual standard of right and wrong and firm mental habits (Mills, *Examination*, 285-86). Stated another way, what utilitarians expected from their efforts was regeneration of mankind "from the effect of educated intellect, enlightening the selfish feelings" (Mill, *Works*, 1:113).

Because Mill was concerned with conduct, he was necessarily concerned with responsibility. Believing that men participated in the formation of their own characters, he found them judgeable, though he did not commend merely retributive justice (Mill, *Examination*, 294). In "Utilitarianism," Mill demonstrated faults in the three basic views on punishment: (1) to punish for a person's own good, (2) to punish for the good of others, (3) not to punish because circumstances rather than individuals are responsible for events. His own conclusion was that punishment must be based on utilitarian expediency (Mill, *Works*, 10:252). Punishment is essentially an extension of utilitarian principles of education. In his essay on Coleridge, Mill explained that society has always depended upon "a system of *education*, beginning with infancy and continued through life, of which, whatever else it might include, one main and incessant ingredient was *restraining discipline*."[13]

In Mill we have a philosopher who, accepting the notion that men have the power to alter their natures, nonetheless classes himself among necessarians, whom he considers wrongheaded fatalists. This flexibility permitted

Mill to argue reasonably for the improvement of mankind in a way that appears contradictory in Godwin and Bray. But there is a real question whether one may admit *any* degree of self-direction and not class oneself among free will advocates. Mill approached this problem from the opposite direction; that is, from the direction of fatalism. In "pure, or Asiatic fatalism . . . our actions do not depend upon our desires. Whatever our wishes may be, a superior power, or an abstract destiny, will overrule them, and compel us to act, not as we desire, but in the manner predestined." In what Mill called Modified Fatalism, "actions are determined by our will, our will by our desires, and our desires by the joint influence of the motives presented to us and of our individual character," but because our character has been made for us and not by us, we are not responsible for it, nor for the actions it leads to. "The true doctrine of the Causation of human actions maintains, in opposition to both, that not only our conduct, but our character, is in part amenable to our will," and hence "we are under a moral obligation to seek the improvement of our moral character" by applying motives that will necessitate us to strive for such improvement (Mill, *Examination*, 298–99).

Mill dreaded the fatalist position that eliminates any possibility of man's shaping his own existence. Individually and in the aggregate, man must have a degree of liberty that gives him hegemony over the elements of which he is composed. He must become a well-run state under the governance of the will, itself ably advised by Reason. To achieve this end, Mill had to admit freedom. But by doing so, he opened the door to the abiding claim of free will proponents. If there is *any* liberty of volition, there must be free will. Summarizing this contradiction, Tulloch said of Mill that he

> maintained to the last that character, like all natural phenomena, is born of circumstance; but he allowed for what he called the action of the will upon circumstance, and seemed to himself in this way to discriminate between his doctrine of necessity and the common interpretation of that doctrine as fatalism. But his reserves were merely sentimental; they were forced upon him by the urgency of facts to which he could not shut his eyes. They did not spring from any change in his point of departure; and his system was really fatalistic, whatever he thought of it.[14]

State metaphors were not uncommon in the moral and psychological literature of the time, as we saw in the previous chapter; Herbert Spencer was certainly not reluctant to employ them. Arguing that human traits such as memory, reason, feeling, and will become apparent only when actions cease to be automatic, Spencer concluded that the aggregate of feelings that constitute the mental *I* do not possess a cohesive force, "but the *I* which continuously survives as the subject of these changing states, is that portion of the

Unknowable Power which is statically conditioned in special nervous structures pervaded by a dynamically-conditioned portion of the Unknowable Power called energy."[15] We have seen that for theists this Unknowable Power is simply called God and that his energy operating through man and creating man's unique identity is will. Spencer secularized the mystery without solving it. In the process, however, he added a clarifying point about the will. Rejecting the doctrine of free will in favor of a determinist position, he pointed out that will is not something separate and identifiable, but merely "the general name given to the special feeling that gains supremacy and determines action. . . . Until there is a *motive* (mark the word) there is no Will. That is to say, Will is no more an existence separate from the predominant feeling, than a king is an existence separate from the man occupying the throne" (Spencer, 503). Drawing upon the philosophical tradition at least from Hume's time, Spencer called attention to the danger of accepting terms of discourse as entities themselves. For Spencer, will is simply the name we give to the *condition* of a predominating emotion.

Though exorcising the spirit of will, Spencer nonetheless appreciated the function of that concept. He offered the developmental hypothesis that individuals and communities, like organisms and states, move from homogeneity to heterogeneity. Existence accordingly becomes more conscious of itself. The emergence of the concept of will, as with those of memory, reason, and feeling—similarly hypostatized terms—represents an elevation of humanity. Thus, in stating his "Results" in *The Principles of Psychology* (1855), Spencer claimed that his philosophy did not degrade mind but elevated matter to a level with mind (Spencer, 620).

Like Mill, Spencer felt able to reconcile material determinism and moral freedom. A later writer, W. K. Clifford, used a similar balance to construct a more complicated, even ironic, design. In "Body and Mind" (1874), he argued that the body must be regarded as an automaton. Following Kant, he described freedom of will as that property which enables us to originate events independently of foreign determining causes. An individual does not make all of his own character, but the human race as a whole, through the process of natural selection, fashions itself over the ages. We are responsible for the future of the race because our actions help to determine what it will become. Employing an argument at least as old as Hume's, Clifford contended that to deny determinism is to deny responsibility and leave the way open for a doctrine of destiny or providence "overruling human efforts and guiding history to a foregone conclusion."[16]

Clifford wanted to dispose of providence, God, or a transcendental ego because these powers were absolutes externally determining causes and therefore depriving men of freedom. Man is a free agent only when his actions arise from within himself. Clifford accepted Henry Sidgwick's assertion in *The Methods of Ethics* (1874) that, despite the almost overwhelming cumulative proof of uniformity in human action, one opposing proof supports our sense of freedom—the immediate affirmation of consciousness in the moment of deliberate volition.[17]

This line of argument led Clifford to the surprising conclusion that it is good for men to become more organic, for, although the body is an automaton incapable of physical spontaneity, the energy that moves it originates in one's self, that is, in the living matter of the body. Clifford restated Kant's definition of freedom as the origination of events independently of foreign determining causes and concluded: "The character of an organic action, then, is freedom—that is to say, *action from within.* The action which has its immediate antecedents within the organism has a tendency, in so far as it alters the organism, to make it more organic or to raise it in the scale.[18] For Clifford, man is most free when he is most organic. He was not bothered by the possibility that all of the forces and influences—chemical and otherwise—playing upon his body might quite reasonably be viewed as "foreign" influences. Clifford's view of the self is thus surprisingly naive. He preferred to see each man not only as an island, but *also* as part of the main. It is a curious, not to say devious, argument that asserts man's freedom by eliminating all conscious authority of the will and assigning it to an entity roughly comparable to Spencer's Unknowable Power, now domesticated, however, within the individual.

Also starting from Kant and Hegel, T. H. Green arrived at similar, yet contrasting, conclusions. Green envisioned a universal scheme wherein free individuals contributed to larger social units in a universe pervaded by an eternal spirit in the process of self-development. Like Kant, Green identified will with rationality. In order to become a spring of moral action, he explained, animal desire or aversion must take a new character through self-consciousness, making it a desire or aversion of a conceived state of the self or an object determined by relation to oneself. Reason, as self-consciousness, is thus the condition of moral activity. Any motive thus issuing in action equals will.[19]

Beginning with some of the same Kantian assumptions that inspired Clifford, Green ended by asserting the identification of will not with organic man but with rationality. Nevertheless, Green did not overlook the inevitable bond between body and will, though he concluded that the will *is* the self-conscious man, not merely a force affecting him from without (Green, *Works*, 2:317).[20] Freedom can exist only for one who is free in the sense that he is the subject that makes the object his through presentation to the self from within, not by external determination. In voicing some reservations about Kant's association of freedom with moral good, Green laid out his own position.

But in men the self-realizing principle, which is the manifestation of God in the world of becoming, in the form which it takes as will at best only *tends* to reconciliation with itself in the form which it takes as reason. Self-satisfaction, the pursuit of which is will, is sought elsewhere than in the realisation of that consciousness of possible perfection, which is reason. In this sense the object of will does not coincide with the object of reason. (Green, *Works*, 2:326-27)

Nonetheless, because in the self-conscious and self-realizing subject self-satisfaction is identifiable with the attainment of perfection, the object of the will tends to become the same as that of reason. "It is this that we express by saying that man is subject to a law of his being which prevents him from finding satisfaction in the objects in which under the pressure of his desires it is his natural impulse to seek it" (Green, *Works*, 2:327).

Thus far, will seems limited to the welfare of the individual alone, but Green was also concerned with individual conduct in its social context. It is through self-conscious individuals that a reconciliation of will and reason is effected because such individuals are the media for a self-realizing principle that establishes a conventional morality which then becomes the standard to which other individuals adjust their self-seeking principles, learning to view their actions as part of a scheme of duty which they recognize as binding upon them. They now choose freely to act according to morality (Green, *Works*, 2:330-31).

This secular pattern resembles the Christian scheme we have already examined where the individual soul, becoming self-conscious through free grace, conversion, or revulsion from sin, yields self-will to God, who then acts through it for good. The Christian's will is freed from sin and selfishness to do his duty. In fact, though Green sometimes expounded his scheme in secular terms,he retained its Christian base. In "The Force of Circumstances," (1860) he admitted that the universal pattern of cause and effect makes us appear to be slaves but added that this inescapable chain may bind us to heaven rather than to earth. The mind may be said to be free because, when a combination of circumstances produces an effect on a given state of mind, the effect may be resistance, not submission. Man has a cancelling power in the will, a freedom not to act under the compulsions of circumstance. When force of circumstance no longer separates us from God, our actions will still be bound and we will not fully realize the impulse of "our purified will," but the good result will be our sense of dependence upon God. Generally, men remain subject to circumstance; individuals are slaves of their own passions, and nations "seem to be the victims of uncontrollable destiny."[21] Nonetheless, even if a small minority of men achieve the necessary freedom to act for good, the consequences are momentous. "The spiritual energy of the liberated few introduces an element of good into the force to which the many are subject." Hence the abolition of serfdom, the reconcilement of nations, and the general recognition of personal equality in modern times. The men whose souls Christianity's positive truths have liberated "exercise a negative influence in removing the most oppressive evils from the outward circumstances of life" (Green, *Works*, 3:9–10).

We have seen that Kant was often cited by English moral philosophers on the issue of the will, though they differed in their interpretations of his philosophy. In a response to W. B. Carpenter's *Principles of Mental Physiology* (1874), which we shall have occasion to discuss in a later chapter, Malcolm Guthrie objected to Carpenter's use of the term "automaton," which Clifford had also used to describe the body, because it seemed to mean the same as universal causation and was thus no proper response to materialists' determinism. To elucidate the issue, Guthrie adverted to Kant, identifying free will with Practical Reason, but he thought that "what is so ardently advocated in the claims of Free Will is really Free Choice, or the unobstructed action of the Practical Reason."[22] Claiming to follow Henry Sidgwick, Guthrie distinguished between the classifying powers of the intellect and Practical Reason. In the latter category, under the heading "Muscular Activity as Controlled," he provided the example of a man seeing a glass of wine before him and being impelled to reach for it because he associates it with previous pleasure but then checking that muscular impulse through Practical Reason's judging, for one reason or another, that it is unwise to take the wine (Guthrie, 30–31).

Referring again to Sidgwick's advocacy of free will, Guthrie introduced the idea of Will Motive as the activity concerned in the phenomena of Effort. It is associated with resolution, firmness, obstinacy, and so forth, whereas the Emotion of Will, or Self Control, "derives pleasure from the effectuation of volitions, and pain from failure" (Guthrie, 48). Guthrie concluded that a man in whom reason is predominant but accompanied by self-control or emotion of will guides his conduct mainly by Practical Reason. Since heredity and environment seem to determine character and consciousness is dependent upon bodily states, will is, for Guthrie, an ordinary human activity following the laws of causation.

Guthrie had objected to Carpenter's confusion in the use of key terms, but his own definitions and his naive examples do very little to clarify the free will versus determinism problem. Henry Sidgwick, from whom Guthrie had appreciatively derived some of his notions, was a far more rigorous and influential thinker. J. B. Schneewind praises Sidgwick for his impartiality in evaluating the three methods of ethics he chose to examine: egoistic hedonism, utilitarianism, and intuitionism.[23] Sidgwick's aim in *The Methods of Ethics* (1874) was to show the methods of obtaining reasoned convictions regarding what ought to be done that are discoverable in the moral consciousness of mankind. He did not wish to obscure the main issues of ethical theory with controversial nonmoral positions; nowhere, says Schneewind, is this aversion more strikingly displayed "than in his claim that the issue of freewill and determinism is simply irrelevant to most moral matters" (Schneewind, 207).[24] In opposition to Kant, Sidgwick said that the sense of freedom involves being free to act wrongly or irrationally as much as it involves acting rightly or rationally, but he found no central ethical issue involved. "An act causing a given result will cause it whether the act itelf is determined or free. It is only if we hold the theological view which makes the reward of virtue depend on free choice of virtuous acts that we should think the question of means affected by the issue. In that case determinism would undermine the belief that virtuous acts are means to the reasonable end of one's own good" (Schneewind, 69).

Sidgwick realized that free will was an essential concept for matters dealing with punishment and responsibility but still considered it essentially irrelevant in the study of ethics. Schneewind provides an illuminating contrast between Sidgwick and a major target of his criticism, James Martineau, explaining that their disagreement is significant in understanding Sidgwick. "It is a disagreement over the issue of whether what is central to a moral theory is consideration of the goodness or badness of the character of moral agents, or consideration of the rightness or wrongness of the acts moral agents perform. We have already seen that Sidgwick assumes the correctness of the second alternative in his attempt to show that the freewill issue is irrelevant to ethics" (Schneewind, 247).

Sidgwick was a specialist at leaving suspended and unresolved important matters that other moral philosophers felt compelled to force to a conclusion. Thus, at the end of the *Methods*, he found that the problem of ethics required the truth of a metaphysical or theological proposition asserting the moral order of the universe but saw no way of proving such a proposition. Similarly, he considered theism a belief that impressed itself upon the living mind as essential to normal life but admitted that such a belief was neither self-evident nor demonstrable (Schneewind, 377).

Sidgwick tried to examine fairly the contrasting views of utilitarian and intuitional schools of philosophy and ended by crediting the one with worthy limits to its methods and the other with noble ideas. He wished to maintain a theistic faith without the means to validate it. Some years later, in *The Foundations of Belief* (1895), A. J. Balfour tried to unify what he considered the untenable views of Naturalists (Mill, Huxley, Spencer) and of Idealists (T. H. Green and his school) by proposing a practical faith encompassing both spirit and matter organized upon a theistic base. He objected to Naturalism's appropriation of science and rejected its premise of the law of causation or uniformity in nature, saying that that premise was unsupportable from personal experience.[25] He did not accept the sensationist approach to the self, finding it an inadequate explanation for the continuity of personality. Of the

Idealists, Balfour remarked that while they attributed free will to the individual, they did not exclude determinism except in the sense of external constraint. Men's actions were thus still strictly prescribed by their antecedents. If this was freedom, Balfour said, it was a kind that eliminated responsibility and resembled the overt determinism of naturalism (Balfour, *Foundations*, 151).

Both schools of thought emphasized reason, but Balfour dismissed reason as a trustworthy basis of human operations because authority will also claim to be derived from reason when challenged by reason. By hindsight men convert mere causes into reasons, thus conclusions are more enduring than premises. Balfour distrusted this "historicization" of reason and reasserted the importance of recognizing that much of experience remains surrounded by mystery. Objecting to Spencer's division of the verities which have to be believed into those relating to the Knowable and those relating to the Unknowable, and his assigning the former to science and the latter to religion, Balfour said: "He has failed to see that if the certitudes of science lost themselves in depths of unfathomable mystery, it may well be that out of these same depths there should emerge the certitudes of religion; and that if the dependence of the 'knowable' upon the 'unknowable' embarrasses us not in the one case, no reason can be assigned why it should embarrass us in the other" (Balfour, *Foundations*, 296).

What Balfour proposed is a world ruled by an unknowable deity whose laws we may never fully comprehend but which we may progressively discover through the scientific method, though the more our knowledge advances, the more the hidden God retreats from us. He postulated a rational God in the interests of science and a moral God in the interests of morality. But his justification for man's ethical needs is the commonplace presumption that there must be a region (the hereafter) where moral impulses will be gratified or God never would have called them into being.

In many ways, Balfour's ethical position sounds like a more sophisticated version of Bray's, though Bray emphasized the moral advantage of necessity. Balfour's philosophy demands some form of freedom in man because it is grounded in a belief in human responsibility, yet, for the greater part of his book, Balfour avoided the subject of free will, finally engaging it in a footnote where he argued that will either acts on matter or it does not. If it does, it is either free or determined will. Free will upsets the uniformity of nature, while determined will implies a mechanical view of the world that makes all will redundant. If the will does not act on matter, volition belongs either to a psychic series running parallel to psychological changes of the brain, or it is a superfluous consequence of physiological changes, in which case, humans become no more than automata. Although his arguments throughout tend to endorse a free will that challenges existing theories of the uniformity of nature, Balfour concluded his note ambivalently by complaining, "None of these alternatives seem very attractive, but one of them would seem to be inevitable" (Balfour, *Foundations*, 312).[26]

Balfour and others, as late as the 1890s, felt able to dismiss scientific approaches to ethical and moral problems as inadequate. By contrast, Thomas Henry Huxley, himself a scientist, had marked views about scientific method and the pursuit of truth and believed that he could defend his views philosophically. He wrote a study of Hume basically supporting Hume's position on necessity while clarifying his definition of volition. Opponents of the doctrine of necessity, who championed man's conciousness of freedom, were wrong-headed, Huxley announced. No one denied that man had a sensation of freedom when he acted, as these disputants claimed. "What they really have to do, if they would upset the necessarian argument, is to prove that they are free to associate any emotion whatever with any idea whatever; to like pain as much as pleasure; vice as much as virtue; in short, to prove, that, whatever may be the fixity of order of the universe of things, that of thought is given over to chance."[27]

But if Huxley fundamentally accepted the doctrine of causation, he had the same misgivings that Mill exhibited about necessity. What he believed in was the uniformity of nature. He argued that science brings the realm of matter and law into greater prominence, driving out spirit and spontaneity, but the result, he insisted, is not materialism and the operative power is not something called necessity. "Fact I know; and Law I know; but what is this Necessity, save an empty shadow of my own mind's throwing?"[28] Huxley asserted in "Science and Morals" (1886) that he was neither materialist nor spiritualist, pessimist nor optimist, but simply an agnostic.[29] Earlier, he had declared himself a scientist with the aim of seeing things as they really are in order to improve man and clear away ignorance and misery. Achieving this required a belief that an order of nature exists that is "ascertainable by our faculties to an extent which is practically unlimited," and "that our volition counts for something as a condition of the course of events."[30] Yet his later definition of free will merely described it as the "absence of any restraint upon doing what one likes within certain limits."[31]

Huxley rejected any concept of free will that made of it an uncaused or self-caused phenomenon, yet, like Mill, argued that man could be improved by education, that the educated individual was, in fact, the cornerstone of all social improvement. Education, he said, promotes morality and refinement by teaching men to discipline themselves and by leading them up from the steaming valley of sense.[32] Like Mill, Huxley rejected "Asiatic" renunciation and fatalism, arguing that man improves through consciousness and will; he escapes from the natural state of evolution to create a state of art called society.[33] But Huxley left the chief question unanswered: by what means does he achieve this condition if he is causally determined?

From philosophical argument to practical application of belief in human conduct may be a large and difficult step, but there was a sizable body of literature throughout the century, increasing toward its close, that simplified some of the attitudes and opinions that we have been exploring and applied them to a general and practical purpose. Ralph Waldo Emerson took the step from elite to popular communication with some ease, establishing a firm and extensive reputation at home in the United States and abroad. Emerson vigorously promoted a philosophy that combined fate and free will. We must accept fate, he said, but are no less compelled to affirm liberty. "We are sure that, though we know not how, necessity does comport with liberty, the individual with the world, my polarity with the spirit of the times."[34] Human existence, he said, is composed of circumstance and life. The two interacting create the drama of our experience. "A man's power is hooped in by a necessity which, by many experiments, he touches on every side until he learns its arc." But "if Fate follows and limits Power, Power attends and antagonizes Fate." Through the interplay of his intellect with circumstance, man may learn to master it. "The right use of Fate," Emerson explained, "is to bring up our conduct to the loftiness of nature." Fate is a name for facts not passed through the fire of thought, for causes as yet unpenetrated (Emerson, *Works*, 6:19–31).[35] Life is a constant striving to master fate.

At first, Emerson located the soul within the self, nature being its exteriorization, but he later came to believe that soul was in nature and man was its supreme product. Stephen E. Whicher summarizes Emerson's position. "As a part of nature, man shared in the Soul; as the only conscious part of nature, he even had the special privilege to see and know the Soul within him; but he was no longer prior to or apart from the world around him."[36] Emerson said, "All power is of one kind, a sharing of the nature of the world" (Emerson, *Works*, 6:56). A breath of will blows eternally through the universe of souls toward right and necessity. Emerson called the law of nature a Beautiful Necessity that educates man to "the perception that there are no contingencies; that law rules throughout existence; a law which is not intelligent but intelligence;—not personal nor impersonal—it disdains words and passes understanding; it dissolves persons; it vivifies nature; yet solicits the pure in heart to draw on all its omnipotence" (Emerson, *Works*, 6:49). In his Divinity School Address, Emerson adjusted his terminology in the direction of traditional theism. The world is the product of one will and one mind and the future will be good for the man who sees himself as the conduit through which the will of God flows. This is the old lesson that man's freedom comes through his submission to God's will, manifest for Emerson in the Law of Nature and its Beautiful Necessity. Obedience is freedom.

Unlike many other thinkers on this subject, however, Emerson, like Carlyle, emphasized the role of the strong individual, conflating the concepts of free will and strength of will. "The one serious and formidable thing in nature is a will," he declared, making the will seem almost palpable (Emerson, *Works*, 6:30). When a strong will appears, it is generally the result of concentration. But if the great man's power comes from concentration, the secret of his influence is that his spirit diffuses itself; he is God's agent and emblem. "Will is the measure of power. . . . he alone is strong and happy who has a will. The rest are herds. He uses; they are used. He is of the Maker; they are of the Made." Will is the miraculous presence of God to men.[37]

At a more popular, less reflective level than Emerson's, Samuel Smiles offered a simplified version of the great man philosophy in his extremely successful *Self-Help* (1859), designed at a mundane level to influence conduct rather than to encourage speculative thought. "It is *will*—force of purpose—that enables a man to do or be whatever he sets his mind on being or doing," Smiles asserted.[38] The long history of the free-will controversy signified little to him. "Whatever theoretical conclusions logicians may have formed as to the freedom of the will, each individual feels that practically he is free to choose between good and evil." The entire conduct of life is founded on this conviction. The freedom of our will "is the only thing that is wholly ours, and it rests solely with ourselves individually whether we give it the right or the wrong direction" (Smiles, 197–98). For Smiles, the will is like an engine driving the ship of self through seas of circumstance, habit, and thought; it might as easily run the ship aground as take it safely to harbor. Napoleon's career illustrates the former case, Josiah Wedgwood's and the Duke of Wellington's the latter.

Though acknowledging the thousand subtle influences molding each individual, Smiles considered man unquestionably responsible for himself; he has the power to construct his own character. To the formation of a strong character, perseverance and attention to detail are essential, the concentration of will upon a single object. "Accident," Smiles shrugged, "does very little towards the production of any great result in life" (Smiles, 108). All of this effort he described in secular and even materialist terms, although his opinions were based upon the Christian virtues we have seen presented at more elevated levels elsewhere. Thus Smiles exalted the virtue of self-denial not after Christ's model of self-sacrifice but because it gave strength to character. Victory over ourselves is the highest virtue. But the purpose of Smiles's self-denial is rather different from F. D. Maurice's, for example. Smiles saw it as "the sacrificing of a present gratification for a future good," and his illustrations of this virtue ran to anecdotes of accumulated wealth (Smiles, 247).

To Smiles, "the crown and glory of life is character" (Smiles, 321). A man with strong character and strong purpose is irresistible. Man's highest achievement is to be deemed a True Gentleman, who is characterized by self-respect, politeness, forebearance, kindness, and charity; who has a keen sense of honor and avoids mean actions; who is, above all, truthful and whose law is rectitude (Smiles, 332ff). Wealth is not a requirement for true gentlemanliness, but it is highly likely, according to Smiles, that he will be English or at least of a Northern European race where self-control and aggressiveness are fostered. For Smiles, will is little more than power and force of personality as manifested in daily conduct; accordingly, he considered speculations on freedom and necessity harmful, because much thought and "much of our reading is but the indulgence of a sort of intellectual dramdrinking" (Smiles, 276). The sober, strong-willed man acts.

W. E. H. Lecky championed a refined version of Smiles's program into the twentieth century. Lecky had a more logical and sophisticated mind even when, as in his *The Map of Life: Conduct and Character* (1902), he was appealing to a general audience. Lecky knew enough to settle the matter of free will at the outset. After summarizing the determinist and free will positions, he lent his authority to the free will side. "The conflict between the will and the desire, the reality of self-restraint and the power of Will to modify character, are among the most familiar facts of moral life," he said. Following Sidgwick's fundamental argument, he added that man's feeling of moral responsibility presupposes a free will. "The best argument in its favor is that it is impossible really to disbelieve it."[39]

Lecky's main purpose in *The Map of Life* was to guide his readers to a rewarding life. He warned in a Carlylean way that man's end is not to achieve peace but "to do his duty and tell the truth" (Lecky, 32). He believed that men would gradually become less introspective, concentrating instead upon useful action. His recommendations about the management of character are all familiar ones. To begin with, a man "must avoid the fatalism which would persuade him that he has no power over his nature, and he must also clearly recognize that his power is not unlimited" (Lecky, 235). Lecky cautioned his readers that the power of the will could be capricious and emphasized the importance of self-restraint and self-sacrifice. Will must establish ascendancy over our thinking and help us to cast away morbid trains of thought and to concentrate the mind vigorously on serious subjects (Lecky, 255).[40] Lecky discussed the function of the will in such practical matters as money and marriage. Men and women, for example, should consider their duty when it comes to the propagation of a proper species and not merely yield to impulses of self-gratification. Lecky concluded that success in life depends more upon character than upon intellect or fortune, upon a careful utilization of time, and reasserting his antifatalist position, upon the focusing of attention upon how to live rather than on how to die.

At one point, Lecky connected the theme of free will with the principal subject of his book—the achievement of a virtuous, rather than a merely happy, life.

According to the doctrine of this book, man comes into the world with a free will. But his free will, though a real thing, acts in a narrower circle and with more numerous limitations than he usually imagines. He can, however, do much so to dispose, regulate and modify the circumstances of his life as to diminish both his sufferings and his temptations, and to secure for himself the external conditions of a happy and upright life, and he can do something by judicious and persevering self-culture to improve those conditions of character on which, more than on any external circumstances, both happiness and virtue depend. (Lecky, 267)

Lecky elevated the will to a position of absolute authority, making it the pilot of reason. This was a strange inversion of Kant's philosophy, where will did not operate upon matter, but was identified with Abstract Reason. With Lecky, character was an ideal within the individual's power to fashion and once that character was shaped, it could alter the world. His was a heartening, if unreflective credo.

Many popular versions of this species of philosophy gushed from the presses around the turn of the century at a time when more serious thinkers were struggling with the specters of determinism and pessimism. The American Frank Channing Haddock's *Power of Will* (1907) is one successful example. Haddock openly declared that the will is higher than the mind, that a strong will can even fashion the plastic gray matter of the brain. Haddock asserted more than he analyzed and never really explored the free will controversy; he considered freedom of will a tautology and bondage of will a contradiction in terms and defined Will as "The Power of Self-Direction."[41] Will is free only when self-caused and it is so when it follows the laws of its own being. "Law is the essence of freedom. Whatever is free is so because it is capable of acting out unhindered the laws of its nature" (Haddock, 13). This position weds Clifford's belief that free will emerges from the organic self to the Individualism championed by Stirner and others that became so fashionable in the late nineteenth century as the demands upon imperialist nations were growing more evident and aggressive self-assertion replaced aggressive self-renunciation. For the most part, Victorians spoke of acquiescing in the designs of providence, but Haddock exclaimed that "man's driving force, conquering fate, is the energy of the free Will" (Haddock, 14).

Like Lecky, Smiles, Carpenter, and others, Haddock centered the power of the will in the capacity for sustained attention to a single aim. He offered examples—Napoleon exhibits strong continuous will, Washington exhibits persistent moral resolution, and Jesus incarnates "the will whose law is holiness" (Haddock, 29–30). Much of Haddock's book, which was not a philosophical treatise but a handbook on the formation of character, reiterated a few basic assumptions about will. He recommended systematic exercises and declared, "The law of right Will is the law of the all-round symmetrical character" (Haddock, 77). Revery is a special enemy of the strong will. Most of part 2 of *Power of Will* describes exercises in attention. *"The secret of Will,"* Haddock asserted, *"is anticipation based on memory,"* crudely echoing Hazlitt's far more subtle claim that the province of the will is the future (Haddock, 254).

It is to such maxims that complex arguments about the will were often reduced. In tracts like Haddock's, the will required no explanation but was assumed. For a large number of serious and uncritical nineteenth-century thinkers on this subject who could not accept materialist determinism, human life was pictured as a temporal road down which each individual moved, establishing a history of decisive voluntary gestures and accordingly requiring an agency capable of projecting his or her identity into a future characterized by spatial dimensions. By the turn of the century, this time scheme had been enclosed with the individual and the landscape of the future was less pictorial than psychological. The past was memory, the future anticipation, and will the mysterious master of both.

Will and the World

CHAPTER FIVE

Progress

SPECULATIONS on the existence or nature of free will and its connection with the larger concepts of the self and the self's relationship to a deity or a natural order were often expounded with a concern for practical applications. These practical applications referred not only to individual human conduct but to the human condition in general. Preceding chapters have been concerned mainly with the individual; those to follow take into consideration larger social structures. The next few chapters consider some intellectual areas that reveal how widespread the concern for will, both as freedom of choice and as force of character, was in the nineteenth century.

Issues of free will, determinism, and providence are prominent in the developmental theories so characteristic of nineteenth-century European thought. Increasing popularity of the concept of progress was facilitated by its alliance with notions of human perfectibility. This perfectibility, in turn, generally assumed mankind's power to alter its condition for the better. What has been a providential view of human development was largely secularized through the speculations of philosophers, historians, scientists, and others. Will as free will and as strength of will was promoted as a central force in the achievement of progress. Because Christian values continued to influence much thinking about progress, the familiar paradox of self-suppression as a means to self-fulfillment found expression in theories of progress as well. In England, a substantial body of opinion concluded that the modern Chris-

tian Englishman stood at the pinnacle of progress because he represented
the highest development of will. Of course, there were many sceptical and
dissenting voices, but where progress was accepted, it was generally bound
to some belief in the power of the human will to shape not only man's individual and communal destiny but the character of the material world itself.

~ ~ ~

Development was one guiding concept in nineteenth-century thought.
We have seen that, as the self was increasingly viewed as progressive, time
became a crucial implement for interpreting individual character. Man was
not merely the plaything of humors; he was a being capable of altering his
own nature and his relationship to external nature. This power of transformation, so evident in the technical changes of the early nineteenth century,
affected men's views of history, which also came to be viewed in developmental terms.[1] The individual pattern of infancy, youth, maturity, and senes-
cence was applied to nations and whole cultures, suggesting pessimism to
some, hope to others.[2] At least one thing seemed clear—beyond the rising
and falling of specific nations was the larger pattern of progress. In *The Ascent of Man* (1894), Henry Drummond expressed a widely held conviction
when he declared, "Love is the final result of Evolution." In fact, Drummond
said, the history of the world revealed not evolution but something higher
that he called involution—"the phenomenal expression of the Divine, the
progressive realization of the Ideal, the Ascent of Love."[3]

We shall look at evolution in its scientific aspect later, but in this chapter
we are concerned with the more amorphous concept of progress, which was,
in the nineteenth century, often associated with one or another attitude
toward evolution. Drummond, for example, enlisted himself among the theists who believed that the will behind evolution was a traditional Supreme
Being. The most familiar form of theist faith in the progress of mankind had
its roots in the eighteenth-century concept of providence. By then, advanced
thinkers, though certainly not the common man, had moved beyond the
idea of "particular" providence to one of general providence. God did not
work directly in the affairs of man, but so arranged things that his overall plan
succeeded.[4] Gradually the argument by design became established as a
proof of God's existence—its most authoritative formulation being that of
Bishop Butler. But as science revealed more and more that seemed inconsistent with Scripture, a doctrine of "progressive revelation" emerged and
proofs of God's role shifted from biblical text to "natural theology."[5] Robert
Chambers and James Hutton quietly tried to preserve a role for providence
in their otherwise revolutionary attitudes about geology. George Cuvier,
Louis Agassiz, and Adam Sedgwick, Darwin's teacher at Cambridge, did the
same thing insistently. Sometimes arguments for providence took a strange

form as when Charles Bray wrote in *The Philosophy of Necessity* (1841) that man had progressed slowly so that by the time human population fills the earth it will have had time to achieve moral maturity. This, he said, is the design of providence and shows that the true history of the world reveals positive advancement and progress, justifying the axiom "whatever is, is right."[6] Providence could assume convenient forms as interpreted by different nations. Thus England in the late eighteenth and early nineteenth centuries could find great comfort in the dispositions of the Almighty: "When providence assigned to England the production of a particular raw material, like wool, it must also have assigned to England its processing into woolens. This reasoning was extended to the acquisition of colonies. Providence had staked out for English acquisition and settlement certain overseas areas of the world; the rival claims of other imperialist countries or of the native inhabitants therefore had no standing."[7]

A surprisingly broad range of individuals accepted this attitude. Goodhearted Thomas Hughes wrote to compliment Benjamin Kidd on his *Social Evolution* (1894), which fortified his faith that British occupation of India and Egypt was part of the cosmic order of things.[8] In practice, most people continued to view Providence in very personal terms, a tendency evident in English fiction at least since Defoe's *Robinson Crusoe* (1719). But providential design suggested another pattern for the developmentally minded nineteenth century, a pattern that came to be known as progress. J. B. Bury long ago provided a basic history of the development of this idea through the eighteenth century, indicating that it prospered in company with a belief in man's perfectibility.[9] But according to John Passmore's more recent study, the concept of human perfectibility has seen great variations in western culture. In Greek and Roman thought, individual men could achieve a relative perfectibility, with self-sufficiency as its chief criterion. By contrast, Christians largely rejected the notion of earthly perfection, locating it instead in the life after death. Christianity was forbidden the consolation of neoplatonism, which allowed for a self-perfection that permitted men a return to the One from which they emanated. Christianity was instead obliged to reject earthly perfection because of its belief in a personal God, who, while remaining distinct from it, created the world by an act of the will and controlled it by the manifestation of that will in the form of grace and miracle.[10] For Christians, fallen man could not lift himself. His will was not to function alone and for his own ends; that would be rebellion. Instead, he must put his will in God's service; that was virtuous resignation. Pelagius and his followers, judged heretical by the established church, rejected original sin, freeing man's will to act in his own behalf. Pelagius's belief was a positive version of which monasticism was the reverse, for it assumed that individual men could achieve perfection through asceticism, in effect, the willed renunciation of the will. Mysticism was the highest development of this tendency.

Though fundamentally opposed, Pelagius and Augustine agreed that only two possibilities existed for man: he could perfect himself through his own free will or he could be perfected through God's grace only. In the seventeenth century, a new possibility emerged that humanity might be perfected by the deliberate intervention of human beings (Passmore, 149). From this point on, numerous schemes promoting human perfectibility surfaced, from legislative reform to eugenics. Increasingly, science replaced divine grace as the agent of perfection, which itself became less a question of sinlessness and virtue than of physical, intellectual, and moral excellence. William Winwood Reade was one of the most prominent spokesmen for human perfectibility through science. Like that more famous champion of human progress, Auguste Comte, Reade posited certain distinct stages of civilization; his were the periods of war, religion, liberty, and finally intellect. In this last period, man would achieve perfection, becoming the idea he had called God, mastering the forces of nature.[11] Through science he would become the architect of systems, the manufacturer of worlds. "Man then will be perfect; he will then be a Creator."[12]

It was with the development of man's third alternative for perfectibility that the concept of progress emerged as an explanatory adjunct. Analogies between nations and individuals became familiar and those between seasons and eras in history were revived. The battle of the ancients and the moderns gradually resolved itself into an armed truce between those who acknowledged the superior material achievements of the moderns while retaining their belief in the values of the ancients, and those who believed that both modern morality and technical advance demonstrated the inadequacy of the pagan past. Progress developed slowly into the single most comfortable assumption of nineteenth-century Europe and America.

Late in the nineteenth century, Henry Maine complained that he had never encountered a satisfactory definition of the term "Progress," used to describe any number of political and social movements.[13] Certainly the term meant many things to many people and covered a multitude of contradictions, yet behind the general concept of progress lay a belief in developmental history, the steady advance from one stage to another through time, and the conviction that the human will, either predominantly, or under the supervision of providence, directed that advance. Robert Nisbet claims that J. B. Bury was wrong to deny the concept of progress to the Greeks, who manifested a strong interest in the idea of growth and of wisdom as the understanding of growth.[14] Though he chronicles the tradition of Greek and Roman thought into modern times, Nisbet does not suggest that the classical view of progress resembled the modern view. Christianity involved a monumental transformation in man's way of viewing his progress. As we have seen in discussing perfectibilty, the Christian religion assumed a permanent set of values instituted by God, yet gradually introduced progressive elements, such as the vision of the unity of all mankind, the role of historical necessity, providential design, and an emphasis upon the spiritual perfection of mankind at the millennium. However, Christianity also forecast a degradation of man that called for descent of God in wrath before the establishment of a blessed reign under Christ.

Plenitude and continuity, Nisbet says, are the fundamental attributes of medieval and modern concepts of progress. "By the first is meant the existence in this world of everything, whether actual and in full realization of itself or potential with realization yet to be, that is necessary to the goodness and the capacity for perfection of mankind. From the second, the idea of continuity, springs the equally important proposition that each condition or state of whatever it is we are interested in contains within it the seeds of the next and higher state or condition" (Nisbet, 91). As we have already seen, this form of progress may emphasize man's free will, as Pelagius argued, or the sovereign will of God shaping history through foreknowledge and the illusion of human free will, as Augustine declared. In both cases, though, a will greater than man's directed the overall course of progress though man participated in it. Most nineteenth-century British writers on the subject found this Christian concentration upon teleology difficult to abandon.

With the seventeenth century, western thinkers became more socially minded, shifting to secular patterns of progress, as we have already noticed in the third alternative of perfectibility—improvement of man by social groups. Bossuet's vision of world history reasserted a providential design located in civilized and uncivilized human institutions. Leibniz and Vico also offered progressive schemes based upon providential design expressed through human institutions. Vico's stages of human history were to be imitated with variations by numerous writers in the nineteenth century from Comte to Reade. In Vico's pattern, human society proceeded from a stage of gods and kinglike priests, to feudalism, to people in conflict with aristocracy, after which a new cycle began.

Robert Nisbet, upon whom I have depended for much of this summary, reminds us that "wherever we turn in the eighteenth century, the religious origins of the 'secular' idea of progress are to be discerned" (Nisbet, 222). Yet most of those ideas promoted an individual or communal freedom rather different from the traditional religious notion of submission to divine purpose. For Adam Smith, that freedom was economic; generally it was political, with an increasing emphasis upon moral and intellectual growth after the beginning of the nineteenth century. Eighteenth-century France was the chief source of progressive thought, though the variety of attitudes was bewildering. For example, Voltaire claimed that the progress of mankind would be rapid if wars and religions were abolished, whereas Turgot argued oppositely that with unreason and injustice there would have been no progress, a view frequently repeated later by theists and nontheists alike (Bury, 149).[15]

Many similar contradictions prevent any simple explanation for the steady acceptance of progress as an article of belief. The influential Rousseau, while stressing the untapped potential of individual humans, considered most social groupings pernicious. Man is characterized by his capacity for self-improvement, Rousseau said. His primeval life fostered this capacity but at the same time encouraged his social instincts, which, as they developed, produced the many liabilities associated with civilization (Bury, 181). We have already seen that Rousseau's opinions stimulated and supported rebellious and individualist inclinations so evident in the literature of the late eighteenth and early nineteenth centuries. But another, more accommodating view was represented by the Count de Volney's popular *Ruins of Empire* (1789), which pictured man's failures as the results of his own errors while promising that his power to shape his own fate was potentially superior to his follies and weaknesses.

The German tradition, though emphasizing different features of human experience, also contributed to the growing acceptance of progress as a reality. Kant emphasized the progressive moral improvement of the human species if not of its individual members, and Fichte detailed five stages of history through which man must pass to the final perfection at which he would approximate reason itself (Passmore, 216–17, 232). Fichte saw man approaching freedom asymptotically, always nearing but never entirely achieving it, since such an achievement would mean the entire suppression of nature and instinct by will and reason. As J. B. Bury describes Fichte's scheme for mankind, it is "to reach a state in which all the relations of life shall be ordered according to reason, not instinctively but with full consciousness and deliberate purpose" (Bury, 251). Herder, while endorsing the overall notion of progress, cautioned that it was not a steady and predictable process. Hegel more modestly disclaimed any ability in the philosopher to predict future conditions, though he considered the historical process a matter of local necessity, and, in *The Philosophy of History*, described a universal progress toward freedom culminating in his time as the embodiment of spirit and will in the State, more specifically for Hegel, the Prussian State. In general, the Germans concerned themselves with the logical and abstract nature of these issues, though some, Herder among them, did try to bind a developmental philosophy to specific details of geographical and climatic influences.[16]

In England, early exponents of progress included David Hartley, Joseph Priestley, and Robert Chambers. Priestley saw history as an illustration of the hand of God, early progress being directly under God's control, later progress more under man's own guidance.[17] In *Vestiges of the Natural History of Creation* (1844), Chambers set forth a consistent developmental theory that accepted progress, with all its apparent inequities, as God's design. He argued that there is a natural tendency to improvement in human society and viewed races as stages of humanity's development toward its highest representation in the Caucasian race, a view persisting in later developmental thought, prominent at the end of the century but dating back at least to the theories of Count Gobineau.

It was a historian, however, rather than a philosopher or scientist, who became England's chief representative of the belief in progress. Thomas Babington Macaulay was extremely influential in fixing English belief in progress, not merely because he was a fine narrator and rhetorician but also because in naming progress the key to history, he located its culmination in the English people. However, if Macaulay placed the English in the vanguard of progress in his own day, he did not automatically assume that they would remain there. His famous reference to the New Zealander of the future visiting the ruins of London indicated his reservations on that matter. Moreover, as Rosemary Jann has argued, Macaulay's conception of history and progress was fundamentally deterministic.[18] Despite Macaulay's skepticism, through the nineteenth century Englishmen increasingly accepted this conviction of their racial superiority. The novelist H. Rider Haggard declared in *Allan Quatermain* (1887) that the highest thing was to be an English gentleman, and Benjamin Kidd asserted that the British (and other Anglo-Saxons) were alone fit to rule the lower races. In "Physics and Politics" (1872), Walter Bagehot considered the British the most advanced people because they had achieved power over nature and themselves and were thus morally superior. In Bagehot's account of man's development to his present high state of civilization, self-restraining morality provided a distinct advantage. Thus it was man's ability to assert his will over the impulsive and instinctive that elevated him to a position of power. But Bagehot also cautioned modern men against the survival of the mere assertion of will through force. "The mistake of military ethics," he said, "is to exaggerate the conception of discipline, and so to present the moral force of the will in a barer form than it ever ought to take. Military morals can direct the axe to cut down the tree, but it knows nothing of the quiet force by which the forest grows."[19]

James Hinton, an advocate of moral progress and the cultivation of the heart, offered dubious evidence for human improvement in the story of Lady Godiva. "Could we *imagine* such a thing done by a lady now?"[20] Hinton suggested that all erroneous opposition to progress would disappear if men realized that it is not simply a supercession of bad by good. We must learn instead to see that "everything that *is* is good and needs to be replaced by the opposite, because it is good, and has therefore prepared for the opposite; that progress is spiral and all things are unipolar and demand their opposite."[21]

James Sully, in an extended assault upon the increasing mood of pessimism he perceived in western society—especially in Germany and

England—offered the fact of progress as an antidote. He accepted the notion that progress grows out of conflict and reasoned that the theory of natural selection did not conflict with the idea of progress. Admitting that the world may once have been overwhelmingly miserable, as Schopenhauer asserted, Sully argued that the balance had shifted in modern times. "The gradual accumulation and transmission of knowledge respecting physical nature and human character, and of the various agencies by which the scope of human action may be enlarged, may be said in a sense to underlie all other modes of progress."[22] What sets modern man above his ancestors is greater command of will. "The civilised man unspeakably surpasses his untaught ancestor in knowledge of the sources of good and ill. Not only so, he surpasses him in the function of self-control, in the power of regulating his thoughts and desires as well as his actions."[23] This largely unprovable assertion passed current with many laypersons of the time. Even an acknowledged agnostic, like Eliza Lynn Linton, justified a life of virtuous self-denial "because of the law of moral evolution, which is just as irresistible as that of the physical. . . . It is the Law of Progress—the law under which all creation lives until it changes into that dispersion of forces we call death and disintegration, to be followed by a nobler reconstruction."[24] W. K. Clifford also argued that the basic direction of human effort was toward the suppression of self and the dedication of the individual to the needs of a larger community, thereby ensuring the upward progress of mankind. Accepting the concept of individual free will, he linked it to the moral imperative of responsibility.[25]

A strange contradiction appears at this point in the argument for progress, a contradiction that is widespread and common to otherwise opposed theories. Man's progress is related to his strength of will, itself a consequence of free will (causative, whether dependent upon or independent from deity or necessity), yet this strength of will takes the primary form of self-suppression in favor of a larger community or an ideal (political, social, or religious). Character becomes the denial of self, free will the suppression of the individual will. Many critics noted this paradox. One late example is the Duke of Argyll's criticism of Kidd's *Social Evolution*. The book, he said, asserts "that the freedom of the individual is the mainspring of all progress. Yet it is constantly asserting in the next breath that the reason and intellect of the individual are always at hopeless variance with the collective welfare." This paradox generally manifests itself as well in practical explanations of causation. Kidd's book "looks upon the most extreme and almost savage competition between individuals in the race for life as the one and only cause and source of all improvement in human society, yet it pronounces not less strongly on the supreme value of that ethical agency which is now technically called 'Altruism.' "[26] Added to this contradiction was another already familiar to us in a different context. If progress was the result of natural law and thus necessary, could it also be considered a consequence of free will? Bruce McPherson declares that English liberals of the nineteenth century more frequently valued liberty over equality in their championing of freedom.[27] In the next chapter, we shall see the Great Man theory of history make some effort to accommodate this conflict, but in general, the question was never answered to the satisfaction of any large consensus. At the end of the century, the issue remained unresolved, and John Beattie Crozier attempted to clarify it in *Civilization and Progress* (1885). Political schemes, he wrote, emphasize either society as a whole or the elevation and expansion of the individual. "Accordingly, the watchword of the one is Order, of the other, Progress; of the one, Despotism (more or less disguised perhaps); of the other, Liberty." His own conclusion was that "*the elevation and expansion of the individual is the goal of civilization, the true aim of Government,* as indeed it is the end to which Nature works."[28]

Although nineteenth-century theories of progress were largely secular, a strong spiritual element persisted. With the exceptions we have already noted, until the eighteenth century, the Christian religion emphasized the essentially static nature of the human condition.[29] Aside from memorable transformations brought about after the Creation itself by such events as the Deluge, the Exodus, and the Atonement, mankind could anticipate mainly striking changes—Apocalypse, the Millennium. But with the secular establishment of the developmental view, religion also incorporated a progressive scheme. One important feature of this scheme was, of course, the conviction that God's providence shaped human destiny. If that destiny was progressive, then so must God's purpose be.[30]

By the last quarter of the nineteenth century, religious progress had adopted and transformed historical, social, and political forms of progressive thought. William Boyd Carpenter wrote in *The Permanent Elements of Religion* (1889) that Progress, along with Dependence and Fellowship, were the three essential elements of religion. Dependence and Fellowship were traditionally accepted elements, but Progress was a relatively novel ingredient which "expresses belief in the forward and upward movement of creation, the belief in personal spiritual progress, and the conviction that not for ourselves alone do the wheels of time move forward, but that they bear all things onward to an age in which the children of men shall be blessed."[31] Only Christianity manifested all three. Carpenter quoted approvingly from John Fiske's *The Destiny of Man* (1884), accepting Fiske's theory that evolution moves through physical, psychical, and moral stages, and his evidence that war "has passed through changes clearly manifesting a movement in a higher direction," and thus proving a divine purpose in evolution.[32]

Fiske was an outright evolutionist who put Darwin to Christian work. The Darwinian theory, he said, "shows us distinctly for the first time how the creation and perfecting of Man is the goal toward which nature's work has all the while been tending."[33] What characterizes man is his improvability.

Fiske admitted that man's improvement in justice and kindness had been very gradual, as had been his growth away from violent strife, but he was hopeful for the future. "The ape and the tiger in human nature will become extinct" (Fiske, 103). Moreover, Fiske found it incredible that, being the object of divine care, man's career would culminate in material existence and concluded that "the more thoroughly we comprehend that process of evolution by which things have come to be what they are, the more are we likely to feel that to deny the everlasting persistence of the spiritual element in Man is to rob the whole process of its meaning" (Fiske, 115–16).

Benjamin Kidd based his entire theory of progress in *Social Evolution* (1894) on the supposition that it was powered largely by Christian impulses, which he opposed to the selfishness of what he called reason. Though little inclined to easy optimism, Kidd presented the superiority of modern civilization as a consequence of man's greater capacity for self-control. Progress itself, he believed, "is a necessity from which there is simply no escape, and from which there has never been any escape since the beginning of life."[34] Against the position represented by Rousseau, Spencer, and Buckle—that reason and conscious choice influenced man's social progress—Kidd insisted that man's social progress "was beyond doubt the result of the conditions of his life, and was made under force of circumstances over which he had no control" (Kidd, 42). Reason, Kidd said, urges man to individualism, not to subordination. The interests of the individual and the social organism—which, like individuals, has definite laws of health and development—are inescapably antagonistic. For Kidd, human history was "the extraordinary spectacle of man, moved by a profound social instinct, continually endeavouring in the interests of his social progress to check and control the tendency of his own reason to suspend and reverse the conditions which are producing this progress" (Kidd, 82). Man's continued progress depends not on increased power of reason but on his becoming more and more religious (Kidd, 245). Social efficiency determines superiority of race, and because the Englishman is notable for his character, probity, humanity, and integrity—in short, his Christianity—he is the natural administrator of inferior peoples. "English rule has tended more and more to involve the conscientious discharge of the duties of our position towards the native races. We have respected their rights, their ideas, their religions, and even their independence to the utmost extent compatible with the efficient administration of the government of the country" (Kidd, 317).

D. P. Crook describes Kidd's *Principles of Western Civilization* (1902) as "a manifesto endorsing an evolutionary teleology against the Darwinian version of evolution as random process. It celebrated purpose as against happenstance."[35] But it was a preordained purpose. Much as Kidd opposed Buckle's theory of progress as the result of man's intellect, he agreed with

Buckle's determinism. As these and other conflicting notions about progress matured and discussion came to involve political institutions, a major issue for a long time hovering just below the surface of dispute emerged openly. As J. B. Bury puts it: "The political question as to the due limits between government and individual freedom was discussed in terms of Progress: is personal liberty or state authority the efficient means of progressing? The metaphysical question of necessity and freewill acquired a new interest; is Progress a fatality, independent of human purposes, determined by general, ineluctable, historical laws?" (Bury, 314).[36]

Kidd's version of progress resembled that of other social theorists like Victor Cousin in honoring Christianity as the highest achievement of human effort; it thus mimicked the providential schemes that we examined earlier. Other adherents of progress placed more value on individual secular institutions. Renan declared that the state was the machine of progress. Saint-Simon and Comte envisioned human progress as best secured in the hands of enlightened savants. Mazzini, influenced by the teachings of Herder and Saint-Simon, remained sympathetic to the providential view but saw nations as the agents of progress. William L. Langer says of this position, "Nationality is the role assigned by God to a people in the work of humanity. It is its mission, its task on earth, to the end that God's thought may be realized in the world."[37] Mazzini accused Carlyle of denying the role of providence in history by rejecting the valuable consequences of the French Revolution, because to Mazzini providence signified progress through the realization of individual and national liberty.[38] J. S. Mill, also thinking of progress as a movement toward greater liberty, found himself in a quandary ultimately expressed in his chapter "The Stationary State," where he had to concede that the object of progress could not be progress itself but must ultimately result in a social system in equilibrium, hence no longer progressing.

If most sentiment in western Europe in the nineteenth century endorsed some theory of progress, there was no lack of cautionary voices. Nietzsche, for example, rejected progress as superstition, emphasizing instead what amounts to a catastrophic theory of human development. The will of the superman overrules the apparent necessity of natural law; he creates himself through his own choice. Moreover, from midcentury on, and especially in France, a belief that Europe was experiencing a decadent rather than a progressive development gained impetus.[39] Some commentators failed to see any evidence of progress. James F. Stephen considered enthusiasm for progress rather odd and drew attention to current theories that warned against too easy an acceptance of unhindered progress.[40] Not sanguine about the enthusiasms of his day, James Anthony Froude also questioned the common opinion that his was an era of progress. He repeated Rousseau's caveat that civilization may be corruptive as well as constructive and wryly noted that he himself saw little improvement in the clergy, education, or government. Popular government, that sets one self-interest against another, "may be called progress, but it is a public confession of despair of human nature."[41] What the world called progress, Froude called change, though he admitted a genuine increase of human command over external things and commended the scientific attitude for its devotion to a high purpose instead of to self. Real progress, he said, would produce citizens growing purer, more just, and more intelligent. He saw no signs of such a movement in human affairs.

Jacob Burckhardt disputed any signs of intellectual or moral progress in the modern world. What moderns regard as moral progress is, he said, the domestication of individuality through the versatility and wealth of culture and by the vast increase in the power of the state over the individual. He dismissed theories of historical progress simply as new versions of the old Christian idea of Special Providence.[42] Unlike Burckhardt, Heinrich von Treitschke, considered the State positively as embodiment of the will to power but nonetheless shared Burckhardt's belief that moral progress was an illusion. The progress of culture may raise the ethical standard of mankind, he said, though it cannot improve the individual, "for man is not controlled by intelligence but by will, of which intelligence is only the servant, and therefore we cannot make it the measure of moral progress."[43] In an impressively mature and objective study, considering its nearness to the issues, Robert Mackintosh argued in 1899 that evolutionary progress could not be taken for granted and that morality and Christianity were still required as safeguards to civilization. The theory of improvement through struggle was insufficient.[44]

Sir Henry Maine expressed his doubts about a general theory of progress cautiously, confining his appreciation of it to what he called the Aryan people. "The natural condition of mankind (if that word 'natural' is used) is not the progressive condition," Maine wrote in "The Age of Progress" (in his *Popular Government*). "It is a condition not of changeableness but of unchangeableness" (Maine, 170). Nonetheless, Maine's principal historical concern was with progress, so much so that J. W. Burrow claims that this concern prevented Maine "from attempting to understand, rather than isolate and condemn, the irrational, popular elements in his own society."[45] Maine was not an evolutionist but focused on the development of institutions. In "The Age of Progress" and elsewhere, he cautioned against too fervently pursuing legislative change, warning that it was an error to identify the advances of science with political "progress" (Maine, 145). Like Maine, Sir Arthur Balfour believed that progress was an exceptional, not a common feature of human history.[46] He asked why the western world should not decay like others. His answer was a hope for the combination of science and industry to improve mankind by improving the conditions of its existence, a view championed as well by figures such as W. W. Reade, Benjamin Kidd, and H. G. Wells.

True reformers had to deal with the question of progress, because, as Patrick Brantlinger has noted, the idea of progress suggested a machine tending itself, whereas the idea of reform suggested that the machine required tending (Brantlinger, *Spirit*, 258). Brantlinger also notes that from a political point of view progress could be seen either as the result of free trade and middle-class industry or as the emergence of the unprivileged into prosperity and respectability (Brantlinger, *Spirit*, 237). J. B. Bury's summary puts the entire issue of progress in the context of a dialectic between the constructive idealists and socialists and the more cautious type that believes in gradual but prolonged movement toward harmony and happiness. The former advocates depend upon a symmetrical system in which the authority of the state is preponderant; the latter emphasize individual liberty (Bury, 236–37).

Despite the commonplace assumption that most intelligent—and not so intelligent—people in the nineteenth century endorsed the concept of progress, there is abundant evidence that a large body of skeptical thought either rejected this concept altogether or seriously modified it. Similarly, though progress is generally associated with technological and social improvement, we have seen that it was rapidly assimilated by champions of moral and religious beliefs. But whether viewed as secular or religious, progress generally implied a teleology and invariably led back to certain central questions. Was progress the result of man's free effort, or the playing out of a predetermined scheme? Did progress increase man's freedom, or appropriate that freedom to a communal function? Underlying one of the most influential "myths" of the nineteenth century is still the rudimentary dilemma—has man free will or not? Does he create his own destiny or act out a role in a long-since-written drama? In an age fascinated by polarities and dualities, the abiding opposition of free will and determinism permeated all critical issues. Progress was only one concept where this opposition surfaced time and again. As we shall see in the next chapter, many nineteenth-century historians found themselves similarly concerned with this crucial theme.

CHAPTER SIX

History

APPROACHES to history in nineteenth-century England may be
roughly divided into two schools—the theistic or providential, and
the positivist or scientific. For simplicity's sake, I have identified
Thomas Carlyle as representative of the former and Henry Thomas Buckle of
the latter. Many assumptions separated these two schools, but fundamental
to their dispute was a different perception of human freedom and of the
nature of the laws governing the universe. One school asserted free will and,
in its more theistic manifestations, a retributive pattern of moral law. The
other perceived men in statistical terms and confined its theories to laws of
cause and effect.

This chapter offers opinions about history and the writing of history as
expressed mainly by historians themselves. There is no attempt to analyze
individual historical texts, tempting as that has been. Mainly, I want to show
how significant the concept of free will was in the nineteenth-century impulse to interpret human action through the shaping power of narrative.

~ ~ ~

Progress was one of the abiding concerns of nineteenth-century thinkers,
whether they accepted or rejected it as a reality. Historians generally felt
obliged to express themselves on the subject. But the issue of will affected
historians in other ways as well. "History is made up of human actions,"

wrote Goldwin Smith in the consequential year of 1859 and added: "Whatever there is in action, therefore, will be everywhere present in history; and the founders of the new physical science of history have to lay the foundations of their science in what seems the quick-sand of free will."[1] Smith then canvassed the ways in which these historians dealt with the free will versus necessity conundrum, summarizing positions that we have already covered and others that will appear in this chapter.

There were at least two clearly definded approaches to history during the nineteenth century in England. One was empirical, concerned with facts and the documentation of events; the other, endorsed by Smith, assumed the existence of a providential design guiding human activities.[2] Two major figures represent the opposed camps, Henry Thomas Buckle and Thomas Carlyle. Buckle, influenced by Comte and the Belgian statistician Quetelet, believed a science of history was possible based on Progress he took for granted. His *History of Civilization in England* (1857-61), which sought to investigate the causes of progress, became the center of controversy because Buckle claimed a great deal for his statistical method of arriving at general conclusions, convinced as he was that social phenomena are as regular as natural phenomena. His opponents included those who accepted the concept of progress, those who deplored his atheism, and those who defended free will against his determinist assumptions.

John Mackinnon Robertson, who carefully examined Buckle's and Buckle's critics' views, explained that Buckle "was proposing, albeit only broadly and not in systematic detail, to begin the reduction of all human affairs to the principle of natural law."[3] Buckle's approach was secular and consciously free of theological premises. Human events arose from two actions—that of external phenomena on the mind and that of mind upon phenomena. The former dominated early, and the latter mature, stages of civilization. All progress in civilizaton resulted from additions to knowledge, not from direct moral teaching.[4] Buckle put aside the whole metaphysical and abstract approach to free will, Robertson said, and treated will instead as "a term of a sequence like any other, peculiar only in respect of its antecedents and activities."[5] In doing so, he followed one of the principal philosophical traditions deriving largely from Hume.

Robertson's object was to vindicate Buckle's method. Admitting that Buckle did not express himself clearly and consistently enough, he considered many of Buckle's critics unfair, reading him incorrectly or from their own specialized areas. Robertson claimed that no one ever proved Buckle wrong in principle and that his method of taking large numbers of individuals and treating them statistically in relation to the influence of geographical location or causal events was workable. Nonhistorians and historians such as G. H. Lewes, Herbert Spencer, Sir Herbert Maine, and E. B. Tylor were similarly eager to prove that the actions of men and societies were subject to natural laws.[6] The tradition of history as an empirical record of fact resembled the utilitarian approach, but there were significant differences. John Stuart Mill himself, dissatisfied with utilitarian accounts of human motives, sought meaning in the philosophy of history, which offered a concept of development and improvement without having to employ a supernatural agency.

It was specifically a supernatural agency, in the form of providence, that constituted the source of energy for the competing philosophy of history best represented by Thomas Carlyle. Carlyle acknowledged an indwelling purpose in human events but was nonetheless especially acute in noting the limits of historians. He saw history as a manifestation of the human impulse to narrate, though he realized that all narration was ultimately a distortion of an unrecoverable reality.[7] Not only is evidence of past events unreliable, narration is itself incapable of approximating the complexity of experience—"so all Narrative is, by its nature, of only one dimension; only travels forward towards one, or toward successive points: Narrative is *linear*, Action is *solid*. Also for our 'chains,' or chainlets, of 'causes and effects,' which we so assiduously track through certain handbreaths of years and square miles, when the whole is a broad, deep Immensity, and each atom is 'chained' and complected with all" (Carlyle, 27:89). Historical narration must ever be an approximation of a past transaction and can never re-create the real historical transaction. In this sense, Carlyle was always inclined to "fictionalize" the past. Furthermore, because he distrusted narrative itself, he promoted the certainty of individual being.[8] Thus the prominent individual in the form of the great man becomes the guidepost to history.

Carlyle wrote "On History" long before Buckle published his statistically based *History of Civilization in England* but had the similarly mechanistic and mathematically minded utilitarians in mind when he objected to their treatment of man as a numerical factor. "Social Life is the aggregate of all the individual men's lives who constitute society; History is the essence of innumerable Biographies" (Carlyle 27:85). Out of individual records by and about individual men, winnowed by the process of memory and forgetting, the process of accident correcting accident (presided over by an "aimful Power"), a suitable result emerges. "History, then, before it can become Universal History, needs of all things to be compressed."[9]

Carlyle placed his trust in a larger purpose working in human events. "The Universe, I say, is made by Law; the great Soul of the World is just and not unjust. Look thou, if thou have eyes or soul left, into this great shoreless Incomprehensible: in the heart of its tumultuous Appearances, Embroilments, and mad Time vortexes, is there not, silent, eternal, an All-just, an All-beautiful; sole Reality and ultimate controlling Power of the Whole?"[10] But the law Carlyle saw in nature was not the law of the utilitarians, Buckle, and others.

Like many of his contemporaries, Carlyle favored emotion and intuition over reason. He understood the degree to which human emotion could alter the manner in which men viewed the past. He considered struggle as a certainty and also as a strong focus for emotions. Thus the past often became, for him, a record of the opposition of an individual will to some contending force. This interest in men of powerful will was a reflection of Caryle's own often-remarked self-will.[11]

It is possible to view Carlyle, as Philip Rosenberg has done in *The Seventh Hero*, as a man unsure of anything *but* the self. At the same time, it is that very self he distrusts, longing instead for a higher power that governs all. "Carlyle is less afraid that the universe is fundamentally a 'dead, immeasurable Steam-engine,' " Rosenberg says, "than he is afraid that it is fundamentally nothing but a projection of himself."[12] Eloise M. Behnken alters this emphasis. Quoting Carlyle's remark "the world of Nature, for every man, is the Phantasy of Himself; this world is the multiplex 'Image of his own Dream,' " she argues that it represents a positive view. "Work as the expression of man's creative imagination lends a subjective quality to the surroundings because man makes things that are uniquely his. This subjective quality leads to emotional satisfaction both because man has something that belongs to him and because he is secure in what has become 'home' instead of a hostile universe."[13] In any case, for Carlyle, man was himself the experimental ground for moral truth. Thus the model for political governance must be the individual's command of the polity of the self. Carlyle said of Abbot Samson, "There is in him what far transcends all apprenticeships; in the man himself there exists a model of governing, something to govern by! There exists in him a heart-abhorrence of whatever is incoherent, pusillanimous, unveracious—that is to say, chaotic, *un*governed; of the Devil, not of God" (Carlyle, 10:88). The self, in its power of will and suppression of self through will, becomes the model of man's dealing with phenomenal existence, while his imagination, his capacity to discover the true laws behind appearances, is itself a proof of the essential unreality of human events. History becomes a record of conflicting good and evil, will and necessity—just as this conflict is the record of individual life.

In "Characteristics" (1831), at the beginning of his career, Carlyle caught the rising sense of a renewed contest between advocates of free will and of rationalist necessarianism. He was familiar with the terms that the Germanico-Coleridgean and Locke-Hartley-Bentham schools of philosophy (as Mill described them) employed. He saw where the precept and equivocations of the time were tending.

Goodness, which was a rule to itself, must not appeal to Precept, and seek strength from Sanctions: the Freewill no longer reigns unquestioned and by divine right, but like a mere earthly sovereign, by expediency, by Rewards and Punishments: or rather, let us say, the Freewill, so far as may be, has abdicated and withdrawn into the dark, and a spectral nightmare of a Necessity usurps its throne; for now that mysterious Self-impulse of the whole man, heaven-inspired, and in all sense partaking of the Infinite, being captiously questioned in a finite dialect, and answering, as it needs must, by silence,—is conceived as non-extant, and only the outward Mechanism of it remains acknowledged: of Volition, except as the synonym of Desire, we hear nothing; or "Motives," without any Mover, more than enough.[14]

Carlyle could not deny necessity, but he conceived it as accommodated to free will. He urged men to transform mechanical necessity into spiritual duty through renunciation and obedience.

Our Life is compassed round with Necessity; yet is the meaning of Life itself no other than Freedom, than Voluntary Force: thus have we a warfare; in the beginning, especially, a hard-fought battle. For the God-given mandate, *Work thou in Welldoing*, lies mysteriously written, in Promethean Prophetic Characters, in our hearts; and leaves us no rest, night or day, till it be deciphered and obeyed; till it burn forth, in our conduct, a visible, acted Gospel of Freedom.[15]

In his essay on "Count Cagliostro" (1833), Carlyle indicated that each man's life resembles a literary composition, focusing on the warfare of Will-strength against Fate. Thus, "the history of an Original Man is always worth knowing" because "will incarnated in a creature of like fashion with ourselves" is so magnificent.[16] Carlyle's interest in free will was bound up with an equally powerful interest in will as the source of action, especially through self-command. The model of triumphant self-command is the hero who instinctively knows not to strive against the underlying realities of human existence but to serve as a conduit for them. His true struggle is against the false impediments of superficial laws created by men. The hero is as great in his refusal to submit to human rules as he is in his submission to the eternal laws of the universe. Moreover, any man may imitate the action of the hero. In doing so, he follows not the hero but the hero's example, rejecting the falseness of human institutions and submitting his will instead to nature's laws. This is the familiar pattern of Christian submission with natural laws standing in for God's will. Extended to the level of political ideology, Carlyle's scheme "takes as its highest ideal a continuous openness to historical action"; it is "a doctrine of permanent revolution."[17] This permanent revolution is not necessarily an overt action but a willingness to adjust the human will to necessity. History is the human account of this conflict.

But Carlyle's conception of history posed problems for the historian. Whereas Macaulay could compose his narratives with a confidence in *events* and their causal relationships, Carlyle's view of experience was too complex for such simple story telling. John D. Rosenberg summarizes his difficulty.

> That no event occurs in isolation but is part of all other events over time and space poses informational, syntactic, and stylistic problems so formidable that in theory history cannot be written, or can be written and understood only by God—conclusions Carlyle later reached in 'On History'. But in practice the historian, like the writer of fiction, circumvents this 'almost incurable defect' in narration by striving to re-create the whole nexus of circumstances— physical, psychological, temporal—of which a given 'event' is only the topical manifestation. Hence Carlyle describes an event as a *"superficies"*, the outermost surface or facet of a vastly larger configuration.[18]

Carlyle felt that his style had to capture the feeling of his world view, hence the complexities of a *Sartor Resartus* and the deviously successful manipulations of tense and narrative voices in *The French Revolution*. Although the later chapters of this book will deal with style in fiction, it is worth noting that an anomalous figure like Carlyle was fully conscious of the relationship of his philosophy to the clothing it wore.

Owen Chadwick comments in *The Secularization of the European Mind in the Nineteenth Century* on the nineteenth-century phenomenon of determinist history, which he describes as a product of the prestige of science and the emergence of statistics as a tool of the social sciences. Before this, history was chiefly viewed as being about people, afterward about laws governing human behavior. Chadwick points to the paradox that troubled historians throughout the century. History owed its new flowering to the Romantic emphasis on sympathy, imagination, and intuition. The Romantics championed individualism and freedom. But the new materialist science of history contradicted that freedom. The old contest between freedom and law took on its characteristic nineteenth-century form in the field of history as well.[19]

Chadwick's generalizations simplify the situation. The Romantics had their own ideas about the strictures of law upon individual freedom and there were determinist historians—like Macaulay—before the new "science" of history developed. Nonetheless, the underlying opposition of individual freedom and governing law was certainly a central concern for historians, though no more so than for other intellectuals, as I hope this study demonstrates.

In England, the chief exponent of the new science was Henry Thomas Buckle. The general introduction to his *History of Civilization in England* (1857-61) in effect threw down the gauntlet to traditional historians. Here Buckle speculated that the concepts of free will and predestination arose from the doctrines of Chance and Necessary Connexion. He assumed that "in the ordinary march of society, an increasing perception of the regularity of nature destroys the doctrine of Chance, and replaces it by that of Necessary Connexion. And it is, I think, highly probable that out of these two doctrines of Chance and Necessity there have respectively arisen the subsequent dogmas of Free Will and Predestination."[20] Free will is a development by metaphysicians and predestination by theologians. Buckle said that these dogmas "supply a safe and simple solution of the obscurity of our being," but they have corrupted knowledge and disturbed society by fostering animosities between religious sects. A scientific historian need accept neither of these beliefs; in fact, he should depend not upon preconceived systems of belief but upon accurate observation. "Rejecting, then, the metaphysical dogma of free will, and the theological dogma of predestined events, we are driven to the conclusion that the actions of men, being determined solely by their antecedents, must have a character of uniformity, that is to say, must, under precisely the same circumstances, always issue in precisely the same results." All variations in the results will be "the fruit of a double action; an action of external phenomena upon the mind, and another action of the mind upon the phenomena" (Buckle, 14-15). External phenomena and the human mind obey natural laws. By careful observation, these laws may be discovered. This is the true object of the philosophical historian.

Many historians in England were to endorse Buckle's emphasis upon law in history, but few were willing to jettison free will. James Fitzjames Stephen, who also believed it possible to discover laws to regulate human society and who praised Buckle for his intellectual and moral courage, argued that "without free will, science would be useless as a guide for social planning and political action."[21] Stephen offered the traditional contention that without free will there could be no responsibility and hence no basis for correcting human behavior. Moreover, he felt that Buckle's claims for a science of history were exaggerated and acutely argued that the motion of law in physical nature was merely a metaphorical description of regularity.

Goldwin Smith, with whom we opened this chapter, was an early opponent of Buckle's, but he also separated himself from the tradition represented by Carlyle. To him, a philosophy of history was impossible until men "thoroughly felt the unity of the human race. That great discovery is one which rebukes the pretentions of individual genius to be the sole source of progress, for it was made not by one man, but by mankind" (Smith, 9). We have already seen that Smith believed in free will and, like Stephen, stressed the significance of human responsibility. Therefore, to him, Buckle's trust in statistics was a major source of error. "Social and criminal statistics are most valuable," he conceded; "the commencement of their accurate registration will probably be a great epoch in the history of legislation and government; but the reason why they are so valuable is that they are not fixed by necessity, as the Necessarians allege or insinuate, but variable, and may be varied for the better by the wisdom of governments" (Smith, 18). Smith also asserted unequivocally that "a complete induction from the facts of history is impossible. History cannot furnish its own inductive law" (Smith, 19). He similarly rejected historians who claimed to perceive a design in history made up of progressive stages. ("How can M. Comte tell that the 'Positive' era is the end of all? How can he tell that the three stages he has before him are anything but a mere segment of a more extensive law?" [Smith, 20].) He warned about crediting metaphorical structures in history, especially the human analogy of youth-maturity-age. He dismissed the theory of nations as stereotypes of ideas and excluded special providence.

Smith believed that history did exhibit moral, intellectual and material progress, and he stipulated "the formation of character by effort" as the end and key of history; hence "effort is the law, if law it is to be called, of History" (Smith, 40, 55). Believing that human justice was identical with divine justice, he did not arrogate to himself a final knowledge of human character. Scientific history seeks authority through analogies with physical science, but the historian who regards history as "the manifestation and improvement of human character through free action is in suspense for want of some sounder and more comprehensive account of human character than has yet been supplied" (Smith, 73).

James Anthony Froude offered an intelligent defense of the Carlylean position, while dismissing the scientific school of history as represented by Buckle. For Froude, the chief flaw in Buckle's system was his inclusion of humanity as subject to the same laws that operate upon the rest of nature, thus making man one more object in a determinist pattern. In fact, said Froude, it is precisely in the doings and characters of human beings that the otherwise rigid laws of nature cease to operate. "In all other things, from a given set of conditions the consequences necessarily followed. With man, the word 'law' changed its meaning: and instead of a fixed order, which he could not choose but follow, it became a moral precept, which he might disobey if he dared."[22] If man is free to choose, he becomes unpredictable and the word 'science' may no longer be applied to the study of his actions. Conversely, if there *is* a science of man, it means that he has no freedom and praise and blame—two important elements in the record of history— become "impertinent and out of place" (Froude, 15-16). But history cannot be a science anyway, Froude argued, because the "facts" upon which it is based come to us from fallible human beings and we must inevitably make a selection from those "facts," thereby creating our own individual designs of what the past may have been. Froude repeated a question attributed to Napoleon—"What is history . . . but a fiction agreed upon?" (Froude, 22) Here we have an obvious echo of Carlyle's distrust of historical narrative and his attempt instead to render vivid the moral significance, not the literal order, of past events. Froude offered his own condensation of Carlyle's practice. "One lesson, and only one, history may be said to repeat with distinctness: that the world is built somehow on moral foundations; that, in the long run, it is well with the good; in the long run, it is ill with the wicked" (Froude, 22).[23] Ultimately, history is addressed less to man's intelligence, Froude claimed, than to his higher emotions, for man's nature will remain a mystery unresolvable by intellect (Froude, 35–36).

Charles Kingsley's *The Limits of Exact Science as Applied to History* (1860) was a restatement of the Carlylean position aimed specifically at scientific historians. These historians, arguing for invariable, immutable, and inevitable laws of history, "blink the whole of the world-old argument between necessity and free-will," Kingsley said.[24] In fact, he contended, the laws of nature compete against one another and man is capable, through his free will, of interfering with those laws as well as the laws of his own nature. Like Carlyle, Kingsley declared that no one can trace the laws of any given progress of events in history because the evidence is partial and contradictory. Like him, he asserted that history is the record of individual men and women, not of masses. The unpredictability of genius cannot be accounted for, and it is the genius rather than the little man who represents the human norm. Moreover, the demoniac element in human nature continually disrupts the apparently regular laws of historical progress. James Martineau, a far more sophisticated thinker than Kingsley, later supported this view, arguing in *The Seat of Authority in Religion* (1890) that history was not merely a pattern of straightforward causation but consisted of paroxysms of change and emergences of outstanding individuals, all showing God working through history. Nature, he said, falls back to an account of "the highest Will." "God is not only in nature, which spreads the scene of history, and in mankind, as natural objects belonging to the furniture of that scene; he is also in those higher endowments of our humanity which transcend the zoologic limits, and enable us to become the actors in history, and to perform its parts."[25]

For Kingsley, the laissez-faire and French Socialist schools of political economy were wrong to dismiss free will, making man the product of circumstance; the French he found self-contradictory in urging that man, lacking free will, nonetheless establish the circumstances that create and thus improve him (Kingsley, 38–39).[26] Free will is at the very core of human progress. Because he is free, man is responsible; because he is responsible, he has a conscience; for Kingsley, the "true subjective history of man is the history not of his thought, but of his conscience; the true objective history of man is not that of his inventions, but of his vices and his virtues" (Kingsley, 55). Nonetheless, Kingsley also acknowledged the existence of laws, order, and progress in history, the most prominent law being retribution—that righteousness will be rewarded and unrighteousness punished. He defines history as "God educating man" (Kingsley, 62).

Kingsley's mentor, F. D. Maurice, was less a historian than a theologian, but his view of history coincided with Carlyle's. Maurice was intensely religious but relatively unconcerned with the 'scientific' details of history. He wrote to his son in 1862 that history, like Scripture, was a revelation of some portion of the Divine mind through facts, and he defended all historical criticism insofar as it tested facts and reverenced them.[27] But earlier, in his sermon on "The Divine Interpretation of History" (1851), Maurice warned that we cannot read history expecting to follow the triumph of a single set of persons. The Hebrew nation, for example, was not specially privileged but simply a model of all history, which must begin with "the belief that there is an Absolute will to all good—an eternal Truth, a living Person—at the foundation of it."[28] History's real purpose is not to chart the career of a selected population but to find evidence of Christ as Lord and King of mankind. To do this, historians must be able to link past to future and determine the patterns of causation. God inspires us with a desire to search out the truths he has concealed from us. Through the gradual disclosure of historical facts, we reveal his design. Maurice hoped that something better than the destiny of ancient as well as modern annalists would become clear as the force governing events. To him that force was "a Will which is compatible with freedom, and which awakens it." Recognizing that will might compel historians "to dread every deviation from truth as no less mischievous to the poetical consistency of their narrative, than to its moral significance." Such a belief will lead to the conviction that, however the design for which a nation exists may have been perverted and concealed by its self-will, that design "will not be sought in vain by the faithful student, and may be fulfilled, within his own sphere, by the faithful citizen."[29]

In championing the pursuit of fact in history, Maurice defended Scripture as history despite its numerous "mistakes," explaining that such circumstantial faults did not affect the Bible's historical reality and veracity. Scriptural texts were not scientific manuals requiring factual precision but revelations of the relationship between God and man that could be conveyed equally by literal or parabolic means.[30] Maurice's attitude echoes Carlyle's distrust of historical facts, a distrust that left him free to create the dramatic scenes of *The French Revolution* without considering that he had falsified the true nature of events.

Many historians, though profoundly religious, nonetheless considered themselves objective students of the past. The Reverend Mandell Creighton, a Church of England divine who wrote a history of the papacy, had a profound belief in personal and historical providence and thus took melioristic progress for granted.[31] As we have seen in our discussion of progress, the British were inclined to consider themselves the favored race of providence. But Creighton was no blind adherent of British superiority. He deplored the Boer War, for example, because he felt that the Teutonic race shared the burden placed on the British by providence. The war was thus a spiritually internecine struggle in violation of divine purpose.[32] A mild-mannered man and accurate historian, Creighton was seldom embroiled in controversy despite his editorship of the *English Historical Review*.

The same could not be said of Baron Acton, a dedicated, if restless, Roman Catholic and an aggressive advocate of unpopular views about history.[33] Unlike his friend Creighton and most of his contemporaries, Acton mistrusted the concept of progress, though he embraced a developmental theory of history derived from the German historian Johann Ignaz von Dollinger, a theory applied mainly to Christianity. Politically conservative, Acton held a gradualist view concerning the evolution of institutions. He defended fixed moral authority because he was pessimistic about the course of human affairs yet maintained faith in an ideal of what man *should* be. "The inflexible authority of the moral code is, to me, the secret of the authority, the dignity, the utility of history," he wrote to Creighton (Himmelfarb, 161).

Acton was as sure of an order operating in history as were Kingsley and Maurice, though lacking their confidence in progress. In this he resembled Carlyle, except that Carlyle placed the burden of human improvement upon the individual, Acton on moral authority. Still, both perceived a willed purpose behind the laws of nature. Acton, as the more precise and more authoritarian historian, was an excellent spokesman for those who opposed the school of thought represented by Buckle. His two essays directly attacking Buckle's methods and underlying assumptions are forceful and lively criticisms.

Acton indicated that a central device in Buckle's "science" of history was to discount individuality and deal with mankind only in terms of large masses. Like other opponents of Buckle, he complained that "it is only to men as persons that free-will belongs: look at them in masses, and they become machines; with their personality you abstract their freedom."[34] Buckle, he objected, thus limited his study of history but did not acknowledge the consequence of that limitation in his practice, rashly discussing the history of civilization without considering its principal ingredient, human free will. In rejecting free will and predestination, Buckle established a hard and fast opposition between fixed laws and free will. But this was a false dilemma, according to Acton. "Freedom is not instability," he said. "True liberty is a self-determined, self-chosen perseverance in the way we deliberately think best. Fixedness, then, is not really opposed to freedom" (Acton, 313). Even if we suppose the existence of an immaterial soul having perfect and even capricious freedom, once that soul is united with material substance, it must obey the laws of matter. "In its inner self-determination it may be perfectly free; yet in the manifestations or results of its free action it is bound by the fixed laws of number, space, and time" (Acton, 314). In any case, Buckle's fixed laws were merely statistical, or numerical, an approach that, for Acton, destroyed history itself by concentrating upon man's works and products, whereas the "true historian takes the individual for his centre" (Acton, 319). Man's actions proceed from his free will, Acton asserted; thus, to deprive man of free will while concentrating upon the consequences of his actions in the mass is illogical.[35]

Even those who considered themselves outside both determinist and Carlylean camps insisted on the role of free will. J. R. Green insisted on the primacy of will and spirit in the historical process.[36] E. A. Freeman, in declaring a science of history impossible because history depended upon uncertain evidence, stipulated the human will as the source of that uncertainty. "We cannot be sure of the future; because, setting aside deeper contingencies, it depends on the human will to fix what shall happen. We cannot be sure of the past, because its evidence depends on human truthfulness; that is, because it depends on the human will to fix what shall be said to have happened."[37]

By now it should be clear that the incompatibility between the positivist (or scientific) and the Carlylean (or theological and providential) schools of historical study rests squarely upon the issue of individual freedom. In the one, there is little room for praise and blame; human events proceed largely as the result of external forces such as climate and disease; human beings resemble atoms moved and assembled by fixed laws of nature. John Theodore Merz credited Laplace's *Théorie analytique des Probabilités* (1812) with the initial stimulus toward this statistical approach. There, he said, "it was proposed, and it has since been carried out, to look upon human beings and human events not as things possessed of an inner world of thought and freewill, but as lifeless units, more uniform and regular than the balls thrown into the urn at an election or the counters in a game of chance."[38] The dominating model in this world view derives from physics, where there is no room for terms such as "purpose," "motive," "ought," and so forth. At mid-century it was characteristic for scientists to view chemical elements themselves in a similarly statistical manner, being more concerned with number and weight than with quality. The drive toward objectivity in science implied a leeching of inner qualities in favor of external, readily measurable attributes. It is not surprising that, with the growing influence of psychology and biology, allied with traditional defenses of man's spiritual nature, numerous reactions against the scientific school would emerge. Both of the broad historical schools we have discussed here accepted a concept they called necessity, but the scientific school identified necessity with fixed laws of nature, whereas the theological school equated that necessity with divine governance.

If men were to remain responsible and man's history to be interpretable as a drama of right and wrong acted out according to the "true" law of Nature—retribution—then man must retain his free will. Even conservative historians like Acton were eager champions of increased human freedom under appropriate governance. For him, religion was the mother of freedom and providence the godparent of progress. However, whereas the liberal born of the Enlightenment associated liberty with the perfectibility of man and the beneficence of nature, Acton, like J. F. Stephen, derived his philosophy of liberty from the corruptibility of man and the maleficence of nature. Man, though always in danger of lapsing into the slavery of evil, retained his capacity for freely electing good. If Buckle and the scientific school tended to reduce human events to predictable mechanical operations, Carlyle and Acton and others like them posited an unpredictable, dramatic world where an existing plot changed with the changing narrative, whose conclusion remained in suspense, a plot, moreover, that came into being through the selecting and shaping power of the human imagination expressed in the time-bound medium of narration. One school sought clarity; the other was content with justice.

Well into the twentieth century, James Ward drew a distinction between science and history that seemed to place the former finally outside the province of historical investigation. The world of science differed from the world of history as mechanism differs from morals, he said. In the former, all is determined. In the latter, spontaneity and purpose are essential, since it is individual motive and preferences concerning the future that beget the pattern of causation that leads to progress or decline. Science concerns what must be, history concerns what ought to be. "Mechanism is conceived as fixed and, so to say, fatally determined: morals imply guidance and control, the choice beforehand of what shall happen."[39] Recognizing the limits of man's free will, Ward still insisted that individual entities determined the development of larger structures—"the agents are first: and law in every sense and evolution are but second" (Ward, 247–48).[40] The scientist views beings as inert, whereas idealists see them as conative.[41] Science, he says, summing up one major argument against the scientific school, has confuted its own naive assumptions. "Setting out in search of matter as that which is alien to mind, it ended up discovering only law and order, which are the sure marks of mind" (Ward, 249). Progress is the way of human trial and error. As a pattern of behavior is repeated, it becomes fixed as habit. What is habit in individual life is heredity for racial life (Ward, 273–74).[42]

Many "scientific" historians, such as James Mill and George Grote, rejected or ignored theological considerations, but many historians considered themselves "scientific" without rejecting the concept of a divine power behind human events. Mommsen, Niebuhr, and Ranke transformed the methods of historical research without abandoning a religious base for their world views. T. W. Heyck designates John Seeley as the first important exponent of history as a science in England, but the Liberal Anglican historians and others, like Acton, also assumed that their approaches were scientific at least in the sense that their methods were based on what they believed to be practical and provable applications of coherent theories.[43]

Behind the apparent dispute between science and history lies the real dispute between acceptance or rejection of human freedom, with or without divine direction. As we shall see in the next chapter, this dispute was more clear-cut in the discourse surrounding the theory of evolution, but it was fully evident in historical debates as well. This dispute surfaced in historical studies because history during the nineteenth century was largely a response to contemporary needs, having serious and immediate political implications and applications.[44] T. H. Green's idealist view of freedom, for example, derived mainly from Kant and asserted the union of reason and will because it described human action as free when man put himself in the service of a law of which he considered himself the author. The resulting union of will and reason advanced human progress by gradually subduing natural impulses to the strictures of this moral law. Hence man's will, or character, was of great importance. For Green, as for Hegel who influenced him, the State itself was an embodiment of Will rather than of Force, and political freedom was man's adjustment to the laws of the State from which he derived his rights.

The German propagandist and theoretician Heinrich von Treitschke carried the implications of Carlylean and Hegelian positions to a Teutonic extreme in his defense of monarchy as the best tangible expression of political power and national unity because it embodies the belief that "history is not the outcome of the brainless power called public opinion, but of the deliberate will of men of action."[45] Treitschke declared that this concentration of will in an individual monarch or a disciplined state is necessary in the struggle to survive. He rejected republican, democratic, and universal suffrage schemes for political organization as incapable of sufficient order. Accompanying his endorsement of the concentrated will of the state was his justification of war, where he believed that superior morality, not superior technical achievement, would provide success (Treitschke, 405). War is the great peacemaker and guarantor of freedom. "There could be no freedom without military power ready to sacrifice itself for freedom's sake" (Treitschke, 396). The State identifies itself with power not for power's sake but in order "to protect and further the higher welfare of the human race, which happens to mean the furtherance of the white, Anglo-Saxon population" (Treitschke, 588).

The State, after all, is supreme above individuals, living by a higher moral-ity. Freedom means being a cooperative citizen, thereby taking advantage of the greatest range of development for the personality. Free will and necessity are not opposed, Treitschke explained, because when a person works ac-cording to his necessary nature, he acts freely. Because man is inevitably fallen (in the manner of original sin), individuals are not improvable, but human society as a whole may progress and improve. There is in Treitschke a confusion of incompatible ideas evident in other historians and theorists we have encountered but here largely derivative from Hegel. Implicit in Treitschke's scheme is a belief in evolutionary struggle for survival without the truly free will to shape the nature of that struggle. Human nature is no more redeemable for him than for a fervent Calvinist; as for the Calvinist, salvation may come through the willed subordination of the will to a higher moral power—in Treitschke's case, the State.

My concentration is upon England, but the English were not unique in the attitudes they held on many of these central issues. Treitschke is merely one extreme case from a possible multitude of varying Continental responses on the questions of freedom, necessity, and history. In England, the struggle to retain a commanding role for the human will in history was intense. Rose-mary Jann, noting that the tension between benevolent determinism and responsible free will structured the treatment of causation in the six histori-ans she treats in *The Art and Science of Victorian History* (1985), tries to explain the Victorian fascination with history. "If the nineteenth century was the age of history, histories themselves were a genre that most efficiently reconciled the contradictory needs of the Victorian consciousness. Victo-rian histories asserted the authority of the real but provided the satisfactions of romance."[46] The Victorian historian offered a history that conformed to the image Victorians wanted to embrace about their own destiny as Teu-tonic, Protestant, middle-class leaders of the western world.

Victorians wished to preserve a role for free will in history because the past thus could remain a romance developing into the present through the effec-tive actions of men who were honed to moral superiority by that effort and those actions. Without free will, there was neither romance nor praise for achievement. Determinist history, despite its advocacy of progress and its many optimistic variants, made history seem little more than a statistical mechanism for describing shifting populations and national boundaries. Thus, underlying the efforts of most historians during the nineteenth cen-tury was the abiding paradox of the age: central to all human endeavor is the exercise of individual human will, yet the highest function of that will is to subordinate itself to some higher power, institutional, moral, or theological. If men were mechanisms, this subordination could be taken for granted and their actions measured and evaluated without praise and blame. But if men were free beings and not automatons, the entire drama of history would require elaborate interpretation. Victorian belief in, and experiments with, narrative were closely related to this interest in the drama of history.

The nineteenth century in England was a great age of story telling and one powerful impulse behind the many narratives it produced—historical, scientific, fictional, and otherwise—was a concern for the way the plot would work out. Chiefly with an eye to the future, writers shaped the story of mankind, Europe, England, or let us say, David Copperfield, so that a guiding power of whatever kind might disclose itself and a discernible relationship between that power and the individual would emerge. Historians sought to construct images of the "real" world they wanted to believe in, and novelists created fictional worlds to endorse a moral design. Behind most of these stories, and characteristic of the age, was a belief in some form of human freedom, most often in the form of an independent individual will.

CHAPTER SEVEN

Evolution

I N chapter 5 we traced one developmental pattern in nineteenth-century thought—progress. Separate from, but inevitably entangled with this historical "myth," was another major theory of development—evolution. To many modern readers evolution means Darwin, but Darwin put forward only one set of theories associated with the larger concept of evolution. This chapter is about evolution, not Darwinism. Though unquestionably there was great difference of opinion between theists and scientists concerning the theory of natural selection and other specific issues, in fact, many theists embraced their own versions of evolution.

This chapter indicates that in much evolutionary thinking a residual teleology remained even among supposedly nontheistic writers and was enthusiastically championed by proponents of religion. All but a few of those who wrote on this subject promoted one or another *plot* or *story* for mankind. Just as historians created histories to reflect their moral assumptions so evolutionists provided differing narratives of biological development according to the moral forces they believed to be operating in the universe. I have offered here a mixture of the soundly scientific and philosophical alongside the apparently eccentric and the transparently propagandistic. My purpose is to provide a sample of various ways in which writers made the broad concept of evolution fit into religious, political, and social ideological modes. I move generally from naturalists to idealists in this discussion and conclude with the work of widely read social theorist, L. T. Hobhouse, who summarized at the end of the century many of the issues that had been prominent during the century, including the new secular defense of altruism. Problems of freedom and law, self and society, responsibility and blame are all related to the defining of self now perceived as multiple, complex, and mutable over time. Belief in evolution for mankind was related to belief in evolution of the self, a subject already touched on in chapter 1. Behind the different evolutionary *plots* there remained the same abiding opposition we have seen elsewhere between freedom and necessity.

~ ~ ~

Early in the twentieth century, Wilfred Ward asked if there had been any great addition to knowledge that belonged to the nineteenth century and promptly answered himself with a yes. The great addition to human knowledge was the idea of evolution in its inorganic, organic, and social manifestations.[1] Ward, though a strong Catholic, found no conflict between his faith and a belief in evolution, despite the furious struggles fought in the name of such an opposition during the century just past. Other religious men were similarly confident that the theory of evolution could be accommodated to faith. Gladstone wrote in 1874: "Indeed, I must say that the doctrine of Evolution, if it be true, enhances in my judgment the proper idea of the greatness of God, for it makes every stage of creation a legible prophecy of all those which are to follow it."[2] R. H. Hutton, referring specifically to the theory of Natural Selection, wrote that "Mr. Darwin's discovery seems to bring back the idea of *luck* into the modification of the forms of vegetable and animal existence."[3] Seen in its proper place in the scheme of the universe, Hutton said, "The Darwinian explanation of the laws of organic progress seems to me to make for the theistic argument instead of against it." Nor did he feel that Darwin's theories in any way invalidated free will in mankind.[4] Peter Morton remarks that earlier Charles Kingsley appropriated Natural Selection as an agency of God's power.[5] Mandell Creighton acknowledged the triumph of evolutionary theory but found it neither troubling nor surprising. "Has it ever struck you," he wrote to a friend in 1889, "that evolution has been the working theory of historians long before Darwin examined it in reference to species? Hegel's 'Philosophie der Geschichte' contained its metaphysical basis, and Ranke's 'Weltgeschichtliche Bewegung' set forth the 'survival of the fittest' in human affairs."[6]

We have already seen that progressive views of human history and beliefs in human perfectibility contributed strongly to the emergence of a theory of development during the late eighteenth and early nineteenth centuries, but it was the establishment of scientific method that provided this developmental theory with its firm base and its arsenal of proofs. Beginning with the geological discoveries of James Hutton and Charles Lyell, men began to realize that the world they knew must have come into existence slowly and over a much longer period of time than had previously been supposed. Robert Chambers, though an amateur, was nonetheless the first to provide a popularly intelligible and coherent theory of development, or evolution, picturing the universe as controlled by natural law under the governance of divine will aiming toward the progress of mankind. His *Vestiges of the Natural History of Creation* (1844) thus offered an early compromise between mechanistic science and theistic religion. Darwin's *Origin of Species* (1859) was by no means the first scientific treatise to set forth a developmental theory, but it did so with such authority and such abundant evidence that it quickly became the focus of evolutionary dispute. Moreover, because of its implications, the book placed Darwin, as William Irvine puts it, "directly athwart almost every great issue in philosophy, ethics, and religion. The old questions of necessity and free will, mechanism and spontaneity, matter and spirit, realism and nominalism, relativism and the absolute were faced all over again and argued in a new light because of *The Origin of Species*."[7] Darwin himself felt hopelessly muddled when called upon to discuss issues of this sort and withdrew from controversy over them, preferring to continue his detailed researches. Others were not so timid. Alfred Russel Wallace, the codiscoverer of the theory of Natural Selection, assumed, as Darwin would not, a teleological purpose in existence and credited man, as Darwin did not, with the power to alter his own condition. Wallace believed that by restraining his animal passions, man could transform the earth into a new paradise. He accepted the Lamarckian notion that beings could progress rapidly through inherited characteristics and pointed to man's large brain as a clear indication that influences beyond natural selection were guiding man toward some higher end.[8] For Wallace, Matter was Force, and Force was Will-Force, hence all of existence was the result of some willing power.

Like many scientists of his day, Wallace was reluctant to scuttle the comfortable notion of man's privileged role in nature, even reviving the old notion that because the earth was located in the center of the universe, it was the best setting for human life. A similar theory had attracted a good deal of attention before Darwin's *Origin* when William Whewell published *The Plurality of Worlds* (1854) to counter speculations about life existing elsewhere in the universe. Whewell had particularly in mind the ideas of Thomas Chalmers, who was already disputing earth's claim as the center of the material and hence of the moral and religious universe.[9] Whewell argued that our solar system "is in a more complete and advanced state, as a system, than many at least of the stellar systems can be; it may be than any other" (Whewell, 175). He described the earth as "the domestic hearth of this Solar System," the only region "fit to be a domestic hearth, a seat of habitation" (Whewell, 229). Without acknowledging a scientific principle of evolution, Whewell projected a developmental view of human nature confined to moral and intellectual progress. The history of life, he said, was not a "repetition of exactly similar cases, but a series of cases perpetually dissimilar. . . . not constancy, but change, perhaps advance" (Whewell, 128).[10] Whewell looked forward to an exalted mankind making manifest ideas that were emanations of the archetypal Ideas of divine purpose.

Despite the introduction of Darwin's theories, then, there were not always distinct differences in the developmental theories before and after 1859. It was not as difficult as historians of the period have sometimes suggested for religious thinkers to incorporate evolutionary ideas into their theistic beliefs. Frank Miller Turner's *Between Science and Religion* provides an excellent account of a group of antipositivist thinkers who were able to retain religious, or at least spiritual, beliefs, while accepting scientific methods for the investigation of natural phenomena. Turner's group includes Wallace as well as George John Romanes, famous for his *Mental Evolution in Man* (1888), Samuel Butler, and James Ward, among others. Moreover, as Peter Morton notes, Darwinians made increasing appeals to teleology over the century because such directionalism made intelligible the spasmodic irregularities in observed frequencies of variation in organic forms.[11]

Some writers already discussed in chapter 4 had pronounced views about evolution, notably Huxley, Clifford, and Spencer. Thomas Henry Huxley maintained the kind of scientific rigor that Darwin respected without withdrawing himself from dispute; in fact, he welcomed controversy as a means of promulgating ideas. Moreover, he was willing to tackle the thorny issues that so muddled Darwin. Among these was the central issue of will. Admitting ignorance about the nature of matter and spirit, Huxley rejected both doctrinaire materialism with its abstraction of necessity, and supernatural intervention, confining himself to the observable laws operating in nature. In "The Physical Basis of Life" (1868), Huxley identifies all life with molecular organization. Even our thoughts are the results of molecular changes and can be tracked, Huxley argued, but left the door open for human will to guide events. However, the central difficulty in Huxley's view is that, while he maintained that man is bound by the laws of nature, he also expected him to alter his own condition, though he offered no designation of where man became capable of thus asserting his will. Huxley defended Hume's conviction that both the physical world and states of human consciousness are subject to a law of causation and reasserted a standard view of the conflict between freedom and necessity. As we saw earlier, for Huxley, free will was merely a sense of volition, the consciousness of having carried a purpose into action, though the power to choose was itself part of the order of nature.

Huxley considered evolution a process operating under a natural law excluding the supernatural and chance. Human volition cannot be self-caused, Huxley wrote in "Science and Morals" (1886), and thus the only sensible meaning of freedom is "the absence of any restraint upon doing what one likes within certain limits."[12] Freedom has a political and social, but not a scientific or metaphysical, significance. Huxley was convinced, as he remarked in "The Struggle for Existence in Human Society" (1888), "that it is desirable that every man should be free to act in every way which does not limit the corresponding freedom of his fellow-man" (Huxley, *Evolution and Ethics*, 227). His position resembles John Stuart Mill's and carries with it the same moral dilemma: if men act as they do because they are particles moved by natural laws, how can they be judged as responsible for those actions? Like Mill, who believed that humanity, not the individual human, could improve itself through education, Huxley believed that mankind as a whole could improve itself ethically.

In "Evolution and Ethics" (1893), a submerged conflict in Huxley's thought surfaced, for there he openly drew the distinction between evolution in nature and evolution in society. The human "state of art"—that is, of humanly fashioned existence—differed from the "state of nature." "The history of civilization details the steps by which men have succeeded in building up an artificial world within the cosmos. Fragile reed as he may be, man, as Pascal says, is a thinking reed: there lies within him a fund of energy, operating intelligently and so far akin to that which pervades the universe, that it is competent to influence and modify the cosmic process." Man's struggle against the amoral force of nature would be difficult, but Huxley concluded, "I see no limit to the extent to which intelligence and will, guided by sound principles of investigation and organized in common effort, may modify the conditions of existence, for a period longer than that now covered by history. And much may be done to change the nature of man himself" (Huxley, *Evolution and Ethics*, 83–85). He ends by quoting the lines from "Ulysses," by his favorite poet, Tennyson, that begin "strong in will / to strive, to seek, to find, and not to yield."

Nineteenth-century thinkers may be forgiven some confusion in dealing with the information that though no more than molecules in a natural world, governed like other molecules by invariable laws, they were expected to take command of the world their ethical nature had shaped and, through the exercise of intelligence and will, fortify that ethical entity known as civilization until the inevitable decay of the natural world brought an end to everything. How, any of them might have asked, does mankind ever manage to grasp the reins of his own existence in the first place, if he is one with the force that impels the steeds of necessity? How, if he had no free will, could man direct that other will that was really just another name for directed action? Huxley had no good answer to this kind of question. A generation later, H. G. Wells would dismiss notions of ethics and the dilemma of free will with the paradigm of a rigid universe in which will, time, and space were only illusions and openly recommend that man shape his future as a poet shapes a poem. For man to believe in directed change, Wells said, is to make directed change possible.[13] But Huxley, despite his avowed agnosticism was very much a product of his age; unlike Darwin, he believed that man was somehow privileged, capable of a life above that of unconscious existence, and though he admitted that human society was probably as much a product of organic necessity as was the society of bees, he still demanded that mankind improve upon necessity (Huxley, *Evolution and Ethics*, 26). Huxley believed in science, the epitome of human intelligence, and he worshiped truth, the object of science. To this ideal he gave the same dedication that other men gave to religion. And he knew it.

There may have been a teleological trace in some of Darwin's observations about natural selection, but Huxley tried to rule out any direction of the process that did not entirely conform to the observed laws of nature. However, it was sometimes difficult not to scratch that teleological itch. William Kingdon Clifford assumed that he was logically pure in his approach to the question of science, evolution, and morality. In "Body and Mind" (1874), Clifford declared man's physical being an automaton. Drawing partly upon Huxley, he explained that consciousness itself was a mechanical process. The mind as mental facts was itself not a force but paralleled physical facts. Will did not influence matter. "The only thing which influences matter is the position of surrounding matter or the motion of surrounding matter."[14] Clifford offered the standard necessarian argument that without a necessary law of cause and effect (i.e., man is an automaton), there can be no responsibility because no act would necessarily lead to a predictable or observable consequence. Once admit the possibility of a break in the law of causation (i.e., free will) and the way is open for the doctrines of destiny, Providence, and other external forces "overruling human efforts and guiding history to a foregone conclusion."[15] Clifford then presented his interpretation of Kant's view that freedom of the will is that property which enables us to originate events independently of foreign determining causes. Although our bodies are automata, he said, we can still do this because we are not puppets (Clifford, 34–35). Elsewhere, he repeated this position, arguing again from Kant and declaring, "I am a free agent when my actions are independent of the control of circumstances outside me," but misunderstanding Kant's exception of will from all phenomenal influence, thereby also preventing it from *operating* in nature. Clifford praised Sidgwick's statement of the question, quoting approvingly this sentence: "No amount of experience of the sway of motives even tends to make me distrust my intuitive consciousness that in resolving, after deliberation, I exercise free choice as to which of the motives acting upon me shall prevail."[16] Huxley understood Kant's assertion of noumenal freedom better than Clifford did, but rejected it because it was of no use at all to men dealing with the phenomenal world.[17] Clifford wanted both worlds—the absoluteness of science, stripped of supernaturalism, and the force of human will contributing to the formation of mankind's own destiny.

Like Huxley, Mill, and others, Clifford admitted that the individual cannot shape the whole of his own character, but like them he also accepted the idea that the human race as a whole had fashioned itself over the ages. Since no consciousness can exist apart from a nervous system, we may not regard the universe or any part of it, he said, "as a vast brain, and therefore the reality which underlies it as a conscious mind" (Clifford, 46). Without revelation of any kind beyond what is available to human consciousness in communication with the phenomenal world, "the only right motive to right action is to be found in the social instincts which have been bred into mankind by hundreds of generations of social life" (Clifford, 49). Here Clifford was unable to resist the teleological itch, for he automatically assumed that the instincts bred in man over these centuries were good.

Possibly Clifford's optimism assumed a relativist view of human history; that is, *whatever* the social instincts evoke is necessarily good. But there is a strong residue of traditional Christian feeling in Clifford's thinking, as his other essays suggest. Rejecting the utilitarian standard of the greatest happiness for the greatest number, Clifford maintained that individuals should not seek their own happiness. Individual happiness is useful only if it increases efficiency. "A man must strive to be a better citizen, a better workman, a better son, husband, or father" (Clifford, 95). Clifford's view of human evolution assumed an increasing capacity not only for self-suppression, as Huxley asserted, but for self-sacrifice as well. Piety was the forgetting of self in the service of the community. Clifford made no mention of the possible sacrifices proposed later by Eugenists that involved the elimination of unwanted human types. Had he been a genuine relativist, he would have had to endorse some such programs in the name of efficiency, but behind Clifford's thinking was an unacknowledged assumption that mankind's evolution was clearly positive and moving toward some favorable end. Winwood Reade, about the same time, while declaring the preeminence of science and rejecting the superstitions of religion, more grandly and unquestioningly affirmed the upward surge of human evolution. For men like this, the hesitations and misgivings of a Darwin or a Huxley were lost. Filled with the visions of science that these leaders made possible, they inadvertently bound those visions to incommensurate moral schemes.

Herbert Spencer, though no Darwinian, was an ardent evolutionist with a complete theory of his own that, without supernatural intervention, accorded a central place to moral conduct as man's best means of adaptation and hence of higher evolution. Satisfactory adaptation also produced personal as well as communal happiness; thus Spencer's theory combined utilitarian aims with scientific laws. Gertrude Himmelfarb explains that for men like

Spencer and Leslie Stephen "morality, happiness, and the evolutionary process were assumed to be different aspects of the same thing."[18] Like Huxley, Spencer put his faith in a complete acceptance of natural law. Though he had tacitly accepted the regularity of such a law in his early writing, he said, it was in 1852, after reading the work of Karl Ernst von Baer, that he became absolutely convinced of it.[19] His entire career may be viewed as an application of this absolute faith in continuity and natural causation of various fields of intellectual investigation. Believing that all phenomena are susceptible of scientific treatment obliged Spencer to accept determinism. As a determinist, Spencer rejected the doctrine of free will. Will, as volition, results when automatic actions become complex and occasion consciousness of them and disappears into habit when they become entirely automatic again, he wrote in *Principles of Psychology* (1855). Man may be free to do as he desires, Spencer allowed, but not to desire as he does. All actions are determined by physical connections, and though man may have the illusion of a self, actions arise from an aggregate of emotions and other impelling forces. Will, Spencer concluded, is only the name given to the special emotion predominating at a specific time.[20] Spencer did not find the elimination of free will disturbing; like Buckle's, his determinism permitted a firm belief in progress. "For Spencer the role of rational choice in the coming millennium [*sic*] is largely supplanted by the built-in habits and instincts which are the product of centuries of adaptation."[21] Thus Spencer could remain a determinist while arguing that men in the aggregate had the power to alter their environment and therefore limit its influence upon them.

In Spencer's evolutionary scheme, only the fit survived; he took credit for establishing the expression "survival of the fittest" as a convenient way of viewing evolutionary development. However, though his scientific theories, especially as applied to society, owed a good deal to laissez-faire economics, an important feature of this thought was founded on a broader concept of cooperation. Spencer thought of evolution as a progression of units from simplicity to complexity; the more advanced the organism, the more diverse and specialized the units it contained. "Evolution is definable as a change from an incoherent homogeneity to a coherent heterogeneity, accompanying the dissipation of motion and integration of matter" (Spencer, *Psychology*, 359). For complex organisms to survive, subordination of the units to the purpose of the whole was essential, therefore Spencer argued that altruism, man's capacity to transcend selfish aims for higher purposes, was an important ingredient in the successful recipe for human evolutionary progress. Moreover, his view was assertively optimistic because he believed that evolution engendered by the persistence of force and consequent cosmic equilibrations would lead toward perfection (Spencer, *Psychology*, 511). Spencer's concept of evolution, which he applied to the natural world, human psychology, and social and political institutions, was heavily moral in

its assumptions, though he posited no underlying force making for righteousness in the universe. He did assume an Ultimate Cause of all things and a
persistent Force that sustained existence but, rejecting theism, asked, "Is it
not just possible that there is a mode of being as much transcending Intelligence and Will, as these transcend mechanical motion?" Pressing the point,
he added, "Does it not follow that the Ultimate cause cannot in any respect
be conceived by us because it is in every respect greater than can be conceived?" (Spencer, *Psychology*, 119).

Spencer referred to the mystery behind the existence of matter and force
as the Unknowable but did not thereby equate that convenient abstraction
with a deity. Samuel Butler, who rejected traditional religious views, and
considered himself a scientist with his own theory of evolution, nonetheless
attempted to combine scientific research with spiritual direction. Butler
called his view a "panzoistic conception of God."[22] Beginning with the same
premise that Huxley used in "The Physical Basis of Life," Butler carried the
idea that all animal and vegetable forms are differentiations of a single
substance—protoplasm—to a different logical conclusion. All living forms,
he said, are in reality one animal or person. "It is in this Person that we may
see the Body of God—and in the evolution of this Person, the mystery of His
Incarnation" (Butler, *Essays*, 35). God is the finite spirit of Life, and men his
embodiment in matter through whom his moral government is exercised.
This notion would be taken up later by various writers, for example, George
Bernard Shaw's vitalism, and perhaps most elaborately, if temporarily, in
H. G. Wells' depiction of God the Invisible King, and more consistently in his
concept of a World Brain.[23] Butler allowed himself to speculate that beyond
this God may be a vaster God of which the one we know is merely a particle
and beyond that God another and another. "We are ourselves the second
concentric sphere of life, we being the constituent cells which unite to form
the body of God. Of the third sphere we know a single member only—the
God of this world; but we see also the stars in heaven, and know their multitude" (Butler, *Essays*, 49).

In *Life and Habit* (1878), Butler reversed the usual conception of the
growth of knowledge, inverting the simple "upward" pattern of understanding from unconscious to conscious; he argued that the pattern correctly
operated from conscious to unconscious. "Knowledge is in an inchoate state
as long as it is capable of logical treatment; it must be transmuted into that
sense or instinct which rises altogether above the sphere in which words can
have being at all, otherwise it is not yet incarnate." In short, "it must become
automatic before we are safe with it."[24] The same is true of willing. "The more
intensely we will, the less is our will deliberate and capable of being recognized as will at all" (Butler, *Works*, 4:36). Perfected actions become unconscious, thus the most important work of our organism is carried on unconsciously. This topsy-turvy evaluation of human effort may seem merely

playful or willfully mischievous, but Butler was making a serious point by challenging the progressivist, rationalist orthodoxy of his time. The challenge was often explicit, as when he chided W. B. Carpenter for restricting the word "scientific" to people who know what they know, that is, who are conscious of what they understand. Those who do not know what they know (those who act upon instinct), he said, also deserved to be called scientists. In fact, those who know they know have *imperfect* knowledge not yet fully incorporated into their being (Butler, *Works*, 4:26ff).

Butler introduced another inversion of customary scientific thinking by arguing that human individuals are compound creatures with an infinite number of distinct centers of sensation and will and intelligence and memory of their own. It is even possible, he said, to suppose that each cell in the human body is a person with an intelligent soul (Butler, *Works*, 4:87ff). Again, one might charge Butler with mere mockery of the biological analogy used by Spencer and others to explain the molecular or atomic nature of human society, where each human is equated with an individual cell contributing to the larger organism. But, in fact, Butler revealed in his eccentric way, the limitations of the Spencerian view, arguing that there was no reason to confine the likeness to mere metaphor, since the metaphor itself was based on a reality that extended beyond conscious human experience in two directions, for if human beings could be viewed as cells in a social organism, they could more "scientifically" be viewed as cells in the one larger creature LIFE. LIFE has come to be what it is through constantly doing the same thing over and over again, "growing till it is first conscious of effort, then conscious of power, then powerful with but little consciousness, and finally, so powerful and so charged with memory as to be absolutely without all self-consciousness whatever," except when faced with new choices and differentiations (Butler, *Works*, 4:105). Each germ, Butler argued, learns by repetition until habit becomes memory so that it can repeat the performance with the slightest necessary variation. Hence the impregnate ovum from which each of us has sprung has "a potential recollection of all that has happened to each one of its ancestors prior to the period at which any such ancestor has issued from the bodies of its progenitors" provided a sufficiently strong and often repeated impression has been made to permit remembering (Butler, *Works*, 4:242).

Butler's theories may sound a good deal like spoofing, but at a time when Mendelian genetics was unknown, Butler had come very close to the modern perception of cells composed of chromasomes bearing inscriptions of DNA like habitual impulses. Our modern metaphor in an age preoccupied with information theory is that of a coded tape or text, but Butler's homely image of cells as sophisticated creatures who have managed to perfect their functions by reducing conscious effort to unconscious instinct serves the purpose too.

That Butler was not merely mocking others with his inversions of orthodox thought is indicated by an important passage in his notebooks, where he attributes free will to atoms.

The element of free-will, spontaneity, individuality, so omnipresent, so essential, yet so unreasonable and so inconsistent with the other element not less omnipresent and not less essential, I mean necessity—this element of free-will which comes from the unseen kingdom within which the writs of our thoughts run not, must be carried down to the most tenuous atoms, whose action is supposed most purely chemical and mechanical; it can never be held as absolutely eliminated, for if it be so held there is no getting it back again, and that it exists even in the lowest forms of life cannot be disputed. Its existence is one of the proofs of the existence of an unseen world, and a means whereby we know the little that we know at all.[25]

Though the terms are commonplace, the notions are not, and they bear a remarkable resemblance to modern quantum physics, which also acknowledges that, despite the predictability (necessity) of subatomic particles in statistical equations dealing with large numbers, no predictions apply to individual particles which remain capable of seemingly capricious behavior. Frank Miller Turner concludes that "through Lamarckianism and a general voluntarism Butler envisioned a world without fixed entities in which all living things, at least in part, created their own essence from the circumstances of their existence."[26] Rejecting the orthodoxies of religion and science, Butler sought to establish a view of existence that allowed for the operation of will at the micro- and macrocosmic levels without abandoning the acknowledged laws of causation. For his time, though his notions were rejected, his achievement was not insignificant.

After its first forceful effect, Darwinism lost much of its persuasive energy, though it had given powerful impetus to the evolutionary theories that gained increased acceptance with time.[27] But if serious scientists became more skeptical of Darwinism and challenged many of its premises, lay writers and philosophers developed their own evolutionary schemes. Many who rejected the theory of natural selection eagerly explored progressive features of evolution. In a lecture delivered at Birmingham entitled "Aspects of Life" (1893), Sir Edwin Arnold, far from a serious scientist, numbered Huxley (mainly as represented in his recently delivered Romanes lecture, "Evolution and Ethics") among the pessimists he deplored. Arnold called attention to the splendors of ordinary life. Look at the common Birmingham artisan, he said, how all the goods of the earth are provided for his purchase, how the means of travel and communication are open to him, how anesthetics and medicine control his pain. Has not human progress made life good? There is, he argued, no good ground for pessimism. Even scientists say that evolution is compatible with faith, for there is no reason why the evolution that shows us advances here on earth should not continue on into another life.[28] Huxley, Arnold charged, was wrong to see man's ethical drives at war with the cosmic process; in truth, man finds contentment in putting himself at one with that process. He quoted Walt Whitman approvingly as one who has learned the secret of harmony with the cosmic process and its purpose (Arnold, 50). Arnold did not doubt that evolution, progress, and improvement were synonomous and he likened the cosmic process to maternal love that sometimes must help us by administering strong medicine. Self-sacrifice was one form of "suffering" that proved the value of apparent evil. Quoting his own essay "Death and—Afterwards," Arnold gave the example of a "sailor leaping from the taffrail of his ship into an angry sea to save his comrade or to perish with him!" The sailor has never read the pessimists Leopardi and Schopenhauer, nor perhaps even the Bible. He leaps not out of argument, but out of love, the generating force of the universe (Arnold, 43).[29]

Arnold's is a naively ecstatic view of human evolution, but it is generally characteristic of one group of exponents who found only hope in the then victorious theory. John Fiske managed to find in Darwinism a proof of Nature's high purpose of designing man.[30] He described man's superior position in the animal world and offered as proofs man's developing consciousness, his growing brain, his command of natural selection itself through the extension of his body in science, and finally the growing predominance of man's psychical life, which in the rude beginnings was only "an appendage to the body," whereas in "fully-developed Humanity the body is but the vehicle for the soul."[31] In the hands of a man like Fiske, evolution no longer bore much resemblance to the procedures in nature that Darwin had called natural selection, the development from simplicity to complexity elucidated by Spencer, or the conflict between human and material nature everywhere implicit in Huxley's speculations.

Henry Drummond acknowledged a debt to Fiske in *The Ascent of Man* (1894), a similarly optimistic interpretation of evolution. Like Alfred Russel Wallace, Drummond argued that man is different from every other product of the evolutionary process because he is *aware* of the process.[32] Moreover, he is the pinnacle of that process, since his species has developed the important functions of maternity and family coherence to their most efficient levels. For Drummond, evolution consisted of two drives—egoism and altruism, or The Struggle for Life and The Struggle for the Life of Others. Gradually altruism will dominate. The most certain prophecy of science, Drummond said, is the amelioration of the struggle for life (Drummond, 212). Like Spencer, Drummond had an optimistic picture of evolution that assumed an increasing degree of specialization and diversification in organisms. But, although he too asserted early in his book that the life of a man or an animal "is set as rigidly as the courses of the stars," Drummond differed from Spencer nonetheless in seeing men as conscious artisans of existence (Drummond, 14). "Henceforth his selection should replace Natural Selection; his judgment guide the struggle for life; his will determine for every plant upon the earth, whether it should bloom or fade, for every animal whether it should increase, or change, or die. So man entered into his Kingdom" (Drummond, 115). Behind this earthly monarch, however, is the divine power that inspires all of life, an Infinite Intelligence and an Eternal Will. "Evolution is not to unfold from within; it is to infold from without. Growth is no mere extension from a root but a taking possession of, or a being possessed by, an ever widening Environment, a continuous process of assimilation of the seen or Unseen, a ceaseless redistribution of energies flowing into the evolving organism from the Universe around it" (Drummond, 324). Drummond concluded: "The Will behind Evolution is not dead; the heart of Nature is not stilled. Love not only was; it is; it moves; it spreads" (Drummond, 345).

I have perhaps quoted more of Drummond than is necessary, but I think it is important to convey the flavor of this rhapsodic affirmation of evolutionary thinking. All that is positive in evolution rests, in this approach, upon the assumption that a conscious Will guides the entire process and has special plans for mankind in its scheme. We have already seen that many theistic commentators argued that man's own will was a portion or tiny replication of that vaster purposive force. Thus the human exertion of will was an endorsement and fulfillment of divine intent. Underlying that endorsement was the additional assumption that will extends itself and grows, establishing empire or hegemony over the things (and ultimately people) of the earth. Von Treitschke offered one expression of this attitude at the political level. We will look at other political ramifications in a moment. But the countervailing force in Drummond's thought is a version of moral doctrine that represents a residuum of Christian thought. Altruism was important to the nonreligious Spencer, and "martyrdom," or suffering for others, was a fundamental assumption in such clearly secular figures as Winwood Reade and H. G. Wells. But altruism was the *keystone* of Drummond's scheme.

In fact, evolutionism could be directed to almost any ideological or political figuration one desired. The social theories of Saint-Simon and Comte are two Continental examples. Englishmen had their own ideological programs of social organization to defend. T. H. Huxley, believing that individual men were not easy to redeem from enslavement to nature's way, like Mill saw education as a means of freeing mankind. A society balanced between anarchy and regimentation appealed to him. Spencer had employed the analogy of body and government, and his ideal society involved elaborate social cooperation through economic division of labor; "social roles, for him, means; specialization of *personnel*."[33] Yet it was a society in which all individuals achieved maximum freedom; limited, as in Mill, only by the liberty of one's neighbor. Huxley rejected Spencer's version of the body analogy, claiming that it overlooked the controlling influence of the brain upon the rest of the physiological organism. Society, he said, is not merely conjunctive but involves conscious renunciation for specific advantages. Every society, he said, resembles a complex molecule, in which the atoms are represented by men, but the social molecule exists through renunciation of some freedom by every individual. "And the great problem of that social chemistry we call politics, is to discover what desires of mankind may be gratified, and what must be suppressed, if the highly complex compound, society, is to avoid decomposition."[34] Society thus requires a constant equilibrium between excesses and control of individuality.

Huxley's statement of this position lacked the bland optimism of Walter Bagehot, who, in "Physics and Politics" sketched a pattern of political evolution from a period when an intelligent elite govern absolutely, to a period of useful progress through conflict (i.e., war), to a period when all the people participate in their own government. Bagehot concluded that the contemporary government of England, which he referred to as the polity of discussion, prevented hasty action and ensured elaborate consideration and thus tended to diminish inherited defects and augment heritable excellences.[35] Huxley may be forgiven for not appreciating the logic of Bagehot's position. His own conclusion was that the natural condition tended to maintain the war of all with each (the negative reading of Spencer's laissez-faire freedom), a condition that did not ensure the success of the morally or physically highest but only of those with the least morality (Huxley, *Essays*, 1:427). Like his combatant in other fields, Matthew Arnold, Huxley approved the State as a mode of discipline to keep citizens from merely doing as they like (Huxley, *Essays*, 1:289).

W. K. Clifford found it easy to sponsor republicanism as the highest form of government on evolutionary grounds. In contrast to Drummond, who argued that evolution was not an unfolding but an infolding, Clifford insisted that natural selection was an example of how freedom (action from within) effects the evolution of organisms. He defined the character of organic action as freedom, "that is to say, *action from within*. The action which has its immediate antecedents within the organism has a tendency, in so far as it alters the organism, to make it more organic, or to raise it in the scale" (Clifford, 290). Crediting Spencer with the idea that the highest of organisms is the social organism, and indifferent to the kind of objection that Huxley raised to Spencer's analogy, Clifford found that a society that could cooperate within itself, independently of foreign determining causes, would act most in accord with the best rule, aiming at freedom rather than anarchy;

"freedom is the organic action of society as such, which is what we call the Republic. The Republic is the visible embodiment and personification of freedom in its highest external type" (Clifford, 295).

By contrast, W. H. Mallock, using evolution to his own ends, found it just as simple to establish firm support for an aristocratic form of government. His arguments are trivial and easily dismissed, but they indicate one extreme to which evolutionary theory and related assumptions about the will could be carried. In his quasi-Carlylean *Aristocracy and Evolution* (1898), Mallock argued that great men—those gifted with the ability to direct other men— are the true causes of power.[36] The great man is distinct from the physically fittest survivor. The one contributes immediately to the welfare of all, the other merely contributes to the gradual physical improvement of the race (Mallock, 92). Mallock disputed social scientists such as Kidd and Spencer who attributed to all men what he felt was really achieved only by the efforts of individuals. Spencer, he said, was especially at fault in seeing men only in greater or lesser aggregates and failing to recognize the crucial instrumentality of the individual (Mallock, 39).

The modern great man, for Mallock, is the large employer. In industry, competition between employers begets progress. Labor plays no motive part in this progress, only enacting the will of the employer (Mallock, 146). This view comfortably suited Mallock's class and political prejudices, reinforcing his belief in some form of aristocracy. Even democrats, he observed, admit the need for exceptional leaders (Mallock, 177). His evolutionary theory supported his conviction that wealth must be protected. If wealth could not be inherited, for example, how could it be accumulated by the great man thence to be expended for the benefit of the many (Mallock, 319)?

Mallock comforted the "ordinary man" by explaining that his condition is not shameful. After all, poets and skilled manual workers are also ordinary, that is, they do not improve the efficiency of their trades (Mallock, 252ff). Though the ordinary or average man does not promote progress, there is no degradation in that. Nor should the average citizen fear that an uneven distribution of wealth will lead to unhappiness. Mallock comforts Benthamites and others with the assurance that the craving for wealth is naturally confined to men with the talent for creating it (Mallock, 368). Only they will suffer pain in failing to attain that wealth.

Like Mill and the libertarians, Mallock approved of increased access to education but at the same time cautioned his readers about the excesses that could follow from such an extension of opportunity, since education sets free and stimulates both sound and unsound intellects. Education could engender an unhealthy desire for wealth and power in those lacking the natural talent to achieve it. The commonest representative of this discontent is the socialist agitator (Mallock, 328ff). There is little about genuine aristocracy and genuine evolution in Mallock's book, which is a transparent and unconvincing piece of propaganda. By carrying the more considered views of Carlyle and even Samuel Smiles to an extreme, the book more obviously demonstrates how fundamental notions about self and will underlie some far-ranging social assumptions.

Although this chapter is devoted mainly to the manner in which evolutionists employed varying concepts of determinism and freedom, it may be useful to point out that, running parallel to the evolutionists, who derived mainly from utilitarian thought, was the group of thinkers referred to as idealists, who owed much to the intuitionist school.[37] Prominent among the English idealists was Thomas Hill Green, whose views we have already examined in another context. Influenced by such figures as Kant, Hegel, Fichte, Carlyle, and Maurice, Green believed that history revealed a developmental pattern of progress interpretable as the self-development of an eternal spirit, with man, the possessor of reason, as its highest manifestation. Freedom was an essential feature of his philosophy. "The idea of a free personality," writes R. L. Nettleship, "exercising its freedom under conditions which it has itself created, formed the meeting-point for his political and religious aspirations."[38] Each individual existence is a manifestation of a single eternal activity characterized by self-consciousness. But the self, in becoming self-conscious and therefore aware of its function as part of the larger life, overcomes the contradiction of its physical/spiritual nature in proportion as it thinks what is true and wills what is unselfish. Thinking makes us free. In politics, Green believed in the power of citizens as a group to make the best of themselves. Private aims, he argued, in an echo of Benthamite theory, were subordinate to the highest good for all. Thus government was justified in interfering with individual freedom where labor, education, health, and similar matters were concerned.

Most necessarians and proponents of the laws of causation nonetheless assumed some form of human freedom, some kind of responsibility, some opportunity for mankind to improve itself. Conversely, most proponents of free will acknowledged that certain universal laws governed human existence. In "The Forces of Circumstances" (1858), Green agreed that men were subject to the influence of circumstance. The recognition of the laws of political economy were an admission that men had "no control over the results of their own combined energies, which operate in a system as independent of human will as that which regulates the motion of heavenly bodies" (Green 3:9). Only the spiritual energy of a liberated few can affect the course of human development.

Green offered different perceptions of human freedom, most of which have been traversed earlier in this study. Rejecting Kant's separation of man's nature into practical and rational features, with his will free only in the latter, Green confined will instead to practical manifestations; the will *is* the self-conscious man, and is not an external force affecting him. On a larger scale, Green argues that man is free in obeying any law of which he feels himself to be the author. He obeys *because* he is author and from an impulse to self-perfection but also because he has drawn his natural impulses into the service of this law and thus is in bondage neither to it nor to the flesh. Mankind, following a similar pattern of self-imposed discipline through law, can attain a great degree of improvement (Green, 2:328–29). The State, as an embodiment of humanly designed law, represents will, not force. Force, Green argued, contradicting the views of such varied thinkers as Bagehot and Treitschke, has only formed states as far as it has operated in and through a preexisting medium of political, tribal, or family rights. Since citizens derive their rights from the State, they do not have the privilege of breaking them except in the interest of the State. Thus Green supported a political position as conservative as it was liberal.

Arthur James Balfour declared himself neither idealist nor naturalist. On the one hand, he declared the absolute spirit free, on the other, he denied the existence of the soul or the absolute.[39] To him, freedom was a reality because he was unwilling to abandon it on ethical grounds, because naturalist arguments against it were incoherent, and because denial of freedom left no room for the self. Yet he recognized the contradictions in believing at the same time in material sequence and states of self-consciousness. "I keep them both," he declared, "conscious of their incompatibility" (Balfour, 107–8).

Balfour made these announcements in a 1911 review of Henri Bergson's *Creative Evolution*, a work that he found seriously flawed. Bergson, said Balfour, claimed that life, will, and consciousness were dependent upon a material organism which they used for releasing energy but failed to describe any mechanism by which to prove that the release of that energy was willed or determined. Balfour considered Bergson's use of science reminiscent of "the familiar theistic argument from design, save that most of the design is left out" (Balfour, 126). He classed Bergson among religious philosophers (by which he meant those who see some suprahuman force *taking sides* in "a moving drama") and was disappointed that Bergson had not carried his "scientific" speculations far enough. "What is it that consciousness strives for? What does it accomplish? It strives to penetrate matter with contingency. Why, I do not know. But concede the worth of the enterprise. What measure of success can it possibly attain?" Consciousness and will can "inflict a few trifling scratches on the outer crust of our world," but most matter remains "the undisputed realm of lifeless determinism. Freedom, when all has happened that can happen, creeps humbly on its fringe" (Balfour, 130–31). Why not, Balfour asked, just call the force of which man is a part God and be done with it? And so we return by a strange path to Samuel Butler's no-longer-eccentric pattern.

Balfour dismissed Bergson's theories but did not appreciate the qualities that made the French writer's work attractive to his contemporaries. He wrote at a time when the naturalist school was temporarily restrained in its assertions of authority, when Darwinism was in ebb, and when spiritual interests of remarkable diversity were popular. He managed to suspend judgment in philosophy just as he managed for a time to hold political decisions in abeyance. Bergson, without Balfour's reservations about human progress, and without his political ambitions, was free to imagine man in very modern terms by stressing what had become a theme of great interest at the end of the century, time. In *Time and Free Will* (1889), Bergson observed that associationist determinism represented the self as a collection of states and that it artificially presented feelings as distinct things. Its great mistake was to convert the concrete phenomena occurring in the mind to artificial reconstructions of them—to present duration as space. But mental states are not spatially discrete; they interpenetrate.[40] The conscious self, as Bergson later averred in *Matter and Memory* (1896), was a subjective juncture of past and present, a union of matter (which retained the physical imprint of past sensation) and soul (the unifying power that knits together past and present sensations).[41] Determinists argue for causation, Bergson said, but leave out the important distinction that space and duration are neither translatable nor equatable. Descartes and Spinoza were closer to the truth in realizing that the whole duration of the universe could be contained in a single moment (Bergson, *Time*, 208).

Bergson concluded that no positive definition of freedom was possible because freedom was the *relation* of the concrete self to the act it performed, a relation indefinable precisely because we are free (Bergson, *Time*, 219-20).[42] The free act takes place in time flowing, which cannot be spatially represented, whereas time flown, which can be spatially represented, is the province of determinism. Although Bergson, like T. H. Green, rejected Kant's removal of free will to the realm of noumena, he retained the subjective emphasis that that removal implied. For Bergson, evolution itself involved subjective growth (what Drummond called an infolding of external experience into the self) but in the dimension of time that is not translatable into space and thence not imperial.

Debates about the nature of evolution continued into the twentieth century and are certainly not extinct in our own day. Evolutionary theory expanded to include most biological and social fields, not least significantly, according to Spencer's early valuation, the social organism itself. Inescapably related to the evolution of the social organism was the role of individual personality and its reflection in social man. George John Romanes had made a major contribution to this area of thought with his *Mental Evolution in Man* (1888). His naturalist investigations later accorded a role to emotions, instinct, imagination, and faith, a tendency in keeping with the revival of respect for the irrational sources of human behavior so characteristic of the late nineteenth and early twentieth centuries. Many advocates of evolution resembled Romanes in his ability to accommodate several apparently incompatible beliefs in a harmonious creed, but I shall examine only one such spokesman.

J. W. Burrow describes L. T. Hobhouse as "virtually the last" evolutionary social theorist.[43] In *Mind in Evolution* (1901), Hobhouse charted the progressive growth of human intelligence from instinctive to reasoned behavior. Beyond mere instinct, animal and human intelligence learns to assimilate and relate experiences, in short, develops conscious memory. What sets men apart from other species is their capacity to develop concepts out of individual ideas. The Universal in thought resembles the Self in psychology. "Generally, the Individual and the Collective Concept resemble the true Universal in detachment from any single sense experience, and in that they group together a mass of experiences on the basis of a common element pervading them all."[44] The recognition of self leads to the recognition of other selves and the concomitant potential for altruistic behavior as reflected in schemes of morality and religion. Reason, or conceptual thinking, emerges as a consequence of the power to relate disparate ideas, and self-consciousness develops as a feature of the mind's evaluation of its own performance. Along with conceptual thought and self-consciousness comes will —the wedding of desire to concrete experience. Will is something higher than focused desire; it is to impulse what the universal is to the idea. "The will is not to be regarded as an additional impulse, or as a force existing outside impulses and operating upon them. It is rather the system or synthesis of impulses, the broad practical bent and tendency of one's nature" (Hobhouse, *Mind*, 350). It may be said that the self achieves *character* through the defining and directing power of the will. "The Will is more than we can feel at any one moment, for it is the whole self, or ourself acting as a whole. This action of the self as a whole is called out and directed by the broad ends of life, and things seen to be bound up therewith. It therefore belongs to the grade of mental development under discussion" (Hobhouse, *Mind*, 350–51). Moral impulses develop into moral will and morality develops now under the governance of man, who has learned to guide the evolution of his own mental life.

Hobhouse believed in the human power of improvement but did not accept the belief in automatic progress so common in his day. He distrusted the application of natural laws to politics, recognizing how easily biological assumptions could be warped to suit a political program. Who, he asked, was to define the term "natural" satisfactorily for such purposes? Nonetheless, he rated communities on their advances in scale, efficiency, freedom, and mutuality. Accepting the Spencerian premise that evolution moved from basic to complicated systems, from homogeneity to heterogeneity, he realized that balancing efficiency and freedom might be difficult but that a high degree of mutuality would surely characterize most successful societies.

Hobhouse was very much in the necessarian tradition concerning what he called the Undetermined Will, viewing it in relation to human responsibility. The "I" cannot be held responsible for a deed unless that deed is the result of a uniform pattern of causation. If free will can alter that causal pattern, it violates the integrity of the self and thus the "I" to be punished is not the equivalent of the "I" that willed.[45] We have seen this argument explored in detail elsewhere and need not follow it up here. Instead, it is interesting to observe that the absence of "free will" does not trouble Hobhouse, for he does not automatically propose the opposite problem of determinism. How is anyone "responsible" for his behavior if all action is inescapably determined? To Hobhouse, the will is a governing power and its force a sort of magnetic charge that preserves the integrity of the self by binding together the volatile elements called desires of which it is constituted. "This action, which we call that of Will, implies a certain inter-relation of the various impulsive and emotional tendencies, which are naturally fostered and strengthened so far as they fall in with the ends which the Will adopts, pressed and re-moulded to adapt them to the course of life which it prescribes, or it may be altogether resisted and, if possible, suppressed" (Hobhouse, *Morals*, 599). In this way, Desire and Will, Pleasure and Happiness come together in a synthesizing Action that constitutes human morality. Following from this social self-consciousness, this rational blending of moral, scientific, and religious spirit, is the "self-conscious evolution of humanity." Until now, man has been the servant of natural law, though slowly the dominance of mind, "the central fact of evolution," was being accomplished. If his view of this process was true, Hobhouse concluded, "it is the germ of a religion and an ethics which are as far removed from materialism as from the optimistic teleology of the metaphysician, or the half naive creeds of the churches. It gives a meaning to human effort, as neither the pawn of an overruling Providence nor the sport of blind force. It is a message of hope to the world, of suffering lessened and strife assuaged, not by fleeing from reason to the bosom of faith, but by the increasing rational control of things by that collective wisdom, the Ειο ξυνδο Λδγοσ, that we directly know of the Divine" (Hobhouse, *Morals*, 637).

For some time after the turn of the century scientific naturalism prevailed throughout western culture. To some degree, subtle arguments of the nineteenth century were reduced to simplistic formulas and discarded. But recently, new challenges have emerged. Philosophers in our time are renegotiating the issue of free will, and scientists are reexamining their assumptions about evolution in the light of new genetic information. Edward O. Wilson, a major spokesman of sociobiology, has provided new but controversial support for optimistic views in his qualified endorsement of altruism as a strong force in cultural evolution. Like Drummond and others, Wilson distinguishes cultural from biological evolution, the one being Lamarckian and swift, the other Darwinian and slow. Wilson rejects the organic analogy for cultures or societies and dismisses our freedom as illusory.[46] Promoting scientific naturalism as an alternative to religion, Wilson recommends "the evolutionary epic" as "probably the best myth we will ever have" (Wilson, 201). The human species (through conventional eugenics and other means) can change its own nature, he says, then concludes with a question that resurrects the very heart of the problem we have been exploring: What will he choose? First, of course, he must be able to choose in any sense that is meaningful. Without will in the nonlogical sense of free will, man can choose nothing but merely move along a course determined forever within the first three minutes of the universe.

From Bentham, to Comte, to Hobhouse, to Wilson, the rejection of free will nonetheless incorporates a belief that man can alter his own nature by wise choice, a contradiction calling for various forms of equivocation and explanation, none entirely satisfactory. From Paley, to Butler, to Drummond, a belief in a guiding force supporting human power to choose required faith in a suprahuman entity that could not be demonstrated by experimental evidence (testimony of spiritualists aside). New conceptions of the self, finding their way into such various fields as psychology, biology, ethics, and fiction, introduced subtle or dramatic variations on the perennial, perhaps unresolvable, quarrel about free will and necessity. Backed up to the utter mystery of existence, men chose the pattern that satisfied them most. This dilemma of freedom and determinism persisted throughout the nineteenth century, taking various forms in various arenas of discussion. But always the question of some form of the human capacity for choice underlay the constant revival of the dilemma. Partly this was because, in a society convinced of the rightness and wrongness of certain forms of conduct, a basis for moral responsibility seemed essential. The exertion of free will provided such a basis for judgment. The next chapter examines this problem of human responsibility in the especially sensitive areas of medicine and law.

CHAPTER EIGHT

Madness

NINETEENTH-century theories about insanity were divided between those emphasizing material and those emphasizing ideal factors. One group assumed a physical basis for insanity; the other focused on moral weakness. Often, but not always, materialists were secular and idealists religious in their aims. Generally, however, all were concerned with the large question of responsibility and stressed discipline as a safeguard against madness. In doing so, these advocates of improved self-government assumed some power in the self, ordinarily defined one way or another as will, that could oversee that process of self-government.

This chapter offers selected attitudes toward madness in nineteenth-century England. It begins with phrenology because early in the century that "science" promised one of the most concrete and measurable theories on human character, specifically for us, on madness. Phrenologists themselves, however, were divided between materialists and idealists, between those who accepted and those who rejected the concept of free will. Mesmerism was another popular if suspect approach to human psychology that featured will as the central human trait. To represent middle and late century attitudes on insanity I have chosen men who were influential and respected in their day. Henry Maudsley promoted a materialist and relativist position, whereas W. B. Carpenter attempted to reconcile determinist physical assumptions with a belief in free will.

Because it must labor to treat, remedy, even cure abnormal conditions, medicine, specifically what we know as psychiatry, must deal theoretically and humanly with the question of free will and responsibility. The situation becomes acute when such responsibility enters the public arena in the form of criminal action. It is here that most human beings encounter the free will versus necessity dilemma in its most extreme and most confusing manifestation, for complicating the familiar dichotomy between libertarian and necessarian beliefs that we have traced through these early chapters was the division among legal actors, themselves obliged to determine the relative importance and relation of criminal acts and the mental states (motives) that prompt them. Because the insanity defense most succinctly concentrates this dilemma, I have concluded part 1 of this study with a brief sketch of nineteenth-century responses to insanity and the law and have suggested that the problem remains unresolved to the present day.

~   ~   ~

If men are free, it is logical to claim that they are responsible for their acts because reason may instruct them. But to what degree are creatures responsible who do not have the full power of reasoning? The question of insanity focuses this issue, extending from the basic relationship of mind and body to the legal attribution of responsibility. But insanity was very little understood during much of the nineteenth century, the prevailing view being that it resulted from an excess of passion or a disruption of reason. This attitude was complicated by the common belief in man's dualistic nature, which located an immaterial soul in a material, and hence corruptible, body. The division between idealists and physicalists, or materialists, continued through most of the century. Idealists concerned themselves mainly with the moral nature of insanity, materialists mainly with physical causes. Vieda Skultans writes that "whereas earlier writers are interested in 'moral force' and 'will,' later writers are interested in 'hereditary endowment' and 'character.' "[1] None, however, denied the physical manifestations of madness.

William Battie was one of the first to attempt a clear new look at madness, which he defined as "deluded imagination." He located the seat of sensation in the medullary substance communicating with the brain and described the cause of madness as "an internal disorder of the nervous substance, which could be *original*, or inherent in the organism, or *consequential*, or occasioned by some external influence."[2] The first form of madness he considered incurable, the second remediable. Battie rejected violent remedies such as purging favored by his contemporaries and argued that much madness was as manageable as other illnesses. His recommendations for therapy included confinement of the patient away from disturbing influences and discipline of unruly appetites. Like the "moral management" exponents of his time, Battie assumed that, even if madness had a physical manifestation in the nervous system, it was susceptible to treatment which involved the recovery of control by a strengthened will.

Battie's program seems rather clear-sighted for 1757, but John Monro, representing what may be called a primitive physicalist position, more determinist in character, quarrelled with it point by point a few months later, concluding that madness will be forever incurable and incomprehensible. Monro rejected Battie's remedies as well, adhering to what he considered "the most adequate and constant cure," evacuation, of which vomiting "is infinitely preferable to any other, if repeated experience is to be depended on."[3] Bleeding was another trustworthy device in Monro's book. These traditional methods were based upon a theory of impurities in the blood and elsewhere in the organism.

The growing interest in insanity among English medical men during the eighteenth century was probably a response to King George III's condition. William F. Bynum, Jr., lists three major positions espoused by British psychiatric literature of the late eighteenth and early nineteenth century: "(1) that insanity is always attended by structural changes and hence is ultimately a physical condition; (2) that insanity is always a mental condition, properly differentiated from any physical disease which secondarily produces mental symptoms; (3) that insanity may be caused by either physical disease or by mental aberrations. The majority of British physicians who expressed themselves on the subject of insanity during our period subscribed themselves to the first position, that insanity is a disease of the body."[4] But for many who believed in the Cartesian divorce of mind, or soul, from brain, understanding madness was a more complicated endeavor. Both groups, however, had to offer some explanation of how insanity affected the patient's moral responsibilities.

Phrenology, one of the more coherent physicalist theories of the early nineteenth century, tried to comprehend the functions and disorders of the mind by rigorously identifying locations in the brain as sources of thought and behavior. For most supporters, phrenology had a strong moral base. George Combe diagramed human faculties under Intellectual Faculties and orders of Feelings (including Propensities and Sentiments), arguing that the former moral and intellectual qualities dominate man's animal appetites.[5] Combe said little about insanity. He attributed brain composition to heredity and thus placed aberrant behavior beyond conscious control; "these causes subsist *independently of the will of the offender*," he said and gave the example of the criminal who "is not the cause of the unfortunate preponderance of the animal organs in his own brain, neither is he the cause of the external excitement which seduces his propensities into abuse, or of the intellectual ignorance in which he is involved."[6] Although this close identification of insanity with brain structure appears to be entirely deterministic, Dr. Johann Spurzheim, the founder of phrenology, assumed the human freedom of willing for or against something.[7] But Spurzheim, too, considered insanity an abeyance of the will and defined it as "*the incapacity of distinguishing the diseased functions of the mind, and the irresistibility of our actions;*" largely, this resulted from too great energy of one power of the brain. "For that reason," he explained, "a genius is so often near insanity; that is, his power is so energetic that it acts independently of the will."[8]

Disagreements among phrenologists about the role of will frequently followed religious lines. William Scott considered Combe's opinions dangerous because they excused man to a great degree from responsibility for his misdeeds. "For Combe the Will was subsumed in behaviourist psychology; for Scott it remained a separate entity, in no way material, decidedly mysterious, and a gift of God."[9] This question of determinism remained a crucial one for phrenologists. Most of them were progressive in their social views and hoped to improve man through education and material advances, but if man's moral nature was determined by his inherited physical qualities, how was he capable of such improvement? This dilemma is one with which we are already familiar among philosophers and moralists, in particular those who espoused Benthamite and utilitarian theories. If will is the key term of responsibility, then free will must somewhere have a place, even if, as with Godwin, it is a useful illusion or, for Mill, a severely limited function. Among medical men, the question was never resolved and, by the end of the century did not matter for phrenology, which was no longer credited as a science.[10]

Like utilitarianism, phrenology was concerned with practical effects based upon fundamental rules derived from what appeared to be natural law. It resembled utilitarianism further in its affection for lists and categories. In its heyday, it had the virtue of being the only thoroughly organized modern theoretical system of psychology. Other contemporary attitudes toward madness and its causes were chaotic and even bizarre by comparison.[11] "Keeping the bowels in free action is indispensable [*sic*] in all cases of insanity," George Man Burrows wrote in 1828, and his view was far from uncommon. As late as 1853, Daniel Noble wrote in *Elements of Psychological Medicine* that "premonitory symptoms of insanity are sometimes dissipated by procuring a free and vigorous action of the large intestines" (Skultans, 120). Purges naturally recommended themselves as satisfactory cures when constipation was acknowledged as a cause of insanity.

Psychologists could not agree about the pathological origins of madness. In 1838, William Willis Moseley asserted "that disease in the organ of the brain, and not in the mind, is the cause of nervous complaints and insanity, is therefore now admitted" (Skultans, 41). But James Sheppard, a few years later, declared with equal certainty "that insanity does not *depend* on disease of the brain" (Skultans, 50). Moseley listed thirty-one exciting causes of insanity including ill-conducted nurseries, strong passions, inebriation, solar heat, onanism, long-continued study, "the fearful associations of being awoke from sound sleep while the house is on fire," and influenza (Skultans, 41ff).[12]

Concern for the pathological features of madness continued, but the nineteenth century also witnessed a growing interest in the moral management of insanity. The concern among advocates of this scheme was discipline of the will. "Through moral management," as Ann C. Colley puts it, "the will would regain its 'supremacy' and control the body and its animal spirits."[13] This approach assumed a moral origin for madness in one or another form of excess; thus "moral factors are seen as forces against insanity. Habit, perseverance, the will and character may each constitute such a counteracting force" (Skultans, 2-3).[14] Advocates of moral management placed a high valuation on self-government and thus accorded well with Victorian political and social authoritarianism. The focus for this movement in England was the Tuke family's model asylum at York called the Retreat. Andrew Scull suggests that the humane methods and domestic arrangements at the Retreat mirrored to some degree the changing economic conditions in England at the time. As the competitive market place made the individual responsible for his own economic success or failure so moral management suggested that the individual, at war with the forces of chaos, was responsible for his own mental condition. The resemblance was strengthened by the systems of reward and punishment employed in asylums.[15] Once institutionalized in other asylums, however, the Tuke system degenerated from the provision of a healthy, stimulating environment to the subordination of inmates to institutional discipline.

The growing interest in treatment of the insane led to many sober as well as zany suggestions. Joseph Mason Cox's swinging machine and the "Tranquillizer," one using enforced motion and the other enforced stillness to effect cures or remission, are examples.[16] Though he was often criticized by colleagues and even satirized in fiction, John Conolly had more reasonable recommendations for medical practitioners.[17] In *An Inquiry concerning the Indications of Insanity with Suggestions for the Better Protection and Care of the Insane* (1830), Conolly noted that all men are interested in the subject of insanity because no man is confident that he can reckon on continued perfect reason in himself. The great error of medical men is in seeking and imagining "a strong and definable boundary between sanity and insanity," thus leading to arbitrary distinctions often detrimental to those classed as insane.[18] Conolly argued that there is no great separation between the sane and the insane, all men being to some degree imperfect. He believed that insanity had a physical basis but that abnormality could be judged only by those who understood the functions of a healthy mind. Most insanity resulted, he said, from excess indulgence of feelings, only relatively few cases from the exercise of the mind.[19] Ordinary life, therefore, differs from the excesses of insanity only in degree and in the existence of social restraint.

The Reverend John Barlow, acknowledging his debt to Conolly, delivered a paper entitled *On Man's Power over Himself to Prevent or Control Insanity* to the Royal Institution in 1843, when he was secretary of that organization. He differentiated insanity, a physical disease, from mental derangement, essentially a failure of will. "Nothing then but an extent of disease which destroys at once all possibility of reasoning, by annihilating, or entirely changing the structure of the organ, can make a man necessarily mad. In all other cases, the being sane or otherwise, notwithstanding considerable disease of brain, depends on the individual himself." Madness followed from a failure to direct intellectual force and to command the bodily organ through habits of calm reasoning. It was thus "a fearful result of an uncultivated childhood."[20]

Barlow argued that the rational will could to some degree control all mental derangement, even mastering many cases where physical degeneration was involved. If people would only exert themselves, he urged, they could be free from such madness. With the poor and uneducated classes, the problem was inefficiency of intellectual force; with the higher ranks, it was misdirection of that force. Questionably claiming that there are no mad mathematicians, Barlow declared that mental derangement can be controlled only through the cultivation of the power of the mind, though he also realized that if the mind once overbalanced in the direction of passion, the intelligent will might temporarily lend its force to that movement.

Barlow's conviction that man's intelligent will could significantly govern the body was supported in an unexpected direction by the studies of James Braid, who, in attempting to verify Baron Reichenbach's experiments in what was called animal magnetism, discovered the principles of hypnotism —or mesmerism, as it came to be known in the nineteenth century—in "the extraordinary power of the mind over the body, and how mental impressions could change physical action."[21] At a practical level, Braid's experiments ended up disproving Reichenbach's theory of a magnetic fluid but in the process demonstrated the power of concentration in controlling physical actions. Braid concluded that he had proved "the *unity* of the *mind*; and the remarkable power of the soul over the body."[22]

Defense of the soul was an important feature in Victorian attempts to understand aberrant behavior. Declaring that insanity arose from corporeal sources, Dr. Johann Spurzheim explained that "the soul cannot fall sick, any more than it can die."[23] George Moore, a doctor who wrote specifically to give religious comfort to sufferers, agreed with Spurzheim's separation of physical and spiritual elements in man and vigorously opposed phrenologists who encouraged materialistic attitudes by equating mind with body; specifically, he objected to Dr. John Elliotson, who suggested that human will was located in the front brain, which then acted on the small brain and spinal system behind.[24] Moore believed that man's body was adapted to his soul and both were designed for instruction in the material universe, the will being disciplined under physical and moral laws that differed in their operations. He explained that mental and physical laws are fixed but moral laws are addressed to the will, which is capable of choosing between good and evil.[25] One law of earthly existence is: "We are formed for moderation" (Moore, *Power*, 205). Inaction and excess are alike destructive to us. Moore said that "insanity is always a bodily malady, although perhaps in most cases moral delinquency is superadded, and the will has been disordered before the body" (Moore, *Power*, 208). Man's hope is in fixing his attention on the higher goals of religious faith and self-less charity. Moore noted the examples of martyrs who submit their wills to God.

More important than the development of a man's brain is his control of it; "instead of mind and memory resulting from brain, that brain, as far as it has relation to the mind is developed and regulated in subserviency to the will" (Moore, *Power*, 138). Will is the master principle, and its moral condition in each man determines his moral destiny. To be free, we must exercise our will for good. Understanding and will, in a religious sense, can proceed only from God; they are included in "selfhood" which signifies the soul. Soul operates through nerve matter, but personality does not reside in one's material being. The soul's threefold order of consciousness (intellect, emotion, and will) corresponds to the body's nervous system (cerebral, cerebrospinal, ganglionic). A proper education will balance these.

Moore believed that man's free will depends upon the consciousness of good and evil. Love, being antagonistic to self-will, is the truest basis for this spiritual knowledge. "If self-control, and the subjection of bodily impulses be not founded on love to others as well as to ourselves," Moore cautioned, "moral derangement is already commenced" (Moore, *Motives*, 121). Like Braid, W. B. Carpenter, and others, Moore considered all attention an effort of will and insisted that man improves himself by fixing his attention on proper objects such as natural beauty and the revealed truth of the Bible (Moore, *Motives*, 150ff).

Moore adopted views we have already seen stated by professional moralists and applied them more specifically and with his own emphases to the issue of mental health. For him, will was volition, or the directive power of the mind to guide bodily functions, but he also conceived of a "higher will," which chose "not merely according to sensation, but according to moral conviction" (Moore, *Motives*, 31). He assumed that volition operates by fixed laws, and the higher will by moral laws, which require that higher will to choose good or evil, hence presuming its freedom. Like many preachers of the time, Moore considered man's will free only when it was able to choose the good; choosing evil meant enslavement by sense. Man was therefore responsible for his insanity, except when physical disease clearly obliterated the operations of the soul. In Moore's scheme, insanity could even be interpreted as a punishment for excess.

Another medical man, Thomas Laycock, had similarly moral and religious aims but propounded a different scheme. His purpose was to justify faith in a providential design through a rational plan demonstrating that apparent imperfections can be interpreted as perfections. He used an argument already familiar to us from earlier chapters that even the laws of physical necessity prove the existence of God by forcing the mind back from event to cause until it arrives at the inevitability of a conscious First Cause.[26] All of the operations of nature are manifestations of soul operating in time and space through matter. Moreover, the ideas of the divine mind revealed in the phenomena of creation are themselves "none other than the fundamental ideas and *a priori* conceptions of the human mind as revealed in consciousness; that the ends aimed at and attained by the Creator are the objects of the instinctive desires of the creature; and that, consequently, the phenomena of nature constitute a reflex of the human mind" (Laycock, 114).

Unlike Moore, Laycock overcame the problem of duality by making all physical events manifestations of spirit and then explaining them as part of a beneficial divine scheme. But just as man must study God and nature to understand that scheme, he must study himself to understand his own purpose. "Perfect freedom is therefore compatible in man only with perfect knowledge of his own nature." Men ignorant of the true nature of the spontaneous "lusts of the flesh," will be enslaved by them, whereas one who understands them may restrain them.

With Laycock, madness became synonymous with loss of free will, itself associated with self-knowledge. Unfortunately, in this order of things, madness is an all too probable outcome in human affairs, for there is much that man does not understand about himself. Laycock himself boasted of having preceded W. B. Carpenter in positing the idea of unconscious cerebral action (Laycock, iii). If new knowledge about man's nature is steadily forthcoming, "perfect knowledge" may be achievable but is very distant. But if man is thus remote from perfect freedom, to what degree may he be held responsible for his failure of knowledge? On this point, Laycock was mute, simply arguing, according to his odd mixture of Kant and Darwin, that man's destiny is full of promise as it follows the evolutionary unfolding of the divine mind's intent.

There are certainly flaws in Laycock's explanation of man's nature and his place in nature, especially in regard to madness and free will, and it was such arguments that Henry Maudsley, representing an entirely different attitude, sought to correct. Maudsley distrusted the metaphysical basis for many of his peers' judgments, though he agreed with some of their conclusions, for example, that having a great purpose in life requiring discipline and self-renunciation contributes to sanity.[27] He agreed, as well, that insanity "is the dethronement of the will, the loss of the power of coordinating the ideas and feelings" but asserted that mental disease is no more than the result of a disordered organ—the brain (Maudsley, *Responsibility*, 77, 15). "I cannot but think," he complained, "that moral philosophers have sometimes exaggerated greatly the direct power of the will, as an abstract entity, over the thoughts and feelings, without at the same time having taken sufficient account of the slow and gradual way in which the concrete will itself must be formed" (Maudsley, *Responsibility*, 273). He objected elsewhere that metaphysicians create an entity of the general term "will" that embraces a multiplicity of volitions.[28]

Maudsley was a materialist, rejecting all spiritual interpretations of man's composition. Praising the Greeks for recognizing madness as a disease, he was hopeful that men were recovering that understanding (Maudsley, *Responsibility*, 9ff). He applied no abstract or predetermined moral laws to man's condition, arguing that "there is no rule to distinguish between true and false but the common judgment of mankind, no rule to distinguish between virtue and vice but the common feeling of mankind" (Maudsley, *Will*, 41–42). He rejected the identification of self as soul and described the Ego as a variable, not a constant. Dismissing the theory of free will, he bound the power of choosing directly to cerebral action. "Theories of freewill," he summarized, "seem to come very much to this—that the will that is swayed by low motives is not free, that the will that is swayed by higher motives is more free, and that the will that is swayed by the highest motives is most free" (Maudsley, *Will*, 234). According to theists, the highest evolution of free will is to lose itself in the Divine Will, but Maudsley objected that man cannot know God's will. Citing Cardinal Newman as a champion of conscience as God's will revealed to man, Maudsley argued that conscience itself is a product of human society and the moral development of the tribe.

Maudsley offered to do what he felt metaphysicians could not do—explain the gradual formation of the concrete will by recurrence. Through repetition, "will remembers and learns to will, exercise building up faculty and conduct character," so that a man is shaped by his circumstances (Maudsley, *Will*, 20). First of all, an individual is what inheritance makes him. No man can escape this elementary truth; education can modify him only within a pattern of inherited capacity (Maudsley, *Responsibility*, 20ff). "There is a destiny made for each one by his inheritance; he is the necessary organic consequent of certain organic antecedents; and it is impossible he should escape the tyranny of his organization" (Skultans, 215). Each man, deep in his heart, believes in this predestination that resembles the "inexorable destiny" of Greek tragedy. And yet necessity is not the same as inexorable fate, it is simply the law of invariable uniformity of cause and effect. And here

Maudsley returned to the standard arguments that, by now, we know so well.

The traditional necessarian position assumes that man is responsible because of the inflexible law of necessity; Maudsley repeated this idea, suggesting that if a man were truly free he would not be responsible for his character because it would not be the product of an ordered causal development. Like Godwin, he admitted that the illusion of free will may be useful against the pressure of a particular passion or motive. Like other delusions, that of free will may do real work in the mind without actually existing. But this small admission raises massive problems. If behavior is altered by a *notion* of free will, what has made that alteration possible? Maudsley was a step beyond Godwin in classifying free will as just one more delusion affecting the mind; however, that does not answer, but merely complicates, the question. How is it that what does not exist may, by altering the operations of the mind, transform external existence as well? Delusions that beget consequences do in some sense exist, though they may exist only as sensations in the human organism. In that, they are like all other sources of stimulation. To examine this subject thoroughly would require a return to the much larger question of the relationship of mind to matter.

Maudsley did not directly engage this question, but his design of human development implies a position. In effect, Maudsley substituted a plan very like providence without a deity. Man is the agent of nature's purpose. "The will of man being the outcome of supreme reason is the highest and latest evolved energy in nature; it is in fact the power by which nature developing through man accomplishes the progressing path of its destiny, the nature-made mean by which nature is made better." It may be described as "the highest instinct of development" (Maudsley, *Will*, 190). Just as the Christian aspires to lose his individual will in that of his God, Maudsley said that the right aim of will is "to escape from the limitation of self and to gain the full freedom of nature by becoming one with it—to surmount self by losing the consciousness of self" (Maudsley, *Will*, 191). Free will is not a relic of a lost human faculty but an ideal toward which man aspires. The present aim of the highest will is social evolution of moral law. The rule of morality is implicit in practice before it becomes explicit in thought and must therefore be sought in conduct. Although we tend to think of will as conscious and individual, it is actually the unconscious, instinctive energy of nature. But, like Huxley and others, Maudsley cautioned that the evolutionary pattern does not guarantee that the morally best will survive; he warned that degeneration is as much a part of nature as generation and that a people or race who no longer aspire to realize the ideal will soon cease to idealize the real and thereby enter into a period of decline or decadence (Maudsley, *Will*, 327).

If man is determined by inheritance and conditioning and is the conduit for the mysterious forces of nature, how may he be viewed as responsible? As we have already seen, Maudsley concluded that men are responsible for their characters because they are the products of interpretable causal patterns. In a passage reminiscent of the Mills' arguments, Maudsley declared that man must improve through education and that the social organization—community, tribe, or race—must do what individuals cannot. Man must cease to labor to know himself in himself and seek instead to know himself in nature. Looking within, he can find no absolute criterion of truth or right, but only self, thus he must seek his standards in the larger experience of the race. "Humanity, not self, is the true concern of the individual who would rise to a higher self." The individual's duty, then, is "to place himself in circumstances of action in which his character will be modified for the better—to *do* in order to *be*; the solemn responsibility under which he is to determine rationally in himself, by help of circumstances, that which may thereby be predetermined in his future conduct, and in some measure in his posterity" (Maudsley, *Will*, 96-97). Echoing Carlyle but lacking his hope for a deity's endorsement, Maudsley harangued his reader, declaring that each atom of society contributes to the whole organism and must do its part. "Not to think and feel only, but to *do*, is the end of being—to act one's part in the becoming of things and to affect for good or ill the common weal by such action" (Maudsley, *Will*, 174).[29] Like medical men who based their beliefs on religion, Maudsley, who did not, arrived at very similar conclusions: Men are responsible for their acts. Self is a barrier to freedom. True freedom is in the submergence of the self in a higher power.

William B. Carpenter began his medical career as a convinced determinist but gradually came to believe that each man may take a part in forming his own character. As a doctor and scientist, Carpenter maintained a thoroughly materialist experimental position that he found compatible with his spiritual belief that a divine purpose supported all. He admitted, for example, that volitional activity operates solely through the instrumentality of the cerebrum but contended that just as the cerebrum controls the automatism of the axial cord so a higher power might govern the automatism of the cerebrum itself.[30] And though he allowed that the physical force exerted by man derived from the oxidation of nutrients, he did not feel that this eliminated the likelihood of a God originating and controlling natural forces by his will (Carpenter, *Nature*, 364). One of Carpenter's central arguments was that matter and force are inseparable yet distinct. His arguments resemble James Martineau's in another context. Matter is the embodiment or instrument of force, which is more akin to mind than to matter and therefore a greater reality than matter. Its apparent purposiveness justifies the attribution of a divine intent. Nature is therefore the embodiment of divine volition.[31]

Carpenter offered several justifications for a theory of free will, none of them novel, all of them based upon the universal existence of a moral consciousness in men—a sense of "ought to" (Carpenter, *Principles*, 300, xxx). In this scheme, man is clearly responsible for his actions, indeed, more responsible the more he controls the automatism of his nature. Like George Moore and others, Carpenter believed that the will operated best when focused on a high ideal, a notion admittedly derived from Carlyle. This high ideal was, as in Maudsley's view, associated with an evolutionary, though not Darwinian, development, a development that promised not only intellectual but also moral growth. Carpenter considered this movement providential and likened it to human patterns of volition. In physiology, he said, voluntary actions do not direct special movements, which remain below consciousness, but simply specify and determine the results. So with God.

For Carpenter, "it is solely by the Volitional *direction of the attention* that the Will exerts its domination; so that the acquirement of this power, which is within the reach of every one, should be the primary object of all mental discipline" (Carpenter, *Principles*, 25). Weakening of this power causes insanity, hence moral management ideas about educating the will appealed to Carpenter. The task for sane and insane alike is unrelenting, since the capacity for attention and the focusing of the will must become habitual through regular exercise (Carpenter, *Principles*, 366). Because men have a limited capacity to master their wills, their degrees of responsibility vary; for the most part, though, men are answerable for their actions, though discipline, not confinement or physical punishment should be the means of curing the insane wherever a cure is possible.

Near the end of the century, James Sully, in *The Human Mind: A Textbook of Psychology* (1892), cited Carpenter as an important source on moral habit and character; the following passage shows his influence.

> To diminish the effect of a hasty impulse by a strenuous effort of attention to ideas of which it took no account, is to assert oneself in a specially emphatic and striking manner, is to strike at the tyrannous monopoly of impulse by a special intensification of consciousness. Hence it begets a particularly clear apprehension, not only of self as agent or cause, but of self as selecting or as freely determining the issue. That is to say, it generates in its most distinct form the consciousness of freedom or free-will.[32]

Sully did not attempt to resolve the metaphysical problem of free will, wanting merely to describe how the ego-enhancing sense of freedom develops in man from the rudimentary sense of unrestrained action, to the ability to restrain impulse, to the deliberations of conscious choice. Largely typical of end-of-the-century attitudes among psychologists and other medical men, Sully was firmly committed to "the scientific position that all action is psycho-physically determined," while at the same time finding a role for man's "alleged freedom."[33] This noncombative reluctance to decide the issue of madness, free will, and responsibility might be sustained where definition and description and perhaps even actual treatment were concerned, but the problem took on a new significance when it entered the arena of the law.

~ ~ ~

Determining the composition of the human psyche and the abstract question of human responsibility was considerably different from the practical problem of deciding what to do with people who behaved insanely, often to the injury of their fellow men. A few prominent cases of harmful madmen kept this issue before the legal community and the general public. James Hadfield's attempt to kill King George III ended with his confinement in Bethlem Asylum following a plea of insanity.[34] Attempts on the young Queen Victoria, followed by Daniel McNaughtan's murder of Edward Drummond, Sir Robert Peel's private secretary, resulted in the legal definition of insanity that remained, until very recently, the apparent standard for English and American law courts.[35]

Before the nineteenth century, the insane were mainly confined in jails because there were so few asylums. However, legal interest in lunacy increased steadily from about 1744, periodically issuing in government acts. In 1744, a select committee seeking to revise the vagrancy laws in order to control antisocial persons such as those "who threaten to run away and leave their Wives and Children to the Parish. . . . [those] found in Forests with Guns. . . . All Minstrels, Jugglers. . . . All Persons pretending to be Gipsies, or wandering about in the Habit or Form of Egyptians," included dangerous lunatics in their report.[36] In 1763, revelations about conditions in private madhouses generated serious efforts at correction which culminated in the ineffective Act for Regulating Private Madhouses of 1774. According to Kathleen Jones, "Lunacy reform began on a national scale with the foundation of the county asylums, following the Act of 1808."[37]

With this increasing interst in lunacy went a greater concern for its sufferers. Emphasis gradually changed from confinement to treatment of the insane, with some hope for remedy. Moreover, as we have already noted, medical men in particular began to stress the moral dimensions of madness, distinguishing them from physical characteristics. Medical commentators of the early nineteenth-century demonstrated an increasing attention to madness as a social rather than simply a clinical matter. Murder is a serious and dramatic consequence of insanity, and nineteenth-century students of medicine and law were understandably concerned about it.[38] I shall examine their attempts to deal with ordinary homicide, but the subject is more complicated than it might first appear. For example, during much of the nineteenth century, women guilty of infanticide were often leniently treated or excused altogether under the assumption that they were suffering from "puerperal psychosis," that is, mental disorder brought on by childbirth. By 1866, the Home Office was routinely commuting the death penalty when a woman was convicted of murdering her own child if it was twelve months or younger, a practice that became law in a Homicide Bill of 1872.[39] This attitude toward female infanticides followed from the prevailing conception of woman's nature. Though women were expected to bear children, a good deal of mystery surrounded the entire subject of procreation, and details about begetting and bearing children were often withheld from them until they were married. Childbirth was paradoxically a shameful and a holy event, associated with sexuality but also signifying the entrance of a new soul into the care of its moral mentors. A woman might well suffer confusion in trying to deal with these conflicting values, but that her distress should lead to infanticide is scarcely a necessary consequence.

In general, the law treated women more leniently than men during the nineteenth century. But they received this lighter treatment because they were considered closer to nature and were associated with passivity, emotion, and irresponsibility. In this sense, they could almost be classed with children. Moreover, for alienists, women were better examples of the body's influence upon the mind, since changes in women's bodies were more apparent. Roger Smith offers the case of a domestic servant who murdered her employer's children.

> This case exemplified the type of logic alienists were trying to establish. They claimed that a physical change associated with menstruation led to a breakdown in the nervous system. This caused the nervous system to operate automatically, without control, under the influence of an idea already present in the mind; the idea served as a stimulus for a complex reflex. Brixey had behaved like a machine, so her violence had meaning only in terms of her body. And since her violence was socially meaningless, retribution was inappropriate. It also followed that if proper institutional arrangements were made the public need have no further worries. To alienists, the violence was a matter for themselves and Brixey.[40]

It would be interesting to explore other aspects of this subject, but for the purposes of the present study, I shall limit myself to the insanity plea for homicide, where the question of freedom and responsibility is most acute.

In the early nineteenth century, criminal law in general was undergoing serious review and reform in England.[41] Godwin, Bentham and his followers, and others recommended more humane forms of punishment than the rather savage laws current through the eighteenth century. Medical men also had strong feelings on this subject. Phrenologists were among the most active reformers. Despite the determinist base of his phrenological thinking, George Combe supported penal confinement in place of execution. "I believe that to an individual whose mind consists chiefly of animal propensities and intellect, confinement, compulsory labor, and the enforcement of moral conduct, will be highly disagreeable, and that is the punishment which the Creator designed should attend that unfortunate combination of mental qualities."[42] Such punishment, he felt, would more effectively teach the sufferer not to infringe the moral law than would pure animal retribution, which Combe considered a vestige of untamed barbarism. Criminals, he said, were not responsible for their mental condition, but nonretributive punishment might nonetheless correct some causes of criminal behavior by creating a respect for restraint (in effect, will-power), by using confinement to eliminate external causes of excitement and by replacing ignorance with instruction. The brain itself Combe considered unalterable. His behaviorist approach did not deal with the criminally insane, but since he did not consider ordinary criminals responsible for their conditions, presumably the insane would not be either. Later in the century, when phrenology had been largely discredited, a similarly physical approach to criminal behavior enjoyed a degree of success. Cesare Lombroso theorized that criminals could be identified by their physiognomy and skull shape and concluded that they were evolutionary throwbacks and hence biologically determined, their crimes being instinctual and not the consequences of willed choice.[43]

Jurists had been struggling with the problem of criminal insanity for some time, but the case that produced a working definition was the McNaughtan case of 1843. Alexander Cockburn, the attorney appointed to represent McNaughtan, drew his information and the rationale of his defense strategy from *A Treatise on the Medical Jurisprudence of Insanity* by Isaac Ray, a young general practitioner of Eastport, Maine. According to Jacques M. Quen, the book remains "a classic of forensic psychiatry" (Quen, 160). Although Cockburn did not use Ray's terms in the trial, his emphasis upon McNaughtan's incapacity to determine right from wrong evoked a verdict of not guilty by reason of insanity. The public outcry was so intense that the House of Lords requested a judicial review of issues raised in the case by a group of judges of the Queen's Bench. Part of the judges' response to the questions set them constitutes what is known as the McNaughtan rule:

> The jurors ought to be told that every man is presumed to be sane, and to possess a sufficient degree of reason to be responsible for his crimes, until the contrary be proved to their satisfaction; and that to establish a defense on the ground of insanity, it must be clearly proved that at the time of the committing of the act, the party accused was labouring under such a defect of reason, from disease of

the mind, as not to know the nature and quality of the act he was
doing; or if he did know it, that he did not know he was doing what
was wrong. (Quen, 162)

Quen comments on the change effected by this new definition. "Present in
the common law before the judges' answers had been an understanding will;
delusion in the presence of reason; mind or will overwhelmed by disease;
ungovernable delusions; controlling disease, the acting power of which
could not be resisted; or an understanding less than that of the ordinary
fourteen year old. All that remained was 'knowledge of the nature and quality of the act' and knowledge of 'wrong' " (Quen, 162).

As Richard Moran points out, McNaughtan himself would have been
judged sane and legally culpable if he had been subject to the standards that
bear his name, for though he may have been otherwise confused, he did
know the difference between right and wrong.[44] Historians have assumed
that McNaughtan was insane, but Moran's review of the case indicates that
the decision was politically convenient, the insanity decree suiting the
prosecution as much as it did the defense. Moran offers evidence for his
conclusion. Whereas the defense supplied several medical specialists, the
prosecution called none. The prosecution overlooked many references to
McNaughtan's political views and to the sources of his money, signs that
McNaughtan was a genuine political protestor, perhaps even in conspiracy
with others. "The defense meanwhile acted to identify the nature of the act
with madness and established this view as the basic position: 'Disease in one
part [of the mind] can make a person 'the slave of uncontrollable impulses'
on a particular subject, and yet not affect his will or behavior in other areas of
social intercourse' " (Moran, 95).

Moran suggests that the prosecution was content to leave McNaughtan
"unpunished" (he was confined in Bethlem Hospital on March 13, 1843, and
moved to the new hospital at Broadmoor in 1864, where he died of diabetes
mellitus on May 3, 1865) because by accepting the notion of his insanity
they discredited him as a political spokesman (Moran, 115). He does not
suggest that this procedure was intentional but rather that it was built into
the political, social, and legal system.[45] Moran's study demonstrates how
easily the focus of a legal case may be blurred or shifted and how the true
character of a crime may be lost sight of through a concern to interpret
human nature.

One serious difficulty between medical and legal parties in cases of criminal insanity was that they employed two different modes of discourse, the one
largely determinist, the other primarily voluntarist. To the one, "responsibility" signified culpability, to the other it denoted traits of character—
dependability and so forth. This problem persists in our own day. William J.
Winslade and Judith Wilson Ross observe in *The Insanity Plea* (1983) that

the prosecution in such cases assumes the existence of human freedom, whereas the defense assumes determinism, mutually exclusive attitudes with which a jury is left to deal.[46] In the nineteenth century as now, alienists (as medical specialists in insanity were called) themselves operated on a dualistic assumption that the body was a species of automaton, though directed by a nonphysical will.[47] At the heart of this issue of legal insanity lies a radical incompatibility. Medicine was and is concerned with the condition of the individual in relationship to pathology and psychology, whereas law was and is concerned with the relationship of the individual to society and society's agreed-upon rules. Pathology and psychology are presumed to be constant, if only we can determine their principles, but the rules of society are patently mutable. How then to reconcile the two and arrive at an agreement about the nature of criminal responsibility?

To believe in criminal responsibility one must first believe in responsibility. Taken in whatever way you like, such a belief assumes that an individual is liable for his or her deeds. This, Carlyle said, was the one certain law of Nature, the inevitability of Justice.[48] To some degree, the responsible individual must be free to make choices, choosing rightly or wrongly as the case may be. He wills this or that action and brings it to pass. Having begotten the deed, he must abide its issue. The man who is not responsible can neither prompt nor restrain his deeds by will, but is overcome by impulse or led to a false choice by delusion. John Charles Bucknill, with legal implications in mind, tried to clarify thus: "*Insanity therefore may be defined as, A condition of the mind in which a false action of conception or judgment, a defective power of the will, or an uncontrollable violence of the emotions and instincts, have separately or conjointly been produced by disease*" (Skultans, 174).

A couple of years after this attempt at definition, the public was still not comfortable with the insanity plea. A writer for the *Saturday Review* declared that, in fact, insanity is no defense or plea. He cited the case of a Mr. Westron who shot a Mr. Waugh. The jury found Westron guilty of the crime but recommended mercy. Justice Wightman interpreted this plea for mercy as a request for acquittal on grounds of insanity. But, the author claimed, leniency of this sort is available to the sane as well if they have acted under a mistaken impression that is comparable to the delusions of those called insane. "We all remember the case of Annette Meyers," he said, "who was not only recommended to mercy, but actually pardoned, on account of the gross provocation she had received from the man she murdered. Suppose her impression had been an insane delusion, what difference would that have made?"[49] In fact, the writer concludes, the law gives no more immunity to madmen than to children and drunkards.

Judgment upon so-called criminal behavior is, except in the most abstract theory, a moral act. Morality depends upon standards of right and wrong.

The choice between them assumes a free will. Many medical men argued, as we have seen, that madness was physically based but nonetheless often held that criminals were culpable for impulsive acts because they had indirectly contributed to their condition through vicious habits, drunkenness being the chief example.[50] Discipline, such men believed, could mediate a condition not too far degenerated. Other medical men were even more vehement about the discipline of the will, defining insanity mainly as a moral fault. For them, some form of punishment was essential so that the weak or refractory will could be drilled into moral order again. They would have agreed in the main with the Reverend John Barlow, who explained that the brain left unmanaged became ungovernable and the individual animalized. When a person in that condition commits a crime, the plea of insanity shelters him from punishment, whereas if he could be persuaded to exert himself he could be freed from his madness.[51] Implicit in nineteenth-century medical thinking was the idea that *free will* was inhibitory, a warden, so to speak, of impulses. By contrast, *freedom* was the release of impulse—doing what one likes. Paradoxically, then, the chief function of free will was to constrain freedom. This attitude was related to the more specifically moral view that describes the will as truly free when it subordinates itself to the larger will of God. Self-will is the freedom that free will must leash to a higher purpose. Although I have been concerned here with the legal and medical quandary over how to deal with the insane, in particular the criminally insane, legal difficulties regarding free will and responsibility extended into many other areas, including that of opium addiction and unjustified confinement.[52]

In this area, the law had to deal with a complication of its own. Law requires two factors to establish guilt—the deed done by the accused (*actus reus*) and the preceding mental state (*mens rea*). This mental state implied, once more, a will free to choose right or wrong. Roger Smith notes that criminal law textbooks assumed that without the consent of the will human acts were not culpable, hence defense pleas had to claim that the defendant's will was not operating (Smith, 72). The paradox here is that where no motive can be determined no mental state may be presumed to exist because the only evidence of a mental state is some act that follows from it. Thus no motive will mean no crime. Comparably, although a delusion constitutes a mental state and may issue in a criminal act, defenses had to argue that the delusion of insanity was somehow different from delusions (misunderstandings) of the sane.[53] Once again the will becomes central. To both medicine and the law, though they could not in the nineteenth century and cannot today come to terms on criminal insanity, the truest definition of the self was of a governing will restraining animal impulse and self-will. Freedom is anarchy; free will is rule.

Neither the McNaughtan rule nor any other rule made cases involving the insanity defense predictable or easy. Much depended, as always, upon the actors, their economic stations, and the social and political circumstances surrounding them. As we have seen the situation of women illustrates this fact. But if the environing circumstances of a case were so influential, some scientific standard for determining responsibility became even more imperative, at least for medical men. Henry Maudsley confidently declared in 1874 that it would become increasingly evident in law cases that determinations of insanity must be made by medical men who had devoted themselves to the study of that disease (Maudsley, *Responsibility*, 77). But, as Roger Smith points out, there was too much general incoherence about mind-body relations among alienists themselves to establish a trustworthy system of rules for judgment. To reconcile the determinism of disease with freedom of the will would be to make cogent both responsibility and exonerating conditions, but alienists could not draw that boundary. The insanity defense was one unsatisfactory attempt to do so (Smith, 167).

Philosophers and moralists could, within the limits of their own systems of logic and morality, identify the self and set limits to its freedom and its responsibilities. These positions could be argued endlessly with little harm. But when it came to the practical matter of saying that an accused person was or was not responsible because of his or her mental condition, such schemes tottered. If the madman was not responsible because he had no strength of will to govern his behavior, was it not also true that all of us, products of innumerable inherited and environmental influences, were similarly handicapped? Were we not all ultimately merely sophisticated automata? In the nineteenth century as now, all the debates about man's freedom came down to this—a being in the shape of man, who acts as no man should because he lacks the governing will that makes for "man-ness" stands before us to be judged.

The ancient Greeks and Romans recognized mental disorder as the source of criminal behavior but did not therefore excuse the perpetrator from penal or social consequences. Insanity was a god-derived affliction but did not remove its sufferer from human justice.[54] As we have seen, the developing modern notion of the self generated many complications and contradictions in interpreting human behavior. The question of legal insanity is merely a particularly acute example. As Nigel Walker asks in his survey of the insanity plea before 1800, "What was the origin of the notion that the mad lack will?"[55] William R. Woodward suggests that the revival of interest in Kant in the late nineteenth century was an effort to save the human will from the determinist implications of evolutionary naturalism. In England the basic intellectual interest was to reconcile the principles of automatic action with a purposeful divine order and human will. At the universities, chairs of philosophy went to persons with psychological interests, and therefore advocates argued for the primacy of consciousness.[56] Darwin himself considered free will equivalent to chance, and in his marginal notes to John Abercrombie's *Inquiries concerning the Intellectual Powers* wrote on the subject of responsibility in crime: "Yes but what determines his [the criminal's] *consideration*? his own previous conduct—& what has determined that? & so on—*Hereditary*character & education & chance. According to all this ones disgust at villain ought to be is nothing more than disgust at one under fowl [*sic*] disease."[57] We have not found any answer to the question of why the mad should be considered to lack will, but in the preceding chapters I hope that I have shown the many ways in which this abiding dilemma of western culture—whether or not men possess the power to shape their selves, their destinies, and ultimately the destiny of the race—affected the judgments, predictions, and actions of thinking men and women in the nineteenth century.

In the chapters that follow, I shall examine the various manifestations in literature of this same commanding issue of free will and determinism. In a study of the insanity defense, Edward Sagarin and Robert J. Kelley write that "in our literary heritage, so rich with severe criticism of injustice, freedom is depicted in terms of choice, and responsibility in terms of the vision of ourselves as free human beings, willing to be held accountable for the choice that is freely made," and they recommend that legal philosophers and social scientists learn from this heritage.[58] But I intend to demonstrate that in the literature of England during the nineteenth century writers were not so naively convinced of human freedom but examined questions of freedom and responsibility with great subtlety and greater seriousness.

PART
TWO

Early Nineteenth-Century English Literature

Introduction to Part 2

PART 1 of this book demonstrates the central importance of a new concept of the self at the opening of the nineteenth century and an increasing awareness of the complexity of that self through the century. It also describes the pervasive moral concern through the nineteenth century with the development of character. Both libertarians and necessarians generally agree upon the importance of improving individuals and society through the subordination of self to some higher purpose. Both generally assumed a direction in human affairs that could be affected to some degree by decisive rather than merely involuntary actions. In fact, nineteenth-century thinkers were very much given to "narratizing" their existence. The chapters on progress, history, and evolution make this apparent, but in other fields that I have not chosen to examine something similar was happening. Higher criticism, for example, was transforming dogma to story. What had been absolute stricture was becoming moral fable, as Tennyson noted in *In Memoriam*. The new discipline of anthropology, with its fascination with myths, was itself mythologizing man's social nature by narratizing prehistory and by plotting contemporary culture from the "beginning" of "primitive" peoples to the middle of civilized nations to the end of "advanced" societies.

Creative writers worked in this same atmosphere of dramatic narratizing that cast strong-willed man in the role of hero. They encountered essays on free will and necessity in the periodicals in which they published their poems and stories. They heard sermons on the will in church. Sometimes, as with Charles Kingsley, they gave the sermon in the church on Sunday and sat down on Monday to tell the same lesson in a novel. They moved among other men and women who consciously dealt with the dilemmas of the will. Dickens was a close friend of John Forster, who served on the Commission for Lunacy, and with Dr. John Elliotson, a prominent medical man with an interest in human psychology who was one of the early promoters of mesmerism. George Eliot lived with George Henry Lewes, one of the most successful and respected scientific popularizers of the day. These writers, and I am chiefly concerned with novelists because story telling is most prominent there, lived in an atmosphere that privileged moral ideologies and teleological interpretations of existence, even when those ideologies and interpretations began with conflicting theses about human behavior as free or necessary. Issues of freedom and necessity were openly discussed in much literature of the century but were also implicit in that era's very manner of story telling.

Part 2 of this study traces in the creative writing of the Victorian period what has been surveyed in part 1. There I showed the widespread awareness of concern about free will and determinism and the offered solutions, most of them presented in developmental terms. But I did not venture to analyze in detail any texts, even where narrative was a central concern, as with history. That kind of analysis is the substance of what follows.

~ ~ ~

In *Sincerity and Authenticity*, Lionel Trilling instanced the pedagogical impulse of the nineteenth-century novel as an example of sincerity. For Victorians, he said, the purpose of art was to induce a sentiment of being, "to recruit the primitive strength that a highly developed culture has diminished." But this sentiment of being and of being strong gives way to the conception of personal authenticity, a change reflected in the acknowledgment of the work of art as "authentic by reason of its entire self-definition."[1] Trilling describes the gradual loss of religious faith that deprived men of a purposive cosmos as a "psychic catastrophe."[2] For Victorians, the universe was a story in the process of being told and men could comfortably anticipate a satisfying conclusion. By contrast, the modern mind no longer trusts narrative largely because it implies an unverifiable rational order. What right, the modern reader—and writer—asks, has an author to govern characters and influence readers?[3]

Many nineteenth-century thinkers did conceive of existence in narrative terms, as earlier chapters on progress, history, and evolution indicate. Carlyle said a person's life was like a literary composition, and Hazlitt connected human freedom with the ability to project the story of life into the future.

Coleridge referred to history as "the great drama of an ever-unfolding Providence," and he meant it literally.[4] He did not, as Trilling says moderns have done, substitute narrative history for God and design.[5] For him, as for James Martineau several years later, human existence was characterized by freedom and drama.[6] Coleridge's "drama" was not the traditional conflict of God and Devil so typical of the Calvinist version of history both supernatural and terrestrial but a more personal drama like the carefully crafted scenario of an artist God who reveals his didactive purpose through human agents acting out a moral tale. Some historians, like Carlyle and Froude saw that story as a vague but discernible pattern of divine law and inevitable justice. Others, like those historians described as Liberal Anglicans, discovered a far more precise narrative unraveling, with clear-cut roles designed for individual nations and men.

But faith in a universal narrative, a tale gradually disclosed through the operations of phenomenal events, was not confined to traditionally religious persons. We have seen how committed many nonreligious, even atheistic, thinkers were to some version of progress, with Winwood Reade perhaps one of the most notable examples. A few, like T. H. Huxley, and H. G. Wells, conceived of human history as a story that man told himself in order to make it true. Most believed that the story was "out there" to be read and interpreted in one fashion or another.

Trilling correctly calls attention to modern artists' distrust of narrative's relationship with concepts such as truth, logic, and rational order. Recognizing the connection between narrative and coercion, they avoid traditional narrative approaches. But, if many modern artists reject the tyranny of narrative (Alain Robbe-Grillet is a widely recognizable example), many others exploit the association as a subject for fictional treatment itself, as Grace Paley does in her short story "Conversations with Father," which overtly explores the relationship of plot and freedom, plot and destiny.[7] Literary artists in the nineteenth century did not embrace narrative out of ignorance. They, too, recognized how intimately story telling was related to a purposive view of the universe and generally preferred to reinforce this association. Sometimes they were absolutely playful in exploring the equation of artist = divinity × narrative = providence. But nineteenth-century writers were also acutely aware of one other integer in this formula, and that was the role of human will.

Susan Sontag has perceptively observed that "the entire history of the various arts could be rewritten as the history of different attitudes toward the will."[8] More specifically, Trilling declared that "a chief subject of the literature of the nineteenth century was the physiology and hygiene of the will, what its normality consisted in, what were its pathologies of excess or deficiency, what were its right and wrong goals."[9] Victorian writers were themselves conscious of this fascination. In *The Gay Science* (1866), E. S. Dallas believed that he was conveying accepted knowledge when he distinguished between fiction of plot and fiction of character.

> Both profess to give us pictures of life, and both have to do with certain characters going through certain actions. The difference between the two lies solely in the relation of the characters portrayed to the actions described. In the novel of character man appears moulding circumstances to his will, directing the action for himself, supreme over incident and plot. In the opposite class of novel man is represented as made and ruled by circumstance; he is the victim of change and the puppet of intrigue.[10]

When we disclose Victorian writers' interest in the will, we are educating ourselves, not revealing a secret unknown to them; part 2 of this book is designed to explore this fact.

In *Nietzsche, Henry James, and the Artistic Will* (1978), Stephen Donadio made a courageous attempt to demonstrate James's consciousness that art was a mode of power employable in ordering experience and, through self-mastery, enabling authorship of one's own being. Though James criticized the looseness of Victorian novels, he shared the impulse of that literature to make experience conform to some version of willed design. But whereas he sought to make himself as artist the work of art, Victorians generally sought to transform an act of will into art. Harold Bloom and Barbara H. Smith and many scholars after them have based their critical methods on the assumption that the artist's state of mind implies a manner of expression and vice versa.[11] The artist's conscious or unconscious presuppositions condition the manner in which he or she is able to *represent* the world. And the available means of representation limit his or her *perception* of the world. This critical assumption operates outside the range of belles lettres. In *Narrative Form*, Leo Braudy demonstrated how history as well as fiction may be viewed as an element of a pattern or as an aesthetic design; variations in this way of perceiving made for considerable differences in the styles and narrative methods of writers such as Hume, Fielding, and Gibbon. J. Hillis Miller has also described the manner in which attitudes about the will influence the nature of narrative in history and in fiction.[12]

Literary and historical scholars have examined this subject extensively, but perhaps it is worthwhile to hear from a practicing novelist on the subject, since, even today, such expositions are as rare as they are valuable. William Gass is fully aware of the larger, often unconscious, assumptions that lie behind the particularities of fictional worlds. "Although fiction, in the manner of its making, is pure philosophy," he says, "no novelist has created a more dashing hero than the handsome Absolute, or conceived more dramatic extrications—the soul's escape from the body for instance, or the will's from cause."[13] His version of the Victorian acknowledgment that novelists are surrogate gods is both modern and perennial. For Gass, the novelist does not govern but allows himself to be governed by a set of principles, "as if God stepped down in favor of moving mass and efficient causes, so to say: 'This is not mine; I do not this; I am not here.' Novels in which the novelist has effaced himself create worlds without gods" (Gass, 20). Nineteenth-century writers were keenly aware of that set of principles but admitted that they were products of their own wills (even, as with Trollope, when characters were presumably allowed to develop their own causal patterns). Nineteenth-century novelists asserted themselves in their fictions because they wished to remind readers of their presence, their will controlling events, and, by analogy, the divine will guiding the providential story.

Ultimately we are all fictionalists. Some of us believe that we are substitute deities with the power to govern the laws that shape the stories of our lives. Some of us do not. Most of us need never consider the issue, but literary artists must. Gass's appreciation of this fact applies to Victorian writers as much as to modern ones.

> Our own minds and our sensory equipment organize our world; it is we who establish these *a priori* connections which we later discover and sometimes describe mistakenly, as natural laws. We are inveterate model makers, imposing on the pure data of sense a vigorously abstract system. The novelist makes a system for us too, although his is composed of a host of particulars, arranged to comply with esthetic conditions, and it both flatters and dismays us when we look at our own life through it because our life appears holy and beautiful always, even when tragic and ruthlessly fated. Still for us it is only "as if." (Gass, 71)

A number of recent books have called attention to the issue of free will and determinism in literature. Philip Drew's *The Meaning of Freedom* (1982) is a history of the theme in English literature, with an emphasis upon the relationship of freedom to politics. Because of its range, the book can offer only isolated instances of close attention to individual writers. Peter L. Thorslev, Jr.'s, *Romantic Contraries: Freedom versus Destiny* (1984) describes the movement during the late eighteenth and early nineteenth centuries from a mechanical to a vital world view where freedom becomes both central and problematic. His descriptions of three competing visions of the universe—organic, Gothic, and open—provide an illuminating chart for organizing the attitudes of major writers of the romantic period. Wendell V. Harris's *The Omnipresent Debate: Empiricism and Transcendentalism in Nineteenth-Century English Prose* (1981) inevitably engages the question of freedom and determinism because that question underlies many of the other disputes between these two schools of thought. Leopold Damrosch, Jr.'s, *God's Plot and Man's Stories: Studies in the Fictional Imagination from Milton to Fielding* (1985) brilliantly demonstrates how assumptions about the nature of providence and God's design affect the way in which different authors— from Puritans, to Defoe and Richardson, to Fielding—constructed their narratives. Thomas Vargish's *The Providential Aesthetic in Victorian Fiction* (1985) examines one aspect of this issue at length in the novels of writers such as Dickens, the Brontës, and George Eliot. Catherine Gallagher explores the influence of ideas about free will and determinism in the context of the industrial revolution and the fiction that took industrialism as a theme in *The Industrial Reformation of English Fiction, 1832-1867* (1985).

It is natural to examine characterization for signs of an author's attitudes toward will, and certainly in succeeding chapters I shall discuss this avenue. It may be less immediately evident that plot, too, is a means of comprehending an author's assumptions about the will. Several years ago, David Goldknopf called attention to the general issue in *The Life of the Novel* (1972) by observing that an interest in linear causation accompanied the rise of the realistic novel. This interest conflicted with traditional providential views implying free will. Darwinian, Marxist, and Freudian determinism resulted, according to Goldknopf, in the modern perception of psychology and the novel as mechanisms. Central to the development of the novel, then, was the perception that plotting reflected metaphysical prejudice.[14] Similar insights concerning the implications of plot have been applied more specifically by other scholars. Robert Caserio observes that "Dickens's sense of plot relies upon a notion that small groups of separate characters or persons are somehow all the same character or person."[15] Put another way, this means that the movement of plot and the consequent arrangement of characters into a moral design, not the revelation of character, generates the power of Dickens's narratives. Caserio says that "Dickens's plots are a kind of curious moral allegory in which the turns of plot rather than the allegorical personifications move the intellectual and the moral design along" (Caserio, 73). Caserio recognizes that "every plot is pervaded by a counterforce that undoes plotting, and that every attempt not to plot or tell a story is pervaded by a stubborn narrative impulse" (Caserio, 282). There are many ways to describe and define these contrasting yet interlocked qualities of plot; Peter Brooks does it elegantly in *Reading for the Plot* (1984). The reading of plot, he says, is a form of desire that carries us forward through the text.[16] All discourse is a signifying chain where meaning, or access to unconscious desire, does not consist in any single link. "Narrative is hence condemned to *saying* other than what it *would mean*, spinning out its movement toward a meaning that would be the end of its movement" (Brooks, 56). Plot diminishes as it realizes itself; narrative desire is inevitably desire for the end.

Read in this manner, plot is a seductive force begetting desire in the reader, and the novelist therefore stands in relation to the reader as a species of psychic panderer. Plot arouses appetency in the reader, who spends energy satisfying it. The reader uses up this desire as he or she consumes the story. With no appreciable change in the dynamics that Brooks describes, I would alter the coordinates, at least as far as nineteenth-century fiction is concerned, and describe plot as the representation of will. The author becomes a guiding, even coercive authority, impelling the reader, who has voluntarily yielded his or her own will for the duration of the story. Paradoxically, the very yielding of that power to the author's authority results in the stimulation of an independent and even contradictory will in the reader. Nineteenth-century authors saw themselves as directive powers and they sought accommodation with their readers. When, in *A Christmas Carol*, the Ghost of Christmas Past appears abruptly at Scrooge's bedside, Dickens remarks that Scrooge was as close to the ghost "as I am now to you and I am standing in the spirit at your elbow," he is toying with an awareness shared by his readers that he is their controlling guide in precisely the same way that the three spirits are Scrooge's.[17] He hopes to enliven their wills and prompt them to some form of exertion, just as the spirits prompt Scrooge to revise his life, which they have "narrated" to him from its beginning past its close.

In the chapters that follow, I approach nineteenth-century literature in a way that I believe explains certain characteristics of that literature and helps us to appreciate its achievment. I shall assume that the preceding chapters of this study have demonstrated how lively and constant interest was during the century in both broad and detailed issues of the free will controversy. I shall examine manifestations in creative literature of this same abiding concern and demonstrate how this concern was reflected in literature's manner of expression.

CHAPTER NINE

Romantic to Victorian Poetry

PART 2 of this book is mainly concerned with the manifestation of attitudes toward free will and necessity in the themes and methods of prose fiction because fiction provides the most convenient means of examining narrative, which is, in the Victorian period, characteristically associated with large assumptions about mankind such as the teleological patterns of development examined in part 1. This chapter, however, indicates some continuities and transformations of opinion from Romantic to Victorian poetry. To begin with, I demonstrate that both Romantics and Victorians were fully alert to the question of free will and determinism. Indeed, some of the Romantic writers were important moralists who wrote essays on the will. Free will and related matters occur regularly in Romantic and Victorian poems which reflect the nineteenth-century fascination with the nature of the self discussed in chapter 1. Even reviews of poetry show an interest in free will, chance, fate, and destiny, and I have included a few samples of this interest. In short, the predominant vision of man as morally free in a world of progressive and evolutionary development that was evident among other writers, as part 1 shows, is evident in the poets of these times as well. Of course, this vision as not exclusive, and I have included examples of writers who did not accept it.

Poetry of this period is more appropriately identified with images than with continuous narrative. Therefore, saving the examination of narrative method for the chapters on fiction that follow, I have here examined a related set of limited images that indicate one change of attitude that took place from the Romantic to the Victorian years of the nineteenth century in England.

~ ~ ~

The earliest major Victorian writers were William Wordsworth and Samuel Taylor Coleridge. By the time Victoria came to the throne, these men represented some of the most prominent defenses of established institutions and moral principles. Wordsworth was Victoria's first appointed laureate. By the time he died, he was as Victorian as Tennyson and more so than Browning. Just a few years after the queen was crowned, John Stuart Mill wrote that Coleridge had been one of the two most important thinkers of his day. The other was Bentham. They were the shapers of nineteenth-century thought. Mill praised both men for grounding speculative thought in the philosophy of mind. The one reasserted the best meaning and purpose of old institutions, while the other wished to eliminate old forms and institute new ones.[1] Though the two thinkers were polar complements, both became Victorian staples. Much of Victorianism is Benthamite, but much is also Romantic, thanks largely to Coleridge and Wordsworth.

If Mill respected Coleridge for providing certain clear and flexible, but conservative, arguments for principles that would become axioms of Victorian thinking, he valued Wordsworth for his cultivation of feelings *under command.* "I needed to be made to feel that there was real, permanent happiness in tranquil contemplation," Mill wrote. Wordsworth, "the poet of unpoetical natures, possessed of quiet and contemplative tastes," did this for him.[2] Later, in introducing a selection of Wordsworth's poetry, Matthew Arnold commended him as a moral poet while warning that Wordsworthians were "apt to praise him for the wrong things, and to lay too much stress upon what they call his philosophy."[13]

Arnold's observation is at the heart of one great difference between the Victorians and their predecessors, for although the Victorian compromise may have begun with the Romantics, there was a clear distinction between those early innovators who founded their beliefs in *philosophy* and the later masters whose values rested in *morality.*[4] Like all generalizations, this one will be found lacking in some specific applications. So will other generalizations I shall make in this chapter. For example, I shall generalize about the contrast between the Romantic urge toward expansion of self and the Victorian tendency toward control and consolidation, and I shall extend those generalizations into some explanations for the different ways in which Romantics and Victorians employ related literary images such as the circle. These generalizations may be risky but are sound enough, I think, to justify examining the relationship between the Romantics and the Victorians from a point of view that is central to philosophy and to morality. Nothing is so crucial to both as the concept of will.

Although I realize that political and social events influenced the philosophical and moral opinions of Romantic and Victorian writers, my purpose is not to examine the external conditions that unite or divide Romantic and Victorian writers but to discover their esthetic and metaphysical kinships or estrangements. There is, after all, no abrupt shift from Romantic to Victorian temper. Wordsworth, Coleridge, and Southey made this transition in their own lifetimes. It can be argued that Keats was inclining that way, young as he was, and it is even possible to see a tendency of this kind in Shelley. One could almost say that one characteristic of English Romanticism was its drift toward what we call Victorianism. From this point of view, the one Romantic who is not a romantic is Byron.[5]

If the agitated Romantics were half in love with easeful Victorianism, Victorian writers often felt the kinship. Arnold seems to have seen himself as a latter-day Wordsworth. We, at least, have seen him as such.[6] Browning began his career as another Shelley, and when he parted from that faith, Swinburne was prepared to take up the mantle. Tennyson admitted his debt to Keats; Rossetti advertised his.[7] In full Victorian fame, Thomas Carlyle was proud to announce himself the direct descendant of the Romantic genius Thomas Carlyle.

Although we have discussed Carlyle earlier in this study, he is worth returning to because he provides an excellent introduction to the linkage between these two major periods of English literature. He *was*, in a sense, his own heir. Born with Keats, he died with Disraeli. Chronologically, he was the last Romantic and first Victorian sage. More importantly, he was a genuine philosopher and he saw the character of his times clearly. Five years before Victoria came to the throne, but after Keats, Shelley, and Byron were dead, Carlyle published his remarkable essay "Characteristics," which, though it seemed novel, was truly a summary of ideas initiated by the great Romantic generation of which he was himself a member. The intellectual struggle that Carlyle described in 1831 involved the same contending forces that had characterized English thought since the end of the eighteenth century and that would abide for nearly a century more. The contest pitted a recognition of the force of the unconscious and a reborn confidence in the power of man's free will against a rationalist necessitarianism. We have seen in earlier chapters how Carlyle argued his case.

Set against the Utilitarian temper was another spirit of the age, represented by Coleridge, Wordsworth, and Carlyle himself. Benthamite philosophy was founded on a belief in the rigorous operation of material law; the major Romantic writers began with necessity too. But having fed upon and digested Hartley and Godwin, these young men now proposed a philosophy assimilating features of the old necessarianism, but offering new sources of value. Accepting the basic notion of a universal natural law, they found room—as Hartley himself had—for a degree of freedom for the human agent. The Romantic spirit renewed faith in the imponderable qualities in man and in nature. Eighteenth-century philosophy had located the springs of motivation outside the self; the Romantics centered the vital principle within man. The mechanistic view emphasizing the ordering power of externals endorsed hierarchical principles of authority, but the Romantics responded by placing fundamental authority in man himself and suggesting that this power extended itself outward to the world at large, uniting eventually with some ultimate law. These writers were conscious of contemporary intellectual changes. Coleridge was himself a major philosophical influence, transmitting the advanced German thought of his day. Hazlitt too wrote philosophical texts. Carlyle provided his own moral schemes, again based on German Romantic thought. Shelley read widely in philosophy and was, of course, intimately associated with Godwin. The ideas and influences described in part 1 of this book were fully present to the imaginations of Romantic writers.

In fact, the agent of the new extension of identity from the self to the non-self was imagination. While reason had been the guiding power for a previous generation, represented notably by Godwin, imagination now usurped that function. Beyond the phenomenal characteristics of man, his role as object, was a transcending noumenal identity which was free, organic, and causal. And if his imagination revealed man to be a causative agent and shaper of reality, behind the imagination there was assumed a yet more fundamental and pervasive force: the will.[8] This assertion of man's creative role revived the well-worn argument of free will and necessity. It is in the working out of this argument that we can trace a powerful Romantic strain through the entire Victorian age.

We have already indicated how openly many of the major Romantic writers engaged the question of necessity and free will. Hazlitt, Coleridge, and Wordsworth ultimately endorsed free will.[9] Shelley was different. He began by accepting Godwin's philosophy that while men consider themselves free, they acknowledge in their conduct that they are determined. Godwin's system was essentially quite simple and absolute. By necessity man was improving according to his dependence upon reason. But John P. Clark has noted that Godwin never explained why mental processes should be subject to the same laws as physical nature.[10] Coleridge, Hazlitt, and Wordsworth did not feel that they were. Shelley worked his way to a similar sentiment. In *Queen Mab* (1813), he followed the necessarian doctrine with certain inconsistencies.[11] He called free will a "delusion" in his notes, and in the poem addressed the "Spirit of Nature" as the "all-sufficing Power, / Necessity! thou mother of the world."[12] Shelley progressed from Godwinian necessity to a Platonism in which necessity ruled the material universe, but "Man's mind, its microcosm, had freedom of will."[13] By the time he published *Prometheus Unbound* (1820), Shelley had come to believe that man could free himself from tyranny of circumstance through the power of his mind.[14] Later, in *The Triumph of Life*, he revealed an attitude more characteristic of the Victorians that human imagination and will are not so free to mold experience as he had hoped and he "much grieved to think how power and will / In opposition rule our mortal day, / And why God made irreconcilable / Good and the means of good" (Shelley, *Poetry and Prose*, 461).

Shelley's view of free will may have been formed partly by his relationship with Byron. Shelley tried to play Coleridge to Byron's Wordsworth, but Byron was a dedicated fatalist.[15] Still, in debating metaphysical issues with Byron, Shelley inevitably refined his own views. In the partly autobiographical "Julian and Maddalo," Shelley said that his characters fell into talk "concerning God, freewill, and destiny," but he never recorded their conversation on these topics, though we know from his preface that Maddalo had "an intense apprehension of the nothingness of human life," while Julian was "passionately attached to those philosophical notions which assert the power of man over his own mind" (Shelley, *Poetry and Prose*, 113-14). The Maniac's case makes Shelley's point that man is the author of his own enslavement. Julian says "it is our will / That thus enchains us to permitted ill— / We might be otherwise." Despite Maddalo's gloomy view of the Maniac's and man's condition, Julian declares "This is not destiny, / But man's own wilful ill" (Shelley, *Poetry and Prose*, 117-18).

Shelley identified human freedom with nature's mutability. Though *Queen Mab* asserts the immutable law of nature, it also states that "throughout this varied and eternal world / Soul is the only element," permeating everything.

> Every grain
> Is sentient both in unity and part,
> and the minutest atom comprehends
> A world of love and hatreds; these beget
> Evil and good: hence truth and falsehood spring;
> Hence will and thought and action, all the germs
> Of pain or pleasure, sympathy or hate,
> That variegate the eternal universe.
> (Shelley, *Works* 1:257-58).

Soul drives the "irresistible law" so that "no atom of this turbulence" can act "but as it must and ought to act" (Shelley, *Works* 1:272). Gradually man will achieve his high purpose, and "with changeless nature coalescing, / Will undertake regeneration's work" (Shelley, *Works* 1:269). By putting himself at one with nature's law, man participates in a recreative power that is progressive. The "Happy Earth! reality of Heaven!" will come into being when man's "blindly-working will" becomes the "elevated will" which has achieved external freedom because it has perceived its necessary unity with the evolutionary force of nature (Shelley, *Works* 1:288, 290). Shelley's confidence in man's shaping power was muted later, as we have seen. Nonetheless, it exhibits one powerful strain of thought examined in part 1—the necessarian belief that man can, though bound by the law of cause and effect, participate in his own progressive growth and that of the race as a whole.

Comparable to Shelley's sentiments are those of Keats, the least openly philosophical of the poets I have named. For example, he described material existence as the medium for a process of soul making, the lending of identity to intelligence.[16] In "Hyperion," Saturn, disanointed by fate, feels he has lost his "strong identity," his "real self."[17] The world has become a vale of soul unmaking for the Titans. It is a necessary process. "We fall by course of Nature's law, not force / Of thunder, or of Jove," Oceanus tells his brethren.[18] Keats valued the poet's capacity to perceive the *actuality* of nature and to be open to it, even to blend with it. Perhaps he felt this article of the Romantic creed more forcefully than any of the others.

Clearly Romantic writers were alert to metaphysical questions and wrote with these large issues in mind. Often they wrote specifically to illustrate them. Yet it is the Victorians who have a reputation as moralists. And this is correct, for, whereas the Romantics proposed their theories in verse, the Victorians, who were equally concerned with metaphysics, extended their interest to practical moral conduct. Though they brooded as much on freedom and necessity, they discussed their matters less openly in their works.

Carlyle labored to bring men to exercise their wills practically, Tennyson studied the will's operations as manifested in conduct. It is this emphasis upon conduct that is typically Victorian. For Tennyson, free will and moral choice were inseparable. Like Carlyle, Tennyson assumed an inexorable law beyond man's control guiding human history.[19] Both felt that men could participate in this process by actively acknowledging the divine immanence in nature.[20] Partly this could be achieved by recognizing the symbolic revelation of that immanence. For Tennyson, God was law and law was the necessity of existence. In *In Memoriam* he described the operations of nature as a "toil cooperant to an end."[21]

Tennyson read as much philosophy as any of the Romantics we have discussed, but he offered little in the way of philosophical discourse. Though some of his later poems are practically sermons, "as a rule," his son wrote, "he knew that poetry must touch on metaphysical topics rather by allusion than systematically."[22] His poetry demonstrates a clear belief in moral responsibility based upon a faith in free will. In his old age, it was a favorite topic of conversation. "Free Will was undoubtedly, he said, the 'main miracle, apparently an act of self-limitation by the Infinite, and yet a revelation by Himself of Himself. . . . Take away the sense of individual responsibility and men sink into pessimism and madness' " (Hallam Tennyson 1:316- 7). In a poem of 1855 entitled "Will," Tennyson contrasted the virtue of "him whose will is strong," with the vice of one who "corrupts the strength of heaven-descended Will" (Tennyson, *Poems*, 1018). This and other examples show that while in many particulars Tennyson was an obvious heir of the Romantics, he placed a Carlylean emphasis on the moral significance of the will revealed in conduct. Like Coleridge and Wordsworth, he saw will as man's central power for supporting faith.

Tennyson's version of the relationship of individual free will to a vaster power resembles what we have seen as typically Romantic. The individual will eventually merges with the Infinite, but after a more elaborate process. It is instructive to compare two accounts of Tennyson's image for the will. Wilfred Ward remembered it this way: "Man is free, but only free in certain narrow limits. His character and his acquired habits limit his freedom. They are like the cage of a bird. The bird can hop at will from one perch to another, and to the floor of the cage, but not beyond its bars."[23] Hallam Tennyson's version is different: "And he wrote for me as to man's will being free but only within certain limits: 'Man's Free-will is but a bird in a cage; he can stop at the lower perch, or he can mount to a higher. Then that which is and knows will enlarge his cage, give him a higher and a higher perch, and at last break off the top of his cage, and let him out to be one with the Free-will of the Universe' " (Hallam Tennyson 1:318- 19). Tennyson's poetry expresses the same sentiment, but as Hallam said, not systematically. *In Memoriam* proper ends with these stanzas:

> O living will that shalt endure
>   When all that seems shall suffer shock,
>   Rise in the spiritual rock,
> Flow through our deeds and make them pure,
>
> That we may lift from out of dust,
>   A voice as unto him that hears,
>   A cry above the conquered years,
> To one that with us works, and trust,
>
> With faith that comes of self-control,
>   The truths that never can be proved
>   Until we close with all we loved,
> And all we flow from, soul in soul. (Poems, 981)

Tennyson's note describes the living will as "that which we know as Free-will in man" (Tennyson, *Poems*, 862). John Tulloch felt that the epilogue to *In Memoriam* summarized the religious teachings of men like Maurice, Kingsley, and Robertson, with all of whom Tennyson discussed religion.[24] But it did more than that. In its very form and movement the poem reflected the belief that men were free to shape life as a poet might shape a poem, or God the universe.

The prologue of Tennyson's poem apostrophizing Christ establishes its keynote. "Our wills are ours, we know not how; / Our wills are ours, to make them thine" (Tennyson, *Poems*, 862). As the poem progresses the poet recovers his belief "That men may rise on stepping-stones / Of their dead selves to higher things" (Tennyson, *Poems*, 864). In the process, his poems grow from "dull narcotics, numbing pain," to an imitation of the providential scheme (Tennyson, *Poems*, 868). "I see in part / That all, as in some piece of art, / Is toil cooperant to an end" (Tennyson, *Poems*, 978). Similarly Arthur Henry Hallam is transformed from a dead friend to a living influence, a surrogate Christ who provides a model for behavior. The love Hallam inspires in the poet produces "the vague desire / That spurs in an imitative will" (Tennyson, *Poems*, 963). His will is confirmed in the shaping of his elegy whose purpose is to embody a great lesson and not present mere beauty "such as lurks / In some wild Poet, when he works, / Without a conscience or an aim" (Tennyson, Poems, 893). If *In Memoriam* is heterodox in some ways, it certainly confirms the widespread belief described in part 1 in a complex self participating in a progressive moral development based on providential design and takes the additional step of likening the work of art itself to that design.

Time and again Tennyson asserted man's need for some high code to muster his will by giving it a high purpose. That code is often embodied in one or more beings—Hallam and King Arthur are the most obvious examples—with Hallam's version of Christianity and Arthur's vows as the necessary codes. Although we could examine these poems in detail for the manner in which will and free will operate, we have room here for no more than a few instructive examples.[25] When *Maud* appeared in 1855, a critic in the *Saturday Review* was unhappy with the substance, though not the craft, of the poem. He disliked its central figure.

> It is the character of a man of high intellect and exquisite sensibility, keenly alive to all impressions, but wanting in the power of action and active sympathies, dependent on the world without him for happiness, and cynical because it is not afforded. Not once throughout the poems is active life painted with real zest. Not once are we called to witness the happiness or the moral cure which result from self-exertion. Everywhere we feel the force of circumstances, nowhere the energy of free will.[26]

The reviewer missed Tennyson's central point. While the narrator's will is divided, while he is at war within himself, he cannot marshal his powers to any good purpose. But love can change that. Moreover, it must be an ideal love transcending mere carnality. When the narrator has lost Maud and suffered madness, he is released from his mental bondage by a vision that provides him with a means of commanding all of his powers for what he believes to be a high purpose. Maud is for him what Arthur and Hallam were, a focus for the will. This focusing of the will in Tennyson's poetry is not for personal salvation. At its best the will yokes itself to serve others. Again King Arthur is the most prominent example, but Tennyson could praise this quality of leadership among his acquaintances as well. So in "To the Duke of Argyll," Tennyson praised the "Patriot Statesman," encouraging him to apply "thy will, a power to make / This ever-changing world of circumstance, / In changing, chime with never-changing law" (Tennyson, *Poems*, 1299).

Despite all that Matthew Arnold wrote about conduct, it is difficult to find references to free will in his prose; yet he was deeply influenced by Spinoza and Coleridge, who, in their different ways, considered it an essential topic.[27] Nonetheless, implicit in his desire to free man from the bondage of history and his own weakness is a confidence that man is free to alter his destiny.[28] In *Culture and Anarchy* (1869) Arnold offered his program for individual freedom: "To walk staunchly by the best light one has, to be strict and sincere with oneself, not to be of the number of those who say and do not, to be in earnest,—this is the discipline by which alone man is enabled to rescue his life from thraldom to the passing moment and to his bodily senses, to ennoble it, and to make it eternal."[29] Still, he cautioned that we cannot simply do as we like, and therefore we require the State, which has the authority for "controlling individual wills in the name of an interest wider than that of individuals" (Arnold, *Works* 5:117). Ultimately, Arnold comes round to a familiar message, "that the only perfect freedom is, as our religion says, a service" (Arnold, *Works* 5:207).

We find clearer indications about Arnold's feelings on the will in his poetry. Like Carlyle and Tennyson, he was more interested in defending faith and defining the self than in examining philosophical ramifications.[30] For him, the self was in a defensive position. It did not extend itself outward to nature. Nonetheless, Arnold time and again averred that man and nature were one. "We learn not to *abuse* or *storm at* the Gods or Fate," he said, because we realize that "the power we would curse is the same as ourselves: the same with the tongue employed to articulate the curse."[31] Still, he frequently reminds us that as though "chartered by some unknown Powers, / We stem across the sea of life by night."[32] In "In Memory of the Author of 'Obermann' " he is more specific:

> We, in some unknown Power's employ,
> Move on a rigorous line;

> Can neither, when we will, enjoy,
> Nor, when we will, resign.
> (Arnold, *Poems*, 136)[33]

Having learned destiny's sentence that he will die in six years, Arnold's Mycerinus speculates that there may be a Force that "Sweeps earth, and heaven, and men, and gods along . . . And the great powers we serve, themselves may be / Slaves of a tyrannous necessity" (Arnold, *Poems*, 28). Arnold's ambivalent attitude appears in the early poem "Written in Emerson's Essays," where the persona marvels at human indifference to Emerson's optimism.

> Yet the will is free;
> Strong is the soul, and wise, and beautiful;
> The seeds of godlike power are in us still;
> Gods are we, bards, saints, heroes if we will!—
> Dumb judges, answer, truth or mockery?
> (Arnold, *Poems*, 53)

The answer is: half-truth. Man is free enough to see the severe limits of his freedom. In "Self-Deception" Arnold explained that men believe they possess capabilities which "a Power beyond our seeing" denies, and in "Empedocles on Etna" he said that while men insist on the right to have their will, Nature does not cooperate (Arnold, *Poems*, 276, 162). "In vain our pent wills fret, / And would the world subdue" (Arnold, *Poems*, 164). In "Courage" Arnold indicated the stoical spirit he felt his times required.

> True, we must tame our rebel will:
> True, we must bow to Nature's law:
> Must bear in silence many an ill;
> Must learn to wait, renounce, withdraw.
>
> Yet now, when boldest wills give place,
> When Fate and Circumstance are strong,
> And in their rush the human race
> Are swept, like huddling sheep, along;
>
> Those sterner spirits let me prize,
> Who, though the tendence of the whole
> They less than us might recognize,
> Kept, more than us, their strength of soul.
>
> Yes, be the second Cato praised!
> Not that he took the course to die—

> But that, when 'gainst himself he raised
> His arm, he raised it dauntlessly.
>
> (Arnold, *Poems*, 141)

We shall see later how Arnold imagined the isolated self discovering its inner sources of strength, but at this point it is safe to say that Arnold made no bold claims for human freedom. Commenting on the poems "Revolution," "Progress," and "The Future" from Arnold's 1852 volume, Patrick J. McCarthy writes:

> Arnold looks at man as both author of his own fate and child of a destiny that determines him—man threatened with the loss of what he values and man lured on to what he has not yet achieved, man continually striving to alter society and to regenerate himself. He is compulsive man, but he acts under the brooding spirit of the age's belief in progress, which in Arnold becomes a subtle belief, guarded, hedged with doubt and committed to the workings of slow time, but there all the same.[34]

Arnold's true solution is to renounce the ego and realize that we are part of the Power that pervades all things. In his *Notebooks*, he wrote, "Faith is allegiance of the moral nature to Universal Reason, or the will of God," and "An approving conscience is the sense of harmony of the personal will of man with that impersonal light which is in him, representative of the Will of God.' "[35] By now this pattern is thoroughly familiar. We have seen it in both religious and secular moralists. Arnold's assumptions are fully in keeping with one of the most pervasive beliefs of his age. But though the message does not vary in essence, there is an important new wrinkle. For Arnold, the self must locate that fragrance of the divine in its own nature; it must almost *create* it for the divine trace is not a still small voice, nor an electrical charge coursing through it. At most it is a faint strain, a haunting echo. But to be free man must discover this essence and unite himself with its power.

A similar view appears in Browning's poetry. Man's will is unquestionably free for Browning and makes its way in an imperfect world by trusting to the ultimate reality called Will which exists behind all things.[36] In a letter to Mrs. Thomas FitzGerald, Browning wrote: "What struck me so much in that Life of Schopenhauer which you gave me, was that doctrine which he considered his grand discovery—and which *I* had been persuaded of from my boyhood—and have based my whole life upon:—that the soul is above and *behind* the intellect which is merely its servant."[37] The soul is one with the will and at its best is the agent of love. The will is capable of evil as well as good, but *correct* human action is at one with divine will. Browning said this many ways in his poetry. In "Rabbi Ben Ezra," man is fixed "mid this dance /

174

Of plastic circumstance" and shaped by God as a potter shapes clay. This process gives his soul its bent and infuses in him the divine spirit.[38] But in "A Death in the Desert," he is also the shaper of life and approximates God's power when, "taking clay, he calls [the desired] shape thereout" in a continuing attempt at a final design (Robert Browning, *Works* 4:288). "A Death in the Desert" is a complicated attempt to suggest a positive solution to the question "What if there be love / Behind the will and might, as real as they?" (Robert Browning, *Works* 4:285). Browning's answer is that there is love behind all things, governing the will which governs might, and man replicates this schema in an imperfect way. His beliefs were surprisingly consistent from *Paracelsus* (1835) to the end of his career. Paracelus learns through love's undoing the proper role of love in man's constitution, "love preceding / Power and with much power, always much more love; / Love still too straightened in his present means, / And earnest for new power to set love free" (Robert Browning, *Works* 1:167). Browning associated love with free will and freedom in general, and he associated all three with Christian faith. Blougram understands this basic fact and explains to Gigadibs that faith can be proven by its power to overcome doubt. "How I know it does? / By life and man's free will, God gave for that! / To mould life as we choose it, shows our choice: / that's our one act, the previous work's his own" (Robert Browning, *Works* 4:146). Elizabeth Barrett Browning shared her husband's faith in free will, and pictured it in similar terms in *Aurora Leigh* (1856), where Aurora presents her views to Romney.

> Let us ponder, friend,
> Whate'er our state, we must have made it first;
> And though the thing displease us, ay, perhaps
> Displease us warrantably, never doubt
> That other states, thought possible once, and then
> Rejected by the instinct of our lives,
> If then adopted, had displeased us more
> Than this in which the choice, the will, the love,
> Has stamped the honor of a patent act
> From henceforth. What we choose may not be good;
> but that we choose it proves it good for *us*
> Potentially, fantastically, now
> Or last year, rather than a thing we saw,
> And saw no need for choosing. Moths will burn
> Their wings,—which proves that light is good for moths,
> Who else had flown not where they agonize.[39]

By the optimistic end of the poem, Romney has absorbed the lesson, declaring, "It is the hour for souls, / That bodies, leavened by the will and love, / Be lightened to redemption" (Elizabeth Barrett Browning, *Poetical Works*, 178).

Browning's opinions remained consistent in his late poems. In *Ferishta's Fancies* (1884), for example, he repeated in "The Sun" that man was an imperfect version of divine will, and, in "A Bean-stripe: Also, Apple-Eating," described the manner in which man's will, not created by himself, must be referred back to the "Prime Sole Will" (Robert Browning, *Works* 10:127). He sums up his view nicely in "Parleying with Christopher Smart."

> Law must be
> Active in earth or nowhere: earth you see,—
> Or there or not at all, Will, Power and Love
> Admit discovery,—as below, above
> Seek next law's confirmation.
>
> (Robert Browning, *Works* 10:188)

Because he believed man is free to shape life, when Browning used the word "fate" he normally referred to circumstances alterable or avoidable through human endeavor. Man is not the slave of a mechanical necessity. Browning trusted in providence as Shelley did in necessity. Both call that high power Love. Like the Victorians, Browning distrusted the material world, but like the Romantics, he felt at home in an imperfect existence.

Browning's beliefs about the will affected the themes and methods of his poems. Some time ago Earl Hilton discussed the tension between human and divine will in *Sordello*, but the best recent study illuminating the connection between Browning's sentiments and his poetics is Herbert F. Tucker, Jr.'s, *Brownings Beginnings: The Art of Disclosure* (1980).[40] Tucker says the central argument of his book is "that Browning's moral doctrine of incompleteness finds a clear aesthetic analogue in his poetics."[41] Later he explains that Browning "makes his style slippery with the consistent purpose of avoiding any structural or semantic enclosure that would dim the sense of the future with which he identifies his poetic mission."[42] Tucker does not emphasize Browning's faith in free will, but his readings of the poems support the approach I offer here. This will become clearer when I discuss Browning's use of the image of the circle.

Edward Dowden accepted in 1867 that though poets like Tennyson and Browning were concerned with the great subjects of "God, and nature, and our relations to them, [of] human character and life and the struggle of will with circumstances," they did not arrive at their conclusions merely by logic.[43] The artistic product is richer than the intellectual because it offers not a view of life but an expression of it; "in proportion as the whole nature of the artist is lost in his work,—his perceptive powers, his sensuous impulses, his reason, his imagination, his emotions, his will,—the conscious activity and unconscious energy interpenetrating one another—his work comes forth full not of speculation, but what is so much better, of life, the open secret of art" (Dowden, 194). Dowden described *Sordello* as Browning's attempt to show the failure to gain full consciousness of one's own existence through mastery over others (Dowden, 235). Lee Erickson has argued that "Browning's poems imply that to project one's will and self upon another . . . is an immoral act."[44] Daniel Karlin has shown that Browning himself, in one of the most important episodes of his life, tried to convey the impression that he was yielding his will at the very time when he was maneuvering Elizabeth Barrett to accept him as lover and then as husband.[45]

The problem in Browning's poems is intriguing, and its successful solution fascinating. The best of the dramatic monologues allow a central figure to attempt to assert his or her will—some succeed, some fail—while permitting the true source of creative energy, the poet composing the poem, to retreat from view. Self-assertion is transferred from author to text. The text speaks, not Robert Browning. And yet, though the poems present themselves as potentially open-ended, they are more nearly iconic in their convincing representativeness of character types. Browning seems to have believed in an underlying consistency of human character—individual differences being merely surface peculiarities. In his prose life of Strafford, Browning wrote: "Infinitely and distinctly various as appear the shifting hues of our common nature when subjected to the prism of CIRCUMSTANCE, each ray into which it is broken is no less in itself a primitive colour, susceptible, indeed, of vast modifications but incapable of further division."[46] Browning's dramatic monologues are experiments in modifying those primary colors, something that Walter Pater grasped in *The Renaissance* (1893) when he noted that Browning's characters were of secondary importance. "His gift is shown by the way in which he accepts such a character, throws it into some situation, or apprehends it in some delicate pause of life, in which for a moment it becomes ideal."[47] Browning was able finally to resolve the opposition between free will and the exertion of will by abandoning the desire for mastery and placing the will's energy freely in the service of the divine will. By unusual avenues, Browning arrived at the most conventional of solutions, but the journey there is exciting and diverting.

Victorian poets generally reveal this pattern of individual will subordinated to a higher power. Even Swinburne believed that man was part of the force that pervaded all existence and was happiest—though never free from pain—when submitting himself to it. Swinburne rejected the Christian faith and embraced his version of paganism, though without accepting its implicit fatalism. Rather, as Chris Snodgrass points out, his poetry reflects the medieval view of self and anima, though Swinburne's anima is the world spirit, Hertha. "In Swinburne's poetry as well, the affirmation of the sacred depends on man's uniting his will with it."[48] In Swinburne as much as in

Browning the free will and the energized will are associated with love. Desire demands an act of will; Swinburne's "scattered cases of burnt-out love can all be traced to a failure of the will."[49] In his championing of freedom for the progress of mankind in "Cosmic Emotion," W. K. Clifford praised Swinburne's expression of faith in *Songs before Sunrise*.[50] His "Hymn on Man" declares that Love engendered the human spirit out of the earth and we may call that Love god, "but God, if a God there be, is the substance of men which is man."[51] Men are the thoughts and the blood enlivening the substance of God. Swinburne's poem praised the reawakening spirit of man prepared to throw off the tyranny of a stale religion. His poem concludes triumphantly.

> And the love-song of earth as thou diest
> Resounds through the wind of her wings—
> Glory to Man in the highest! for Man is
> Master of things. (Swinburne, 174)

"Hertha" makes the same point, asserting man's identification with the spirit of Love that moves the universe and applauding his incipient freedom. Indeed, this is the underlying message of most of Swinburne's poetry, and the repeated patterns of his imagery reinforce it.[52]

Swinburne was not the only poet to affirm the optimistic view that the human spirit was free and capable of directing itself to some higher state manifested in the practical liberation of politically oppressed peoples such as the Italians. George Meredith also endorsed an evolutionary scheme describing the ascent of man individually and as a race from blood to brain to spirit, paradoxically asserting man's need to exert himself in order to renounce the Self and to recognize his affinity with nature. One of Meredith's clearest expressions of this position is in "The Woods of Westermain," where he exclaims that the once dragonish Self of man is becoming more refined. "Change is on the wing to bud / Rose in brain from rose in blood." "Mind that with deep Earth unites" may ascend in endless improvement. Many minor poets offered their versions of this evolutionary ascent, but one sample is perhaps more than enough to make the point. Mathilde Blind's *The Ascent of Man* (1899) provides a summary of human evolution and shows how man's ability to work in social groups gave his puny efforts a powerful combined will. Man can rise above the "immemorial strife" of existence through visionary thought. The poet's role is to assist man in this effort and Love is the force that will help man to achieve a higher destiny. Through man's will, life will achieve its highest form.[53] Like many theorists of the day, some of whom were discussed in chapter 7, poets embraced the affirming notions of progress and evolution in their most comforting teleological patterns. They read the story of mankind as a triumph and constructed their poems accordingly.

But if there were many poets willing to accept such a faith in the eventual triumph of human freedom, of course there were others who were not so clear in their estimates of the freedom of the will. Edward Robert Bulwer-Lytton, who wrote under the name Owen Meredith, believed as a young man that the time was ripe for a rebirth of religious feeling and had hopes for material progress's part in elevating the human soul.[54] He shared these sentiments with his friends the Brownings. However, this optimism cooled. By the time he wrote *The Wanderer* (1857), he was already concerned, as he confided to John Forster, with "the point where the mind, having experienced faiure within and imperfection without is brought to reconsider its own relation with the world, put itself more soberly in unison with life as it is, and establish for itself a moral code for practical use in future action."[55] He still insisted that "God's will is good," and that "good is life's predestined end," but he was uncertain that man's nature could fathom that will and that goodness.[56] He also seemed uncertain about the degree to which man was free to direct his own life. Writing to Theodor Gompperz in 1866, Meredith speculated, "Perhaps life with all its various experiences is no more, in the inscrutable purpose of Providence, than so much stuff of different kinds for the spirit to work upon, and thereby prove its power, putting itself as it were in evidence before the great spirit of all . . . kindling, showing, and setting itself free" (Bulwer-Lytton, *Literary Letters* 1:210–11). In one of his poems, a character examines the concept of liberty and finds it illusory because it can exist for man only when he is free from the flesh.[57] Meredith believed that nature was a manifestation of God's will, ensuring all organisms happiness as a means of achieving its ends, and that the human endeavor toward happiness was a duty, but he also acknowledged that man could not escape sorrow because he could not escape circumstance (Bulwer-Lytton, *Literary Letters* 1:150–51).

A great part of Meredith's poetry deals with the sorrow that circumstance brings. *Lucile* (1860), the poem that brought him fame, is a good example. Mainly it deals with the mischances of love, but "fate" is a word often used by the characters of this novel in verse. At a climactic point in the narrative, the Duc de Luvois encounters Lucile de Nevers, once his love, whom he disappointed. He excuses his failure with a familiar plea. "By the laws / Of a fate I can neither control nor dispute, / I am what I am." But Lucile replies:

> "We are our own fates. Our own deeds
> Are our doomsmen. Man's life was made not for men's creeds,
> But men's actions"
>
> (Meredith, Poems, 121)

Yet the twists and turns of the narrative, its accidents and coincidences, suggest that men's deeds are not entirely at their command, though in the end all works out for the general if not the individual good in the disclosure that "our life is but love / In act" (Meredith, *Poems*, 149).

The conflict between a conviction that man's fate is determined by his deed and a belief in providential determinism found expression in a peculiar late poem entitled *Glenaveril; or The Metamorphoses* (1885). By the time he wrote this poem, Meredith had spent many years as a public official. His friend Betty Balfour theorized that his later poetry became more and more fanciful because it represented more and more an escape from "an uncongenial world of fact." For Meredith, poetry was "a land of refuge; an ideal world of consolation, where the 'Inevitable No' of destiny was avoided and he could frame things anew, not as they were, but as they might have been" (Bulwer-Lytton, *Literary Letters* 1:83).

It would not be worth the effort to explain the many involutions of *Glenaveril*'s narrative, but the core of the story is simple. Two young men, born on the same day, mature in different ways—one as a sports-loving, noble-mannered fellow, the other as a bookish young man with democratic sentiments. The puzzling feature is that the first grows up as a humble pastor's son, the other as the heir of a Scottish lord. From the outset, everything indicates that the two have somehow been exchanged. But at the very end of the tale that issue remains unresolved. They might have been substituted for one another through a nurse's blunder. Such a substitution would explain many things—the boys' temperaments suitable to their stations, the young woman Cordelia's instinctive love for the man she thinks is the pastor's son, Emanuel, but who is really Ivor, and other similar instances. But Meredith abandons speculation. "Think what thou wilt, then, Reader! For my part, / There is no theory about love, I care / To prove, or *dis*prove." He offers his reader the opportunity to find in his story a moral that softens "The harshness of untoward circumstance," but presents no such comforting conclusion himself (Meredith, *Glenaveril* 2:304).

As though confusions were not great enough, Meredith compounded them by having the young men exchange identities. Ivor, believed to be Emanuel, dies by a fall in the Alps not long after he has declared there is no chance in Nature but that chance is merely our name for what we do not understand. Ironically, his death confirms chance as mystery rather than accident because it fulfills the Glenaveril tradition of death by accident. When Lord Glenaveril, Ivor's father, suffers such a death, the mild scholar Ludwig Edelrath muses on the apparent truth of the strange tradition.

> What are accidents?
> A causeless accident there cannot be.
> And what excludes transmitted influence

From such a series? Character is fate;
Men's dispositions do their dooms dictate.
(Meredith, *Glenaveril* 1:24)

Throughout the poem, accident and circumstance are superseded by a providential scheme. The two young men work out their appropriate destinies. The real Ivor is dead, and Emanuel will go to America with Cordelia to lead a Utopian community. But in thus endorsing providence, Meredith seems to have canceled freedom of the will, for act as the characters may, the overriding design works out as it must. Near the end of the poem, Meredith used a familiar metaphor to explain this situation. It is Edelrath who offers the suggestion that all of circumstance constitutes the substance for dramatic art. " 'The poem whereby each is most affected / The drama of his own life needs must be.' " All men have the capacity to appreciate the unfolding of their own life stories, and Meredith asks if this innate narratizing inclination is not a reference

For the Great Author of this Human Plot,
Who both created and controls it all?
To Him, whose will doth to each act allot
An end that by its actor is unknown,
We abdicate the guidance of our own!
(Meredith, *Glenaveril* 2:239)

Meredith himself claims that his role as poet merely resembles nature in being a vehicle for a higher will. He says that he has withheld nothing from the reader but writes what "A Presence" compels him to:

viii

As some unseen dictatress (who but stays
    Till all is said, impatient to be gone)
Her strong injunction on his spirit lays:
    What she reveals not, is to him unknown,
    And only what she bids him say, he says.
    Nought may he add thereto, that is his own;
Nor stop, as he delivers them, to guess
The sense of her imperious messages.

ix

But all the images thou dost behold
    Reflected here, whate'er they seem to be,

> Are Life's reflections. And Life leaves untold
> The greater part of all she does: for she,
> Ever propounding problems manifold,
> Keeps in her own unopened hand their key.
> Even Law, herself, declines the impossible task
> Of answering the question thou wouldst ask.
> (Meredith, *Glenaveril* 2:302–3)

The poem is not designed by the poet; its intricacies and involutions are not his, but simply a reflection of Life. Hence life's mysteries, and we might say apparent evils and inconsistencies, are also misleading, for behind the mysteries of a material world dominated by circumstance and the inscrutable workings of nature is a Great Author who has planned and executed the whole like a work of art. Other authors offered themselves as miniature imitations of god himself creating their miniature worlds, but Meredith presents his miniature world as a full-size transposition of the real thing and himself as God's pencil.

What then becomes of individual free will in this sorrowful world secretly working toward good? It is a question that Meredith can answer only with the explanation that character is fate, though there is a hint that he may himself have consciously or unconsciously understood that his scheme of God, the benign but unforthcoming artist, was insufficient. At the beginning of book 2 of *Glenaveril*, we are told that trivialities make life seem comic, but behind the mask it is tragic, "A constant train of tragical events / Moving to one immense catastrophe" (Meredith, *Glenaveril* 2:108). These lines read very like the dark alter ego of lines by Meredith's greatly admired Tennyson that conclude his most famous poem—"And one far-off divine event, / To which the whole creation moves" (Tennyson, *Poems*, 988).

If Meredith's poem is overcomplicated and largely unresolved, it is because he saw human existence in those terms; his faith in a divine purpose keeps a higher will active, though man's will seems less and less free the more precise providence's scenario becomes. Meredith consciously clung to a kindly providence, but other poets could not credit providence with benignity if they credited it at all.

Perhaps the most famous Victorian poem announcing the dominion of fate in human affairs is Edward FitzGerald's *The Rubáiyát of Omar Khayyám* (1859), a poem that remained unnoticed by the general public for most of the poet's life but which increased in popularity after his death. Contrasting the *Rubáiyát* with *In Memoriam*, D. C. Somervell assumed that the former poem "appealed to a generation tired of the struggle between faith and doubt," a generation that grew up in the shadow of Darwin's *Origin of Species*, and was prepared to embrace a carpe deim philosophy.[58] This may be too simple an explanation for the poem's popularity, though it is probably true that the poem conformed more to the mood prevailing at the end than to that of the middle of the century.

FitzGerald's poem has often been read as a pagan, atheistic statement, but that shrewd and surprising observer of literature and culture G. K. Chesterton proferred an equally plausible view. FitzGerald's, he said, "is that terrible theism which can imagine nothing else but deity, and which denies altogether the outlines of human personality and human will."[59] Chesterton added that a Christian reader would naturally object to the absence of free will in FitzGerald's scheme. Of course, the scheme as such was not FitzGerald's, but Khayyám's, and in a less than entirely candid preface to his "translation," FitzGerald dumped the blame for its content entirely on the Persian poet. "Having failed (however mistakenly) of finding any Providence but Destiny, and any world but this, he set about making the most of it," he explained. Khayyám was unwilling to conceive of the universe as a Lucretian drama of "homeless Necessity, [and so] flung his own Genius and Learning with a bitter or humorous jest into the general Ruin which their insufficient glimpses only served to reveal; and pretending sensual pleasure as the serious purpose of Life, only *diverted* himself with speculative problems of Deity, Destiny, Matter and Spirit, Good and Evil, and other such questions, easier to start than to run down, and the pursuit of which becomes a very weary sport at last!"[60]

FitzGerald hinted here that the poem does not express theistic sentiments but that theistic language is merely a convenient mode for a more general indictment. Better to give a god a bad name if you mean to beat him. And so the analogy of mankind to so many damaged clay pots does not really assume the existence of an inept deity but is a way of conveying the meaninglessness of existence. The poem spreads blame broadly to plural powers elsewhere.

73

With Earth's first Clay they did the Last Man knead,
And there of the last Harvest sow'd the Seed:
And the first Morning of Creation wrote
What the last Dawn of Reckoning shall read.

(FitzGerald, 147)

Still, the fiction of a single accusable author was useful, as in these two notorious stanzas.

80

Oh Thou, who didst with pitfall and with gin
Beset the Road I was to wander in,

Thou wilt not with Predestined Evil round
Enmesh, and then impute my Fall to Sin!

81

Oh Thou, who Man of baser Earth didst make,
An ev'n with Paradise devise the Snake;
For all the Sin wherewith the Face of Man
Is blacken'd—Man's forgiveness give—and take!
(FitzGerald, 149-50)

These are less the words of a Persian poet in the eleventh century than of a disillusioned Calvinist in the nineteenth. It is not surprising that a modern poet who had much to say himself about a universe of chance and who himself used God as a convenient target of abuse, should have asked, as Thomas Hardy is said to have done, that stanza 81 of the *Rubáiyát* be read to him on his deathbed.[61]

~ ~ ~

Up to this point I have mainly described the common occupation with the theme of the will among Romantic and Victorian poets. Now I shall mention some differences. The Romantics were struck by the limitless improvability of man's nature; the Victorians believed in human progress, almost a second faith for many of them. But these two notions were not identical. At the same time that scientific studies were lending apparent proof to the theory that man was on an ascending plane of progress, they were presenting unwelcome evidences of man's bondage to the earth. For example, investigations of the human brain were gradually succeeding in localizing mental functions. Eventually such investigations produced grave doubts about man's freedom.[62] Similarly, the increased intellectual activity prompted by a revival of moral and religious interest in Victorian years paradoxically bred an increasing skepticism as scientific investigations aided the higher criticism in breaking down convictions so recently regained. Just as the Romantic revival of philosophical optimism was gradually modified in the direction of more conservative moral thinking, Victorian religious enthusiasm tempered itself to a secular sobriety or divided into thorough idealism or determined pessimism. The Victorians represent both an extension of Romantic ideas and a defensive consolidation of them. I do not intend to offer a history of ideas for the nineteenth century, but I believe that a selective examination of certain rudimentary images will help to demonstrate what I mean.

It is often by spatial conceptualizations that men reveal their basic assumptions, and I believe that images of expansion and encirclement provide a way of stipulating some changes between Romantic and Victorian outlooks. Let us begin with Carlyle because his writings combine Romantic and Victorian feelings about the will. For him, as for the Romantics, existence is definable as action; it is dynamic. The will everywhere touches an agitating reality, manifested as force of one kind or another. It is a Newtonian picture animated. "Our whole Universe is but an infinite Complex of Forces; thousandfold, from Gravitation up to Thought and Will; *man's Freedom environed with Necessity of Nature*: in all which nothing at any moment slumbers, but all is forever awake and busy."[63] There is a teleology in all of this movement. "All grows, and seeks and endures its destinies." Is it not plain truth, Carlyle asks, "that human things wholly are in continual movement, and action and reaction; working continually forward, phasis after phasis, by unalterable laws toward prescribed issues?" (Carlyle, *Works* 3:103).

Carlyle's scheme presents two apparently incompatible ideas. If man is environed by necessity and moves by unalterable laws to prescribed issues, how is he free? Also, if his freedom is viewed as a point surrounded by necessity, how does he move linearly toward some designed destiny? These incompatibilities are only apparent, for Carlyle elsewhere offered explanations for them. In *Sartor Resartus*, Teufelsdrockh describes the mixed felicity and care of his childhood. "Among the rainbow colours that glowed on my horizon, lay even in childhood a dark ring of Care. . . . It was the ring of Necessity whereby we are all begirt; happy he for whom a kind heavenly Sun brightens it into a ring of Duty, and plays round it with beautiful prismatic diffractions; yet ever, as basis and as bourne for our whole being, it is there" (Carlyle, *Works* 1:78). Man is free when the ring that encircles him becomes a brace and not a bond. Since the human will cannot alter imprisoning circumstance, it must transform itself into an agent at one with circumstance. This scheme resembles the pattern we have already described in which the will finds its freedom in submission to a higher power. But there is an important distinction here. The individual will does not blend with a higher purpose, does not lose its individuality. Instead, its sense of uniqueness is enhanced. It finds its particular place in a vast scheme, like an atom in its larger organism.

If there is no inconsistency between free center and environing necessity, there is likewise no real contradiction for Carlyle between the implied stasis of the circle and the onward flow of destiny. He characterized time as a mystery and illusion. All that man perceives as action through matter is the "Time-vesture of God" (Carlyle, *Works* 1:210). If man could transcend the limitations of his own faculties, he would see that God is the force that sustains everything, that *is* everything; hence progress from point to point is a human perception, not a reality. The circle and the line need not be incompatible. To one whose will is obedient to the inexorable law of nature this truth is evident.

Coleridge's outlook is like and unlike Carlyle's in a way that makes the continuum of transition from Romantic to Victorian clear. Like Carlyle, Coleridge employed the images of center and circumference to describe man's place in nature. He asserted that "the true object of Natural Philosophy is to discover a central Phaenomenon in Nature," which in turn "requires and supposes a central Thought in the Mind." Although a finite universe composed of atoms is notionally true, it merely reveals the limits of man's imagination and understanding and is not necessarily true in nature. Because the mind requires a center, or conceptual starting place, Coleridge says, every whole "must be conceived as a possible centre in itself, and at the same time as having a centre out of itself and common to it with all other parts of the same System." This abstract pattern works in nature too. Coleridge asks what the conditions are for a unit "to be the centre of a system and (as, in dynamics, the power of the centre acts in every point of the area contained in the circumference) be the centre and the copula (*principium unitatis in unoquoque Toto*) of a System," and concludes that it must have a center outside itself and yet be a center or cohesive force for a system of its own, with a perpetual tendency to include whatever exists relative to it into itself and to repel what it cannot include.[64] Every such unit, like human intelligence, may thus be pictured as an expanding circle. Explaining that nature is the Universal Principle of Life of which man is a part, Coleridge describes how man functions as such an expanding center through the operation of his will, by which he means more than voluntary power. He repeats the image borrowed from dynamics, picturing man as a plenum pressing outward from his own center against the circumference that is the boundary of his identity, the world of circumstance not himself. Man can do this because he has imagined a center in himself which we may loosely term the self. "Man must have an object in himself, an object which he himself has constituted, which is at one and the same moment the subject and the legislator, the law and the act of obedience."[65] By an inward act of discovery, man gains the power to transcend the boundaries of the self.[66]

Coleridge's description of the imagination is germane. The primary imagination is "a repetition in the finite mind of the eternal act of creation in the infinite I AM." Man thus is a unit in a system whose center is outside of himself. The secondary imagination is an echo of the primary imagination "co-existing with the conscious will" and differing only in degree and mode of operation from it. "It dissolves, diffuses, dissipates, in order to recreate" or idealize and unify.[67] Man now becomes a unit whose center is his secondary imagination assimilating to it whatever it can include, and creating, through a process of dissolution or unification, new systems of perceiving. Outward from this center of energy his conscious will exerts pressure upon the circumference or boundary of his being, but ultimately he seeks something vaster.

Coleridge had explained that self-consciousness is impossible except by and in a will that is free. Self-consciousness begins in the center of the system known as the self and reaches to the center of the most inclusive system outside the self. "We begin," he says, "with the I KNOW MYSELF, in order to end with the absolute I AM. We proceed from the SELF, in order to lose and find all self in God" (Coleridge, *Biographia* 1:185).[68] Like Carlyle, Coleridge sees man confined by a "ring-fence" or even a series of ring-fences, of necessity. He cannot disentangle himself from this "skein of necessity . . . which surrounds with subtlest intertwine the slenderest fibres of his Being, while it binds the whole frame with chains of adamant," until, by realizing that this necessity is himself and must "in all its directions and labyrinthine folds belong to his Being, and evolve out of his essences," he discovers that he is the shaper, not the thing shaped and he is free to extend himself *into* the ring-fence of which he is himself the fabric.[69] Where Carlyle sees the encircling necessity as a not-self that defines the self, Coleridge imagines man *becoming* his encirclement in a process of growth. The will's energy, for Carlyle, is held bound in its iron circle of necessity, or duty, for the duration, and this is good. It is an aid, like any discipline. But Coleridge sees the will capable of dissolving or extending the circle. To pause and admit a discipline or unbreachable boundary is to lose the freedom of imagination and will which permits the eventual merging into the will of God.

Shelley's philosophy is similar to but simpler than Coleridge's. In "On Life," he included himself among those who believe "that nothing exists but as it is perceived," making imagination the creative power. Shelley explained that after a youthful fascination with materialism, he realized that man was a dynamic and creative being. "Whatever may be his true and final destination, there is a spirit within him at enmity with nothingness and dissolution. This is the character of all life and being. Each is at once the center and the circumference; the point to which all things are referred, and the line in which all things are contained" (Shelley, *Poetry and Prose*, 476). And just as each individual is both center and circumference, so is his highest achievement—poetry. In *A Defence of Poetry*, Shelley wrote that "poetry is indeed something divine. It is at once the centre and circumference of knowledge." It is a moral agent as well because "poetry enlarges the circumference of the imagination by replenishing it with thoughts of ever new delight, which have the power of attracting and assimilating to their own nature all other thoughts, and which form new intervals and interstices whose void for ever craves fresh food" (Shelley, *Poetry and Prose*, 503, 488).

In his poetry this attention to encirclement takes many forms. The symbol of the boat adrift on a "circumfluous Ocean" suggests many things (Shelley, *Poetry and Prose*, 357). It may be a symbol of the soul or self carried by the spirit of nature not yet a part of that force but guided by it. Islands in Shelley's poetry may be read as loci of unification. Like the boat, the island is surrounded by ocean. The redemptive, quiet isle is in harmonious relation with the ocean that represents its boundaries, though finally, like man's soul and the All, isle and sea are one. Neville Rogers reminds us that Shelley's image of the "one warring with the Evil Principle" was the ouroboros, the serpent biting its tail and thereby forming a circle representing eternity.[70] Shelley resembled Coleridge, then, in conceiving of the self as a willed force moving out from a center to a circumference which is the temporary limit of its own force, thus suggesting an infinite and eternal expansion into the all-encompassing Will.

But not all Romantics went this far. Wordsworth, also an apostate of necessarianism, proposed mediating boundaries between man and nature. This was a common theme in philosophy. In the same year that Wordsworth completed *The Prelude*, William Drummond published *Academical Questions* (1805). Drummond was interested in the subject of boundaries, citing Aristotle on man's perception not of primary matter but only of its boundary or form. Men conceive of individuality by outline, determining those points at which a unit touches what impinges upon it. A being is not merely its outline and is "different from its bounds, as a whole is different from any of its parts. . . . But we cannot conceive a whole without all its parts, nor a body without its bounds."[71] Although Drummond went on to discuss the subject of extension and matter, he had touched upon our main motif—the relationship of central identity to what confines or surrounds it. Wordsworth's speculations on this theme were more profound than Drummond's.

Even after he began to value duty more than self-assertion, Wordsworth was unwilling to accept a thorough control; "Denial and restraint I prize / No farther than they breed a second Will more wise."[72] He had always been unwilling to yield authority over his own identity. Wordsworth wished to achieve a balance between the self in itself and as perceived form. Geoffrey Hartman says that Wordsworth's "ultimate figure remains a borderer, at once natural and human," on the edge of the supernatural.[73] While admitting the unity of nature, Wordsworth was reluctant to be lost in it. He praised Coleridge for not being deceived into thinking "that our puny boundaries [described by science] are things / That we perceive, and not that we have made," and, yet, he found in the study of geometry "a type, for finite natures, of the one / Supreme Existence" incapable of change "to the boundaries of space and time."[74] Wordsworth presents man, Hartman says, as "a mesocosm: at the boundary of all realms, and himself their boundary. Wordsworth preserves the self from all (including mythic) encroachments because the self is not this or that but *between*. He guarantees man his own realm without separating him fatally from nature or supernature."[75]

Wordsworth believed in the unity of all life but valued individuality highly and hence was forced, as Drummond saw, to preserve an acute sense of boundaries. Man's center is his free will, but he is always sensitive to his peripheries. "Points have we all of us within our souls / Where all stand single" (Wordsworth, *Prelude*, 81). Coleridge too believed that man had to conceive a center for his identity, but while Coleridge encouraged indefinite expansion outward, Wordsworth suggested a pattern more like Carlyle's. Moments of insight are likened to spots of time or islands in the river of time. Man's will shapes these moments through memory and imagination. The "efficacious spirit" associated with these spots of time "lurks / Among those passages of life that give / Profoundest knowledge to what point, and how, / The mind is lord and master—outward sense / The obedient servant of her will" (Wordsworth, *Prelude*, 445-47). Instead of the self merging with the world of circumstance, it preserves a measure of separation. Wordsworth is midway between Shelley and Carlyle. The former's islands were havens at one with the sea; the latter's circle of necessity was a confining boundary in a linear progression. For Wordsworth the contiguity is delicately proportioned.

If Wordsworth saw the self consolidated by a consciousness of its boundaries, never permitting itself to flow into the circumambient will, Keats saw the poet's self refined by becoming others. He estheticized what had been philosophical. There is, in his motion of negative capability, the suggestion of Shelley's dissolving power and Coleridge's infinite extension of the center into the circumference. But for Keats the process ended with the self and art and did not extend to a transcendent principle of love and divine will.

The Romantics associated the will with self-conscious identity extending outward toward a mystery that they trusted because they were a part of the mystery.[76] They were willing to risk this expansion because they sensed that the self was composed of a multiplicity of traits that could be reshaped; it was a self-created form. The existence of distinct individual minds was a delusion, Shelley wrote. "The words *I, you, they,* are not signs of any actual difference subsisting between the assemblage of thoughts thus indicated, but are merely marks employed to denote the different modifications of the one mind."[77] To Coleridge, individual personality was the achievement of the highest sense of certainty through reason, but this personality was part of a larger whole. "There is one heart for the whole mighty mass of Humanity, and every pulse in each particular vessel strives to beat in concert with it."[78]

Carlyle understood this sense of the interconnectedness of all things, as his chapter "Organic Filaments" in *Sartor Resartus* shows. And yet he emphasized not the yearning of the self toward assimilation with the whole but the consolidation of the self through renunciation. The Victorians were like him in this. They valued individual identity and were uncomfortable with mysteries and divisions of the self.[79] Looking back on the Romantics, Victorian writers often respected them as poets but were critical of them as men. Walter Bagehot dubbed Shelley an impulsive child who did not understand the internal struggles of complex characters. He lacked the "characteristic action of the will—namely, self-control."[80] When Bagehot styled Shelley as "undivided," he was not praising him. Arnold found little that was first-rate among the Romantics. Though he admired Wordsworth's ability to render a sense of joy in nature and Byron's power of personality, he felt that Keats produced little and was immature, while Coleridge was a "poet and philosopher wrecked in a mist of opium," and Shelley was a "beautiful and ineffectual angel."[81] Leslie Stephen saw Coleridge as an example of vast powers running to waste. Like Arnold, he could not always condone the conduct of that earlier generation.[82]

The Victorians believed they possessed what the Romantics lacked. Inheriting strong passions, love of nature, and a yearning to escape the limitations of material life from the Romantics, they brought to these impulses a firm will and self-discipline, which, though it left them with warring selves, made them, in their own estimation, finer men. Where the Romantics dared to extend themselves indefinitely into the mysterious necessity encircling them, Victorians focused their wills upon the centers of their beings, closing off an alien circumambience.

If isles were Shelley's points of resolution held in an amniotic sea, for Arnold they were symbols of isolation.

> Yes! in the sea of life enisled,
> With echoing straights between us thrown,
> Dotting the shoreless watery wild,
> We mortal millions live *alone.*
> The islands feel the ensclasping flow,
> And then their endless bounds they know.
> (Arnold, *Poems,* 124)

Arnold's "endless bounds" might more accurately read "unending." The "unplumbed, salt, estranging sea" will forever separate individuals. The agitations at the boundaries of the self reassured Wordsworth; for Arnold they were torture. The "enclasping flow" is a constant reminder that the will is limited, communication beyond the self minimal. The great nature toward which the Romantics yearned here proves hostile or indifferent.[83] Man cannot vitalize it with his imagination. That illusion is lost. Shelley could trust the sea on which his soul was borne, but Arnold knows that "our bane . . . is weakness, is a faltering course. . . . We stem across the sea of life by night" (Arnold, *Poems,* 140–41). "For most men in a brazen prison live. . . . And while they try to stem / The waves of mournful thought by which they are pressed, / Death in their prison reaches them, / Unfreed, having seen nothing, still unblest." The few who escape "depart / On the wide ocean of life anew," only to drift without directions where "tradewinds which cross it from eternity" prevail, until they are swamped, "still standing for some false, impossible shore" (Arnold, *Poems*, 269–70).

Arnold's sea of life is crueler than any we have seen. At least for Carlyle the environing necessity was deadening, not, like Arnold's, invasive. Romantics pressed out into the world of material necessity; Arnold felt the world threatening to flow in upon him in "waves of mournful thought." Attempts at freedom mean shipwreck in an elemental power. At the end of "A Summer Night" Arnold looks to the "untroubled and unpassionate" depths of the sky for hope (Arnold, *Poems*, 271). Man cannot reach the divine will through a submergence in the life of this world. He must subdue himself to nature's law, which he cannot alter, and then leap to the divine. It is as though he put on Daedalus's wings to escape Coleridge's ring-fence of necessity—and with about as much hope of success.

It is not that man does not wish to be a part of nature, but, as Empedocles unhappily admits, mind and thought "keep us prisoners of our consciousness" (Arnold, *Poems*, 189). The Scholar-Gipsy had "*one* aim, *one* business, *one* desire," and thus could return to nature. But the ordinary mortal "half-lives a hundred different lives," and has "never deeply felt, nor clearly willed" (Arnold, *Poems*, 339–40). Man is time's prisoner because his passions urge him toward a peace he cannot have. Only the poet subdues the energy of his heart to view the whole course of man.

> In the day's life, whose iron round
> Hems us all in, he is not bound;
> He leaves his kind, o'erleaps their pen,
> And flees the common life of men.
> He escapes thence, but we abide—
> Not deep the poet sees, but wide.
> (Arnold, *Poems*, 92)

Man's only course is resignation; they "who await / No gifts from chance, have conquered fate." They may calmly draw near "the general life" (Arnold, *Poems*, 94).

Arnold was a cankered Romantic. His longings were the same, but the ideals and passions they represented were unattainable for him. He believed that man was one with the Principle of Life and that his individuality was borne along with the general life of nature, but he did not believe that modern man had the will to expand his central self outward to other centers, let alone through environing necessity. Instead, that center itself was hidden. Man's nature is fragmented and his "genuine self" buried, following "his being's law" in secret like a subterranean river, while the superficial selves might "seem to be / Eddying at large in blind uncertainty, / Though driving on with it eternally" (Arnold, *Poems*, 272-73).[84] Behind Arnold's isolated islands, his circling, eddying, weak-willed spirits, is a confidence in a general life of which man is a part. Unfortunately, that life is mainly inaccessible. The iron boundary made by time is rarely breachable and then only by the greatest poetic spirits.

For Tennyson, the circle is usually time. It is the "round of time," and the circling seasons, the cycle of nature, or the circle of the year. He mentions "cycled times" and "a cycle of Cathay" (Tennyson, *Poems*, 728, 1216, 716, 933, 699). *In Memoriam* and *Idylls of the King* follow the cycle of seasonal movement, thereby exploiting a tension between the confinement of the circle and the potential release from that repeated round; for while the circle of time confines man, the action of each poem points toward an ultimate transcendence of time. Time is the circle binding man, but seen from the perspective of eternity it is an illusory circle, and man is not caught in it, but ascending spirally.

Tennyson pictured man's free will as a caged bird rising from perch to perch until it is freed. His poems reveal this faith in the ascent of spirit. He said of the dead Hallam, "Thy spirit . . . Did ever rise from high to higher," and wishes that he could wing his "will with might / To leap the grades of life and light, / And flash at once, my friend, to thee" (Tennyson, *Poems*, 899). All of *In Memoriam* is a testimony to this ascent, as are the symbolic statues at Camelot that indicate progressive stages from lowest beasts slaying men up to Arthur "with a crown / And peaked wings pointed to the Northern Star" (Tennyson, *Poems*, 1669).

Because time is a function of matter, Tennyson associated circling seasons with the "circle of the hills," the "circle of earth," and the "phantom circle of a moaning sea" (Tennyson, *Poems*, 954, 317, 1745). Thus the material world is still that circle of necessity binding man to life and entrapping a will which yearns to be free. Sometimes the menace of this circle is stated more particularly. In "The Vision of Sin," the central character finds himself in a place of sin with "low voluptuous music . . . woven in circles" which the company of libertines imitates in dance, "wheeling with precipitate paces." Later in the poem this bacchanal is mimicked in a *Totentanz* when, "trooping from their mouldy dens / The chap-fallen circle" of corpses capers (Tennyson, *Poems*, 719, 723). The circle of sin becomes the corrupting circle of the earth, binding the soul. Lucretius, too, infected by an aphrodisiac, dreams of "girls, Hetairi, curious in their art, / Hired animalisms," who "yelled and round me drove / In narrowing circles till I yelled again / Half-suffocated." Earthly passion presses in upon Lucretius who wishes to be "centered in eternal calm," married to the "passionless bride, divine Tranquillity." He feels some monster has laid his "vast and filthy hands upon [his] will," depriving him of his "power to shape," and driving him to suicide (Tennyson, *Poems*, 1207–17). He is the antipode of Arnold's Empedocles, for while the latter philosopher fears the extinction of feeling by too much thought, Lucretius dreads the overthrow of mind by passion. A subtler materiality always threatens to invade the mind. The central voice of "The Two Voices," who suffers from a "divided will," discovers that doubt may become an imprisoning ring. "In the same circle we revolve. / Assurance only breeds resolve," he says, sensing that the will itself must solve the problem of doubt, since argument cannot (Tennyson, *Poems*, 106, 535).

Escape from the encircling barrier of material life is possible through the exertion of free will, but it is a laborious task, not at all like the merging into nature described by the Romantics. It begins with discipline. "Self-reverence, self-knowledge, self-control, / These three alone lead life to sovereign power," Pallas Athene tells Paris in "Oenone," then promises:

> my vigour, wedded to thy blood,
> Shall strike within thy pulses, like a God's,
> To push thee forward through a life of shocks,
> Dangers, and deeds, until endurance grow
> Sinewed with action, and the full-grown will,
> Circled through all experiences, pure law,
> Commeasure perfect freedom.
>   (Tennyson, *Poems*, 393–94)[85]

In "The Ancient Sage," the message, though more mystical, is the same. The Sage informs his young companion that "all that breathe are one / Slight ripple on the boundless deep," but that ripple "feels that the deep is boundless, and itself / For ever changing form, but evermore / One with the boundless motion of the deep." Men may sometimes escape "the mortal limit of the Self," and pass "into the Nameless, as a cloud / Melts into Heaven," but this is a rare forecast of eventual union with the deep (Tennyson, *Poems*, 1355–56). Man's duty as long as he is flesh is to work in the world, as Arthur instructed the seekers of the Grail. Time is an illusion by which man is bound, though he can master it. "But thou be wise," the Sage advises, "in this dream world of ours, / Nor take thy dial for thy deity, / But make the passing shadow serve thy will." To do this you must dive

> Into the Temple-cave of thine own self,
> There, brooding by the central altar, thou
> Mayst haply learn the Nameless hath a voice,
> By which thou wilt abide, if thou be wise.
>   (Tennyson, *Poems*, 1353, 1351)

Tennyson's belief in free will and will power is similar to Carlyle's. Human will is part of a larger, transcendent will that, in life, can lose itself in that larger force only for fleeting moments. Man's task is to shape his individuality through a disciplined will. In "The Golden Year" Tennyson toyed with an image of human endeavor which he rejected. Leonard, having decided that it is not man's nature to "fix a point, to rest," and that "to be resolved into the all . . . [is] to lose [himself]," wonders what alternative there is:

> And here, methought he seemed to grasp
> A pair of shadowy compasses, with these
> To plant a centre and about it round
> A wide and wider circle.
>
> (Tennyson, *Poems*, 717)

Tennyson discarded this Romantic image of a widening circumference out from a central point and chose instead, in other poems, the image of ascent, perhaps in spiral or by steps, but upward, above the ring-fence of necessity. He never forgot that the ring-fence was always there.

Browning was more energetic in his faith, but he too began with doubts. "Pauline," derivative from Shelley, shows his working out of our familiar metaphors. Browning's persona says that though his "soul had floated from its sphere / Of wild dominion into the dim orb / Of self—that it was strong and free as ever! / It has conformed itself to that dim orb." He has an intense consciousness of self linked to "self-supremacy, / Existing as a centre to all things / Most potent to create and rule and call / Upon all things to minister to it" through his vivid imagination, but his soul "will not rest / In its clay prison, this most narrow sphere." When the persona controls his restless passion through "commanding will," he realizes that earthly life is not his only sphere and that his imperious soul hungers for God in whom he puts his trust. "No more of the past!" he exclaims, "I'll look within no more" (Robert Browning, *Works* 1:5-6, 20-21, 31). With this cry Browning sets himself apart from most of his contemporaries, who, like Tennyson, Arnold, Clough, and others, brooded on that center of energy, nurturing it for its leap beyond necessity. Nonetheless, Browning believed as much as any that truth rose out of man. "There is an inmost centre in us all, / Where truth abides in fulness; and around, / Wall upon wall the gross flesh hems it in," says Paracelsus (Robert Browning, *Works*, 1:61). The flesh had to be made servant, not enslaver. Man must not retreat within, but thrust outward. Browning was unwilling to let his own inmost self express itself outwardly but eagerly stripped off the encircling layers of his imagined characters or of truth itself, as in *The Ring and the Book*.[86]

Browning approved the aggressive Romantic stance but yoked that assertion to a Victorian belief in the imperfection of the material world and the consequent need for self-discipline. As Abt Vogler says, summing up an entire phase of Browning's thought, "On earth the broken arcs; in the heaven, a perfect round" (Robert Browning, *Works* 4:258). For Browning, man encircles himself with fate. If "we draw a circle premature . . . Bad is our bargain," he advised. We should trust God, for it is his "task to make the heavenly period / Perfect the earthen" (Robert Browning, *Works* 3:378). Daniel Karlin points out that although Browning was willing to allow a spherical excellence to others—Shelley's circles, the perfect orb of Dante's poetry, Giotto's O—he appears to have believed that his own poetry was aspiration toward, not achievement of, adequate expression.[87] For Browning, the circle image was risky. "The circle is the symbol of infinity, but also of zero, a nothingness which encompasses everything in a form of terminal closure." In "Old Pictures in Florence," Browning noted the irony of Giotto's achievement—the O he drew was perfect, but the campanile he was to construct remains unfinished.[88]

In the late poem "Numpholeptos," Browning described a nymph, who may represent the absolute or some ideal, as a whiteness from which rays spread out "from centre to circumference, / Shaft upon coloured shaft" (Robert Browning, *Works* 9:50).[89] He, the nymph's devotee and pilgrim, can never reach her; nonetheless, all those who wish to retain her love must "go boldly on adventure, break through bounds / O' the quintessential whiteness that surrounds" her feet (Robert Browning, *Works* 9:51). The pilgrim in the world of Time cannot attain the center, for he is a point on the circumference, mimicking in the prison of his own orbed self the freedom of that vaster circle. It is a planetary design not unlike Coleridge's picture of self and infinite centers.[90] J. Hillis Miller's is the best summary I know of the broader importance of the circle metaphor in Browning's poetry:

> The creation is a circle, but it is an infinite circle, or, rather, an "eternal circle" (I, 165), for its most important dimension is the perpetual motion of time. The transcendent God is the perfect sun at the center and the creation proceeds eternally onward in its ever-renewed approach toward God. At this moment of universal history man is "completion of this sphere / Of life" (I, 162), but man has not yet achieved his full humanity, and, even when he does, he will only be a steppingstone to higher forms which will go still closer to God.[91]

An Owen Meredith might call out for perfection—"O sphere my soul," but other Victorian poets were less confident of that achievement (Meredith, *Poems*, 167). Swinburne, who felt the same impulse to transcendence that Shelley did was skeptical enough to hold back at the very margin of his own circumference, perceiving the limits of opposing realms of experience. "This consciousness of limits drives Swinburne to haunt boundary lines," Jerome J. McGann aptly puts it before going on to examine Swinburne's poetic practice.[92] In Swinburne, man is described as the transient foam-flower cast up by the eternal sea—more alone and fragile in his individuality than Arnold's isolated isles, less hopeful than Shelley's sea-lovers.

By the end of the century, the characteristic Victorian retreat into the protective yet imprisoning circle of the self became an opportunity for luxury. Pater wrote in the "Conclusion" to *The Renaissance*:

> Experience, already reduced to a swarm of impressions, is ringed round for each one of us by that thick wall of personality through which no real voice has ever pierced on its way to us, or from us to that which we can only conjecture to be without. Every one of those impressions is the impression of the individual in his isolation, each mind keeping as a solitary prisoner its own dream of a world.[93]

Pater inverted the Romantic image of the central self permeating the circumference that surrounds it and conceived instead a central personality that absorbs and transforms impressions much as organic tissue absorbs and transforms its nutrients. At the same time, Pater altered the typical Victorian image of the free self environed by necessity and offered in its place a self that is by nature separated from a world of "impressions" ordered not by a law of necessity but by the aesthetic impulses of that very personality.

Earlier, in *The Gay Science* (1866), E. S. Dallas had offered a prosier variant model of the self. For him an inner ring of human consciousness was surrounded by a ring of the unconscious.[94] Dallas's scheme falls midway between Carlyle's freedom bounded by necessity and Pater's thick wall of personality. But again it is human imagination that represents man's capacity for freedom because it exists as the free play of thought. Both Romantic and Victorian poets associated free will with the imagination. This power replaced or was identified with the intuition or conscience that moralists more characteristically designated as man's link with a higher will.

In general, I believe that we can trace a change from a prevailing, but not exclusive, attitude among the Romantics that man's nature was in some important sense free and capable of altering the world of which it was a part, to a prevailing, but not exclusive, attitude among Victorians that, though man's will was ultimately free, it was so liable to injury and invalidism that its wisest posture was one of defense. Andrew Griffin presents an appealing image for this change.

> For the Victorian imagination in general, it follows that the search for strength and selfhood in Nature can no longer be an escape or an enfranchisement but must become a troubled retreat: a con-

centration of forces, a defensive turning-inward toward hidden or guarded sources. What the park or garden was to the Victorian city, the soul or vital self might be to the active self, to what is called "life in the world."[95]

Free will in the nineteenth century may be defined as man's capacity to put himself at one with some transcendent law. The movement from Romantic to Victorian is largely an emendation of this attitude. The Romantics were influenced by necessarianism through Hartley, Godwin, and others but modified their views to accommodate and even to stress free will. In making this adjustment, Coleridge and Wordsworth revived religious faith and set the tone for a characteristic Victorian outlook. Carlyle, having been through the turmoil of the Romantic generation, settled down to disturb the nineteenth century with news that there was free will and that it needed what nourishing it could get in a world largely confined by habit and necessity. His plea for action was the lively twin of Coleridge's and Wordsworth's more contemplative views. The generation that heard Carlyle's call found themselves on a darkling plain where some battle had been won and a freedom achieved at great expense. They inherited not exuberant victory but, with exceptions, a brooding examination of the survivors and the dead. Convinced that no final triumph was possible in a world seeming more and more alien to man's spiritual core, they assumed a defensive stand without abandoning the essential beliefs of their predecessors. The Romantic skirmishing was over; Victorians prepared to endure a siege.

To a great extent, the Romantics were atheistic, agnostic, necessarian, and positive. The Victorians revived providence, faith, and skepticism. But the distinctions were blurred. One generation sought to lose self in nature, necessity, or love; the other preached subordination to an abiding law that was God's design, a "power not ourselves that makes for righteousness," the Unknowable, or "an end toward which all creation moves." The Romantics sought to merge individuality and All through expansion of the self; Victorians believed they must shape distinct identities thereafter subdued to a higher purpose often called duty. The Romantic struggle was toward that moment of illumination when the self blended with the law in a profligate abandonment of personality. Although the more prudent Victorians valued this experience, they preferred to constrain internal force to some principle, even at the risk of quelling that force. The one saw union as release; the other feared the loss of self. Romantics welcomed mystery in nature and themselves; Victorians longed for impossible certainties. Still, the ground of their conflict, though differently traversed, was largely the same.

The Romantics seemed agreed in perceiving existence in holistic terms. They recognized no radical separation between self and nature. Certainly their individual was part of a larger reality of which his or her interaction was an integral function. Most felt as well that meaning originated in the self, not in external things, and that the font of creation was imagination, not reason. The highest function of the imagination was the reconceiving of the world, made possible by its intimate affinity with life, nature, God, the unseen power, or whatever else the principle of creation might be called.

The Victorians, while maintaining the Romantic conviction that values were preserved in man's feelings and that external nature offered rejuvenating power, nonetheless perceived man as embattled, his feelings and intelligence surrounded by threatening forces which obliged him to close off his inner self even while encouraging an aggressive, expansive outer self. They associated the will more with intelligence than with imagination. Like Coleridge, most saw it as divided or diseased; therefore, its premier function was to maintain discipline and then to manifest that self-control in conduct. Free will became internal restraint, external ambition. "Hence," wrote Samuel Smiles, the spokesman of Victorian values at their most approachable level, "energy of will may be defined to be the very central power of character in a man—in a word, it is the man himself."[96] Freedom of the will was not spontaneous but achieved through self-scrutiny and self-control. To possess free will was henceforth to subordinate the power of the will to the duty ordained by God. Renunciation of the self could come only when that self was well-defined. For the Victorians the boundaries were clear.

CHAPTER TEN

Early Nineteenth-Century Fiction

I N part 1, we noted an increasing trust in feeling over reason from the eighteenth to the nineteenth centuries among commentators on free will and necessity. With novelists, this change of emphasis had consequences for the way stories were told and the sentiments appealed to in their readers. This chapter demonstrates briefly how novelists with different outlooks reveal the influence of philosophical assumptions on narrative practices. In Godwin's *Caleb Williams*, the guiding force of the narrative is necessity, but in Robert Plumer Ward's *Tremaine*, it is providence. James Hogg uses narrative to satirize a theological point of view, thereby revealing the artist's awareness of the relationship between narrative strategies and philosophical premises.

In dealing openly with the connections between story telling and free will, necessity, and providence, these works indicate that some authors were conscious of the implications for narrative of philosophical or religious beliefs. Of course, many writers had no such self consciousness. Nonetheless, popular domestic and adventure novels by writers like Susan Ferrier and William Harrison Ainsworth reveal underlying values, especially regarding free will, manifesting themselves clearly or confusedly in thematic and structural ways. Essentially, the nineteenth century accepted a providential view of human history. Whether writers of fiction acknowledged this openly or not, their stories were likely to reflect a providential pattern.

~   ~   ~

In *Philosophy and the Novel*, Peter Jones selects a passage from George Henry Lewes's *Comte's Philosophy of the Sciences* (1853) to epitomize the major change in nineteenth-century thinking from an Augustan faith in reason to a Victorian confidence in feeling. "There never will be a Philosophy capable of satisfying the demands of Humanity," Lewes wrote, "until the truth be recognized that man is moved by his emotions, not by his ideas: using his Intellect only as an eye to *see the way*. . . . Intellect is the servant, not the lord of the Heart."[1] Much literature of the nineteenth century is concerned precisely with the conflict implicit in this reorganization of values. From one point of view, the authentication of feeling is a means of affirming intuition and counteracting the pessimistic implications of logic, which were increasingly identified with a necessarian creed. From another point of view, the endorsement of feeling is an escape from the flat landscape of reason into the more picturesque ambience of risk.

To begin with the second of these possibilities, we may consider the Gothic novel. These fictions emphasize dominant male figures characterized by strength of will who are generally rebels against the ethical or social codes that confine them, like Melmoth and Montoni, or are outright embodiments of uncontrolled self-indulgence like Lewis's Monk. The heroines in these tales are essentially powerless, manipulable beings whose exertions cannot materially alter the course of events. However, the illusion of male power and female impotence is corrupted by the coincidences and accidents of plot. Thus Montoni's power in *The Mysteries of Udolpho* (1794) dissolves quickly once the pattern of causation that places Emily St. Aubert in his power is comprehended and resisted, something that is possible only through the fortuitous exchange of information. Accident or coincidence may be the result of chance or the revelation of a providential order. The former situation breeds an atmosphere of dread. No event can be trusted, no action properly interpreted. If events are not accidental, but part of a covert order, they may be considered diabolic, thus stoking the paranoia and supernatural anxiety that characterize Gothic narratives, or providential and benign, thus ultimately justifying both suffering and deprivation. The heroine's meek vulnerability triumphs over the villain's spurious authority through her submission to a higher power. In a novel like *The Mysteries of Udolpho*, individual destiny is determined by conscious forces beyond the human will, and thus the significance of characters' fates rests more in their design than in any inner moral struggles; character is often submerged in setting and obscured by vague mood painting. An elaborate, involved prose style masks the real direction of narrative meaning as effectively as do the many complications of plot.

This is not the case in Godwin's *Caleb Williams* (1794), which appropriates Gothic mannerisms to a different purpose. In the opening pages of the novel, Williams attributes his misfortunes to his own curiosity. He was inquisitive about human solutions to the phenomena of the universe, a methodological impulse. A more pernicious manifestation of his curiosity was teleological. Williams says that his curiosity "produced in me an invincible attachment to books of narrative and romance. I panted for the unravelling of an adventure."[2] This thirst for narrative sequence and solutions mirrors Godwin's own impulses, for, if Williams looks outward to the linear movement of narrative with all of its magnetic power of attracting incidents to an ultimate focus, Godwin's craving was to analyze the *origins* of human actions. He transformed his narrative from third to first person, explaining in his preface to the novel that it best allowed him "the analysis of the private and internal operations of the mind, employing my metaphysical dissecting knife in tracing and laying bare the involutions of motive, and recording the gradually accumulating impulses" that led his personages to act as they did (Godwin, *Williams*, xxviii).

Near the end of his narrative, Williams cries out in dismay, "Great God! what is man? Is he thus blind to the future, thus totalling unsuspecting of what is to occur in the next moment of his existence?" (Godwin, *Williams*, 324) The fault lies with Williams himself. Despite Falkland's declaration that the incidents of his own history illustrate that "all are but links of one chain," Williams fails to recognize the tightening chain of cause and effect in his own story (Godwin, *Williams*, 156). He sounds very like Victor Frankenstein when he says, "My offence had been merely a mistaken thirst for knowledge" (Godwin, *Williams*, 154). He has yielded time and again to his curiosity about Falkland's secret and admits that his "choice" to spy upon his patron involved serious risk; yet later, when persecuted by Falkland, he complains that "one circumstance was sufficient to blast" his free spirit and heart (Godwin, *Williams*, 124, 296). This one circumstance is, however, part of a long sequence of events that Williams does not comprehend until he sets about shaping that sequence into a story. Though he refers to an "uncontrollable destiny" that has prompted his actions, Williams does not see himself as a victim of necessity (Godwin, *Williams*, 151). Near the end of the novel, to protect himself, he threatens: "I will tell a tale—!" (Godwin, *Williams*, 364) He does so, unaware of the difference between the forces that shape men's lives and the men who shape stories of those lives. Only at the very conclusion of his narrative does Williams realize that narration itself has been a dangerous illusion; his true story is discredited by the law and only the liar Falkland's obsession with his good name provokes him perversely to admit to his old crime and verify Williams's account. Yet after Falkland's death, Williams devotes himself to correcting one narrative with another, and his story ends with these words: "I began these memoirs with the idea of vindicating my character. I have now no character that I wish to vindicate: but I will finish them that thy [Falkland's] story may be fully understood, and that if those errors of thy life be known, which thou so ardently desirdst to conceal, the world may at least not hear and repeat a half-told and mangled tale" (Godwin, *Williams*, 378).

For Godwin, men had no free will but were creatures of circumstance capable of understanding their lamentable condition. Through the conflict of inherited nature and social context, Williams finds himself in a situation he can never control. His apparent choices are volitional but not really expressions of free will. The life story he lives is already inscribed, his living it is the equivalent of narration, and only when he reaches its end can he properly comprehend it. The force behind narrative in Radcliffe was providence, in Godwin it is necessity. Injustice is not the willed, conscious violation of the rights of others but an imbalance between the unalterable law of nature and the capricious rules of man. This transformation in the sense of moral responsibility affects the manner in which narratives present values.

Novels of the late eighteenth and early nineteenth century often had a strong moral purpose. Robert Plumer Ward's *Tremaine* (1825) is an example. Though it passes as a novel, this account of a fastidious hero who falls in love with a pious young woman is more like a sermon and proud of it, as the opening of Chapter 31 indicates. The reader addresses the author directly.

> "An important question that, with which you concluded the last chapter."
> " 'Tis therefore I concluded, for surely to answer it requires a chapter by itself. And yet much will depend upon the life, character, and education, to say nothing of the sex of the person, who may be at this moment honouring this essay—"
> "Essay? surely, Sir, in begins to be a novel!—"
> "By no means! and I will maintain it before any bishop, professor, or critic in Christendom, that it still is that treatise of moral philosophy I intended when I set out. I am to relate facts, and if love be a subject of moral philosophy, how can I help it?"[3]

The greater part of Ward's book consists of conversations between the skeptical Tremaine and the intelligent and good-hearted rector and squire Dr. Evelyn. These conversations gradually clear Tremaine's mind of error. At first, Evelyn opposes the romance between Tremaine and his daughter, Georgina, but after a marathon discussion on providence concluding with a definitive statement on free will, Tremaine confesses himself won back to his traditional faith and soon after he and Georgina marry.

Ward's chapters on providence review a series of standard arguments, such as those we have seen expressed by other religious moralists in chapter 3. Interesting for our purpose of relating philosophical and theological assumptions to fiction is the resemblance between Ward's convictions about man's relationship to providence and his attitudes toward fiction. Life and art are shaped by moral designs. Men and fictional characters may examine moral questions and make moral choices, but their actions proceed under the confining rule of providence and author. God, like the novelist, may guide the "story line" of outward circumstance, but the final decisions of his characters are the results of their own free will exercised according to good reason. This is a rough sketch of a pattern that we will see elaborated later. It may strike us today as amazing that a novel like *Tremaine* was a popular favorite in its season, but that success demonstrates that many readers were prepared to accept and appreciate overt discussions of religious and philosophical issues in the fiction they read and approved. Readers and authors were entirely conscious of significant moral issues such as the free will debate and were perhaps as capable of drawing analogies between providence or necessity and narrative.

One remarkable novel of this period derives much of its liveliness from its ability to enact a standard Christian topos in its story and in its form. James Hogg's *The Private Memoirs and Confessions of a Justified Sinner* (1824) satirizes extreme predestinarian religious zeal. Lady Dalcastle, uncomfortably married to a very ordinary, life-loving laird is such a zealot. She exclaims to her tutelary minister, "How delightful to think that a justified person can do no wrong! Who would not envy the liberty wherewith we are made free?"[4] The laird gives readers a moral viewpoint on this faith when he denounces the Reverend Robert Wringhim for "splitting the doctrines of Calvin [and] setting up a system of justifying-grace against all breaches of all laws, moral or divine" (Hogg, 145).

The central narrative of Hogg's novel is the confession of young Robert Wringhim, the legal son of Laird and Lady Dalcastle, but probably the illegitimate product of the Reverend Wringhim's intimacy with the lady. He grows up under the protection of these two zealots and is bred to the faith. On the day his foster father welcomes him "into the community of the just upon earth," Robert encounters a strange young man who ultimately proves to be the devil (Hogg, 205). Robert thinks of him as a powerful foreign prince— which he is, though his domain is that of Darkness. The devil encourages Robert's belief that whatever he does is alright because he is of the elect and cannot suffer retribution. He interprets the sins to which he prompts Robert, including the murder of his older brother, as religious duties.

Robert is an intelligent young man with a poor character given to lying and malicious behavior. Hogg suggests that this combination suits the predestinarian creed well. Robert is happy with this faith because it excuses his conduct, though he acknowledges that "it made the economy of the Christian world appear to me as an absolute contradiction" (Hogg, 210). Extreme Calvinism is the real contradiction, as numerous passages in the novel reveal, from Robert's own comments to the reported story of the devil's use of Christian doctrine in attempting to corrupt the entire village of Auchtermuchty. And the contradiction turns on the pivot of freedom. Robert and his kind believe themselves free from retribution and thus *free* in another sense because they are predestined to redemption. But, in fact, this freedom is slavery to sin. In Robert's case, literally slavery to the devil, for he admits that he and Gil-Martin (as the devil calls himself) are disciple and master, and even inseparable, "incorporated together," and the devil agrees (Hogg, 247, 275). In short, Robert is a living example of the lesson so often presented by the religious moralists we examined in chapter 3. In imagining himself free, he is enslaved by sin. Only in submission to God—not to a humanly concocted creed—can real freedom be achieved.

Hogg's story is all the more interesting because it consciously exploits the sensitivity to a complex or multiple self so central to the nineteenth-century fascination with the will. Robert is so preoccupied with his self, is, indeed, so self*ish*, that he loses himself. The more he falls under Gil-Martin's influence, the less he knows of what he is doing, even concluding that he has "two souls, which take possession of my bodily frame by turns, the one being all unconscious of what the other performs" (Hogg, 253). This suggestion finds clearer and more complete expression in Hogg's fellow Scotsman's *The Strange Case of Dr. Jekyll and Mr. Hyde* (1886), which also shares structural features with the *Confessions*, for both are divided narratives, a relatively "objective" first-person narration standing against the contained first-person confession.

The division of narration into two distinct voices mirrors the other doublings in the novel—especially mirrorings of Robert in George, his opposite, and Gil-Martin, his familiar. But the two narratives have another relationship. The editor is intrigued by the "Confession," but does not depend upon it for his own narrative, which attempts an accurate historical account of documentable events. His story thus creates a form of historical necessity within which Robert's narrative occurs, in a sense predetermining what that narrative can convey. Robert's account is highly subjective and interprets events differently, but by the time we reach his disclosures of motivation, we already know the inevitable conclusion toward which all his supposedly "free" struggles are tending.

If the editor wonders what the "Confession" is, speculating that it may be an allegory or "religious PARABLE, showing the dreadful danger of self-righteousness," Robert himself wants to preserve his story in print for the benefit of those who come after (Hogg, 282, 272). He even speculates on what future readers may think of some of his statements and believes that when he is gone the sons of men will "ponder on the events of my life; wonder and tremble, and tremble and wonder how such things should be" (Hogg, 206). He shapes the reader's interpretation of his life history by stipulating the moment that transformed the "monotonous *farrago*" of his existence into "a relation of great and terrible actions, done in the might, and by the commission of heaven" (Hogg, 204). Robert believes that he controls the narrative of his life, but ironically the editor's frame provides another and opposite interpretation. Despite all assertions to the contrary, Robert has consulted only self-interest not the lessons of providence. Read it as he may, we see the story of his life differently.

Of course, Hogg wants his readers to get his joke and offers several clues to the reading of the whole text. The anonymous editor even voices his distrust of James Hogg, the chief means of his acquiring the printed pamphlet of the "Confession." But making the joke an open one changes nothing about the narrative game that Hogg has played. The delusions of freedom and the character of the inscribed stories we live are still vividly portrayed.

I have suggested that fiction at the turn of the century emphasized the liberating force of feeling as opposed to the ordering power of intellect. Gothic fiction played with concepts of human freedom in its own curious manner. Godwin, though faithful to reason, mistrusted any thinking that overlooked the power of human impulses. Ward, by contrast, put his faith in common sense and intuition—a uniting of mind and heart that was the acceptable mode in much Victorian fiction. Hogg mocked the extremes of emotional and intellectual religious zeal in favor of the golden rule. These three novelists made philosophical and theological issues prominent in their work. But other novelists early in the century were equally alert to the importance of will as a theme, though they were less alert to its implications for narrative. They were more interested in relating tales of domestic difficulties and dazzling adventures.

The titles of her novels summarize Susan Ferrier's interests: *Marriage* (1818), *The Inheritance* (1824), and *Destiny, or The Chief's Daughter* (1831). The central actions of her stories involve expectations and disappointments concerning love, marriage, and money. Characters are clearly contrasted as moral and immoral, generous and selfish, and so on. Although there are very few passages where issues such as providence and free will are discussed, the tensions of the narratives assume that characters are working out their individual fates within a larger moral design. In *Marriage*, Mary Douglas, a good-hearted, self-sacrificing young woman, refuses the attentions and proposals of men she cannot love and also of Charles Lennox out of pride, though she does love him. Eventually, the two young people acknowledge their love over the deathbed of Charles's mother. In this moment of utter humility and self-forgetfulness before death, these two good people capable of patience and restraint recognize their compatibility. Charles proves his character in an obvious way open to men—soldiership at Waterloo. Mary, like so many women, more passively endures. In the end, the lovers marry. By contrast, Mary's self-indulgent sister, Adelaide, marries for money and station instead of love but, accustomed to yielding to her own desires, soon runs off with a lover. Her disgrace and shame are the direct consequences of her selfish nature. Larger patterns of justice and charity are evident throughout *Marriage*. Ferrier made certain that her narrative imitated the "story" of providence, with the usual expectation that a well-regulated mind submits itself to divine will.

The plot of *The Inheritance* takes Gertrude St. Clair from a youthful fascination with romance to a calm acceptance of true affection and duty in marriage. She eventually marries Edward Lyndsay who has patiently encouraged her to give more time to charity, less to the things of this world. He is like Austen's Mr. Knightley just as Gertrude slightly resembles Emma Woodhouse. But unlike Austen, Ferrier regularly urges attention to providential design rather than to simple prudence. Captain Malcolm in *Destiny* expresses her view simply: "We have indeed little control over circumstances—these are regulated by a higher power; but as rational and reflecting beings, we are accountable for the exercise of our faculties."[5]

Dealing with thoroughly traditional materials of English fiction, Ferrier wove them into an obvious structure of moral values that is clear from the outset. God's providence is the network within which men and women make their choices. They are free to choose ill or well, but when they do, they know it. Finally, all are *accountable*.

Susan Ferrier's novels qualify as serious fiction. William Harrison Ainsworth's do not. Nor is the reasoning in his hastily produced romances clear and consistent. Nonetheless, underlying his melodramatic plots is a discernible belief about the nature of human freedom. This belief rarely surfaces as direct discussion but is implicit in the plot lines. Occasionally it finds in moments of crisis. In *Jack Sheppard* (1839–40), Sir Rowland Trenchard has tried unsuccessfully to dispose of his young nephew Thames Darrell. Now the notorious Jonathan Wild offers to undertake the same task. " 'No,' replied Sir Rowland, who appeared completely prostrated. 'I will struggle no longer with destiny. Too much blood has been shed already.' "[6] When Wild later urges Sir Rowland at least to hide the boy so that he will not be recognized and endanger the nobleman's claim to the Trenchard estate, Sir Rowland once more replies: "Heaven has decreed it otherwise. . . . I yield to fate." Wild presses him, telling him to yield to nothing. "Man's fate is in his own hands. You are your nephew's executioner, or he is yours. Cast off this weakness. The next hour makes or / mars you for ever" (Ainsworth, *Sheppard*, 111). Wild again urges Trenchard to murder Darrell, driving the distraught aristocrat to respond: "Do you think you can shackle my free will, villian?" Wild replies affirmatively, since he has power over the weaker man (Ainsworth, *Sheppard*, 194).

Sir Rowland refers to "free will," "fate," and "destiny," but these terms are very loosely employed in Ainsworth's fiction. In *Crichton* (1837), for example, there is much talk of fate, but it signifies no intellectual engagement with ideas of necessity and free will. Crichton, warned of Catherine de Medici's plan to poison him, says he will accept the fate assigned by heaven, but feels that his destiny is not yet fulfilled. At least, he explains to Marguerite de Valois, "I can have no foreknowledge, though your mother's starry lore would tell you otherwise—nor, it may be, free agency."[7] But it doesn't matter because his aim is fixed, his purpose firm. If Crichton rejects the powers of astrology, the plot inconsistently seems to verify them at times. The simple fact is that Ainsworth, working with historical events, was content to render already confirmed incidents as saleable spectacle. His stories concentrate on action and superficial description. They do not plumb character or ascend to metaphysical speculation.

Ainsworth's characters have fixed destinies. Sir Rowland is a good example. But these destinies arise from the characters' deeds and are not preordained. Destiny, understood as the culmination of one's life, is the reward or retribution for one's acts. Man is free to commit crimes, but these crimes invariably fix him in a network of circumstances the outcome of which is called his fate. Thus one potent character may influence the so-called destiny of another. Jonathan Wild helps to shape Jack Sheppard's fate and to influence Sir Rowland's. He is a secular destiny, a parody of divine governance. But if Wild is forceful enough to succeed in his plans for others, especially in regard to Jack Sheppard's career, an obvious destiny shadows his own existence. Wild's prefigured fate is to die on the gibbet, a plot detail reinforced by his vows to bring others to that end. Ainsworth's villains imitate the role of Milton's Satan. They may tamper with the lives of free beings, but they can never alter God's design. Always, their evil finds a place in the providential scheme. Ainsworth uses the Gothic device of the omen to enhance the inevitability of his villains' fates. Jack's hanging is accurately predicted by Galgebrok. Cruikshank's illustrations of young Sheppard symbolically establish his eventual fate.[8] Omens are true, but not always precise. Sir Rowland's horse falls in front of Newgate prison, an apparent sign that he will hang there for his offenses. Instead, he dies in the Well Hole at Wild's house.

If evil persons weave the web of their own fates through the iron law of the inevitable consequences of their deeds and are thus "pursued" by destiny, virtuous characters enjoy the benevolent direction of providence. Thames Darrell is spectacularly preserved from death in the Thames River and again later from drowning in the North Sea. He is protected by the Marquis de Chatillon, who, by coincidence, turns out to be his relation. Despite the many plots against him, Darrell is able to survive his ordeals at home and abroad and return to England, where he is eventually recognized as the true heir of the Trenchard estate. Thames has never forfeited the protection of providence, for he has always acted according to divine injunction. Jack Sheppard may initiate actions that alter the course of Darrell's misfortunes, but he cannot correct the pattern of his own destiny. His interference in Darrell's life may complicate, but not negate, the virtuous young man's destiny. Each of his acts is, however, another strand in his own noose. An early chapter depicting Jack's initiation into a life of crime is entitled "The First Step toward the Ladder," and suggests the inevitable pattern that will end with Sheppard ascending the ladder to the gibbet.

Ainsworth's adventure narrative gains energy from its simplified creed. The events of the plot move smoothly because they stand in immediate causal relation to one another not because they are credible. One sequence moves in an upward, salvational direction (despite temporary setbacks), the other in a downward, damnational direction (despite temporary successes). If cause and effect are untwined, the pattern is more obvious, revealing how, through the use of coincidence, the evil characters are made to participate in the ultimate salvation of their virtuous antagonists. But Ainsworth's narratives have radical inconsistencies in them and are ultimately unsatisfying as coherent works of art because the expressed philosophy in them is not inherent in their structures. The stories are patched together, the characters unexamined. Narrator and characters alike seem to make little distinction between providence, destiny, and fate. These are stories with little depth because they do not manifest any clear assumptions about human existence upon which they operate.

A common plot design of nineteenth-century literature involves the displacement of a central character from his or her just line of development and depends upon the coherent vision of justice that Ainsworth lacks. Often a usurper consciously or unconsciously drives the just person into hardship and suffering. Inevitably, the wickedness or weakness of the usurper undermines his position, the virtuous hero or heroine is reinstated, and the story line advances rapidly to a satisfying close. This is the basic plot line of *Jack Sheppard* as it is of *Oliver Twist* and many other novels of the time. Samuel Warren's *Ten Thousand A-Year* (1841) is a lengthy example. Christian endurance is the chief lesson of these novels. In Warren's story, despite poverty, suffering, various humiliations, and dangers along the way, Charles Aubrey never loses faith. "Still pressed, as indeed he was, his spirit had by no means lost its elasticity, supported as he was by a powerful, an unconquerable WILL—and also by a devout reliance upon the protection of Providence."[9] Throughout the novel, the reader is encouraged to believe that, just as the narrator guides him through the complexities of plot with occasional sermons, explanations, and evaluations, so a Divine Power guides the complex story of his life with occasional signs, which, if he has faith, he will read correctly. But not all references to providence are so secure. As far back as

Robinson Crusoe, Defoe played with the notion that each man discovers the providence he needs. In nineteenth-century novels, individual expectations of providential help are often unfounded. A marked instance occurs in Henry Cockton's *Valentine Vox* (1840) when Goodman confidentially asserts his trust that providence will aid him to escape from the lunatic asylum in which he is unjustly confined. Despite his trust, Goodman's escape attempt fails. Generally, however, the reader of a nineteenth-century novel could be confident that, even if individuals were disappointed in this way, a providential design guided the events of the narrative, reinforcing his confidence that author and deity were partners in the laying out and interpreting of the human story.[10]

The connection between fiction and providence was well established before the Victorian period, as Leopold Damrosch, Jr., has splendidly demonstrated in *God's Plot and Man's Stories* (1985). Damrosch shows how different beliefs manifested themselves in different narrative methods. Thus Defoe's Puritan outlook in *Robinson Crusoe* (1719) ignores elaboration of plot in favor of amplified detail, whereas Fielding's Anglicanism calls for greater attention to the pattern of events. In *Tom Jones* (1749), an "omniscient and affectionate narrator acts as the disposing deity of the fictional universe, instructing the reader, by means of a plot whose coherence is only gradually revealed, to understand the operations of a Providence that subsumes all of the apparent accidents of chance or Fortune." Fielding believes "not only that life is providentially ordered (most novelists for the next century and a half believed that) but also that the shape of a fictional work can directly imitate that order."[11] Victorian novelists were conscious of their roles as surrogate deities, and their novels demonstrated as much as Fielding's the effects of philosophical and religious beliefs upon narrative method.

CHAPTER ELEVEN

Mary Shelley

C HAPTER 10 compared novels where a consciousness of the free will question affected form with novels where incoherent attitudes about the will resulted in uninteresting narrative structures. This chapter discusses Mary Shelley's *Frankenstein*, a novel that takes will as one of its major themes. But whereas chapter 10 emphasized narrative structure, this chapter concentrates on characterization.

As the early chapters of part 1 show, a new consciousness of the self at the turn of the century led to revived philosophical discussions about the nature of human freedom. A work like Hogg's *Confessions* explored the religious ramifications of a predestinarian fascination with moral freedom arising from an absolute spiritual determinism. Mary Shelley's novel examines the problems arising from man's capacity to create the illusion of freedom in a determined world. Imagination, honored by most Romantic writers, here becomes a potentially dangerous power that, by aspiring to transcend the laws of nature, enslaves itself to the necessary consequences of the acts it engenders. The substance of the many philosophical and religious texts that we explored earlier in its forensic role is here dramatized and embodied in a cautionary fable.

~ ~ ~

Mary Shelley's *Frankenstein* (1818) represents a significant transition point between Romantic and Victorian thinking about the will. In many ways, the novel may be read as a treatise on the subject of free will and fate. The theme is stated early and repeated often; moreover, Shelley's intellectual background offers ample evidence that this issue concerned her deeply.

When Captain Walton, asserting his confidence that he will succeed in discovering the North Pole, exclaims, "What can stop the determined heart and resolved will of man?" his optimism, strongly resembling Victor Frankenstein's youthful assurance, must be measured against Frankenstein's final estimate of his own career: "Nothing can alter my destiny: listen to my history, and you will perceive how irrevocably it is determined."[1] Thus, in the first pages of Mary Shelley's novel, a belief in free will and the power of man to impose his will upon nature opposes a conviction that human life is determined by circumstance and therefore follows a necessary and irreversible pattern. Ironically, it is the man who has succeeded in demonstrating an entirely unique power who feels destined, whereas Walton, who has as yet achieved nothing, remains confident of man's limitless freedom. In a tale which seems to describe the triumph of human will, the true theme is self-enslavement; its ostensible subject is the pursuit of knowledge, but its real concern is human ignorance and folly. Characters with ambitious plans lack breadth of vision and become victims of unforeseen events. More painfully, those who act out their ambitions suffer the deepest agony of unfulfillment.

Frankenstein dramatizes the intellectual controversy so vigorously conducted throughout the nineteenth century in England that is surveyed in part 1 of this book. But while taking up this controversy as a theme, it also embodies that theme in the characters and structure of the novel. Each of the narrators in Mary Shelley's novel—Walton, Victor, and the Creature—is a self-enslaver and victim of impulse who rivets his chains through his own blindness. Mary Shelley may have meant to emphasize the importance of this theme of self-enslavement by mentioning Count de Volney's famous *Les Ruines; ou, Méditation sur les révolutions des empires* (1791) as a prominent part of the Creature's education. Volney's work took up the grand subject of mankind's struggle for improvement against the limitations of his own nature, a fashionable subject at the turn of the century greatly influencing Romantic writers, as we have seen in part 1. Self-love, wrote Volney, is the source of happiness and perfection when it is equivalent to self-respect, but, when disordered, it is the source of all sorrow as well. Volney concluded that the primordial basis of law was in the natural truth that all men are equal, free, and independent and that therefore liberty and equality are the foundations of happiness in society. While convinced that man was improving and could achieve a better world, he believed that man was inveterately his own enslaver because he could not control his impulses. Using religion as an example, Volney demonstrated how readily man relinquished authority to a force beyond himself, thereby insuring the servile condition his impulsiveness engendered. "But such is the human heart. A little success intoxicates man with confidence; a reverse overturns and confounds him. Always given up to the sensation of the moment, he seldom judges things from their nature, but from the impulse of his passion."[2] These words could easily be taken to describe Victor Frankenstein. But all three narrators of *Frankenstein* are self-involved, ambitious, and beset by illusions. The foundation of their ambitions and illusions is self-love. All three are egoists who, in varying degrees, ignore the truths of natural law. Volney argued that man's waywardness, the failure to accept a steady and patient improvement of human circumstances, brought him to grief. Freedom came with the recognition of equality. This steady but constant change is the immutable law that Elizabeth comprehends. Craving to exceed that law is the rudimentary sin which leads to sorrow. The aspiring will becomes its own jailer.

Ambitious self-love was a familiar characteristic of the Romantic hero and was challenged by sober critics, among them Mary Shelley's father. In *Thoughts on Man* (1831), William Godwin condemned the irrational selfishness of undisciplined humanity. "The original impulse of man is uncontrollableness. When the spirit of life first descends upon us, we desire and attempt to be as free as air. We are impatient of restraint. This is the period of the empire of will."[3] Godwin felt that man's native wildness arose from his restless sense of the incompatibility of mind and body. "The human mind," he wrote, "is a creature of celestial origin, shut up and confined in a wall of flesh. We feel a kind of proud impatience of the degradation to which we are condemned" (Godwin, *Thoughts*, 99). This proud impatience, he added, might lead to revery, castle building, and pursuits of hidden knowledge, including "necromancy, sorcery and magic" (Godwin, *Thoughts*, 104). It was the business of education to tame man's recklessness.

As we have seen in part 1, Godwin's views were those of the necessarian camp, to which he and Percy Shelley declared allegiance, but if influenced by their views, Mary Shelley approached the problem of adequately defining and applying the powers of the self in her own manner. The three narrators of *Frankenstein* are all impatient, self-willed, and eager for knowledge. As we meet them, they are progressively outlandish. Walton is the first and most nearly normal. His aims are humanly approachable, though eccentric. He admits to his sister that "there is a love for the marvellous, a belief in the marvellous, intertwined in all my projects" (Mary Shelley, 21–22), which he himself describes as "day dreams," admitting that they lack discipline. With little reasoned evidence, he assumes that the North Pole will be a region of "beauty and delight," not the "seat of frost and desolation," and imagines that its wonders will be as splendid "as the phenomena of the heavenly bodies undoubtedly are in those undiscovered solitudes" (Mary Shelley, 15–16). *Undoubtedly*, Walton says, revealing that his anticipations are projections of desire, not conclusions based on examination of facts. He has no way of determining the state of the heavenly bodies; no more can he predict a world of beauty at the North Pole.[4]

Walton's quest for the Pole is as arbitrary as some of his earlier ambitions. "I also became a poet," he says, "and for one year lived in a Paradise of my own creation." (Mary Shelley, 17).[5] Disillusioned at the end of that year, he abandoned his aim to find a place among the Homers and Shakespeares of the past. In truth, Walton has no genuine aim but is driven by a vague, impulsive will to excel, to make his mark in the world, to signify. While cataloguing the jumbled motives for undertaking his journey—the discovery of new knowledge, the satisfaction of curiosity, the glory of being the first to tread the hidden world, the desire to benefit mankind—he incidentally states what is perhaps the most significant reason when he says, "nothing contributes so much to tranquillise the mind as a steady purpose—a point on which the soul may fix its intellectual eye" (Mary Shelley, 16).

Walton is instinctively aware that his daydreams require regulation. His perception is correct; it is his aim that is outrageous. There is a dark but unperceived caveat in his declaration that his resolutions to discover the Pole "are as fixed as fate" (Mary Shelley, 21). By binding his will in this manner he creates his fate. Fate is fixed because men of inflexible intent make it so. But Walton is not as committed as he seems. He fondly remembers the domestic comforts of home and regrets the lack of any sympathetic mind to understand his yearning. And, just as Mephistopheles promptly attends Faust when that heartsick mage expresses his desire for release from the triviality of his world, so Walton's alter ego miraculously responds to his summons amidst the wastelands of the Northern Sea.[6] Unlike Mephistopheles, Walton's companion comes not to encourage him in his quest but to warn him against it, using his own history of "occurrences which are usually deemed marvellous," to provide Walton with an apt cautionary tale (Mary Shelley, 30). His has become that fixed fate that Walton only contemplates.

Victor Frankenstein is far more exceptional than Walton in his gifts and his ambitions. He is more forceful and more profound. Nonetheless, he is a victim of the same wilfulness and egotism that he wishes to correct in his naive companion. Walton has not deeply pondered his contest with Nature; Frankenstein has eagerly examined his. While his childhood companion, Elizabeth, was content with the appearances of things, he precociously delighted "in investigating their causes," desiring "to learn the hidden laws of nature" (Mary Shelley, 36). But his "bright visions of extensive usefulness," prompted by a sense of man's dominating will, were gradually transformed "into gloomy and narrow reflections upon self," until now Frankenstein regrets "the birth of that passion, which afterwards ruled my destiny" (Mary Shelley, 38). Frankenstein's "passion" was, of course, his desire to discover the secret of life, a project immeasurably greater than Walton's and on an entirely different scale. Walton's is geographical, Franken-stein's metaphysical. Walton seeks an answer in the world of matter; Frankenstein aims to penetrate beyond matter to its animating source. Both men, by creating specific goals to which they dedicate themselves, fix their own fates.

Frankenstein claims that he made the choices which set him in his course but at the same time implies that that course was unavoidable. This apparent contradiction concerning free will and fate is partly resolved by a passage in chapter ten that summarizes Frankenstein's dismay. Torn by remorse, he finds relief in contemplating the magnificent scenes of nature near the glac-ier of Chamonix. His pride chastened and his grief temporarily subdued, he reflects upon the unique character of man: "Alas! why does man boast of sensibilities superior to those apparent in the brute; it only renders them more necessary beings. If our impulses were confined to hunger, thirst, and desire, we might be nearly free; but now we are moved by every wind that blows, and a chance word or scene that that word may convey to us" (Mary Shelley, 97). At first Victor's conclusion seems paradoxical, making reason-ing man less free than unreflecting animals, but necessarian arguments that William Godwin put forth in his *Enquiry concerning Political Justice* (1793), which Mary had read in the fall of 1814 and again in April 1817 when she was revising her novel, make Victor's assessment more intelligible. We have already seen, in chapters 2 and 10, that Godwin assumed an absolute rigor in the law of cause and effect but distinguished between the operation of that law in physical nature and in the human mind.[7] His reasoning is in some ways peculiar, for while he argues that "the actions and dispositions of mankind are the offspring of circumstances and events, and not of any orig-inal determination that they bring into the world," he also insists that "the great stream of voluntary actions essentially depends, not upon the direct and immediate impulses of sense, but upon the decisions of understand-ing."[8] All of nature is governed by a law of necessity, but this law has more than one manifestation, since actions can be both voluntary and involun-tary. Unreflective life is driven by impulse alone; its actions are involuntary. Only man is capable of voluntary actions because these actions depend upon choice, a determination of the intellect. And yet, being the results of preceding acts, the voluntary actions prompted by thought are themselves necessary. Hence, whereas material nature is determined by material causes only, man, who is both mind and body, is determined by mental as well as physical causes. He is therefore less free because subject to a greater number of determining forces. An animal's necessity follows from its physical im-pulses, but a man can create a destiny from his own mind. The true dilemma of Mary Shelley's novel resides in the complex irony that the mind which creates the illusion of freedom is at the same time the source of man's most acute agony through its ability to perceive a bondage that it has itself begotten.

But the cure for that agony also resides in the human imagination. Victor Frankenstein's vision of human frustration is appropriately staged at Chamonix, for it was in this same location that Percy Shelley offered a speculation that might have ameliorated Frankenstein's suffering.[10] In "Mont Blanc," Shelley pictured the great power of human imagination. "The everlasting universe of things / Flows through the mind," much as the forces of nature flow through the Ravine of Arve (Percy Shelley, *Poetry and Prose*, 89). He sees in the mountain rising above the turmoil where he stands a symbol of power and serenity "which teaches awful doubt, or faith so mild, / So solemn, so serene, that man may be, / But for such faith, with nature reconciled" (Percy Shelley, *Poetry and Prose*, 91). This power dwells apart "in its tranquillity, / Remote, serene, and inaccessible" (Percy Shelley, *Poetry and Prose*, 92). Not only can the human mind imitate this grandeur but the grandeur itself does not exist without the power of imagination to figure it.

> The secret Strength of things
> Which governs thought, and to the infinite dome
> Of heaven is as a law, inhabits thee!
> And what were thou, and earth, and stars, and sea,
> If to the human mind's imaginings
> Silence and solitude were vacancy?
> (Percy Shelley, *Poetry and Prose*, 93)[11]

Victor Frankenstein's great error is that, though he can feel the force of life ranging through the world below, he never lifts his eyes aloft to learn the lesson waiting there for men. Bitterly aware of his own contributions to his dreadful destiny, he never fully comprehends his failings. Near the end of his life, he says to Walton: "From my infancy I was imbued with high hopes and a lofty ambition. . . . Despondency rarely visited my heart; a high destiny seemed to bear me on, until I fell, never, never again to rise" (Mary Shelley, 211). There was no more reason for him to have believed in that high destiny than later to believe in an evil one, just as, at a more immediate level, there is no more reason for Walton to believe in an edenic North Pole than to assume that the stars are filled with wonders. Both men, out of their unrestrained imaginations, have concocted dangerous illusions. Both have been driven by an intellectual impulse, but neither has considered the simple fact that mental as well as physical actions have their inevitable consequences. They have not realized that their imaginings beget acts and that their acts beget results which they name fate. This is the immutable law.

Frankenstein desired to search out the "secrets of heaven and earth" in "the outward substance of things, or the inner spirit of nature and the mysterious soul of man" (Mary Shelley, 37).[12] While he succeeded in understanding the one, he never fathomed the other. It is the soul of man that he cannot comprehend, as his account of his own life shows. Frankenstein is never certain where choice and chance separate. As his story continues, he more frequently and overtly pictures external influences guiding his destiny.[13] At one point, he suggests that his ideas might "never have received the fatal impulse that led to my ruin," if his father had explained that Cornelius Agrippa's occult writings, by which young Victor was fascinated, were obsolete (Mary Shelley, 29). Missing the important lesson that he has feverishly pursued secrets that men have long since found false, he responds with anger, not humility. He is not chastened to recognize the limits upon men's minds and the dangers of the unregulated imagination.

Victor seems almost perverse in resisting invitations to a kinder fate. Witnessing a tree shattered by a thunderbolt, itself almost a providential sign, Victor experiences a temporary revulsion from occult interests, turning instead to mathematics, which gives him a sense of "tranquillity and gladness of soul" that should indicate the correctness of this new choice. Frankenstein describes this event as the last effort by the "spirit of preservation" to avert the impending evil. But, he adds, "Destiny was too potent, and her immutable laws had decreed my utter and terrible destruction" (Mary Shelley, 42). Victor has now come to locate the forces driving him entirely outside himself in an imagined spirit of preservation and a destiny. He declares that when he went to Ingoldstadt to continue his studies, "Chance—or rather the evil influence, the Angel of Destruction," held sway over his life and led him to M. Krempe (Mary Shelley, 45). But Professor Krempe merely corrected Victor's impressions about the outdated writers in whom he had been so interested. Next Frankenstein claims that it was Professor Waldman who spoke "the words of fate" inimical to him, and which "decided my future destiny" (Mary Shelley, 48–49). In fact, Victor has no clear perception of the causes of his fate, which are mainly within himself, not in external things. He himself says that his "temper was sometimes violent, and my passions vehement" and given to caprice (Mary Shelley, 37). He is as changeable as Walton till he strikes on his dominating scheme.

It is ironic that Frankenstein, often taken as the archetypal scientist, should destroy himself by ignoring the principle of cause and effect, which is the very basis of scientific method. Richard Hengist Horne recognized this fact in 1844: "The Monster created by Frankenstein is also an illustration of the embodied consequences of our action. As he, when formed and endowed with life, became to his imaginary creator an everlasting, ever-present curse, so may one single action, nay a word, or it may be a thought, thrown upon the tide of time, become to its originator a curse, never to be recovered, never to be shaken off."[14] By failing to recognize the elementary reality of consequences, Frankenstein blinds himself to the inevitable pattern of cause and effect within himself and to relations in the external world as well.

He converts necessity into malign fate. Looking back, he can instruct Walton that a "human being in perfection ought always to preserve a calm and peaceful mind, and never to allow passion or a transitory desire to disturb his tranquillity" (Mary Shelley, 55–56). But, though he can give this advice, he remains incapable of abiding by it himself. Though he can recognize the law of being, he does not submit to it.

In *An Enquiry concerning Political Justice* (1793) and in *Thoughts on Man* (1831), Godwin argued that man's true freedom lies in his ability to achieve a condition of equality and equability among his kind. His daughter seems to have agreed with this view, and her novel demonstrates the folly of those who do not.[15] Frankenstein had every opportunity to succeed in this way. By his own testimony, he enjoyed a perfect childhood and was surrounded by models of benevolence in his generous and thoughtful parents. It was through no rejection of or by his family that he turned to arcane researches but solely through the impulse of his imagination. Provided with the intelligence, abilities, and resources to contribute to the welfare of his kind, Frankenstein is impelled instead to go beyond the normal channels of improvement which attract his sensible counterpart, Clerval. It is with this break from the normative human community that Frankenstein begins to fashion his destiny, for the act of separation is itself alien to the natural laws that govern man.[16]

Frankenstein violates the principles of useful behavior set down by Volney and Godwin, for though he declares that his ambitions will benefit mankind, it is clear that what he craves is selfish gratification. In an early experiment, he sets out to discover the philosopher's stone (capable of transmuting lead to gold) and the elixir of life but quickly abandons the first in favor of the second. "Wealth," he explains, "was an inferior object; but what glory would attend the discovery, if I could banish disease from the human frame, and render man invulnerable to any but a violent death!" (Mary Shelley, 40).[17] Lust for fame drives Victor Frankenstein just as it drives the inferior Walton and is the source of Victor's subsequent desire to control the forces of life and death. "A new species would bless me as its creator and source; many happy and excellent natures would owe their being to me. No father could claim the gratitude of his child so completely as I should deserve theirs" (Mary Shelley, 54). In fact, Victor's relationship with his gruesome offspring is a perversion of parenthood.

Mary Shelley's novel offers several models to encourage the renunciation of extraordinary ambition in favor of communality. Clerval, Victor's level-headed friend, is one spokesman, but it is Elizabeth, the novel's central representative of placidity, who provides Victor with an image that could save him. In a letter urging Victor to return home, Elizabeth recounts the promising history of Justine Moritz—an ominous note, since Justine's fate will soon demonstrate the injustice and sorrow that are a part of man's condition.

Elizabeth's letter also contains a significant testament to the proper order of society. "The blue lake, and snow clad mountains, they never change;—and I think our placid home, and our contented hearts are regulated by the same immutable laws" (Mary Shelley, 64). In "Mont Blanc" the snow-clad mountain symbolized the power of intellectual and emotional serenity above the ruck of the world. On a more modest level, similar images from nature provide Elizabeth with models for regulation extending from the individual and family to society at large. "The republican institutions of our country have produced simpler and happier manners than those which prevail in the great monarchies that surround it," Elizabeth writes, adding that the elimination of severe class distinctions has refined the manners and morals of the common people (Mary Shelley, 65).[18] She implies that the Swiss suffer no great pains and injustices because they have governed their ambitions and aspirations and determined to live in reasoned restraint with one another.

The day of Frankenstein's marriage, which he says "was to fulfill my wishes and my destiny," provides another emblem of the proper course for men and nations (Mary Shelley, 192). Again it is presented in terms of Switzerland's natural setting and its placid, egalitarian principles. Looking across Lake Geneva, the newlyweds "saw the mighty Jura opposing its dark side to the ambition that would quit its native country, and an almost insurmountable barrier to the invader who should wish to enslave it" (Mary Shelley, 193). The caution to restrain undue ambition is clearly written in nature. But very shortly Elizabeth will be dead and Victor's "enslavement" complete, the outcome of his overweening ambition and his inability to read the signs of nature and of man correctly. Victor has looked *into* nature but not *at* it. When obsessed by his experiment, Victor's "eyes were insensible to the charms of nature," and he became indifferent to his closest friends and relatives (Mary Shelley, 55). All the horror that followed stemmed from that ignorance of natural law. Frankenstein's mighty act of will, because it opposes him to the natural course of things, inevitably leads to frustration and enslavement. In a more destructive version of Walton's pattern, he flees from domestic communality to the icy wastelands of human emptiness.

Having set out to be master of nature, Frankenstein becomes the vassal of his ambition embodied in the Creature who is the product of his successful experiment. Through his intellect, Frankenstein sought to subdue nature, but now his mind is fettered by the material consequences of his own imaginative effort.[19] The Creature is the necessary effect of that mental act. It is literally the fate that Victor has made for himself. The high destiny he once imagined for himself, the benevolent and positive act of creating life, has turned into its opposite. "All my speculations and hopes," he laments, "are as nothing; and, like the archangel who aspired to omnipotence, I am chained in an eternal hell" (Mary Shelley, 211).[20] Whereas he once sought to create life, he now is determined to destroy it. Whereas the distant goal that led him on contained the promise of improvement, affection, and fulfillment, it now promises only annihilation. Frankenstein's single purpose becomes the need to cancel out his lone achievement: "I must pursue and destroy the being to whom I gave existence; then my lot on earth will be fulfilled, and I may die" (Mary Shelley, 212). Frankenstein's career is a parody of the optimistic picture so common in Mary Shelley's day and characterized in part 1, that a complex and free human self could, through the power of the imagination, so govern the course of nature that a pattern of progress would lead to the eventual perfection of mankind. This fine dream assumed free will or at least "freedom" and an uncorrupted imagination.

Like Frankenstein, Walton and the Creature have models of tranquillity. Walton respects his sister Margaret's domesticity, and the Creature cannot forget the idyllic contentment of the DeLaceys, which he was instrumental in destroying. But none of these three adventurers can rest in tranquillity. Walton rejects a life of comfort and luxury for a material quest. Frankenstein, turning from his best influences, seeks a metaphysical adventure. The Creature, eager to rest in calm and peace with the DeLaceys, ends in a pursuit of his own origins. It is longing that makes him approach the DeLaceys, thereby ending his secret happiness among them, and longing that impels him to seek out his creator. Different as their individual circumstances may be, each of these figures turns most decidedly from tranquillity toward the turmoil of a quest and in doing so calls in question the nature of the human will.

Frankenstein ends as the slave of his creation, impelled toward utter negation, but the Creature is no more free than his doomed creator. Walton was an example of an ordinary man possessed by a humanly extreme objective; Frankenstein exemplified a superhuman craving for transcendental knowledge and power; but the Creature is an almost allegorical abstraction. He may be seen as a pure experiment to test Godwin's theory that men are fashioned by circumstance.[21] The Creature begins as neither monster nor man and he remains appropriately unnamed. He is brute creation forced to an ontological pursuit. He is as much grander and more vicious than Frankenstein as Frankenstein was more brilliant and unwise than Walton. More obviously than Walton or Frankenstein, the Creature has been open equally to free choice and to determining circumstance. After an initial apprenticeship of the senses, the Creature enjoys a crude type of education by observing the DeLaceys. While the Creature is free to elect the conditions of his education, he passively accepts the information available. Walton and Frankenstein, more subject to the advice and guidance of others, willfully choose their own ways but encounter their determining ideas in an equally haphazard fashion. "My education was neglected," Walton declares, explaining that he came upon histories of voyages that enchanted him by accident in his uncle's library (Mary Shelley, 16). Frankenstein "chanced to find a volume of the works of Cornelius Agrippa" at an inn where his family was detained by bad weather. His father "was not scientific" and left his son to educate himself in the studies that interested him most (Mary Shelley, 39–40).

The Creature actually receives the most organized education of the three. Like Frankenstein and Walton, he develops "dreams of virtue, of fame, and of enjoyment" (Mary Shelley, 221). When he attempts to take control of his life, however, he discovers the elementary human fact that individual men do not control their destinies. The Creature can never join the human community because of what he *is*. What Walton and Frankenstein have consciously rejected, he could never have had. He is born outcast, no matter how much he yearns for the sympathy of fellow beings. Denied this sympathy, he turns his considerable powers to destruction, a living lesson correcting the fundamental error of his creator and demonstrating what existence is outside the human community. Walton clings by a thread of correspondence to his beloved sister. Frankenstein has his family, Clerval, and Elizabeth. The Creature makes the final point of absolute isolation. He is identified with mountain and arctic waste and sterility because he represents the power and distance associated with these symbols, but he is the reverse of what Mont Blanc should be. He is Mont Blanc conceived by a madman.

But at what point has the Creature determined his own fate? In a review (published posthumously in 1832) of his wife's novel, Shelley pictured the Creature's crimes as "the children, as it were, of Necessity and Human Nature" and described the Creature himself as "an abortion and an anomaly," with a mind early framed for affection and moral sensibility, and a character capable of benefiting society. Shelley concluded that the Creature's "original goodness was gradually turned into inextinguishable misanthropy and revenge."[22] Beginning in what appears to be utter freedom, the Creature soon demonstrates how like iron those frequently mentioned immutable laws of nature are. Like Frankenstein, he recognizes moral rule, but he does not act by it. Like Frankenstein, he is forced to admit that despite his superb intelligence, he "was the slave, not the master, of an impulse, which [he] detested, yet could not disobey" (Mary Shelley, 220). And like Frankenstein, he compares himself to Milton's fallen creatures (Mary Shelley, 221, 129).

The misfortunes of Lucifer and Adam, which Mary Shelley made a significant part of her story, are aptly analogous to the fates of Frankenstein and his Creature, for they are the results of unwise ambition.[23] Unsatisfied with God's order, Lucifer aspired beyond his station and was cast into Hell, being doomed thereafter to work only through negation, knowing that his destructive acts would always serve the ends of Providence. Like Lucifer, Adam fell by presuming to a power forbidden him by God. Raphael specifically tells Adam that God has left him the power of perseverance in good, "ordained thy will / By nature free, not over-ruled by fate / Inextricable, or strict necessity."[24] Through his free will, Adam opposes his will to God's rule. In doing so, he begets his fate. Once made, Adam's choice engenders a necessity unalterable except by divine intervention. In *Frankenstein*, there is no divine intervention. Because Frankenstein seeks knowledge beyond the range of his tranquil and domestic Eden, he destroys that Eden and himself. The Creature, a victim of disrupted order, begins his career after the Fall. In other respects, his history resembles his creator's and is a comment upon it.

The pathos of these similar careers lies in the fact that Victor and his Creature believe that their destinies should have been other than they are. "I was formed for peaceful happiness," Frankenstein says at the same time that he declares, "I am a blasted tree; the bolt has entered my soul."[25] The foreshadowed doom has come to pass and a high destiny has been replaced by grief. The Creature also laments: "My heart was fashioned to be susceptible of love and sympathy; and, when wrenched by misery to vice and hatred, it did not endure the violence of the change, without torture such as you cannot even imagine" (Mary Shelley, 219–20). Both believe that there were other careers that they could have followed, thus assuming that their free wills could have transformed their lives. At the same time, both believe that their fates are determined conclusively.

These incompatible views are not unresolvable. Several characters in *Frankenstein* demonstrate an ability to choose courses that are beneficial to others. Elizabeth is one. Clerval is another. And the master of Walton's ship, who sacrifices his personal desires and wealth to the happiness of others, is one more. Man can exercise choice freely within the limits of natural and social law, for then his actions accord with the regular and orderly process of things and are based upon a clear perception of the relationships of cause and effect. Man abandons freedom when he exerts his will against the law of nature, when he sets his own desire above the welfare of mankind and therefore acts irresponsibly. Self-love, not resignation, is then his driving force.[26]

For Mary Shelley, extreme self-assertion leads to inevitable dismay, since man's condition does not permit the operation of will against the natural order. Her attitude is made clear in a later novel, *The Last Man* (1826). She describes the character Raymond, based upon Byron, in terms equally applicable to Victor Frankenstein. "Thus, while Raymond had been wrapt in visions of power and fame, while he looked forward to entire dominion over the elements and the mind of man, the territory of his own heart escaped his notice; and from that un-thought of source arose the mighty torrent that overwhelmed his will, and carried to the oblivious sea, fame, hope, and happiness."[27] Like Frankenstein, Raymond feels hounded by an inescapable fate or destiny once he realizes that his fortunes have turned. What he does not realize is that the source of his destiny is in his own mind, the one province that he has not mastered.

Later in this novel, the narrator, Verney, fleeing with a small band of survivors from the ravages of a plague, reflects upon the sad contrast between mankind's former aspirations and its present fate. Verney is overwhelmed by the realization of human fragility, then acknowledges that human destiny has never really been in doubt.

> Sudden an internal voice, articulate and clear, seemed to say:— Thus from eternity, it was decreed: the steeds that bear Time onwards had this hour and this fulfilment enchained to them, since the void brought forth its burthen. Would you read backwards the unchangeable laws of Necessity?
>
> Mother of the world! Servant of the Omnipotent! eternal, changeless Necessity! who with busy fingers sittest ever weaving the indissoluble chain of events!—I will not murmur at thy acts. If my human mind cannot acknowledge that all that is, is right; yet since what is, must be, I will sit amidst the ruins and smile. Truly we were not born to enjoy, but to submit, and to hope. (Mary Shelley, *Man*, 290–91)

Although man is bound by necessity, he is not therefore helpless; he has only to put himself at one with the great Power in nature whose "immutable laws" are beneficial when properly perceived. To do this, he must free himself from the self-imposed enslavements of what Shelley in "Mont Blanc" called "large codes of fraud and woe."[28]

In his note to *Queen Mab*, which Mary Shelley had read as early as 1814, Shelley argued the doctrine of necessity, asserting that "every human being is irresistibly impelled to act precisely as he does act: in the eternity which preceded his birth a chain of causes was generated which, operating under the name of motives, makes it impossible that any thought of his mind, or any action of his life, should be other than it is."[29] Free will he called a delusion, a position similar to Godwin's. Mary Shelley, the lover of one and daughter of the other, was probably influenced by them. Even so, when commenting on *Queen Mab* years later, she was reluctant to endorse Shelley's notes, which she reprinted "not because they are models of reasoning or lessons of truth, but because Shelley wrote them" (Percy Shelley, *Poetical Works*, 338). Moreover, as part 2 of this book demonstrates, there were sufficient presentations of this lively and prominent subject for Mary Shelley to form her own conclusions about free will and necessity.

Shelley, like Godwin, concluded that the doctrine of necessity would spare men the follies of religion, its schemes of retribution, and the wasteful and destructive passions of hatred and contempt religion engendered. They hoped that a thorough-going humanism would follow the recognition that "there is neither good nor evil in the universe, otherwise than as the events to which we apply these epithets have relation to our own peculiar mode of being" (Percy Shelley, *Poetical Works*, 309). But *Frankenstein* is not a tale of hope, nor does it end with suggestions of improvement in man's state. Percy Shelley and Godwin urged that man could still shape his course by choices that were consistent with natural laws working toward equality and hence good, but Mary Shelley emphasized man's failure to recognize the nature of the laws to which all men must ultimately conform. For her, no dominion over the elements and over men could succeed if the heart of man remained unexamined and undisciplined. She showed that man's highest aspirations, viewed in the long perspective of time, were folly. One doom awaits them all. And she displayed the agony of minds capable of envisioning the highest ends but cast down to the greatest misery, all the more acute because these sufferers were aware that the very powers of intellect that rendered their visions possible made their slavery lucidly evident to them. *Frankenstein* is a picture of the human intellect tortured by the Nessus shirt of its own highest power, the imagination.

Since Mary Shelley referred directly to Prometheus in the title of her novel, it is important to consider the significance of that mythological figure. Heroically against the forces of the gods, he brought fire and life to mankind. But mankind might have responded to this gift in the words of Milton's Adam, which Mary quoted immediately following the title of her novel:

> Did I request thee, Maker, from my clay
> To mould Me man? Did I solicit thee
> From darkness to promote me?
> (Milton, 10, lines 743–45)

In his notes to *Queen Mab*, Shelley had pictured Prometheus as the destroyer of man's healthy innocence by his doubtful gift that brought disease and suffering, not joy. "All vice rose from the ruin of healthful innocence. Tyranny, superstition, commerce, and inequality were then first known, when reason vainly attempted to guide the wanderings of exacerbated passion" (Percey Shelley, *Poetical Works*, 327).

In *Frankenstein*, the gift of life is a dubious gift. Certainly it brings only pain and sorrow to Frankenstein's Creature, who must long for that which he can never have and who is evil against his own will. He reflects the case of man in general, who, as Godwin pointed out, is characterized by a restless craving for something beyond his mortal condition. This craving, often taking the form of a pursuit of occult knowledge, can lead only to disaster. In *An Enquiry concerning Political Justice*, Godwin described free will as an illusion; later, in *Thoughts on Man*, he admitted that this illusion might nonetheless be useful in giving rise to moral energies and enthusiasms and hence creating for man a mood of hope and conceptions of nobility and greatness. *Frankenstein* is a history of the loss of that illusion.

. Frankenstein, Walton, and the Creature all assert the superiority of man, but Percy Shelley had offered a sobering view of that superiority in his notes to *Queen Mab*.

> The supereminence of man is like Satan's, a supereminence of pain; and the majority of his species, doomed to penury, disease, and crime, have reason to curse the untoward event that, by enabling him to communicate his sensations, raised him above the level of his fellow-animals. But the steps that have been taken are irrevocable. The whole of human science is comprised in one question:—How can the advantages of intellect and civilization be reconciled with the liberty and pure pleasures of natural life? How can we take the benefits and reject the evils of the system, which is now interwoven with all the fibres of our being? (Percy Shelley, *Poetical Works*, 328)

Shelley recommended vegetarianism as a first step in the right direction, but Mary Shelley had no such remedies. Despite the benevolence of the best man and the benevolent wishes of the most energetic, the world is not a province of joy. In creating life out of an uncontrolled egoistic impulse, a gesture of rebellion against natural law, Frankenstein replicates the conditions brought about by the original Prometheus. He leaves his Creature alone in a frustrating world where his preeminence can lead only to annihilation, and he destroys the healthful innocence represented by Elizabeth, William, and Justine. To the very end, Frankenstein, while seeing his error, cannot act differently. "Farewell, Walton! Seek happiness in tranquillity, and avoid ambition," he cries, and then immediately relapses into his old illusion, speculating that "another may succeed" where he has failed (Mary Shelley, 217–18).

Mary Shelley suggests that like Justine, who accepts her unjust fate, and like Elizabeth, who acknowledges nature as a model for behavior, and like Clerval, whose reasonable aspirations coincide with the expanding activities of society, all men would be happiest if they conformed their wills to the laws of nature. Although she does not directly state a doctrine of necessity, she depicts the failure of schemes based upon the dangerous illusion that men have the freedom to govern their own destinies. And yet there is a contradiction in this moving and troubling story which makes it more moving and troubling still, for while the exercise of man's will is defeated by the forces of circumstance, it is nonetheless true that man has proved capable of challenging those laws that bind unthinking nature. Perhaps this novel was Mary's answer to "Mont Blanc." There Shelley pictured a serene and tranquil strength for the imagination to emulate. Mary Shelley showed the results of diseased, fevered imagination. In her story that very power to conceive an action that subdues or alters natural law is also the source of man's greatest agony. Frankenstein's tragedy is a magnified version of the dilemma facing any man but perhaps chiefly the poet. The imagination that has made him singular draws its power from his emotions which are expressed in the egoistic self-assertion of his will that sets him at odds with the equalizing laws of nature. He has the genius to imagine a fate other than the one he lives, but though he may seem to alter the course of events, he cannot control that fate. He can forever picture a destiny which he knows he cannot achieve, and as the consequences of his acts move further and further from his ideal, that destiny becomes a horrid, mocking phantom that haunts him, spoiling all happiness, peace, and love.

CHAPTER TWELVE

Edward George Bulwer-Lytton

B ULWER was an extremely successful and prominent novelist of the nineteenth century. Though he was often mocked for his excesses (Thackeray did his share), he was also admired by, and influential with, fine writers, Dickens among them. We have seen in the last couple of chapters various degrees of responsiveness to the issue of free will in fiction of the early nineteenth century in England. Clearly, writers like Godwin and Mary Shelley took it as a central theme and examined its implications for narrative and characterization. In Bulwer, we have a novelist who not only made freedom and necessity themes in his novels but who also elaborated his theories about their relationship to the rhetoric of narrative.

Like Mary Shelley, Bulwer warned against the abuses of the selfish will, but he emphasized, beyond Shelley's resignation, an active effort of love and a conviction of divine guidance. In his novels, we can see a transformation of Romantic fervor into Victorian earnestness. The self, for him, is correctly identified with soul. He is especially instructive for his conscious idealizing and allegorizing and his willingness to defend his literary methods. I have chosen examples of his romances, his historical fiction, and his realistic novels, but Bulwer attempted other forms with equal success among his reading public. His career thus provides a forecast of several types of fiction that we shall encounter in later chapters. He was in advance of most of his contemporaries in translating some of the characteristically Victorian features of the free will versus necessity debate into fictional narrative because he was entirely conscious of the many analogies that existed between the roles of author and providence and expressed himself directly concerning them.

~ ~ ~

Edward George Bulwer-Lytton was one of the most aggressively philosophical novelists among those who achieved fame during the nineteenth century. He read widely in historical, philosophical, metaphysical, and occult literature. His values remained stable throughout his life and his views on history and society changed only slightly. Bulwer poured his extensive learning into his imaginative writing as one might pour vat wine into bottles, sometimes stirring its sediment and clouding its substance. His beliefs clearly and confessedly guided his manner of constructing his fictions and poems. I shall be concerned here with his ideas about free will, immortality, the temporary enslavement of the soul in the body, and the importance of action in pursuit of the ideal. In *Zanoni* (1842), a highly symbolic novel, the hero asserts an opinion for a young aspirant to the life of the ideal that could be Bulwer's own. "Young man," Zanoni explains, "Destiny is less inexorable than it appears. The resources of the great Ruler of the Universe are not so scanty and so stern as to deny to men the divine privilege of Free Will; all of us can carve out our own way, and God can make our very contradictions harmonise with His solemn ends."[1] We must keep this assertion in mind, because, like many novelists at the time, Bulwer frequently used words like "fate" and "destiny" in a less than rigorous manner.

As a Christian apologist, Bulwer had to reconcile man's free will with the concept of divine providence. Many of his narratives take up this issue directly. *Eugene Aram* (1832) is an example. Its titular protagonist is one of Bulwer's most destiny-ridden characters. Guilty of participating in a murder when a young man, he has remained a solitary scholar abjuring fame until he meets Madeline Lester, when the vicious incident of his past returns to haunt him as he yearns for human society and Madeline's love. Early in the novel, Aram asserts a determinist opinion. Contemplating the appointed order of the heavenly bodies, he asks, are men too not "the poorest puppets of an all-pervading and resistless destiny? Shall we see throughout creation each marvel fulfilling its pre-ordained fate—no wandering from its orbit, no variation in its seasons—and yet imagine that the Arch-ordainer will hold back the tides He has sent from their unseen source, at our miserable bidding? Shall we think that our prayers can avert a doom woven with the skeins of events? To change a particle of our fate, might change the destiny of millions." Aram concludes that "the eternal and all-seeing Ruler of the Universe, Destiny or God, had here fixed the moment of our birth and the limits of our career. What, then, is crime? Fate! What life? Submission!"[2] Like Victor Frankenstein, Aram is an example of the rebellious will discussed in chapter

2 that contends against circumstance in order to assert its own preeminence. Like Frankenstein, when Aram sees that self frustrated, he capitulates entirely and blames the offenses of self-will on fate.

Aram restates his view of fate several times in the novel, asking "Who is answerable for his nature? Who can say, 'I controlled all the circumstances which made me what I am?' " (Bulwer-Lytton, *Novels* 1:49) He declares that man cannot alter God's scheme. "What is writ is writ" (Bulwer-Lytton, *Novels* 1:196, 364). Bulwer does not endorse this view, though he acknowledges the importance of circumstances in shaping character; had early circumstances been different, Aram's nature might have "fitted him for worldly superiority and command" (Bulwer-Lytton, *Novels* 1:45). But in his preface to the 1840 edition of the novel, Bulwer lists the "influence of circumstance upon deeds," as only one element in Aram's fate. Others are the entanglements of human reasoning, the perversion of man's finest gifts through "self-paltering with the Fiend," and the secret way that conscience frustrates the ends for which crime is committed (Bulwer-Lytton, *Novels* 1:vii).

Bulwer's first novel, *Falkland* (1827), explored a similar type. Falkland too withdraws from the world, though out of disgust and sorrow, not guilt. Like Aram, he feels that a man is free and secure only when he is independent of other men. In the first letter of this epistolary novel, Falkland explains to his friend Frederick Monckton that he has chosen to live in solitude. "I rather gather around myself, link after link, the chains that connected me with the world . . . and I make, like the Chinese, my map of the universe consist of a circle in a square,—the circle is my own empire of thought *and self*; and it is to the scanty corners which it leaves without, that I banish whatever belongs to the remainder of mankind."[3] Like Aram, Falkland finally admits that withdrawal is not possible. Just before his death, Falkland imagines himself about to become either a link in a new concatenation of heavenly beings "redeemed, regenerate, immortal, or—*dust!*" (Bulwer-Lytton, *Falkland*, 292). Similar images of enchainment are common throughout the literature of the period.

Both Falkland and Aram are wrong in attempting to withdraw into a world of selfish contemplation, because such a withdrawal is a false use of their powers and unnatural.[4] Zanoni provides an extreme example. His withdrawal from ordinary humanity and renunciation of ordinary human affections gives him supernatural powers that he may employ in nature or in society. This isolation must be corrected by involvement. Love for Viola Pisani deprives Zanoni of some of his marvellous powers; however, the narrator explains in his Introduction that Zanoni's career and the novel's plot describe a Platonic return to the soul's first divinity and happiness, an ascent by various stages to "the enthusiasm of Love" (Bulwer-Lytton, *Novels* 22:xvii).

Falkland and Aram are guilty of committing their strength of mind and will to an imperialism of the spirit. Falkland likens his subjective world to an empire; Aram seeks to dominate the world of knowledge. But without the tempering power of love, these intellectual aims are invalid. In *Zanoni,* it is Mejnour, the symbol of intensely rational examination of nature, hence science, who entertains imperial designs. His hope is

> to form a mighty and numerous race with a force and power suffi-
> cient to permit them to acknowledge to mankind their majestic
> conquests and dominion—to become the true lords of this
> planet—invaders, perchance of others,—masters of the inimical
> and malignant tribes by which at this moment we are sur-
> rounded,—a race that may proceed, in their deathless destinies,
> from stage to stage of celestial glory, and rank at last amongst the
> nearest ministrants and agents gathered round the Throne of
> Thrones What [*sic*] matter a thousand victims for one convert to
> our band? (Bulwer-Lytton, *Novels* 22:181)

This pattern of progress is not unlike Bulwer's own scheme for individual or racial improvement, but in Mejnour it lacks the important ingredient of self-less idealism. Restless conquest, restless activity, even of the mind, is not the end that Bulwer favors. Instead he promotes equilibrium of the will. In his narrative poem *The New Timon* (1846), Bulwer described a tortured, Byronic hero disappointed by society and frustrated in love, who wanders restlessly through the world, railing against the nastiness of life. Finally, he retreats into his soul. "Within, the gates unbar, the airs expand, / No bound but Heaven confines the spirit's land."[5] However it is not until Morvale, the Indian protagonist, learns Christ's message of bringing love into the heart that his soul finds rest.

Zanoni teaches a similar lesson to his beloved Viola moments before facing death in the turmoil of the French Revolution. Their imprisonment ironically constitutes a calm haven amidst the surrounding turbulence, but it also represents bondage of the flesh from which they will escape through death and ascend to Heaven. Zanoni can meet death calmly because his learning serves God not material things; thus his soul can find joy in its own sense of the Beautiful "in the serenity of its will, its power; in its sympathy with the youthfulness of the Infinite Creation, of which itself is an essence and a part, the secrets that embalm the very clay they consecrate, and renew the strength of life with the ambrosia of mysterious and celestial sleep" (Bulwer-Lytton, *Novels* 22:397). At the end of *The Disowned* (1828), the dying Algernon Mordaunt asks if men after death will be "the exiled from a home, or the escaped from a dungeon?" Bulwer makes clear that death is man's friend because it frees him. Virtue and valor strengthen man to accept suffering and death. "The soul, into which *that* spirit has breathed its glory, is not only above Fate—it profits by her assaults!" Thus, even on "the last sands of life, and encircled by the advancing waters of Darkness and Eternity, it becomes in its expiring effort doubly the Victor and the King!" (Bulwer-Lytton, *Novels* 9:432).[6]

A landscape of the spirit emerges from these recurring images in Bulwer's writings. His spiritual geography shows the movement from the optimistic Romantic image of an expanding central self to the skeptical Victorian image of protective encirclement. Man withdraws from the struggle of human society into the protected realm of his own mind or soul. But that realm is never free from the assaults of material existence so long as it is bound in flesh. In fact, it becomes another sort of imprisonment unless love enters, uniting the soul with the larger purposes of God as manifest in nature and nature's laws. The will subdues not only physical and intellectual appetite but itself as well, accepting death as a gift and a release, not as a penalty. The will's true object exists nowhere in this world; it achieves serenity by accepting this truth and anticipating joy in the life to come. Man's will is free to learn strength of will so that he may discipline himself to the hope of redemption. This was the common message of many of the religious and secular moralists surveyed in part 1. But Bulwer embodies his message in a variety of tales.

The long poem *King Arthur* (1848, revised 1870) is practically a treatise on man's discovery and fulfillment of his high duty. In his preface of 1870, Bulwer wrote:

> Neither men nor nations . . . can adequately fit themselves for great destinies unless to practical energies they add spiritual and intellectual freedom; nor can any beneficent conquest be achieved over the brute forces of nature without moral subjugation of the superstitious terrors and false desire that assail the mind. It is then only that the guardian and guiding instinct of a noble purpose assumes definite form, and is clothed with human loveliness, as Duty becomes Beauty in the successful completion of a life truly heroic.[7]

King Arthur has a "stern will," but a will greater than his shows him a vision of the task that he must undertake. His obligation is vaguely assigned to the Fates, but early in the poem we have a hint of what those Fates may be. In a passage describing the rising of the sun, Bulwer writes:

> Life, in each source, leaps rushing forth anew,
> Fills every grain in Nature's boundless plan,
> And wakes some fate in each desire of Man. . . .
> (Bulwer-Lytton, *Arthur*, 36)

The fates are nature working through man. To the uninformed populace, their king's departure on his quest is frightening, like the entrance of "some monster Chance," but Arthur's quest will ultimately secure him the wisdom to rule and defend his nation (Bulwer-Lytton, *Arthur*, 41). It is also allegorical of man's conquest of nature and himself in the service of a high ideal. Eventually, Arthur discovers that fate is nature's power over soulless matter, the fixed laws that the brute world obeys, the immutable laws to which Mary Shelley advised men submit. But, for Bulwer, man, though bound in the world of matter, has a unique power of his own, "in the Soul / Of Man the Supernatural lodged reveals / The God whom Nature—Matter's Fate—conceals" (Bulwer-Lytton, *Arthur*, 296).[8] In a lecture to Lancelot, Merlin suggests the limits of man's intellect: "can the human judgment gauge the worth / Of the least link in Fate's harmonious chain?" (Bulwer-Lytton, *Arthur*, 318) Fate is now God's Providence operating as a harmonious pattern of cause and effect that is necessity in matter but open to choice in man. Arthur regularly makes consequential choices, in one instance selecting a future life of struggle and service over one of ease and pleasure.

Man's duty is to nourish the divine seed in him, but he is free to make or mar his destiny through selfishness, error, or weakness. Being mortal, man can never know true happiness, but being more than mortal, the shadow of heaven falls upon him (Bulwer-Lytton, *Arthur*, 149). Man can arm himself with the strength of high purposes. Thus Arthur remains firm in the most dismal waste places. "Believe thou hast a mission to fulfil, And human valour grows a Godhead's will" (Bulwer-Lytton, *Arthur*, 235). By the end of the poem, Arthur discovers his destiny as the champion of political freedom, though freedom from materialism is implicit, as is freedom from self-indulgence. "Men to be free must free themselves," Arthur says (Bulwer-Lytton, *Arthur*, 269).

In selecting the meter for his long narrative poem, Bulwer wanted a familiar but not overworked form, one that combined alternate rhyme for its nobleness with an end rhyming couplet to clinch the sense. The appeal of the stanza form he selected (*a b a b c c* in iambic pentameter) was "its peculiar melodies of rhythm and cadence, as well as the just and measured facilities it affords to expression, neither too diffuse, nor too restricted" (Bulwer-Lytton, *Arthur*, xiii). A comparable union of order and freedom characterizes the narrative. From time to time we are given clear indications of the direction of the action (for example, the stating of the quest's objectives, Arthur's choice of his future, or his decision to leave the woman he loves and return to his kingdom), but within that ordering scheme, the events of the story develop with apparent spontaneity. This scheme of freedom within a binding frame replicates man's freedom within the providential scheme. I might seem to be forcing this connection if Bulwer had not himself called attention to the relationship of narrative and providence in a comic interlude. Gawaine complainingly narrates the bizarre adventures he has endured because of a raven, but Arthur explains that, had it not been for the sequence of events initiated by the raven, Gawaine never would have ended up the leader of a band of Eskimos in the northern seas just at the place and time necessary to rescue him from catastrophe. "In every ill which gives thee such offence, / Thou see'st the raven, I the Providence!" Arthur exclaims (Bulwer-Lytton, *Arthur*, 248). The apparently accidental events of Gawaine's tale are not accidental for Arthur, who believes in a design that contains them and shapes them to an intelligible purpose. So Bulwer's poem embodies the nature of human existence as Bulwer perceived it—surprising and only partially predictable events occurring in what appears to be a random manner, that, when viewed in retrospect, reveal the orderly form of a providential design. All true art is ethical, Bulwer said. "Art, in fact, is the effort of man to express the idea which Nature suggests to him of a power above Nature, whether that power be within the recesses of his own being, or in the Great First Cause of which Nature, like himself, is but the effect."[9] A true work of art involves a spiritual creation not producible in nature. Just as "virtue consists in a voluntary obedience to moral law, so genius consists in a voluntary obedience to artistic law. And the freedom of either is this, that the law is pleasing to it—has become its second nature." Each great artist makes his own technical rules and fits his freedom to "those elements of truth and beauty which constitute the law."[10] The artist's case is man's case—limited freedom within a binding law.

Bulwer believed that his narratives should have a coherent moral scheme and admitted his tendency to impose a conceptual order upon his fictions.[11] He described *Zanoni* as the next thing to an allegory, and in his 1853 preface to the novel, ranked it as his highest achievement in prose fiction, equating it with *King Arthur*, his highest achievement in verse. He valued these works largely because they embodied the lesson they were meant to convey. His description of *King Arthur* applies as well to *Zanoni*.

> As man has two lives—that of action and that of thought—so I conceive that work to be the truest representation of Humanity which faithfully delineates both, and opens some elevating glimpse into the sublimest mysteries of our being, by establishing the inevitable union that exists between the plain things of the day, in which our earthly bodies perform their allotted part, and the latent, often uncultivated, often invisible, affinities of the soul with all the powers that externally breathe and move throughout the Universe of Spirit. (Bulwer-Lytton, *Novels* 22:ix)

Introducing marvels and supernatural forces into a story allows for behavior and events not bound by an absolute necessity. In narratives like *King Arthur, Zanoni*, and *A Strange Story* (1862), Bulwer felt free to explore directly his most profound philosophical beliefs. He wrote to his son in 1853, "I incline to believe that the future is not predecreed to individuals, and that is why it cannot be ascertained; that it varies from week to week according to the change of circumstance and our own conduct, Providence working out the same grand results, no matter what we do, how we prosper or how we suffer."[12] His role as novelist in his marvellous narratives resembles providence, for he establishes a moral scheme with typical figures to trace the principal lines of action, though within that framework circumstantial details remain unpredictable, even miraculous, and hence free.[13]

In his preface to *A Strange Story*, Bulwer used Maine de Biran's theory of the three lives of man as a foundation for his story. According to Biran, man's first life is animal, organic, ruled by necessity; his second life includes free-will and self-consciousness (the union of mind and matter); third is the life of man's soul.[14] This third life aspires to intellectual and moral perfection. Drawing upon the philosopher Jacobi, Bulwer asserted that "without some gleam of the supernatural, Man is not man, nor Nature, nature" (Bulwer-Lytton, *Novels* 13:vii). Man reveals God by his capacity to rise above nature and by opposing and conquering it. Bulwer believed that man's immortality was proven by his special capacity to comprehend abstract ideas connected with immortality (Lytton 2:247). In a letter discussing *A Strange Story*, he wrote: "Nature only gives to each organized life capacities to receive instincts or ideas which are suited to its destiny. . . . Each thing after its kind has the capacity to receive ideas or impressions *that correspond with its destination*." Man alone receives ideas that carry his being into a life beyond this world, thus he must be destined for such a life (Lytton 2:403). This is the philosophical underpinning for *A Strange Story*, but lest the reader miss the heat behind its supernatural fire, Bulwer spelled it out.

But when the reader lays down this Strange Story, perhaps he will detect, through all the haze of Romance, the outlines of these images suggested to his reason: Firstly, the image of sensuous, soulless Nature, such as the Materialist had conceived it. Secondly, the image of Intellect, obstinately separating all its inquiries from the belief in the spiritual essence and destiny of man, and incurring all kinds of perplexity and resorting to all kinds of visionary speculation before it settles at last into the simple faith which unites the philosopher and the infant. And, Thirdly, the image of the erring but pure-thoughted visionary, seeking over-much on this earth to separate soul from mind, till innocence itself is led astray by a phantom, and reason is lost in the space between earth and the stars. (Bulwer-Lytton, *Novels* 13:viii)

In the novel, Dr. Allen Fenwick is a student of science, a materialist. Margrave represents animal power or what Allan Christensen calls the "amoral will."[15] The former does not credit the existence of soul, the latter has sacrificed it to enjoy complete engagement in material life. Lilian is unworldly spirit yearning for immaterial existence. Dr. Julius Faber, Fenwick's wise friend, says of Lilian and Fenwick, "I would draw somewhat more downward her fancy, raise somewhat more upward your reason" (Bulwer-Lytton, Novels 13:250). Eventually that is what happens and through their mutual love these two learn the intense reality of the soul and the importance of its working in this world.

Bulwer defined the soul as "a something in man that lives on, and in truth soul really means the living principle" (Lytton 2:406). It was neither mind nor will but underlay both. Intelligence could err by neglecting the spiritual, and will could act for good or evil, but soul was the trustworthy guide that identified moral ends and the kernel of individual identity.[16] If man could identify his true purpose in life, he would discover the nature of his self and employ his will to noble ends. This is the story of *King Arthur* without the Romance. Without recognition of the soul, there is only the powerful materialism of a Mejnour or Fenwick, or worse, of a Margrave or the Cagliostro of "The Haunted and the Haunters" whose will is so powerful that, in a parody of the soul's immortality, it lives on after him, creating fearsome images and events. The skeptical narrator of this short story agreeing to stay in the haunted house, feels the evil presence. "I was aware that there was a WILL, and a will of intense, creative, working evil, which might crush down my own."[17] This power is maintained by physical means—a compass floating in a clear liquid—and a curse. When the material device is smashed, the haunting ends.

Bulwer's romantic narratives, with their supernaturalism and mystery, are the most convenient vehicles for the ideas we are discussing here, but Bulwer wrote novels of ordinary life as well, either melodramatic, like *Paul Clifford* and *Eugene Aram*, or realistic, like *The Caxtons* and *My Novel*. We have discussed *Aram* already, but before going on to the Caxton novels, I would like to look at an intermediate form, the historical novel. In *Zanoni* and *A Strange Story*, Bulwer outlined the moral framework of his narratives. He does not do that for *The Last Days of Pompeii* (1834), but it is there. The narrative rises out of certain important conflicts—true and false religion, Christian and Pagan values, selfish and unselfish love, idealism and materialism. Arbaces, a learned Egyptian, is the chief villain. Though outwardly a champion of the worship of Isis, he is a materialist who, like a modern scientist, uses reason to examine the force of necessity as manifested in nature. His discoveries provide comforts for the masses, and he allows himself extraordinary sensuous delights.

Arbaces is a combination of extreme cerebration and extreme sensual indulgence. At the opposite extreme is Apaecides, a young religious enthusiast, eager to deny the claims of the body in a commitment to the life of the spirit. Associated with him and set against Arbaces, is Olinthus, a Christian missionary who represents an active faith. Glaucus and Ione are expatriate Greeks who cherish the cultural tradition of their land and people. Both are handsome and intelligent, with a strong sense of social decorum. They are superior to the mechanical and pedantic Romans who, Glaucus says, "mimic my Athenian ancestors [but] do everything so heavily."[18] Filling out this diagram of spirit, intelligence, and flesh is the loving Nydia, the blind flower girl whose wholly physical attraction to Glaucus occasions both disasters and rescues.

As in any historical tale based upon a real situation, Bulwer's novel follows a preordained set of conditions. Whatever else may happen, on a given day Vesuvius will erupt and Pompeii will be destroyed. Our foreknowledge of this outcome does not extinguish our interest in the events of the plot but heightens it as we become intrigued with the fates of individual characters. The general, inescapable direction of events is toward a cataclysm of which the characters are unaware. Like divinity, we and the narrator see men impotent to change the course of providence and ignorant of its design make moral choices that nonetheless reveal their roles in that larger scheme.

Arbaces is the figure most clearly associated with the notion of destiny. The Egyptian is "one of those haughty and powerful spirits accustomed to master others" (Bulwer-Lytton, *Pompeii*, 57). In him, the passion of power "corresponded exactly to his character." His conscience "was solely of the intellect; it was awed by no moral laws" (Bulwer-Lytton, *Pompeii*, 159). His arcane studies have led him past scientific certainties to mysteries of nature. He believes that he has eluded the one danger to him that he has read in the stars and exults: "I have passed, I have subdued the latest danger of my destiny. Now I have but to lay out the gardens of my future fate, unterrified and secure" (Bulwer-Lytton, *Pompeii*, 237). But later, he has a troubling dream in which a terrible embodiment of nature warns him that he is a puppet unwisely vain about his knowledge. A wind, calling itself Necessity, rushes Arbaces off toward the Unknown. He asks if it will be to happiness or woe. Necessity replies:

"As thou hast sown, so shalt thou reap."
"Dread thing, not so! If thou art the Ruler of Life, *thine* are my misdeeds, not mine."
"I am but the breath of God!" answered the mighty WIND.
"Then is my wisdom vain!" groaned the dreamer.
"The husbandman accuses not fate, when, having sown thistles, he reaps not corn. Thou hast sown crime, accuse not fate if thou reapest not the harvest of virtue." (Bulwer-Lytton, *Pompeii*, 421)

And so it transpires. During the chaotic attempt of the crowds to flee from the wrath of Vesuvius, Arbaces and Glaucus confront one another. As Arbaces steps forward to seize Ione from Glaucus, lightning strikes a bronze statue, shivering it and its column. The fragments crash down upon Arbaces, and the narrator remarks laconically, "The prophecy of the stars was fulfilled" (Bulwer-Lytton, *Pompeii*, 479).

If Arbaces, in selfishly arrogating power over events without concern for good or evil, sows the seeds of his own destiny through the law of necessity, Nydia commits a more innocent but just as fatal an error. When the proud daughter of a wealthy Roman acquires what she believes to be a love potion by which she hopes to secure Glaucus's affection, Nydia, herself desperately in love with the handsome Greek, takes it for her own use. But the potion is a mind-destroying drug, not the aphrodisiac that Arbaces promised to supply, and when Glaucus drinks wine tainted with the drug, he suffers a mental confusion lasting long enough for him to wander the streets and by coincidence come upon Arbaces murdering Apaecides. Apparently insane, he is charged with the crime and imprisoned. Nydia's attempt to alter destiny has unfortunate immediate consequences but does not prevent the eventual union of the true lovers, Glaucus and Ione. Having helped to save the pair and realizing that she can never share Glaucus's love, Nydia drowns herself.

Before meeting Ione, Glaucus is an ordinary young heathen, but his love for this exceptional woman transforms him into an idealist. "He felt that henceforth it was his destiny to look upward and to soar" (Bulwer-Lytton, *Pompeii*, 52). True love, based on the virtues of sympathy and self-suppression, sows seeds of eventual joy, just as the seeds of lust and selfish desire breed sorrow. After describing the two lovers laying out "the chart of their destiny to come," that is, projecting their hopes for the future, the narrator intrudes surprisingly, explaining that he has purposely refrained from developing their characters.

> But in dwelling so much on their bright and bird-like existence, I am influenced almost insensibly by the forethought of the changes that await them, and for which they were so ill prepared. It was this very softness and gaiety of life that contrasted most strongly the vicissitudes of their coming fate. For the oak without fruit or blossom, whose hard and rugged heart is fitted for the storm, there is less fear than for the delicate branches of the myrtle, and the laughing clusters of the vine. (Bulwer-Lytton, *Pompeii*, 202–3)

And yet, as he writes this, the narrator knows that the vicissitudes will be overcome and the lovers will enjoy at last the species of destiny they anticipated. They plotted their destination correctly, though their map to show the way was faulty, illustrating again that though the providential design remains secure, there is much room within it for the play of free will and circumstance.

The happiness that Glaucus and Ione find is not merely personal; returned once more to their beloved Athens, the ancient source of philosophy, they espouse Christianity, which teaches them a higher faith than reason alone could supply. Frustration at their nation's enslavement by Rome is relieved by their growing power of resignation. Glaucus writes to his friend Sallust, "the glory of a few years matters little in the vast space of eternity . . . There is no perfect freedom till the chains of clay fall from the soul, and all space, all time, become its heritage and domain" (Bulwer-Lytton, *Pompeii*, 491).

In *The Last Days of Pompeii*, Bulwer made his familiar scheme clear, though not explicit. Spirit, itself supported by love and faith, must guide intellect through the will that overcomes mere animal impulses. Only in this way does man achieve his high destiny. While there is a providential design that governs the lives of all men, that design is grand in its aims, leaving individuals to create their own fates by the choices they make. A world of perfect order encloses one of contingency, and Bulwer's narrative method reflects this. A mood of inevitability pervades *Pompeii*, intensified by references to predicted destinies such as Arbaces's. Nonetheless, characters make decisions that violate the apparent direction of the plot. Nydia's appropriation of the love potion is only one example. Even the narrative intrusions serve a double purpose. By interrupting the story line, they encourage a sense that real events are subject to similarly surprising disjunctions. At the same time, the existence of a narrator who knows the whole story of which we know only a portion, confirms our trust in an overall design, even though that narrative voice sends us down false trails in the story (examples include the subplot involving the gladiator Lydon and the involuted account of Nydia's attempts to escape from Arbaces's palace) and offer pronouncements that transcend the safely finished world of the novel and bleed into the contemporary reader's world, as in the following: "Italy, Italy, while I write, your skies are over me, your seas flow beneath my feet; listen not to the blind policy which would unite all your crested cities, mourning for their republics, into one empire; false, pernicious delusion! your only hope of regeneration is in division. Florence, Milan, Venice, Genoa, may be free once more if each is free" (Bulwer-Lytton, *Pompei*, 124).

Ultimately Bulwer's narrative method reinforces the picture of a world of individual freedom within a larger providence. But this world is not confined to the realm of fiction, since fiction at its highest is simply a means of reasserting this world view by linking fictive and real worlds through the immutable human affections. Bulwer explained this relationship in the context of historical fiction, but it applies more broadly.

In the tale of human passion, in past ages, there is something of interest even in the remoteness of the time. We love to feel within us the bond which unites the most distant eras—men, nations, customs perish; THE AFFECTIONS ARE IMMORTAL! they are the sympathies which unite the ceaseless generations. the past lives again, when we look upon its emotions; it lives in our own! That which was, ever is! The magician's gift, that revives the dead, that animates the dust of forgotten graves, is not in the author's skill; it is in the heart of the reader. (Bulwer-Lytton, *Pompeii*, 187)

At its best, fiction seizes attention through the affections, intrigues the reason through the unraveling of plot and the exposition of ideas and inspires the spirit through the eventual resolution of conflicts and an endorsement of faith.

All of Bulwer's writing was moral even when it was not allegorical. His characters accordingly were developed or typical to greater or lesser degrees. Andrew Brown explains how Bulwer distorted history in *Rienzi* (1835) in order to fashion a suitably moral type out of what had been a rather deplorable Roman leader.[19] Margaret F. King and Elliot Engel argue that there is a developing pattern in Bulwer's heroes from the Byronic rebels against established order, to the intermediate figures in a novel like *Pompeii*, who learn moderation, to the Carlylean figure who can adjust his aims to the social realities of his time, as in *Ernest Maltravers* (1837).[20] However, Bulwer had anticipated his more accommodating types in the figure of Henry Pelham, who, while playing a role that makes him shine in society, is actually a strong and admirable figure. As Reginald Glanville says near the end of the novel, "I know, amidst all your worldly ambition, and the encrusted artificiality of your exterior, how warm and generous your real heart—how noble and intellectual is your real mind; and were my sister tenfold more perfect than I believe her, I do not desire to find on earth one more deserving of her than yourself."[21] Allan Christensen notes that Pelham's union with Ellen represents the embracing of the anima figure who withdraws him not only from the superficial world of levities and follies" but from his own self-absorptions.[22] This union is a credible version of the more overtly symbolic union of Fenwick and Lilian in *A Strange Story* or the historically transposed version involving Glaucus and Ione in *Pompeii*.

Much of Bulwer's early writing is concerned with discovery of the real self. Clarence Linden in *The Disowned* (1828) and Paul Clifford literally search for personal origins and legal identities. Falkland and Eugene Aram discover the real but appalling selves concealed within their otherwise worthy beings. The exploration of self takes on a new and milder form in *The Caxtons* (1849) and *My Novel* (1850–53), obvious attempts by Bulwer to deal with the mundane. He returned to the melodramatic and metaphysical again but for a time sought to peddle his abiding beliefs in a less intoxicating brew.

In his preface to *The Caxtons*, Bulwer stressed the ordinariness of his characters and observed that the novel's "plot is extremely slight, the incidents are few [and] such as may be found in the records of ordinary life."[23] Apparently Bulwer wanted to free his characters from the philosophical uniforms he so often forced them to wear. Drawing his inspiration, at least at the outset, from *Tristram Shandy*, he created a fictional world emphasizing spontaneity and contingency. At the same time, like *Shandy*, Bulwer's novel describes individuals faced with circumstances resulting from events they cannot control. Pisistratus Caxton's education is an example, for it illustrates that character is largely formed in childhood and that nature and love, rather than rule and punishment, should govern that training (Bulwer-Lytton, *Novels* 7:13).[24] These influences do not absolutely determine character. The scoundrel Francis Vivian declares man to be the slave of nature and heredity, but Bulwer and Pisistratus reject this determinist view of a world without moral laws (Bulwer-Lytton, *Novels* 7:107). When Francis Vivian is frustrated in his ambitions and humiliated, the desolation of his grief reminds Pisistratus of what the earth would be "were man abandoned to his passions, and the CHANCE of the atheist reigned alone in the merciless heaven" (Bulwer-Lytton, *Novels* 7:393).

Bulwer could not help seeing life as a shaped contest, no matter how loosely he organized its form or left his characters room to do as they pleased. More than once, he likened life to the stylized conflict of theatrical presentation. Here is Austin Caxton, Pisistratus's father:

> "Life is a drama, not a monologue," pursued my father. " 'Drama' is derived from a Greek verb signifying 'to do.' Every actor in the drama has something to do, which helps on the progress of the whole: that is the object for which the author created him. Do your part, and let the Great Play get on." (Bulwer-Lytton, *Novels* 7:134)

Later, the narrator appropriates theatrical language to describe his own effort. "The stage-scene has dropped," he says. Several years must be supposed to pass before action resumes. Meanwhile critics in the audience pass judgments. After a suitable time has passed for the actors to have changed their costumes, the narrator exclaims, "Play up, O ye fiddles and kettle drums! the time is elapsed. Stop that cat-call, young gentleman; heads down in the pit there! Now the flourish is over, the scene draws up: look before" (Bulwer-Lytton, *Novels* 7:448). And the story resumes.

The conceit is amusing, if unoriginal, but Bulwer meant it to be instructive as well, emphasizing the parallel between the drama of life and the drama of fiction. Each character in the novel has a higher purpose than his own selfish ends, performing a part in what will be the instructive pattern of the whole. Fiction's aim is to transcend itself and become knowledge, an aim paralleling Austin Caxton's explanation that "it is an inevitable law that a man, in spite of himself, should live for something higher than his own happiness. He cannot live in himself or for himself, however egotistical he may try to be. Every desire he has links him with others. Man is not a machine,—he is a part of one" (Bulwer-Lytton, *Novels* 7:134). And so, with Pisistratus's help, Francis Vivian must learn, as more sensational figures such as Aram and Zanoni learned in their own ways. Broken and disgraced, Vivian regenerates himself through hard work and a heroic death.

Pisistratus and his cousin both learn that the classic advice, "Know thyself," is no longer adequate. The new demand is a Carlylean, "Improve thyself" (Bulwer-Lytton, *Novels* 7:445). And Pisistratus does act to improve himself, electing the difficult course of hard labor as an agriculturalist in Australia. Although he thought fortune cruel to him when it withheld Fanny Trevanion, his soberer view dismisses the image of a chance-driven universe and embraces Dante's championship of Fortune. "And I think, if one looked narrowly at her operations, one might perceive that she gives every man a chance at least once in his life: if he take and make the best of it, she will renew her visits; if not, *itur ad astra.*" (Bulwer-Lytton, *Novels* 7:351).

Pisistratus seizes fortune's offer that takes him to Australia, where he becomes wealthy enough to return home and help his uncle Roland revive the ancestral property. Yet his freely chosen deeds may be seen as part of a larger design, as he himself suggests. Praising Australia, he says:

> And this land has become the heritage of our people! Methinks I see, as I gaze around, the scheme of the All-beneficent Father disentangling itself clear through the troubled history of mankind. How mysteriously, while Europe rears its populations and fulfils its civilizing mission, these realms have been concealed from its eyes,—divulged to us just as civilization needs the solution to its problems; a vent for feverish energies, baffled in the crowd; offering bread to the famished, hope to the desperate; in very truth enabling the "New World to redress the balance of the Old." (Bulwer-Lytton, *Novels* 7:460–61)

Like so many of his contemporaries, some of whom we have already touched upon in part 1, Bulwer could accept the English appropriation of a continent because it appeared to fulfill so comfortably—for Europeans—the progressive design moved forward by the engine of providence.

The Caxtons owed much to Sterne, but its sequel, *My Novel* was partially inspired by Fielding, especially in its narrative structure, for the playful, intrusive narrator is even more in evidence here than in *The Caxtons*.[25] Each book of the novel begins with a chapter directly presenting the narrator himself. The first of these tells how Pisistratus was urged to write his novel. The second is entitled "Informing the Reader How This Book Came to Have Initial Chapters." In it, Mr. Caxton recommends Fielding's practice because it allows the reader to begin the story on page five rather than on page one. Initial chapters, he says, allow a certain repose in novels as landings do on staircases. Pisistratus objects that this practice brings the author too prominently before his readers. So what, his father responds; everyone knows a book must have an author. Besides, he adds, you may always use a chorus if you don't wish to come forward in your own person.[26] Pisistratus's chorus consists of his father, his wife, and his uncle Roland. The teller of the tale in his milieu thus becomes a part of the tale he tells and is influenced in the manner of his telling by his audience. But both teller and audience are, of course, fictional creations themselves and it is Bulwer, not Pisistratus, who, while enjoying the blessings of initial chapters and much more, hides behind the chorus.

All of this may seem rather stale to modern readers, brought up on sophisticated narratives and the critical interpretations that illuminate them, but it was surely unusual in its day, being an advance upon Thackeray's innovative approach in *Vanity Fair* (1847–48) and *Pendennis* (1848–50), and influenced his approach in *The Newcomes* (1853–55).[27] Bulwer was not as skillful as Thackeray and sometimes his narrator's intrusiveness is clumsy. In one instance, Pisistratus observes: "In my next chapter I shall give a picture of the squire, but first" and then launches into another subject (Bulwer-Lytton, *Novels* 17:37). Some interruptions enhance the spontaneous character of the story, as do the numerous abrupt plot developments and the sudden additions of minor characters who are only partially worked into the plot lines. Others seem entirely gratuitous. For example, when Leonard Fairfield asks the bookseller Mr. Prickett what John Burley has written, Pisistratus steps in, saying, let me answer that question, since I know far more about Burley than Prickett can. But even these apparently pointless narrative usurpations contribute to a larger purpose.

We have already seen how elaborately Bulwer structured his novels and how insistent he was that they convey a moral. *My Novel* holds to the latter requirement, but like *The Caxtons*, is purposely loose in architecture to give the impression that characters direct their own fates. The book's lesson is that knowledge, intellect, and will in themselves are no guarantee of virtue or good conduct. Randal Leslie, who consciously determines to seek knowledge as power and thereby fuel his ambition to rise out of near-poverty to wealth, is the central example of this error. Bulwer describes him as a representative of "Intellectual Evil" (Bulwer-Lytton) *Novels* 18:287). Here is what his strength amounts to. "Untempted by wine, dead to love, unamused by pleasure, indifferent to the arts, despising literature save as a means to some end of power, Randal Leslie was the incarnation of thought hatched out of the corruption of will" (Bulwer-Lytton, *Novels* 18:418).

Randal's opposite number is Leonard Fairfield, less shrewd, but with uncorrupted feelings. We are told in an initial chapter that he typifies Genius passing through the Practical in order to influence the world (Bulwer-Lytton, *Novels* 17:359). Later he is described as simplicity refined by intelligence, passing through knowledge unsoiled (Bulwer-Lytton, *Novels* 18:137). He owes this immunity to the good counseling of Parson Dale and Dr. Riccabocca. Dale feels that men are too much occupied with mind and not enough with simple heart. He and the learned Riccabocca teach Leonard that knowledge is only one kind of power and not the greatest. In fact, intellectual cultivation is not necessary for virtue, which is available to the humblest intellect. Knowledge is a trust to be used in the service of faith. The model is the New Testament (Bulwer-Lytton, *Novels* 17:277). Leonard acts on this lesson, becoming a poet and novelist who can move and inspire his readers with noble feelings.

Randal and Leonard make clear-cut choices that determine their fates. A providential scheme sees that the evil choice is punished, the wise one rewarded. There are other variations on this warning. Audley Egerton, a dedicated and scrupulously honorable political leader, suffers from the knowledge that he has betrayed his best friend, secretly marrying the woman they both love, then abandoning her to obscurity and death. He is tormented by this secret and eventually wears down through a combination of hard work and the strain of this hidden offense until his heart fails him. The man he injured, Harley L'Estrange, has wasted his life in melancholy wandering, though innately he has "that gift which belongs to the genius of Action. He inspired others with the light of his own spirit and the force of his own will" (Bulwer-Lytton, *Novels* 18:385). Having supposed Egerton to be his faithful friend, L'Estrange yearns for vengeance when he learns the truth. Parson Dale warns Harley against revenge and the narrator intrudes to support the Parson's view. "He who has once done a base thing is never again wholly reconciled to honour" (Bulwer-Lytton, *Novels* 18:522). It is his beloved Violante's "heroic will," her determination to leave him despite her love for him if he does anything ignoble, that saves L'Estrange (Bulwer-Lytton, *Novels* 18:527).

Many characters in the novel manifest weakness of will and lack of control. Their cases are easy. What fascinated Bulwer was the dilemma of *corrupted* will, for in man's inevitable struggle against destiny a strong will is a two-edged weapon. Strength of will, when guided by moral purpose, ensures success in life because struggle is life's way of evoking the virtues that unite man with providence.[28] The wisely strong-willed man may contend against circumstance and shape his own fate.

Bulwer saw the design of his novel as directly related to this metaphysical pattern. In the initial chapter of book 12, the Caxtons speculate on the fates of the characters, recommending their own preferences for the development of the story. Besieged by these suggestions, Pisistratus responds.

> "Silence!" cried Pisistratus, clapping his hand to both ears. "I can no more alter the fate allotted to each of the personages whom you honour with your interest than I can change your own; like you, they must go where events lead them, urged on by their own characters and the agencies of others. Providence so pervadingly governs the universe, that you cannot strike it even out of a book. The author may beget a character, but the moment the character comes into action, it escapes from his hands—plays its own part, and fulfils its own inevitable doom." (Bulwer-Lytton, *Novels* 18:359)

Bulwer here emphasizes the manner in which his fiction replicates man's condition in the world, even if his analogy is humorously drawn. Bulwer has another amusing twist in store near the end of the novel. Chapter 34 ends with Egerton's death and the revelation that Leonard is his son. Then comes the "Final Chapter."

> PISISTRATUS.—"What remains to do?"
>
> MR. CAXTON.—"What! why, the *Final Chapter!*—the last news you can give us of those whom you have introduced to our liking or dislike."
>
> PISISTRATUS.—"Surely it is more dramatic to close the work with a scene that completes the main design of the plot, and leave it to the prophetic imagination of all whose flattering curiosity is still not wholly satisfied, to trace the streams of each several existence, when they branch off again from the lake in which their waters converge, and by which the sibyl has confirmed and made clear the decree that 'Conduct is Fate.' "
>
> MR. CAXTON.—"More dramatic, I grant; but you have not written a drama. A novelist should be a comfortable, garrulous, communicative, gossiping fortune-teller; not a grim, laconical, oracular sibyl. I like a novel that adopts all the old-fashioned customs prescribed to its art by the rules of the Masters,—more especially a novel which you style 'My Novel' *par* emphasis." (Bulwer-Lytton, *Novels* 18:580)

Everyone agrees that Pisistratus must add a conventional last chapter to tidy up plot lines and provide an account of his characters' fates. Suspecting some such demand, Pisistratus has come prepared with a supplementary manuscript and proceeds to relate what happens to the major characters.

This foolery may seem unnecessary, except that it serves an instructive purpose. If the "Final Chapter" that Pisistratus reads is that which appears in the novel as we read it, it includes the exchange between Pisistratus and his relatives, which means that that too had been foreseen. As in the libertarian view of God, foreknowledge does not mean foreordained. In fact, only at this point do we realize definitively that the true Author exists beyond and independently of his creation and thus cannot be Pisistratus, who is himself a creature of the fiction. Bulwer is the analog for God, his creation the field in duration where beings endowed with freedom work out by their choices the destinies they will endure or enjoy and which nonetheless fall within the larger design of the Author of existence, who knows beforehand how the story will end.

CHAPTER THIRTEEN

CHARLES DICKENS

B ULWER often discussed his artistic aims, but when it came to embodying them he was neither subtle nor entirely successful. Dickens rarely elaborated on his artistic objectives, but many of his novels are hugely successful incorporations of certain of his recoverable attitudes. In many ways his novels incarnate the more commonplace moral defenses of free will examined in their expository form in part 1. Dickens was not sentimental about the will. He had friends, Bulwer among them, who wrote on the subject and others who dealt with the problem in their professional lives—John Forster and Dr. John Elliotson, for example. Dickens was sensitive to the free will versus determinism problem. For him, strength of will and free will were closely connected, often, perhaps, confused. Ultimately, his picture of the will was a familiar one—that the will is untrustworthy because it can be corrupted by selfishness; hence he sanctioned self-renunciation as the true course to freedom. The free and strong will subordinates itself to duty.

What is significant about Dickens is the way his story-telling gradually comes to embody his valuation of the will. Like Carlyle, Dickens assumed a strong power of necessity in human life. But though life might seem an interlocking, disabling fabric, the individual was still free to move through it. Dickens's mature novels embody in their narrative methods the drama of free will opposing necessity. The conflict between determined and free existence is rendered in the dynamics of narrative itself.

~ ~ ~

In many ways, Charles Dickens is the best representative of changing attitudes toward narration and characterization from early to middle nineteenth century because he is so prominent and his views on these subjects are so much more implicit in his works than explicit in his comments about them. Dickens had far less to say about the rational basis for his techniques than did Bulwer or Eliot, and his practice shows a conflict in his underlying assumptions that both clarifies his methods and makes them more difficult to deal with.

Dickens saw the world as coincidental and yet ordered. John Forster wrote: "On the coincidences, resemblances, and surprises of life, Dickens liked especially to dwell, and few things moved his fancy so pleasantly. The world, he would say, was so much smaller than we thought it; we were all connected by fate without knowing it; people supposed to be far apart were constantly elbowing each other, and to-morrow bore so close a resemblance to nothing half so much as yesterday."[1] Chris Brooks argues that Dickens shared Carlyle's typological approach to experience. Carlyle's key was the Bible, but Dickens generated his symbols from the immediate context of his central image; his symbolic realism is semantically self-sufficient.[2] "By retaining realism, but at the same time, forcing us to recognise meaning *as an integral part* of that reality, Dickens establishes a symbolic dimension in the very stuff of the real world."[3] If symbolic meaning is implicit in the world, then experience is a true syntax from whose elements these symbols are derived and new expressions of the "sentence" of life made possible by their reassemblage. A syntax of experience thus discoverable and ultimately interpretable must be predetermined and unalterable. Dickens's world therefore appears to be understandable only if determined.

J. Hillis Miller, approaching this subject from another direction, sees a connection between Dickens's metonymic realism and a determinist view of existence. "There is a close relation," he says, "between metonomy and this form of narrative [about the progress of decline]. The story of a man's degeneration 'impelled by sheer necessity' constitutes a spreading out of a diachronic scale of the determinism implied synchronically in saying that each man is defined by what is around him."[4] Robert Barnard goes so far as to say that Dickens's novels may themselves be taken as symbols of destiny.[5]

But, if Dickens inclined to narrative structures that suggest causal determinism, he also recommended a view of individual human beings that promoted the concepts of freedom and responsibility, though the freedom part became more restricted as Dickens matured and "darkened." From his earliest days as a writer, Dickens was aware of, if not serious about, the dilemma of freedom and determinism. In *Sketches by Boz*, he constantly called attention to the causal relations that bring about transformations of character, as though change in the individual results not from inner motives but from external action. In "Horatio Sparkins," the comic protagonist, although meant to be absurd, nonetheless poses a serious problem when he asks "Is effect the consequence of cause? Is cause the precursor of effect?"[6]

Fred Kaplan has documented Dickens's strong interest in mesmerism, a practice emphasizing a "characteristic Victorian triad—energy, will, and power."[7] However, whereas Dickens's friend Dr. John Elliotson, one of the most prominent exponents of mesmerism and phrenology in England, approached his subject from the scientific materialist's position, Dickens never lost his belief in man's spiritual nature. He became an accomplished mesmerist without claiming to understand the power that was to him a manifestation of cosmic energy and order. Mesmerism was one more tool for understanding human nature and grappling with the mystery of the self. Surely will power and strength of will were important ingredients of character, ingredients that Dickens himself possessed in abundance. Kaplan describes Dickens as "a novelist of the will who warned against the will's excess" (Kaplan, 236). According to Kaplan, Dickens believed that, in creating his self-identity and self-worth, man establishes a connection between internal and external cosmic forces "but that this energy has as its agent the human will, which can use the force for good or for evil ends." Good ends call for love and self-sacrifice; ends that are evil involve manipulation and brutality (Kaplan, 240).[8]

The Romantics championed a heroic will struggling against a stultifying environment. But like Mary Shelley and Bulwer, Dickens distrusted the will because "despite the potential beneficial uses of this energy those who had extraordinary powers of will were more likely than not to use them for self-serving ends. So the Dickens world is populated with the threats of domination and exploitation" (Kaplan, 237).

But if Dickens recognized the potential power of the human will for good and for evil and if he recognized the need for man to restrain his will in the service of others, did he at the same time believe that man was *free* to govern his will? I have already suggested that Dickens conceived of the human condition largely in terms of interlocking fates. If destiny directed human careers, in what way could man be viewed as free and thus at liberty to exercise his will power?

In the abstract to her dissertation, *Division in Dickens: Determinism and Free Will in the Novels through Bleak House*, Rhonda Wilcox Nelms writes:

> Dickens's suspension of thought on the subject of free will directly affects his treatment of character and structure. Repeatedly, separate worlds for the deterministic and the free are set up within a single novel, and the former characters seem much more effec-

tive than the latter. The grounding in detailed causes which Dickens uses to justify or explain the psychology of his deterministic characters makes them vivid, while the characters of free will, whether by default or design, are generally left without this specificity and thus without this degree of reality.[9]

In effect, Nelms argues that Dickens never reconciled the paradox that men can be free in a determined world. But I think it is possible to find a pattern similar to that in Bulwer's writing, more skillfully presented in fiction but rarely articulated beyond the novels. I do not intend to go through all of Dickens's novels demonstrating and reiterating a few basic points, but a representative examination of the novels is necessary to establish a consistent argument.

The Pickwick Papers (1836–37) is early and not seriously concerned with metaphysical issues. The characters seem free in a largely undetermined world and people are held accountable for their deeds.[10] On the other hand, they do not have developed characters, and their actions seem as accidental as the world in which they move. The same cannot be said of Oliver Twist (1838), where a clear moral scheme emerges. Various scholars have accepted Oliver as a representation of the human spirit freely electing the true Christian path, a variation upon Christian in Pilgrim's Progress or a representative of free will.[11] His struggle against evil surely suggests man's power to persevere in virtue. Endangered at the workhouse and more under Fagin's control, Oliver remains uncorrupted. But his goodness is highly improbable, given the conditions into which he is born, though Dickens's Wordsworthian assumptions allow for this power. In Nicholas Nickleby, Dickens likened the human soul to a coin freshly minted in heaven from which the emblems may all too quickly be abraded by use. Oliver is such a well-minted coin of true metal. Conceivably he has inherited his mother's goodness. His training in struggle—beginning with his very first breaths—prepares him for a life of endurance. In the end, this combination of inborn virtue and training in hardship triumphs.

Rhoda Nelms objects that the people in the supposedly free world of Oliver Twist "seem paradoxically determined and flat as characters, while those in the determined world have more fully developed identities and give the effect of greater freedom, since the most basic element of free will is the ability to determine one's own identity" (Nelms, 37). But, as we have seen in earlier chapters, Victorians had a different view of the correct application of free will. True freedom involves renunciation of self-will and submission to the will of God. The function of free will is to choose right. Those who do so resemble one another and appear more predictable in their behavior, whereas those who selfishly resist the will of God and try to impose their own will in place of God's providence become interesting for the peculiarities of their

individual hungers and desires, though they are gradually enslaving themselves to their vices and losing their free will, not increasing it. In distinctly
particular ways each of the major villains in *Oliver Twist* suffers the fate he
has bred for himself—Sikes in violence, Monks in madness, Fagin in legal
extermination. The illusion of their freedom becomes the reality of destinies
they have forged like chains. Steven Marcus has noted that the population of
Oliver Twist consists only of persons involved with Oliver's fate; "in a world
where there is no accidental population, no encounter can be called in
coincidence" (Marcus, 78-79). This is not a determined but a fabular or
providential world. It is filled with meaning and purpose but must be deciphered and the solution acted upon. Like the Old Testament God, Dickens
attributes freedom and the consequent responsibility to all of his characters
but hardens the hearts of those who do evil against his own grace.

In chapter 3 of *Master Humphrey's Clock*, the old gentleman narrator
gives a clue to his creator's impulses when he says that he often succeeds in
"diverting the current of some mournful reflections, by conjuring up a
number of fanciful associations with the objects that surround me, and dwelling upon the scenes and characters they suggest." For example, he imagines
the lives of persons who might have occupied the various rooms of his house.
"With such materials as these," he explains, "I work out many a little drama,
whose chief merit is, that I can bring it to a happy end at will."[12] It is in such a
mood of pensive melancholy that Master Humphrey opens the narrative that
becomes *The Old Curiosity Shop* (1840-41). He is "speculating on the
characters and occupations of those who fill the streets" of London and is
troubled especially by the sight of children exposed to evil contact, when he
comes upon young Nell who seems an angel in the midst of wickedness. It is
as though his need to create a fable to counteract the dreadful scene around
him evokes this manifestation of innocence, as though Nell is simply the
necessary principle of good in a narrative that is to end well at Master
Humphrey's will. Like the deity in which he believes and trusts, he wants to
create a sequence of events in time embodying the truths of providential
design and divine justice. This impulse toward happy endings that compels
Master Humphrey to impose his own creative readings upon a recalcitrant
world is more succinctly and powerfully rendered when he sees Nell in her
bed, surrounded by the "fantastic things" her grandfather has accumulated.
To him, she exists "in a kind of allegory" and therefore seizes his imagination. " 'It would be a curious speculation,' said I, after some restless turns
across and across the room, 'to imagine her in her future life, holding her
solitary way among a crowd of wild grotesque companions; the only pure,
fresh, youthful object in the throng. It would be curious to find—.' "[13]

Master Humphrey breaks off his meditation at this point because he is
anticipating the very story he is about to tell. But he has said enough to let us
know that what follows is a species of allegory, a modernized version of *Pil-*

grim's Progress. Although the elements of this allegory are open to various interpretations, I think we may view Nell's passage through many constricting and confining settings to a region where her spirit is freed from fear and ultimately from flesh as a rendering of the free will's struggle against the limitations of material necessity. When the pure and self-less will achieve its objective of uniting itself with the divine purpose, it fulfills its earthly role. Quilp is the will gone wrong, attempting to compel all things to obey and yield; Nell's grandfather lacks will and is the dangerous toy of circumstance, but Nell represents endurance on behalf of others and achieves her final freedom in death, leaving her "will and testament" to those who survive and can benefit from the lesson of her being. Earlier in the story, Nell herself found comfort in thinking that the little scholar who died young went to a better existence. Her own death amplifies that lesson as "a mighty, universal Truth. When Death strikes down the innocent and young, for every fragile form from which he lets the panting spirit free, a hundred virtues rise. . . . In the Destroyer's steps there spring up bright creations that defy his power, and his dark path becomes a way of light to Heaven" (Dickens, *Shop*, 544).

Nell's career has changed much. Evil has been defeated (at least for a time), and many whose lives were touched by her have been greatly improved; Kit treasures her memory and has improved his life, Dick Swiveller has undergone a healthy but painful transformation. Dick's is an interesting case where will is concerned. Like a mockery of the classical hero, Dick rails against the "fate or destiny" that has reduced him to poverty and servitude and assigns responsibility for his acts and deeds to "his unlucky destiny" (Dickens, *Shop*, 254, 260). But Dick's condition is the consequence of his own failings, not of an impersonal destiny. From being a creature who swivels one way or another depending upon the winds of circumstance, Dick learns to take command of his own existence. The Marchioness, a distorted reflection of Nell, is the apparent source of his change. Amazed by her capacity to control her own limited environment, Dick marvels "can these things be her destiny, or has some unknown person started an opposition to the decrees of fate?" (Dickens, *Shop*, 432) Ultimately, it is Nell who represents resistance to the seeming decrees of fate and who asserts the principle of individual freedom. There is, perhaps, some sly significance in the name Dick assigns to the Marchioness when he undertakes to educate and improve her. Like an Oedipus spared the tragic consequences of destiny, Dick marries his own Sophronia Sphynx, who masks no evil future but unveils the mystery of love, self-sacrifice, and self-discipline.

This allegorical novel's "one common tale" ends in a cemetery, where the sexton, so conscious of the uncertainty of life yet so sure of his own immortality, is the "type of all mankind" (Dickens, *Shop*, 397). When our narrator has brought his good characters to their happy conclusion through the power of his own creative will, he reminds us that so in life "do things pass away, like a tale that is told" (Dickens, *Shop*, 555). In his narrator and in his allusion to the Bible, Dickens identifies tale telling as a way of understanding and dealing with the world. Human life is like a story, but at the same time man's free will enables him to shape the story of his will. As we have seen in part 1, Victorian attitudes were primarily teleological and will was associated, as in Hazlitt, with projection of a narrative pattern into the future. Gradually Dickens refined his manner of expressing this developmental attitude.

The *Old Curiosity Shop* depends very little upon the realities of quotidian existence. In later novels, Dickens made greater use of realistic details; they too carry a heavy symbolic weight but, except for *Hard Times*, do not again assume the diagrammatic order of this novel. *The Old Curiosity Shop* is a sermon, *Hard Times* is a harangue. But from early in his career, Dickens was trying to come to terms with problems of human freedom and responsibility. In the first novels he did not clearly distinguish how some men might be determined and others free. I believe that Rhonda Wilcox Nelms is right to focus on *Barnaby Rudge* as a work in which the complexity of Dickens's attitude becomes manifest. In *Pickwick* and *Oliver*, free will and determinism are opposed to one another in separate portions of the novel. "In *Barnaby*, however, the early free will section is set up carefully to be gradually undermined in the second part, moving from individuals, to social forces, to, ultimately, the providential power behind it all which is so overwhelmingly apparent in the penultimate chapter of the book." This pattern will "develop into the exquisite interplay of the two halves of *Bleak House*" (Nelms, 124).

But a third integral is required in this moral calculus—providence, the purposive movement of the story of life. Alexander Welsh sees *Martin Chuzzlewit* (1843–44) as the first text to teach "providence according to Dickens. The false and the misled in the novel foolishly believe that they are the children of Providence; to surprise and punish them Dickens has Martin Chuzzlewit senior play the role of God." Bringing that judgment upon Pecksniff, old Martin reminds him that the evil he did he did "of his own free will and agency."[14] Marley's Ghost in *A Christmas Carol* (1844) offers a graphic image of man's self-enslavement in wickedness when he responds to Scrooge's question of why he is fettered. " 'I wear the chain I forged in life,' replied the Ghost. 'I made it link by link, and yard by yard; I girded it on of my own free will, and of my own free will I wore it.' "[15] Scrooge has the opportunity to ungird himself of his chains and by his own free will release himself from the fetters of circumstance. But Scrooge's case is emphatically exceptional. Generally men must live with the consequences of their acts.

Dombey and Son (1846–48) intimates the relentlessness of this largely determinist sentiment. Steven Marcus explains that Mr. Dombey begins as a "worshipper of the will and idolator of his self-appointed destiny" and in this arrogant view "embodies in part the ethos of the nineteenth-century businessman, who conceived of the world as a kind of neutral material to be acted upon and fashioned to one's design" (Marcus, 323). But a heavy sense of the power of circumstance broods over the book. Little Paul's extinction, Edith Dombey's humiliating acceptance of an unwanted, mercenary marriage, Mr. Morfin's habituation to familiar conditions, John Carker's prolonged debasement for a single error, Solomon Gills's stagnant business—these and other elements of the story suggest a world where escape from determining conditions is all but impossible.

This world seems to be governed by men with power, like Dombey and Carker, one by inherited right, the other through craft. But neither of these representatives of power and control recognizes the design that guides human existence, and by placing themselves in opposition to it they bring about their own collapses. By contrast, those who are guided by love and self-sacrifice learn to see that higher pattern and their influence spreads. Florence gradually attracts to her a band of faithful believers, ultimately including her desperate father. These people are generally powerless but good of heart—Susan Nipper, Mr. Toots, Captain Cuttlefish, Walter Gay. But it is they who slowly turn the tide of the novel.

Dombey and Son teaches us not to confuse free will and strength of will. There are powerful ironies in the uneven contest represented in the natures of Carker and Florence. His abilities are numerous, his strength of will prodigious, and yet, because he is a slave to his impulses and ambitions, his will is not free. He is on the track that leads to death from the outset.[16] His course is determined precisely because he cannot free his will from what John Bunyan would easily have described as Satan. Mr. Dombey is no more free, being a servant of Mammon and his own gigantic pride. He has power but no true freedom. Only those who can picture to themselves what it means to go beyond the self are truly free. Despite external constraints, they are free because moral alternatives are open to them. All of this is implicit in *Dombey and Son.* It becomes far more evident in *David Copperfield.*

Like all of Dickens's novels, *David Copperfield* calls attention to such powerful dichotomies as freedom and constraint, charity and acquisition, order and chaos. But these dichotomies, though often obvious, are seldom simple. So it is possible to say that in *Copperfield* Steerforth, the agent of so much disorder and suffering, is irresponsible because his mother has spoiled him. His will is undisciplined, and yet, when stirred, Steerforth can channel it to whatever end he seeks. Steerforth does not lack will; he lacks an object for the action of his will. But, in a more significant way, he lacks *free* will because he is so *self*-willed. Steerforth needs a pilot to teach his will its limits and its appropriate goal.

Steerforth is only one of many characters in the novel who could have benefited from a *proper* guidance. Dora and Em'ly have also been spoiled.

David, who has suffered under a malign and a benign "tyranny," begins his married life unprepared for the special discipline and forebearance it requires. The Murdstones were no model of hymeneal harmony but neither was Aunt Betsey. Puzzled by the incomplete joy of his marriage, David muses, "I did feel, sometimes, for a little while, that I could have wished my wife had been my counsellor: had had more character and purpose, to sustain me, and improve me by; had been endowed with power to fill up the void which somewhere seemed to be about me; but I felt as if this were an unearthly consummation of my happiness, that never had been meant to be, and never could have been."[17] David's most important recognition is the danger of his own "undisciplined heart."[18] *David Copperfield* may be more about the heart than it is about the will, but the two cannot be separated in Dickens's scheme of values, and in this novel, Dickens discovered that he could embody his lesson about human nature in the way that he told his tale, and to do this he boldly made his narrator a storyteller composing the story of his own life.

Chris Brooks has suggested that inserting David as narrator between himself and his reader allowed Dickens to reveal David's understanding of his life along with the technique by which he does this.[19] That technique is very complex, for David's story is told in retrospect by a trained author of fiction. Many artful devices are evident in David's telling, most notably, perhaps, the foreshadowings relating to Em'ly's fall and Steerforth's death. Patterns of imagery are clearly flagged; thus related images of sea and storm culminate in a chapter entitled "Tempest," where inner and outer storms are brought to a simultaneous climax.

Felicity Hughes argues that Dickens the novelist self-consciously commented upon David Copperfield the novelist. She says that "David offers a naive, unphilosophical view of his own experience; that adult David offers, at the same time, a systematic interpretation of that experience behind young David's back as it were; and that Charles Dickens simultaneously suggests a critique of that systematic interpretation offered by adult Copperfield, behind *his* back."[20] Hughes claims that David is attracted to evil characters because he cannot resist their mesmeric powers, but David is equally drawn to good characters like Betsey, Mr. Peggotty, Agnes, and so forth. In fact, young David is attracted to others because he has not located a source of strength within himself. He learns gradually to exert his will upon the world around him by discovering the true meaning of that world through his capacity for narration. Hughes indicates that David's progress—reflected in young David, adult David, and Dickens as narrator—is from fairy tale and fable, to romance, to the biblical truth of allegory.[21] David's source of power appears very early. As a melancholy child, he has recourse to great fictions as a form of escape. While traveling from home to school, he makes up stories about the potentially happy homes he imagines along the way. At school, he establishes himself as Steerforth's favorite by playing the story telling Scheherazade to his demanding Sultan (Dickens, *Copperfield*, 93).

David's capacity to imagine a pattern in his life as coherent as those in fiction and with as great a meaning proves his salvation. By contrast, Steerforth considers narratives merely as amusements and diversions, though at one seriously low and revealing point in his history, he discloses a lingering wish that moral tales were true. " 'I wish with all my soul I had been better guided,' he exclaimed. 'I wish with all my soul I could guide myself better.' " This is Steerforth's lament to David even as he is planning to ruin Em'ly and betray his friend. He explains his blue mood as the *aberglaube* of childhood moralizing tales. " 'At odd dull times, nursery tales come up into the memory, unrecognized for what they are. I believe I have been confounding myself with the bad boy who "didn't care," and became food for lions—a grander kind of going to the dogs, I suppose' " (Dickens, *Copperfield*, 322). The passage ends with Steerforth's wish that he had had a steadfast and judicious father, but the very point of *David Copperfield* is that we all do have a steadfast and judicious Father, if we will only listen to his story and take the meaning into our lives.

David is slow to do so. He begins by noting parallels between his own life and the famous secular stories he has read, from *The Arabian Nights* to *Robinson Crusoe*. The mature version of this practice resembles F. D. Maurice's view of history in which all historical events are analogous because they all direct our attention to the same few truths. Thus the model of ancient Israel is repeated in Christian Rome and modern England. For Dickens, the parallels are both simpler and more complex. Ham and Em'ly forgiving the fallen Martha reflects Christ's pardoning of Magdalene, a fact emphasized by Brown's illustration, which places a picture of Christ's act directly above the kneeling Martha. Behind the door in this illustration is a picture of Eve tempted by the serpent, suggesting an even older model of human behavior repeated endlessly. Such direct or implied analogies recur throughout Dickens's mature writings.[22] What makes them stand out in *Copperfield* is that David himself is a self-conscious narrator aware of the methods he is using to influence his audience. David arrogates to himself the powers of a deity in shaping the story of his life as though he exists in a timeless region where he may choose any perspective he likes. Hence, the astonishing statement that opens chapter 40, "The Tempest": "I now approach an event in my life, so indelible, so awful, so bound by an infinite variety of ties to all that has preceded it in these pages, that, from the beginning of my narrative, I have seen it growing larger and larger as I advanced, like a great tower in a plain, and throwing its fore-cast shadow even on the incidents of my childish days" (Dickens, *Copperfield*, 784). If the events of childhood really felt the shadow of later events falling upon them, then the later events are predetermined, if only in the artist's retrospect and they mimick God's universal knowledge. In any case, David admits that his narrative has been composd of an infinite variety of ties and of foreshadowings. He has transformed the flat plain that Steerforth used as a metaphor for purposeless human existence into a landscape to set in relief the monumental event that organizes that waste space. Experience receives moral form, a story like those haunted Steerforth and could have saved him had he believed in a Divine Author.

David begins his last chapter, "And now my written story ends," and ends it with an emblem. He has learned to discipline his heart, to subordinate his desires to a larger purpose, to free his will by putting it in the service of a greater good. There is ambiguity in his opening line because the end of his written story is his end as a character as well. Thus the real author, Dickens, brings his character's story to a close, as God will bring each living creature's to a close. At this close we may all hope to approximate David's condition. Throughout his narration, Agnes, the lamb of God, has been the abiding model of the self-sacrifice David has learned so arduously. Now she stands beside him, both human and spiritual guide, the tutelary spirit of the tale he concludes and the tale that he is.

> I turn my head, and see it, in its beautiful serenity, beside me. My lamp burns low, and I have written far into the night; but the dear presence, without which I were nothing, bears me company.
>
> Oh Agnes, oh my soul, so may thy face be by me when I close my life indeed; so may I, when realities are melting from me like the shadows which I now dismiss, still find thee near me, pointing upwards! (Dickens, *Copperfield*, 877)

David Copperfield reveals Dickens's attentive relation of narrative to what we may call his philosophical convictions, but the novel that most obviously demonstrates self-conscious narrative technique in the service of intellectual beliefs is *Bleak House* (1852–53). The double narration of this novel has generated a great deal of discussion, but for present purposes, one chief distinction seems clear. The harsh third-person narrator presents a determinist view of social and individual destiny that conflicts with Esther Summerson's cordial assumption that man has the capacity to decide his fate. In working out this submerged dispute between determinism and free will, both narrators assume a larger design of which all men are only a part. To one voice, that greater design is an irreversible fate, while to the other, it is a providential opportunity. Through the unusual device of double narration, Dickens conveys the belief that if man has faith in the central human qualities embodied in the teachings of Christ—love and self-discipline—he can participate in directing his fate.[23]

Bleak House operates at two levels. Esther's is the private, subjective view; the third-person narrator's is the historical, objective view. While the novel dramatizes values for individual behavior, it is also a parabolic version of Dickens's larger social and historical attitudes made clear both through biblical and historical allusions and in the novel's very form. Dickens's hopes for the future were based upon a faith in individual effort. From early in his career he championed political and social reform, but his support of reform was not theoretical, for he counted more on the forceful application of individual human will to bring about favorable change than he did on any political scheme. He distrusted politicians because they valued programs over individuals. The organized philanthropies in *Bleak House* are samples of the failure of this approach. Esther's personal sympathy to immediate need is far preferable.

In his early novels, Dickens viewed evil in individual terms, but the later works reveal a growing sense that, while good is a product of individual exertion, evil is mainly the consequence of inept institutions or unhealthy social conditions. *David Copperfield* represents the climax of Dickens's belief in the individual's power to effect good; *Hard Times* was the first of his novels to state clearly the dangers to that free spirit from the imposition of system. Between these two novels, *Bleak House* presents a world balanced between individual affirmation and materialist negation, between the individual power to bring about useful change and environmental forces operating to prevent that change. The novel exhibits Dickens's confidence in man's power to make a better world but soberly indicates the limitations of that power. Ultimately, the voice of freedom overcomes the voice of determinism, but it is a long and weary contest. *Bleak House* may be seen as Dickens's first conscious working out of a dilemma that continued to occupy him—the need to believe in the power of individual will in the face of a growing conviction that the forces shaping man all but extinguish that power.

As we have seen, Dickens realized that freedom and power of the will could be applied malevolently as well as beneficially. The powerful wills of such rascals as Quilp, Ralph Nickleby, and Uriah Heep are inevitably frustrated because their exertions are self-serving and therefore self-destructive. While strong will is often an attribute of wicked characters who abuse it, strength of will is essential for successful heroes and heroines who achieve love and tranquillity through their ability to forget themselves and to sympathize with others. However, as Fred Kaplan suggests, first they must "establish an active identity through the exertion of energy under the control of will. Without such self-identity one is at the mercy of external forces that may diminish one even more."[24]

Like Carlyle, Dickens believed that the illusion of a determined existence results from a failure of the will or a false conviction that fate or destiny directs events. In one case, men abdicate control and find satisfaction in assuming that things are as they must be; in the other, shrewd men conclude that destiny may be comprehended but not altered. Tulkinghorn and the whole institution of the Law illustrate this latter condition, for both, while bound to work out official processes to the last detail, do not presume to alter an inevitable destiny that concerns them very little. Only strong-willed but selfless and therefore free individuals can overcome the belief in a determined existence. Esther, as disciplined as Tulkinghorn, has a faith that his cold, dispassionate mind lacks. She too believes in a scheme, but it is the benevolent scheme revealed in the teachings of the Bible and specifically in the words of Christ. She does not hoard human mysteries but sees the divine mysteries revealed.

While the third-person narrator describes a society lamed in its will and devoted to the mechanical support of the status quo and to the frustration of change, Esther offers a promise of useful action. The gloomy anonymous growler presents detached views of a determined world; Esther's cheerful voice counters with subjective responses conveying the sense of a world open to modification. The third-person narrator never participates, never acts, but Esther is integral to her tale and her reactions are positive, not denunciatory or ironic. Failings in others prompt her sympathy, not her scorn. Her selflessness frequently evokes a similar altruism in others. Her greatest frustration is with those who, having the understanding and opportunity to do so, refuse to employ their wills to any good end. She deplores Skimpole's parasitical idleness, Mrs. Pardiggle's misdirected vigor, and Richard Carstone's aimlessness, because she believes that beneath all human activity lies the power of the disciplined will to change things for the better. Hence, while the Dedlocks, Tulkinghorns, Smallweeds, and even Richard seem involved in a puzzling "net of destiny" which limits their ability to transform the world, Esther conceives of her life as fulfilling an equally strict, but more positive design, a design instilled in her youth and fostered by her mentor, John Jarndyce.

From her earliest days, Esther was trained to view life in terms of spiritual authority. Although her godmother's version of this code was unduly harsh, Esther reconceived it in terms compatible with the forgiving and sympathetic practices of John Jarndyce. Godmother, Jarndyce, and Esther all believe that there is a spiritual scheme to which individuals must accommodate themselves, but there is a characteristic difference in the way in which each perceives that scheme. For the godmother, human acts beget unalterable retributions; for Jarndyce, men are free to follow the providential design, but are generally too weak or blind to do so; for Esther, the essence of human nature is to make one's acts conform to the greater design.

An important scene occurring early in the novel establishes a model for understanding the design that Esther follows and the structural pattern upon which Dickens constructed his tale. One evening, as Esther is reading to her godmother from the Bible, she comes upon a passage which the godmother recognizes as acutely apt. It is the passage in John 8:6–7 quoting Christ's caution to the tormentors of the adulterous woman: "He that is without sin among you, let him cast the first stone at her."[25] Esther's godmother realizes that she has played the role of accuser, for she has condemned Esther's mother for violating the sexual code and has let the child understand that she is morally compromised from birth, though she does not disclose her illegitimacy. Esther's godmother assumes a predetermined fate for Esther because of her mother's sin, but that is not the message of the creed she claims to follow. Torn between her interpretation of Christian duty and the words of Christ implicitly condemning her unsympathetic attitude toward the fallen, she responds with another quotation from Christ that seems to justify her. Springing up, with her hands to her head as though in agony or confusion, the godmother cries out "in an awful voice, from quite another part of the book: 'Watch ye therefore! lest coming suddenly he find you sleeping. And what I say unto you I say unto all, Watch!' " (Dickens, *House*, 19).[26] This passage lacks the first's compassion but is equally concerned with justice. It is Christ's response, in Mark 13, to his apostles' question concerning the fulfillment of their savior's predictions. After a long account of the many events that will transpire before that time, a time known only to the Father, Christ concludes with the following words.

> Take ye heed, watch and pray: for ye know not when the time is. For the Son of man is a man taking a far journey, who left his house, and gave authority to his servants, and to every man his work, and commanded the porter to watch. Watch ye therefore: for ye know not when the master of the house cometh, at even, or at midnight, or at the cock-crowing, or in the morning: Lest coming suddenly he find you sleeping. And what I say unto you I say unto all, Watch. (Mark 13:33–37)

Despite the godmother's attempted vindication, Christ's warning does not support her but clearly signifies that men determine their own destinies. They are given the power to labor for good. If they fail, they do so freely. Dickens enlisted Christ's words to emphasize his conviction that man is free, thereby signaling that Esther has the power to shape her character, just as mankind has the power to shape its destiny.

The scriptural passage from Mark contains motifs of sleeping, waking, work, and idleness that recur throughout *Bleak House*, extending the significance of Christ's message from a personal to a broadly social application. The house that the Son of Man has left in mankind's care is typified in Bleak House and caricatured in Chesney Wold, but finally it is the entire world of men, represented in this novel as English society. Events at Bleak House provide a miniature example of the proper fulfillment of Christ's advice; John Jarndyce is watchful, not only attending to the actual property with which he is entrusted but careful as well for the persons with whom his responsibilities involve him. Esther quickly assumes the caretaking duties of Bleak House because she too is conscious of the trust placed in her and knows how to care for others. She need never fear the Master's coming. Everything at Bleak House is done promptly and according to rule and order, yet with love. In this it is the absolute contrast to the Court of Chancery.

Chesney Wold, the other major house in *Bleak House*, is only superficially patterned on the model recommended by Christ. Although Sir Leicester is a good steward of his property and is attentive to the family name, he has forgotten that he holds his estate merely in trust and that his duty is to keep it in readiness for his Master, not to appropriate it for his own pleasures and purposes. Sir Leicester's quarrel with Boythorn turns upon this issue of ownership as opposed to use; his abiding fear of a revenant Wat Tyler communicates his vague recognition that his appropriation is not fully authorized.[27] In contrast to Bleak House, there is no feeling of human brotherhood or even family love at Chesney Wold. There, all interest in propriety and order is founded on material concerns. It is, therefore, doubly ironic that his finest possession, Honoria, is beyond Sir Leicester's possession in any but a legal sense. Her feelings are fixed elsewhere. Their marriage mirrors Sir Leicester's relationship to his other property.

If Bleak House is a model of God's house well kept, English society is an example of God's house neglected. The Court of Chancery represents the stewards who have not remained alert but have slumbered at their tasks or wandered from their duties. The fog that encompasses London emanates from the Court and does not merely pervade it. Opening references to mud emphasize the Court's occupation with material concerns at the expense of human feelings. From the very outset, the Court is associated with sleepiness, ineptitude, and waste, and both the third-person narrator and Esther convey the sense that a judgment is building against these unwise stewards. The nature of that judgment is intimated by references to Wat Tyler and especially by the fate of Krook, the mock Lord Chancellor. Though befogged and besotted, he considers himself shrewd yet cannot keep his house in order and lapses constantly into stupor, finally meeting his end in a horrifying foretaste of brimstone and hellfire. In the case of Chancery, the returning Master will find his stewards sleeping and judge them for their dereliction, a judgment adumbrated by Miss Flight who repeats with the insistence of a death knell that she expects justice in her case on "the Day of Judgment." Her statement masks a sad irony concerning her own expectations but also reveals the larger irony that true judgment will fall upon her tormentors, not upon her.

Krook's gruesome fate is described by the third-person narrator; the more compassionate Esther presents a comparable, though milder, example of punishment for misguided interest. Like Sir Leicester and the Court of

Chancery, Richard Carstone has mistaken the object for the task assigned. Instead of seeking a service to perform, he lays claim to a material estate. In so doing, he disregards the excellent model provided by John Jarndyce. In the end, Richard realizes that he has selfishly neglected his proper duty and asks forgiveness of his guardian, admitting that his hopes for the resolution of his case were a dream. "And you, being a good man, can pass it as such, and forgive and pity the dreamer, and be lenient and encouraging when he wakes?" (Dickens, *House*, 870) But the dreamer must wake betimes. Richard has awakened only in time to recognize his folly.[28] The judgment that has been anticipated throughout the novel with consummate narrative skill has come down. But it is not the judgment expected. Justice has been meted out but not by the Court of Chancery. And the significance of Esther's establishment of a new Bleak House, where the lessons of Christ will be put into effect, where the stewards will see their duties and carry them out even into the world at large, is that a further judgment impends still over the entire nation.[29]

This further judgment is indicated by a fairy-tale amplification of the scriptural advice underlying the morality of the novel. Both narrators in *Bleak House* recognize the importance of fables. The third-person narrator notes the distorting effect upon the Smallweeds of a neglect of "all story-books, fairy tales, fictions, and fables" (Dickens, *House*, 288). Esther, following the example of the New Testament, constantly employs fables and fairy tales to instruct children. Utilizing fairy tales requires an imaginative sympathy that views them as models of morality, like Christ's parables, not as mere diversions. Dickens clearly approved this method of education, which resembled his own narrative method of interpreting the world.[30]

Early in *Bleak House*, Dickens suggests a fairy-tale structure that foreshadows the New Testament pattern that appears a few pages later.[31] Having already indicted Chancery for its failures, the narrator observes that Sir Leicester approves the tedious operations of the Court with which his social sphere, the world of fashion, is closely allied and thus condemned by association: "Both the world of fashion and the court of Chancery are things of precedent and usage; oversleeping Rip Van Winkles, who have played at strange games through a deal of thundery weather; sleeping beauties, whom the Knight will wake oneday, when all the stopped spits in the kitchen shall begin to turn prodigiously!" (Dickens, *House*, 8). The worlds of Chancery and of fashion, both composed of neglectful leaders of society, are filled with sleepers who will one day be rudely awakened by a Knight with a capital *K* who will come on no romantic mission but as a judge.[32] The Knight is the Son of Man, the master of the house who returns from his journey to find the servants sleeping. From this point of view, the spits that turn prodigiously suggest a lurid Last Judgment scene. Krook's demise is analogous to this prophetic event.

The worlds of fashion and Chancery are associated with fairy tales, but Esther sets herself off from fanciful and unreal realms. Early in her story, she says that she was brought up "—like some of the princesses in fairy stories, only I was not charming—by my godmother" (Dickens, *House*, 15). Esther's life does not have the preordained symmetry of the fairy tale princess who lives in a largely determined world. Sleeping Beauty, for example, simply waits to be awakened. Esther must actively shape her own life. Chesney Wold, so alluring to the young and ambitious Honoria, is a "Fairy-land to visit, but a desert to live in" (Dickens, *House*, 11). It is as though Cinderella marries her Prince only to find his castle stale and ungratifying. Though using fairy tales to instruct the young, Esther knows better than to live in fable, for she believes in the greater scheme of God's providence. Unlike David Copperfield, who calls attention to his skills in shaping the story of his life, Esther the storyteller must make her story seem free from such shaping devices. David is the medium of his experience, but Esther assumes that we will see through her to the significance of her subject, hence her embarrassment when she withholds information. Precisely because she knows the rhetorical power of story telling, she must not seem to be using it when she tells her own story. Hers is an utterly realistic perception of earthly life, scrupulously renouncing even the most innocent illusions and thereby helping her to escape the fates of those who live primarily in the service of one illusion or another. She believes in the interconnectedness of men and events but does not pretend to comprehend the whole design. She acts out her individual part, believing that her free and unselfish exertions serve the purpose of providence.

Bleak House is outstanding for the manner in which apparently disparate parts serve a larger design. I believe that Dickens consciously embodied one important teaching of his novel in its very form, for there is a contest between predetermined pattern and free detail throughout *Bleak House*. John Forster, who knew very well how intriguing the notion of coincidence was to Dickens, pointed out the relevance of all details to the story in *Bleak House*, asserting that "nothing is introduced at random, everything tends to the catastrophe."[33] As though to emphasize the deterministic nature of the complexly interrelated events, Forster referred to the "chain" of small incidents leading to Lady Dedlock's death and the "chain" of interest that binds the inhabitants of Chesney Wold, Bleak House, and Chancery together.

The binding of detail to design by the device of coincidence has continued to intrigue readers of *Bleak House*. George Gissing, a devoted admirer, complained that because "arbitrary coincidence" replaces "well-contrived motive" in the novel, it resembles "a mechanical puzzle rather than the complications of human life."[34] Others have convincingly argued that the "unlikely chance, accident, coincidence . . . links of fate, crossed lines of destiny, secret moral alliances," and so forth, succeed in creating a powerful moral fable.[35] Some critics have modestly defended the coincidences as plausible, while others have demonstrated that Dickens's use of coincidence in *Bleak House* ultimately conveys a "sense that real life blends the casual and the causal, that things are connected and contingent, patterned and random, that we are both free and determined."[36] E. D. H. Johnson asserts that in Dickens's world, "the apparent randomness of existence conceals an underlying providence," and both he and W. J. Harvey emphasize John Jarndyce's words of advice to Richard Carstone: "Trust in nothing but Providence and your own efforts." Johnson provides evidence that Dickens himself viewed the structures of his fictions as imitations of divine providence.[37]

What is clear in all of these arguments is that the coincidental complexity of Dickens's plots makes *Bleak House* itself a model of a world in which design transcends individual character. Robert Caserio says that "Dickens's sense of plot relies upon a notion that small groups of separate characters or persons are somehow all the same character or person."[38] Karen Chase develops this line of thought, observing that "the movement of the Dickensian plot is the complex adjustment of an expressive system struggling to tame aggression, to relieve guilt, to modify desire, and to preserve innocence." In fact, she argues, the plot may be considered *Bleak House*'s most interesting character.[39] To transcend character, however, is not to dismiss or underrate it. Chase says it is still the task of characters in the novel to restore their independent wills and recover the ability to direct the course of events.[40] And Caserio finds that "the possibility of plot, of creatively wilful and purposeful action, is for Dickens and his characters the hope of rescue and release from this circle of pain."[41] That Dickens imitated providence in the construction of his tales does not mean that he was confident of all the moral rules governing his created world. In fact, beginning with *Bleak House*, it is more and more evident that complications of plot in Dickens's novels become a means of confronting the density of existence. J. Hillis Miller wisely suggests that "everywhere in *Bleak House* we see characters who are engaged in an attempt to vanquish the chaos of a merely phenomenal world"; the true detective becomes the narrator, who attempts, "through mere passive perception and the exercise of constructive intelligence to discover the laws of the world he sees."[42] In *Bleak House*, detection is a conspicuous part of the story, ultimately focusing in a genuine detective. "But unlike the Dickensian narrator, Bucket belongs to the fictional universe and participates in its dramatic action. In this way, the detective becomes an incarnation of the divine narrative privilege that Dickens usually reserves for himself. He brings the plot's agency down to a human scale."[43] We must remember, however, that while the third-person narrator analyzes an offensive world of stagnation, idleness, pride, and folly, another observer is composing a totally different picture of that same world. Moreover, where the third-person narrator is detached, ironic, and passive before the very forces he scorns for their passivity and negation, Esther Summerson is intimately engaged in the events of the story. She is changed by them, but more importantly, she changes them. Dickens employs a species of dialectic to examine two fundamentally opposed methods of interpreting existence. From the beginning, he provides signals to indicate which of these methods he prefers. But that does not invalidate, nor should it diminish, the significance of his exploration.

The third-person narrator pictures a dehumanized world that is both atomized and causally necessary. All of matter is composed of isolated units that nonetheless impinge upon one another in a sequence of causes and consequences in which there is apparently neither meaning nor feeling. Thus, in the opening passage of the novel, human characteristics are subordinated to qualities of the London fog. In the third-person narrator's world, human powers are subject to material forces beyond human control, forces which move in a direction generally unfavorable for mankind. And yet this world abounds with suggestions of intent: the prophetic legend of the Ghost's Walk at Chesney Wold, and the apparently inescapable fates of Nemo at the personal level and Tom-all-Alone's at the social level imply a nemesis or destiny operating within a dimension of purpose and not mere mechanicalness. Always the third-person narrator emphasizes the inevitability of events, the causal necessity that leads from small crimes to major consequences. The cold and frozen world of the Dedlocks, the reiterated hint of revolution, the relentless success of the Man of Iron, the ominous allegory hanging over Tulkinghorn, and the futility evident in the machinations of the Smallweeds all contribute to a sense of fatality. The greatest instance of this pattern is the case of Jarndyce and Jarndyce itself, for the many complications of this case have tempted those involved "into a loose way of letting bad things alone to take their own bad course, and a loose belief that if the world go wrong, it was, in some off-hand manner, never meant to go right" (Dickens, *House*, 5).

The world pictured by the third-person narrator is cold, stagnant, and determined because it describes isolation, selfishness, and idleness leading to the entrapment of human purpose in the apparent causal sequence of events. A good deal of will is expressed by Tulkinghorn, Lady Dedlock, Mademoiselle Hortense, and the Smallweeds, but all of these exertions of will lead toward stasis. Similarly, loss of will follows from an unthinking commitment to material circumstances, while freedom rests in the rejection of system for the reality of individual purpose. George Ford has demonstrated that Dickens believed "that human energy, responsibly directed, can be potent" and "that to admit the potential potency of human will in society is to eliminate the bleakness that we feel pervading the atmosphere" of the novel. He shows that Dickens's characters can be divided into those who are dedicated and hardworking and those who are "selfish or weak-willed indolent amateur dabblers."[44] Some are fully capable of aiding themselves, some are not, while others, though capable of self-help, refuse to act.

Richard Carstone, who abandons a rewarding human situation in favor of a corrupt system, is the principal example of man subordinating his will to a false external design. Richard creates his own nemesis and destroys himself. The huge, malign system of Chancery persists because men believe in it. Gridley is the smaller, Richard the larger embodiment of this fact. In these and other examples, Dickens particularizes Coleridge's observation that when men concentrate their wills upon themselves or upon material conditions, they soon come to believe that their lives are guided by an inescapable destiny or fate. The third-person narrator in *Bleak House* presents a world of men who have subordinated their wills to the wrong purposes or who have failed to employ their wills to any purpose at all: he depicts an existence that appears determined, fated, and inescapably destined because of selfishness—precisely the picture that Coleridge had rendered in *Aids to Reflection* and that is everywhere suggested in Carlyle's works, especially *Sartor Resartus*. Clearly, misdirected will and the failure of will constitute two major sources of suffering in *Bleak House*.

If there is any force that dispels the bleakness of *Bleak House*, it is Esther Summerson, who is able to achieve this reclamation of the world through her conviction that human will matters, and that, being free, it can change circumstances for the better. The third-person narrator shows a world deadened by submission to an existing material system, whereas Esther presents one in which individual effort can release men from the tyranny of circumstances and create an atmosphere of hope and joy. Esther has been described as the principal flaw in an otherwise powerful novel, but Robert A. Donovan has cautioned that we must distinguish Esther's function as narrator from her ostensible role as heroine. Though Esther does not explicitly state a rule of behavior, her observations constitute a "simple, traditional, and predictable system of moral values." Donovan adds that while Esther may seem sentimental to us, "we must recall her function to provide a sane and wholesome standard of morality in a topsy-turvy world."[45] Esther is not "static, consistent, passive," but acts upon the world and develops in her own character.[46] Like his other first-person narrators, she demonstrates Dickens's interest in psychological development and is an accurate psychological study. From the beginning, Esther guides her conduct according to a set of positive moral rules which modify her stern godmother's code. While that forceful woman impressed upon Esther the importance of "submission, self-denial, diligent work," she transforms the model to something far more benign, hoping to become, "industrious, contented, and kind-hearted."[47]

Prostration before a wrathful God is not the same as willed submission of self to a loving God's design.

If the third-person narrator is essentially pessimistic and inclined to describe events as necessary elements in a causal sequence, Esther is optimistic, recording circumstances that display the human potential for freedom and the reasons for hope. Esther succeeds in transforming the lives of unfortunate youngsters like Caddy Jellyby and Charley Neckett. In trying to help Jo, she transforms her own life. This transformation represents a monumental exertion of will. With the exception of figures like Jo and Guster, Esther Summerson is potentially the most determined character in *Bleak House*, for the conditions of her birth make escape from, or alteration of her fate, unlikely. However, while literally a "diseased" element of society, Esther becomes one of the principal healers in that society. Like her very appropriate partner, Allan Woodcourt, Esther believes that evil conditions can be changed, and she is willing to make the necessary sacrifice to bring about that change.

Esther's sacrifice is significant socially and personally. Attempting to succor Jo and Charley, Esther contracts a malady that symbolizes the interrelatedness of all humanity. At a more personal level, her ordeal frees Esther from the chain of destiny. Before her illness, Esther's beauty linked her inescapably with Lady Dedlock, her secret mother. Esther's physical transformation signals a profound change, suggesting that, in reaching out to her fellow man, she separates herself from Lady Dedlock's loveless fate. Esther suffers in order that others may be saved, and her Christ-like selflessness liberates her from the determined world of those who remain bound to the fates their own selfishness has created. During her illness, Esther dreams that she is one bead upon a flaming necklace strung together somewhere in a great black space. She prays to be taken off the circle of "inexplicable agony and misery," and her illness does remove her from this ring of destiny (Dickens, *House*, 489).[48] She will never more be bound to that circle of frustration. After her illness, Esther is freed from all that her mother represents. She has the power to make a new life.

The unusual device of double narration calls attention to the construction and purpose of *Bleak House*, which remains a richly complex work, but though *Bleak House* is more "constructed" than Dickens's earlier novels, though there is less free play in it, it does not greatly differ from works that had immediately preceded it. We have seen how the storm and water references in *David Copperfield* reveal the manner of Steerforth's death that is foreshadowed throughout the novel.[49] Equally clear is David's own need to tame his undisciplined heart. Other novels reveal a similar though unelaborated contention between the need for order and discipline and the relentlessness of events according to a system of mechanical causation. This contention is more apparent in *Bleak House* because the system of causation is more conspicuous (the connection between Tom-all-Alone's, Chancery, and Bleak House is an example), and because the two sides in the contest have separate representatives.

In the world of *Bleak House*, large forces draw individual lives together into an integrated pattern, but it remains with the individual will to perceive that pattern as destiny or providence.[50] The larger scheme may be benign and not dismally deterministic. A sign that we are meant to take the more hopeful view is the chilly third-person narrator's gradual allowance for exceptions to the determinist pattern under the pressure of Esther's persistent faith. For example, the happy release of Captain George from the entanglements that threaten him is recorded by the third-person narrator, who thus acknowledges at least one instance of the human ability to escape the limitations of society that men misconstrue as fate or destiny. Gradually, then, the two narratives approach one another until the third-person narrator concludes with a balanced picture of peace and stupor at Chesney Wold. But it is the happy and energetic Esther who has the last and hopeful word in her new Bleak House dedicated to service.

Both narratives suggest that, by ignoring their true roles in life, men construct a force in circumstance that acts against them and which they perceive as destiny—a fatal inevitability in a hostile world. Knowing their true Christian functions in life, on the other hand, men may discover joy by fulfilling their parts in a providential pattern that is the bright counterpart of bitter destiny. The intellect, roughly represented by the third-person narrator, cannot provide hope, for it fixes its attention on material, measurable objects. But the subjective self, the sympathetic heart, penetrates beneath the surface of things to the substance of reality, which is spiritual and unmeasurable. This lesson we have already seen propounded in the simpler and more obvious morality tale, *A Christmas Carol.* As long as his mind is turned to material things, Scrooge lacks joy, and his life seems bound by an iron chain of necessity. Once his heart is instructed, he is able to reconstitute his world, and the destiny that seemed so inescapable and so necessary changes too. A new, hopeful pattern of providence replaces it. In a complex and less exuberant manner, Dickens presents the same argument in *Bleak House.* Now, however, we are in Scrooge's place and we must listen to the ominous or inspiriting narrators of the novel as Scrooge listened to the different Christmas voices. Like Scrooge, we are meant to choose the hopeful way in which men are free to shape their lives toward a happy purpose.

There is a design governing events in *Bleak House.* Those who resist the true purpose of existence feel imprisoned and fated, while those who comply with that purpose feel free and blessed. If we suppose that the world is fated and that we are not free, it is because we are asleep, we dream, failing to attend to our appointed tasks. We are blind to providence. Awakened, we shake off the dream of fate and put our blindness behind us, as Esther does, and take our fates in our own hands. Only through willed selflessness and love can men recognize the providential design offered in the teachings of Christ.[51] Watch, and do your duty, Christ had said. That way lies contentment. It is Esther's voice that keeps the value of simple acceptance, resignation, and willed goodness before us. By setting her voice against that of the more penetrating and bitter third-person narrator, Dickens renders all the more sharply his view of the true nature of human freedom.

I do not intend to follow this subject out through the remainder of Dickens's novels, but it is worthwhile to glance at his treatment of it in the latter part of his career. Will is an important theme in *Little Dorrit* (1855–57), for example. Near the beginning of the novel, Arthur Clennam, the novel's protagonist, has a conversation in Marseilles with his new friend Mr. Meagles, who is returning to England and who encourages Clennam to do the same. Clennam says he might do so, and Meagles replies that he means that Clennam should return "with a will." Clennam's response paints a stark picture of a type of character more common to the later fiction than to Dickens's early, more positive novels.

> "I have no will. That is to say," he coloured a little, "next to none that I can put in action now. Trained by main force; broken, not bent; heavily ironed with an object on which I was never consulted and which was never mine; shipped away to the other end of the world before I was of age, and exiled there until my father's death there, a year ago; always grinding in a mill I always hated; what is to be expected from *me* in middle life? Will, purpose, hope? All those lights were extinguished before I could sound the words."
> "Light 'em up again!" said Mr. Meagles.[52]

But Clennam cannot so easily assert command over his life because he lacks the self-confidence of those who trust in their own power to guide events. He actively distrusts his inner self. Insecure in his hopes regarding Pet Meagles, he displaces his feelings, telling himself that his sore heart and his "weakness" of loving "was nobody's, nobody's within his knowledge, why should it trouble him? And yet it did trouble him" (Dickens, *Dorrit*, 200). Throughout the novel, this sense of nonentity haunts Clennam, keeping him at odds with the world. Shaped by confining and disfiguring influences, he lacks the will to alter himself because he cannot believe in himself.

The same chapter that introduces Clennam introduces Miss Wade. She does not, like Clennam, lack a sense of her own worth, but like him she sees herself as a victim. Her paranoia, however, is extreme and Dickens later describes her as a "self-tormentor." She is proud, with "an unsubduable nature," and she is a fatalist. When the small company brought together accidentally by the quarantine at Marseilles is set at liberty and is separating, Miss Wade responds to Mr. Meagles's farewell by saying: "In our course through life we shall meet the people who are coming to meet us, from many strange places and by many strange roads . . . and what it is set to us to do to them, and what it is set to them to do to us, will all be done" (Dickens, *Dorrit*, 25). She sounds this notes more than once, but Dickens, as he concludes the chapter, reminds us that there is another way of taking Miss Wade's vision.

> The day passed on; and again the wide stare stared itself out; and the hot night was on Marseilles; and through it the caravan of the morning, all dispersed, went their appointed ways. And thus ever, by day and night, under the sun and under the stars, climbing the dusty hills and toiling along the weary plains, journeying by land and journeying by sea, coming and going so strangely, to meet and to act and react on one another, move all we restless travellers through the pilgrimage of life. (Dickens, *Dorrit*, 27)

The important word is "pilgrimage." There is a road for us to follow that passes down the vista of time. But the landscape is not meaningless; it is charged with significance for those who understand. Life is not an aimless wandering, but whether we realize or not, a series of choices we make in prosecuting our way.

Little Dorrit is both a practical and a metaphysical examination of imprisonment. Lionel Trilling in his preface to *Little Dorrit* noted that the novel was "about society in relation to the individual will," and that in an age that honored the creative will, prison was an apt image of all that tended to frustrate that will (Dickens, *Dorrit*, vi-vii). Trilling said that, like Freud, Dickens recognized the primacy of the will in his conception of the human mind, realizing "that the organization of the internal life is in the form, often fantastically parodic, of a criminal process in which the mind is at once the criminal, the victim, the police, the judge, and the executioner" (Dickens, *Dorrit*, viii). I have mentioned the "will-lessness" and self-punishment in Clennam and Miss Wade, but *Little Dorrit* is populated with many versions of these character traits. Mrs. Clennam and Mr. Dorrit cannot escape the psychological enclosures of their own imaginations. The careers of selfish beings like Merdle and Blandois reveal that their apparent liberty masks a real entrapment. Merdle always seems to be taking himself into custody and Blandois follows out his doom from prison cell to death in the collapse of the Clennam house.

Dickens believed that men imprisoned themselves. He would have understood Shelley's Prometheus. Submission alone deprived a man of freedom.

One's surroundings, though influential, cannot deprive man of free will. Each man chooses enslavement or freedom.[53] Only one character in *Little Dorrit* fully exhibits this truth, and it is Amy Dorrit herself. Amy has grown up in the unpropitious atmosphere of the Marshalsea Prison and yet hers is a truly free spirit. She has not yielded to environmental influences; "she was inspired to be something which was not what the rest were and to be that something, different and laborious, for the sake of the rest" (Dickens, *Dorrit*, 71).

Amy recognizes the degree to which her father and the people she meets in society remain imprisoned and how they enslave themselves to material things, as for example, the appurtenances of wealth in the Merdle and Dorrit families. But she never wavers, and in the end, her unassailable love and virtue redeem Clennam, who has fallen ill yearning for freedom from a tawdry, unjust world. When he returns to consciousness, he sees Amy Dorrit's compassionate eyes turned toward him. Her readiness to pour out her "inexhaustible wealth of goodness upon him, did not steady Clennam's trembling voice or hand, or strengthen him in weakness. Yet, it inspired him with an inward fortitude that rose with his love" (Dickens, *Dorrit*, 758).

Dickens uses no obvious narrative technique to embody the theme of freedom and confinement, aside from the intensely interwoven plot lines suggesting an existence more like a net than some rich tapestry, yet the theme is clearly central throughout the novel, and Amy Dorrit, the one truly free because truly unselfish person in the book, is the fulcrum upon which the plot turns.[54] *Little Dorrit* is not a moral fable like *Old Curiosity Shop*, but its message inscribed in the world of credible events, is similar. Chris Brooks argues that *Little Dorrit* "is a symbolic narrative which enacts processes of entrapment and frustration in the reader's consciousness through the very act of reading."[55] I would not carry my argument that far but would repeat that, as author of a world composed mainly of misapplied will, Dickens carefully wrought his tale to show both the inextricable linking of human destinies and the power of selflessness in overcoming the power of events. He so shapes the lives of his characters that, in retrospect, we see not aimless voyaging in a labyrinth or trackless sea but a guided pilgrimage along a path for which the signs are clear to those who can read.

There is less a sense of providential guidance in *Little Dorrit* than in *Copperfield* and *Bleak House*, but this providential key returns with full orchestration in *A Tale of Two Cities* (1859), the inspiration for which Dickens credited to Carlyle's historical vision. Dickens's novel, like Carlyle's *French Revolution*, insists that historical events follow a course set down by divine justice, a course unalterable by individual human choices. Man's free will cannot change the ultimate aims of providence, though it may affect the manner in which those aims are brought about. At first Dickens creates a strong impression or inevitability in events—that men are mere leaves in a sea of causation. Fate, we are told early in the story, has already singled out the tree that will become the guillotine.[56] The narrator, in a striking passage about the essentially secret and mysterious nature of each human being refers to events as "appointed" (Dickens, *Tale*, 10). Madame DeFarge menacingly hopes for Lucie's sake that "destiny" will keep her husband out of France (Dickens, *Tale*, 176). Her very knitting is a parody of the Fates who determine the lives of men by spinning and cutting the threads of their existence. Mr. Lorry is described as having been cut out as a bachelor from his cradle (Dickens, *Tale*, 184). All such references suggest a world borne forward on a stream of necessity.

At the same time, deeds and their consequences are assignable to men. The sufferings of the French peasants follow from the crimes and abuses of the French aristocracy. Revolution follows upon repression. The Revolution itself may be seen both as an act of freedom or as a determined, inevitable consequence. And yet individual men and women can resist the impelling force of destiny. Carton is the outstanding example, but Miss Pross, Mr. Lorry, and Jerry Cruncher participate to some degree. Carton shares Clennam's self-denigration but is a harder case. Although he cannot muster the will to change his own life, he channels his will in selfless service of a principle, embodied by Lucie, that he worships. His act "revises" history.

The events of this novel are as intricately interwoven as those in other of Dickens's mature novels, again suggesting the web of destiny so frequently alluded to in these novels. But *A Tale of Two Cities* more forcefully explores destiny's double face; hence the novel's balanced style, emphasized by its opening lines and the many doublings and mirrorings of the story. Ultimately, the golden thread of love, self-sacrifice, and compassion shines through the knitted web of fate. The end of the novel discloses the brighter vision of order guiding human events revealed (Dickens, *Tale*, 357–58).

The narrator of *A Tale of Two Cities* obtrudes the story telling techniques that guide his readers' consciousnesses, conspicuously signaling foreshadowings and reverberations of events and marking important motifs—like resurrection—in an unmistakable way. Readers are made to feel that they are hearing a story, not being offered the illusion of witnessing historical events. This constant emphasis upon a shaped story evokes both the sense of necessity associated with fate and the sense of security associated with providence. We are given a clue to the proper understanding of this creative shaping power in Carton's reflections before his death when, in imagining the beneficial effects of his sacrifice, he composes the "story" of the future, which necessarily becomes the true conclusion of the novel. We cannot be meant to think that Carton is deceiving himself with a fable but must accept his vision of a time to come when Lucie's grandchild will visit his grave and remember him with respect and later tell his child Carton's "story" (Dickens, *Tale*, 358). Like Carton, Dickens tells a story that reshapes the known and therefore determined past and gives it a new design by projecting its plot lines into the future—the time of his telling, when all the forces he has described can be understood as part of God's providence. Men are free to shape their lives in the same way that authors shape their fictions. Both take the things of this world, reconceive them in their minds, and marshal them to God's purpose.

In *Great Expectations* (1861), Pip must retell the story of his life to make it coincide with the plot lines of providence. This novel, like all the late novels, gives great weight to determinist arguments and shows the powerful influence of environment. In fact, Pip is one of the most notable examples of such influence in Dickens's novels and Magwitch and Stella are not much less prominent. The theme of imprisonment is not so pervasive here as it is in *Little Dorrit*, but the same sense of constraint and self-confinement is amply evident. Throughout the novel we are made to reflect on "the long chain of iron or gold, of thorns or flowers" that life can be depending on the turn of one significant event.[57]

Pip is another first-person narrator, but unlike David Copperfield, who consciously shapes a life, the design of which he believes he can comprehend in retrospect, and unlike Esther, who wishes us to see the story she believed herself to have lived, he must *retell* his story because he spent so much of it living the wrong plot. If Carton achieved "freedom" by projecting the story of his life beyond his death, Pip is entrapped by a similar projection of his story into the future. While Pip is acting out circumstances that he interprets as a coherent plot, these circumstances are in reality assembling into a far different story. Only with the reappearance and death of Magwitch does Pip learn what story he had been living, only when he has relived it can he retell it as part of the greater design in which all life participates. Like Esther, he has a prolonged fever dream that symbolically indicates his desire to be freed from the determinist scheme in which he feels caught. "I was a brick in the house wall, and yet entreating to be released from the giddy place where the builders had set me. . . . I was a steel beam of a vast engine, clashing and whirling over a gulf, and yet . . . I implored in my own person to have the engine stopped and my part in it hammered off" (Dickens, *Expectations*, 500). When he revives from his illness, he takes command of his life, and when he has come full circle to Satis House and Stella, he can begin to tell to us the story he has now the self-discipline and humility to comprehend.

Dickens often commented on the discipline needed to be a successful author. He wrote about the picture of an author that an imaginary Voluntary Correspondent to *Household Words* might have. "It would amaze his incredulity beyond all measure to be told such elements as patience, study, punctuality, determination, self-denial, training of mind and body, hours of application and seclusion to produce what he reads in seconds, enter into such a career. He has no more conception of the necessity of entire devotion to it, than he has of an eternity from the beginning."[58] Part of Dickens's animus against idlers like Henry Gowan and Eugene Wrayburn arose from his conviction that men have an obligation to shape their lives. As an occupation, literature was such a shaping for the artist himself through discipline and self-denial, but as literary art it also resembled the divine direction of human purpose.

The reader of *Our Mutual Friend* (1864–65) and any other Dickens novel may be assured, Robert Morse said, in calling attention to the interrelated fates of Dickens's characters, that "however remote from each other they may at first appear, [they] will interlock in a tightening pattern and each make his influence felt by the others, as in a folk tale the ragged old woman casually befriended by the third son is sure to reappear in his hour of need." Morse observed that modern novelists (he was writing in 1949) have been willing to forego the advantages of such well-meshed plots.[59] My point is that Victorian novelists like Dickens, who firmly believed in a providential scheme where God's and man's wills were important, found the model of strict plotting congenial in a way unavailable to most modern writers, who may appreciate the metaphor of a providential author but cannot accept a literal correlation.

Our Mutual Friend draws much of its energy from the opposition so graphically presented in *Bleak House*, between a belief that individual and social life may be reconstituted through disciplined and selfless effort and the contrary notion that individual roles have been unalterably established by stern necessity from the beginnings of time. Dickens complicated his task by employing a bewildering range of characters who wish to "make themselves." At first, it is difficult to draw distinctions among them. Wrayburn and Lightwood are obvious examples of men who have not chosen their own courses in life but are doing what is expected of them. Wrayburn, in particular, is acutely aware that he is living out a preordained narrative composed by his father, and he resents it. Set against these apparent flaneurs are the determined self-improvers Bradley Headstone and Charley Hexam, who wish to rise in life by shedding their origins. Some apparently well-established men are frauds—Veneering and Fledgeby fit this category in different ways. Some men who seem to have been made, have really made themselves. Boffin and John Harmon are the examples here, but Harmon is a special case and the focus of the novel.

Beyond all individual identity in *Our Mutual Friend* is the mutual identity of the mud and water—the primal origins of man's physical being. "Dust thou art," might be the thoroughbass to the novel's counterpoint of characters, all of whom are bound together not only by plot and its coincidences and crossings but by imagery and allusion as well. From Hexam's river bottom to Boffin's mounds, to the muddy weir, to the "dust" cart into which Sloppy pitches Wegg near the end of the novel, the characters are united in their relationship to waste, death, and their emblems. From this basal slime, men come into being. Harmon has been submerged and has been "recalled to life" in a pattern familiar from *A Tale of Two Cities*. To make himself a new man, he reverses Arthur Clennam's role as a will-less "nobody," and assumes a new active identity. As John Rokesmith, Harmon is content to lose the riches supposedly due to him in order to gain possession of his own soul. Not by forgetting or denying the past but by stripping himself of its chains, Rokesmith, like Pip, frees himself to make a new life by honest effort. His symbolic loss of self is reflected in his general selfless interest in others, a feature set off all the more clearly against Bella Wilfer's announced aim of making her fortunes by marrying wealth.

G. W. Kennedy observed that one means of controlling the self in *Our Mutual Friend* is through the capacity for naming, and certainly naming is important to characters like Harmon, Headstone, Rogue Riderhood, and others.[60] But it is conspicuously important to the narrator of the story as well. Offering false identities and withholding real ones is a major activity in this novel. Moreover, these identities are seldom left in peace but are incorporated into stories beyond the control of those who form their subject. Thus the central character of the novel is first introduced incidentally at a dinner party as a figure in a diverting narrative. Boffin comes on the scene in a similar way. So men might easily be viewed as puppets destined to act out the events of a preinscribed fable. But against this form of story telling, Dickens sets the constructive fables that Lizzie Hexam sees in the fire. Like Carton in his last moments, Lizzie "reads" the future. It is the only way to give shape to past and present. Wegg may read *The Decline and Fall*, but he understands nothing of its larger import (that all things pass away) nor its personal application (that a man who rises in the world may just as easily fall again). The past is a lesson, not a mold or a model. But it is also undeniable. The ambitious Charley Hexam is a curious mixture "of uncompleted savagery, and uncompleted civilization."[61] He will never fully lose the one, nor gain the other. Likewise, his mentor Bradley Headstone's "savage" past will rise up internally as passionate jealousy and externally as Rogue Riderhood, whose appearance he assumes to commit evil. Bradley significantly erases his name before he sets out on the brief excursion that will leave him and Riderhood locked together in death in the mud at the bottom of the river lock. Dust thou art. If life is a river flowing from an irreversible source toward a determined end, men need not plunge themselves into its mire but may, through effort, make their journey upon its surface.

Lizzie's habit of extending the present into possibilities through story is contagious. When Bella begins to suspect her true inclinations, she imagines a script in which somebody on one of the boats out on the river would come to her and direct the course of her "romance." That somebody, already brought to shore, is John Harmon, and their child will later be another such arrival. Bella constructs plot lines for her life but does not understand them until Harmon and Boffin interpret them for her (Dickens, *Friend*, 774). Ironically, the story she hears is a retelling of the story so indifferently related by Lightwood early in the novel—the story of Harmon and his prescribed bride. These two people complete the original diagram of the story, as though it were a destiny fulfilled, but they have shaped its meaning to their own purpose, rinsing it of Old Harmon's sour intent and imbuing it with the sweetness of genuine love. So are we all born into lives that must have a certain design with certain inescapable features, but we have freedom of will and strength of will to live that design in a way that will serve ourselves and others.

To command the story of our lives, we cannot deny our origins. Headstone learns this lesson. Harmon embraces what was positive in his childhood and builds upon it. Nor should we live according to another's dictates as Wrayburn and Twemlow do—an alternative comparable to existential bad faith or Heidegger's "inauthentic life." Nor should we try to mimic the past. The Boffins realize that they cannot re-create little John Harmon. Each life is unique and valuable. They take into their care instead the highly volatile Sloppy, resistant to any external shaping force. Man escapes himself by losing himself, he gains freedom by willing not to be other than he is but to make the most of what he is. Harmon embraces what was positive in his childhood and builds on that strong affection, while letting the features represented by wealth, which have accidentally been stripped from him, disappear. He has the opportunity to remake himself on the ground of what he is, not of what others expect him to be. He escapes the anecdotal role assigned him at the opening of the novel and reenters that narrative on his own terms.

As narrator, Dickens enacts the gestures he wants his readers to experience. His complicated story is the story of story making. He is the providence who names his creations and gives them courses to follow. But they are free within the larger story to rename themselves and retell the story of their lives. In the end it will all be as the author has intended, down to the least thread in the pattern (as Dickens indicates in his postscript), but while the characters live in our mind, their interlocked existences, their tensions and efforts, constitute a real freedom in a real design. For Dickens, mankind's story is ever making until in some remote time, the Great Author puts down his pen and all the plots, with the individual actors whose lives made a difference while they lived and beyond, will come together in a gorgeous tapestry of truth.

Midcentury Fiction

CHAPTER FOURTEEN

Certainty and Ambivalence

C HAPTER 3 of part 1 sampled the various degrees by which religious moralists of the nineteenth century reconciled free will with the concepts of providence and necessity. This chapter discusses mid-Victorian novelists who, while accepting a providential scheme, offered varying presentations of free will.

Many novelists employed the most basic and forthright conventional Christian diagram of submission of the will as true freedom; others, like Charles Kingsley, tried to balance and reconcile self-assertion with self-annihilation. Many writers were ambivalent about the relationship of free will to some form of necessary governance or prescription. Wilkie Collins's novels frequently show the strain of this doubt and are most successful when they employ a narrative strategy expressing that ambivalence without requiring authorial resolution. Perhaps the most subtle and skillful stylist in this regard was Thackeray, whose narrative manipulations consciously elude the certainty of philosophical assertion while embodying the ambiguity of ordinary human perception about the effect of free will upon circumstance. The human capacity for story telling was itself the measure, largely illusory, of human freedom. In advance of contemporary historians discussed in chapter 6, Thackeray realized that history was also a form of fabling and toyed with that theme in *Henry Esmond*. With less passion and conviction, Trollope tamed Thackeray's approach. All of these writers reveal in their manner of telling stories and creating characters the nature of their assumptions about the will's place in a world of circumstance overseen by a power that made for righteousness.

~ ~ ~

Dickens's attitudes about the will were commonplace in fiction of the middle Victorian years, but his ways of incorporating those attitudes in his narrative presentations were ingenious. He was concerned with strength of character, the necessity for submission of the will to a higher power, and the recognition that ultimately that power operated according to a scheme of absolute justice. This was the prevailing outlook during the Victorian years, but there were wide variations in the acceptance of this scheme. Some novelists presented the design unquestioningly, others revealed serious doubts and reservations in the manner of their representing human experience.

Charlotte Brontë's strength as a novelists derives partly from the powerful sense of conviction and emotional sincerity in her writing. Her views on the will are conventional, and her narrative methods relative to those views are not problematic. Strength of will is important in Charlotte Brontë's characters, from Caroline Vernon in the early tales, through Rochester and Jane Eyre, to Lucy Snowe. Caroline Vernon crosses the line from will to willfulness, but later figures learn to subordinate their wills to providential intent.[1] *Jane Eyre* (1847) is largely a detailed examination of the process by which a strong-willed woman learns to subdue her own desires and channel her will toward a more "reasonable," that is to say, "moral," end. Lucy Snowe's experience is certainly more complicated and the conclusion of her story more problematic. I believe that Thomas Vargish exaggerates when he says that in *Villette* (1853) the rules of life have undergone "sinister modifications," with the individual will "deprived of its power to control circumstances," and transformed into an agent of its own pain.[2] These are definitely novels in which strength of will is central, but they do not engage the question of free will in the same way, for example, that Dickens and Thackeray do. Brontë's literary methods are innovative, but her treatment of the will is traditional. Like Dickens and others, Brontë asserts that humans are free to shape themselves and similarly believes that self-will is fundamentally wrong. St. John Rivers is admirable in his willed suppression of erotic yearnings in favor of his severe religious calling, but Brontë does not encourage such an extreme instance of self-suppression. It is enough that Jane can control her impulse to yield to Rochester and bow to divine strictures instead. The punishment for self-indulgence is obvious in Rochester himself and more so in his mad wife. Freedom of will is unquestioned in Brontë's novels, which are more concerned about the achievement of liberty and independence than with freedom from destiny or necessity. Despite the subtleties of narrative in both and the intriguing use of allusion and imagery, neither of the Brontë novels I have mentioned extends concepts of the will into the nature of its narration in ways different from those we have already examined.

In Mrs. Gaskell's novels, strength of character is again important, as is subordination of that will to providential aims. Catherine Gallagher examines *Mary Barton* (1845–47) as a novel complicated by mixed modes (tragic and melodramatic) and competing metaphysics (free will and determinism). Gaskell was writing, she says, "in the determinist tradition as it had been adapted by critics of industrialism, but her writing was also infused with the new Unitarian emphasis on free will," especially as represented in the thinking of James Martineau, whose opinions we examined in chapter 3.[3] Thus John Barton's tragedy is presented in terms of cause and effect, whereas the domestic tales "aim at showing how to circumvent tragic cause-and-effect logic by simply acting, doing one's immediate duty, without stopping to ponder all the consequences" (Gallagher, 82). This pattern is not far from the dichotomy that Dickens highlighted in the two voices of *Bleak House*. Gallagher feels that the conclusion of John Barton's story "points to narrative as an instrument of God's Providence without having to sort out the tangle of its own narrative threads" (Gallagher, 87). Given the emphasis upon the connection between narration and will that we have witnessed in so many writers of her time, I am not sure that Gaskell was as uncertain of her approach as Gallagher suggests. *North and South* (1854–55) is a good example of her methods.

Both Margaret Hale and John Thorton are strong-willed and proud of their self-control. Both believe that they can control their lives and shape their destinies despite increasing evidence that they are not in full command of their futures, cannot maintain absolute self-mastery, and are dependent on their fellow men. Once they have learned humility and faith in a guiding force above them, they reassert their belief that, together, they can control the direction of their lives. The man of cause-and-effect materialism unites with the woman of domestic freedom to form a bond that will serve both spiritual and material existence. Two stories intertwine to prove the likelihood of providential benevolence. But all depends upon humility. Margaret's acknowledgment that her own strength is insufficient without divine support is a highly conventional scene characteristic of much Victorian literature. She had thought that she had only to will to achieve a life without reproach. "And now she had learnt that not only to will, but also to pray, was a necessary condition in the truly heroic. Trusting to herself, she had fallen. It was a just consequence of her sin, that all excuses for it, all temptation to it, should remain for ever unknown to the person in whose opinion it had sunk her lowest."[4]

The narrator's endorsement of this traditional view of the relationship between individual and divine will occurs in the scene immediately following the death of Margaret's mother. The penultimate paragraph of the chapter begins: "Then Margaret rose from her trembling and despondency, and became as a strong angel of comfort to her father and brother." Her strength responds to her well-trained will. She assumes authority over the suffering household, especially her brother's passionate grief that is so different from the sorrow of adulthood "when we become inured to grief, and dare not be rebellious against the inexorable doom, knowing who it is that decrees" (Gaskell, *North and South*, 316–17). The paragraph closes, showing Margaret as an individual capable of dealing with the suffering and mystery that are a part of the great design she cannot fully understand. The last paragraph of this chapter entitled "Home at Last" offers its own interpretation of the meaning of individual death. The narrator describes Mr. Hale's quiet suffering and Margaret's sympathy for him, then concludes: "The night was wearing away, and the day was at hand, when, without a word of preparation, Margaret's voice broke upon the stillness of the room, with a clearness of sound that startled even herself: 'Let not your heart be troubled,' it said; and she went steadily on through all that chapter of unspeakable consolation" (Gaskell, *North and South*, 317). The New Testament, with its message of salvation and hope through suffering provides the text to which all secular texts submit, just as Margaret will herself submit the "romance" of her life to the true model of Christian heroism, acquiescence in the purpose of God.

Andrew Sanders has shown how important this contradiction is in Mrs. Gaskell's historical novel, *Sylvia's Lovers* (1863–64), where the initial refusal to submit to the will of God creates a later more painful necessity of doing so.[5] Not fate but human confusion brings ruin upon the characters of this tale. Here as elsewhere, Mrs. Gaskell offers trust in a providential design as the main solution for human distress. We have already had ample evidence that much of Victorian literature does not question this axiomatic belief.

One writer who followed the traditional mode, but gave it a few variations of his own, was Charles Kingsley. We have already discussed his role as a moralist and need not dwell long on his fiction, because to a certain degree Brenda Colloms is correct in saying that Kingsley's novels are extensions of his sermons.[6] In both, Kingsley was a champion of will understood as strength of character. This binding power of the self was prominent in his own nature. John Martineau wrote that Kingsley was so many-sided "that he seemed to unite in himself more types and varieties of mind and character . . . [and] to be filled with more thoughts, hopes, fears, interests, aspirations, temptations than could co-exist in any one man, all subdued or clenched into union and harmony by the force of one iron will, which had learnt to rule after many fierce and bitter struggles."[7] That Kingsley was able to express all sides of his nature argues that he saw the self as a polity in which one overall authority permitted a certain freedom to its individual subordinates. This was also his model of authority in church and national structures (Kingsley, *Life* 1:67). He did not, like many of his contemporaries, denounce self, but declared that self is "only wrong in proportion as you try to be something in and for yourself, and not the child of a father, the servant of a lord, the soldier of a general" (Kingsley, *Life* 1:319). Evil had no existence in itself but was the consequence of this error about the self, for "men can and do resist God's will, and break the law, which is appointed for them, and so punish themselves by getting into disharmony with their own constitution and that of the universe." God's providence is a means of baffling this "lawlessness and self-will" and turning it into a means of education for the violators (Kingsley, *Life* 2:28)

This pattern is evident in Kingsley's novels, all of which incorporate the principle that men may be educated by their errors if they read the consequences aright. However, men may not passively assume that God's will guides them; they must actively seek it out. In *Water Babies* (1863), Kingsley suggested that creatures may evolve through exertion of will or degenerate through a lack of exertion.[8] The same message of learning to channel one's strength of will into the purpose assigned by God operates in all of Kingsley's fiction, taking different forms in the different plots. For example, both *Yeast* (1848) and *Westward Ho!* (1855) end with the central character content to be humbled by God's apparent will. Two other novels more explicitly touch upon the question of free will, however, and I shall examine them more closely.

Alton Locke (1850) is the first-person account of a narrator who passes from religious training, to skeptical opposition, to faith in a personal Christ and a loving God. Shedding the severe Calvinist religion of his childhood, Locke develops a forceful self-will, helpful in educating himself but dangerous insofar as it tempts him to trust himself alone for his fate.[9] Locke is temporarily attracted by Mr. Windrush's "Emersonian" preaching that disputes "the advocates of free-will and of sin," arguing instead that man cannot disobey his Maker, that "all things fulfill their destiny." He recommends total abnegation of will and denial of self. "God is circumstance, and thou his creature! Be content! Fear not, strive not, change not, repent not! Thou art nothing! Be nothing, and thou becomest a part of all things" (Kingsley, *Locke*, 231–32). Though allured by Windrush's eloquence, Locke avoids his unitarian principle of letting each man believe as he sees fit.

Meanwhile, Locke, who has been laboring at his poetry as well as his trade of tailoring, achieves some degree of fame when his book of poems is published. At the same time, he becomes involved in questionable political activities associated with the Chartist movement. Unjustly imprisoned, Locke is released in time to witness the political betrayal of the Reform Bill in Parliament and the April 10 failure of the Chartist demonstration in London. Immediately following these intellectual humiliations, Locke sinks to his lowest moral level when he incorrectly accuses his cousin of stealing the woman he loves and is struck down for his insolence and loses his "honour, self-respect, strength of will [and] faith in my own destiny—the inner hope that God had called me to do a work for him" (Kingsley, *Locke*, 366). Locke collapses and, in the conventional pattern of much Victorian fiction, undergoes an illness that leaves him weakened but purified.[10] During his illness, a hallucinatory dream carries him along the whole path of animal evolution to a beautiful vision of man's future where all people perform their parts for the good of the whole community, worshiping in common the All-Father of the world. In this dream, Locke learns to cease tormenting the world "with talk about liberty, equality, and brotherhood; for they never were, and never will be, on this earth" (Kingsley, *Locke*, 386). Instead, he discovers that true freedom is in meekness, true strength in weakness. Mankind was an equal brotherhood when it left the All-Father and will be so again when it returns to him, Locke concludes in his dream. He wakes to find himself tended by his friend Crossthwaite and his patroness, Lady Eleanor Ellerton, who tells him how she overcame self-will and learned selflessness and how Locke's heroes— Strauss, Emerson, and such—cannot offer the simple and true faith that Jesus of Nazareth can. Locke objects that he must continue to strive for freedom among men of his class and she replies: "You are free; God has made you free. . . . He is your king who has bought for you the rights of sons of God" (Kingsley, *Locke*, 403). Locke accepts this equivocating message as symbolized in the angelic Lady Ellerton herself. She dies, having arranged Locke's passage to the New World, and he expires on the way, having just composed a hopeful poem calling all men to strive for a better world under God.

Catherine Gallagher says that in *Alton Locke* Kingsley "chose a form that expressed his Romantic faith in a free will benevolently reconciled with God-given circumstances" though his reforming purpose "led him to add incongruous elements, suggestions of negative environmental determinism, to that form" (Gallagher, 89). The form of the book makes the free will versus determinism controversy inescapable. First-person narration operates here, as elsewhere in the fiction of the time, to leave many causal connections unspecified, therefore encouraging a faith in free will. This narrative approach "licenses inconsistencies in all aspects of the narrative. Alton need not detail motives or trace a coherent plot" (Gallagher, 95).

Alton never emerges as a coherent character but blends into the authorial voice to become a representative of a writer who stands for writing itself. Lacking a distinctive voice and character, he becomes indistinguishable from the authorial voice and "turns the narrative into a work preeminently about writing" (Gallagher, 104). Gallagher explains that "God is the agent in making Alton a poet, but Alton is in turn the agent of God's willed social regeneration. Here, as in other poets' stories, God's hand directs the poet's destiny, but in *Alton Locke* the poetry itself is not the reigning telos. It is, rather, merely an instrument of social reform" (Gallagher, 92). Gallagher reveals the confusion in Kingsley's strategy, a confusion that is characteristic of his metaphysical and political-social position. The confusion is masked in *Alton Locke* by the first-person narration but becomes more evident in objective narration.

Tom Thurnall in *Two Years Ago* (1857) is a less complex variant of the Alton Locke figure. He is an adventurer, good-natured, honest, and self-assured, but "godless" in that he does not think a deity guides him. Early in the novel, when he has been shipwrecked returning to England after years of wandering, Grace Harvey, echoing the Evangelist tracts of the time, tells him that God has so spared him because he has great plans for him. Later, in trying to convince Grace that fighting an outbreak of cholera in their community is not resistance to God's will, Tom admits that he believes in a God who made this world and who offers man new opportunities in the world hereafter the suffering of this one.[11]

Like Alton Locke, Thurnall thoroughly enjoys the material world. Beautiful scenery preaches to him a sermon of hope. The narrator likens Tom to Ulysses, also a self-helpful, cheerful, fate-defiant wanderer, but adds that Tom is more of a pagan than the Greek, "for he knew not what Ulysses knew, that a heavenly guide was with him in his wanderings; still less what Ulysses knew not, that what he called the malicious sport of fortune was, in truth, the earnest education of a father" (Kingsley, *Two Years* 1:372). In his struggle against fortune, Tom has placed his confidence in himself and his own self-education. Near the end of the novel, the narrator passes judgment on Tom's misguided faith. "What refuge, then, in self-education; when a man feels himself powerless in the grip of some unseen and inevitable power, and knows not whether it be chance, or necessity, or a devouring fiend? To wrap himself sternly in himself, and cry, 'I will endure, though all the universe be against me;' how fine it sounds! But who has done it?" (Kingsley, *Two Years* 2:344). Self-education is impossible; only God, through earthquakes, storms, and other miseries visited upon man, can educate man in his own weakness and the greater unity and purpose of God.

Tom remains vain about his own strength. "All the miraculous escapes of his past years, instead of making him believe in a living, guiding, protecting Father, have become to that proud heart the excuse for a deliberate, though unconscious, atheism. His fall is surely near," the narrator explains with all the subtlety of a stage whisper (Kingsley, *Two Years* 2:376). And, indeed, when Tom sets out on his adventures again, his vanity causes his imprisonment for over eighteen months, during which time he learns humility. Returning home to his blind father and faithful Grace Harvey on Christmas Eve, he declares that he will never part from Grace again and asks her to teach him how best to place himself in the hands of his heavenly Father. Even allowing for my extreme simplification of Kingsley's narrative, it should be apparent that determinism is a straw man in this novel when it appears and Tom's salvation is prefigured in signs that he is capable of directing his free will and force of will in the service of others. Narrative method does not notably reinforce Kingsley's theme but in its extreme casualness is compatible with his faith in free will. Jerome Hamilton Buckley confidently summarizes Kingsley's novel: "The moral of the novel is pointed beyond mistake; however strong man's particular will, his whole power lies in his dependence upon the universal Will; self-assertion has meaning only when the self acts humbly in accordance with the laws of God and nature."[12] As we shall see, the main difficulties with this equation arise when writers begin to perceive disparities between the laws of nature and the laws of God.

Unlike some of the writers we have discussed, Kingsley earnestly advocated self-expression and action, even violent action. He eagerly supported war when he believed it just and championed vigorous political activity. Admitting that some of these actions might prove wrongheaded, he did not fear such errors, convinced as he was that a loving Father would use them to reveal the right way and believing that he lived in an *alterable* and therefore *remediable* world. Kingsley did not deny the self but gloried in the uniqueness of individuals and applauded strength of will. Nonetheless, he insisted upon the need for traditional Christian self-sacrifice, valuing it as an intensification of moral awareness. He felt that mystics wrongly asserted that self-sacrifice is attained by self-annihilation. "Self-sacrifice, instead of destroying the sense of personality, perfects it; while self-annihilation is, in reality, only relinquishing one selfish pleasure for another" (Kingsley, *Life* 1:102).

His belief that the expression of personality was consistent with subordination to God and that God acted directly to educate individual men as well as mankind at large is reflected in Kingsley's attitude toward fiction. His narratives are filled with forward and backward looking passages that emphasize the overall moral design of the story. He insisted that creation of characters (through description and appropriate dialogue) was essential and that influences on these characters should be clearly presented so that they stood out as believable figures. He also insisted that the author-narrator had the right to announce his views directly to his reader. "People are too stupid and in too great a hurry, to interpret the most puzzling facts for themselves, and the author must now and then act as showman, and do it for them. Whether it's according to 'Art' or not, I don't care a fig." The important thing, he concluded, is that such passages please and instruct (Kingsley, *Life* 2:39–40). Norman Vance calls attention to the resemblance between Kingsley's fictional structures and the subjects they present. "Formal anarchy and imaginative extravagance are as characteristic of Kingsley's art as the brilliant descriptive passages or the scenes of furious dramatic action. His method of writing accounts for the disorganized vigour of his narrative: he would compose isolated fragments in his head, 'a bit here and a bit there', working himself into a frenzy of excitement as he stormed round his garden before dashing into the study to commit it all to paper."[13] Kingsley wanted to make his point that men were free to choose freedom; the disorder of his narratives demonstrates his personal belief in the power to shape purpose in life not by external prearranged structures but by the energy of faith supported by a mastering will.

In *Alton Locke*, the first-person narrator, after exhorting his readers to familiarize themselves with the working man's condition, corrects himself, saying that declamation is of little use. "I had much better simply tell my story, and leave my readers to judge of the facts if, indeed, they will be so far courteous as to believe them" (Kingsley, *Locke*, 89). But neither Locke nor Kingsley is capable of renouncing declamation, for Kingsley did not really want his readers to make of his narratives what they would. He shaped his characters with a stern hand, placed them in circumstances that would test their natures, and let them prove the abiding lesson according to which his fables were constructed in the first place. His characters were "free" insofar as they "came alive" to the reader by fulfilling their assigned roles. They were not meant to stray as Thackeray's did, or be perverse like Meredith's or Hardy's. As a narrator, Kingsley wished to be what he conceived God to be—not the wrathful leader of a tribe who might punish and reward but the sternly compassionate Victorian father who liked his children to manifest some spirit before he birched them and showed them the proper way a thing was done.

Though the basic world view among Victorian novelists was providential, a sense of pagan destiny or fate often entered their fictions, as it did their philosophical disputes (part 1). I have already mentioned Carlyle's struggle with the concept of necessity as fated or as providential. The issue reappears in various guises, particularly in novels concerned with the discovery of religious or philosophical truth. Most of these novels appeared after the 1870s, but the issue was alive throughout the century, carried over from Romantic preoccupations. Edward Fowler, the central character in James Anthony Froude's "The Spirit's Trial," undergoes a severe test of his Christian faith. He is a weak-willed young man who suffers the rule of a domineering father and separation from the woman he loves. He determines to reclaim his character, not with religious and moral implements but through reason. "With a haughty stoicism he resolved to cauterize his wounds or cut them out. If fate, as he called it, chose to go on persecuting him, he would rule fate; and a sternness of purpose, now wholly worldly and irreligious, came to his help, which enabled him to despise opinion and once more rise and exert himself."[14] Fowler succeeds in his conquest of self and wins the friendship of his lost love, her husband, and especially their child. This reconciliation follows his discovery that divinity is immanent in the material world. After Edward's early death, his friend Arthur concludes from the documents Edward has left that "a profound belief in God and God's providence, lay at the very core of his soul; but all beyond it seemed but shifting cloud, at a distance forming into temples and mountains, and skyey palaces, but seen close and examined, all fog and choking vapour" (Froude, 180–81). Edward Fowler abandoned conventional Christianity but retained a sense of divine regulation in the universe. His life remained meaningful as symbolized by his coincidental rescue of his old love's child.

Not all novelists accepted this traditional attitude, though they were generally subtle in counteracting it. Sheridan Le Fanu was deeply interested in the power of the will, especially as expressed in forms of tyranny and domination. Charlotte Brontë certainly recognized that unconscious impulses could move men and women to act in strange ways but also believed that ultimately faith and reason could harness those impulses. If they did not, degeneration and even madness might follow, as in Bertha Mason Rochester's case. Le Fanu inverted this program, ironically using the environment of insanity to illustrate the power of will derived not from reason but from emotion. In *The Rose and the Key* (1871), Maud Vernon is unjustly confined in an asylum. Though already a strong-willed young woman, she learns from the abridgment of her liberty. Because it is essentially strong, her character is improved rather than broken by the experience. "It is well," the narrator remarks, "when, even in after-life, we can see that our sufferings have made us better, and that God has purged the tree, and not cursed it."[15]

Maud's mother is also strong-willed but viciously so. She has the appearance of coldness but is secretly passionate and violent. She is moved by no fixed principles, no maxims of duty, but only by impulse (Le Fanu, 126). The narrator's comments on Mrs. Vernon apply to mankind in general. "It is not belief that forms the desire, but the desire that shapes the belief. Little originates in the head. Nearly all has its inception in the heart. The brain is its slave, and does task work. . . . There is another occult force, a mechanical power, as it were, always formidably at the service of the devil and the soul. . . . It is the desire that governs the will, and the will the intellect. Let every man keep his heart, then, as he would his house, and beware how he admits a villain to live in it" (Le Fanu, 192–93).[16]

This metaphor is the working principle of other stories by Le Fanu. In "Carmilla," the heroine's father unknowingly admits a dangerous female vampire into his home and nearly loses his daughter to her. The story, though presented in Le Fanu's characteristic nouveau Gothic style, may also be read as a parable of the imperiled will, for Carmilla threatens complete possession of the young woman whose blood she drinks. The strong-willed, virile father, aided by the experienced General Spieldorf, manages to frustrate the vampiress's powerful but selfish will. By contrast, "Green Tea" describes the decay of will in a minister who slowly yields to an obsessive hallucination about a monkey. In *Uncle Silas* (1864), Maud Ruthyn's liberty and personality are threatened by three bizarre figures—her governess, Madame de la Rougierre; her Uncle Silas; and her cousin Dudley. Silas is the guiding force behind the others, his motive being control of Maud's inheritance. Though the novel abounds in Gothic trappings, it is a rudimentary contest of wills, with a documentary will at its center. We shall return to this congruence and its significance later, but here it is enough to note that Le Fanu's narrative structures fail generally to exploit the drama of wills that he describes. Outside the short stories, there is little narrative ingenuity. But Le Fanu may have preferred this approach. Jack Sullivan says that especially in the late stories "Le Fanu gives us a basic pattern, then twists and distorts it in different stories so that the reader is surprised in a variety of unpleasant ways even though he knows basically what is going to happen" (Sullivan, 53). Later he describes a "mixture of hesitating indirection and stark precision" as the characteristic of Le Fanu's prose style (Sullivan, 59). The sense of frustration in not being able to focus the will precisely on what, in a starkly precise and basically familiar world, occasions one's sensations of dread and discomfort, is fully in keeping with Le Fanu's apparent belief that although man's will may be free, he lacks sufficient comprehension of his world to employ it effectively in action.

Other writers exhibit similar equivocations in prose style, plotting, and attitudes toward the will. Wilkie Collins is an interesting example of a writer who, while suggesting providential schemes to his conventional readers both in the plot-focused nature of his stories and in their direct treatment of poetic justice, seems to have believed more in a pre-Christian destiny than in providence, if he believed in any such overarching design. H. J. W. Milley singled out Collins's regular use of the motif of fatality, where a malignant force directs characters to a predestined end.[17] Sue Lonoff points out that, especially in his best-known novels, Collins often plays games with plot, characters, readers, and texts (Lonoff, 117). Like Dickens, he recognized the resemblance between novelist and providence. However, lacking Dickens's firm belief in that providence, Collins fabricated a world in which moral schemes are scarcely more certain than amoral schemes. Ultimately, his concern for audience forced him to provide the expected distribution of punishment and reward, but this outlay of pain and largesse often operates against the apparent generating forces of his novels. In *The Moonstone* (1868), a non-Christian fate attaches to the moonstone itself, and the pattern of moral justice it fulfills is Oriental, not Christian. Betteredge's faith in *Robinson Crusoe* as a providential guide is all the more ironic in that Defoe's novel is itself conspicuously preoccupied with providential design. But, as Sue Lonoff remarks, in *The Moonstone*, providence "has become a vehicle of irony exposing the absurdities of those who invoke it, or it has degenerated into coincidence. It may be providential that Murthwaite appears just in time to explain the Indians' behavior, or that Jennings crosses Franklin's path just when his services are needed: but clearly the hand behind these events is the author's and not the Almighty's" (Lonoff, 221-22).

The Moonstone is intricately plotted like many other of Collins's novels, but the plot seems to reveal a causal necessity approaching pagan superstition and veering away from the resolutions of providence. The machinery of earlier novels also lacks a providential base. In The Dead Secret (1857), threadbare Gothic devices—a hidden note of great importance, a remote, half-ruined estate, a secret marriage, an inheritance, among other nineteenth-century literary conventions—produce a plot line so contorted that characters must be hustled here and about in varying guises and altered natures in order to adjust to it. Take Leonard Frankland, for example. He is an agreeable young man of the upper class who fully accepts notions of good birth and class distinctions, yet when he discovers that his beloved young bride not only lacks the reputable heritage he supposed but is actually illegitimate, he blithely and abruptly modifies his views, acknowledging that the highest honors are not those of family but those conferred by Love and Truth.

It may be argued that in this novel, Collins simply had not yet learned his trade, though it is certainly an improvement upon the hidden identities, coincidental encounters, unexplained disappearances of characters, strangely distributed inheritances, and so forth of the poorly contrived Hide and Seek (1854). By contrast, the success of The Woman in White (1859-60) is attributable to Collins's clear mastery of a complicated plot and a notably improved power of characterization. In fact, character becomes as significant as plot in this novel. In his "Preamble" to the novel, Collins wrote: "This is the story of what a woman's patience can endure, and of what a man's resolution can achieve," thereby implying that his story would demonstrate the power of human will to overcome evil forces bearing upon it.[18] One force against which these heroic figures must contend is the equally powerful and noticeably more subtle will of Count Fosco; another is the machinery of the Law. Collins probably intended no metaphysical implications about a greater determinist Law operating in the universe, and Fosco and Glyde probably do not embody a Gnostic underpower against the light and truth of Walter Hartright, Marion Halcombe, and Laura Fairlie, but there is, nonetheless, an opposition here of good and evil that suggests a menacing regularity to evil that must be opposed by free and spontaneous invention. Fosco is an artist of evil. He weaves a plot. Hartright is creative for good; he must interpret Fosco's scheme and rewrite its conclusion. Fosco's name in Italian means "dark" or "obscure." Walter must illuminate that darkness. To some extent, The Woman in White recalls Caleb Williams, where a good man slowly deciphers the nature and design of a superior, but corrupt, man.

Caleb Williams is told in the first person, so we have only the narrator's sense of the design by which he feels himself entrapped. Collins was justly proud of his innovation of multiple narration. In his preface to the 1860 edition of his novel, Collins explained his achievement in terms of his craft (Collins, *Woman*, 499). Yet the technique has other implications. Because the story unfolds from various perspectives, the reader must construct his or her own developing pattern. It is in the silent interstices of the plot that Collins plays his games of expectation and reversal. The characters assume an apparently free and independent existence, helping to shape the scheme of which they are a part.

In his preface to the 1861 edition of *The Woman in White*, Collins asserted that the primary object of a work of fiction was to tell a story, then added, "it may be possible in novel-writing, to present characters successfully without telling a story; but it is not possible to tell a story successfully without presenting characters: their existence, as recognisable realities, being the sole condition on which the story can be effectively told" (Collins, *Woman*, 501-2).

Collins seems to suggest that the characters *do* imitate real persons and evoke the readers' sympathies, presumably because their struggles are believable. But there is a concealed irony in Collins's method. Although a portion of the narrative is composed contemporaneously with the events it records, most of the story is presented in retrospect, the greater part of it by Walter Hartright, a man who believes that life has a design. Marian, who shares his feeling, with important differences, records one such expression of his belief. "The night, when I met the lost Woman on the highway," he tells her, "was the night which set my life apart to be the instrument of a Design that is yet unseen. Here, lost in the wilderness, or there, welcomed back in the land of my birth, I am still walking on the dark road which leads me, and you, and the sister of your love and mine, to the unknown Retribution and the inevitable End" (Collins, *Woman*, 212). How different would the story be if told mainly by Count Fosco, with his contempt for law and cynicism about human nature? "Mind, they say, rules the world. But what rules the mind? The body. The body (follow me closely here) lies at the mercy of the most omnipotent of all moral potentates—the Chemist" (Collins, *Woman*, 477-78). The intricacies of plot are interpreted for us by Hartright, and Collins does not contest his interpretation. The happy conclusion of the novel seems to endorse that interpretation, but a sneaking suspicion lingers that no moral design overarches existence. Men follow their impulses and make their fates. Glyde dies as a consequence of his greed. Fosco hesitates to do his worst because he admires Marian; he dies because he has violated a trust and has been found out by men as relentless as himself. The cheery conditions of the novel's close obscure Marian's lack of a reward commensurate with her virtue. She too would have liked her Walter as a prize.

Marian Halcombe has resolution and strength of character. In this she far outstrips Laura and other characters in the novel. Kenneth Robinson claims that Marian represents Collins's "most deeply felt tribute to the qualities he admired in woman."[19] And yet he leaves her essentially unrewarded and unfulfilled. In *No Name* (1862), Collins distributed between two heroines the qualities that he combined in Marian. Magdalen Vanstone has a forceful mind, a strong will, ingenuity, and the power of resolute and even aggressive action. Viewing human behavior as theatrical performance (a theme emphasized by Collins's division of his narrative into "scenes"), Magdalen believes that she can revise the outcome of the play by creating new roles or assuming roles assigned to others. She is an accomplished amateur actress and achieves many of her aims through her skill at disguise. Richard Barickman, Susan MacDonald, and Myra Stark observe that Magdalen both rejects options or the lack of them in other women's lives and tests them by impersonation; the "theme of acting is thus very closely related to the theme of willing or choosing, as opposed to submitting and accepting."[20] But despite her cleverness and her forceful character, Magdalen is stymied and frustrated at each important stage of her plan to recover an inheritance that she believes has been unjustly withheld from her and her sister, Norah. Though she is willing to use unscrupulous means to gain justice, in moments of crisis Magdalen's "indomitable earnestness" and "inborn nobility" rise above the "perverted nature" that tempts her to use deceit and trickery.[21] If Magdalen is inherently strong, noble, and earnest, Norah's form of resolution calls for patience and "the courage of resignation," which ultimately prove superior to all of Magdalen's scheming (Collins, *No Name*, 468). Norah marries honorably for love and steps gracefully and legitimately into the inheritance that Magdalen has so deviously struggled to recover, thereby revealing to Magdalen the folly of such methods.

In his preface to *No Name*, Collins described his novel as depicting, in the character of Magdalen, "the struggle of a human creature, under those opposing influences of Good and Evil, which we have all felt, which we have all known" (Collins, *No Name*, 5). The contest of the human will in the theater of moral obligation is Collins's central concern; accordingly, mystery and suspense become less important. Neither reader nor characters require a secret to urge them to anticipate and formulate the shape the future will take. Collins explained, "The only Secret contained in this book is revealed midway in the first volume. From that point, all the main events of the story are purposely foreshadowed before they take place—my present design being to rouse the reader's interest in following the train of circumstances by which these foreseen events are brought about" (Collins, *No Name*, 6). The complexity of events, not their mysterious connections, is what Collins wants to emphasize. But more directly than in *The Woman in White*, Collins here seems to commend the idea that there *is* an overarching design governing men's actions as though they were actors in a play long since composed, whose ending is already foreknown. Evidence for such a view comes when

Captain Kirke, who has loved Magdalen in vain, returns from a sea journey on a ship called *The Deliverance* just in time to happen upon a feverish, impoverished Magdalen and provide for her recovery. "What mysterious destiny had guided him to the last refuge of her poverty and despair, in the hour of her sorest need? 'If it is ordered that I am to see her again, I *shall* see her.' Those words came back to him now—the memorable words that he had spoken to his sister at parting" (Collins, *No Name*, 434). Kirke's faith helps him to decipher the meaning of this event. " 'What has brought me here?' he said to himself in a whisper. 'The mercy of Chance? No. The mercy of God' " (Collins, *No Name*, 435).[22]

Magdalen has tried to alter the great design of providence. She has struggled to make events conform to her will and desire but has forgotten that to exert one's will in this selfish way is to lose true freedom of the will. A sign of her false position is her own apparent enslavement to chance. Magdalen decides whether or not to commit suicide merely by the chance of an even rather than an odd number of boats passing her window in a given time. By contrast, Norah, submitting her will to a higher purpose, never suffers Magdalen's harrowing emotions and never places her salvation in the hands of chance. Her strength is in her self-regard.

It is difficult to determine how sincere Collins was in the sentiments he expressed. One major problem with his fiction, a problem that ultimately vitiated the later novels, is a latent insincerity. This insincerity becomes conscious, I believe, in *Armadale* (1864–65, 1866) where Collins purposely generated the narrative energy of his story from the progressive fulfillment of an unusual dream. The novel's basic narrative premise is improbable. One Allan Armadale has caused the death of another man by the same name who was his rival in love and material inheritance. Both have offspring with similar names, though in temperament and appearance they are opposite, one being blondly handsome, naive and open, the other being dark, melancholic, and private. The first does not know the secret of their relationship; the second, assuming the name Ozias Midwinter, does. Allan Armadale has a peculiar dream aboard the ship named *La Grace de Dieu*, the ship on which his father died. He dismisses the dream, but Midwinter, to whom Armadale is inexplicably attracted, accepts it as an authentic forecast of events.

Kenneth Robinson says that "the mainspring of the story is the idea of fatality. Wilkie's obsession with Doom is given full reign."[23] In fact, the plot of the story, with its many involutions, reversals, coincidences, and so forth, is a form of purposely ambiguous representation that exploits both pagan and Christian expectations about the meaning of existence. In an "Appendix" to the novel, Collins explained that he had purposely left the interpretation of the dream open. His readers could view it as a portent or as a rationally explicable event, he said, and offered samples of coincidences occurring in real life that justified the realism of his involved plot and its assumptions. The novel itself ends on a note of ambiguity. For example, although almost all other steps in the plot fulfill Armadale's dream, its worst and concluding incidents never come to pass. Was the dream prophetic, half-prophetic, coincidental? What message is the reader to derive from the fact that the dream is trustworthy until its end? It cannot be dismissed, but it cannot be fully certified either. Midwinter, who has loved the villainess of the story and lost her, assumes that there has been a positive purpose in the suffering he has undergone and witnessed. He explains to Armadale that he cannot accept his rational view of the dream, but he has learned to view its purpose with a new mind. "I once believed that it was sent to rouse your distrust of the friendless man whom you had taken as a brother to your heart. I now *know* that it came to you as a timely warning to take him closer still. Does this help to satisfy you that I, too, am standing hopefully on the brink of a new life, and that while we live, brother, your love and mine will never be divided again?"[24]

The Reverend Decimus Brock is a good, conservative minister who affirms the providential view that "no evil exists out of which, in obedience to his [God's] laws, Good may not come" (Collins, *Armadale*, 300). In a posthumous letter, he tells Midwinter that he is "the man whom the providence of God has appointed to save" Armadale, whose father's life was taken by Midwinter's father (Collins, *Armadale*, 302). But Brock's view about good and evil is not entirely confirmed by other *voices* in the novel. The third-person narrator himself comments earlier that "suffering can, and does, develop the latent evil that there is in humanity, as well as the latent good" (Collins, *Armadale*, 525). And the plot, though it brings together the relatively uninteresting Armadale and Neelie Milroy, leaves some disturbing loose ends. Midwinter survives alone and shaken. Lydia Gwilt, who has plotted great mischief throughout the novel dies saving him from the death she had plotted for Armadale. Love and decency coexist in her with greed and hatred. Meanwhile, the confirmed scamp Mrs. Oldershaw profits from a bogus conversion, making a virtuous name for herself in public preaching.

In his article "Reading Detection in *The Woman in White*," Mark M. Hennelly, Jr., shrewdly remarks that "besides appearing to be prosaic and predictable . . . life also seems to be mysterious and chaotic; and detective fiction vicariously solves life's mysteries by providing a perfect paradigm for imposing rational order on an irrational universe: 'the conviction of an unseen Design in the long series of complications which . . . fastened round us.' "[25] In *Armadale*, the elaborations of the plot increasingly resemble the perversities of human existence, not a scheme laid out for man's salvation, a labyrinth for him to labor through, not a pathway to redemption. The characters seem doomed, time and again defeating themselves as they struggle to assert their wills against a prefigured doom. Midwinter is the chief example of this tendency. Miss Gwilt resembles Magdalen Vanstone in trying to make the future conform to her will by means of deceit and crime. She is similarly, but more definitively, frustrated. Reason and raw will seem unable to deflect the forces that shape men's lives. Sins of the fathers are inherited by the sons, but no other causal scheme seems to relate human deeds to human rewards and punishments. Whatever power controls men's destinies, it is impervious to individual exercises of human will. Winifred Hughes says that in *Armadale* fate or providence has lost its effectiveness as a controlling mechanism in a predictable universe. "The rigid pattern of the dream and its fulfillment disconcertingly contradicts the evidence of the rest of the novel, in which "Retribution," like everything else, has to take its chances. Unlike the melodramatists of the popular stage, Collins no longer equates plot with moral content or with the ultimate meaning of human destiny."[26] Human existence resembles the complicated plot of a novel in which the author may introduce a curse that abides, allow proleptic glimpses of the story to be unfolded, and set his characters in motion against one another, while always retaining the power to introduce unexpected incidents and convenient coincidences. Collins appears to be turning the equation of authorial approximation of providence on its head. The characters in his fiction perceive as providential what is merely the novelist's exercise in control of his craft. And just as the novelist does not pretend that his fictions are rational constructions but mainly controlled expressions of emotion, so human existence seems less the result of an organized rational plan than the plaything of a mysterious power. Collins is coming close to implying that men project their stories into the mind of a hypothetical deity as a means of authorizing an arbitrary organized perception of their lives. Life is not a play to be re-scripted or a dream to wake from. What we know is that we play our parts in a mystery and give them meaning by the life stories we compose according to our temperaments and our desires. This is a negative version of Hazlitt's more positive designation of the future as the playground of the free will.

We have already seen that in *The Moonstone*, Collins's finest novel and the one that immediately followed *Armadale*, the emphasis upon false providential patterns, the inadequacy of reason, and the dependence upon inexplicable sources of human behavior is overt. If Dickens's Buckett is readable as a divine agent tracing the providential scheme with his forefinger, Collins's Cuff, by contrast, represents the refined but nonetheless faulty human intelligence tracing a rational pattern in human events but coming to conclusions often no more correct than those Betteredge derives from his *Crusoe*.

Ross C. Murfin has indicated that "the theme of the mysterious power of the written is everywhere in *The Moonstone*." The "action" of the novel is writing insofar as the events are all recalled by writers.[27] From this perspective, Cuff assumes an authorial role since it is he who reveals in writing the name of the true thief, Godfrey Abelwhite, on the same page where Collins too first reveals the secret. Murfin further indicates that we may read *The*

Moonstone as a study of the "duplicity" (or duality) of human identity—one manifestation of which is the division between conscious and unconscious self. From this point of view, the re-creation of Franklin Blake's "crime" is the best representation the narrative offers of itself, and Jennings assumes the authorial role as he restages the event. Collins is thus a man of two minds.

> One mind views the novel as creative play, an escapist's drug, and thinks the final results of that play less interesting than the play itself, the ink visions enjoyed along the way. Collins, when of this entertainer's mind, suggests that ink liberates, that it liberates non-rational thought, and that it liberates fiction, which is our life. The other mind of Collins thinks that the significant secrets, both of life and of his novel, are the inter-involvement of unconscious and conscious life, the fact that our identifications of guilt and innocence are simplistic fictions, and that the most revealing glimpses of reality look, to the world that wishes to know only simple truths, like fictions. This Collins sees truth and romance as being strangely and strikingly similar, and he takes as his authorial figure a man who takes drugs out of dire necessity.[28]

But there is no reason to confine Collins's perception of himself or others to dualities. I have already suggested that he saw human nature as multiple and relative with no trustworthy order perceivable by which to govern its responses. An honest literary fiction must therefore reflect this pervasive ambiguity and even persist in obscuring authorial authority, lending credibility to one outlook and then to another. Mysteries may be resolved, Collins implies, but not therefore understood.

It is no accident, I think, that Collins's two genuine achievements both avoid an objective narrator and convey their stories by means of multiple and often contradictory narrators. Only in this way could Collins approximate his own outlook—that life has no inherent design to be fathomed by the interpretation of this or that set of signs but is a complex union of human motive and external circumstance guiding a very limited yet free will to make choices in the face of mystery. The reviewer for the *Times* of 30 October 1860 was extremely acute in judging where Collins was heading. Character, he said, was true to itself whether a story was unfolding or not. As character becomes the focus of a fiction, story is in danger of being neglected. But the opposite is also true. "We shall not afflict the readers by dwelling on the fashionable German jargon as to the relations of the subjective and the objective in fiction—as to the doctrine of freewill, or to the victory of man over circumstance, implied in a feeble plot; and as to the doctrine of necessity, or the conquest of man by circumstance, implied in a good plot" (Collins, *Woman*, Appendix B, 503). What the reviewer wants to know is why good character development cannot be compatible with elaborate plot development, concluding that it is not so in *The Woman in White*.

The reviewer does not consider that a man who writes for a living might feel the need to construct a novel that satisfies his audience's expectations yet also accords with his own, perhaps uncomprehended, psychological needs. After *The Moonstone*, Collins seems to have given up the struggle and decided to write what he thought would sell. At the same time he seemed, as author, to want to force a pattern upon experience that he could not himself endorse. He opens *The Fallen Leaves* (1878), a novel that travesties his methods, thus: "The resistless influences which are one day to reign supreme over our poor hearts, and to shape the sad short course of our lives, are sometimes of mysteriously remote origin, and find their devious ways to us through the hearts and the lives of strangers."[29] This passage resembles many where Dickens speculates on the strange comings together of disparate fates. But Dickens can believe that a providence guides these many tributary paths into a highroad to salvation. Collins seems to have no such conviction, though the lingering need to believe in a pattern that is not merely psychological haunts him.[30] *The Fallen Leaves* reads like a program to resolve this mood, but its coincidences are preposterous. The rascal Jervy appears in London coincidentally acquainted with the only two persons who know the details about Mr. and Mrs. Farnaby's secret concerning a lost child. The improbably named Claude Amelius Goldenheart (Collins was given to this kind of unusual naming) on his very first visit to London, encounters that lost child on a stroll through the slums! In the later novels, the characters degenerate into melodramatic but quirky figures. The plots have little impetus. *The Fallen Leaves* was not Collins's last novel, but what followed revealed a writer writing to write, a consciousness divorced from any coherent embodying power.

William Makepeace Thackeray represents a yet greater withdrawal from confidence in providential design. Nonetheless, like Collins, he hankered after some sense that man was not abandoned to the mechanical consequences of his own acts. Gordon Ray quotes an important passage where Thackeray faces the dilemma of such responsibility.

Who has not felt how he works, the dreadful, conquering Spirit of Ill? Who cannot see, in the circle of his own society, the fated and foredoomed to woe and evil? Some call the doctrine of destiny a dark creed; but, for me, I would fain try and think it a consolatory one. It is better, with all one's sins upon one's head, to deem oneself in the hands of Fate than to think, with our fierce passions and weak repentances, with our resolves so loud, so vain, so ludicrously, despicably weak and frail, with our dim, wavering, wretched conceits about virtue, and our irresistible propensity to wrong, that we are the workers of our future sorrow or happiness.[31]

Despite the serious tone of this passage, an ironic flavor remains, a flavor reflected in Thackeray's fictional practice.

Thackeray told John Cordy Jeaffreson that he had no control over his characters, but that, on the contrary, he was in their hands.[32] And yet he described his characters as puppets and himself as puppet master. Nonetheless, his novels present strongly realized characters, who interact spontaneously and without the constraint of elaborate plotting, a shaping power governs, or at least discloses, the stories of their lives. Despite his aloof manner, Thackeray was a moralizing and didactic novelist, as his letter to Mark Lemon of 24 February 1847 indicates. There he spoke of the "vast multitude of readers whom we not only amuse but teach. And indeed, a solemn prayer to God Almighty was in my thoughts that we may never forget truth & Justice and kindness as the great ends of our professional. . . . our profession seems to me to be as serious as the parson's own."[33]

If Thackeray was a moralist and a believer in an Almighty God, he was also convinced that man did not live in a simple providential world whose schemes were easily traced. Unlike Collins, who retained both design and ambiguity in his novels, Thackeray rejected conventional patterns. Justice, for Thackeray, was capricious and obscure, not certain and reassuring as for Dickens or Carlyle. Man lives amid moral confusion, lost in Vanity Fair. He may construct plots of his life, but Thackeray realized that these plots were illusions, as did Trollope, who remarked candidly, "In our lives we are always weaving plots."[34] As novelist, he *plays* at Fate but a fate that projects no more design than the puppets who suffer its dictates. Geoffrey Tillotson pointed out that apparently fated incidents in Thackeray are no more than normal developments of events; they are not special accidents or coincidences.[35] Fate may be no more than what happens. If so, it presents no special check upon human action. Characters are free to choose, though their choices will not make them free.

Thackeray's characters do not develop in significant ways but have typical significance, and the patterns for Thackeray's narratives are conspicuously traditional "old stories"—the Bible, classical literature, *The Arabian Nights*, fairy tales—all offered at the same zero level of allusion or parable. Moreover, the patterns are as ironically pointed as one would expect from the master of Vanity Fair. Jack P. Rawlins connects this use of old story formulas with Thackeray's sermonizing through "its attempt to achieve universal moral relevance at the expense of dramatic intensity."[36] But if characters are simple and plots dissipated, their substructure essentially fabular anyway, what drives the narrative and what holds the reader? And, for our present purposes, how do the tests people face demonstrate and embody an attitude regarding will or determinism? I shall have to approach these questions by taking a step or two backward.

Sir Henry Maine may have stumbled on a significant truth when he declared that whereas Dickens derived his ideas and moral aims from Bentham, Thackeray's opinions resembled Rousseau's, which were in reaction against an excessive veneration of civilization and progress. "Theoretically, at any rate," Maine says, "Thackeray hated the artificialities of civilisation, and it must be owned that some of his favorite personages have about them something of Rousseau's natural man as he would have shown himself if he had mixed in real life—something, that is, of the violent blackguard."[37] In his antidemocratic mood, Maine exaggerated the case, but it is true that Thackeray reflected human character more realistically than many of his contemporaries as a tangle of good and evil impulses rather than artificially isolating benevolence from greed and virtue from malice.

I do not mean to suggest that Thackeray is a penetrating analyst of human motives. The characters in *Vanity Fair* are simple, but their *behavior* is a mixture of good and evil, caring and carelessness. Amelia is dear and loving but also weak and self-indulgent. George is vain and selfish but responsive to moral goading on occasion. Dobbin is noble but susceptible; heroic but also foolish. Even Becky has her moments of compassion. Becky is also the character who seems most in control of her destiny. Thackeray does not talk about free will and determinism, but he describes patterns of consequence that lead to certain conclusions. From the first time we meet her, Becky is in revolt against circumstances. She struggles to change those circumstances and seems to succeed. But accompanying that pattern of success is a parallel pattern of failure, like a ghostly nemesis. She becomes friendly with the Sedleys but fails to capture Jos; she marries into the Crawley family but misses the wealthy father and picks up the impecunious son; she enchants the Marquis of Steyne but loses her husband and her social caste. The acts of rebellious freedom that constitute her effort at liberation are at the same time egoistic deeds that drive her along an inevitable path toward doom, though it must be admitted that just as her crimes are far slighter than Clytemnestra's, so her doom is comparably innocuous.

Perhaps it is the pathetically banal nature of human destiny that most intrigued Thackeray. He was not much given to bountifully rewarding his heroes and heroines, let alone his scamps and rascals. He was generous to Arthur Pendennis, who, at the end of *Pendennis* (1848–50), is a successful novelist and a happily married man. But Pen is not the best man in this story. George Warrington is. Reflecting on how desirable Laura would be as a wife, George concludes that he has no chance with her because fate has ruled otherwise. He imagines what he could have achieved had Laura been his ideal, then chides himself. "Psha, what a fool I am to brag of what I would have done! We are the slaves of destiny. Our lots are shaped for us, and mine is ordained long ago."[38] Later, however, when confessing to Pendennis the folly of his early marriage, he admits, "My fate is such as I made it, and not lucky for me or for others involved in it" (Thackeray, *Works* 2:248).

If fate is the consequence of our own deeds, Thackeray nonetheless struggles against that notion, yearning, as the passage quoted earlier suggests, to locate the blame on some power beyond the self. "We alter little," the narrator comments in *Pendennis*. "When we talk of this man or that woman being no longer the same person whom we remember in youth, and remark (of course to deplore) changes in our friends, we don't, perhaps calculate that circumstance only brings out the latent defect or quality, and does not create it" (Thackeray, *Works* 2:280). Jack P. Rawlins argues that, unlike Fielding in *Tom Jones*, Thackeray places little obligation on his heroes to make their own fates and gives the instance of Philip who "does not earn his good fortune, either by actions that bring it about or by actions that demonstrate to us his deserving it." He adds that "this freedom from consequence" is made clear by the exception of Colonel Newcome who suffers needlessly, insisting on "living out his novel" (Rawlins, 219–20). But we have seen that Warrington is aware of his tendency to shape his life according to a Greek tragedy, where fate has determined the bitter outcome. Warrington has the strength of character to see what he is doing and revise the estimate of the plot of his life. The significance of his critical power is brilliantly represented also in his editing Pen's life as represented in his romantic tale, *Walter Lorraine*. George teaches Pen to revise his life story. Sentiment and melodrama are modified to a romance and skepticism that, combined, provide the substance of a successful novel. Craig Howes has recently suggested that once Thackeray had established Pen as a successful novelist, he transformed his narrative manner and became Pen in the fiction that followed.[39] One might as easily say that Thackeray combined in himself the qualities of Pen and Warrington. What is important here is Thackeray's awareness that all of life is a process of fictionalizing but that to believe the romances or tragedies we concoct is a serious error. As Rawlins points out, Thackeray meant to produce fiction that did not obey the conventions and which violated expectations about plot development precisely because he wished to teach his readers that simple fictions are dangerous. Above all, we must not trust to the traditional resolutions of poetic justice. To suffer, for example, is not a guarantee of reward.

In Dickens and others, suffering strengthens virtue; Collins recognizes that it may degrade as well as ennoble. But Thackeray can see no merit in suffering. Only resigned defeat awaits those who are disappointed in their aims. "Lucky he who can bear his failure so generously," the narrator of *Pendennis* exclaims, "and give up his broken sword to Fate the Conqueror with a manly and humble heart!" (Thackeray, *Works* 2:281). Men do not create but only interpret their lives. The Power that has made the earth and the sky has also ordered a world of weariness, sickness, failure, and success (Thackeray, *Works* 2:85). Thackeray makes this point clear at the very end of his novel.

> If Mr. Pen's works have procured him more reputation than has been acquired by his abler friend, whom no one knows, George lives contented without the fame. If the best men do not draw the great prizes in life, we know it has been so settled by the Ordainer of the lottery. We own, and see daily, how the false and worthless live and prosper, while the good are called away, and the dear and young perish untimely,—we perceive in every man's life the maimed happiness, the frequent falling, the bootless endeavour, the struggle of Right and Wrong, in which the strong often succumb and the swift fail: we see flowers of good blooming in foul places, as, in the most lofty and splendid fortunes, flaws of vice and meanness, and stains of evil; and, knowing how mean the best of us is, let us give a hand of charity to Arthur Pendennis, with all his faults and shortcomings, who does not claim to be a hero, but only a man and a brother. (Thackeray, *Works* 2:495)

Despite Thackeray's apparent acceptance of fate, he seems to keep George Warrington's admission in mind and acknowledge that men may control their destinies. Pendennis's growth from self-indulgence (his early romances and careless social habits) to self-denial (sparing the infatuated Fanny), to self-discipline (his commitment to serious authorship), although it proceeds with the help of his tutelary spirits Laura and George, nonetheless represents a significant application of will. That the effect of such application changes his life implies that strength of will assumes freedom of will. Perhaps we need not give up our broken sword to fate but may beat him down like any other enemy.

It is no accident, I think, that Pendennis is both a survivor in the battle with fate and a successful novelist. Men imagine a story for their lives and then live out the tale. George Warrington believes his plot line is written and that he must live it out, but Pendennis has the imagination to realize that the future is not written. Thackeray did not wish to prescribe the future and seems to have preferred the efficacy of imaginative will over imaginative reason. Geoffrey Tillotson remarked the oneness of Thackeray's material, tone, and form and concluded that the "lack of edged shape in his novels is not a negative thing, but deliberate and positive, the achievement of an aspiration towards rendering the vastness of the world and the never-endingness of time. . . . Instead of design Thackeray's novels give us continuity."[40] He also wanted to demonstrate the folly of breaking narratives up into credible stories. If characters reappear from one story to another, then *their* stories cannot be simplified and concluded. Pendennis, as narrator of *The Newcomes*, continues to tell his own story, along with those of other characters; it did not end with the conclusion of *Pendennis*. On this vast time scale, the causes and consequences of actions can never be definitely assigned. A new version of a sequence of events could readjust our interpretation and our assignment of values. Thackeray often calls attention to this likelihood, as he does near the end of the *Adventures of Philip* when the narrator admits that if a biography were written from the point of view of characters he has depicted as meanhearted, "some other novelist might show how Philip and his biography were a pair of selfish worldlings unworthy of credit."[41]

The Newcomes (1853–55) makes Thackeray's method obvious. It opens with "a farrago of old fables" in which animals debate their various faults. This toying with Aesopian moral fables is deplored by a putative critic, himself presented by the narrator as a Solomon who sits in judgment upon the author's "children" and chops them up.[42] The animals are all self-involved, critical of others without seeing their own limitations, presuming that they are free to guide their own lives until the appearance of an ass in a lion's skin frightens them, proving their confidence false and leading to their demise. The narrator explains that his own story is just such another animal fable, designed to elaborate a similar lesson. The story proceeds, however, with the frequent assistance of several other sets of allusions to biblical stories, Christian hagiography, tales from *The Arabian Nights*, and classical myth. These allusions seldom establish regular patterns to suggest meaning in the characters' lives but appear so frequently and are so regularly equated with contemporary circumstances that they manifestly suggest that human experience is a complex replaying of a few archetypal patterns. Men and women believe themselves to be free and capable of shaping their destinies by their reason and their will, but little stretches of their life stories are actually stamped out into patterns like dough by a cookie cutter. In a chapter appropriately entitled "An Old Story," Ethel Newcome is likened to a princess, and her aunt, who wishes to place her well in the marriage market begins "to look more and more like the wicked fairy of the stories who is not invited to the Princess's Christening Feast" (Thackeray, *Works* 6:33). When Ethel decides not to marry Lord Farintosh, whom she does not love, the allusion becomes classical, the refusal occurring in a chapter entitled "In Which Achilles Loses Briseis."

This allusiveness to recognizable plot fragments from the western cultural heritage does not consist of straightforward comparisons. All have an ironic flavor, for the characters in this story are not heroic (neither, the suggestion is, were many of the originals of these stories). For example, after the numerous references to the parable of the Good Samaritan, Ethel emerges as the best representative of that role. Why should a woman not be the Samaritan? Other characters play parts that do not entirely suit them. Throughout the novel allusions to conventional roles establish parallels between mundane contemporary events and famous sequences of the past but also present an ironic comment on all fabling. Some characters openly liken themselves to figures in a fiction. Mrs. Mackenzie tells Pendennis, the author of this story, that novelists stop at the third and marriage volume but that her third volume ended when she was sixteen. "Do you think all our adventures ended then, and that we lived happy ever after?" (Thackeray, *Works* 5:292). Thackeray's joke is evident here because the third volume of Pendennis's own life "ended" with the prospect of a satisfying marriage, yet here he is, beyond marriage and the fiction of his own life, constructing the fiction of other lives.

Pendennis, once the central figure of a novel, now composes the story of the Newcomes, further blurring the significance of narration and compromising the "truthfulness" of what he has to say simply because he is a novelist, a professional fabler. By making Pen his narrator, a device he said he "borrowed from Pisistratus Bulwer," Thackeray provided himself with a mask, as he claimed, but also specifically replaced an omniscient providential artist with a fallible story teller.[43] By this and other narrative devices (Esmond's first-person account, etc.), Thackeray drove home his point that in the fictional world as in the real world, we cannot count on a dependable scheme measurable in moral values. In both worlds men are free and make free choices but can never fully know what influenced these choices or what their "final" outcome will be. Moreover, the perception of such causes and consequences changes over time, even the time of the telling. Bulwer's Pisistratus Caxton claimed that he could not govern his characters, who were free; Thackeray suggests that the "freedom" of characters has little significance in the way we actually live. Pen moves in and out of the events of his narrative, creating a sense that he is as much a part of the world he is describing as are his characters and that they are both constrained by the circumstantiality of that world. At the conclusion of the novel, however, when the good characters have been cleansed of their follies and made humble, the narrator steps forward to rend his own fiction, noting some of his own mistakes in telling the story, and reminding us of the animal fable with which he began. Now the novelist abandons his fiction and invites his readers to sustain it on their own. "You may settle your Fable-land in your own fashion. Anything you like happens in Fable-land." The poet of Fable-land is all powerful and morality pervades his domain, the narrator says, but it is clear that such regular and satisfying patterns exist *only* in Fable-land. "Ah, happy, harmless, Fable-land, where these things are! Friendly reader! may you and the author meet there on some future day" (Thackeray, *Works* 6:505–6). But this Fable-land exists *within* the structure of Pen's and Thackeray's narrative, it is not coequal with it. In fact, the narrator specifically refuses to conclude his story, forcing the reader to do that and create his or her own story.[44] Thackeray was deliberate in his refusal to provide the usual comforting closure in his novels. In an 1848 letter to Robert Bell, he wrote of *Vanity Fair*: "I want to leave everybody dissatisfied and unhappy at the end of the story—we ought all to be with our own and all other stories."[45] It was a position he adhered to throughout his career.

Men are free when they are fabricating fictions but only when those fictions are stories removed from life. The narrator of *The Newcomes* establishes the allusive parallels between his characters' lives and notable personalities from Fable-land. This is an ironical rendering of the theological explanation of contemporary historical events as reenactments of biblical archetypes so acceptable to F. D. Maurice and his school discussed in chapter 3. Faith supports the theological analogues; skepticism undermines any satisfaction in fables. In the one, man is free within the larger pattern of providence; in the other, the patterns are created by men who cannot believe them but who must still believe themselves free in their power to imagine patterns.

Pendennis is a skeptical intelligence yearning for the comfort of some order—divine or otherwise. His solution is to fabricate that order and make himself the immanent deity of the world he has created, walking about in it as the Greek gods were wont to do and as inept as they often were in understanding or guiding their mystifying world. The same is true of *The Adventures of Philip* (1861–62), even more bluntly based on the pattern of analogues that we have seen operating in *The Newcomes*. The full title calls attention once more to the story of the Good Samaritan. But something altogether more sly and intriguing happens in *Henry Esmond* (1852).

We have seen that it makes a difference in novels such as *David Copperfield* and *Alton Locke* that the first-person narrators are themselves writers. Authorship is even more important with Esmond. He is not merely the narrator of his own story, but the chronicler of historical "fact." We have already seen that introducing historical "reality" into fiction adds the narrative stricture that certain events *must* occur because we know them to have occurred. This does not mean that events we do not know not to have occurred did not occur. This is the realm of freedom. Although *Henry Esmond* is not as allusive as Pendennis's novels, it depends upon at least one chief conventional pattern—the story of Jacob, the patriarch who waited patiently to win his Rachel. Esmond himself calls attention to this analogy, though he applies the analogy to himself and Beatrix. Beatrix rightly interprets it in reference to Esmond and her mother, whose name, after all, is Rachel.[46]

Andrew Sanders claims that there is no authorial voice in *Henry Esmond* to interpret Esmond's historical account.[47] But Esmond himself attempts the role of objective author by recounting his personal history in the third person as though to establish a sense of destiny and historical inevitability where there is only individual invention. Esmond's artfulness reveals his distrust of history as recoverable truth. "In *Henry Esmond*," Sanders says, "Thackeray presents a scrupulously 'invented' picture of life, yet the invention itself represents the arbitrary and ambiguous nature of human experience." Nonetheless, Thackeray's rendering of history as the subjective account of one individual is more "realistic" than the work of historical novelists, and, one might add, historians, who wrote to illustrate a moral or providential pattern operative in history.[48]

Thackeray was in advance of most historical thinking in his day because he rejected providential or progressive history, instead rendering the past as a collection of arbitrary events given meaning through the shaping power of art. A further irony in *Esmond* is that the artistic shaper of history, who asserts his freedom of will by constructing the world in which he must live, is himself a fiction. Esmond may imitate a deity designing human time and circumstances and descending into the world of his creation; he may alter history to his needs and reap the benefits of his free acts; but he remains a fiction. For the true creator, Thackeray, freedom is in Fable-land only, but there it is complete. Recounting his story with the advantage of retrospect, Edmond does the opposite of what an objective historian would do—he bestows free will upon himself and mutes the power of circumstance. Even Carlyle's heroes of history are not free in this sense but only insofar as they become the willing channels of divine purpose. Esmond is misled, however. He is a creature of fable who does not realize, or only partially realizes, that his reshaping of events is consolation, not truth. In this he resembles any artist who may find freedom in Fable-land but must return to a world where chance or fate surrounds him once he leaves the safety of his fiction.

Esmond is not as free as he himself supposes. Disguised identities and coincidences aside, certain features of his narrative suggest that he is living out a destiny foreordained not only by his own choices but by the deliberate control of his own author. For example, whereas Esmond uses the Jacob typology casually in reference to Beatrix, Thackeray demonstrates that Esmond's entire life is a working out of that stereotype with a perverse twist in it. Esmond is not entirely forthright in attempting to force the events of his life into a consistent design. Early in his tale he boasts that now, as an old man sitting and recalling "in tranquility the happy and busy scenes of [his youth], he can think, not ungratefully, that he has been faithful to that early vow" of fidelity to his mistress, Lady Castlewood (Thackeray, *Works* 7:92). This passage suggests many things but not that fidelity and obedient service will take the form of marriage, and especially marriage to Rachel only after Esmond's passionate love for her daughter, Beatrix, has been rejected. Was it fidelity all along that Esmond felt, and, if so, the same kind of fidelity? Or is this passage, like so many others, a warning for the reader to be wary of Esmond's version of history?

Thackeray was a compulsive gambler in his youth and suffered hugely from the capriciousness of luck. He was doubtful to what degree men could govern themselves and therefore to what degree they were accountable for their acts. In "A Gambler's Death," he connected his own weakness with one possible story line his life might have taken. He tells of encountering an old fellow student and lending him five pounds, with which Attwood, the friend, achieves spectacular gaming success before fortune turns again. Thackeray remarks, "I dare not think of his fate, for except in the fact of his poverty and desperation was he worse than any of us, his companions, who had shared his debauches, and marched with him up to the very brink of the grave?"[49]

Esmond's account of personal and national past is doomed to error insofar as it attempts to create a coherent story of past events, for the general law that gives coherence to his serialization of past events is his own love, largely misunderstood by himself through much of his history. Thackeray called Esmond a "prig," indicating that his rendering of the past is not authoritative.[50] Thackeray did not approve of such plotting; plots themselves were falsifications, though enduringly attractive because they carry the flavor of explanation and justification with them. Jack P. Rawlins says that "those events that potentially have consequences in the scheme of the main plot—the love interest, for instance,—are made ostentatiously artificial by Thackeray. He makes us see that those elements that make up a plot in *The Newcomes* are the creation of an author who desires to make a plot" (Rawlins, 109).

In a moment of reflectiveness, Thackeray said that life would be more comfortable if it were fated, because then we would not be responsible for our deeds. But he apparently believed that we *were* responsible and fate was only one or another plot got up to excuse or justify our condition. Life was too complex to be understood in these terms. Though men and women were free, the consequences of that freedom were uncertain. Real freedom existed only in Fable-land. That is why Thackeray was so reluctant to trace the destinies of his characters and preferred to have them continuing to exist in an achronological milieu. When Thackeray composed a novel, it was, as he said, "the destiny of his narrative," that he pursued, for fictive narrative was the only reality over which he as author had any real control (Thackeray, *Works Newcomes* 1:506).

Near the end of his career, Thackeray acknowledged the direct influence of an author's world view upon his fictions; "our books are diaries," he wrote, "in which our own feelings must of necessity be set down."[51] He admired authors like Alexander Dumas who could sketch an entire plot in their minds before beginning to write but confessed that his own stories *must* go a certain way, in spite of themselves. "I have been surprised at the observations made by some of my characters. It seems as if an occult Power was moving the pen." And he wondered if other novelists experienced this "fatalism" (Thackeray, *Works* 22:260). But, of course, there is an irony even here, for the Dumas-style novel that is fixed from the outset is the truly fated because the characters must do as the author has foreordained, whereas in Thackeray's fictions, the author is as much surprised by the "free" actions of his characters as they themselves must be and thus the occult power that energizes author and characters alike leaves them a measure of freedom within the uninterpretable design.

Thackeray said of his fiction writing, "What I want is to make a set of people living without God in the world."[52] By this he could have meant without the moral order or the providential scheme implied by God's presence. He did his best to strip providence from his fiction, but the moral stand remains strong. Like Thackeray, Anthony Trollope described his art as essentially moral. "I have ever thought of myself as a preacher of sermons, and my pulpit as one which I could make both salutary and agreeable to my audience."[53] But in Trollope's novels the moral positions are less evident than in Thackeray's.[54] Trollope more than Thackeray gives us a human world where no god intervenes, not even that substitute god, the author. Trollope is a Thackeray without anguish. He too assumes a world without clear design yet trusts that matters will work out well if we make an effort. Unlike Thackeray, who could not see that strength of will guarantees success or happiness and did not want to accept the responsibility that attends free will, Trollope was content to grant mankind free will and its consequences but never openly placed acts and their consequences in a metaphysical context. Even in Trollope's prose style, the hidden retractions and reversals so common to Thackeray are reduced to clarity and a straightforward march of evidence. Events occur and, in so happening, beget other events. Men are the initiators of deeds and the inheritors of consequences. For Trollope, men are free because fate, providence, and necessity are superfluous. Accordingly, Trollope makes himself as unnecessary as he can as author. Like Thackeray, he claims simply to have written with a basic sense of good and evil to be worked out. "As to the incidents of the story, the circumstances by which these personages were to be effected, I knew nothing. They were created for the most part as they were described. I never could arrange a set of events before me" (Trollope, *Autobiography*, 291). Trollope did not wish to imitate God but to live in the world of circumstantiality with his characters, to let them develop their own identities and shape their own courses. Trollope's fictional world is comfortably circumscribed. His famous recipe for the novel is instructive in this regard. It must "give a picture of common life enlivened by humour and sweetened by pathos." It must be peopled by "real portraits . . . of created personages impregnated with traits of characters which are known." These characters are far more important than plot, though there must, of course, be a story (Trollope, *Autobiography*, 116).

Trollope's fictional world is a world taken for granted. It deals with what is "common" and "traits of character which are known." Notions of fate, providence, and destiny do not intrude because our perception of the human condition rarely rises above the collision of individual character. Trollope's world is plotless because his characters are hypothetically free to alter the story at any moment. Yet their world is ordered because their natures and their acts are limited to the familiar precincts and predictable ranges of average human experience. Trollope could write so abundantly and with such ease because in his fictional world there was no conflict between free will and a determining force. Either he disbelieved in any such force or he conveniently excluded it from the world in which he wished to bring rewards to the good and to embarrass the wicked.

As in Thackeray's novels, Trollope's characters move freely over the range of his fictions, similarly suggesting the existence of a thriving community beyond the limits of individual plot lines. Moreover, plots and subplots sometimes come into conflict with one another, providing the multiple perspectives on characters' actions that Thackeray so prized. James Kincaid says that "The complexity of Trollope's novels arises mainly from the fact that this coherence is both attacked and supported. Trollope writes a plot with one hand, while with the other he knifes at it."[55] Kincaid demonstrates, too, that Trollope utilized conventions while intent upon subverting them. "We are urged, on the one hand, to find full meaning in pattern suggested by the action, but there is a concurrent sense of the artificiality, even falseness of that pattern, a sense that genuine life is to be found only outside all pattern."[56]

In his youthful commonplace book, Trollope expressed opinions that remained essentially unchanged for the rest of his life. From the start, he was interested in depicting real human nature and deplored Bulwer's inability to do so. Interest in Bulwer's novels attached to the stories, but Trollope was not interested in the basic impulse of story, what he described in an estimate of a G. P. R. James romance as that very poor charm, "the desire to know what becomes of the people."[57] More interesting for the theme of the present study is one of Trollope's objections to Pope's *Essay on Man*.

> Again Pope would make us destitute of free will—a sort of metaphysical Calvinist—a rational predestinarian—man is with him nothing—his movements are ordained—he should move, implies the author, as his impulses direct—& not complain—he is nothing—a tool used by some power—a puppet not only of his passions (which is true enough) but of the workings of a system. And I fleece my brother that the chain of a preordained system might not be broken.
>
> He says rightly that we should submit to God [—] he inculcates rightful obedience but he induces it from such a reason, that a bad

man should not be discontented with and fight off his own vice—we may not strive to improve morality.[58]

I see no reason to doubt that Trollope assumed human free will and the importance of submission to God's will, but he clearly did not support or exhibit a providential scheme in his fiction. Trollope is concerned with strength of will but seems to distrust it as an inauthentic expression of human freedom. In a novel like *He Knew He Was Right* (1868–69), the trouble between Louis Trevelyan and his wife Emily arises largely from each insisting on having his or her own way. Trollope shows a contrasting ability in strong-willed characters like Nora Rowley and Jemima Stanbury to accede to reasonable restraints upon their desires. He prefers characters like Arabin and Eleanor Bold, or Frank Greystock, or Mrs. Max Goesler, or Phineas Finn, who have an underlying integrity of character, though subject to lapses in judgment, behavior, or absolute rectitude. Trollope wants his attractive characters to be middling; the more energetic figures like Lizzie Eustace, Lopez, Melmotte, Fisker, Slope, and Mrs. Proudie are chastised. And, like Thackeray, he wanted his narratives to be shorn of the excessive energies of romance. He even pretended to amputate that strongest of narrative lures, suspense. In *Barchester Towers* (1857), he calms the anxious reader concerning Eleanor Bold's future.

> But let the gentle-hearted reader be under no apprehension whatsoever. It is not destined that Eleanor shall marry Mr. Slope or Bertie Stanhope. And here, perhaps, it may be allowed to the novelist to explain his views on a very important point in the art of telling tales. He ventures to reprobate that system which goes so far to violate all proper confidence between the author and his readers, by maintaining nearly to the end of the third volume a mystery as to the fate of their favourite personage.

He deplores this use of suspense and considers it ultimately unsatisfying for author and reader alike, then adds, "Our doctrine is, that the author and the reader should move along together in full confidence with each other."[59]

Trollope similarly abandoned suspense in *Dr. Wortle's School* (1881) as an attraction and recommends the proper audience response. He says he'll abandon the usual principles of story telling and put "the horse of my romance before the cart. There is a mystery respecting Mr. and Mrs. Peacocke which, according to all laws recognized in such matters, ought not to be elucidated till . . . so near the end that there should be left only space for those little arrangements which are necessary for the well-being, or perhaps for the evil-being, of our personages."[60] But Trollope is not quite candid in passages of this sort. For example, though he tells us who Eleanor Bold will not marry, he doesn't mention who she *will* marry, if anyone at all. Nonetheless, the object of such authorial passages is to create an illusion of low-tension narrative so very like our actual experience that the fictional characters will appear real.

Trollope did not take that additional, complicated step that Thackeray took—to make the narrative voice a means of divorcing fictional and real worlds by emphasizing the former's artifice. He was content to allow his authorial intrusions to *reinforce* the connection between fiction and reality. Both writers wished to present a fictional world ungoverned by a providential or an artistic design. To them, the real world contained beings who, for better or worse, controlled their lives through free will. How they exercised that freedom was the interesting thing. By emphasizing the freedom of their characters, both novelists relaxed the structure of their narratives to such a degree that the reader him or herself was invited to participate in the fiction making, with Trollope as a form of entertainment and mild instruction, with Thackeray as a warning not to be duped into accepting the stories all men are deceived into composing of their lives.

CHAPTER FIFTEEN

George Eliot

T HE last chapter examined some novelists whose basic outlook resembled the dominant outlook among the religious moralists surveyed in chapter 3. George Eliot's nontheological position is more in keeping with the necessarians discussed in chapter 4. But what could be presented clearly in expository prose was less pliable in fiction. Eliot wanted to represent a world governed by the laws of invariant causation unaffected by any supernatural power. It was, therefore, presumably a Godwinian world where free will was a useful but illusory notion. Eliot wanted to retain some measure of freedom in her characters and apparently wanted to embody that freedom in the form of her novels. The highly formulaic nature of some of her novels aptly renders a world in which necessity is the overarching force, but it seems to falsify genuine individual freedom in a circumstantial world. The less rigorously designed novels, *Mill on the Floss* and especially *Middlemarch*, better incorporate the possibility of freedom and necessity operating together. In any case, Eliot was less concerned with exploring the question of free will and more intrigued by the proper application of the will as power for action. Her conclusion was the familiar recommendations that we suppress our self will in the interest of a higher good.

~ ~ ~

Unlike most of the novelists I have discussed so far, who were reticient about the relationship of their philosophies to their fictions, George Eliot was a consciously philosophical novelist, aware of the implications of her thinking in her fictional approach. George Bernard Shaw claimed that Eliot "was broken by the fatalism that ensued when she discarded God. In her most famous novel *Middlemarch* . . . there is not a ray of hope: the characters have no more volition than billiard balls: they are moved only by circumstances and heredity."[1] Recent critics have been more temperate in their assessments. George Levine wrote of Eliot, "Determinism informed her artistic vision," adding the qualification that "determinism was for her not a rigid and depressing system but an aspect of the world which she saw and dramatized."[2] The editors of Eliot's notebook for *Middlemarch* suggest that her main question was how free any person was to shape his own or another's destiny.[3] Shaw implied that an author who believed in determinism would be unable to create a convincing and intriguing world of human action, but Gillian Beer says that "George Eliot's creativity escapes from the dilemma of determinism by invoking the multiple and the latent."[4] Eliot's determinism is not a simple matter; as with Mill and other necessarians, it leaves the door of individual freedom ajar. It cannot be said that for Eliot the will is ultimately free, but her determinism is far from absolute.[5]

In some ways, Eliot is the best example for the present study because critics have so consistently identified the philosophical significance of her novels. The outline of her intellectual development has long since been schematized. Mary Anne Evans began as an earnest Evangelical but soon substituted for Christian injunctions to submit the independent will to the will of God a nontheistic variation on that theme—the suppression of self for the good of mankind. Bernard J. Paris describes an intermediate stage of this development in which, influenced by the ideas of Spinoza, Hennell, and Bray, Evans could "accept the determinism of science without sacrificing her belief that a spiritual principle governs the universe" and is discoverable "through man's own mind contemplating itself and the course of nature."[6] Ultimately, Eliot arrived at the positivist creed that sustained her for the rest of her life.[7] For Paris, Eliot's task is "envisioning the implications for human existence of the order of things and of the subjective and objective approaches to reality."[8] U. C. Knoepflmacher offers another dichotomy, describing two conflicting impulses that operate in Eliot's fiction—the desire to depict temporal actuality as she saw it, along with a need to assure her readers "that man's inescapable subjection to the flux of time did not invalidate a trust in justice, perfectibility, and order."[9] Felicia Bonaparte less positively sees Eliot applying the universal symbol of Greek tragedy to individual cases. "The Greek gods and modern science, Eliot claimed, disclose the same absurd universe and the same tragic confrontation. The Greeks called it hybris and nemesis; Eliot calls it will and destiny."[10] Behind these and similar interpretations lies the basic question of whether man is free or determined.

Eliot anchored her view of human conduct on the principle that men inevitably reap the consequences of their actions, a view that her contemporaries quickly grasped. Edward Dowden applauded her scientific approach. "The assurance that we live under a reign of natural law enforces upon us with a solemn joy and an abiding fear the truth that what a man soweth, that shall he also reap; and if he sow for others (and who does not?) others must reap of his sowing, tares of tares, and wheat of wheat."[11] Baron Acton wrote that "the doctrine that neither contrition nor sacrifice can appease Nemesis, or avert the consequences of our wrong-doing from ourselves and others, filled a very large space indeed in her scheme of life and literature; she believed the world would be better if men could be made to feel that there is no escape from the inexorable law that we reap what we have sown."[12] An interesting expression of this inexorable law occurs in *Adam Bede* (1859) when Arthur Donnithorne appeals to the Reverend Mr. Irwine for advice in his romantic quandary. Arthur argues that even a man of strong character may be overcome by love. Mr. Irwine responds: "I daresay, now, even a man fortified with a knowledge of the classics might be lured into an imprudent marriage, in spite of the warning given him in the Prometheus."[13]

Aeschylus's *Prometheus Bound* is scarcely about marriage; it mainly treats the Titan's suffering as a consequence of his sympathetic consideration for mankind. Prometheus's lament is more characteristic of the play's central theme.

> So must I bear, as lightly as I can,
> the destiny that fate has given me;
> for know well against necessity,
> against its strength, no one can fight and win.[14]

Arthur does not pick up Mr. Irwine's allusion, complaining instead that despite their careful deliberations, men should be ruled by moods after all. Mr. Irwine does not relent but more precisely restates his point, saying that moods are just as much a part of a man's nature as his reflections. "A man can never do anything at variance with his own nature. He carries within him the germ of his most exceptional action." Arthur objects that a man may be betrayed by a combination of circumstances, and though he uses the word "circumstances" casually, in the context of this conversation it carries for the reader the philosophical implication of "determining influences." Thus whereas Arthur depicts himself as a creature at the mercy of wayward events, hoping to excuse his impulses, Irwine perceives his dilemma in classical and philosophical terms where human responsibility is implicit. A man's struggles against temptation, he says, "foreshadow the inward suffering which is the worst form of Nemesis," then elaborates a necessarian creed. "Consequences are unpitying. Our deeds carry their terrible consequences, quite apart from any fluctuations that went before—consequences that are hardly ever confined to ourselves" (Eliot, *Bede*, 147). It is just such a nemesis that Eliot charts in Arthur's and Hetty's careers.

Ian Adam says that "man's free will and his consequent responsibility for his actions are emphasized at several points in *Adam Bede*," and claims that " 'Nature' cooperates to a large extent with that set of values which George Eliot shares with Carlyle and with that view of responsibility and free will which she emphasizes more than he."[15] But, if this is so, free will means simply that the individual can choose the better over the worse course if his motives, themselves determined, are strong enough.

Adam Bede is an early dramatization of Eliot's dilemma. Without crediting the existence of a Supreme Being or providentially directed spiritual and supernatural world, she believes in determinism or invariability of sequence in nature. At the same time, like the utilitarians, she requires some quality in mankind that makes it capable of improvement, a quality that, arising from within man, resembles what others might call free will, though for Eliot that term is forbidden. Man must improve upon nature because nature, by itself, is amoral. U. C. Knoepflmacher points out that Eliot's ambivalent attitude toward nature is exemplified in *Adam Bede* through Dinah and Hetty, the one representing higher, the other lower, nature (Knoepflmacher, 119ff). But if there is no supernatural reality, how does man, himself a part of nature, come to be moral in a nonmoral universe? This, of course, was a problem that T. H. Huxley and others like him tried to address, as we saw in part 1. Eliot asserted that the universe was merely causal and nonteleological, but she could not refrain from establishing a moral pattern in her fiction.[16] Ironically, the more she affirmed human freedom, the more rigorous her fictional structure became, whereas, when her characters are most constrained, their fictional frameworks are more relaxed.

Representing a nonsymbolic universe realistically would presumably exclude the serious use of symbols, but Eliot encouraged symbolic readings in *Adam Bede*, even elevating its characters through allusions to *Paradise Lost*.[17] Moreover, the novel is almost formulaic in its ordering. Calvin Bedient, more severe than most critics, complains that the novel's "realism . . . can be reduced to a moral formula or two." What's more, the novel is static, he says. "George Eliot's moral mind rules the book, and this mind itself is fixed and self-referring."[18]

Nor can the novel, for Eliot, genuinely approximate tragedy. A passage from *Felix Holt* (1866) echoes the conventional terms of Greek tragedy. "For there is seldom any wrong-doing which does not carry along with it some downfall of blindly-climbing hopes . . . some tragic mark of kinship in the one brief life to the far-stretching life that went before, and to the life that is to come after, such as has raised the pity and terror of men ever since they began to discern between will and destiny."[19] But if Eliot's opposition of will and destiny restates the Greek conflict of hybris and nemesis, her retreat from heroic to common action diminishes tragic force. Jeanette King says that Eliot's fidelity to life deliberately undermines the movement of her novels toward tragedy.[20] Though tragedy is a part of human life, it is *only* a part and does not encompass individual existence. Bedient too rejects Eliot's attempt to create a common tragedy. "Positivist tragedy, a tragedy of broad daylight, is a contradiction in terms."[21]

Eliot's themes call for tragedy, but her commitment to realism and her solution for human suffering forbid it, hence there is bound to be some imperfection in the forms she employs, unless, as in *Silas Marner* (1861), she suspends her absolute commitment to realism and modifies her strict application of causal invariance. U. C. Knoepflmacher explains that *Silas Marner* succeeds so well as a work of art because it is concerned more with its own coherence than with its lessons. Freedom and accident may be at odds in other novels; in *Silas Marner* they are smoothly allowed to blend. This is no realist novel but a moral fable.[22] Thus the many references to luck and chance, the several gambles and risks that characters suffer or initiate, are credible. That they should ultimately prove to be causally related is not surprising either. Godfrey Cass, for example, sees that the life he interpreted in terms of chance and luck is actually governed by strict rules of consequence and that he is responsible for every deed. He knows this early in his career but forgets the truth of it when his brother, Dunstan, "providentially" disappears. Dunstan is blackmailing Godfrey, who must give him what he asks. The narrator remarks: "And if Godfrey could have felt himself simply a victim, the iron bit that destiny had put in his mouth would have chafed him less intolerably." But he knows that it is his own "vicious folly" that has thus saddled him.[23] Ultimately, Godfrey's luck collapses and he suffers an ironic reversal when he is frustrated in his attempt to recover the daughter he long ago abandoned. His wife, Nancy, decides that adopting Eppie would contradict the will of providence, and Godfrey is forced to abandon all hope of recovering his child.

Only in a fable or a fairy tale could such neat reversals seem acceptable. And *Silas Marner* is filled with them. Silas himself, disenchanted with the religious brotherhood of Lantern Yard, abandons it and his spiritual life together, committing himself instead to solitude and gold. The chance that subsequently deprives him of his gold also brings him Eppie. Brian Swann notes that as soon as Silas accepts responsibility for himself, chance ceases to be inimical.[24] Thus, although Silas will not raise "his own will" as an obstacle to Eppie's good fortune of adoption into the Cass household, he is "providentially" rewarded when Nancy decides that such a move would oppose providence.

Of course there is no providence in the novel. There is only the pattern that arises from men's actions interacting with circumstance. But a willingness to face the consequences of one's deeds and to recognize the limits of circumstance teaches humility to the wise and puts them in harmony with the natural order of things. Dolly Winthrop is the spokeswoman for this view, though she states it in an old-fashioned theistic form. "It's the will of Them above as a many things should be dark to us," but that "all as we've got to do is to trusten, Master Marner—to do the right thing as fur as we know, and to trusten" (Eliot, *Marner*, 204).

Silas Marner avoids the problem of resolving belief and expression by concentrating on esthetic form, but most of Eliot's novels try to reconcile contending assumptions, among them, and most pertinent here, the assumption that all existence is subject to the law of invariance of consequence and that because man can alter his condition he is morally responsible.[25] Eliot wrote to Frederick Harrison: "I think aesthetic teaching is the highest of all teaching because it deals with life in its highest complexity. But if it ceases to be purely aesthetic—if it lapses anywhere from the picture to the diagram—it becomes the most offensive of all teaching" (Eliot, *Letters* 6:600). Yet it was precisely such didactic diagramming that hostile critics objected to in her novels. W. H. Mallock described her fiction as "a gradual setting forth of a philosophy and religion of life illustrated by a continuous succession of diagrams" (Knoepflmacher, 165). Like other authors I have discussed, Eliot wanted her fiction to teach as well as to entertain, but she had a more detailed philosophy to expound and therefore was more seriously challenged to accommodate form and style to the ideas she wanted her art to embody. She did not always succeed.

Romola (1862–63) is perhaps the most obvious lapse of picture to diagram among Eliot's novels. She read encyclopedically to prepare for this historical tale, being, as usual, greatly concerned with accuracy of detail.[26] She read Bulwer's *Rienzi*, but apparently his very successful *The Last Days of Pompeii* was also not far from her mind when she composed the romantic plot of her novel.[27] Tito, a handsome Greek in Italian Florence, except for his corruptibility, resembles Glaucus, the high-minded Greek in Roman Pompeii. Both men fall in love with compassionate and intellectual women of high birth and unusual learning. Both are loved in a more animal way by humble women. Tito succumbs to Tessa's innocent charms, thereby setting one evil train of consequences afoot, whereas Glaucus never knows of Nydia's passion, though she is likewise instrumental in altering his destiny— almost fatally. In both novels, the noble-natured heroines are contrasted with religiously fanatical brothers who die. There are other similarities indicating that Eliot was searching for a proven pattern of romance to bear the weight of her lesson.

She did not succeed according to an early representative estimate in the *Westminster Review*. Praising Eliot for her minute analysis of moral growth, the reviewer isolates the achievement of the book: "No one has so fully seized the great truth that we can none of us escape the consequences of our conduct, that each action has not only a character of its own, but also an influence on the character of the actor from which there is no escape." But he goes on to deprecate the actual structure of the novel: "the external machinery of the tale is but the means by which it shall be set in an adequate light, considerations of probability are comparatively small matters, and the most fortuitous coincidences are accepted without a pang so that they do but aid in the display of that which is of more importance to the author than any superficial likelihood."[28] She might have avoided this weakness by setting her tale in the contemporary world, he says. But it is likely that Eliot chose a remote time precisely so that she could simplify her moral lesson without obviously belying experience.

George Levine has shown that *Romola* and *Daniel Deronda* sustain the moral schematism of *Silas Marner*. All approach moral fable to a greater or lesser degree. But the stories of the two main characters of *Romola* are in tension because one is in the tradition of realism, the other in the tradition of romance.[29] *Romola* thus hovers between novel and fable. Possibly Eliot intended this. Her failure was one of experiment, not ineptitude.

The coincidences that beset Tito Melema exceed all probability. Fra Luca, the monk who knows the story of Tito's obligation to his foster father, turns out to be Romola's brother, Dino. Escaping from his guards while being marched through Florence, Baldassarre, the injured foster father, runs headlong into none other than Tito himself. Baldassarre already suspects betrayal because he chanced to see the ring he had given to Tito on the finger of a man he encountered casually in Genoa! Seeking refuge, Baldassarre ends up at the same place where Tessa, the mother of Tito's child, lives, and she innocently reveals some of Tito's story to him. These are only a few samples, but the crowning coincidence is in Tito's death. Escaping from an angry crowd, he leaps into the Arno and comes ashore precisely where Baldassarre has stationed himself to wait for discarded food. He leaps upon Tito and murders him then dies himself. This is a fable embodying nemesis in an actual character. Far from disguising her method, Eliot underscores it with Piero di Cosimo's premonitory painting of Tito as a man alarmed and terrified by some sudden revelation. Of course, Piero gets Baldassarre to model as the threatening figure in this painting. Piero's picture is a diagram with a vengeance.

Romola's story is equally governed by coincidence. Ironically, when she sees Piero's sketch of Tito and the wild prisoner, she dismisses it as a mere coincidence. Attempting flight from Florence in disguise, Romola encounters Savonarola on the road out of town. He persuades her to return home, claiming that he is God's messenger to save her from lapsing into a selfish life with no rule but her own will.[30] Are we to accept his explanation? How else does he chance to be there? If we apply the author-providence model here, we can say that Savonarola is Eliot's messenger to Romola, but that is no more than to say that Eliot so created her fictional world as to allow its characters no true freedom. Wherever Romola goes and whatever she does, circumstances conspire to involve her in predetermined plot lines. For example, when she is tending the sick, Romola revives none other than Baldassarre, who has been given up for dead. Later Romola happens upon a child wandering in the street and helps it to find its home. Whose home is this but Tessa's, whose child but Tito's? And so it goes. In a universe so tightly woven, how is an individual free to interlace her own thread as she chooses?

And yet *Romola* is about strength of will. Tito's moral degeneration follows from his selfishness. At the crisis of his meeting with Baldassarre, he loses his usual self-command. The narrator explains: "Tito was experiencing that inexorable law of human souls, that we prepare ourselves for sudden deeds by the reiterated choice of good or evil that gradually determines character" (Eliot, *Romola* 1:211).[31] For Tito, life is a game and his part in it an acted role. He cannot be sincere but falls into a pattern of deceit that ultimately weakens him. This inexorable law applies not only to individuals but to whole nations. "Our lives make a moral tradition for our individual selves, as the life of mankind at large makes a moral tradition for the race; and to have once acted greatly seems to make a reason why we should always be noble. But Tito was feeling the effect of an opposite tradition; he had won no memories of self-conquest and perfect faithfulness from which he could have a sense of falling" (Eliot, *Romola* 2:58).

By contrast, Savonarola exerts his "mighty and generous will" for a higher purpose (Eliot, *Romola* 1:199). He sincerely means to subordinate his own selfish interests to the common good and preaches this lesson unhypocritically. Moreover, his preaching wakens a slumbering intent among the people and gives "the vague desires of that majority the character of a determinate will" (Eliot, *Romola* 2:27). Romola, who begins with an "imperious will," learns to bow before a higher law (Eliot, *Romola* 1:59; 2:70). Paradoxically, she throws "all the energy of her will into renunciation" (Eliot, *Romola* 2:75). In doing so, Romola realizes "what a length of road she had travelled through" since first meeting Savonarola. She appreciates how greatly she has changed and what a distance there is between her past and present selves and turns her attention to the future. She is freed from the self that wished to control the past and senses the liberating dedication of selfless acceptance of the changes to come. The scene embodies an idea implicit in Hegelian thought—that man's will is with the future until it becomes his personal past and assumes form through reflective thought. It was an idea present in Bulwer's very different philosophy as well. Thus Romola renounces the past self that has assumed a rigorous and even dangerous form and commits her will to the unfolding future, whereas Tito is entangled in the past, his future ransomed to an increasingly rigid destiny. Believing that he retains control of the past, Tito loses the future. Romola accepts the inevitability of the past and inherits the future. She has learned what has never become apparent to Tito—that, as the narrator explains, "Our deeds are like children that are born to us; they live and act apart from our own will" (Eliot, *Romola* 1:156). Eliot wants to demonstrate that freedom and destiny may be reconciled. Her solution sounds very like the traditional Christian answer—to sink the individual will in a higher law. But whereas the Christian may abandon mere reason and comfortably take his God on faith, Eliot can offer no such security. In *Romola* Eliot tries by an effort of her own will to create a fictional world in which that higher law credibly operates. Within the world of *Romola* the consequences of unwise moral choices are glaringly obvious, but they do not translate into the living world of real men. Eliot recognized *Silas Marner* as a "sort of legendary tale," whose moral formulas might apply to real life in the way that the slogans of fairy tales do—provisionally.[32] In *Romola*, Eliot seems to have wanted the formulas to apply directly, but in the real world the evidences for Eliot's higher law are not so easily demonstrable. The form Eliot's novel takes embodies her intellectual quandary. She wants to believe that human existence has a moral shape, but she can provide no evidence for that shape aside from the law of necessity. Her highly contrived fictional world can provide the design only by appropriating conventions of supernatural governance that Eliot herself rejected as a true explanation. Her characters thus do not appear free and responsible since all that they do is so patently arranged by a prescient, omnipotent author.

Eliot made another attempt to resolve this disjunction between moral pattern and unpatterned circumstantiality in *Daniel Deronda* (1876). Part of her difficulty in *Romola* was that her heroine was too ideal—a goddess, not a woman (Eliot, *Letters* 4:103–4). Her powerful will served a noble purpose. By contrast, as Martin Price suggests, Gwendolyn Harleth's "assertion of will is imperious in tone, but it has no high object."[33] Gwendolyn's selfish will has no anchor and therefore fluctuates with fear. What she needs is the moral certainty of a Deronda. What she evokes instead is Grandcourt, a connoisseur of tyranny, "the nemesis her nature calls up by its very lack of any object beyond herself."[34] So Faust's cry for greater power similarly evokes the demonic spirit of denial because the selfish desire for power is founded not on creation but negation. Inverted prayers are answered by fallen angels. Each man or woman evokes the appropriate demon by his or her selfish desire. Gwendolyn's belief that the homage of men proves the dominion of her will is a delusion, because it is founded not on discipline or self-mastery, but on a mere impression of authority. Gwendolyn is a gambler with existence, as the repeated references to her gambling and risk taking suggest. She believes in her will but trusts to chance. By contrast, Daniel Deronda has the governed will so energetically championed by Samuel Smiles and others, but he lacks an appropriate object for his will. Unlike Tito, he has trained himself in virtuous habits; hence he is prepared for his crisis and makes Romola's choice to devote himself to a cause that transcends his individual will.

Eliot's narrative is an effort at mastery very like Deronda's. Her long submission to her craft prepared her for a supreme test at creating a fictional world that describes the manner in which humans exert their wills and participate in the formation of their characters and thus direct their fates. At the same time, that world must convey a sense of moral law without the obtrusive fabling of *Romola*. Eliot must give evidence both of man's power to compel events and also of the justification of worthy events to compel. Her narrative must assume the properties of a sacred text. Mary Wilson Carpenter has suggested that Eliot may have patterned her novel on the scriptural Book of Daniel and the design of Apocalypse.[35] She believes that Eliot exploited the theological controversy about the Book of Daniel active in the nineteenth century and reversed the traditional Christian interpretation by having Jewish Daniel convert Christian Gwendolyn. The novel's chapters suggest a balanced numerical significance that establishes an unobtrusive sense of inevitability. Eliot has retreated beyond fable and legend to myth—insofar as the biblical accounts may be viewed as myth. Rather than reviving old myth, however, Eliot seeks to transform the machinery of myth into living history. Mordecai, in advocating Zionism, does not ask simply that the old Hebraic *rule* be reinstituted but that the Jewish *spirit* be revivified. "I believe in a growth, a passage, and a new unfolding of life whereof the seed is more perfect, more charged with the elements that are pregnant with diviner form."[36]

Though *Deronda* has gained in stature recently, general readers as well as scholars have consistently preferred *The Mill on the Floss* (1860) and *Middlemarch* (1871-72) among Eliot's novels, and this is probably because these novels make greater concessions to the circumstantial world. *The Mill on the Floss* (1860) owes much of its savor to its strong sense of contingency, of the sense of real existence conveyed, for example, in the conversations of Maggie Tulliver's aunts and the ebullient monologues of Bob Jakin. Without getting into the issue of literary realism's dependence upon illusion, it is still possible to assert that realism is served by an apparent redundance of specific detail, such as Mrs. Glegg's judgments upon her relatives. Still, the many details about Florentine life that Eliot packed into *Romola* as though she were making sausage instead of fiction remain so much dead matter, whereas those about St. Ogg's vivify *The Mill on the Floss*. Perhaps Eliot wrote more convincingly of St. Ogg's because she drew upon personal recollection, whereas Renaissance Florence was only the setting of a programmatic fable. However, *The Mill on the Floss* is not without its program too.

Felicia Bonaparte has discussed the determining effect of genetic patterns in the main characters.[37] By heredity, Tom is inclined to strength of will and Maggie to impulsiveness. In this sense, both are predetermined to follow a certain general course of action. Character is destiny, the narrator comments, quoting Novalis, then adds: "But not the whole of destiny."[38] We cannot predict behavior adequately because character combines with external circumstance to produce mystery and the impression of chance activity or coincidence. Thus the narrator, refusing to reveal what is presumably available to him since he is narrating a story already completed in the past, creates an artificial sense of the mystery of presentness by remarking at one point, "Maggie's destiny, then, is at present, hidden and we must wait for it to reveal itself like the course of an unmapped river: we only know that the river is full and rapid, and that for all rivers there is the same final home" (Eliot, *Mill*, 351). But the narrator's simile, joined with the many intimations of flooding and drowning in the novel, covertly suggests that the Floss is an embodiment of Maggie's foreordained destiny. Just as she may learn the lesson of renunciation yet be unable to follow it, so the river inevitably overflows when the rains fall and swell it. The banks of the river are circumstance, Maggie's impulsive character the flowing current.

The narrator says that the lonely, dreaming Maggie was "quite without that knowledge of the irreversible laws within and without her, which, governing habits becomes morality, and, developing the feelings of submission and dependence, becomes religion" (Eliot, *Mill*, 253). From Thomas à Kempis she accepts the principle of submission and tries to live by it, surprising her relatives by her ability to constrain her willfulness. She claims to have found peace by this method. "Our life is determined for us—and it makes the mind very free when we give up wishing, and only think of bearing what is laid upon us, and doing what is given us to do" (Eliot, *Mill*, 264). But, in the crisis of her attraction to Stephen Guest, she passively yields to the current of the river in a parody of renunciation. The tide of her destiny overwhelms her rational purpose. Shortly after this sequence, she herself admits that she had not fully understood renunciation, which she conceived as "quiet ecstasy" but which Philip Wakem more correctly describes as "that sad patient loving strength which holds the clue of life" (Eliot, *Mill*, 413).

Maggie's is not the only destiny with which the novel concerns itself. All of the Tullivers have destinies to fulfill which remain mysteries to them because they do not understand those "irreversible laws within and without" each individual. Moreover, for Eliot each individual destiny is unpredictable because it is a combination of individual character (including heredity) and external circumstance. Thus when Mr. Tulliver angrily decides to borrow money in order to return Mrs. Glegg's loan and thereby initiates his financial ruin, we are told that he is unable to manage the loan as he wishes, "not because [his] will was feeble, but because external fact was stronger. . . . Mr. Tulliver had a destiny as well as Oedipus, and in this case he might plead, like Oedipus, that his deed was inflicted on him rather than committed by him" (Eliot, *Mill*, 117). Like his father, Tom Tulliver has congenital deficiencies which first appear as an inaptitude to deal with "signs and abstractions" under Mr. Stelling's tutelage but extend to a lack of human sympathy (Eliot, *Mill*, 150). Tom's necessary return to his tutor's home is described as a "severe phase of his destiny," because it represents a career path uncongenial to his native qualities (Eliot, *Mill*, 142). Yet, because Tom represents a boy of flesh and blood and is not merely the author's abstraction designed to illustrate the evils of mistaken education, he is "not entirely at the mercy of circumstances" (Eliot, *Mill*, 152).

Maggie is destroyed because she does not comprehend that her opiumlike dream of refashioning the world to her taste is the seed of disaster. She cannot attain the unity she yearns for in the world. Tom, too, hopes to reshape the world to his design, though he expresses his will not in dreams, but in the realm of actuality and seems to succeed. But the strength of will that comes from Tom's integrity of self excludes compassion and flexibility. Moreover, his strength of will has little to do with freedom of will. Once he forms an opinion or establishes a purpose, he will not change. His concept of duty is noble, and he fulfills his father's dream, but more than his sister, he is ignorant of nature's irreversible laws. "Tom, like all of us," the narrator says, "was imprisoned within the limits of his own nature" (Eliot, *Mill*, 437).

The thingness of the world and of ourselves defeats us. The Floss is therefore a superb image of human submergence in the flux of existence. We invite disaster when we try to escape from contingency. Uncle Pullet has a simple system. He "had a programme for all great social occasions, and in this way fenced himself in from much painful confusion and perplexing freedom of will" (Eliot, *Mill*, 84). Aunt Pullet's program is explaining events in relation to providence. But for those who rise above this level of submission to ordinary existence, life can never be so easy. We are warned early on that this is precisely the situation for Tom and Maggie and that their situation is representative of more exalted cases. The narrator explains that the oppressive narrowness characteristic of dull and worldly St. Ogg's

> has acted on young natures in many generations, that in the onward tendency of human things have risen above the mental level of the generation before them, to which they have been nevertheless tied by the strongest fibres of their hearts. The suffering, whether of martyr or victim, which belongs to every historical advance of mankind, is represented in this way in every town, and by hundreds of obscure hearths; and we need not shrink from this comparison of small things with great; for does not science tell us that its highest striving is after the ascertainment of a unity which shall bind the smallest things with the greatest? (Eliot, Mill, 238-39)

Eliot's purpose is to demonstrate this binding of one thing to another. She wants to show that both obscure and prominent human destinies operate according to the same laws that function in all matter. Her novel is an attempt to manifest those laws at work—in heredity, in external nature, in social institutions.

As a girl, Maggie is a creature eager for beauty and knowledge, already unconsciously "yearning for something that would link together the wonderful impressions of this mysterious life, and give her soul a sense of home in it" (Eliot, *Mill*, 205). In the real world, this yearning must be frustrated. The linkage Maggie craves may have two faces—the benign smile of providence or the grim frown of determinism. The individual must submit to both. Only one being may escape destiny—the being who is himself providence. In *The Mill on the Floss*, that being is the narrator. J. Hillis Miller describes the narrator of *Middlemarch* as a Feuerbachian "divine knowledge, sympathy, and power of judgment which has arisen from the encounters of individual men with their fellows."[39] But Eliot's narrator there and in *The Mill on the Floss* is also capable of irony. At one point he pauses to caution us about composing stories of our lives that take on a providential shape. "If we only look far enough off for the consequence of our actions, we can always find some point in the combination of results by which those actions can be justified: by adopting the point of view of a Providence who arranges results, or of a philosopher who traces them, we shall find it possible to obtain perfect complacency in choosing to do what is most agreeable to us in the present moment" (Eliot, *Mill*, 288-89).

Life has no real pattern discernible to men. Maggie idealizes renunciation and ironically renounces discipline, bringing on what then appears to be the predetermined fate of her passionate nature. She has learned the lesson of human imprisonment, but she cannot escape the prison. Tom has aspired to material well being and the possession of property through discipline and the exertion of his will, but it is precisely this inflexibility that constitutes the weakness of his character. And the narrator, having warned against the human tendency to convert mysterious existence into a story, renders the events of the Tulliver family into a narrative buttressed by coded signs, moved forward by a strong teleological current, and ending in a symbolic and "satisfying" dramatic conclusion. Except that literary critics have not been happy with this stunningly complete mode of closure. There have been more than enough explanations for this dissatisfaction, but surely one is that the certainty and "fittingness" of the flood, following from numerous foreshadowings, conflicts with the implicit message of the novel that in the tumble of existence, in the complicated interlocking of human nature with the world's contingency, no such design can emerge except by the human impulse to render experience into narratized patterns. In the metaphysical world implied by Eliot's beliefs, only an opening into opportunities of further interrelations would be suitable, something more like the rebelliously incomplete ending Thackeray held to in *The Newcomes.* Eliot employed a solution something like this in *Middlemarch.*

Contingency defeats the tiny "heroes" of St. Ogg's, but the contest of self and world is more evenly waged in the world of Middlemarch where there are no St. Theresas, it is true, but where there is a Dorothea Brooke. Maggie Tulliver represents an onward step in human consciousness from self-concern to selflessness. The meaning of her sacrifice survives her. But she was doomed from the start by her character and by the design of Eliot's narration. The situation is different in *Middlemarch,* where characters have a fighting chance. Mark Schorer has written: "It is through the great scenes of the book, then, where 'choice' and 'circumstance', or, if you wish, idealism and fact, love and money—where these become 'enmeshed', where the plot gradually closes down on the characters, that the book derives its real movement and life."[40]

Ironically, in this novel where individual freedom has freer play, the narrator more frequently calls our attention to destiny and coincidence. Comparing Dorothea's attributes to Rosamond's early in his acquaintance with the two women, Lydgate finds them insufficiently feminine and so is indifferent to her turn of mind. The narrator comments: "But any one watching keenly the stealthy convergence of human lots, sees a slow preparation of effects from one life on another, which tells like a calculated irony on the indifference or the frozen stare with which we look at our unintroduced neighbor. Destiny stands by sarcastic with our *dramatis personae* folded in her hand."[41] In *Middlemarch,* the narrator holds those dramatis personae and disposes their lives according to his design, though he claims that he is doing no more than tracing them. "I at least have so much to do in unravelling certain human lots, and seeing how they were woven and interwoven, that all the light I can command must be concentrated on this particular web, and not dispersed over that tempting range of relevancies called the universe" (Eliot, *Middlemarch,* 105). He even excuses the operations of apparent coincidence by another sort of appeal to the intricate interweaving of human events. In this way, he explains the improbable detail of Raffles's acquiring the slip of paper incriminating Bulstrode. By placing the incident in a cosmic scale, he diminishes its improbability. It's no more unlikely, he says, than the process by which a scholar may come upon a historically significant stone. "To Uriel watching the progress of planetary history from the Sun, the one result would be just as much of a coincidence as the other" (Eliot, *Middlemarch,* 302). But there are coincidences not easily dismissed—that Raffles should be not only Bulstrode's "accomplice" but also the partner of Will Ladislaw's mother; that Dorothea, trying not to believe in Will's moral weakness, should arrive at the Lydgate household precisely at that one moment when Will and Rosamond are in a compromising attitude, and so forth.

The narrator solicits our indulgence in accepting the coincidences of his narrative as natural conjunctions likely in the elaborately tangled web of human existence.[42] At the same time, he provides object lessons in the error of presuming that a special providence protects us. For example, Fred Vincy's naive confidence that "the wisdom of providence or the folly of our friends, the mysteries of luck or the still greater mystery of our high individual value in the universe, will bring about agreeable issues."[43] Fred is held captive by his faith in luck and providence much as Dickens's Pip is enslaved by his great expectations. For Fred, old Featherstone's will is an ironic representation of special providence. Fred figures he does not need strength of will or exertion of his volitional powers because his *will* exists outside himself, benevolently preparing his destiny. When this dream proves untrustworthy, it also shatters Fred's confidence in providence. Only when he determines to fashion his own life through hard work does Fred free himself from the egoistic fantasy of providential care. Bulstrode's uneasy faith in a special providence governing his existence is mocked when Raffles refers to the incriminating letter as "a providential thing" (Eliot, *Middlemarch*, 383). Bulstrode is forced to feel that his past "is not simply a dead history, an outworn preparation of the present," but "a still quivering part of himself." He is trapped in "the train of causes in which he had locked himself" (Eliot, *Middlemarch*, 450).

The fiction of special providence complements the fiction of coincidences. Both imply a world open to modification of the law of invariant consequence. Eliot's contemporary readers understood the nature of human fate as she presented it. This is from the *Atlantic Monthly* review of *Middlemarch*. "The destiny which surrounds her characters . . . is the compounded description of natural laws, character, and accident which we call life. It leaves nothing out of view; neither the material nor the moral forces; neither the immutable fixity of physical succession, nor the will. Man is, in these novels, neither a creature who controls . . . nor who is controlled by nature; he is himself part of nature."[44]

More strongly than in her other novels, Eliot here emphasized the role of human will. I am not the first to notice, for example, that Will Ladislaw is appropriately named, for the burden of his development is that he learns to discipline his talents to a worthy purpose. He achieves this control by taking Dorothea as his model and by learning to look beyond his own immediate desires. Dorothea notices an important positive trait that will free him eventually; "he was a creature who entered into every one's feelings, and could take the pressure of their thought instead of urging his own with iron resistance" (Eliot, *Middlemarch*, 364). Dorothea influences an important decision in Will's career. In their interview in Rome, Will declares that he will "renounce the liberty" that Casaubon's allowance to him has permitted and return to England "to work my own way" (Eliot, *Middlemarch*, 165). To a great degree, Dorothea concentrates and focuses Will's will. To some degree, he is her will—the putting into action in the larger world of her high aspirations.

Dorothea sets Will on the path from false to true liberty. But ironically it is liberty that she herself is at first content to renounce. In the familiar pattern of Christian renunciation, she likes "giving up," as her sister, Celia, puts it (Eliot, *Middlemarch*, 13). Dorothea openly champions "submergence of self in communion with Divine perfection" (Eliot, *Middlemarch*, 18). And in a human analogy for the divine relationship, she anticipates a marriage union that will "give her the freedom of voluntary submission to a guide who would take her along the grandest path" (Eliot, *Middlemarch*, 21). Unfortunately, her guide is Mr. Casaubon who leads her out of the "labyrinth of petty courses, a walled-in maze of small paths that led no whither," which is how she sees ordinary social life, into the "anterooms and winding passages" where he carries "his taper among the tombs" (Eliot, *Middlemarch*, 21, 145, 308). Will is quick to observe how confining Dorothea's life with Casaubon will be. "And now you will go and be shut up in that stone prison at Lowick: you will be buried alive" (Eliot, *Middlemarch*, 163). Dorothea does soon come to feel "in a virtual tomb" at Lowick where "the mere chance of seeing Will occasionally was like a lunette opening in the wall of her prison" (Eliot, *Middlemarch*, 348, 265).

Dorothea learns not to convert all of her strength of will into "resolute submission," and tries instead to save others with her strength, yearning "towards the perfect right, that it might make a throne within her, and rule her errant will" (Eliot, *Middlemarch*, 391, 577). But most characters in *Middlemarch* remain enslaved and entrapped. Lydgate imagines himself free and in control of his destiny but soon discovers how easily slavery begins. An early forecast of his fate occurs when the narrator summarizes his professional ambitions. Among middle-aged men dully going about their vocations, he says, "there is always a good number who once meant to shape their own deeds and alter the world a little." But they are fitted gradually into the average, perhaps the subtle change beginning in them "with the vibrations from a woman's glance" (Eliot, *Middlemarch*, 107). Rosamond is a significant factor in Lydgate's transformation into the average. Leaving the Vincy house an engaged man, Lydgate's "soul was not his own, but the woman's to whom he had bound himself" (Eliot, *Middlemarch*, 223). This enslavement is a secular version of the Christian picture of the spirit's enslavement to the animal self. Before Lydgate's meeting with Rosamond, the narrator has already pictured him as having two selves, one idealist, one impulsive amorist. The latter self triumphs. In the Christian paradigm, the will is enslaved when it serves the animal self; similarly Lydgate's will is only superficially his own as he falls more and more under Rosamond's authority. He soon discovers his powerlessness over her. The germ of his attraction to

Rosamond soon becomes a full-blown disease through Lydgate's weak habit of yielding to his wife (Eliot, *Middlemarch*, 431). "It always remains true," the narrator observes, "that if we had been greater, circumstance would have been less strong against us" (Eliot, *Middlemarch*, 428). Eventually, Lydgate admits the failure of his intellectual ambitions and accepts "his narrowed lot with sad resignation" (Eliot, *Middlemarch*, 586). Near the end of the novel, a disappointed Will Ladislaw is also prepared to "cross his small boundary ditch . . . [to] . . . discontented subjection." (Eliot, *Middlemarch*, 588). Dorothea's high-minded love spares him.

Some characters are entrapped by their self-assertion, like the strong-willed Bulstrode, who cannot escape the consequences of his early treachery, and Rosamond, who is frozen into the role she acts. Others achieve a degree of liberty by learning to suppress their own desires for some greater aim. Fred Vincy is a rudimentary example, the Reverend Farebrother, a more admirable one. In *Middlemarch*, Eliot tries to show that there is a middle way between self-assertion and self-repression, that will is a complex attribute in human nature. Just as men must learn to balance the influences of character and circumstance, the dream of free will and the certainty of invariable consequence, they must also learn to balance their own natures between impulse and restraint. Bulstrode's "self-preserving will" does not preserve him in the end, while Farebrother's "infirmity of will" yields him a minor victory (Eliot, *Middlemarch*, 534, 139).

Eliot offers two ironic examples of how selfish will is inevitably frustrated—the documentary wills of Casaubon and Featherstone by which they seek to extend their authority beyond the grave. Casaubon makes it a condition of his will that Dorothea not marry Will, but it is precisely his rude association of the two with the idea of marriage that makes it a possibility for them—at first only ideally but eventually in fact. Featherstone's apparently strong will proves to have been a divided will as his nature and private life were also apparently divided—a glancing echo of Lydgate and Bulstrode. He has two wills, and anticipating his death, begs Mary Garth to destroy one. She, obeying a higher principle and strong of will herself, refuses. As a consequence, Joshua Rigg, Featherstone's "side-slip of a son" from his "other" life, inherits Stone Court and does the one thing Featherstone most feared; he sells it.

In effect, the "good" characters have learned to do what Dorothea stated as an ideal at the outset—submerge their selves in something higher. As I have already noted, this is a variation on the familiar Christian pattern of renunciation of self-will to achieve true freedom in accepting divine will. Nor has Eliot's narrator tried to disguise the equation, though his story offers mankind and mankind's ideal as the greater entity to which individual men should submit themselves. With the same attention to the contingency of the world prominent in *The Mill on the Floss*, but with greater allowance for the genuine interplay of character and circumstance, he fashions a more credible story, one that seems less a fable than a picture from life. In describing Lydgate's aims in his research, he describes his own aims.

> He for his part had tossed away all cheap inventions where ignorance finds itself able and at ease: he was enamoured of that arduous invention which is the very eye of research, provisionally framing its object and correcting it to more and more exactness of relation; he wanted to pierce the obscurity of those minute thoroughfares which are the first lurking-places of anguish, mania, and crime, that delicate poise and transition which determine the growth of happy or unhappy consciousness. (Eliot, *Middlemarch*, 122)

Eliot's task as a novelist was to convey her largely determinist philosophy in a manner that would not merely describe that philosophy but make it evident in the experience of reading her narrative. She chose an objective narrator describing past events so that her sentences have a profound historical weight to them, suggesting the manner in which accumulating events inevitably prepare incidents that are to come. Furthermore, by the illusion of a narrator's limited information, she suggested the small opportunities by which individuals might direct the flow of their experiences. At her worst, Eliot undermined her expressed belief that human destiny was a result of character and circumstance by overworking coincidence. Her more diagrammatic stories propose a universe almost as strict and inevitable as Calvin's or Jonathan Edwards's, and with a similar downward slant, excepting the few elect. She stylized that strictly governed world to good effect in *Daniel Deronda* and excused it as a legendary world in *Silas Marner*, but it was still a world at odds with her declared beliefs. In *The Mill on the Floss*, and particularly in *Middlemarch*, she came closest to approximating her vision of a world where a small degree of human effort combines with the powerful flood of circumstance to alter the world. Her narratives are complex interweavings of various individual histories united through the analytic powers of a narrator more human sage than divine power, who understands, and in understanding shapes, the dynamics of the world he describes, thereby himself becoming a model of how each individual human being may frame his story to conform to all the other stories that men and women are constructing for themselves and eventually compose a harmonious and true history of them all. Her characters' destinies may be predicted and guessed at but not foreseen as inevitable. The most intriguing of them—those who live in a dense world of materiality, filled with Mr. Brookeses and other garrulous gossips whose stories are uncreative anecdotes—seem to share in the direction of their destinies as Eliot believed we all can, with the result that when the novel ends, the characters' story does not.

Eliot understood that if the past embodied the palpitating reality of our acts, as Bulstrode's and Tito's cases demonstrate, the future represents opportunity and hence the only province of freedom. Some people may try to inscribe their wills on the future by means of legal documents. Thus Causabon's and Featherstone's wills become parodies of the true projection of the self into the future. The good thing about the future is that it is not, or cannot be proven to be, fixed. To attempt to fix it by posthumous edict is therefore an inversion of nature's way. *Will* is the future tense and those who commit their powers to some high but uncircumscribed purpose in the future approximate free will and find the proper application for their strength of will. In *Middlemarch*, Eliot captured her own insight best in the manner of rendering it, and so the novel seems most satisfying as a true picture of existence as she understood it.

CHAPTER SIXTEEN

George Meredith, Samuel Butler, Thomas Hardy, and Theodore Watts-Dunton

D ISCURSIVE secular writers on the subject of the will offered a widening range of opinion in the latter half of the nineteenth century as science introduced new avenues for examining man's self, his nature, and his freedom. Chief among these new avenues was the broad theory (or set of theories) covered by the term "evolution," reviewed in chapter 7 of this study. The present chapter looks at some representative novelists who incorporated new thinking about human nature in a wide range of attitudes reflected in the manner of their narrations.

George Meredith believed in free will and progress. Balancing a trust in reason with a respect for intuition and imagination, he located freedom in the latter with its power of liberation through language, especially metaphor. For Meredith, to learn to read life was to imagine it into being. Life was art and narration. But to the artist of art and of life alike, conquest of self was the first step toward reading the text of life correctly. Samuel Butler had less faith in reason, more in the unconscious motive powers. He proposed his own theory of evolution, in which heredity severely limited human freedom. His method was to shock his readers into awareness. Shock was, in his theory, the one way out of a simple and rigorous determinism. For Thomas Hardy, the human power for imagining life as a story was a prominent source of human misery, because most people aspire to circumstances that the conditions of natural life will not permit. They do not realize that they project false stories from their own unexamined desires. Hardy's narrative method suggests that the only safe place for fictions is in art. Finally, Theodore Watts-Dunton's *Aylwin* contains a hodgepodge of many of the contending attitudes toward free will and the prison of circumstance prevalent at the end of the century and cavalierly offers the conclusion that man is free in a wonderful, mysterious, and inexplicable world. All of these writers reflect the growing complexity of views about the free will versus determinism dispute, and their narrative strategies indicate conscious or unconscious efforts to render philosophical assumptions in appropriate vehicles.

~ ~ ~

Three important writers of the late nineteenth century rejected theism and were unwilling to retain the Christian structure of morality. The philosophical assumptions underlying their novels provide an instructive gradation. George Meredith was frankly optimistic, progressive, and vitalistic; Samuel Butler was more guarded and even sardonic but nonetheless generally inclined to accept an evolutionary and progressive design for humanity; and Thomas Hardy, while claiming to be a meliorist, generally pictured man as an incompetent antagonist against fate, whose few successes were brief and limited.

Meredith was a champion of idealist progressive evolution, believing that man was a creature lodged in matter but constituted of spirit, itself connected with the Earth Spirit or Spirit of Life, an idea he derived from Goethe's writings and that he shared with other writers of the period, notably his friend Swinburne.[1] Positive in his anticipation of man's future, he placed great value on comedy as a means of assisting human improvement. For civilized communities in particular, Meredith believed that comedy was the true specific of social ills because it had as its chief target human egoism. So long as egoism is useful to society and the nation, the imps of comedy forebear, but in a place like England in the late nineteenth century, where great valor is seldom required, idle egoism is open game.[2]

Game is what Meredith calls comedy, and games and gamelike activities (for example, the chase or hunt) abound in a novel like *The Egoist* (1879) to illustrate that the rules by which men live may be viewed as play and thus under his control. Even the laws of nature may be realigned to suit human designs. What else is technical progress? Meredith had as little faith in science as he did in religion. "We have little to learn of apes," he said, offering art as the true means of educating mankind (Meredith, *Egoist*, 4). Art, too, is gamelike. Meredith's artist sets his own rules within the general necessity of language and its communicating function, then makes his created world live, not by playing the part of a detached providence but by entering and informing the very being and substance of his characters and their world. His method for achieving this union is to submerge author and characters in a bath of language that, in calling attention to itself, presumably distracts the reader from the barriers that *telling* normally constructs. Robert M. Adams notes the antistory function of the willow pattern allusion underlying the narrative of *The Egoist*, the abandonment of an authoritative moral voice in the novel and the absence of other expected devices. "Poetic justice simply doesn't happen in the book; virtue doesn't get much rewarded, vice is hardly punished. Apart from divine providence, it doesn't look as if the author believes in that other special dispensation of the Victorian novelist, bilateral symmetry."[3] Meredith is not as innovative as Adams makes him sound, for Thackeray had anticipated him in many ways. Both employed narrative methods that presented man as neither trapped nor driven by a necessary scheme of God, fate, or causal invariance but as confined by his own petrified desires. Comedy could dissolve these "mind-forged manacles" and allow man his freedom once more and also keep him on his guard against the process of ossification. Like Shelley's Prometheus confronting a tyrannical Zeus, Meredith believed that man would be able to throw off the dominion of false ideas once he realized that their force rests in his own submission to them. Walter Wright says that "putting man in some outer region of the spiritual universe or making him a deterministic creature was contradictory to Meredith's belief in the significance of individual spirituality. At the same time, he believed that the individual mind reached its highest form only when in intimate concord with nature and when self-forgetfully participating in a community of ideas. It was a function of literature to illustrate this truth and to show how affinity of human minds was to be achieved."[4]

Meredith was not content merely to create characters and set them moving in a plot. Language itself had to test the rules by which information was communicated. Though man's freedom was not unlimited, it was ample and growing. If man's ideas were to expand and increase that freedom, the medium by which those ideas were transmitted would have to change as well. We cannot examine the many devices that Meredith used to effect his purpose, but a glance at one or two might make the point.

Though he had a good deal of faith in exposition and allowed himself many opportunities to lecture his readers, Meredith had much greater confidence in metaphor.[5] Gillian Beer says of *Beauchamp's Career* (1875) that Meredith used metaphor to show his characters waking to imaginative life.[6] Beer believes that it is with this novel that Meredith achieves his distinctive style. Whether or not that is so, Meredith had long experimented with metaphoric and other stylistic variations and considered himself an innovator with language.[7] In much of his fiction, for example, he used certain basic image patterns to carry moral values. Thus clothed/unclothed frequently suggests truth/disguise, and mountain/lowland suggests spiritual ascent as opposed to sensuous indulgence. Meredith customarily used organic metaphors to develop positive associations and often selected other metaphorical patterns for the significance of their vehicles. In the opening chapter of *Beauchamp's Career*, Meredith characterized the British fear of invasion with a series of metaphorical forms from personifications of Panic, the Press, the Government, and the People, to a complex analogy of a squire who has been frightened by a Robin Hood figure into vowing an investment in self-protection. At the end of this long passage, Meredith seems to dismiss his similitudes in favor of direct statement. "Similes are all very well in their way. None can be sufficient in this case without levelling a finger at the taxpayer—nay directly mentioning him."[8] Meredith could have told us directly that the invasion panic was contrived by government and effected through the press in order to frighten taxpayers into financing military improvements. His verbal fireworks seem gratuitous, since their main purpose is to provide an introduction for the hero of his novel. When Meredith does introduce Neville Beauchamp a paragraph later, he relates him to the substance, but not the tropes, of the elaborate disquisition on panic. "Young Mr. Beauchamp at that period of the panic had not the slightest feeling for the taxpayer. He was therefore unable to penetrate the mystery of our roundabout way of enlivening him" (Meredith, *Career*, 6). Beauchamp does not have the subtle, metaphoric, and intuitive intellect necessary—along with reason—to grasp an issue so volatile and so complex. Thus he remains perplexed about the threatened conflict. His rudimentary solution is to address a letter to the French Guard personally taking up their challenge. Of course he is absurd, but he is absurd because he cannot understand that human motives and actions are not overt and logical, and that though intimately interwoven, human lives are affiliated by largely inexpressible feelings, not matured ideas. Meredith's metaphorical language demonstrates this point, then opposes to it Beauchamp's bare, literal, and vulnerable mind.

Beauchamp's great fault is that he lacks a subtle enough intelligence; he is not adept at fathoming the unexpressed. He has "not the faculty of reading inside men"; he "has no *bend* in him" (Meredith, *Career*, 355, 437). He wants life to be simple, direct and rational, though his own spoiled romances might have shown him how false such a hope is. Meredith ironically uses a coagulation of metaphors to describe Beauchamp's obsession with a single idea. Such an obsession, he says, "is at once a devouring dragon, and an intractable steam-force; it is a tyrant that has eaten up a senate, and a prophet with a message. Inspired of solitariness and gigantic size, it claims divine origin. The world can have no peace for it" (Meredith, *Career*, 355). In a novel about political controversy and the struggle of a young man to achieve heroic ends, these metaphors, the steam engine aside perhaps, are extremely fitting.

Dedicated to reason, Beauchamp is inadequately appreciative of other modes of understanding, but he is educable. He learns patience himself and recommends it to others (Meredith, *Career*, 510). In the novel's last chapter, entitled "The Last of Neville Beauchamp," Lady Romfrey looks upon the young man not as one who has failed but "as one in mid career, in mid forest, who, by force of character, advancing in self-conquest, strikes his impress right and left around him, because of his aim at stars" (Meredith, *Career*, 515). Beauchamp achieves only half the necessary education before his early death, but his career compares favorably with others who lack his willingness to challenge accepted conditions, especially his early love Renée, whose chief liability is "her sense of submission to destiny" (Meredith, *Career*, 57). Beauchamp does not achieve the full freedom and self-comprehension that Meredith would wish for men, but he learns Dr. Shrapnel's lesson that "the victory over the world, as over nature, is over self" (Meredith, *Career*, 401). His death attempting to save another life is an emblematic proof of that.

Metaphor is for Meredith a means to help his readers experience the consciousness of his characters and a marking device of values. But metaphor also provides the organic filaments that weave his narratives together in imitation of the binding power of the Spirit of Life, filaments sometimes almost invisible but operative nonetheless. Between his reference to the English taxpayer and his presentation of Beauchamp's naiveté in the first chapter of *Beauchamp's Career*, Meredith offers a striking image of his own role as story teller. He says that he will paint "what is, not what I imagine." Immediate experience, its politics, and the ideas of men will be his themes which he will keep "at blood-heat, and myself calm as a statue of Memnon in prostrate Egypt! He sits there waiting for the sunlight; I here, and readier to be musical than you think. I can at any rate be impartial; and do but fix your eyes on the sunlight striking him and swallowing the day in rounding him, and you have an image of the passive receptivity of shine and shade I hold it good to aim at, if at the same time I may keep my characters at blood heat" (Meredith, *Career*, 6). Meredith asserts his artistic self-command while ironically identifying his role as essentially passive, an identification not to be trusted, as the immediately succeeding metaphor of himself as warrior or hunter suggests. His apparent immobility is belied in his power to create, to be "musical." Moreover, Meredith cloaks himself with the mystery and authority of magic and the supernatural by appropriating the Memnon allusion.[9] Metaphors of magic and wizardry recur throughout the novel, interlacing the mundane with the mystery of creativity. Lamenting that he can not write simple tales of mystery and adventure, Meredith says his narrative manner is "like a Rhone island in the summer drought, stony, unattractive and difficult between two forceful streams of the unreal and the over-real which delight mankind—honour to the conjurers!" (Meredith, *Career*, 461). But if he is statuesque, stony, and difficult, he still sings, and what he sings is change. If Beauchamp never becomes a singing Memnon, at least he escapes what Lord Romfrey calls the national scourge of being "a statue turned out by an English chisel" (Meredith, *Career*, 514). Statues, like novels, are memorial works of art, but if they do not "sing" with the sunrise of each succeeding generation, there are mere museum pieces or urban decorations. Beauchamp does not achieve Meredith's aims, but he has proven his freedom from the stultification of changeless obedience to tradition.

Meredith had dealt with incomplete careers before. *The Ordeal of Richard Feverel* (1859) introduced a young hero with such natural gifts and such inherently positive impulses that his success in self-fulfillment should be easy. Unfortunately, his father takes charge of his education and systematically unsuits the young man for the life he must face. Even this early novel is supported by a tissue of metaphors supporting the central notion that human impulses must be guided, not balked, that self-control, not theoretical compulsion leads to healthy adult activity.[10] Sir Austen's misguided system leads Richard into error that causes the early death of his wife, Lucy, and his own psychic shipwreck. Lady Blandish charges Sir Austen with a double-sided crime in destroying the prospects of these two promising young people. In his arrogance "he wished to take Providence out of God's hands" by substituting his own concept of Science. Looking on the wrecked young lives, Lady Blandish says, "I shall hate the name of Science till the day I die."[11]

Meredith trusted neither religion nor science as dogmatic systems. He sympathized with spontaneity and naturalness and made these sympathies evident in his novel, though spicing them with irony in the chapter that describes the blossoming love of Richard and Lucy. "Away with Systems! Away with a corrupt world! Let us breathe the air of the Enchanted Island!" he begins, then presents the young lovers as inhabitants of a prelapsarian garden. "They have outflown Philosophy. Their Instinct has shot beyond the ken of Science. Imperiously they know we were made for Eden: and would you gainsay them who are outside the Gates, and argue from the Fall?" (Meredith, *Ordeal*, 192, 194). This enchanted world will have its own disastrous Fall when Richard's father usurps providential authority.

The Ordeal of Richard Feverel is not a tightly constructed narrative. Meredith did not aim at tightly constructed narratives, wanting his novels to convey the same sense of natural unpredictability and potential for development that he saw as a part of life. Gillian Beer has made this point succinctly.

> Meredith's open discussion of technique within his novels is a part of his belief in free will. This belief expresses itself in a number of ways: he gives character pre-eminence over shapeliness of plot; he flouts the analogues and expectations he has built up in the reader; he exploits comedy (with its emphasis on the accountability of individuals) and he invokes the comic spirit, which insists on observation rather than involvement from reader and narrator alike. He seeks our free assent to the implications of what he shows

rather than a passing emotional submission to fiction. (Beer, 38–39)

She adds that, though Meredith may discuss his techniques and comment on the events and characters of his novels, he "never suggests that he is in command of the fate of his characters or that he can alter the direction of the story. By his narrative interventions he breaks the illusion that there is one absolute way of rendering the world: the interventions complicate what may appear simple" (Beer, 39). Meredith avoided careful plotting because he recognized that plots were akin to fatalism, and he was not a fatalist. As we have seen, these narrative preferences were already a part of the tradition of English fiction when Meredith began to write.

Meredith's first novel gave an indication of his tendency to liberate characters from plot. He called it *The Shaving of Shagpat: An Arabian Entertainment* (1855), and, as George Eliot remarked, its narrative combined the episodic quality of Eastern fiction with the intellectual aspirations of Western literature.[12] This allegorical fantasy embodied Meredith's moral aspirations; in it, the ordinary citizen Shibli Bagarag learns to "master the event"; that is, take command of himself and hence of the world around him. "Shagpat represents the pretentions of the modern social system, and Shibli Bagarag is the naive young reformer tested and toughened by a series of perils and temptations that represent the chief forces of worldliness and self-indulgence."[13] Unlike so many of Meredith's central figures, Shibli is entirely successful in his effort.

Harry Richmond, for example, must face a world as challenging as, if more forgiving than, those of Richard Feverel and Neville Beauchamp. As he finishes telling his own story, Harry admits that he is still "subject to the relapses of a not perfectly right nature, as I perceived when glancing back at my thought of 'An odd series of accidents!' Which was but a disguised fashion of attributing to Providence the particular concern in my fortunes: an impiety and a folly!"[14] It is Austen Feverel's offense more prominently developed. *The Adventures of Harry Richmond* (1871) is largely about the folly of assuming a providential design, in Richmond Roy's case, special providence. But to be free, men must strip away all illusions of fate and destiny and take the responsibility of their lives upon themselves. The husband in *Modern Love* (1862) refuses the cowardly displacement of responsibility for his situation on others.

> I am not one of those miserable males
> Who sniff at vice, and daring not to snap,
> Do therefore hope for heaven. I take the hap
> Of all my deeds. The wind that fills my sails
> Propels; but I am helmsman. Am I wrecked,

I know the devil has sufficient weight
To bear: I lay it not on him, or fate.
Besides, he's damned. That man I do suspect
A coward, who would burden the poor deuce
With what ensues from his own slipperiness.[15]

Meredith wanted no blaming of the devil, or God, and so renounced providential control and urged his readers to accept the blood heat of his creations as their own, while he provided the music of their story as naturally and as magically as the statue of Memnon when the morning sun strikes upon it.

Sometimes Meredith's themes and methods come together in a particularly happy manner, as in his finest novel, *The Egoist*. A major concern of the novel is liberation, in particular, Clara Middleton's release from her engagement to Sir Willoughby Patterne. As she begins to feel the discomfort of being treated like one of Willoughby's possessions, she craves liberty, blaming "herself and him, and the world he abused, and destiny into the bargain" (Meredith, *Egoist*, 51). At first, mental liberty is her immediate need; "She asked for some little, only some little, free play of mind in a house that seemed to wear, as it were, a cap of iron" (Meredith, *Egoist*, 67). But before long she is yearning for a Perseus to rescue her, a comrade or lover (Meredith, *Egoist*, 85). However, she gradually learns that to free herself she must educate herself to the use of her free will. She can do this by learning to read the world and herself.[16] In one of his notebooks, Meredith advised himself, "The book of our common humanity lies in our own bosoms / To know ourselves is more a matter of will than of insight" (Beer, quoting Meredith's notebook, 109).

Willoughby exclaims to Clara, "You have me, you have me like an open book, you, and only you!" (Meredith, *Egoist*, 52). Unfortunately for Willoughby, it is true that Clara shares with other captives "that power to read their tyrant" (Meredith, *Egoist*, 120). Though she has a moment of doubt that she has "misread" Willoughby, she soon revives confidence in her assessment of him and does not give way to the editing of herself that the narrator describes as woman's usual protective behavior.

Maidens are commonly reduced to read the masters of their destinies by their instincts; and when these have been edged by overactivity, they must hoodwink their maidenliness to suffer themselves to read: and then they must dupe their minds, else men would soon see they were gifted to discern. Total ignorance being their pledge of purity to men, they have to expunge the writing of their perceptives on the tablets of the brain: they have to know not when they do know. The instinct of seeking to know, crossed by the task of blotting knowledge out, creates that conflict of the natural with the artificial creature to which their ultimately-revealed double-face, complained of by ever-dissatisfied men, is owing. (Meredith, *Egoist*, 170)

In planning her escape from Willoughby, Clara feels driven by necessity and appalled that this act will transform her into a legible object. "She was one of the creatures who are written about" (Meredith, *Egoist*, 126). Even Clara's father, understandably for a scholar, sees her as a text. "She has no history," he reassures Willoughby. "You are the first heading of the chapter" (Meredith, *Egoist*, 161). But she is not the legible tale either of them can inscribe or read. "There was no reading of her or the mystery" of her changed mood for Willoughby (Meredith, *Egoist*, 119).

Willoughby is doubly disqualified for interpreting Clara. To begin with, he assumes that "Providence, otherwise the discriminating dispensation of the good things of life," has arranged everything to suit him (Meredith, *Egoist*, 243; also 91, 370, 236). Complicating this false assumption about how the story lines of existence are actually disposed is Willoughby's reservoir of usable texts. Willoughby's lexicon of tender language and his expectations about story derive from his "favourite reading . . . , popular romances" (Meredith, *Egoist*, 187). He even believes that his education in these romances has given him a predictive power (Meredith, *Egoist*, 196). He must suffer the bitter irony later, when he has lost Clara and fallen back upon the faded and toughened Laetitia Dale, of being told that Society is in his debt for a "lovely romance" (Meredith, *Egoist*, 398). By this time, Willoughby has "learnt to read the world," and is not happy with the information it provides (Meredith, *Egoist*, 399). He knows too late that he has concocted a parody of his Providential Romance.

But if Willoughby's reading expectations falsely cast him as the hero of a splendid romance, he cannot help belittling Vernon Whitford's sordid history of love. Vernon married his landlord's daughter, who proved disreputable before her early death. "The story's a proof that romantic spirits do not furnish the most romantic history," Willoughby intones to Clara (Meredith, *Egoist*, 319). But Clara has already fallen under the spell of Vernon's alpine imagery for freedom, and when Meredith's novel ends, these two find themselves the proud owners of the happy ending originally designated as Willoughby's property. This outcome is possible, however, only because Clara decides to follow some stern advice from Vernon at a crisis in her life. Like Savonarola in *Romola*, Vernon meets his heroine in flight from her unwanted lover and the life he promises and advises her to return and face her situation. The London train leaves without her. "She had acted of her free will: she could say that." Returning to Patterne Hall, Clara is downcast. "She could have accused Vernon of a treacherous cunning for imposing it on her free will to decide her fate" (Meredith, *Egoist*, 229, 232). But it is precisely this act of free will that allows for the happy conclusion to her story. The tyrant Willoughby who seemed the master of his fate ends up the captive, betrayed by his egotism, whereas his dependents are liberated through their capacity to read themselves and others not as preinscribed texts but as mysterious elements of a narrative in the process of unfolding.

Bondage, confinement, and restraint of all kinds preoccupy Meredith's writing and are closely associated with his preoccupation with clothes, masking, and disguise. Meredith drives his narratives insistently toward disclosure and release, through a narrative method of indirection, elision, and withheld information. In a sense, Meredith throws the responsibility for liberation on the characters themselves and upon the readers. Characters often enslave themselves by accepting rules set down by others. We have already noted this fault in Renée, Beauchamp's early love. Sometimes characters believe themselves to be free but are subtly imprisoned by their own errors, as with Sir Willoughby Patterne or the central figures of *The Tragic Comedians* (1880). The seventeen-year-old Clotilde von Rudiger is enchanted by Alvan, a promising young politician. Both mistake her originality for independence and courage and their tragedy follows from the discovery that she lacks the fortitude to throw off the shackles of social and class convention. Alvan has flaws of his own. He does not realize that he gradually commits himself to codes that he does not endorse. He makes such concessions when trying to gain acceptance by Clotilde's family and in the management of his political career. The narrator summarizes concisely: "Ceasing to be a social rebel, he conceived himself as a recognized dignitary, and he passed under the bondage of that position."[17] Any man who makes Respectability his Zeus must look to his liver.

One of Meredith's most elaborate and serious examinations of self-liberation is *Diana of the Crossways* (1885). Early in the novel we are made aware of Diana's yearning for "the glittering fields of freedom."[18] Her escape from her husband's control is the first manifestation of this freedom, a liberty she fears to lose by returning to him or by being caught by any other man. But Diana has not fully learned the lesson that "by closely reading herself . . . she gathered an increasing knowledge of our human constitution, and stored matter for the brain" (Meredith, *Diana*, 113). She has yet to accept the injunction of her beloved friend Emma who tells her that we may be happy if we "but keep passion sober, a trotter in harness" (Meredith, *Diana*, 180). Like other characters in the novel, especially Sir Lukin Dunstane, she cannot abandon notions of providence, destiny, and fate. She is particularly willing to accept Percy Dacier's trust in fortune when he pleads with her to run away with him. "Fortune is blind," he says. "She may be kind to us. The blindness of Fortune is her one merit, and fools accuse her of it, and they profit by it! I fear we all of us have our own turn of folly: we throw the stake for good luck" (Meredith, *Diana*, 238). Like Eliot's unwise characters who willingly gamble because they assume a world governed by chance, Diana accepts this world view and its argument in a moment of weakness. Preparing for flight with Dacier, Diana "thought of herself as another person, whom she observed, not counselling her because it was a creature visibly pushed by the Fates'" (Meredith, *Diana*, 241). At this moment her faithful admirer Thomas Redford appears, calling Diana to Emma's sickbed. Something stronger than fate intervenes, though Diana continues to feel that "hand resembling the palpable interposition of Fate had swept" her and Dacier apart (Meredith, *Diana*, 246). But the fates are mere excuses that men make for their own confusion and lack of command, as Meredith suggests ironically when the consequences of Diana's revelation to the press about the prime minister's impending change of policy about the Corn Laws become apparent. "She heard also of heavy failures and convulsions in the City of London, quite unconscious that the Fates, or agents of the Providence she invoked to precipitate the catastrophe, were then beginning cavernously their performance of the part of villain in Diana's history" (Meredith, *Diana*, 258). When Emma Dunstane comments to Redworth on the irony of fate that has affected Diana's life, he replies heatedly.

> "Upon my word," he burst out, "I should like to write a book of Fables, showing how donkeys get into grinding harness, and dogs lose their bones, and fools have their sconces cracked, and all run jabbering of the irony of Fate, to escape the annoyance of tracing the causes. And what are they? Nine times out of ten, plain want of patience, or some debt for indulgence. There's a subject:—let some one write, Fables in illustration of the irony of Fate: and I'll undertake to tack-on my grandmother's maxims for a moral to each of 'em. We prate of that irony when we slink away from the lesson—the rod we conjure. And you to talk of Fate! It's the seed we sow, individually or collectively." (Meredith, *Diana*, 356)

Diana herself finally accepts this truth and in coolly assessing her own errors remarks, "Ah! let never Necessity draw the bow of our weakness: it is the soul that is winged to its perdition" (Meredith, *Diana*, 360). She learns self-mastery, as her meeting with Dacier and his new bride shows. She discovers the "laws of life" and confidently submits to marriage again, realizing that with Redworth it need not be a form of bondage.

Diana spends a good part of her time in disguise because she feels it necessary to play a role. Acting images abound in this novel. But Diana has another form of disguise. "Metaphors were her refuge. Metaphorically she could allow her mind to distinguish the struggle she was undergoing, sinking under it. The banished of Eden had to put on metaphors, and the common use of them has helped largely to civilize us" (Meredith, *Diana*, 231). In a fallen world, roles and metaphors are necessary to communicate sentiments not acceptable as naked fact. But if Diana cloaks herself in protective metaphors, in this novel and all of his others Meredith himself employed metaphor precisely to unclothe illusions by calling attention to the habits of language that create them. Something similar happens with the rich complex of allusions imbedded in the title of this novel.[19] This Diana is neither goddess nor witch but a woman who needs to discover the laws of nature by which she may control her own life and find happiness. Meredith is subversive in his use of the metaphor and resistant to literary convention as well. Refusing the role of theatrical stage manager demanded by his English audience that calls for a tidy nuptial chapter, Meredith says, "Rogues and a policeman, or a hurried change of front of all the actors, are not a part of our slow machinery" (Meredith, *Diana*, 371). Meredith is not, like Thackeray, a puppet master calling attention to the puppet nature of his creations but has the same aim of permitting his characters to achieve their own freedom. Thackeray distracted his readers to free his characters; Meredith makes the opposite choice of intimacy.

Meredith's last novel, *The Amazing Marriage* (1895), simplifies the themes of freedom and bondage. Carinthia, the book's heroine, represents individual integrity, "I hate anything that robs me of my will," she says.[20] And nothing does. Her main contest is with Lord Fleetwood, who himself has a determined but "shifty will" (Meredith, *Marriage*, 254). Smitten by Carinthia, he fears subjection to her. He recognizes her strength of will and fears that she will appropriate the masculine role. Still, he proposes to her and feels honor-bound to marry her. He thinks of her as a witch who has entrapped him but admits that Carinthia has not duped him; "he had done it for himself—acted on by a particular agency" (Meredith, *Marriage*, 197). Though she must suffer, Carinthia retains her integrity and independence much as Aminta does in related circumstances in *Lord Ormont and His Aminta* (1894). She remains secure in her belief in her own freedom, she feels that she shapes her own destiny. By contrast, Lord Fleetwood feels his life dogged by the fates. Moreover, like other unattractive figures in this novel, he is a gambler. Such slaves of fortune, Meredith explains, are "feverish worshippers of the phantasmal deity called the Present; a god reigning over the Past, appreciable only in the Future; whose whiff of actual being is composed of the embryo idea of the union of these two periods." This sort of character counts on luck, but the Black Goddess of gambling corrupts as it enslaves her devotees. "Their faith as to sowing and reaping has gone; and so has their capacity to see the actual as it is" (Meredith, *Marriage*, 112). In a world of change, all causal relations are called in question. Free will loses significance except as a random act. But for Meredith, strength of will is strength of purpose too, and only those who believe themselves free to alter events can have a settled purpose that is not renunciation and submission.

For Meredith, as for other novelists in nineteenth-century England, gambling served as a metaphor for chance. But he believed the correct attitude toward life was to view it as orderly, not random; as subject to certain laws, not directed by capricious fates. Eliot placed her faith in the invariable law of consequence and trusted in a steady advance of human intellect and moral strength. Meredith, without examining such complicated issues as first causes and scientific determinism, asserted that men, and perhaps more particularly women, were capable of controlling their own lives. The metaphor for that control was art. Like Clara Middleton, women and men must learn to read the world and themselves so that they may participate in the ongoing narrative. They would not look to a providential author to make their stories for them. Unlike most novelists of his time, Meredith attempted to leave control in the hands of his characters, though ironically, his elaborate style led many readers to suppose that he was dominating rather than liberating them. Meredith's philosophy abandoned dualism between matter and spirit, and his literary method sought a comparable erasure of the boundary between idea and its medium, language.[21] Language was to idea as blood was to spirit through the medium of brain. Text was the word made flesh.

Meredith rather easily overlooked many difficult issues that prevented other non-Christian writers from so bracingly and whole-heartedly endorsing freedom of the will. We have already had a taste of Samuel Butler's more dour views as they appeared in his expository works, but those views bear upon his fictional methods as well. Not only was Butler aware of the logical difficulties in definitely asserting belief in free will or determinism, he was astonishingly clever in toying with these beliefs. *Erewhon* (1872) is a satire with serpentine developments on many of the ideas with which we are concerned. Much of this satire depends upon elaborate reversal, hence the Erewhonians do not perceive a pocket watch as evidence of creator, according to Paley's analogy but regard it as the "designer of himself and of the universe; or as at any rate one of the great first causes of all things."[22] Similarly, for Erewhonians, progress means preventing the evolution of machines, which they perceive as a competing species (Butler, *Erewhon*, 81–2). Other sly reversals in which the Erewhonians punish ill health as a crime and worship ideals instead of an anthropomorphic God also have their obvious bite. A more surprising reversal has to do with the Erewhonian mythology of the unborn who live in a pleasant preterrestrial spiritual state. Only the most foolish of them choose to die in that world in order to be born into ours. The unborn are warned of the risks of such a passage, for example the possibility of being born to wicked, foolish, or unsympathetic parents. Their perception of human freedom is interestingly skewed. Advisors warn the unborn: "if you go into the world you will have free will; that you will be obliged to have it; that there is no escaping it; that you will be fettered to it during your whole life, and must on every occasion do that which on the whole seems best to you at any given time, no matter whether you are right or wrong in choosing it." They add that heredity and environment will bias the nature of such choices and will most likely incline to misery, after which they conclude: "Reflect on this, and remember that should the ill come upon you, you will have yourself to thank, for it is your own choice to be born, and there is no compulsion in the matter" (Butler, *Erewhon*, 186–87).

Man, in this view, has a free will that does not differ at all from determinist impulse except that the creature is free to choose birth, something denied to humans, who presume that everything afterward is free. Learning about the evolutionary threat to humans posed by machinery, the narrator develops an analogy that demonstrates how very like determinism the Erewhonian view of free will is. Responding to the charge that machines cannot evolve because they lack a will, he argues that "a man is the resultant and exponent of all the forces that have been brought to bear upon him, whether before his birth or afterwards. His action at any moment depends solely upon his constitution, and on the intensity and direction of the various agencies to which he is, and has been, subjected. Some of these will counteract each other; but as he is by nature, and as he has been acted on, and is now acted on from without, so will he do, as certainly and regularly as though he were a machine" (Butler, *Erewhon*, 245).

Other Erewhonian theories are Butler's own notions carried to extremes. Some Erewhonians propose that animals, because they so resemble man, also have rights; these proponents argue in favor of vegetarianism until another subtle argument demonstrates that plants are intelligent as well, perhaps even superior. They feed themselves, protect themselves and know what they want as much as any human embryo does. "The rose-seed did what it now does in the persons of its ancestors—to whom it has been so linked as to be able to remember what those ancestors did when they were placed as the rose-seed now is. Each stage of development brings back the recollection of the course taken in the preceding stage, and the development has been so often repeated, that all doubt—and with all doubt, all consciousness of action—is suspended" (Butler, *Erewhon*, 278). This pattern is, of course, the same scheme that Butler would later advance seriously in *Life and Habit* and other works.[23]

Butler's skills in *Erewhon* are only partly novelistic. It might be more accurate to call him a fabulist here. His narrator, an amateur writer, recognizes the difficulty, admitting, "I should never come to an end were I to keep to a strictly narrative form, and detail the infinite absurdities with which I daily come in contact" (Butler, *Erewhon*, 105). The first six or seven chapters, however, constitute a smooth narrative much in the manner of travel and adventure literature of the time. But reader expectations are set up for a reversal when the tale shifts suddenly into an expository form containing other narratives and texts within it. In a crude and unpolished way, the form of Butler's narrative reflects its import, though it would be rash to claim much more than this, especially since Butler himself mocks the purpose of his narrative by having his narrator present it as a fund-raiser to finance a missionary trip back to Erewhon.

The Way of All Flesh (1872-84; published 1903) is a novel and a carefully considered one, and its form follows the pattern implied in Butler's philosophical theories, though the novel itself rarely takes up the touchy issue of free will and determinism directly. Butler's concept of heredity is central to the novel, which rehearses in the history of the Pontifex family, the ideas set forth in Life and Habit (1878) and elsewhere. Heredity is another name for the memory of matter, and just as cells or rose-seeds "remember" earlier cells and rose-seeds, so humans carry an unconscious memory of their progenitors. Ernest Pontifex carries the "information" of preceding generations, information that is released through trauma. His grandfather was a creative, impulsive, constructive man. Ernest's father was a priggish, unimaginative man. Ernest outgrows the cowardice instilled in him by his immediate family and, through a series of fortunate disasters, discovers qualities more like those of his grandfather, though his form of creativity—writing—is less practical and not immediately effective. Peter Morton explains that Ernest is passive because survival for him requires camouflage, not conflict. "For in each Lamarckian generation each person bodies forth the total experience of his forebears and even of the totality of life itself; for he is in truth frighteningly free, almost in the existential sense of being forced to raise himself by his own moral bootstraps."[24] Elsewhere, Morton says that Butler "is profoundly optimistic about the individual's freedom to choose a destiny and melioristic in his attitude to the family organism" (Morton 175). But I suspect that this is too positive an assertion of Butler's position. After all, most of mankind goes about its business entrapped, like Theobald and Christina Pontifex, in one or another set of prohibitions. They create their own images of sin and doom and then learn to fear them. Ernest, though he does break out of this pattern, scarcely exerts a determined will in the process. His disasters come from his impulse to imitate others—as with his zeal for the College of Spiritual Pathology that ultimately leads to his arrest for accosting a young woman and his loss of money to an embezzling friend. Ernest's good fortune results mainly from luck in the form of his Aunt Alethea and his godfather, Overton, the narrator of the novel.[25]

Other Victorian novelists—Eliot and Meredith are notable examples—deplored the dependence on lucky chance exhibited by their weaker characters, but Butler saw chance as an inevitable part of life. Biological inheritance itself is a throw of the dice. After that, luck is predictable. Early in the novel, Butler made his position clear.

Fortune, we are told, is a blind and fickle foster-mother, who showers her gifts at random upon her nurslings. But we do her a grave injustice if we believe such an accusation. Trace a man's career from his cradle to his grave and mark how Fortune has treated him. You will find that when he is once dead she can for the most part be vindicated from the charge of any but very superficial fickleness. Her blindness is the merest fable; she can espy her favorites long before they are born.[26]

Butler satirizes human dependency in Theobald Pontifex's courtship. Ernest's father earns his university fellowship, is ordained, and takes a place with Mr. Allaby, the rector of Crampsford, who has five unwed daughters. As soon as they have met Theobald, the girls quarrel over which is to become his wife. Mr. Allaby recommends gambling as a solution and the next chapter opens with "the Miss Allabys in the eldest Miss Allaby's bedroom playing at cards, with Theobald for the stakes" (Butler, *Flesh*, 52). Christina wins, and, though Theobald is not the man she hoped for, she accepts the challenge and snares him. Theobald has very little control of this most important decision.

Once luck and external circumstance have had their play, the individual possesses sufficient freedom to react to events and is more likely to do so if some shock frees him from the bondage of convention. "Every change is a shock," the narrator explains; "every shock is *pro tanto* death. What we call death is only a shock great enough to destroy your power to recognize a past and a present as resembling one another" (Butler, *Flesh*, 283). After a series of such shocks, Ernest decides to abandon the respectability associated with his past and begin again at the bottom. This pattern is repeated in full at least one more time. Gradually Ernest becomes self-confident enough in handling his "inheritance" to deserve the financial inheritance left to him by his aunt and supervised by Overton.

Theobald, seeing himself as representative of paternal authority, demanded complete obedience of his children, insisting that the "first signs of self-will must be carefully looked for, and plucked up by the roots at once before they had time to grow" (Butler, *Flesh*, 106). But what is a weed to Theobald is a flowering plant to Butler. For example, he insists on the value of pleasure. In *Erewhon* this notion was expressed by the Erewhonians punishing their citizens for bad health. We owe it to ourselves, Butler says, to follow our wills. We should not deny but indulge ourselves. "All animals, except man, know that the principal business of life is to enjoy it—and they do enjoy it as much as man and other circumstances will allow. He has spent his life best who has enjoyed it most; God will take care that we do not enjoy it any more than is good for us" (Butler, *Flesh*, 98).

It is in this clear turning away from the traditional Christian pattern of self-denial, self-control, and self-sacrifice that Butler offers his own radical pattern of freedom. Most champions of freedom had hitherto agreed to the need for self-suppression in one form or another. True freedom came only through the reining in of wildness. But Butler had less confidence than Meredith in man's conscious powers and more explicitly sided with those who argued for a subtler, secret motive force. "I fancy," he writes early in the novel, "that there is some truth in the view which is being put forward now-adays, that it is our less conscious thoughts and our less conscious actions which mainly mold our lives and the lives of those who spring from us" (Butler, *Flesh*, 27).

The Way of All Flesh does not depart from the pattern of the late nine-teenth-century English novel in appearance, but it embodies assumptions that make it something of a sport. Like all of Butler's works, from *Erewhon* and *Luck or Cunning* to *The Authoress of the Odyssey, The Way of All Flesh* aims to violate expectations, to educate by means of a salubrious shock. His novel employs standard narrative means, but his narrative, in effect, goes nowhere. At the end of the novel, Ernest, his main character, has achieved nothing special. He has earned his right to survive through luck and a little cunning. Characters are set forth as though they have comprehensible mo-tives, though our narrator regularly suggests that men's motives cannot be known, not even by themselves. Ultimately, this example of novelistic art, conventionally expected to present a history of development, an endorse-ment of social structure, and a moral, offers none of these. Instead it pre-sents the embodiment of a thesis. The novel itself is the flesh of Butler's theory by which that theory can be known, and because Butler believed that intellectual schemes were relative and idiosyncratic, the embodiment of his theory becomes the transcription of his self, something he admits openly.

> Every man's work, whether it be literature or music or pictures or architecture or anything else, is always a portrait of himself, and the more he tries to conceal himself the more clearly will his char-acter appear in spite of him. I may very likely be condemning my-self, all the time that I am writing this book, for I know that whether I like it or no I am portraying myself more surely than I am portray-ing any of the characters whom I set before the reader. (Butler, *Flesh*, 74–75)

Man is free for Butler but free to utilize only what luck (heredity and circumstance) and cunning (his decisions prompted by unconscious im-pulses) have provided. He must suffer and grow, though beside him a benevo-lent force may be waiting to reward him for bungling into self-awareness. Like the novelist who sets out to tell a tale and must work with language and personal experience, the free man writes the text that was encoded in him long ago.

So much has been written about tragedy, fate, and chance in Hardy's fiction that I need not devote as much time to Hardy as he would otherwise deserve here. It is clear from his poetry, especially *The Dynasts*, that Hardy had a secure, if not entirely coherent, philosophy encompassing the notion of will. To some degree he simply secularized the Christian view while draining it of its high valuation on self-sacrifice. Human will is a part of the Immanent Will—a power more positively viewed by Swinburne and Meredith as the Life or Earth Force—that energizes the universe. Supposedly unaware of Von Hartmann's writings, Hardy assumed that he was innovative in suggesting that the Unconscious Will was "becoming conscious with the flux of time."[27] Otherwise, the Immanent Will was very like an unconscious or thoughtless deity, a characterization that appears comically in several of Hardy's poems, such as "God-Forgotten," "God's Education," and "God's Funeral." Instead of asserting the traditional view that man discovers his unity through the spark of intelligence or soul within himself, Hardy reversed the process and made the unconscious will capable of acquiring the consciousness already evident in man. Moreover, whereas the good Christian discovered his freedom in submitting his will to God's, Hardy's individual was freest when least exposed to the notice of the forces that impel life. Nonetheless, as J. Hillis Miller has noted, man still remained only a part of the Great Will.

> Even when the individual will acts with the paradoxical freedom of a self-acting finger it is still no more than a portion of the universal Will. As a result, the more powerfully a man wills or desires, the more surely he becomes the puppet of an all-shaping energy, and the quicker he encompasses his own destruction. As soon as he engages himself in life he joins a vast streaming movement urging him on toward death and the failure of his desires.[28]

Bert Hornback says that, for Schopenhauer, "though man '*acts* with strict necessity,' he '*exists* and is what [he] is by virtue of [his] *freedom*.' In Hardy, this freedom is the freedom of character, of what the dramatist deals with as being. The necessity is the moral necessity of consequence, an 'incessant impulse' which shows itself dramatically in patterns of intense coincidental recurrence in the lives of free men."[29] Coincidence, Hornback continues, is the artistic device Hardy uses to reveal the moral drama in the lives and situations that he constructs. In this, Hardy would then resemble Eliot in her unabashed use of coincidence to regulate and unite the various story lines her characters follow. Peter Morton, approaching *Tess of the d'Urbervilles* with inheritance theory in mind, concludes that the novel asserts a rigid determinism and a total pessimism, with its numerous coincidences reinforcing a sense of character as fate (Morton, 206).[30]

Hardy may be read in many ways, the emphasis on freedom or its lack varying with the reader. Nor can Hardy himself be trusted entirely in what he said about his philosophical notions. Hardy did not consider himself a philosopher and often denied that he held settled views.[31] Nonetheless, he did make broad assertions helpful for anyone trying to understand his art, which is what interested him most. Hardy said that nonrationality was the principle of the universe, thus excluding any theistic assumptions (Florence Hardy, *Later Years*, 90). He dismissed both chance and purpose as the guides of human life, asserting the primacy of necessity (Florence Hardy, *Later Years*, 128). Life to him was an interlocking web, all things merging into one another.[32] In referring to his "prematurely afflicted century," Hardy looked down the future hoping that whatever transpired for the human race, pain for it and its companion animals would be kept to a minimum by "loving-kindness, operating through scientific knowledge, and actuated by the modicum of free will conjecturally possessed by organic life when the mighty necessitating forces—unconscious or other—that have 'the balancing of the clouds', happen to be in equilibrium, which may or may not be often."[33]

Hardy expressed these general views and felt free to judge the philosophies of others, but he never presumed to render a consistent philosophy in his own writing.[34] He said that his works of art offered not a system of philosophy but provisional impressions, and I believe that we must accept this demurrer (Florence Hardy, *Later Years*, 175).[35] Hardy wanted his art to intensify the expression of things (Florence Hardy, *Early Years*, 231). This intensification inevitably involved the distorting and shaping of circumstances, and since Hardy also believed that art was the expression of idiosyncracy, such shaping inevitably mirrored the artist's nature (Florence Hardy, *Early Years*, 294). Hardy went so far as to declare that each individual artist discovers anew the design of nature, implying that the design is peculiar to his own method of perceiving, not abiding in nature itself (Florence Hardy, *Early Years*, 198).[36]

In a very intelligent and adventurous essay on *Tess of the d'Urbervilles*, Charlotte Thompson, beginning with the assumption that Hardy believed that the mind has the power to alter the material world, demonstrates how words become things in the novel, how ideas receive literal form.[37] Although the narrator can manipulate language, he is not entirely in command of the world he describes. Thompson's reading reinforces Hardy's own assertion that transformations in the natural world take place through an interpreting mind mediating between the realms of substance and idea largely by means of simile. F. D. Maurice and others had argued the case for the embodiment of ideas in matter on the model of the incarnation of Christ.[38] And Meredith self-consciously complicated language, forcing his readers to recognize just how difficult the process of converting ideas into substance was. Hardy stressed how language often entraps and occasionally frees human beings, how traditions embodied in language hold the human spirit in fee.

Tess of the d'Urbervilles is founded on the bitter irony that a foolishly proud attempt to recover the inheritance of a family name leads, by way of the false possessor of that name, to a much older, natural, and painful inheritance. The superficial significance of a name is trivial in comparison with genetic inheritance. Moreover, the Durbeyfields are degenerate in name and character from their notable forebears. Tess's trump card is not her d'Urberville blood, but her face.[39] She is attractive not because of her history but because of what she is and may be. Her characteristic mode of thought is future directed. Only as her sufferings accumulate does she feel the weight of the past. Though intelligent, Tess is moved primarily by emotion and imagination, and it is partly her failure to control these traits of her nature that brings about her misfortune. Hardy takes pains to indicate how much Tess is a victim of her imagination. After her fall, when she goes out walking alone at night, she is hypersensitive to her surroundings. "At times her whimsical fancy would intensify natural processes around her till they seemed a part of her own story. Rather they became a part of it; for the world is only a psychological phenomenon, and what they seemed they were" (Hardy, *Tess*, 72). Tess also suffers from the imagined disapproval of her companions, though the narrator specifically indicates that her associates are sympathetic rather than hostile. Her misery is "founded on an illusion. She was not an existence, an experience, a passion, a structure of sensations, to anybody but herself. To all humankind besides Tess was only a passing thought." Tess has broken a social law but not one recognized among the harvesters nor, for that matter by her own instincts. "Most of the misery had been generated by her conventional aspect, and not by her innate sensations" (Hardy, *Tess*, 77).

The law that does matter is the "irresistible law" that draws Tess and Angel together, the same "cruel Nature's law" that makes the other milkmaids feverish with desire (Hardy, *Tess*, 109 and 124). And Tess is much closer to this law than Angel is, for he lives largely in his mind, a dupe to the illusions generated there. Tess cannot see the world simply as it is; instead it becomes a scheme of values, of gifts and debts. When Angel declares that he has taken a marriage license not requiring Church publication of the banns, Tess is relieved, but fears "this good fortune may be scourged out of me afterwards by a lot of ill" (Hardy, *Tess*, 173). Ill follows partly because Tess tries to repay the debt to fate, first by leaving a note for Angel explaining her situation and later by confessing to him on their bridal night. She feels that it "was wicked of her to take all without paying. She would pay to the uttermost farthing; she would tell, there and then" (Hardy, *Tess*, 188). But the oral version of Tess's history creates an important change between the newlyweds; "the complexion even of external things seemed to suffer transmutation as her announcement progressed. . . . And yet nothing had changed since the moments when he had been kissing her; or rather, nothing in the substance of things. But the essence of things had changed" (Hardy, *Tess*, 190-91). We shape the world subjectively and then live with the consequences. For Hardy, the imagination that Romantics heralded for its capacity to fashion a pattern or story for existence, becomes dangerous in the way Mary Shelley had suggested because it can construct a story remote from the real incidents of life. It is even worse if the story is beyond the individual's control. Unlike her mother, for whom Tess's marital misfortune is like a crop failure, "a thing which had come upon them irrespective of desert or folly; a chance external impingement to be borne with; not a lesson," Tess sees intent, almost narrative purpose in events. "How unexpected were the attacks of destiny!" she thinks when she learns that her parents doubt her story of being married (Hardy, *Tess*, 215-16). This placing herself at the center of a "story" in which forces beyond her control direct her destiny occasions much of Tess's suffering. The same, on a different level, is true of Angel too.

Hardy did not condemn his characters for their poetic fancies but simply showed how out of keeping such high-minded poetry was with daily life. Tess insists upon justice operating in her universe; she believes she has moral debts to pay. As Hardy sees it, this and her idealism make her virtuous. He argued that, despite her failings, Tess maintains an innate purity, though her outward purity left her with the murder of Alec. "I regarded her then as being in the hands of circumstances, not normally responsible, a mere corpse drifting with a current to her end."[40]

Joseph Warren Beach described Hardy as a determinist rather than a fatalist. Both types, he explained, agree on the helplessness of the individual will against the will in things. "Only the determinist conceives the will in things as the sum of natural forces with which we have to cope, whereas the fatalist tends to a more religious interpretation of that will as truly and literally a *will*, an arbitrary power, a personal force like our own. Sometimes Mr. Hardy allows his characters the bitter comfort of that personal interpretation."[41] Actually, Hardy may be described as a determinist writer of fatalists' tales, his characters' sufferings often arising from their confusion of the two attitudes. Though fatalism may be their bitter comfort, it is also the source of their pain.

No narrative intrusion summarizes the philosophical structure of Hardy's fictional universe. So dependent is that structure upon individual perception that the novelist can only illustrate how characters create their worlds and suffer the consequences. But Hardy knew how significant the shaping power of the artist is, how important that that shaping power should appear to be esthetic and not an imitation of providence.[42] In his early fiction Hardy was apparently less concerned with art finished according to a coherent esthetic creed than with simple success as a writer. His invitation of suggestions on what he should write and his ready yielding to editorial alterations of his tests indicate that trade considerations were dominant in his early works. But from the beginning, Hardy was fascinated by the mechanics of consequence. Bathsheba Everdene impulsively sends a valentine to Boldwood as a joke, unaware of the possible consequences of her act. The valentine excites Boldwood's love and initiates a sequence of events leading to tragedy. Boldwood cannot conceive a lack of serious motivation behind the valentine. "The vast difference between starting a train of events, and directing into a particular groove a series already started, is rarely apparent to the person confounded by the issue," Hardy coolly remarks.[43]

Dale Kramer sees Bathsheba's act as a "directionless act of free will" and Boldwood as caught up "in a chain of events consequent upon his own unintentional act of free will."[44] For Kramer's purpose of showing the tragic pattern developing in the narrative this description is adequate, but it seems doubtful that "free will" is exactly the word to use for what Hardy depicts. Impulsiveness depends upon character traits inherited or bred; the nature of the consequences that follow from impulsive acts depends upon circumstance. Gabriel Oak, a man careful to control his impulses, is nonetheless unfortunate, but he responds to his misfortune calmly with "that indifference to fate which, though it often makes a villain of a man, is the basis of his sublimity when it does not" (Hardy, *Crowd*, 46).

Hardy explained that in *Two on a Tower* he attempted "to set the emotional history of two infinitesimal lives against the stupendous background of the stellar universe and to impart to readers the sentiment that of these contrasting magnitudes the smaller might be the greater to them as men."[45] This was also the mature Hardy's central objective, as the insignificance of human life was his constant theme. *The Return of the Native* is a forthright embodiment of this view. Speaking in his own voice, the narrator describes Clym Yeobright's face as "the typical countenance of the future," recording a new attitude toward existence, "the view of life as a thing to be put up with, replacing the zest for existence which was so intense in early civilizations." Long centuries of disillusion have instructed man. "That old-fashioned revelling in the general situation grows less and less possible as we uncover the defects of natural laws and see the quandary that man is in by their operation."[46] Clym has returned to Egdon Heath discontented with his life in fashionable but superficial Paris and hoping to improve the educational circumstances of the country population. He feels a deep kinship with the Heath, a kinship subtly reinforced by the resemblance between his face and the face of Egdon Heath. "It was at present a place perfectly accordant with man's nature—neither ghastly, hateful, nor ugly; neither commonplace, unmeaning, nor tame; but, like man, slighted and enduring; and withal singularly colossal and mysterious in its swarthy monotony. As with some persons who have long lived apart, solitude seemed to look out of its countenance. It had a lonely face, suggesting tragical possibilities" (Hardy, *Return*, 4). The enemy of the Heath is civilization, yet civilization is what Clym wishes to bring to it. He thus inadvertently betrays the Heath despite his kinship to it because he wants it to be other and "better" than it is. Clym's is an aspiration of the mind, prompted by selfless generosity, but based upon a fundamental illusion according to the "laws" of Hardy's novel. Eustacia Vye is the conscious antagonist of the Heath. She considers herself "above" the Heath and its denizens and longs to escape, craving the very civilization that is opposed to all that the Heath represents.

Eustacia is proud of her power, which has a magical quality in her own eyes. Johnny Nunsuch tending her fire is a "little slave" who "seemed a mere automaton, galvinized into moving and speaking by the wayward Eustacia's will." He resembles a statue magically animated by Albertus Magnus (Hardy, *Return*, 47). Eustacia compares her power to summon Damon Wildeve to the Witch of Endor's summoning of Samuel (Hardy, *Return*, 52). She is rebellious but directs her resentment "less against human beings than against certain creatures of her mind, the chief of these being Destiny" (Hardy, *Return*, 56). She is dangerous because having "lost the godlike conceit that we may do what we will," she has not "acquired a homely zest for doing what we can" (Hardy, *Return*, 57). Such a condition may lend grandeur to a character but also betokens mischief. Eustacia's allusions suggest that she views herself heroically, placing the blame for her misfortune on a consciously hostile force. She thinks herself worthy of a Saul or Bonaparte yet finds herself linked to two inferior men. " 'How I have tried and tried to be a splendid woman, and how destiny has been against me! . . . I do not deserve my lot!' she cried in a frenzy of bitter revolt. 'O, the cruelty of putting me into this ill-conceived world! I was capable of much; but I have been injured and blighted and crushed by things beyond my control! O, how hard it is of Heaven to devise such tortures for me, who have done no harm to Heaven at all' " (Hardy, *Return*, 236).

Like Tess Durbeyfield, Eustacia makes herself the chief character in a drama. Her attitude is pagan, projecting a fate so interested in her life that it actively thwarts her ambitions. She wishes to rise above the level of the Heath and is boldly associated with the Rainbarrow and other elevated places. But she comes to rest at the lowest point available, in the depths of the pond, as does Wildeve, her male counterpart, who also aspires to a fortune far above what the Heath can offer. What life teaches man above all else is the folly of aspiring on the basis of vain illusions. Here again the Heath is instructive. Just after Clym and Eustacia agree to marry, Clym looks out at the Heath. "There was something in its oppressive horizontality which too much reminded him of the arena of life; it gave him a sense of bare equality with, and no superiority to, a single living thing under the sun" (Hardy, *Return*, 164).

Later, forced by his impaired vision to work as a furze cutter on the Heath, Clym begins to understand the lesson of its horizontality. He tells Eustacia that he could rage against the fates like Prometheus, but "the more I see of life the more do I perceive that there is nothing particularly great in its greatest walks and therefore nothing particularly small in mine of furze-cutting" (Hardy, *Return*, 199).

Furze growing ruggedly close to the ground provides a model for human existence, whereas the fir trees by Clym's cottage signify the danger of aspiring. This clump of trees thrusts up so high it appears "as a black spot in the air above the crown of the hill." After her walk to Clym's house, Mrs. Yeobright rests beneath these trees and notices that they are "singularly battered, rude, and wild." Forgetting her own "storm broken and exhausted state," she observes in detail how the weather has splintered, lopped, distorted, blasted, and split the trees. Even with no wind blowing, the trees keep up "a perpetual moan" (Hardy, *Return*, 217). They are a monitory emblem of the suffering that comes to those who try to rise above the natural conditions around them. Heights symbolize danger in other novels as well—a tower with an observatory in it that leads to an unwise romance in *Two on a Tower*, a church tower that collapses, an emblem of the collapse of Henry Knight's unrealistic idealism about the woman he loves in *A Pair of Blue Eyes*, and elsewhere, as in *The Mayor of Casterbridge* or *Jude the Obscure*, the aspiring to a metaphorically "higher" social condition.[47] Perhaps one of the saddest instances is Tess's elevation to the ritual stones at Stonehenge because of her parents' yen for a possible rise in their social condition.

Hardy does not condemn ambition but cautions that it is often based upon illusions about oneself and the world, upon interpretations of the world that are shaped by one's own emotional and intellectual cravings. The Heath is an antidote to such fancies, and Thomasin, the embodiment of a sensible approach to life.

> To her there were not, as to Eustacia, demons in the air, and malice in every bush and bough. The drops which lashed her face were not scorpions, but prosy rain; Egdon in the mass was no monster whatever, but impersonal open ground. Her fears of the place were rational, her dislikes of its worst moods reasonable. At this time it was in her view a windy, wet place, in which a person might experience much discomfort, lose the path without care, and possibly catch cold. (Hardy, *Return*, 283)

In *The Mayor of Casterbridge* (1886), Hardy provided two contrasting types of character, one almost certainly doomed, the other capable of some satisfaction in life; one struggling to assert himself, the other content to hold her own against destiny. Michael Henchard is a man of great vigor whose failing is to allow his temper to affect his judgment.[48] His misfortunes generally follow from his own errors—very notably his wilful sale of his wife and child when under the influence of drink. Henchard is volcanic and aggressive. Contrasting him with the Jacob-like, patient, and humble Donald Farfrae, the narrator says that the latter's success was probably not due to luck. "Character is Fate, said Novalis, and Farfrae's character was just the reverse of Henchard's, who might not inaptly be described as Faust has been described—as a vehemently gloomy being who had quitted the ways of vulgar men without light to guide him on a better way" (Hardy, *Mayor*, 88).[49] Henchard's misery stems from his own actions and from his obstinate impulse to locate the source of his trouble outside himself. "Henchard, like all his kind, was superstitious, and he could not help thinking that the concatenation of events this evening had produced was the scheme of some sinister intelligence bent on punishing him. Yet they had developed naturally" (Hardy, *Mayor*, 96–97). By the time Henchard learns the lesson of his sufferings, he lacks the zest to engage the struggle of life again. The "ingenious machinery contrived by the Gods for reducing human possibilities of amelioration to a minimum" has fashioned life this way (Hardy, *Mayor*, 244).

Elizabeth-Jane's career follows a different pattern. She has intelligence and good looks, but what serves her best is a certain cast of temperament. "Like all people who have known rough times, light-heartedness seemed to her too irrational and inconsequent to be indulged in except as a reckless dram now and then." She has a healthy fear of destiny common to thoughtful people who have suffered. Because she expects little, what comes to her seems much—a serene married life wherein she can instruct others in the secret "of making limited opportunities endurable" (Hardy, *Mayor*, 255).

Most critical attention has correctly focused on Henchard; after all, the novel specifically singles him out and provokes additional curiosity by its subtitle, "A Story of a Man of Character." As we have seen in part 1, character in Hardy's day was understood to include strength of will. Hardy demonstrates how faulty this kind of character may be when it is unreflective. Henchard has a strong character, but Hardy scarcely could have meant to recommend that character as a moral model. From his selling his wife to his violence toward Farfrae, Henchard is a forceful but not an admirable character. Literary allusions indicate a tragic dimension to Henchard's life, but they are so complex and even contradictory that they must be sifted carefully. As Frederick R. Karl has indicated, in *The Mayor of Casterbridge* "Greek tragedy now serves modern sensibilities, and its external determinism is now internalized and seen as of man's own making" (Hardy, *Mayor*, 383). But this novel is not only about tragedy. Hardy was right to insist that he should not facilely be labeled a pessimist. He wrote to William Archer that he was not a pessimist. "On the contrary, my practical philosophy is distinctly meliorist. What are my books but one plea against 'man's inhumanity to man'—to woman—and to the lower animals? . . . Whatever may be the inherent good or evil of life, it is certain that men make it much worse than it need be. When we have got rid of a thousand remediable ills, it will be time enough to determine whether the ill that is irremediable outweighs the good."[50] Elizabeth-Jane's modest but real achievement of content is an example. She has no illusions and cannot therefore easily be led into folly. She will not forge the links of her own chain of evil destiny.

Jude the Obscure (1895) offers little hope of contentment and less grandeur of tragedy. Suffering and frustration in this book are relentless. Many of its thematic lines come together in the sequence of Father Time's murder of his siblings and his own suicide. Sue Bridehead reacts bitterly. "There is something external to us which says, 'You shan't.' "[51] As a young woman, Sue saw existence as a melody or dream with a First Cause working somnambulistically. She felt then "that at the framing of the terrestrial conditions there seemed never to have been contemplated such a development of emotional perceptiveness among the creatures subject to those conditions as that reached by thinking and educated humanity. But affliction makes opposing forces loom anthropomorphous; and those ideas were now exchanged for a sense of Jude and herself fleeing from a persecutor" (Hardy, *Jude*, 270). This rendering is similar to Mary Shelley's description of selfish imagination begetting a destiny that returns to haunt it. If the imagination is the agent and proof of man's free will projecting his freedom into the future, then that freedom is a kind of curse because it makes possible an agony of frustration by creating unrealizable dreams.

Both Jude and Sue picture themselves as figures in mental landscapes that they have created. Jude's improbable dream of achieving a university degree and Sue's pagan enthusiasm for a life of intellectual and emotional independence both overlook the liabilities within themselves and the social inertia ranged against them. They persist, from the highest motives, in making decisions that invariably put them at odds with the general community. In addition, they have not understood their own most elementary impulses of sexuality and comradeship, and worst of all they have fabricated false images of one another. Ironically their initial false images become the real ones, the two lovers changing places and remaining as remote from one another as they were at the start. Surely circumstance is hard on Jude and Sue, but they themselves have oiled the ingenious machinery that will crush them.

Hardy seems to have remained undecided about just what freedom meant to human beings. In "The Profitable Reading of Fiction," he said that the novels having the best effect on a healthy mind show character and environment combining to work out individual destiny, but he did not explain precisely what character was and whether it was entirely shaped by a force such as inheritance.[52] Roy Morrell suggests a parallel with the Existential philosophy of Sartre, arguing that the lack of causal psychological backgrounds in Hardy's people "is a measure of their freedom." They are determined by environment but only temporarily.[53] As J. T. Laird asserts, Morrell is surely right to emphasize the role of choice in Hardy's narratives, but I believe that he exaggerates the degree of "freedom" these characters enjoy.[54] Henchard's sometimes perverse choices are conscious but determined by ungovernable impulses beneath his conscious mind, yet Morrell singles him out as one who could have done otherwise.[55] Hardy's poetry frequently illustrates the ironic consequences of "wrong" choices, though it does not suggest that "right" choices were possible, or, in a long perspective, "better." Perhaps Laird's position is safest. Hardy does not offer a world of "complete natural determinism," but certain attitudes are linked—at the inactive range, passivity, fatalism and the life of nature, at the active range, precipitancy and recklessness. Thus Hardy isolates a limited ground for sane achievement. His "championing of will and its concomitants, foresight, alertness, and dependability, is accompanied by a healthy respect for stoicism."[56] What was clear to Hardy was that man's gifts of intelligence and sensibility were out of keeping with the forces of nature. In a variation of Mary Shelley's message in *Frankenstein*, Hardy indicates that man's highest qualities are doomed to frustration because they are based upon illusions of purpose and order that cannot be proven to exist. If man is free, his freedom consists in imagining an illusory world. Those characters who make no attempt to bend the "laws" of nature or society to their needs—like Thomasin and Elizabeth-Jane—discover that it is possible to live in accommodation with the forces around them.

Just as man shapes his destiny through the fictions he creates, Hardy shapes his fiction by making destinies obviously contrived. He believed from his earliest attempts at fiction that unusual incidents were necessary to gain a reader's interest. He used coincidence, sometimes improbable coincidence purposely to show the shaping power of the narrator, to indicate how incidents with no special significance in themselves—a note slipped accidentally under a carpet, a Furmity woman reappearing at an inconvenient time—resemble malign gestures of fate only because human beings have made decisions and created illusions that charge these events with an ultimately specious significance. Love itself is one of the most damaging illusions, and most of Hardy's stories turn on the workings of human passion.[57]

Like other novelists we have examined, Hardy insisted that his characters shaped their own destinies.[58] Michael Millgate writes of *The Mayor of Casterbridge*, where Elizabeth-Jane serves as onlooker and reader representative, that it is "almost as though Hardy shrank from the responsibilities of omniscience, from the necessity for moral judgments and firm intellectual commitments, and found a certain security in adopting—usually quite inconsistently and on a scene-to-scene basis—the limited but essentially human perspectives available to particular characters."[59] But Hardy is most faithful to his own view when muting the role of the narrator, just as a writer like Collins could best embody his views in multiple narrative, where the author need not assert any definitive opinion. The great power of Hardy's narratives is in the contrast between the stories his characters shape for themselves and the one that Hardy is shaping for them. Marlene Springer has suggested that, through his elaborate use of allusion, Hardy "requires of his readers that they bring to his novels an imaginative effort, that they read as connoisseurs."[60] Just as Meredith used difficult metaphorical language to compel his readers to engage in the imaginative act which he saw as the apex of human freedom—the liberation of the creative mind—Hardy sought to compel his readers, by his use of allusion and other narrative devices, to recognize how easily the patchwork heritage of human intelligence could provide images and ideals dangerous when taken seriously and applied to life. Eustacia Vye likens herself to the Witch of Endor, believing she is an exalted and powerful person. The narrator likens her to numerous avatars but consciously mixes his classical, biblical, and popular dramatic references, thus demonstrating his own power of enlarging Eustacia's character. But he immediately shrinks that character back to its proper dimension when he asks simply, "Why did a woman of this sort live on Egdon Heath?" (Hardy, *Return*, 54). It is instructive when a novelist enhances character by allusion but dangerous when a character does the same, as when Sue Bridehead pictures herself as a pagan antagonist of Christian civilization. The artist employs his allusions in a narrative under his control; the living being (or the character figuring that being) has no such control and cannot depend upon the operational effectiveness of such allusions and other fancies.

Hardy's generally unobtrusive narrator does not seem to be shaping the events of his story, but it is *his* fiction that will prevail, not those of his characters. Behind the strange circumstances of his stories there is a design, but it is that of the author's self-conscious fiction, that is, his art. The characters who take such fictions for realities see themselves as actors in a story created by powers who scheme out their destinies, but in thus believing in a design behind their own projections they lose the very power of their will by investing all of its energy in an illusion. The artist does not mimic providence; instead, providence merely resembles a faulty artist. In fact, there is neither artist nor artistry beyond the realm of human fictions. The freedom of man's will rests only in his power to create fictions, and only in art is it possible to indulge this gift without suffering the unpredictable consequences such fiction making engenders. Hardy the artist assumed not the role of providential creator but of representative humanity utilizing its fictionalizing power to illustrate the very dangers that power entails.

Perhaps a fitting way to bring this section to a close is by discussing a novel that, while looking back to the marvels of Romanticism, incorporated many of the issues familiar to late-Victorian writers. Theodore Watts-Dunton's

Aylwin (1898) was a surprising best-seller, exploiting certain late-century fascinations—as with gypsies and Wales—and promoting a renewed nature worship that Watts-Dunton himself wrote of elsewhere as the Renascence of Wonder. The novel is not well made. It was composed over a number of years and never did mend its seams appropriately. The basic plot is simple—Henry Aylwin, the narrator, falls in love with Winifred Wynne but is separated from her by the death of her father, who has violated the tomb of Aylwin's father and presumably suffered his curse. This incident drives Winifred into a hysterical madness and she disappears. The remainder of the story is Henry's account of his efforts to recover her.

Henry's chief contest is between his desire and the frustrations of circumstance. This theme is stated early in the novel when Henry recounts how, upon departing for Cambridge, he thought of all that he intended to do for Winifred though fate itself should say no. "I did not know then, as I know now," he reflects, "how weak is human will enmeshed in that web of Circumstance that has been a-weaving since the beginning of the world."[61] Annoyed by the superstitions of his ancestors both Romany and English (his father's first wife was a gypsy), Henry turns instead to "the wonderful revelations of modern science, my attitude towards superstition—towards all supernaturalism—oscillated between anger and simple contempt" (Watts-Dunton, *Aylwin*, 45). And yet he is snared in a world where Christian mystical belief and gypsy superstition bedevil him. His father's curse is effective; the fateful sign that guides Winifred in her madness proves actual, not merely a figment of her distorted mind. Henry is angered to find his own logical mind yielding to superstitious interpretations of events. His dilemma is typified by two paintings and the world views they present. On the one hand is the mystical painting "Faith and Love" by Wilderspin, a disciple of Henry's father; on the other is Cyril Aylwin's caricature of this painting. The first represents Isis unveiled as a joyful maiden flanked by Faith and Love, a symbol of "the true cosmology" of Henry's father and is the opposite of "that base Darwinian cosmogony which Carlyle spits at, and the great and good John Ruskin scorns," Wilderspin explains (Watts-Dunton, *Aylwin*, 189). The cynical Cyril's mockery of this painting uses the lower-class, crude, and vulgar Mrs. Gudgeon as model for an Isis grinning beneath a veil held by two figures, one resembling Darwin, the other Wilderspin. She is the Goddess of the Joke, Cyril explains, "who, when she had the chance of making a rational and common-sense universe, preferred amusing herself with flamingoes, dromedaries, ring-tailed monkeys, and men" (Watts-Dunton, *Aylwin*, 245). This contrast is intensified by the fact that Winifred, supposed to be Mrs. Gudgeon's daughter, is the model for Wilderspin's Isis. Two widely opposite types of women stand for two views of the world. The conflicting values expressed in the two paintings spill over into life, for when Henry discovers that Winifred was the model for Wilderspin's painting, Mrs. Gudgeon, her opposite, tells him that Winifred has died and been buried in a pauper's grave. The Goddess of the Joke announces the triumph of nihilistic philosophy. Henry collapses in agony. "And there at the feet of the awful jesting hag, Circumstance, I could only cry 'Winnie! my poor Winnie!' while over my head seemed to pass Necessity and her black ages of despair (Watts-Dunton, *Aylwin*, 301).

The next chapter is entitled "The Revolving Cage of Circumstance," and simply pursues the consequences of Henry's grief, his encounter with his remorseful mother, and his reading of his father's mystical writings. Desperate in his longing for some sense of Winifred, he goes to Mount Snowden, a place associated with her in his mind, accompanied by his gypsy friend Sinfi Lovell. In that beautiful natural setting, Henry *sees* Winifred but immediately regards the vision as a hallucination—the consequence of his own prostration and Sinfi's mesmerically powerful will that has enslaved "his will and his senses" (Watts-Dunton, *Aylwin*, 358). But even believing the vision false, identifying Winifred's face with the beauty of nature helps Henry to shed his morose view of the world as a charnel house and to recover instead a sense of the world's beauty.

Henry stays some weeks in the vicinity of Snowdon and then is surprised by Sinfi's return with a live and healthy Winifred, explaining that with the help of the painter D'Arcy (patterned on D. G. Rossetti), Winifred's curse was transferred magnetically to Sinfi, who was able to overcome it. D'Arcy's letter to Henry summarizes this solution to his problem. "As Job's faith was tried by Heaven, so has your love been tried by the power which you call 'circumstance' and which Wilderspin calls 'the spiritual world.' All that death has to teach the mind and the heart of man you have learnt to the very full, and yet she you love is restored to you, and will soon be in your arms" (Watts-Dunton, *Aylwin*, 442). Henry could find no consolation in materialism for the loss of his great love, D'Arcy says. He himself underwent a similar suffering, discovering his consolation in a power that transcends death.

> Yes, my dear Aylwin, I knew that when the issues of Life are greatly beyond the common, and when our hearts are torn as yours has been torn, and when our souls are on fire with a flame such as that which I saw was consuming you, the awful possibilities of this universe—of which we, civilized men or savages, know nothing—will come before us, and tease our hearts with strange wild hopes, though all the "proofs" of all the logicians should hold them up to scorn. (Watts-Dunton, *Aylwin*, 444)

Sinfi, in making Winifred's *dukkeripen* (or fate-sign) come true, has also conquered her own. Winifred's fate is to marry Henry; Sinfi's was to love him in vain. The story ends happily with the loving pair viewing the symbol of

their happiness—a cross-shaped, rose-colored cloud and light over Snowdon.
Watts-Dunton's novel must be read with considerable suspension of disbelief. The philosophy it expresses appears to be direct, but in fact is clouded by
unresolved issues on the questionable margin of "philosophical" thought.
Henry Aylwin's greatest torment is that he finds no satisfaction in materialism, yet can only fear the teaching of traditional faith. He cannot decide for
certain if man's destiny is shaped by heredity, malign fate, supernatural
powers recognized by the gypsies, or only by random circumstance. Like
Henry, the reader too must juggle a complex of competing beliefs, because
he knows no more than the first-person narrator, except for a few forecasts of
events to come and backward reflections. Unlike Henry, the reader does not
have a recovered sweetheart to help him affirm his trust in the prevailing
power of love in the universe. We must trust not Henry himself but D'Arcy,
who interprets Henry's story for him. D'Arcy sees life the way he sees paintings—as symbolic renderings of the veil of nature. Watts-Dunton's romance
aspires to this same condition. There are enough symbolic hints and structural clues for us to interpret *Aylwin* as Watts-Dunton intended, but that interpretation can never be reduced to a summary or epitome. William Sharp
wrote to Watts-Dunton that he might have called his novel *Destiny* if the title
had not already been used by a famous author (probably Susan Ferrier).
"The irresistibility of Fate, the overwhelming power of Circumstance, find
genuine expression in your pages. As through Aeschylus, as through Omar
Khayyam, there is beyond the general light an ominous shadow—of inevitable descent."[62] There is no ignoring that shadow in the novel, but ultimately
it is the light that triumphs. The novel is called *Aylwin*, not *Destiny*; it names
its central character and transfers emphasis from destiny to individual will.
There are fates, but they may be altered and even overcome. Man lives in the
face of mystery and must exert his will as though he is free because to yield to
materialist determinism is to abandon that freedom. Just as the reader follows a bizarre tale with many strange turnings, discontinuities, and coincidences, trusting that a narrative design will finally emerge, so man must
assume a design arising out of his experiences in a manner he will never be
able to define but in which he can place his trust. Watts-Dunton's narrative
leaps to its conclusion by inexplicable events that override the relentless
approach of destiny. The inexplicable cancels fate because it suspends causation. It is miracle brought within reach of those eager to believe. Whereas
Hardy declared all interpretations of cosmic designs temporary fictions that
men individually and as communities create for themselves and recommended none of them, urging only a faith in the admitted fiction of creative
art, Watts-Dunton suggested that, although the story of existence could not
be fully known as a work of art may be, it is there to be viewed with all its
symbols awaiting our hopeful interpretation.

Late Victorian Fiction

CHAPTER SEVENTEEN

Anti-materialists

IN part 1, we saw that many religious skeptics in the later part of the nineteenth century tried to preserve the moral scheme constructed upon the tenets of Christianity, even overhauling theories of development and evolution to their purposes. This desire to preserve a moral framework for conduct in a skeptical age was commonplace in the literature of the later nineteenth century. For example, novelists like Eliot and Meredith sought to retain moral values by urging control of the selfish will. This chapter presents selected responses by late nineteenth-century novelists to the challenges of materialism and doubt, from the severely chastened fiction of William Hale White to the aesthetic uncertainty of J. H. Shorthouse and the moral certitude of Mrs. Humphry Ward. Common to these atheological moralists was a recognition of how significantly religious faith had become internalized rather than located in a separate deity. Godhead now was in the self and manifested in the power of the will, itself assuming a free will, though, as with Shorthouse, that free will might be no more than a necessary illusion.

Another response to religious skepticism was direct affirmation, and this took some striking forms near the end of the century. If Shorthouse presented the world as dreamlike, George MacDonald offered dream as the positive mode of understanding the mystery of God's universe. Like Meredith, he suggested that man learn to *read* the world, but for him, what man read were true signs placed in this world by God legible to man once he had educated himself to the language of symbols. As with Dickens, the world's story is sketched in outline and mankind's task is to interpret, and, in so doing, act out its individual and communal roles. If MacDonald offered belief through interpretation, Marie Corelli asked for trust in the freedom and power of the will with no reasoned defense, and George Du Maurier described a world of absolute freedom only within a self infinitely expandable in time, a shapeable dream world opening even the past to the power of the will.

Each of these novelists uses a different narrative approach to embody his or her perception of human freedom. All present existence as a mystery and recommend the will and imagination as the chief means for interpreting that mystery. Narrative plots and structures are loose or rigorous according to the freedom or constraint expressed in the "philosophy" they espouse. Some, as with White and Du Maurier, show little awareness of this connection, but others, as with Shorthouse and MacDonald, actually discuss it in their texts. Having lost a sense of clear providential design, but unwilling to abandon a belief in some scheme supporting moral conduct, these authors employed both familiar and novel narrative means to make such a scheme credible.

~　~　~

Rider Haggard praised Eliza Lynn Linton, after Mrs. Linton's death on 14 July 1898, as "one of the ablest and keenest intellects of her time."[1] Mrs. Linton was born in 1822, began publishing fiction in her twenties, and was the first paid woman writer on an English newspaper, *The Morning Chronicle*. She remained a controversial novelist and journalist throughout her life, knew most of the important people of the Victorian era, and spoke out on many of its major issues. She was not religious but defended morality and human progress. Though certain of the distinction between right and wrong, she had reservations about human self-direction characteristic of much writing of the late Victorian period. Shortly before her death, Mrs. Linton wrote to her sister, "We follow the law of our physical being so closely, and when we are well things all look bright, and when we are not well they look dark. But also, we have a *certain* amount of free will and a *certain* amount of power over ourselves, and as we resolutely set ourselves to *be* and to *think* and to live, so we can, up to a certain point."[2]

Several minor novelists at the end of the century consciously took up the issue of human conduct in the face of failed religious faith and uncertain control of individual destiny. Like Mrs. Linton, these authors promoted a belief in human freedom while dismantling many old pillars of that freedom. William Hale White's *The Autobiography of Mark Rutherford* (1881), for example, chronicles a young man's routine passage into the dissenting ministry lacking rudimentary facts about sex and basic methods for a rational appreciation of religious beliefs. Gradually he loses his religious faith but replaces its values with parallel values of his own. He comes to see Christ's atonement as "a sublime summing up as it were of what sublime men have to do for their race; an exemplification rather than a contradiction, of Nature herself, as we know her in our own experience."[3] Christ's suffering and self-denial are mirrored in the daughter of Rutherford's atheist friend, Edward Gibbon Mardon. Mary Mardon is a model of self-denial and patience, foregoing the opportunity to marry in order to attend to her father's needs and dying soon after him. Rutherford rejects the Church's God, substituting a God that is an abstraction of nature. Abandoning concepts such as resurrection and immortality, he believes that mankind is improvable on earth and longs to devote himself to helping his fellow man toward some worthy ideal. He avoids metaphysical speculation and extreme self-analysis, preferring to occupy his mind with more immediate concerns of actual conduct.

Rutherford wants the fruits of faith in human conduct without the tenets of faith. In a world becoming more and more directly equated with the law of the survival of the fittest, he craves supports for altruistic self-sacrifice. It is small wonder that, lacking the dogma that justified earlier models of self-sacrifice, Rutherford finds metaphysical speculation and self-analysis uncomfortable.[4] His romantic involvements demonstrate the enormous influence of physiological impulses on behavior, but like Mrs. Linton, Rutherford still believes that he has sufficient free will to shape his own course in life and even guide his fellow man. By the end of the novel, he finds a modest but appropriate role working for a free-thinking London publisher.

J. Henry Shorthouse's *John Inglesant* (1881) appeared in the same year as White's novel. Although set in the seventeenth century, it too chronicles the movement of its central character from a religion of obedience to one of independent thought.[5] John Inglesant begins as a Catholic and Royalist and, after adventures among Jesuits and Quietists, comes to rest in the Church of England. Like Rutherford, Inglesant places his faith not in dogma but in conduct and in the image of a Christ of Atonement. He tells a Roman cardinal, "We must *suffer* with Christ whether we *believe* in Him or not. . . . Sin and suffering for sin; a sacrifice, itself mysterious, offered mysteriously to the Divine Nemesis or Law of Sin,—dread, undefined, unknown, yet sure and irresistible, with the iron necessity of law."[6] Inglesant's faith is a love of humanity for what it is, with all its weakness, not for what it should be. Like Rutherford, Inglesant patterns his life on Christ's; this Christian pattern also determines the framework of Shorthouse's novel, which is not tightly plotted. Just as the characters—especially Inglesant—have difficulty in asserting any strong and acceptable dogma and thus fall back upon rules of conduct, so the novel focuses on a central image of salvation but allows its plot lines to cross oddly or unravel carelessly. In his preface, Shorthouse admits this feature of his narrative: "Amid the tangled web of a life's story I have endeavoured to trace some distinct threads," he says and names some central themes of the book (Shorthouse, x).

There is another feature of Shorthouse's narrative that makes elaborate plotting unlikely. Although the novel eschews supernaturalism, it contains some surprising coincidences and occult events. For example, Inglesant's great nemesis, the Cavaliere Malvolti, whom he releases from his vengeance, returns to his home to discover that his beloved sister has been coincidentally ruined by his erstwhile companion in sin. Both he and Inglesant recognize this "coincidence" as a sample of "justice at work among the affairs of men" (Shorthouse, 393). Also, Inglesant witnesses the future death of his brother, Eustace, in a crystal ball. The novel's phantasmagoric quality is intensified by Inglesant's periodic mental confusion that makes the world seem dreamlike and unreal and by the many images likening life to a theatrical performance and men to conventional types playing out their assigned roles.[7]

If life is dreamlike and theatrical, it is both beyond and within man's power. Dream suggests a world where will is suspended and determinist law gives way to chance. Theater suggests apparent freedom within a rigidly scripted sequence of events. Twice in the novel, Shorthouse openly explores the quandary of crediting free will in a world of chance or of mechanical law. In one instance, the Catholic Cardinal Rinuccini tries to draw Inglesant out of monastic seclusion into an engaged, active existence. His Paterian rhetoric pictures life as a work of art to be fashioned by individual power.

> The freewill, the reason, and the power of self-command, struggle perpetually with an array of chance incidents, of mechanical forces, of material causes, beyond foresight or control, but not beyond skilful management. This gives a delicate zest and point to life, which it would surely want if we had the power to frame it as we would. We did not make the world, and are not responsible for its state; but we can make life a fine art, and, taking things as we find them, like wise men, mould them as may best serve our own ends. (Shorthouse, 254)

The second discussion of free will comes near the end of the novel, when Inglesant has made his choice against the kind of authority represented by the Jesuits and for the individual freedom of thought represented by Molinos and the Quietists. Inglesant has been a seeker wavering between the competing desires for authority and for freedom from authority. Finally he turns to the Church of England as the protector of cultural as well as religious freedom. For Shorthouse, culture "represented the mean, a proper balance of the world and the spirit, of freedom and authority, of self-denial and self-fulfilment."[8] Because Absolute Truth has not been revealed to man, he must depend to some degree upon his intuition. "We find ourselves immersed in physical and psychical laws, in accordance with which we act, or from which we diverge. Whether we are free to act or not, we can at least fancy that we resolve. Let us cheat ourselves, if it be a cheat, with this fancy, for we shall find that by so doing we actually attain the end we seek" (Shorthouse, 444). Men merely imagine they are free to be virtuous, yet in their deluded action they do achieve virtue. Shorthouse sounds a little like Max Beerbohm in "The Happy Hypocrite," where to wear the mask of virtue is to become virtuous, or like H. G. Wells in his frequent assertions that if man acts as though he is free, he actually frees himself to shape his destiny. But Shorthouse comes to no clear-cut decision, and his narrative method reflects this indecisiveness. He crudely exploits his "editor," Geoffrey Monk's inadequate documentary resources to justify jumps and breaks in the narrative. Massive gouts of detail do not advance the narrative, characters are introduced and forgotten or disposed of cavalierly, and motivation seems important only for the central character. But since Inglesant's world is not governed by a linear providential force, it may pause or advance as its characters perceive new meaning in the mysterious world around them.[9] Shorthouse described life as a moral game of make-believe; it should not be surprising that his novel resembles a dream.

Mrs. Humphry Ward's *Robert Elsmere* (1888), by contrast, declares that life is no theatrical performance and no dream (though certain of her characters use the images). She herself, while rejecting traditional theology, retained belief in an unchangeable moral law. William S. Peterson says that the major theme of her fiction is "the immutability of Divine law . . . and the futility of human rebellion against it." Her combination of conservative morality and revolutionary theology, he says, was not unusual among eminent Victorians.[10] Elsmere is another serious young man who, like his author, outgrows the religious faith of his youth. In its place he establishes a "New Brotherhood of Christ" that aims to reconstitute the figure of Christ for its own time. From his boyhood, Elsmere had a natural gift of sympathy, "at the bottom of the lad, all the time, there was a strength of will, a force and even tyranny of conscience, which kept his charm and pliancy from degenerating into weakness, and made it not only delightful, but profitable to love him."[11] Elsmere's career is patterned on St. Augustine's *Confessions*. Scrupulous in his intellectual search for truth, he discards the traditional faith to which his wife remains committed. He fears that he has lost all ground for a belief in God, but Mr. Grey, described as a Hegelian who "had broken with the popular Christianity, but [for whom] God, Consciousness, Duty were the only realities," comforts him with the assertion that all religions are true and false (Ward, 62). In all of them "man grasps at the one thing needful—self forsaken, God laid hold of" (Ward, 267). Elsmere is described as a modern

"Man of Feeling" free from the burden of self, but he cannot accept the fervent High Churchman the Reverend Mr. Newcome's advice to abandon doubt and escape the perniciousness of freedom by becoming Christ's slave. Elsmere considers an unreasoned faith worthless and thus for him "only the *habit* of faith held, the close instinctive clinging to a Power beyond sense—a Goodness, a Will not man's. The soul had been stripped of its old defences, but at his worst there was never a moment when Elsmere felt himself utterly forsaken" (Ward, 347).

Mr. Grey provides Elsmere with the consolation he requires. "Love and imagination built up religion,—shall reason destroy it?" he asks rhetorically and immediately replies: "No!—reason is God's like the rest! Trust it,—trust him. . . . learn to seek God, not in any single event of past history, *but in your own soul,*—in the constant verifications of experience, in the life of Christian love" (Ward, 356). Elsmere comes to resemble the great religious leaders of the past. He is a vehicle for the spirit of devotion and can lead the poor and the friendless because he embodies spiritual idealism. His admirer Hugh Flaxman explains that "there is no approaching the idea for the masses except through the human life; there is no lasting power for the man except as the slave of the idea" (Ward, 577-78).

Elsmere ends, then, not as the slave of Christ and unreasoning belief but as the slave of reason itself, which, according to Mr. Grey, will more surely put him in the service of the *idea* of Christ. And yet the old scheme remains. Only through abandoning self will does man achieve freedom. It is no longer an anthropomorphic deity or a sacred text to which he must bow his head but a Hegelian idea. Beyond man's will, there still abides a Will to which we must submit, for it has a purpose and a plan. But to submit requires great strength of will. Self-sacrifice demands a powerful effort of self-control. Elsmere repeats in a modernized form the old paradox that man achieves freedom by subordinating his impulses to his will and then offering that will in the service of something greater.[12] The effort is more difficult for Elsmere than for earlier heroes and heroines because now there is no Father to whom this service may be rendered, only an Idea. At the end of the novel we get some idea of how difficult this service is when Elsmere dies, worn out in his care for the poor and suffering.

Mrs. Ward referred to her novel as an "unpretending history," but it is more than that (Ward, 151). Unlike the other novels we have just been discussing, Mrs. Ward's is carefully constructed.[13] The characters are rich and complicated beings with credible motives acting in a shaped plot suggesting inevitable progress toward a foreseeable end. Emphasizing the positive lesson of Elsmere's career is a complex set of foils. His wife, Catherine, lacks his intellectual liberty, but her traditional faith is liberalized through his example. More dramatically contrasted with Elsmere is Edward Langham, who has little strength of will and is energized by no ideal; he sees only "the uselessness of utterance, the futility of enthusiasm, the inaccessibility of the ideal, [and] the practical absurdity of trying to realise any of the mind's inward dreams" (Ward 53). If St. Augustine is the model for Elsmere's struggle, that for Langham's is Amiel.[14] The one represents intellectual spirituality, the other intellectual aestheticism. Langham is as much drawn to the artistically accomplished Rose Leyburn as Elsmere is to her religious sister, Catherine. But whereas Elsmere and Catherine create a satisfying married life together, Langham is too divided in mind, too lacking in confidence and purpose to fulfill his marriage engagement to Rose. His life is a waste and a proof that aesthetic indulgence by itself brings no real gratification. Even Rose, a gifted violinist, though she can interpret the art of the subtlest moderns, such as Wagner, Brahms, and Rubenstein, has no ideal beyond art to sustain her. It is she who laments the human habit of attitudinizing. With her habit of esthetic perception, she pictures life as "one long dramatic performance, in which one half of us is for ever posing to the other half" (Ward, 488).

But Mrs. Ward is not recommending Shorthouse's ambivalent solution—to treat life as though it were malleable to the human will and make it, like an art, serve our pleasure. Her advice is to train the will in seeking truth, then submit it to the something beyond ourselves that makes for righteousness, as her uncle Matthew Arnold might have put it.[15] The truth rises from within us not because we have chosen to give life—even faith—style but because that is the true dwelling place of God. Man submits his will to what is highest within himself. He bows down to the godhead in himself.

In contrast to the earnest doubters who wanted to preserve the Christian ethos without religion were those writers who sought to renew traditional Christian values along novel and exciting avenues. As early as *The Portent* (1860 in *The Cornhill Magazine*, 1864 in book), George MacDonald had indicated the significance of will in his beliefs, but this significance is fully manifest in the intriguing late novel *Lilith* (1895).[16] The first-person narrator, Mr. Vane, exploring his old family house rich with memories, steps through an unusual mirror into a strange land where his guide, Mr. Raven (who later proves to be Adam), educates him in the mysteries of his allegorical realm that can be described only indirectly because ordinary language cannot approximate the forms that rise in the narrator's mind.[17] The narrator asks if his guide could help him with explanatory definitions and categories. Mr. Raven replies: " 'I could not. But if I could, what better would you be? You would not know it of *your*self and *it*self! Why know the name of a thing when the thing itself you do not know? Whose work is it but your own to open your eyes? But indeed the business of the universe is to make such a fool of you that you will know yourself for one, and so begin to be wise' " (MacDonald, *Lilith*, 25). Inadequate as language is for communicating the nature of the narrator's experience, it is the only medium available for a narrative presentation. Language is a system of ambivalent signs that creates meaning according to acknowledged rules and relationships. MacDonald's narrative tries to create its own "language" with far more puzzling signs. Thus Mr. Raven is sometimes a man, sometimes the bird his name signifies, and sometimes the original embodiment of humanity, Adam. Forms, land-scapes, time relationships all fluctuate constantly, as do the names for them. The language of words is only one form of communication, though the most social. But to effect social intercourse, one must know his or her own nature. Just as a dreamer must convert his dream images to language or an artist his inspiration to words if either wants others to comprehend what he has felt, so ideas and beliefs must receive a communicable form if they are to be shared. From this point of view, right naming is the first human necessity, as Adam's history illustrates. But few humans realize that to name is already to begin the process of creation, even of fictionalizing, because real existence is not a story following a temporal line, but simply experience awaiting the potential meaning conveyable through interpretable signs. This is the same percep-tion so evident in Hardy and other writers but converted here into a fable that enacts the very procedure it describes. When Mr. Raven tells Vane that people in the mirror land do not know their names, the young man consid-ers it very strange. "Perhaps so," his guide replies, "but hardly anyone any-where knows his own name. It would make many a fine gentleman stare to hear himself addressed by what is really his name" (MacDonald, *Lilith*, 78).

Mr. Raven says that the universe is a riddle to be solved and that Vane is resisting the solution. Vane admits that until now, lacking self-confidence, he has made small use of his life, but to give his life purpose he must give it a shape and to do that he must act and choose. An early exchange between Vane and Mr. Raven is especially instructive on this issue. Vane complains about the puzzling world into which he has been led.

"What right have you to treat me so, Mr. Raven?" I said with deep offense. "Am I, or am I not, a free agent?"

"A man is as free as he chooses to make himself, never an atom freer," answered the raven.

"You have no right to make me do things against my will."

"When you have a will, you will find that no one can."

"You wrong me in the very essence of my individuality," I per-sisted.

"If you were an individual I could not, therefore now I do not. You are but beginning to become an individual." (MacDonald, *Lil-ith*, 19)

The message is cryptic at this point, but MacDonald's narrative method soon demonstrates that the mirror land is the battlefield of the narrator's personality. Its peculiarities are manifestations of his longings and anxieties, and since these are largely unformulated, they appear fluid and unfixed. Finding himself on a flat, barren plain, reminiscent of Browning's "Childe Roland" or Carlyle's Center of Indifference, the narrator intuits his relationship to the mirror world. Though he longs for some prominence of hope, he realizes that no elevation of the landscape will alter his condition "while *everywhere* was the same as *nowhere*. I had not yet, by doing something in it, made *anywhere* into a place" (MacDonald, *Lilith*, 87). He comprehends that the source of formulation is within man. To use the terminology of our study, man is not predestined or determined by external laws but free to shape his own destiny. "That which is within a man, not that which lies beyond his vision, is the main factor in what is about to befall him: the operation upon him is the event. Foreseeing is not understanding, else surely the prophecy latent in man would oftener come to the surface" (MacDonald, *Lilith*, 86).

The universe is a complex riddle composed of ambiguous signs that are the expression of God's thoughts. A man consolidates his nature by articulating those signs.[18] Ultimately, the meaning of existence arises from some inner font, which is identified with individuality and will, but here as so often before, the fundamental paradox reappears—to discover one's individuality and free one's will, one must submit to a greater power. Vane's most serious error is his free decision to reject Adam's advice and run away from the dead beings of the mirror world. He does not yet realize that one must "die" metaphorically in order to be saved and that in the mirror land metaphors are real.[19] The narrative itself progresses according to this principle, operating on levels of metaphor, analogy, symbolism, even allegory, but constantly plunging back into mundane reality until the reader is forced to distrust or accept the validity of all. The entire novel may also be read as a fable of literary creation, its spiritual concepts gradually being reduced to textual forms representing an essentially unutterable experience.[20]

But dreamlike as these appearances seem, there is a reality behind them and it is intimately associated with the will, a point made clear in a dramatic scene between the loving and sympathetic Lady Mara, woman of sorrow, and the evil princess Lilith, whose great sin is selfishness. Lilith imagines herself utterly free. "No one ever made me" she exclaims. "I defy that Power to unmake me from a free woman. You are his slave, and I defy you! You may be able to torture me—I do not know, but you shall not compel me to anything against my will." Mara explains that there is a light that goes deeper than the will, that can free it from the selfish will which is not really one's own but "the Shadow's." "Into the created can pour itself the creating will, and so redeem it." Lilith replies that Mara is simply a slave of that light, but Mara answers, "I am no slave, for I love that light, and will with the deeper will which created mine. There is no slave but the creature that wills against its creator. Who is a slave but her who cries, 'I am free,' yet cannot cease to exist" (MacDonald, *Lilith*, 217). Lilith insists that, though she may suffer for her rebellious stand, she will nonetheless remain free. But Mara tells Lilith that she is not free because she wishes to enslave others. Lilith needs to feel her power through the domination of others and is therefore the slave of every slave she has made. "She alone is free who would make free" (MacDonald, *Lilith*, 218). After this scene, the narrator becomes conscious of "a horrible Nothingness, a Negation" surrounding Lilith. But even Lilith may be saved through God's mercy.

For MacDonald, the traditional equation takes a novel form, but its import remains unchanged. All human creativity derives from a creator. Man's true freedom of will is in recognizing that source of his strength. Once he submits to that power it flows through him into acts of generosity and selflessness. But man may confuse his strength of will with freedom of will. This is Lilith's error. She is a slave of the Shadow. It can beget nothing but exists only as the negation of light. Assuming this stance, one may feel the power of self-assertion but only through acts of suppression and destruction. Lilith is the true slave, and her supposed strength of will is nothing but an iron cage to imprison her.

Near the end of *Lilith*, when the narrator dies symbolically into life, Adam tells him that henceforth "the more you live, the stronger you become to live." He responds, "But shall I not grow weary with living so strong? . . . What if I cease to live with all my might?" And The Mother reassures him, "It needs but the will, and the strength is there. . . . *The* Life keeps generating ours" (MacDonald, *Lilith*, 260). Though the term suffers some equivocation through the novel, true *will* is that in the human soul which emanates from God. Strength of will is a trait of human character that may operate for good or ill. The great task is to place strength of will in service of the higher will, to be a creative, not a negating, force. At the end of the novel, the narrator still lives in a region that imperfectly traverses the two worlds of spirit and matter, though he hopes to progress in a positive manner, ultimately converting life into dream. His allusion to Novalis may suggest that, after his pilgrimage in the world of images, the narrator, as novelist, has reemerged to do his creative work. The truth implanted in his soul has become discoverable and hence transmissible because he has scattered the cloud of self and freed himself to communicate in a language he can share with all mankind.[21] In this reading, *Lilith* is not only the history, but also the embodiment and product, of the free will in service of a spiritual ideal through the creation of an enabling object. The author and the narrator are not one but *stand for* one another, thus neither can be providential and prescient because the telling of the story is always underway and open to transformation and at its conclusion projects into an undetermined future.

MacDonald's novel describes and represents a God-directed world where men are nonetheless entirely free.

If George MacDonald's *Lilith* unfolds as a dreamlike narrative, enforcing the notion that human experience is malleable to human spirit, much as language is to the writer, Marie Corelli's *A Romance of Two Worlds* (1886) develops like the kind of musical improvisation for which the narrator is so famous. Corelli's explanation that she wrote her novel to counter the twin dangers of materialism and spiritualism allies it with MacDonald's. Love for God is the truth she wished to promote. "For the distinguishing mark of the true spiritualist is what I may call Self-rejection. Self stands on one side, as it were, and is no longer allowed to obscure the Soul's view of the splendid universe to which it belongs."[22]

Corelli's book presents a familiar outline: a central character suffering emotional discontent encounters a group of people led by a wise spiritual man that guides her into novel spiritual states from which she emerges strengthened to act for the good. Like MacDonald, Corelli puts her faith in intuition, not reason. Her heroine is specifically instructed to "mistrust that volatile thing called Human Reason" (Corelli, 325). The nameless heroine is a piano improvisator suffering from spiritual and bodily malaise when a friend introduces her to Casimir Heliobas, a sage who has studied the control of human electricity. Heliobas's theory of electricity owes much to nineteenth-century interest in animal magnetism and to newer theories of electrical transmission by ether or by wave action. Corelli's electrical imagery is a modernization of the traditional light imagery MacDonald was still using some nine years later. Heliobas explains that "every human being is provided *internally* and *externally* with a certain amount of electricity." Internally it is the germ of a soul or spirit, that, if neglected, will remain a germ and migrate elsewhere at the body's death. "If, on the contrary, its growth is fostered by a persevering, resolute WILL, it becomes a spiritual creature, glorious and supremely powerful, for which a new brilliant, and endless existence commences when its clay chrysalis perishes. So much for the *internal* electric force. The *external* binds us all by fixed laws, with which our wills have nothing whatever to do" (Corelli, 144–45).

The heroine places herself under Heliobas's tutelage and eventually is sent off on a disembodied tour of the universe where she discovers that the body is a prison to the soul; learns that, of all the planets, only earth harbors unbelievers in God's purpose; and encounters the central world, the origin of all creation and the source of electricity. When she returns from this excursion, the heroine recounts her experiences to Heliobas, who declares, "It proves to me more than ever the omnipotence of will" (Corelli, 247). A modern reader might distrust Heliobas's expositions on the power of seeing spirits in the air, on the methods of separating souls, and on the moon as an electric photograph. But these details are subordinate to his main message that all of existence is connected by electrical current—much as Carlyle's was interpenetrated by organic filaments—and that man has the power to direct that current. "Why the very essence of our belief is in the strength of Will-power. What we will to do, especially if it be any act of spiritual progress, we can accomplish" (Corelli, 257). At first Corelli seems to be advancing a new radical freedom of the will, but eventually a familiar pattern emerges when the heroine arrives at Heliobas's rooms just in time to prevent him from killing Prince Ivan Petroffsky, who has attacked the wizard, believing him responsible for his beloved Zara's death. Heliobas tells her that she has fulfilled a destined mission. But if her actions have been part of a larger pattern, to what degree and in what manner has will been free? Corelli does not engage this problem but concludes her novel with the heroine adjuring the reader to think about his or her life and believe in free will and a universe powered by life.

Corelli's novel is not a polemic, but a series of assertions. Following her own character's advice, she eschews reason in favor of spiritual intuition. She does not explore her image of the soul as germlike in the way that MacDonald anatomizes his symbols of faith but is content merely to offer it as a concrete description. Believing that individuals are free and that freedom originates in the soul, Corelli cares most about her characters' passions, the testing of one will against another and spirit against matter. Her plot is a sequence of improvisatory rhapsodies spun out with the apparent confidence that an overall design will reveal itself because the inspiration impelling the narrative derives ultimately from some higher power. In a clumsier and cruder fashion, Corelli's novel like MacDonald's draws the world of matter closer to the boundaries of spirit and dream, but whereas MacDonald offered his work of art as a symbolic rendering of his belief, Corelli presents her story as a form of fictional documentary evidence.

Another novel of this same period did not hesitate at the boundary of matter and spirit but ventured into an amazingly rich world of dream, a world opening up all history to those who gain admittance. In George Du Maurier's *Peter Ibbetson* (1892), the first-person narrator tells of his youthful disbelief in theism and his faith in human progress. Cruelty was the only sin young Peter Ibbetson acknowledged. He was a dedicated materialist. "Free will was impossible. We could only *seem* to will freely, and that only within the limits of a small triangle, whose sides were heredity, education, and circumstance. . . . That is, we could will fast enough—*too* fast; but could not will *how* to will: fortunately, for we were not fit as yet, and for a long time to come, to be trusted, constituted as we are!"[23] Lacking free will, mankind was nonetheless borne upward by an evolutionary force that inclined it to exert its will to achieve what little was possible until it should learn to control circumstance, adapt education to a consistent end, and guide heredity.

Young Peter believes in no afterlife and no spiritual consolations and thus determines that he must make the most of the one life he has. I do not intend to trace Du Maurier's narrative at length; it is enough to note that Peter falls in love with a married and inaccessible woman, in an angry moment kills his uncle, and is eventually placed in a lunatic asylum. Here the woman he loves visits him in his dreams, gradually convincing him that it is possible for the two of them to *actually* live in their shared dreams and to control those dreams according to their own and inherited memories (which, with some practice, takes them back to prehistoric times). They transcend the limits of time and return to any past event they please. After many exciting and pleasurable adventures, the dreams suddenly change and Peter learns that his beloved has died in the material world. But she returns to him once more in a dream, promising a future transcendence equal to the past transcendence they have shared.

Du Maurier ends his novel ambiguously. Ibbetson's writings may be the mere hallucinations of a madman or the visions of a seer. In any case, he has lived believing that, while his physical being has remained confined in an asylum, his spirit has been free to range over all of history. His condition is an elaborate extrapolation of the nineteenth-century conception of the self as an immaterial spirit bound in a prison of flesh. But it goes on to explore the Kantian implications of that condition. In the world governed by material laws, man is not free, but in the world of spirit, no material laws constrain him. As with Henri Bergson's philosophy, *Peter Ibbetson* suggests a means of reimporting freedom of the will through the new dimension of time.

Du Maurier's narrative method reflects this set of ideas. A slight frame surrounds the central narrative. Written by Ibbetson's cousin Madge Plunkett, it confirms the material historical facts. This frame represents the "real" world of daily existence, but the memoir it encloses signifies the free interior regions of the self. The memoir's first-person narration focuses on human desires and fears. The plot is extremely sketchy, a mere framework to establish the necessary complicating circumstances before the body of the novel, consisting of dream excursions, takes over. No overall moral design governs this fictional universe, nor is one evident in the architecture of the novel or in passages of exposition. An impressionistic report of a heavenlike afterlife reaches us by way of Peter's dead love. No relentless accumulation of events, no dreadful advance of cause and effect, dooms Peter to suffering. He escapes from the determinist material world where such things happen into the free world of dreams. The greater part of the novel is dedicated to an exaltation of his freedom from necessity's chain of events. If the past is fixed and therefore determined, the ability of the human mind to recover it still represents the kind of freedom a God might feel in being omniscient. Du Maurier is reifying here Butler's image of heredity as the memory of units in the Body of the Universe. Human freedom seems to be guaranteed in the hint that because no future exists in the dream world, it remains open to the free action of the will. A God that does not know the end of things is not bound to end them in any given way. Du Maurier makes none of this explicit. Unlike MacDonald and Corelli, he was not much interested in conveying any theory of the will and was more interested in telling an exotic story. Still, at the close of this unusual narrative we are invited to believe not only that life, rightly known, is a dream or phantasmagoria but that it is one potentially within the power of man to shape, much as Peter shapes his memories into the text he leaves, or as any artist shapes the fable we read.

CHAPTER EIGHTEEN

Walter Pater and the Nineties

T HE previous chapter examined novelists who removed the preserve of
divinity to the individual self, where the will could reconstruct justifications for moral standards with or without a theological base. Walter
Pater more intensely situated freedom in the self and made self-communion
the basis for values. However, his self was not an ark to contain divinity; it was
itself all the divinity men could know. Although determinist thinking seemed
to be triumphant at the end of the century, many writers did not submit to a
simple pessimism but asserted the freedom of the will, even if that freedom
was little more than a consciousness of not submitting. Pater is the subtlest
and most artful exponent of this tendency. For him, the very power of perception, the ability to assemble sensations into structures of meaning and
emotion, was the truest freedom available to men. And it was freest when
most suspended. To choose a direction and fix a destination was to imitate
the certainties of destiny. As he himself realized, his artistic style was his
surest manifestation and guarantor of his freedom.

~ ~ ~

By now it should be difficult to talk of the last two decades of the nineteenth
century simply, even dismissingly, as "The Decadence." As Holbrook Jackson pointed out in *The Eighteen-Nineties* (1913), this was a period of complex fecundity. Yet the simplifying spirit always yearns to make a historical

period more graspable by making it less reticulate. Even accomplished literary critics have this tendency. John A. Lester, Jr., over-emphasizes the pessimism of the 1880-1914 period and its concentration upon the development of the self.[1] Though mentioning some optimistic attitudes of writers during this period, he remains convinced that pessimism dominated because "Darwin left no room whatever for purpose in the world, human or divine, or for any free will to pursue such a purpose if there was one" (Lester, 84ff). Lester says that the concept of chance in the universe came to outweigh that of determinism and that man's mind seemed less a tool to discover truth than a mechanism for survival (Lester, 46-47).

We have already seen that many efforts were made to revoke or modify Darwin's theories. Darwin himself accepted some of these modifications.[2] It is certainly true that a grimmer mood emerged at the end of the century, but it was far from all-pervasive. May Sinclair wrote in *Audrey Craven* (1897) that "in our modern mythology, Custom, Circumstance, and Heredity are the three fates that weave the web of human fate."[3] Max Beerbohm expressed the resigned negativism of the time in his satirical "A Defence of Cosmetics." "No martyrdom, however fine, nor satire, however splendidly bitter, has changed by a little tittle the known tendency of things. It is the times that can perfect us, not we the times, and so let all of us wisely acquiesce. Like the little wired marionettes, let us acquiesce in the dance."[4] The inability to control existence through exercise of the will may constitute one late-century attitude, but there were other attitudes as well. Osbert Burdett judged Lionel Johnson and John Davidson for their failure of will but also noted Thompson's call for energy of will.[5] Holbrook Jackson also indicated that will was a consciously important issue for John Davidson, and James G. Nelson describes his Davidson's *Fleet Street Ecologues* (1893, 1896) as a "dramatization of an inner conflict between his will and his esthetic temperament."[6] If Davidson ultimately failed in his will, he placed it centrally, as did others with more hope. Arthur Symons wrote, "We can get anything we want if we will it."[7] In evaluating another character, Edmund Wotton in Vernon Lee's *Miss Brown* (1884) expresses a typical "decadent" pessimism. " 'I don't believe in praise and blame' he answered; 'I believe merely in fate. Some people are born noble, truthful, chaste—others just the reverse. It is the fault of neither; and each, in its way, is equally interesting and valuable to the artist or the psychologist.' "[8] But the whole force of Lee's novel is against the emptiness associated with this etiolated aestheticism, a force boldly concentrated in her heroine, Anne Brown. She, too, begins with pessimism.

> But in Anne this purely negative creed speedily became positive; pessimism produced not a desire to abandon the odious reality and take refuge in mere imaginary happiness, but a frightful moral tension, a constant battle of her aspirations with her belief, of her con-

science with her reason, a strain of rebellion against the inevitable. So, to the weight of the knowledge of evil, to the weight of the consciousness of the deadness of soul which surrounded her, was added in Anne the terrible sense of the injustice and callousness of nature and of fate, of the groundlessness of those instincts of good which left her no peace (Lee, 223–24).

Anne perseveres in her desire to achieve something positive and, in the end, marries the dispirited poet and painter Walter Hamlin to save him from another woman and to revive his creative energies. In a more direct vein, Alfred Orage used Nietzsche's writings to argue the importance of the aggressive will especially in the artist as creator of new imaginative values.[9]

It was this fascination with the central role of will that Holbrook Jackson had in mind when he defined "Decadence" as "imperialism of the spirit," the assertion of I will over merely I am.[10] Such otherwise contrary figures as Oscar Wilde and William Ernest Henley champion the same kind of individualism, one that rejected subordination of the self and fostered self-development. Wilde described perfection as individualism, picturing the socialist future as a society of free individuals fully developed.[11] Jerome Hamilton Buckley, contrasting Charles Kingsley's Victorian activism with Henley's, explains that the former's sermons called for the assertion of a powerful personality defying circumstance under the care of a divine Benevolence, whereas " 'Invictus' rests on no such faith; the poet stands alone, a defiant agnostic, exultant in his strong free will, whatever gods may be" (Buckley, 21). Nonetheless, Henley's final accommodation, according to Buckley, sounds much like the secularized Christianity of many another late Victorian. "In the manifold achievement of his time he saw a last resolution of the conflict between fate and free will. The clutch of circumstance remained an inescapable reality; but the unconquerable soul asserting its intrinsic divinity found fulfillment within the laws preordained for its existence" (Buckley, 207). This is a freedom that is no freedom but a mood.

One major writer of this period typifying the subjective retreat before the ominous rule of material determinism is Walter Pater, who offered an especially subtle solution to the dilemma. Donald D. Stone claims rather surprisingly that "Nietzsche and Pater, the two major philosophers of the 1880s, both proclaimed the freedom of the will—freedom from all past theories and systems—and the preeminent value of art."[12] Peter Dale clarifies this opinion by demonstrating how art offers freedom from the web of natural forces in Pater's The Renaissance.[13] But Pater's solution was not divorced from past theories and systems. Beyond Nietzsche, Pater depended heavily upon traditions of English and German philosophy for his formulations. Billie Andrew Inman has shown in Walter Pater's Reading that Pater may easily have appropriated the notion of Art's superiority to nature from Hegel, whose writings he knew well.[14] He may also have adopted certain concepts from Fichte's philosophy, for example, the educational pattern of Fichte's *Vocation of Man* that follows the three stages of doubt, knowledge, and faith. Doubt begins with a questioning of individual freedom of the will that results in the sense that freedom is an illusion and that individuals are merely part of a linked deterministic chain. The way out of this barren belief is, Fichte says, to trust one's deepest impulse which will reveal one's true purpose or destiny. "According to Fichte, one finds freedom in cultivating oneself for the performance of one's vocation" (Inman, 17). Self-culture leads in turn to a recognition of the free self in others; "by being conscious of self and cultivating self, we participate in the One, or God, which is the total of all consciousness" (Inman, 18).

Pater's debt to Fichte is plausible, but he could have found similar patterns of education in Carlyle, Matthew Arnold, or many other contemporaries, as part 1 of this study demonstrates. The general spiritual progress described here is not far removed from the traditional pattern of Christian salvation and much closer to its secularized Victorian manifestations. Edmund Gosse reported that by the time Pater had written *Studies in the History of the Renaissance*, he "had gradually lost all belief in the Christian religion."[15] So evidently was this work an assertion "that no fixed principles either of religion or morality can be regarded as certain," that it caused the alienation of old friends and the evocation of new opponents.[16] But Pater remained interested in morality and the consolation of some faith. The years, Gosse said, brought "a greater and greater longing for the supporting solace of a creed" (Gosse, 260). But Pater remained reluctant to accept anything so firm as a "creed." Pater is supposed to have said that he wrote *Marius the Epicurean* to show the necessity of religion and elsewhere supported the notion of a "fourth religious phase" of skeptical hope.[17] But his attitude toward religion remained ambiguous. In a letter to Mary Ward in 1885, he wrote: "To my mind, the beliefs, and the functions in the world, of the historic church, form just one of those obscure but all-important possibilities, which the human mind is powerless effectively to dismiss from itself; and might wisely accept, in the first place, as a workable hypothesis."[18] U. C. Knoepflmacher makes a convincing case that Pater's Platonism represented an attempt "to recover a 'positive' creed for the nineteenth century through an imaginative reinterpretation of this creed's historic 'origins.' "[19] Preserving much of the outline and moral import of traditional Christianity, Pater aestheticized it in a manner different from most of his contemporaries.

Pater did not recommend that art retreat into an ivory tower, the artist solipsistically ignoring the world and his fellow men. In the "Wincklemann" essay of *The Renaissance*, he clearly declared that art should serve culture. "What modern art has to do in the service of culture," he wrote, "is so to rearrange the details of modern life, so to reflect it, that it may satisfy the spirit." That spirit craves a sense of freedom. This need brings Pater immediately to the problem of conveying that sense of freedom in the modern world.

> That naive, rough sense of freedom, which supposes man's will to be limited, if at all, only by a will stronger than his, he can never have again. The attempt to represent it in art would have so little verisimilitude that it would be flat and uninteresting. The chief factor in the thoughts of the modern mind concerning itself in the intricacy, the universality of natural law, even in the moral order. For us, necessity is not, as of old, a sort of mythological personage without us, with whom we can do warfare. It is rather a magic web woven through and through us, like that magnetic system of which modern science speaks, penetrating us with a network, subtler than our subtlest nerves, yet bearing in it the central forces of the world.[20]

Given this complexity, can art provide the spirit with an equivalent for the sense of freedom? "Natural laws we shall never modify, embarrass us as they may," Pater acknowledges, "but there is still something in the nobler or less noble attitude with which we watch their fatal combination." In the romances of Goethe, Hugo, and others, this network of natural laws becomes the tragic situation within which noble characters work out their supreme denouement. "Who," Pater asks, "if he saw through all, would fret against the chain of circumstance which endows one at the end with those great experiences?" (Pater, *Renaissance*, 185).

It is not possible to alter the course of natural events, but art offers a different form of freedom, an intensification of experience that enlarges the "space" of our existence, "in getting as many pulsations as possible into the given time" (Pater, *Renaissance*, 190). The world is a Heraclitian flux, but through art, man may freely organize his mode of perceiving that flux. Pater's is a far more sophisticated version of Henley's truculent adherence to a personal assertion of will in the face of unalterable circumstance and is related to Meredith, Hardy, and other writers in the acute perception that the "reading" and "story making" that individuals indulge in create a sense of freedom because they are arbitrary. Pater proposes a very limited form of free will, but its product, if limited to this world, is an enviable one—"to give nothing but the highest quality to your moments as they pass, and simply for those moments' sake" (Pater, *Renaissance*, 190).[21]

Given this open acknowledgment of art's role—both for artist and perceiver of art—as an education to ecstasy through engagement in the world, it is not surprising to find Pater assuming the narrative role not of a deity who creates characters and places them in circumstances where they may work out their fates through contests of action but of an anatomist who slowly lays bare the stages by which his subjects achieve their highest states of self-awareness. To make this anatomy credible, the subject of his analysis is ordinarily some version of himself. He is, to a great degree, in the position of the Giordano Bruno of *Gaston de Latour* (1896), who, in analyzing the natural world as identical with the body of God, succeeds in analyzing himself and vice versa. If God is in all things, then to appreciate any minutest detail is to appreciate him. To explore the self and its wonders is to worship divinity.

In *Marius the Epicurean* (1885), Marius is awakened to the relationship of "outward imagery identifying itself with unseen moralities" after a visit to a temple of Aesculapius.[22] This association of idealism and attention to the healthy body increases as Marius conceives, through the tale of Cupid and Psyche, an ideal of perfect imaginative love. When his friend Flavius dies, Marius turns to philosophy, absorbing the Heraclitian concept of the world as constant change. Self-culture becomes his aim, the achieving of a constantly renewed mobility of character that will keep him in harmony with the perpetual motion of the world.

> And towards such a full or complete life, a life of various yet select sensation, the most direct and effective auxiliary must be, in a word, Insight. Liberty of soul, freedom from all partial and misrepresentative doctrine which does but relieve one element in our experience at the cost of another, freedom from all embarrassment alike or regret for the past and of calculation on the future: this would be but preliminary to the real business of education— insight, insight through culture, into all that the present moment holds in trust for us, as we stand so briefly in its presence. From that maxim of *Life as the end of life*, followed, as a practical consequence, the desirableness of refining all the instruments of inward and outward intuition, of developing all their capacities, of testing and exercising one's self in them, till one's whole nature became one complex medium of reception, towards the vision—the "beatific vision," if we really cared to make it such—of our actual experience in the world. Not the conveyance of an abstract body of trusts or principles, would be the aim of the right education of one's self, or of another, but the conveyance of an art—an art in some degree peculiar to each individual character; with the modifications, that is, due to its special constitution, and the peculiar circumstances of its growth, inasmuch as no one of us is like another, all in all. (Pater, *Marius*, 117–18)

Marius tests many novel sensations and ideas, including the attractive new religion of Christianity, without rejecting or accepting any creed, but maintaining a keen ability to appreciate the small share of existence allotted him. Before his death his receptivity of soul has reached its zenith, and dying is the equivalent of an apotheosis. The ever editing and commenting narrator steps in to interpret for us. "Surely, the aim of true philosophy must lie, not in futile efforts towards the complete accommodation of man to the circumstances in which he chances to find himself but in the maintenance of a kind of candid discontent, in the face of the very highest achievement; the unclouded and receptive soul quitting the world finally, with the same fresh wonder with which it had entered the world still unimpaired, and going on its blind way at last with the consciousness of some profound enigma in things, as but a pledge of something further to come" (Pater, *Marius*, 380).

The power of Pater's will is paradoxically to achieve the highest degree of receptivity to experience while remaining untainted by it. Free will is the ability to disengage the self from the world of consequence and circumstance not materially but imaginatively. The self is inescapably "ringed round . . . [by] a thick wall of personality"; it is bound in flesh and must suffer the rule of natural law (Pater, *Renaissance*, 187). But if we cannot fashion our external being, we can shape our internal self like artists, refining its facets until it burns with a hard gemlike flame. The will is most free, then, when it least commits itself to any final objective. Once bound to a specific form or object, it loses the freedom of its subjective suspension. The will remains free as long as it remains untouched by conscious teleology. To take aim is to lose direction.

Pater's novels are not straightforward narratives. Where would they go? They are, instead, assemblages of historical vignettes, extracts from literature, portraits of historical figures, philosophical or literary essays, and so forth, all brought to bear upon a hypothetical sensibility that may be read not as a believable independent character but as a manifestation of Pater's own ideal self. The style itself becomes as important as plot or character—a mind setting itself free in the act of setting minds free.

The "Unfinished Romance," *Gaston de Latour*, is especially clear in this regard; Gaston's stages of development remain more diagrammatic because they are incomplete. Like Marius, he early responds to the beauty of the earth and the charm of ceremony. Introduced to the poetry of Ronsard, Gaston discovers a new and higher delight; "the visible was more visible than ever before, just because soul had come to its surface."[23] Exposure to this poetry and to Ronsard the man reveals a division in Gaston himself between the ideals of material and spiritual beauty. The next fashioning force upon him is Montaigne, who teaches him the value of doubt and the incredible diversity within the self. Truth, he explains, "lies if anywhere in the minute and particular" (Pater, *Gaston*, 93). Once assemble those particulars into a scheme and you offer not truth but opinion, itself simply "the projection of individual *will*, of a native original predilection. Opinions!—they are like the clothes we wear, which warm us not with their heat, but with ours" (Pater, *Gaston*, 92). Implicit in this statement is Pater's own belief that man's freedom of will is exactly in the fashioning of a fine suit of clothes for his self to wear from the weave of the universe, without falling into the error of making it a uniform. Pater's Montaigne, fascinated by chance and fortune in men's affairs, offers no theory of destiny or providence but glories in his own responses to such mysterious transformations. His self is his ultimate subject.

Hints of Gaston's suffering in the world of "real" events precede the next and last offered model for his development, that of Giordano Bruno, who, as I have already mentioned, conceived of the universe pantheistically as the body of God. Prompting his philosophy is the thought of liberty. "God the Spirit had made all things indifferently, with a largeness, a beneficence, impiously belied by any theory of restrictions, distinctions, of absolute limitations. Touch! see! listen! eat freely of all the trees of the garden of Paradise, with the voice of the Lord God literally everywhere!—here was the final counsel of perfection. The world was even larger than youthful appetite, youthful capacity" (Pater, *Gaston*, 152–53). The ultimate development of this philosophy is a freedom not only from physical restraints but from moral restraints that does, in fact, bear a family resemblance to Nietzsche's philosophy. Pater has Bruno argue that "in proportion as man raised himself to the ampler survey of the divine work around him, just in that proportion did the very notion of evil disappear. There were no weeds, no 'tares,' in the endless field. The truly illuminated mind, discerning spiritually, might do what it would" (Pater, *Gaston*, 160).

Truly a liberating philosophy with an apparent licensing of an unchained will! But Pater felt, if he did not fully exhibit, the limitations of his scheme. Gaston suspected in his youth that his thoughts might not be his own but came to him through the mediation of others (Pater, *Gaston*, 40). And his entire education in what we have of this novel is precisely that process of mediation through outstanding representatives of Gaston's time. Even as Pater narrates Gaston's progress to a greater freedom and intensity of spirit, the very nature of his narration reinforces the boundaries within which Gaston will achieve such freedom. The chapters are set in place like huge blocks of stone elegantly decorated resembling Gaston's beloved Chateau of Deux-manoirs, which may be taken to symbolize the bond that love can create between ideal and material but also the confinement that the material ultimately represents for the ideal. The body may not be a prison house, but the spirit must live within its confines, no matter how well furnished. Pater offers a Kantian freedom, having currency, like Bergson's, only in another realm of experience, another order of time. He offers seriously what du Maurier toyed with sensationally in *Peter Ibbetson*.

His method of composition, as described by Edmund Gosse, seems to image Pater's approach to experience; it surely images the piecemeal assemblage of his novels. Pater would begin with loose notes on small squares of paper which he would set out before him like a puzzle, "and when the right moment came the proper square would serve as a monitor or as a guide." Then Pater would begin his composition on lined paper, using every other line so that he could insert "descriptive or parenthetical clauses, other adjectives, more exquisitely related adverbs until the space was filled" (Pater, Gosse, 263–64). Here is the skeptical fashioner, anticipating no final object for his narration or exposition, but always refining and enriching until the textual space is filled. This chastened method of enlargement is the same procedure he recommends for subjective experience. The labor of composition is at the same time the liberation of the spirit. In the material world volition and expression join only here.

Pater's very sentences enact his delight in suspended judgment and reluctance to conclude as the subordinate clauses hold back fulfillment and abrupt exclamations are gradually reabsorbed into the long rhythms of the paragraphs. This connection was fully conscious because Pater believed that style was the expression of a specific identity through the exertion of will. "Literary art, that is, like all art which is any way imitative or reproductive of fact—form, or colour, or incident—is the representation of such fact as connected with soul, of a specific personality, in its preferences, its volition and power."[24] Braced by the restraints of art, the master artist vindicates his liberty by fashioning "his own true manner" (Pater, *Works* 5:14). But literary architecture cannot work merely to a pattern. If it is to be rich and expressive, it "involves not only foresight of the end in the beginning, but also development or growth of design, in the process of execution, with many irregularities, surprises, and afterthoughts; the contingent as well as the necessary being subsumed under the unity of the whole" (Pater, *Works* 5:23). The method of creation thus imitates the subject—the development of a unique consciousness—and also the increased awareness of the artist. Somewhere in those labored literary constructions a spirit delights in its freedom, though the body of language binds it to the page and we are free to read with delight or annoyance as our individual natures variously dictate.

Pater and a few others like him found a means of countering the increasing sense of determinist necessity that Lester correctly associates with the end of the nineteenth century. They did so by removing the arena of freedom to a world where whatever could be called action was entirely internal. At the same time, another breed of writers sought to preserve a *sense* of freedom, without necessarily accepting the *fact* of freedom, by turning that activity outward into extreme and even improbable adventure.

CHAPTER NINETEEN

Adventure Fiction

W ALTER Pater's fiction represents the introspective and subjective response to the issue of free will and necessity. Action is unimportant in his treatment of the theme. But if free will could be viewed by some as an internal dilemma, for others, it had an important bearing upon real action in the world. The action or adventure literature at the end of the century reveals an equally strong sense of the new concept of the multiple self as that found in "aesthetic" fiction. The popularity of adventure stories late in the century indicates that readers wanted a rendering of the world that allowed for independent and determining action on the part of individual heroes and heroines. Generally, adventure fiction avoided direct discussion of philosophical issues. Robert Louis Stevenson made this clear in his comments on fiction, and his views are reflected in the work of Rudyard Kipling. But some adventure writers consciously engaged the question of freedom and necessity in their novels. Their narrative methods reveal a good deal about their approach to this subject. These approaches to the self and to narrative accounts of the self's confrontation with the world are related to the nineteenth-century British sense that an imperialist creed was justifiable in terms of the moral organization of the material world.

~ ~ ~

The dismay and energy of the late nineteenth century may be identified with aestheticism and with stoic activism, two prominent tendencies of the period, which, according to David Daiches, may be seen as "opposite sides of the same medal," since they both "represent attempts to compensate for a lost world of absolute values."[1] James Sully interpreted this apparent conflict in the late decades of his century as a combat of pessimism and optimism, the former occasioned by religious skepticism, "the apparent failure of a social and political ideal, [and] the collapse of the extravagant aspirations and endeavours of certain aesthetic schools;" the latter by a desire to transcend personal consideration for the larger needs of the human race.[2]

Growing out of the existing literary tradition, but imbued with the moods and sentiments of its time, was a body of writing in late nineteenth-century England manifesting the complexity of the struggle between pessimism and optimism, or aestheticism and activism, through the reassertion of human will. Popular adventure tales, romances, and fantasies, while fortified by elements of traditional beliefs, nonetheless sought a means of asserting man's freedom which could transcend discredited religious beliefs as well as the everyday experience that science seemed ever more convincingly to proclaim as the standard of reality.

Hardy and writers like him, by associating modern life with Greek tragedy, rendered aesthetically endurable for them what would, without the consolations of traditional faith, otherwise be a mere mechanistic, degraded existence. This aestheticizing impulse exhibits itself in Richard Jeffries's futuristic romance *After London* (1885) where Aurora Thyma preserves Sophocles' *Antigone* in an age returned to a worse than medieval barbarism. She has selected this great tragedy because "in some indefinable manner the spirit of the ancient Greeks seemed to her in accord with the times, for men had, or appeared to have, so little control over their own lives that they might well imagine themselves overruled by destiny." Ruled by tyrants, these men could neither govern their daily lives nor believe in any chance for personal advancement, and thus the notion of Fate was all too germane to their lives. "The workings of destiny, the Irresistible overpowering both the good and the evil-disposed, such as were traced in the Greek drama were paralleled in the lives of many a miserable slave at that day."[3]

The parallel is important because Jeffries was writing a parable not merely of an England wild again in a distant future but for his own day, a day in which those unfavored by caste and family had little hope to advance themselves and where a growing tyranny of industrialism and law seemed to reduce life to a cog in a necessarian machine. Much of the popular literature of the time contains a similar conservative energy revealing a genuine concern for an expiring freedom before the reductive forces of science and atheism.

In the romances of the late nineteenth century there is a struggle to reaffirm human will and to identify it with a form of destiny that may ennoble, rather than demean man. Behind this effort lies a long tradition in which domination of the material world signifies power and, by implication, freedom of the will. In *Dreams of Adventure, Deeds of Empire*, Martin Green describes the emergence of the hegemonic attitude among merchants of the core countries England and Holland. Their economic system developed an anti-imperialist ideology in which freedom and morality were the main values. "The new empire was, or felt like a community of freely competing equals, and called itself a nonempire to draw attention to that difference. Its means and values flourished in the core states, and their gospel was taken to the periphery and beyond, in all confidence that they could take root there, by an act of will. When they did not take root, that was attributed to a failure of will."[4]

It could be argued, at least in the nineteenth century, that the values Green described failed to take root because they were radically hypocritical, since the transporters of those values believed themselves racially superior to those among whom they hoped to spread their beliefs. Nonwhite, nonwestern peoples were seen as childlike, primitive, or worse. Fiction of the period, exploiting themes of survival of the fittest and social evolution, reinforced these assumptions.[5] In these tales, foreign lands are the appropriate setting for the strong-willed English adventurer to express his dominating character positively, freed from the petty constraints of normal Christian society. Other more serious novelists, like Joseph Conrad, suggested that the European adventurer met his nemesis in the outlands of empire, because his success fostered fantasies of power that blinded him to reality.[6] Conrad considered action "the illusion of a mastered destiny" by which fears of the future are stilled.[7] An underlying insincerity betrays the certainty of much imperial adventure literature. Alan Sandison comments that Conrad, Kipling, and Buchan offered no solid faith but only an ideal of competence, "the illusion of a universe that is not insusceptible to human control and a destiny which it may yet be possible to master. In all three authors we therefore find the same autocratic thirst for power and an admiration of resolute, imperious action" (Sandison, 139). Sandison may overstate the case, ignoring these writers' own awareness of the illusions they described.[8] They knew that behind assertions of the will lay serious doubts about the will's freedom to alter destiny.

I am less concerned with writers of accepted literary merit than with a subgroup that openly concerned itself with issues of free will, providence, and destiny. But to clarify the role of adventure literature in the scheme of this study, it may be worthwhile to glance at some masters of the genre. In "A Humble Remonstrance," Robert Louis Stevenson responded to Henry James's requirements for the novel by explaining that art can never be true to life but turns creatively away from it. All of the sentences, pages, and chapters of a well-written novel echo and re-echo "its one creative and controlling thought."[9] In defending his own adventure tale *Treasure Island* against James's friendly criticism, Stevenson argued that there are many kinds of novels, not just one, and each exists by and for itelf. Emphasizing action in *Treasure Island,* Stevenson admitted to circumscribing character. "To add more traits, to be too clever, to start the hare of moral or intellectual interest while we are running the fox of material interest, is not to enrich but to stultify your tale" (Stevenson, *Works* 13:352).

Stevenson acted upon this principle as did most serious adventure writers of his time. Though he surely held certain views about human nature and its possible freedom, he was unwilling to cumber his adventure plots with expositions of these views. At the same time, he was fully aware that "in all works of art, widely speaking, it is first of all the author's attitude that is narrated, though in the attitude there be implied a whole experience of life."[10] Moreover, he realized that the very complexity and character of modern narrative embodied philosophical assumptions, the admission of great detail in the novel signifying, for example, a more ample contemplation of man's circumstantial existence (Stevenson, *Works* 22:248, 267). It is the artist's task to "drive and coax" his ideal conception and the material tools for its expression "to effect his will" (Stevenson, *Works* 22:270).

Stevenson was not reluctant to express his views about human nature; he was simply reluctant to include those views in his adventure stories. In *Lay Morals,* for example, he developed his theory of man's twofold nature. In the same body with his conscious self "dwell other powers, tributary but independent."[11] These powers may often becloud the central self whose chief aim is what Stevenson calls "*righteousness*," a yearning for unity of purpose (Stevenson, *Works* 22:558, 561). In the mystery of God's universe man must ever be wrong, but he must be right to himself (Stevenson, *Works* 22:566).

These assertions are clear enough, but only rarely did Stevenson permit himself the luxury of introducing them directly in his fiction. In the tale "Markheim," the titular character has murdered an antique dealer for his money when the devil appears to assist him. Markheim rejects his help and insists that he is better than his actions suggest. Circumstances have driven him to wicked deeds, but he and all men, he asserts, "are better than the disguise that grows about and stifles them."[12] He says that now with money he will be able to reform his life, but the devil replies that Markheim has made his own fate and adds "content yourself with what you are, for you will never change; and the words of your part on this stage are irrevocably written down." Markheim retorts that there is "one door of freedom open," and has his victim's maidservant go for the police to arrest him" (Stevenson, *Works* 7:125–26).

The Master of Ballantrae (1889) comes closest among the full-length adventure stories to openly probing the mysteries of human identity and the force of human will. But the assertion of human will is here equated with the selfish James Durie's wickedness. He is characterized by such statements as

"I have always done exactly as I felt inclined," and "I go my way with inevitable motion."[13] He is so gifted that he seems diabolically fortunate, except that his schemes ultimately fail. He explains, "my life has been a series of unmerited cast-backs," but he overlooks his betrayals, deceptions, and crimes that have brought about his several discomfitures (Stevenson, *Works* 9:236). James Durie has a cynical view of human existence and admits that what he desires is submission by others to his "kingly nature" (Stevenson, *Works* 9:219). But he has no moral order, no sense of selflessness to support his life. Important decisions in his life are determined by the spin of a coin. He is a gamester of life who cannot see that some laws may not be violated with impunity forever.

Set against James is his dull younger brother, Henry, who is the better man, suffering from James's financial claims and personal insults. Henry is capable of great self-suppression, but it earns him few rewards—material or moral. Ultimately, goaded by James's impudence, he turns to his brother's more direct methods. He fights James and runs him through with his sword, but James survives and returns to harass him. Meanwhile, his own character has altered. He becomes obsessed with injuring James in return and even plots his death. In the end, they die moments apart in the barren wilderness of northern New York.

This story may be read as a simple adventure tale or as a morality fable about the contention between two aspects of human nature—the craving for assertion and self-gratification and the capacity for stoical restraint and concern for others. But no simple Christian scheme results. The demonic and the mundane destroy one another. That the novel is in some sense a study of the divided self is suggested by Stevenson's preface, which opens with a paragraph distinguishing between his self that identifies with his native city and the self associated with the life he has made elsewhere. Appropriately, the narrative that follows is presented by a man whose whole life has been one of moral rectitude and service, Henry's servant, Ephraim Mackellar, and his story incorporates the narratives of Chevalier Burke and John Mountain. As we have seen earlier, especially with Wilkie Collins, multiple narration is an ideal narrative mode for an author who wishes to leave philosophical issues unresolved.

The most famous of Stevenson's stories is also a multiple narration and again opposes a man of restraint and reason against one of indulgence and appetite. The lawyer Utterson introduces *The Strange Case of Dr. Jekyll and Mr. Hyde* (1886), but enclosed in his narrative is Dr. Lanyon's document and Henry Jekyll's own full statement of the case. We approach the true facts much as we might enter Jekyll's home by its sordid back entrance with its wall like "a blind forehead" and proceed through the decent interior to the private workroom at its center. Jekyll himself explains his profound duplicity and how it taught him that man is truly two not one. He even hazards the guess "that man will be ultimately known for a mere polity of multifarious, incongruous and independent denizens" (Stevenson, *Works* 7:351).

Jekyll's story is too familiar to rehearse here, but we can at least note that Stevenson suited his fractured narrative to the divided nature of his central figure and, in doing so, left us the choice of interpreting existence along Utterson's abstemious lines or Jekyll's indulgent ways. In one, the will is strong but free only insofar as it restrains what is waiting inside to do harm. In the other, the will is set free to gratify its impulses but in doing so enslaves itself to its lowest drives. Free will and strength of will here become problematic, and the issue of freedom is left unresolved as the story ends with the posthumous voice of Henry Jekyll.

Jekyll and Hyde is something of an anomaly in Stevenson's writing career because he so openly imports philosophical and psychological issues into his narrative. But, as we have seen, he did not hesitate to take up those issues elsewhere, for our purposes, nowhere as interestingly as in the fragment "Reflections and Remarks on Human Life," where two characters in a serial novel dispute their relationship to the author and the degree of freedom they have in the design of his story. The priest warns that the author disapproves of Count Spada and has some appalling judgment in store for him. But Spada replies that he sees no evidence that the author is a friend to good since so many good characters have suffered in the story. The priest contends that the purposes of the serial story are necessarily hidden to the characters in it. But Spada argues freedom from responsibility under those conditions: "How can you, for one instant, suppose the existence of free will in puppets situated as we are in the thick of a novel which we do not even understand?" (Stevenson, *Works* 22:625). The priest contends for "a sort of empire or independence of our own characters when once created, which the author cannot or at least does not choose to violate" (Stevenson, *Works* 22:626). The dispute ends as the characters are obliged to resume their parts in the serial with chapter 35, "The Count's Chastisement."

Stevenson was obviously aware of the by-this-time conventional analogy of author and providence and in this fragment explored it humorously. But in his fiction, the larger questions of free will and necessity are rarely touched upon except in the nature of their characters and the manner of their telling. Other important writers at the end of the century also contemplated philosophical issues without introducing them directly into their adventure tales. As *The Jungle Books* (1894–95) show, Kipling credited The Law of the Jungle, by which, beyond the social regulations of the animals, he meant the Laws of Nature. But, though his characters often show the ability to understand and therefore successfully act in accordance with those laws, he rarely deals explicitly with the question of free will or fate, though some of the stories call such issues to mind. *Kim* (1901) is an elaborate exploration of forces shaping a young boy of mixed genetic and cultural inheritance. It raises the question of identity. But when Kim asks himself, "Who is Kim—Kim—Kim?" he gets no answer and his mind turns, as always, to the external things of the world.[14] He is, however, a companion to the kindly Lama who does believe in the Great Wheel governing human existence. The Lama seeks to free himself from the Wheel of Things—reminiscent of Watts-Dunton's Wheel of Circumstance—through the discovery of the River that will cleanse him of materiality. But though the novel toys with ideas of predestination and human independence, these ideas play no significant role and do not affect its straightforward narrative methods. Like Stevenson, Kipling knew that too much exploration of such matters could be deadly to his story.[15] But there was an unusual group of writers at the end of the century who overlooked that rule of adventure novelists and made discussions of fate, providence, and freedom important features of their romances.

Kipling's friend Rider Haggard was prominent among those popular writers who manifested in their fiction a concept of fate or destiny which, while not endorsing genuine freedom of the will, left man situations in which his choices were significant. Haggard felt that events in his own life had been guided by "the hand of Destiny" and considered belief in destiny a traditional attitude in mankind. "The alternative," he remarked, "would seem to be the acceptance of a doctrine of blind chance which I confess I find hideous."[16] Destiny is everywhere in Haggard's fiction. In *She* (1887), Leo Vincy seeks to fulfill a destiny that he only vaguely comprehends. Resolved to carry out a mission entrusted to him as the representative of an ancient family, Leo discovers the remote African country where Ayesha, ruler of the lost city of Kôr, anticipates his arrival, believing him to be the reincarnation of Kallikrates, the man she loved and murdered centuries before. Leo's fate seems inescapable. He cannot resist Ayesha, who wants him to share her near-eternal life on earth. There is, however, an overarching design of which the marvelous destinies of Leo and Ayesha are only a part. In demonstrating the source of her power for Leo, Ayesha destroys herself. The moral recorder of these events, Ludwig Holly, promptly declares, "Thus she opposed herself to the eternal law, and, strong though she was, by it was swept back into nothingness—swept back with shame and hideous mockery!"[17]

By strength of will, Ayesha controls men and occult forces; but strength of will and freedom of will are not the same. Nonetheless, exerting her will elevates Ayesha well above the commonplace, nor is she crushed by a banal determinism. Instead, a mysterious force, interpretable as a manifestation of divine purpose, intervenes spectacularly. In this depiction of overweening pride chastised by divinity, Haggard mixes Christian and pagan notions. Leo's and Ayesha's fates appear to have been predetermined, and their destinies pursue them as in a Greek tragedy, but as in a Christian moral fable, only the uncharitable party suffers death. Leo survives, chastened, prepared to seek an elusive truth wherever it may be found, his will presumably at one with the ruling plan of the universe.

Destiny plays a similar part in many of Haggard's tales. His early realistic novel *Jess* (1887), based on his experiences in Pretoria, takes up directly the themes of human transience, free will, strength of will, renunciation, and God's providence. Virtuous Silas Croft believes "there is a Power that looks after the helpless," while the wicked Boer Frank Muller is convinced that "chance is the only god." Confident in his own strength, he adds: "But there are men who ride chance as one rides a young colt. . . . I, Frank Muller, am one of those men."[18] John Niel, the hero of the novel, has moments when he questions the nature of existence, though fundamentally he trusts in what he cannot understand. Jess, having decided to hide her love for John to protect her sister's romance with him considers it an "illustration of her impotence in the hands of Fate" when she meets him accidentally. She feels that she is the instrument of a superior power to whom her individual fate is insignificant. The narrator intrudes.

> It was inconclusive reasoning and perilous doctrine, but it must be allowed that the circumstances gave it the color of truth. And, after all, the border-line between fatalism and free-will has never been quite authoritatively settled, even by St. Paul, so perhaps she was right. Mankind does not like to admit it, but it is, at the least, a question whether we can oppose our little wills against the forces of the universal law, or derange the details of the unvarying plan to suit the petty wants and hopes of individual mortality. Jess was a clever woman, but it would take a wiser head than hers to know where or when to draw that red line across the writings of our life. (Haggard, *Jess*, 122–23)

The writing of Jess's life is as muddled as Haggard's own prose. It is not bad prose and it gets its story told, but it suffers from some of the same radical uncertainty as his doubts about providence and fate. The confusion is typified in one sentence, when Jess, knowing she has the power to evoke Niel's love, determines to use that power. "And now she yielded to an overmastering impulse and chose," Haggard writes (Haggard, *Jess*, 134). But what kind of *choosing* is involved when an *overmastering* impulse moves us? The narrative manner reflects this uncertainty, sometimes probing easily into the minds of characters, commanding their pasts and futures, at other times declaring its own inadequacy without irony.[19]

The same may be said of much clumsy fiction of this and other periods, but interesting here is the conjunction of method with essential and expressed opinions about human freedom or the lack of it, more significant considering Haggard's description of the imagination as "a power which comes from we know not where. Perhaps it is existent but ungrasped truth, a gap in the curtain of the unseen which sometimes presses so nearly upon us . . . it may be that those who possess it are gates through which the forces of good and evil flow down in strength upon the world: instruments innocent of their destiny."[20] The novelist, then, is himself an actor in a large destiny of which he himself is not aware. Like the active heroes of adventure tales, he can only do what seems right, believing himself the agent of a benign purpose. Like other writers we have studied, but with less sophistication, Haggard saw life as a form of inscription, a story that may or may not already be written out to the end but which we can know only in the process of the telling. None of us knows where to draw the red line across the writing of our lives.

The realistic novel *Jess* implies that a benevolent design does prevail, though it works out ill for Jess herself. Still, no central figure asserts a coherent philosophical belief. In *King Solomon's Mines* (1885), on the other hand, Allan Quatermain often muses on the nature of existence. Though an avowed fatalist, he nonetheless believes that a merciful Power intercedes to spare his life.[21] He is not a passive but firmly believes in the need of a forceful will to survive the rigors of the African wilds. Sir Henry Curtis, a man of heroic dimensions, is more direct in his allegiance. Facing a dangerous march into the desert, he suggests: "And now before we start let us for a moment pray to the Power who shapes the destinies of men, and who ages since has marked out our paths, that it may please him to direct our steps in accordance with his will" (Haggard, *Mines*, 72). Later, in *Allan Quatermain* (1887), the aging adventurer's philosophy becomes clearer yet. Learning of the death of his son, Allan falls back upon his stoical nature. "Who am I that I should complain? The great wheel of Fate rolls on like a Juggernaut, and crushes us all in turn, some soon, some late—it does not matter when, in the end it crushes us all."[22] In the most dangerous circumstances, Allan keeps a cool head because he believes we never can know what will happen to us next, even in moments when we feel most secure. "It is all arranged for us, my sons, so what is the use of bothering?" (Haggard, *Allan*, 108).

In *Montezuma's Daughter* (1893), Thomas Wingfield, the Elizabethan narrator of the tale, comments that his friend and benefactor, Andres de Fonseca, was a fatalist, then adds that it is "a belief which I do not altogether share, holding as I do that within certain limits we are allowed to shape our own characters and destinies."[23] With Carlylean vigor, Haggard affirms the law of inevitable justice; Wingfield declares that life has taught him the lesson "that no wrong can ever bring about a right, that wrong will breed wrong at last, and be it in man or people, will fall upon the brain that thought it and the hand that wrought it" (Haggard, *Daughter*, 2).

And yet Haggard's works are filled with coincidences, with great events turning upon "trivial and apparently accidental circumstances" (Haggard, *Allan*, 230). Haggard wants it all ways—characters who have some power to shape their own natures and thereby *earn* reward or punishment acting within a preordained scheme that allows for the interposition of a merciful power. Such a mélange demands less than rigorous logic, as we have seen in the concise example from *Jess*. And yet in this bouillabaisse of paganism and Christianity, there is a distorted mirror image of the suspended judgment characteristic of Pater. Meditating on an impending battle in which thousands of men will die, the Allan Quatermain of *King Solomon's Mines* reflects: "Truly the universe is full of ghosts; not sheeted, churchyard spectres, but the inextinguishable and immortal elements of life, which, having once been, can never *die*, though they blend and change and change again forever" (Haggard, *Mines*, 181). This is no accidental reflection. It reappears, refined, in *Allan Quatermain*, when Allan again muses that human nature "is like an iron ring" that may be polished or flattened on one side, but whose total circumference will never change, then goes on from this image to a surprisingly different one (Haggard, *Allan*, 5). "Human nature is God's kaleidoscope, and the little bits of coloured glass which represent our passions, hopes, fears, joys, aspirations towards good and evil and what not, are turned in His mighty hand as surely and as certainly as it turns the stars, and continually fall into new patterns and combinations. But the composing elements remain the same, nor will there be one more bit of coloured glass nor one less for ever and ever" (Haggard, *Allan*, 6).

For Pater, a closed material system is manipulated by the individual consciousness to the best, that is, the most intense, effect—gemstones exquisitely shaped. But these gems become for Haggard bits of colored glass, part of a toy for God's diversion. Haggard's image is an inadvertent parody of Pater's, yet the world views that bred these images were not so remote as they may seem. Both men sought to establish some degree of freedom by suspending judgment, Pater through a refusal to commit, Haggard by an indiscriminate acceptance.[24] Hoping that man was capable of spiritual as well as material improvement, Haggard yet supposed that history moved in cycles. Alan Sandison concludes that, for Haggard, "action is still pragmatic, man's existence being guaranteed by a transcendental power." But he cannot dismiss a deepening fear that humanity "might yet turn out to be the helpless subject of a vast mechanistic process, ungoverned and ungovernable" (Sandison, viii).

The relationship of man's will to his destiny is most schematically described in the allegorical tale that he wrote with Andrew Lang, *The World's Desire* (1890).[25] In this continuation of the Odysseus story, the wandering hero travels to Egypt where he hopes to possess his true love, Helen of Troy, but where instead he is duped into infidelity by Meriamun, the selfish and violent wife of the Pharaoh, who has foreseen Odysseus's arrival. In Meriamun's vision, the gods describe the eternal pattern which she, Odysseus, and Helen must embody. They are ideal types condemned to descend to earth and exert their powers through numerous lives, enacting their destiny, "till the hours of punishment are outworn, and, at the word of Fate, the unaltering circle meets, and the veil of blindness falls from your eyes, and, as a scroll, your folly is unrolled, and the hid purpose of your sorrow is accomplished and once more ye are Twain and One."[26]

Throughout the story, fate is the force that determines events, the trappings of ancient fable constituting a paradigm of man's circumstances on earth. Though he quest after his heart's desire, he may not achieve the ideal in this world but may enjoy only simulacra of it. The ideal is good and pure, its types corrupt and even evil. By accepting the simulacra as genuine, man is shut off from his ideal. The notion is at least as old as Plato, and in Haggard's more immediate past, writers like Byron, Keats, Tennyson, and Rossetti, had employed it.[27] That this condition should be presented as mankind's inescapable fate, however, makes human life a sore trial and the exertion of human will forever impossible of fulfillment, except insofar as it resigns itself to the inevitable design. For Haggard, man's heroic striving to reach beyond normal experience is a grand achievement of the human will, but always that will is doomed to a crushing check when it strikes the borders of human possibility. The iron ring of human nature cannot change.

Haggard preferred to keep open several possibilities for explaining the human condition, always assuming that a just God governed somehow. His writing method reflects this reckless trust that a power beyond the self supervises the course of our lives, for Haggard simply waited until his imaginative idea took possession of him and then surrendered absolutely to it until he had bodied it forth.[28] His prose style is direct but not graceful, aiming straight forward as though the end of the tale is inevitable yet becoming cluttered with narrative intrusions and comic digressions. Rarely does it pause to reflect upon itself with subordinate clauses, balanced sentences, and so forth. It is a style suited to improbabilities, where reflection spells disaster. Haggard claimed not to be concerned with tricks of style but, in his best work, knew how to please a wide and varied audience. Perhaps this style worked so well because it suited the nature of the narratives it recounted. For Haggard, interpreting life was like unrolling the scroll of fate. Representing it was like inscribing that scroll as it unrolled.

Bram Stoker was another popular novelist whose tales combined free will and destiny in a peculiar fashion. He was not as popular as Haggard, but his works manifest similar preoccupations. Count Dracula, in Stoker's most famous tale, *Dracula* (1897), is characterized by his powerful will dedicated to utter selfishness. Ayesha had been imposing, even threatening, but Dracula is a menace to all mankind. At first he succeeds in his predatory aims because he has the occult power to master the wills of others and to transform himself from one physical shape to another or convey his spirit from place to place regardless of material or spatial obstacles. Despite Professor Van Helsing's precautions, Dracula repeatedly assaults Lucy Wetenra until it seems that nothing can resist his evil. Van Helsing raises his arms in frustration "as though appealing to the whole universe. 'God! God! God!' he said. 'What have we done, what has this poor thing done, that we are so sore beset? Is there fate amongst us still, sent down from the pagan world of old that such things must be, and in such a way?' " Even the unsuperstitious Dr. Seward laments, "Surely there is some horrible doom hanging over us that every possible accident should thwart us in all we try to do."[29] Maintaining its faith in providence and combining its power through love, dedication, and self-sacrifice, the small band of friends led by Van Helsing conquers Dracula by turning his overweening selfish will against him.[30] The group may even be read as an allegory of the elements of human personality. Mina is the soul, Seward the intellect, Godalming nerve, Quincey muscle, and Van Helsing the will that unifies them in their high purpose. *Dracula* is a parable against materialistic nihilism, showing that the selfish exaggeration of individual will does not free the individual from the ultimate pattern of justice that God's providence imbeds in human experience.

A similar contest occurs in *The Lair of the White Worm* (1911), which, though an abysmally bad narrative, reveals some of Stoker's continuing preoccupations. The evil characters in this tale are reincarnations, or continuations of, evil presences identified with the Mercian landscape. Edgar Caswall has all the attributes of his Roman ancestors who were "cold, selfish, dominant, reckless of consequences in pursuit of their own will."[31] More than once he finds himself in a contest of wills with Mimi Watford, the representative of innocence. Each time he is foiled by her power for good; ultimately he goes mad, believing himself the Almighty directing the elements by the force of his will.

If Caswall resembles Dracula in his ruthless selfishness, Lady Arabella March resembles him in her taste for blood and her ability to transform herself into an enormous white worm. Like *Dracula*, this novel has broad implications of doom for modern man. Dracula threatened to create a race of soulless Undead—an apt image for the spread of modern materialistic atheism that Stoker feared. In *The Lair of the White Worm*, Caswall's kite, representing his fascination with the power of his own will, "seemed like a new misanthropic belief which had fallen on human beings, carrying with it the negation of all hope" (Stoker, *Worm*, 74). Lady Arabella repeats the danger implied both in Haggard's superintelligent Ayesha, and in Dracula, for she offers the prospect of a world enslaved by selfish amorality.

In *The Jewel of Seven Stars* (1904) Stoker also examined the capacity, evident first in Dracula, of controlling both physical and psychic elements of the self through incredible strength of will. This novel recounts the efforts of a group of antiquarians to revive the mummy of an ancient Egyptian queen. Abel Trelawny speculates that the ancient Egyptian theory of a multiple self divided into the Ka, or Double; Ba, or soul; Khu, or spiritual intelligence, and so on, explains Queen Tera's ability to control the elements and direct the movements of her physical substance, particle by particle, through the power of "an unimprisonable will or intelligence."[32]

When these adventurers attempt the actual revitalization of the mummy, almost all are destroyed by a mysterious natural uproar, implying that Tera's ancient power has been overwhelmed by the Christian God. Queen Tera's mighty will and her pagan gods cannot pass the limits set by providence. As in *Dracula*, pagan destiny is contained by Christian authority. Still, Tera, like Dracula, though originally mortal, has been able to increase her will to an almost godlike level. It is even possible that Trelawny's daughter, born from a dead mother, may have been dead herself but reanimated through Queen Tera's power and thus not "an individual at all, but simply a phase of Queen Tera herself; an astral body obedient to her will" (Stoker, *Jewel*, 260). Stoker can satisfy the yearning for extraordinary exertion of the will so common to adventure tales like his, Haggard's, and others', while also providing the consoling message that no such exertion can go beyond set limits. Human will, though in its apparent freedom capable of supernatural achievements, is nevertheless limited.

Stoker encourages an open mind concerning the unexplained; his introduction of occult or spiritual details in his stories reveals an outlook sympathetic to the spiritualism prominent in the intellectual climate of late nineteenth-century England. In *The Mystery of the Sea* (1902), primarily a mystery-adventure tale, Archibald Hunter discovers, through clairvoyant powers, that he is doomed to act out his destiny in a centuries-old mystery. Hunter doubts the old crone Gormala MacNiel's explanation of his clairvoyant gift. " 'Am I to take it' I asked, 'that Second Sight is but a little bit of some great purpose which has to be wrought out by means of many kinds; and that whoso sees the Vision or hears the Voice is but the blind unconscious instrument of Fate?' "[33] Though Gormala's reply is ambiguous, the answer to Hunter's question comes soon enough from his own experiences. He realizes that the material world is a mere "film or crust which hides the deeper moving powers or forces," and is convinced "that there [is] somewhere a purposeful cause of universal action" (Stoker, *Sea*, 28).

As the incidents of the tale unravel, Hunter realizes that the woman he has fallen in love with is also a part of the ancient fate. "Once more," he says, "the sense of impotence grew upon me. We were all as shuttlecocks, buffeted to and fro without power to alter our course." But this recognition has its own compensation. "With the thought," Hunter adds, "came that measure of resignation which is the anodyne of despair" (Stoker, *Sea*, 178). It is Allan Quatermain's stoicism over again, the determination to face frightening prospects calmly because they cannot be altered. But Hunter's resignation gives way to action, and though the fate involving him is consummated, its resolution brings happiness for him and Margaret, he having employed his Second Sight to outwit the commonplace villains of the tale.

There is a dark cast to the novels of Haggard and Stoker, despite their occasionally hopeful conclusions. Invariably a spiritual or superhuman agency spares specific individuals or mankind in general from irresponsible gigantisms of the will. But over these tales hovers the implication that men alone do not have the will to combat determined malignity. Only when they align themselves with higher spiritual forces can they participate in mastering evil. There is an all-or-nothing Manichean air to these fables. If Dracula is not stopped, the world will be emptied of life and populated instead by zombielike Undead, who, if one pursues the idea to its end, would ultimately die out for lack of the very prey they had transformed to members of their cult. There is no hindrance to Ayesha's power until suddenly she is cast back into nothingness, into the void. These stories require either plenitude or nothingness. Existence appears to be a doubtful crust over an unknown center. Either that center wells forth benignant energy, or the crust threatens to collapse into a central vacuity. Even nature is ambiguous, being subject both to evil and divine control. Some extraordinary power must both support man's will and confine it, must shatter the contending power of evil which ultimately drives on to mindless self-gratification and nothingness. The concept of fate or destiny provides a handy framework for the contest of superhuman forces recounted in fiction of this sort. It is the scheme out of which the hero cannot break but against which he may exert his will, finally to discover that he is obliged, as are the superhuman predators, to bend that will to an overriding Will encompassing all things. Despite the obvious similarity to the traditional Christian pattern of resignation in the service of divine will, these fictional climates suggest a pessimism that James Sully attributed partly to the influence of philosophers like Schopenhauer and Hartmann, a pessimism that, while giving lip service to a benevolent power, looks upon life as an unpredictable and malign mystery in which the illusion of free will is projected largely in the swollen wills of evil figures, while a real fatalism operates within the shadowy strictures of divine approval. One romance-adventure novel directly illustrates the Schopenhauerian undertone of much of this literature of power.

In Robert Cromie's *The Crack of Doom* (1895), the incredibly bright scientist Herbert Brande is leader of an organization called the *Cui Bono* Society, whose members share the belief that existence is permeated not by God or by universal good but by evil. Their aim is "the restoration of a local etheric tumour to its original formation." In other words, they "mean to attempt the reduction of the solar system to its elemental ether."[34] Brande is characterized by his powerful will and extreme intelligence. He and certain of his associates can read minds and communicate telepathically over long distances. Furthermore, Brande has controlled his beautiful and intelligent sister, Natalie, by a form of mesmerism, using her to involve Arthur Marcel, the narrator of the tale, in the Society's venture. It is ultimately Marcel who frustrates Brande's scheme of splitting the atom and starting a chain reaction to unravel the painful network of existence and return the solar system to a state of rest. "The optimistic notion," Brande says, "that Nature is an all-wise designer, in whose work order, system, wisdom, and beauty are prominent," is wrong. Instead, "wholesale murder is Nature's first law. She creates only to kill"; Brande intends to stop that killing and suffering by one great destructive act (Cromie, 86).

Schopenhauer argued that only by a refusal to will to live can man oppose the overriding Will of existence to beget itself endlessly in a meaningless and painful replication. Refusing to be is man's only true act of free will; all other actions merely enable the greater Will. Cromie's Brande transforms Schopenhauer's private act into a cosmic gesture of resignation, for by renouncing being, Brande hopes to cancel the Will of existence itself and erase forever the mistake of eternal begetting. By accident, Brande's powerful will is impaired sufficiently for Marcel to frustrate his plan. When Brande dies, Natalie dies too because her brother's superior brain has absorbed hers and consumed her mental vitality. Her parting words, later confirmed by signs of her continued existence beyond death, provide the slight optimistic message of the novel. "Existence as we know it is ephemeral. Suffering is ephemeral. There is nothing everlasting but love. There is nothing eternal but mind" (Cromie, 206).

There is in Cromie's tale a perplexing dynamism common to other romances of the time. While human will is obviously free enough to contend against a natural or destined order, it cannot succeed in its selfish and mistaken ends. Man must strive, but he must also fail. Cromie closes his story with the suggestion that another party of the *Cui Bono* Society may succeed in its similarly destructive mission in the future, a continuing threat characteristic of stories of this kind to the present day. The possibility that rampant destructive will might revive itself suggests a fatality in man's condition. He cannot resist striving against what he sees as a futile and melancholy destiny. Yet in straining to overcome or elude his fate, viewed in negative, materialistic, even pagan terms, he plunges beyond the proper dimensions of human will and must therefore be punished by some force representing a neutral, if not benevolent and Christian, power. Even those who have struggled against evil, like Marcel, or Haggard's Leo Vincy, are left saddened by their experiences, though Stoker's heroes sometimes attain physical or material rewards. Resignation to providence suggests that the yearning for true fulfillment of the will, the achievement of the ideal, as in *The World's Desire*, cannot be satisfied in this world, but only in some other. At this point, the energy and dismay of the vitalist and the aesthetic currents of the late century join in the peculiar recipe of popular romance.

A last example takes us into the twentieth century and strangely combines aesthetic sensibility and vitalist adventure. Adam Jeffson, the last man on earth in M. P. Shiel's *The Purple Cloud* (1901), travels the depopulated world acting out the same destructive impulse exhibited in Cromie's novel by burning down as many major cities as he can. Jeffson, too, believes that a hostile destiny or fate guides man's existence. In a scene replete with nineties iconography, Jeffson comes upon a beautiful, long-haired, voluptuous woman in a ruined settlement overgrown by wild nature. Although he is gradually drawn back to something like humanity from the monster he had become, he determines not to make love with this woman. By thus negatively exerting his will, he believes he can defeat the Schopenhauerian Will that drives all living things to mindless begetting and endless grief. By the end of the novel, however, Jeffson concludes that God knows best.

Among the popular adventure romances of the late nineteenth century, energetic optimism and sorrowful doubt openly combine. Like the Aesthetes, who saw the ideal as the only objective of value while recognizing that it was unachievable, writers such as Haggard and Cromie presented situations in which the longed-for ideal—often in the form of a beautiful woman—is unattainable. In this world there is mainly energetic striving and unappeased desire; in the next only is there hope. Some writers offered the possibility of possessing the ideal in this world, but for them as well the knowledge of this possibility created an atmosphere not of joy but of melancholy, as with Du Maurier and Corelli.

Popular romances, in attempting to gratify certain imprecise desires in their readers, revealed a concept of human will which is curiously paradoxical. Man is fated, destined, or ruled by providence and yet is free to struggle against these dominating forces. In the knowledge that his life is determined there is frustration, even grief, but the knowledge that the force determining his life, though not always the traditional fatherly God, is yet a benevolent power tending to good is his source of assurance and content. These tales of men and women overcoming natural obstacles, sometimes superhuman obstacles, only to be stymied by a preordained purpose, demonstrate a serious yearning characteristic of their time. They display a confidence in man's ability to progress, to command the world of matter, to alter phenomenal existence. At the same time, they disclose a deep-seated dread of that existence as a charade beyond which imponderable forces act. The confidence that urged imperial and scientific advance was balanced by a dread that that advance went forth unto a fragile shell of appearance which might at any moment collapse, dropping all into an unpeopled void, where all human exertion ends.

Unlike the carefully constructed aesthetic narratives of a Pater with their relentless revisions and increments or the lean, well-made, and purposeful adventure tales of a Stevenson, these narratives are characterized by a headlong impulsiveness that depends upon the reader's interest in the final unseating of an evil power by agents of good. It is as though the authors trust more to the willed energy of their tale than to any design they might themselves construct. If they tell the tale through, what matter if its form came to them as a product of imagination or as an embodiment of some Purpose working through them?

Conclusion and Afterword

T HIS chapter offers first a concise summary of the chief issues and conclusions of the study as a whole. An afterword then indicates that this general topic is important as well in European and American literature of the nineteenth and twentieth centuries. It reviews some recent philosophical writings on free will and determinism and suggests that, despite new scientific concepts and attitudes toward the treatment of the self, the dispute is still deeply concerned with questions of responsibility and moral values and remains unresolved. In following the movement of this large theme into the twentieth century by references to a few prominent writers at the turn of the century, it argues that, if contemporary novelists are less immediately alive to the issues we have discussed here, many of them still embody in the nature of their narratives—some very aggressively, as with John Fowles—their underlying assumptions about human freedom. The point of this book has been to show how variously and profoundly world views, even when not directly presented, infiltrate and shape the manner in which we convert experience—real or imagined—into the stories we wish to hear.

~ ~ ~

I have tried to show how ideas about a specific set of related concepts—free will, determinism, chance, fate, and their concomitants—manifested themselves in the culture, and especially the creative literature, of nineteenth-century England. The primary reasoned positions were: (1) materialist determinism or necessarianism, which concentrated on the law of invariable consequence, or cause and effect; (2) providential order, which allowed varying degrees of human freedom; (3) predestinarianism, which was confined mainly to the more aggressive dissenting religious sects; (4) fatalism, which allowed for the existence of a malign or indifferent principle active in the universe against which free will might or might not be operable; and (5) chance, which assumed no necessary concatenation of events (usually, however, believers in chance and luck did not reason out the consequences of their thought, and they incorporated the possibility of chance into some other, more regular concept of the order of existence).

Despite the wide range of these beliefs and the numerous subtle variations within each category, recommended conduct was surprisingly uniform. Though the traditional Christian assumed free will, he believed that that will was only properly free in submitting itself to the will of God. The secular determinist, not accepting free will, counseled self-restraint in the service of some high cause. Even the fatalist was likely to advise stoic endurance, his version of resignation. True believers in luck or chance rarely offered or even intimated advice. Romantic writers, no matter if they championed free will or accepted a determinist doctrine, proposed a more active and aggressive will, in the sense of a self expressed through volition. Byron is a good example. It is amusing to learn from John Malcolm Ludlow of Harold Westergard's conversion from being " 'a complete unbeliever and materialist,' " through a reading of Byron's *Cain*, which "revealed to him the reality of the human will."[1]

I have assumed that a genuine revision occurred some time during the eighteenth century concerning the way human beings perceived and defined the *self*. Related to this new conception of human nature was a revived interest in man's capacity to control his own and external nature, a capacity that seemed to require something like free will. However, a long tradition of inconclusive philosophical debate allowed for another opinion—that human nature, though bound by invariable laws of cause and effect, might still alter itself for the better. In the nineteenth century, this view was necessarian and utilitarian. Opposed to this secular position was the liberal religious stand that man was improvable because free and responsible. Under providential guidance—which was, during the century, less and less identified with divine intervention and more and more associated with the mysterious scheme of the universe—individuals acted out their roles, making free choices in a larger pattern of justice and mercy. Some views, such as extreme Calvinism, argued for an absolute divine scheme in which human action did not signify, but though these views had wide popular circulation, they rarely appeared in the creative literature of the time unless as subjects of mockery.

Many writers openly endorsed free will or necessity; just as many tried to adapt elements of both in their philosophies. Shelley called himself a necessarian, but all of his sentiment seems to proclaim man's ability to alter the circumstances of his life. Godwin rejected free will as a truth but welcomed it as a useful illusion. Champions of free will still found it necessary to reconcile human freedom with the absolute authority of God or the absolute regularity of natural law. The venerable old quarrel continued in lively fashion through the century without any conclusive positions being established, but in the process, many new areas of discourse contributed to this ongoing debate. The notion of progress—that there was an overall movement over time that, through regular improvement, promised a far superior future world on earth—was acceptable to theological and nontheological disputants alike, though there were always many ready to question such a comfortable hypothesis. The appropriation of teleological schemes to history and the justification of moral attitudes and actions (when it came to empire building) demonstrated the power of narrative schemes in the assertion either of free will or determinism as the operative power in human events. What at first seemed to be a hard blow both to progressive thinking and optimistic teleological interpretations of the human story was quickly averted when theological writers appropriated evolutionary theory to their own purposes.

Behind much of this struggle to assert human independence from or uniformity with strict causality was a powerful nostalgia for the moral code of Christianity as understood in nineteenth-century England. Thus believers and nonbelievers alike engaged the knotty issue of human responsibility. Man must be free to be responsible, said the one side. Whether man is responsible or not, he must be taught to behave in a given way, replied the other. In many areas, these concerns could generally be ignored, but in certain ones—such as medicine (later psychology) and the law—they had to be confronted. In these arenas, we still live with the confusion of unresolved definitions of man's self, his moral nature, and his responsibility.

What most characterized the renewed free will versus determinism dispute in the nineteenth century was its location in a developmental setting that focused on the growth of a dynamic self in a dynamic society. This developmentalism was best understood when disciplined by narrative. In short, it was necessary to reduce experience to an intelligible story. If historians, theologians, biologists, and anthropologists tried to compose "real" stories of human experience, artists set about instead to creative fictive stories. But just as those "real" stories were predetermined by the intellectual presuppositions their architects brought to them, so fictional narratives were influenced by the "stories" that their authors already assumed to be a part of human existence and models for human action.

Therefore, in the creative literature of the nineteenth century, but especially in its novels, it is possible to discover certain methods of characterization and strategies of narration that coincide with certain underlying beliefs about man's freedom or the lack of it. I have discussed works of fiction that were well-known in their own day or that have since been valued for one reason or another in an attempt to show that writers, especially novelists, not only were very much aware of the free will versus necessity debate and its implications for human behavior but also consciously or unconsciously employed artistic techniques to support their own outlook. In narrative we can find implicit (sometimes explicit) signs of the degree of certainty or doubt an author felt, or wished to indicate, about human freedom in the web of causation. I have limited this study to nineteenth-century England because that is the cultural setting that I know best, but I believe the methods used in this study apply more broadly as well.

Concern with the will was by no means confined to England and the nineteenth century. Much of the new thinking on this subject in the late eighteenth century came from Europe, especially among German Romantic philosophers. Will as volition was an important theme everywhere. Balzac's novels are examples, especially *Louis Lambert* (1834–35).[2] I suspect that careful research would show a roughly parallel development of ideas and their expression in Continental and English literature through the century. Certainly by the end of the century, a common sense of determined existence had increased markedly. William Eickhorst notes that decadent characters in German literature at the end of the century are signaled by their conviction that they have no free will and are mastered by nerves, life, or fate.[3] There is a materialist emphasis on heredity in these books. According to A. E. Carter, the pursuit of the abnormal among French Decadent writers "is linked to the main characteristic of decadent sensibility: its intellectualism, its will-power."[4] But that will power is often confined to the operations of art or is applied as Schopenhauerian denial, as in Villiers de l'Isle-Adam's *Axël* (1890), where will, necessity, and the occult are all bound up together and conclude with self-extermination of the principals.[5] Huysmans, looking back on the time when he was writing *A rebours* (1884) confessed "I did not take into account the fact that everything is mysterious, that we live only in mystery, and that if such a thing as chance existed, it would be still more mysterious than Providence."[6] He chose providence and the Catholic Church because he wanted order, freedom, and hope. "No," he declared, "faith in Our Lord is not fatalism. Free will remains intact."[7]

R. H. Thomas, discussing the atmosphere in which Thomas Mann developed as a novelist, writes:

> Nietzsche described the nineteenth century as "honest but sombre," more "submissive to reality" than the eighteenth, "weak of will . . . and fatalistic." Mann found this criticism "magnificently apt." He also attached importance to the fact that it was the nine-

teenth century that "first produced and developed the sense of history." The doctrine of evolution, combining the notion of determinism and progress, embraces both aspects. The century which witnessed the triumph of the idea of evolution also saw the rise of the genealogical novel.[8]

There is a good deal about Nietzsche, fatalism, and genealogy in *Buddenbrooks* (1901), and humanity's relationship to large determinist forces is never out of sight in Mann's other writings. It becomes a central topic of discussion in *Dr. Faustus* (1947), where Adrian Leverkuhn's complicated music represents the achievement of freedom through complete determination, and in *Felix Krull* (1955), where Felix's ability to transform life into theater echoes Mann's interpretation of Schopenhauer's ideas.

> The pregnant and mysterious idea [developed by Schopenhauer in "Transcendent Speculations on Apparent Design in the Fate of the Individual"] is briefly this: that precisely as in a dream it is our own will that unconsciously appears as inexorable objective destiny, everything in its proceeding out of ourselves and each of us being the secret theatre-manager of our own dreams, so also in reality the great dream that a single essence, the will itself, dreams with us all, our fate, may be the product of our inmost selves, of our wills, and we are actually ourselves bringing about what seems to be happening to us.[9]

The general movement from providential to determinist thinking during the nineteenth century was not confined to Europe. In the United States, Emersonian confidence in the will, which so buoyed Walt Whitman's aggressive expression of freedom, lost ground to the determinist thinking of such different writers as Twain and Dreiser.[10] Melville's skeptical fiction, especially in such overt instances as the "Mat Maker" chapter of *Moby Dick* (1851), indicates an intellectual, if not chronological, pivot point in the American tradition. Defense of free will became more and more a matter for specialists to debate, though William James's chapter on determinism in *The Will to Believe* (1896) was a refreshing assertion that that debate was still an even game if the two sides could acknowledge some basic ground rules.[11]

The game has continued on into the twentieth century with no noticeable increase in mutual sympathy. The prevailing view today seems to be deterministic, and therefore interesting defenses of free will call attention to themselves as exceptions. D. J. O'Conner's very accessible popular study *Free Will* (1971) provides a general summary of the modern situation and offers a useful bibliography of works defending the concept of free will to one degree or another. Most statements assuming determinism are not contentious; they are generally scientific rather than philosophical explanations. Thus Dean H. Kenyon and Gary Steinman's *Biochemical Predestination* (1969) does not set out to challenge free will, and never approaches issues of moral responsibility, but simply wants to prove "that the association of units toward the ultimate development of the living cell is determined by the physicochemical properties possessed by the simplest starting compounds from which these systems evolved," which means that "the ultimate characteristics of the living cell can be traced back to the nature of the starting compounds from which it was produced."[12] In short, cellular structure is what it had to be, given its origins.

J. Z. Young seems to be asserting a similar determinism when he argues in *Programs of the Brain* (1978) that the lives of human beings and other animals are governed by programs written in the genes and brains. The fundamental program is in DNA, the second language is embodied in the structure of the brain. But Young preserves some flexibility for his argument by allowing for the limits of human information, explaining that "the causes of the actions of a given man will include not only all the genetic variables and the choices made in his past but also all those operations of the brain that go on as he exercises the special human capacities of choice between many alternatives, which we ordinarily call his free will."[13] W. H. Thorpe, pursuing a similar issue, is concerned with the problem of tracing the movement from nonliving systems to very different living systems that have internal self-representation which could only occur, he says, at the molecular level.[14] The puzzle is how the cell developed the capacity to decode DNA messages it generates itself. Life, Thorpe says, is both programed and self-programing (Thorpe, 24).[15] But he is willing to assume something different from the mechanical determinism of the physicists. He discusses purpose in nature; life is purposive insofar as it demonstrates an intention to attain some end. Man is not only purposive, he is "a self-experiencing animal in a way transcending the experience of other animals" (Thorpe, 77). From the uniqueness of man's experiencing self arise all the other characteristics in which he can be considered as unique: imagination, art, a sense of values, "the free will to choose between values, the moral sense in all its ramifications, philosophy (including scientific theories), religion, the concepts of the soul and of deity, and the knowledge of death" (Thorpe, 78). Thorpe maintains a pragmatic dualism based on the fact that an entity is a subject to itself but to us is an object. Subjectivity is posited because it is necessary for an entity to exist, and the evolution of subjectivity becomes a central issue. Man's mental complexity allows for a hierarchy that permits a belief in freedom of the will because the higher the level to which a decision is referred the less predictable the choice; "if we climb upwards towards the top of the hierarchy and try to understand the human mind with its freedom of the will, we find the universe dissolving into an infinity of mind which is, and can only be, the sole way of understanding 'the universe' " (Thorpe, 115).

John Thorp seems to be going a step further, as the title of his book suggests: *Free Will: A Defence against Neurophysiological Determinism* (1980). He proposes that man is capable of freedom of decision while admitting that freedom of action is a more complicated matter.[16] The self, he says, is a self-activating agent because, although the neural system generates events, neural and mental states are not identical. Moreover, neural events may be prompted by the hegemony of the brain. As a libertarian, he defends the idea of metaphysical responsibility but considers responsibility relative in a moral form because morality has to do with external and contingent situations.[17]

Karl Popper argues more precisely against determinism than for free will, but his picture of an open universe, evidenced by the asymmetry of past and future and determinism's inability to predict the future, allows for something like what others call free will.[18] "We are 'free' (or whatever you want to call it), not because we are subject to chance rather than to strict natural laws, but because the progressive rationalization of the world—the attempt to catch the world in the net of knowledge—has limits, at any moment, in the growth of knowledge itself, which, of course, is also a process that belongs to the world" (Popper, 181). Popper's argument is against scientific determinism, but it also undermines any theory of metaphysical determinism, about which arguments must always, he says, remain inconclusive. Popper recalls that in his discussion with Einstein about metaphysical determinism, he founded his negative position on the subjectivity of the arrow of time. If nothing else changes, human consciousness of what it perceives does (Popper, 89ff). Bulwer had long ago proposed a similar notion. And the general orientation of free will with the unconcluded future was a central concern in the intellectual prose and fiction of the nineteenth century. Popper's position, like the others I have discussed in the last few pages, is equipped with very sophisticated scientific information, but that information has not resolved the dispute. In fact, science itself provides new ammunition against the determinist position from Heisenberg's indication that the measurer and examiner of data alters what he measures and examines in the process of doing so to the surprising possibilities of quantum mechanics, which Popper says, "introduced, in spite of the protests of Einstein, what he described as 'the dice-playing God' " (Popper, 125).[19] Popper concludes by positing an open universe where men are dealing with emergent properties and thus must always expand their knowledge.

It may seem from my sketchy and random survey that at least some of the more unusual views about human freedom have been deleted from the store of intelligent modern proposals—such as the suggestion that associated human will with animal magnetism, electric force, or phrenological configuration. But many contemporary views of human nature suggest similar schemes. Theories of body types imply a genetic determinism, just as serious investigation of parapsychology suggests free will. Arthur Koestler's *The Roots of Coincidence* (1972) is perhaps the most prominent appeal for a serious study of parapsychology. Koestler praised Heisenberg for putting an end to causal determinism in physics and listed many instances suggesting that noncausal, nonphysical factors operate in nature. For Koestler, the discoveries of Schrödinger, Pauli, and others have brought a rapprochement between parapsychology and modern physics that has dismissed the clockwork universe of nineteenth-century physics.[20]

Modern interest in free will is no more casual than was the intense concern of the Victorians we have studied, because implicit always in the idea of free will is the idea of responsibility. In short, it is a question of morality. Austen Farrer tried to make some helpful distinctions between determinism and libertarianism by restricting the provinces of their authority. Decision thinking and causal construction are different idioms, thus for the purposes of his discussion, Farrer said, "we define determinism as a doctrine which restricts the idiom of decision as closely as possible to the sphere of action, libertarianism as a doctrine which extends it into the realm of theory. The libertarian, that is, takes the way we think in the mood of decision as evidence for a theoretical belief, belief in a sort of agency undetermined by natural law. The determinist disallows the inference; in his opinion, our action exemplifies natural law as much as anything does; only the mood of decision employs an idiom unable to express the thought of its own subjection to laws."[21] The determinist depends upon operations and connections, whereas the libertarian draws conclusions based on larger patterns. If the determinist says that man's area for decision is a mere spot in the causal pattern of the universe, the libertarian replies that "the whole mass of natural fact, as we men have put it together, is the product of an enterprise which knows itself as free" (Farrer, 171). Farrer argues for examining action patterns in individual behavior as well as in the larger context of natural events. The libertarian needs a world of causal necessity, but he perceives it in larger terms than unit relations. Determinism, Farrer says, is the child of mathematics, which cannot help with psychology (Farrer, 196).

Farrer's position resembles the nineteenth-century view that founds human freedom on the immeasurability of subjective experience. His conclusion about man's nature and place in the universe will not sound unfamiliar either. Determinism and libertarianism are, Farrer says, faiths, but bare libertarianism is an empty faith without the additional commitment to responsibility that can be founded only in the concept of human will, which Farrer does not conceive of as divided into volition and free will, but as being "action itself" (Farrer 106). He wonders if human will "does not spring continually out of a deeper source of will, the wellspring of the world" (Farrer, 315). To some, this may sound like a benign version of Schopenhauer's view that human will is no more than a manifestation of the Will which moves all existence to continue in being.

Some philosophers are more concerned with the broad idea of human freedom than with free will, thus Stuart Hampshire says in *Freedom of the Individual* (1965), "I have avoided the word 'determinism,' and I have not even stated, even less tried to refute, a thesis of determinism. I have tried to specify a distinction between the observed natural course of events and man's decisions about the natural course of events."[22] Oversimplified, Hampshire's contention is that man has the power to plan and to do things. He is capable of reflection and can therefore make decisions that are clear formulations of his desires. Because he can know what he will do and what will happen, he is free, and the more he can know about himself and about the world around him, the freer he is. Hampshire concludes that "a thesis of determinism, which entails that the commonplace scheme of explanation of conduct is replaceable by a neutral vocabulary of natural law, seems to me unacceptable. But it is possible that some other thesis of determinism, which does not claim that a neutral vocabulary of natural law might 'replace' the existing vocabulary, might be untouched by the arguments of these lectures."[23]

Hampshire's is a common-sense approach, purposely avoiding the more complicated metaphysical issues. He is concerned less with implications about the universe, as someone like Popper is, than with the conduct of men. A. J. Ayer is similarly occupied with the moral consequences of belief in free will. In *The Central Questions of Philosophy* (1973), he is especially interested in the point at which free will is so attenuated that responsibility can no longer be assigned, as in cases where a physical impossibility or psychological law prevents action.[24] Ayer's approach is based upon logical analysis, but he accepts a position about free will that, though tenable, he says, departs considerably from our ordinary way of thinking. It is a view we have heard several times and which Ayer himself associates with Locke.

> Free actions can then be characterized, in the way that Locke and others have proposed, as those in which the agent is not prevented from doing what he chooses, no matter how his choices are themselves determined, and the justification of reward and punishment will be that they exert a causal influence upon the agent's future choices as well as on the choices of others who may be expected to learn from the example.[25]

Modern emphasis upon human freedom tends to depart from specific attention to free will and to deal instead with larger units. Rollo May comments, " 'Free will,' in its traditional sense, seems to be a concept that has been the cause of years of fruitless arguments. It is the *whole human being* who is free, not a *part* of him or her such as will."[26] Speaking as an analyst, May claims that man may renounce freedom through neurosis or repression of anger. He suggests that modern western man has conceded to destiny the power over illness largely because of the technological claims of modern medicine and has divested himself of the responsibility to fight his own disease (May, 204ff). For May, freedom is "the capacity to pause in the midst of stimuli from all directions, and in this pause to throw our weight toward this response rather than that one" (May, 163). Such a pause breaks the rigid chain of cause and effect. May recommends a greater attention to destiny, because freedom comes alive only when confronted with its opposite. "Freedom and determinism give birth to each other. Every advance in freedom gives birth to a new determinism, and every advance in determinism gives birth to a new freedom. Freedom is a circle within a larger circle of determinism, which is, in turn, surrounded by a larger circle of freedom. And so on *ad infinitum*" (May, 84).

May is concerned with individual and communal well-being and sees modern illness, both physical and mental, as the product of selfishness and mechanistic thinking. Jonathan Glover, also concerned with well-being and responsibility, is less optimistic and inspirational in tone than May, but his approach is compatible. He does not propose a theory of free will, but instead challenges determinism as applied to human beings, citing almost universal agreement among contemporary philosophers "that we need no longer worry about determinism" because "a sufficient explanation of a human action can never be given in causal terms."[27] He concludes that except for extreme cases of the mentally ill, "determinism does not entail that we are always unable to act differently from how we do act."[28]

William H. Davis touches on the most prominent features of the free will question in his survey of the subject. Determinism should be able to predict the future, if it cannot, it remains as theoretical as free will. But essential to free will is the operation of reason. Davis falls back upon a way of conceiving the self as a structure of entities or faculties.

> The *reason* depends upon the *will*, upon the faculty of self-control, in order to free its results of emotional and logical irrelevancies. In ordinary affairs of life, the *will* depends upon the *reason* to show it the world of possibilities. . . . By the moral and aesthetic sensitivities the good and lovely are *felt*. The reason opens up for us the world of possibilities and consequences; the sensitivity gives us a clue to the relative values of these possibilities; the will enables the self to select which possibility to actualize.[29]

Edward D'Angelo reviews what he considers the four possible positions on the free will controversy: libertarianism, soft determinism (free will and determinism are both true), hard determinism, and disbelief in free will and determinism. D'Angelo remains objective himself but cites explanations that man feels free though his acts are caused, because his choices are made toward the future. In the end, he concludes that differences of opinion, especially between soft and hard determinists, the one accepting concepts of responsibility and blame that the other rejects, are linguistic because they define terms like "free" and "moral responsibility" differently.[30]

The modern debate on the will goes on less popularly and less fiercely than did the Victorian contest, but it does go on and no doubt *will* go on because its essentials remain unprovable. We do not all accept a divine revelation that the world is consciously designed and that we do or do not have freedom to contradict the will of the designer. Science cannot present enough detailed evidence to predict the future accurately, especially the future of human behavior. Some of its findings even seem to challenge a strict determinism. Our chief hope on either side of the dispute is greater knowledge and application of reason. And at the heart of the dispute is still the question of moral responsibility and the way we interpret events according to some causal pattern.

I have limited myself to a study of nineteenth-century literature and culture, but the free will question has definite bearing on the twentieth century too. In *The Natural History of H. G. Wells* (1982), I discussed the differing views of Wells and some of his associates, including Conrad and Gissing, all of whom had express, but differing, views. Wells accepted the physicists' determinist, blocklike, four-dimensional universe yet believed at the same time that man had free will—or, what amounted to the same thing, the workable illusion of it.[31] Conrad conceived of the universe as a soulless mechanism and himself as a helpless spectator. Gissing had a similar opinion purged of Conrad's pleasure in the spectacle and his respect for the more decent human illusions.[32] The dilemma at the end of the nineteenth century was to reconcile an increasing sense of determinism with the continuing sense of human responsibility. J. A. Symonds's poem "The Will" renders the sentiment concisely.

> Blame not the times in which we live,
> Nor Fortune frail and fugitive;
> Blame not thy parents, nor the rule
> Of vice or wrong once learned at school;
> But blame thyself, O man!
>
> Although both heaven and earth combined
> To mould thy flesh and form thy mind,

Though every thought, word, action, will;
Was framed by powers beyond thee, still
  Thou art thyself, O man!

And self to take or leave is free,
Feeling its own sufficiency:
In spite of science, spite of fate,
The judge within thee soon or late
  Will blame but thee, O man!

Say not, 'I would, but could not—;He
'Should bear the blame, who fashioned me—
'Call you mere change of motive choice?'
Scorning such pleas, the inner voice
  Cries, 'Thine the deed, O man!'[33]

Man's governing power is not his own but is fashioned by an unknown power beyond him, yet he is responsible for his deeds. Responsible to himself. The struggle now is located *within* man. The condition cries out for a remedy, but Symonds offers only the illness, not its palliative. Man's consciousness of volitional power imprisons him in guilt and inevitable dismay. All philosophical dispute is drowned by personal sensation. What does it matter if man's actions may be explained away by environment and heredity? If man *feels* responsible for his deeds, he *is* responsible.[34]

Richard Le Gallienne took a different approach to the problem. In *The Religion of a Literary Man* (1895), he declared free will a dogma we can do without. "Life," he said, "is a reality governed by illusions, and 'free will' is one of the illusions that govern it."[35] Most of our existence is ruled by external forces and accident. Our problem is the human assumption that the universe is made for us; but, Le Gallienne suggested, we are more like flowers that God has planted here. He welcomed the loss of "free will" as a means of diminishing an excessive concern for "individualities." Symonds felt that a sense of freedom would intensify his sense of being; Le Gallienne seemed almost weary of that clinging attention to self.

When I began this study, I had planned a concluding chapter dealing with the strangely similar-yet-different attitudes toward free will and necessity of Wells and Yeats. The Wells research went its own way and became a book by itself and other scholars have said enough about Yeats by now for me to make only a brief reference to him here. Robert Snukal has written that Yeats's "philosophical defence against modern determinist thought was Kant's analysis of the role of freedom of the will in the antinomies."[36] Yeats had nothing new to offer on this subject, but he was conscious of how one's opinion about free will affected how one interpreted people, history, art, and politics. For Yeats, "The central human activity is to find and create order and purpose, to make art, and so determine, in a temporary and limited fashion, human history" (Snukal, 126). In the later poetry, art is "the supreme example of our 'self-begotten' freedom from necessity" (Snukal, 135). In his poems about his friends, Yeats described the willed creation of individuality. This is in the late poetry. In his earlier work, Yeats rejected the will.[37] In "The Symbolism of Poetry" (1900), he recommended deleting from serious poetry "those energetic rhythms . . . which are the invention of the will with its eyes always on something to be done or undone," and concentrating on more monotonous rhythms "to keep us in that state of perhaps real trance, in which the mind liberated from the pressure of the will is unfolded in symbols."[38] Of course Yeats is here discussing will as volition, not free will. But the subject becomes confused once he has established the design of *A Vision* (1937), for there Will and Mask interact with Creative Mind and the Body of Fate in a historically rigid pattern that seems to exclude freedom. Here is a sample passage where terms familiar to us throughout this study seem cavalierly stirred together in a philosophical mulligan stew.

> The *Will* looks into a painted picture, the *Creative Mind* looks into a photograph, but both look into something that is the opposite of themselves. The *Creative Mind* contains all the universals in so far as its memory permits their employment, whereas the photograph is heterogeneous. The picture is chosen, the photograph is fated, because by Fate and Necessity—for I need both words—is understood that which comes from without, whereas the *Mask* is predestined, Destiny being that which comes to us from within.[39]

There are, however, points when men can achieve freedom, and, in a reprise of the Christian scheme we have seen now in so many guises, they involve surrender of the will.

> Between Phase 4 and Phase 5 the *tinctures* ceased to be drowned in the One, and reflection begins. Between Phases 25, 26 and Phases 4, 5, there is an approach to absolute surrender of the *Will*, first to God, then, as Phase 1 passes away, to Nature, and the surrender is the most complete form of the freedom of the *Body of Fate* which has been increasing since Phase 22. When Man identifies himself with his Fate, when he is able to say "Thy Will is our freedom" or when he is perfectly natural, that is to say, perfectly a portion of his surroundings, he is free even though all his actions can be foreseen, even though every action is a logical deduction from all that went before it.[40]

Yeats seems to have believed in a largely determinist scheme from which men could escape through the will as expressed by human creativity. If, for Wells, human history was the story man shaped for himself out of necessity and the future was the dream of free will, for Yeats, history was a symbolic design from which the individual escaped in a moment of lyric intensity by yielding his will in this world to will as artistic creation. As we have seen in Pater and other writers, this was not a unique view at the end of the nineteenth century.

The subject of the will remained lively in the arts. Arthur Waugh, producing a manifesto for "The New Realism" in *The Fortnightly* in 1916, declared that this new school of art rejected determinism and championed life.[41] Bernard Shaw ebulliently promoted a vitalism that assumed free will. But we cannot pursue that history. More time will give us perspective, but my impression of current writing is that, except among a few thoughtful artists, the issue of free will and necessity plays a very small part. Jean Paul Sartre and Albert Camus were as much philosophers as novelists, and so it is not strange to discover the theme in their work. Some writers are willing to discuss these subjects forthrightly. Saul Bellow is one. Others imply a genetic determinism, like John Irving in *The World according to Garp* (1976). But there are not many novelists who self-consciously manifest their philosophical opinions in the very structure of their fictions. John Fowles is an exception. In *The Aristos* (1970, rev.) he openly declared freedom of will "the highest human good," but he had some curious variations to play on his theme. One was political. "Freedom of will in a world without freedom is like a fish in a world without water," he said. "It cannot exist because it cannot use itself."[42] The whole purpose of *The Aristos* was "to preserve the freedom of the individual against all those pressures-to-conform that threaten our century."[43]

True to his faith, Fowles has been willing to allow his characters a degree of freedom from his own command so that they may encounter the contingency of the fictional worlds in which they live. This technique is especially effective in Fowles's "historical" novels. In *The French Lieutenant's Woman* (1969), Charles's story seems to be going along a conventional track when he virtuously decides not to stop at Exeter to visit Sara but to return to his fianceé. Fowles allows us to pursue this story for some distance before letting us know that Charles has broken through conventional plotting and conventional morality. He *has* made a visit to Sara and it has changed his life. At the end of the novel, Fowles leaves us, as readers, with two possible conclusions to his fiction, and then, as a character in his own novel, departs, leaving the ultimate choice to us, or to his characters.

In a more bizarre and elaborate exploration of human freedom, Fowles provides the readers of *A Maggot* (1985) with some pointed clues that his characters, especially his Lordship, alias Mr. Bartholomew, see themselves as characters in a play. As I read Fowles's novel, Mr. Bartholomew is both an eighteenth-century nobleman disgusted with the unfreedom of his age and a character resentful of having to do what an author directs. "I am born with a fixed destiny," he tells the actor Lacey. "I am, as you might be, offered a part in a history, and I am not forgiven for refusing to play it."[44] Mr. Bartholomew is on his way "to meet one I desire to know, and respect, as much as I would a bride—or a Muse indeed, were I a poet" (Fowles, *Maggot*, 36). But Fowles never lets us know just who this is—Fowles himself, the imagination that makes his characters possible, or some unnamed being or essence. We know, however, that the being he seeks exists in another temporal dimension and the secondhand account we receive of his fate suggests that he has been carried into the remote future by a space-time vehicle. In any case, he escapes from eighteenth-century England, from the determinism of Fowles's novel, and from us. The final act of his play, Mr. Bartholomew explains to Lacey, "is not yet written" (Fowles, *Maggot*, 39). And that is why he can escape. But he has an advantage over other characters. These "are like most of us, still today, equal victims in the debtors' prison of History, and equally unable to leave it" (Fowles, *Maggot*, 235). Of a minor character, Fowles says:

> John Lee *is*, of course; but as a tool or a beast is, in a world so entirely pre-ordained it might be written, like this book. He laboriously reads the bible, and so does he hear of and comprehend the living outside world around him—not as something to be approved of or disapproved, to be acted for or against; but as it simply is, which is as it always would or must be, an inalienably fixed narrative. (Fowles, *Maggot*, 393)

But Mr. Bartholomew wants to *be* in another sense, to renounce the debt of history. He refuses to be "like the personages of a tale" and thus aligns himself with the builders of Stonehenge who lived "before the tale began . . . in a present that had no past, such as we may hardly imagine to ourselves" (Fowles, *Maggot*, 145). Like so many proponents of free will, he exploits the one avenue of exit open to him—the future, but with the additional irony that his future must go beyond ours and the narrator's present. Although Mr. Bartholomew mysteriously escapes the fiction of history, he continues to exist there as a supporting spirit for Rebecca Lee, in effect his convert, who will become the mother of Ann Lee, a great voice for change in her time.

Fowles is not alone in permitting his stated philosophy to shape the matter, form, and style of his fiction (Gabriel Garcia Marquez, especially in *One Hundred Years of Solitude* [1967], is another), but we are perhaps less capable of appreciating this kind of achievement in our own day unless we can see the complex manner in which this process of embodied ideas had been established over the preceding generations. This study has been an attempt to describe that process.

Writers like Fowles and Marquez are acutely conscious of the relationship of narrative and time. We have seen that writers from Hazlitt, to Carlyle, to recent philosophers writing on free will mentioned in this chapter have identified belief in free will with future-oriented thought. The nineteenth century was preeminently a period in which historical thinking prospered and when much of that thinking assumed a developmental and progressive form. Many of the best writers mentioned in the preceding chapters were alert to this fascination with history and saw its bearing on their manner of composing. Arthur C. Danto writes that "to exist *historically* is to perceive the events one lives through as part of a story later to be told."[45] Danto explains that for a historian to ask the historical significance of an event requires an answer available only in the context of a story (Danto, 11). This is so largely because our knowledge of the past is limited by what we do or do not know of the future, because the significance of past events changes as the consequences of these events unfold into the future (Danto, 18). Thus "what we select as the beginning of a narrative is determined by the end, a claim borne out by the legitimacy of narrative descriptions of the beginning with reference to the end" (Danto, 248).[46] When we read a narrative, we expect that each thing mentioned is going to be important. Victorian writers overwhelmingly acknowledged and served that expectation. A modern writer like Fowles, who is resisting the imprisoning effect of narrative, might be expected to introduce a good deal that is redundant or untagged for value. But he will inevitably encounter another difficulty, for the language with which a writer tries to wrest freedom from circumstance is itself constrained by its syntactical and grammatical structures, especially its tenses. Danto, who devotes some time to this issue, comments concisely that we acquire our concept of the past as we acquire our language (Danto, 91).

Danto is a philosopher of history; I have concentrated on fiction, whose great advantage is that it is, in a sense, irresponsible history. It *can* know the future of its history. As with *A Maggot*, it can even create a future beyond the present time of the author. What must be a real operating power—providence, necessity, chance—in the stories that historians tell, may be metaphorical in fiction. Thus life may often be represented as a drama, a story, a work of art, and the author is only analogically an omniscient deity. Frank Kermode writes that the "*as if* of the novel consists in a . . . negation of determinism, the establishment of an accepted freedom by magic."[47] But I hope that it has become apparent through this study that, at least in nineteenth-century England, writers could make their *as if* world resemble the world as they perceived it and that, as they constructed the sentences and paragraphs constituting their narratives, they very often replicated in the very nature of their telling the kind of world they believed themselves to live in—open to the full operation of the human will or absolutely constrained by a god or natural necessity. To the degree that this practice was unconscious or inescapable, even the magical *as if* of imaginative literature was no true exercise of free will, but a trick window in the locked and barred house of fiction.

Notes

Notes to Introduction to Part 1

1. Albrecht Dilhe, *The Theory of Will in Classical Antiquity* (Berkeley: University of California Press, 1982), 26. Subsequent references appear in the text.
2. Oskar Walzel, *German Romanticism*, trans. Alma Elise Lussky (New York: Capricorn Books, 1966), 266–67.
3. Friedrich von Schlegel, *Lectures on the History of Literature, Ancient and Modern* (London: Bell and Sons, 1896), 106.
4. Friedrich von Schiller, *Naive and Sentimental Poetry and On the Sublime: Two Essays*, trans. Julius A. Elias (New York: Frederick Ungar Publishing Co., 1966), 195ff.
5. Andrew Lang, *Modern Mythology* (New York: AMS Press, 1968, reprint), xi–xii.
6. William Hazlitt, "On Gusto," in *The Complete Works of William Hazlitt*, ed. P. P. Howe (London and Toronto: J. M. Dent and Sons, Ltd., 1930), 78. See chapter 4 for Hazlitt's views about free will and necessity.
7. Jacob Burckhardt, *Force and Freedom: Reflections on History*, ed. James Hastings Nichols (Boston: Beacon Press, 1964), 316ff; Thomas Hill Green, *The Works of Thomas Hill Green*, ed. R. L. Nettleship (New York: Kraus Reprints, 1969), *Miscellanies and Memoir* 3:11ff.
8. Karl Kroeber, *Romantic Narrative Art* (Madison: University of Wisconsin Press, 1960), 120–21 and 190–92.
9. Two works dealing with the Romantic concern for the will are Michael G. Cooke's *The Romantic Will* (New Haven: Yale University Press, 1976) and Peter L. Thor-

NOTES

slev, Jr.'s, *Romantic Contraries: Freedom versus Destiny* (New Haven: Yale University Press, 1984).

10. David B. Greene, *Temporal Processes in Beethoven's Music* (New York: Gordon and Breach Science Publishers, 1982), 29. Subsequent references appear in the text.

11. Morse Peckham, *Beyond the Tragic Vision: The Quest for Identity in the Nineteenth Century* (New York: George Braziller, 1962), chaps. 8, 9. See also Friedrich Blume, *Classic and Romantic Music: A Comprehensive Survey*, trans. M. D. Herter Norton (New York: W. W. Norton and Co., 1970), 122.

12. Martin Meisel, *Realizations: Narrative, Pictorial, and Theatrical Arts in Nineteenth-Century England* (Princeton: Princeton University Press, 1983), 71. See also Jacques Barzun, *Darwin, Marx, Wagner* (Garden City, N. Y.: Doubleday and Co., 1958), 264.

13. Stefan Jarocinski, *Debussy: Impressionism and Symbolism*, trans. by Rollo Myers (London: Eulenburg Books, 1976), chaps. 4, 5, conclusion.

14. Hugh Macdonald, *Skryabin* (London: Oxford University Press, 1978), 49.

15. Thomas Carlyle, *Sartor Resartus: The Life and Opinions of Herr Teufelsdröckh*, ed. Charles Frederick Harrold (New York: The Odyssey Press, 1937), 192.

16. William Ewart Gladstone, *Correspondence on Church and Religion*, ed. D. C. Lathbury, 2 vols. (New York: The Macmillan Company, 1910), 2:150–51.

17. F. B. Smith's *Florence Nightingale: Reputation and Power* (New York: St. Martin's Press, 1982) shows how forcefully Nightingale exerted her will to get her own way. According to Smith, she was far more a hegemonic than a renunciatory figure.

18. G. D. H. Cole, *The Life of William Cobbett* (New York: Harcourt, Brace, and Co., n.d.), 431.

19. Cole, 315–16.

20. *The Life of William Cobbett* (Philadelphia: E. L. Cary & A. Hart, 1835), 199. The *Life* says of Cobbett's behavior: "We trace in Cobbett's conduct evidences of *industry, independence, impetuosity* (considered as the force of impulse), *ambition, disobedience, obstinacy, pride, perseverance, impatience of control, sobriety, the power of will, judgment, frugality, generosity, foresight, moral reasoning power,* and *strong common sense*" (55–56).

21. The best recent study of physiognomy in nineteenth-century literature is Graeme Tytler's *Physiognomy in the European Novel: Faces and Fortunes* (Princeton: Princeton University Press, 1982).

22. Ibid., 73.

23. James W. Redfield, *Comparative Physiognomy or Resemblances between Men and Animals* (New York: W. J. Widdleton, 1866), 293.

24. In *The Annotated Dracula* (New York: Clarkson, N. Potter, 1975), Leonard Wolff suggests that Stoker may have had Lombroso's identifying criminal features in mind when describing Count Dracula (300).

25. John Abercrombie, *The Philosophy of the Moral Feelings* (Boston: T. H. Carter, 1836), 123ff.

26. Ibid., 222–23.

27. Catherine Crowe, *The Night Side of Nature: Or, Ghosts and Ghost Seers* (London: G. Routledge and Co., 1852), 491.

28. Arthur Henry Hallam, *The Letters of Arthur Henry Hallam*, ed. Jack Kolb (Columbus: Ohio State University Press, 1981), 311. Subsequent references appear in the text.

29. *Remarkable Escapes from Peril* (London: The Religious Tract Society, n.d.), 9.

30. Ibid., 74.

31. "The Vanity and Glory of Literature," *Edinburgh Review*, 180 (April 1849), 318-19.

32. A fine recent study of the moral significance of English fiction is Leopold Damrosch, Jr.'s, *God's Plot and Man's Stories: Studies in the Fictional Imagination from Milton to Fielding* (Chicago: University of Chicago Press, 1985). A standard study of the moral fiction of the nineteenth century is Robert Colby's *Fiction with a Purpose: Major and Minor Nineteenth-Century Novels* (Bloomington: Indiana University Press, 1967). Kenneth Graham discusses Victorian ideas about the moral obligation of fiction in *Criticism of the Novel, 1865-1900* (Oxford: The Clarendon Press, 1965), 78ff.

33. Leo Braudy, *Narrative Form in History and Fiction* (Princeton: Princeton University Press, 1970), 50.

34. Ibid., 216.

35. Paul Ricoeur, *Time and Narrative*, trans. Kathleen McLaughlin and David Pellauer (Chicago: University of Chicago Press, 1984), 3.

36. Ibid., 52.

37. Edward Dowden, *Studies in Literature, 1789-1877* (London: Kegan Paul, Trench and Co., 1889), 163.

38. W. L. Burn, *The Age of Equipoise: A Study of the Mid-Victorian Generation* (New York: W. W. Norton and Co., 1965), 21.

39. It would have been possible to examine the whole field of religious fiction for the attitudes and beliefs about the will imbedded in its narratives. For some idea of how many of these novels appeared during the nineteenth century, see Margaret M. Maison's *The Victorian Vision: Studies in the Religious Novel* (New York: Sheed and Ward, 1961) and Robert Lee Wolff's *Gains and Losses: Novels of Faith and Doubt in Victorian England* (1977). Whole areas of fiction that I have not treated for economy's sake are open to similar interpretation. See, for example, Catherine Gallagher's examination of the themes of free will and determinism in industrial novels in *The Industrial Reformation of English Fiction, 1832-1867* (Chicago: University of Chicago Press, 1985).

Notes to Chapter 1: The Self

1. Walter Kaufmann, *Hegel: A Reinterpretation* (Garden City, N.Y.: Anchor Books, 1965), 20-21.

2. Karl Löwith, *From Hegel to Nietzsche: The Revolution in Nineteenth-Century Thought*, trans. David E. Green (Garden City, N. Y.: Anchor Books, 1967), 31. See also G. W. F. Hegel, *The Philosophy of History*, trans. J. Sibree (New York: Dover Publications, Inc., 1956), 319ff.

3. Edward Bulwer-Lytton, "Self-Control," in *Caxtoniana: A Series of Essays on Life, Literature, and Manners* (New York: Harper and Brothers, 1864), 210–11.

4. Arthur Henry Hallam, *The Letters of Arthur Henry Hallom*, ed. Jack Kolb (Columbus: Ohio State University Press, 1981), 317.

5. Wylie Sypher, *Loss of Self in Modern Literature and Art* (New York: Random House, 1962), 19. Subsequent references appear in the text.

6. Wayne Shumaker, *English Autobiography: Its Emergence, Materials, and Form* (Berkeley and Los Angeles: University of California Press, 1954), 22, 29.

7. John O. Lyons, *The Invention of the Self: The Hinge of Consciousness in the Eighteenth Century* (Carbondale and Edwardsville: Southern Illinois University Press, 1978), 9. Much of what follows draws upon Lyons's book. Subsequent references appear in the text.

8. William H. Marshall, *The World of the Victorian Novel* (South Brunswick, N.J. and New York: A. S. Barnes and Company, 1967), 27.

9. Frederick Garber, *The Autonomy of the Self from Richardson to Huysmans* (Princeton: Princeton University Press, 1982), 40. Subsequent references appear in the text. Much of what follows draws upon Garber's book.

10. Löwith, 10.

11. Leopold Damrosch, Jr., *God's Plot and Man's Stories: Studies in the Fictional Imagination from Milton to Fielding* (Chicago: University of Chicago Press, 1985), 4.

12. However, love is the dominant passion in Conrad's nature, and he upholds his own ethical standard. He will not murder a sleeping enemy. Also, courtesy finds a place in Conrad's world in the person of Gulnare.

13. David Morse, *Perspectives on Romanticism: A Transformational Analysis* (Totowa: N.J.: Barnes and Noble Books, 1981), 213.

14. See Löwith concerning Hegel's views, p. 84.

15. Shumaker, 89–90.

16. William K. Clifford, "On the Scientific Basis of Morals," in *Lectures and Essays*, ed. Leslie Stephen and Sir Frederick Pollock, 2 vols. (London: Macmillan and Co., 1901), 2:79. One must keep in mind the tradition of Hartleyan associationism, too.

17. Ibid., 80ff. Clifford's view, based on Hegel, might be compared with James Ward's, which appears later in this chapter.

18. Clifford, "Right and Wrong: The Scientific Ground of their Distinction," in *Lectures and Essays* 2:138–39.

19. Frederick Denison Maurice, *Theological Essays*, 2d ed. (Cambridge: Macmillan and Co., 1853), 52.

20. William Boyd Carpenter, *The Permanent Elements of Religion* (London: Macmillan and Co., 1889), 255. Carpenter admits that the sense of freedom thus achieved may be illusory but argues that it serves its purpose nonetheless.

21. James Hinton, *Man and His Dwelling Place* (New York: D. Appleton and Co., 1872), 138.

22. Hinton, *Philosophy and Religion: Selections from the Manuscripts of the Late James Hinton*, ed. Caroline Haddon (London: Kegan Paul, Trench and Co., 1881), 163.

23. Ibid., 165–66, 201.

24. Hinton, *Dwelling Place*, 152–53.
25. Hinton, *Life in Nature* (London: Smith Elder and Co., 1862), 85.
26. Hinton, *Philosophy and Religion*, 216.
27. Hinton, *Life in Nature*, 104.
28. Ibid., 140, quoting Coleridge.
29. Samuel Butler, *Samuel Butler's Notebooks*, ed. Geoffrey Keynes and Brian Hill (London: Jonathan Cape, 1951), 197.
30. Butler, *Life and Habit: The Works of Samuel Butler* (New York: E. P. Dutton and and Co., 1923), 4:85.
31. Ibid., 64. See also the theories of self presented by F. W. Myers, discussed in John R. Reed, *Victorian Conventions* (Athens: Ohio University Press, 1975), 339.
32. Butler, *Life and Habit*, 85.
33. See the discussion of this theme of enclosure and extension of the self in chapter 9.
34. James F. Ferrier, *Institutes of Metaphysic: The Theory of Knowing and Being* (Edinburgh: William Blackwood and Sons, 1854), 111, 134. Subsequent references appear in the text.
35. But see Frederick Copleston's objection that the true conclusion to Ferrier's epistemological premises is solipsism.

> And Ferrier escapes from this conclusion only by an appeal to com-
> mon sense and to our knowledge of historical facts. That is to say, as I
> cannot seriously suppose that the material universe is simply object for
> me as subject, I must postulate an eternal, infinite subject, God. But on
> Ferrier's premises it appears to follow that God Himself, as thought by
> me, must be object-for-a-subject, the subject being myself (*A History of
> Philosophy*, [Garden City, N.Y.: Doubleday and Co., Inc., 1967],
> 8:186).

36. *The Life and Letters of Mandell Creighton by his Wife* (London: Longmans, Green, and Co., 1904), 2:211.
37. James Ward, "Psychology," in *Significant Contributions to the History of Psychology, 1750–1920: Series A: Orientations*, vol. 8; James Ward, ed. Daniel N. Robinson (Washington D.C.: University Publications of America, 1977), 167.
38. Ward, "Psychological Principles," in *Significant Contributions*, 370-71. Subsequent references appear in the text.
39. Compare Ward's definition with John Stuart Mill's: "A person whose desires and impulses are his own—are the expression of his own nature, as it has been developed and modified by his own culture—is said to have a character. One whose desires and impulses are not his own, has no character, no more than a steam-engine has a character" ("On Liberty," in *Collected Works of John Stuart Mill*, ed. J. M. Robson [1977], vol. 18, *Essays on Politics and Society*, 264).

Notes to Chapter 2: A Short History of the Free Will Controversy

1. James Martineau, *Essays, Reviews, and Addresses* (London: Longmans, Green and Co., 1891), vol. 4, *Academical, Religious*, 4. Subsequent references appear in the text.

2. There have already been satisfactory contributions to the study of this perennial controversy. See, for example, Archibald Alexander's early and impressive *Theories of the Will in the History of Philosophy* (New York: Charles Scribner's Sons, 1898).

3. Thomas Hobbes, "Leviathan," in *British Moralists 1650–1800*, 2 vols., ed. D. D. Raphael (Oxford: The Clarendon Press, 1969), 1:55.

4. Elsewhere Hobbes defines the will as the last in a succession of deliberations and contrary appetites before the doing of an action ("Of Liberty and Necessity," in *British Moralists* 1:67). Archibald Alexander says Hobbes was the first philosopher to investigate train of thought in relation to will (*Theories*, 164).

5. Ralph Cudworth, "A Treatise of Freewill," in *British Moralists* 1:128.

6. Ibid., 132.

7. John Locke, "Essay Concerning Human Understanding," in *British Moralists* 1:144.

8. Ibid., 153.

9. Samuel Clarke, "A Discourse," in *British Moralists* 1:199.

10. David Hume, *A Treatise of Human Nature*, 2 vols., ed. T. H. Green and T. H. Grose (London, 1886); reprint ed. Aalen (West Germany: Scientia Verlag, 1964), 2:181.

11. Ibid., 188.

12. T. H. Huxley, *Collected Essays* (London: Macmillan and Co., 1894), vol. 6, *Hume: With Helps to the Study of Berkeley*, 222.

13. This was to be Godwin's argument as well.

14. Joseph Butler, *The Analogy of Religion, Natural and Revealed, to the Constitution and Course of Nature*, 2 vols. (Oxford: Clarendon Press, 1874), 1:13. Subsequent references appear in the text. See Mozley and Popper for later examples of extensions of this method.

15. William Godwin, *Enquiry concerning Political Justice and its Influence on Morals and Happiness*, 3d ed., facsimile, intro. and notes F. E. L. Priestley, 3 vols. (Toronto: University of Toronto Press, 1946), 1:382–83. Subsequent references appear in the text.

16. Godwin, *Thoughts on Man: His Nature, Productions, and Discoveries* (London: Effingham Wilson, 1831), 228–29. Subsequent references appear in the text.

17. Near the end of *Thoughts on Man*, Godwin distinguishes between the "speculator in his closet," who proves logically that he is a passive instrument of necessary forces, and the same man when he leaves his study for the daily intercourse with society, who then regards himself as endowed with liberty of action and initiative power. Perversely, Godwin declares this illusory sense of freedom as the source of all greatness in men (pp. 437–38). We shall examine the subject of phrenology later in this work from a different point of view.

18. David Hartley, *Observations on Man, His Frame, His Duty, and His Expectations*, 2 vols. in 1, facsimile, intro. Theodore L. Huguelet (Gainesville, Fla.: Scholars' Facsimiles and Reprints, 1966), 2:68. Subsequent references appear in the text.

19. David Bower, *David Hartley and James Mill* (New York: G. P. Putnam's Sons, 1881), 175.

20. "Though Mill does not specifically refer to the questions of Free Will and Necessity, which have so vexed the minds of moralists at different times, there can be little doubt—judging from his analysis of Volition—that he would have adopted what Hartley calls the theory of the Mechanism of the Human Mind, as opposed to that of Free Will, in any but the popular use of the word" (ibid., 174).

21. William Drummond, *Academical Questions* (London: Cadell and Davies, 1805), 1:350. Drummond indicates Spinoza's as the most celebrated philosophy of materialism (p. 217).

22. Joseph Priestley, "Disquisition Relating to Matter and Spirit," in *Joseph Priestley: Selections from His Writings*, ed. Ira V. Brown (University Park: Pennsylvania State University Press, 1962), 265–66.

23. Ibid., 276–77.

24. William Belsham, *Essays, Philosophical, Historical, and Literary* (London: G. G. and J. Robinson, 1799; facsimile, New York: Garland Publishing, Inc., 1971), 1:15.

25. See Bertrand Russell, *A History of Western Philosophy* (New York: Simon and Schuster, 1945), for a simple summary of Saint Augustine's position (p. 365). For discussion of Paul and the doctrine of predestination, see E. J. Bicknell, *A Theological Introduction to the Thirty-Nine Articles of the Church of England*, 3d ed., rev. H. J. Carpenter (London: Longmans, 1963), 220–21.

26. Bicknell, 218.

27. Hannah Arendt, *The Life of the Mind: Willing* (New York: Harcourt, Brace, Jovanovich, 1978), 70, 68.

28. Jonathan Edwards, *The Works of Jonathan Edwards*, ed. Paul Ramsey (New Haven: Yale University Press, 1957), vol. 1, *Freedom of the Will*, 9.

Notes to Chapter 3: The Religious Moralists

1. John Tulloch began his important *Movements of Religious Thought in Britain during the Nineteenth Century* (1885) with Coleridge. He said that Coleridge restored harmony between reason and religion and located the will as the root of spirituality in man and as the synonym for the self.

> This "intelligent self" is a fundamental conception lying at the root of his system of thought. Sin is an attribute of it, and cannot be conceived apart from it, and conscience, or the original sense of right and wrong, governing the will. Apart from these internal realities there is no religion, and the function of the Christian Revelation is to build up the spiritual life out of these realities—to remedy the evil, to enlighten the conscience, to educate the will. This effective power of religion comes directly from God in Christ. ([Leicester: Leicester University Press, 1885; reprint, New York: Humanities Press, 1971], 16)

Many studies have indicated Coleridge's importance in the tradition of English religious and philosophical thought. One of the standard accounts is Charles Richard Sanders's *Coleridge and the Broad Church Movement* (Durham, N.C.: Duke University Press, 1942), and one of the more recent is Wendell V. Harris's

The Omnipresent Debate: Empiricism and Transcendentalism in Nineteenth-Century English Prose (Dekalb: Northern Illinois University Press, 1981).

2. Samuel Taylor Coleridge, *Biographia Literaria*, ed. J. Shawcross, 2 vols. (London: Oxford University Press, 1962), 1:80.

3. Quoted from *Unpublished Letters* by Sanders, p. 52.

4. Coleridge, *The Statesman's Manual, The Collected Works*, ed. R. J. White (Princeton: Princeton University Press, 1972), Appendix C, p. 65.

5. Ibid., Appendix A, p. 55.

6. Quoted from *Literary Remains* by Sanders, p. 44.

7. In *On the Constitution of the Church and State*, Coleridge wrote: "Even in man *will* is deeper than *mind*: for mind does not cease to be *mind* by having an antecedent; but Will is either the first . . . or it is not WILL at all" (*The Collected Works*, ed. John Colmer [Princeton: Princeton University Press, 1976], 10:182).

8. Coleridge, *Aids to Reflection*, prelim. essay James Marsh, ed. Nelson Coleridge (1825: reprint, Port Washington, N.Y.: Kennikat Press, 1971), 107–8. Subsequent references appear in the text.

9. In chapter 1, I mentioned John O. Lyons's explanation of how the new concept of the self, emerging about the middle of the eighteenth century, placed the self in opposition to what is because it viewed self as willed assertion. Hence the self is always charged with revolutionary sentiment (Lyons, *The Invention of the Self: The Hinge of Consciousness in the Eighteenth Century* [Carbondale and Edwardsville: Southern Illinois University Press, 1978], 197ff).

10. Julius Charles Hare, *Sermons Preacht in Herstmonceux Church* (London: John W. Parker, 1841), 25–26. Subsequent references appear in the text.

11. Frederick Denison Maurice, *Theological Essays* (Cambridge: Macmillan and Co., 1853), 41. Subsequent references appear in the text.

12. Olive J. Brose, *Frederick Denison Maurice: Rebellious Conformist* (Athens: Ohio University Press, 1971), 72.

13. Maurice, *The Religion of Rome, and Its Influence on Modern Civilization* (Cambridge: Macmillan and Co., 1855), 298.

14. Ernest W. Bacon, *Spurgeon: Heir of the Puritans* (London: George Allen & Unwin, 1967), 80.

15. See Norman Vance's *The Sinews of the Spirit: The Idea of Christian Manliness in Victorian Literature and Religious Thought* (London: Cambridge University Press, 1985) for an account of the influence especially of Maurice, Kingsley, and Hughes in their own time and after.

16. Charles Kingsley, *The Works of Charles Kingsley* (London: Macmillan and Co., 1884; facsimile, Hildescheim, West Germany: George Olms Verlagsbuchhandlung, 1969), 26:257. Subsequent references appear in the text.

17. See, for example, Kingsley, vol. 18, "Heroism," and vol. 24, Sermon 14.

18. Kingsley asserted in "Heroism" that "true heroism must involve self-sacrifice" (18:233).

19. Thomas Hughes, *The Manliness of Christ* (New York: John B. Alden, 1887), 587–88.

20. Bacon, 85. It is surprising to learn that John Ruskin was warmly attached to

Spurgeon. Tim Hilton suggests that some of their views are not dissimilar (*Ruskin: The Early Years* [New Haven and London: Yale University Press, 1985], 262ff.

21. Charles Haddon Spurgeon, *Sermons, Fifth Series* (New York: Sheldon and Co., 1865), 101. Subsequent references appear in the text.

22. Spurgeon, *Sermons, Tenth Series* (New York: Robert Carter and Brothers, 1883), 191. Subsequent references appear in the text.

23. Spurgeon, *Sermons, Sixth Series* (New York: Sheldon and Co., 1865), 86. Subsequent references appear in the text.

24. Spurgeon, *Sermons, Fourth Series* (New York: Sheldon and Co., 1864), 414-15.

25. John Henry Newman, *Apologia Pro Vita Sua*, ed. David J. DeLaura (New York: W. W. Norton and Company, 1986), 187. Subsequent references appear in the text.

26. Thomas Vargish, *Newman: The Contemplation of Mind* (Oxford: The Clarendon Press, 1970), 35, 82. Vargish refers to *Loss and Gain* and to Newman's letters. See also Sermon 14 in Newman, *Sermons, Chiefly on the Theory of Religious Belief, Preached before the University of Oxford* (London: Francis and John Rivington; Oxford: J. H. Parker, 1844), esp. 353-54. Subsequent references appear in the text.

27. Quoted in A. Dwight Culler's *The Imperial Intellect: A Study of Cardinal Newman's Educational Ideal* (New Haven and London: Yale University Press, 1955), 268-69.

28. Newman, *An Essay in Aid of A Grammar of Assent*, ed. and intro. I. T. Ker (Oxford: Clarendon Press, 1985), 232. Subsequent references appear in the text.

29. M. Jamie Ferreira, *Doubt and Religious Commitment: The Role of the Will in Newman's Thought* (Oxford: Clarendon Press, 1980), 71ff, 59.

30. Newman, *Sermons and Discourses (1839-57)*, ed. Charles Frederick Harrold (New York: Longmans, Green and Co., 1949), 154. Subsequent references appear in the text.

31. Culler, 86-87.

32. Newman, *Sermons*, 125-26. Subsequent references appear in the text.

33. Wilfrid Ward, *William George Ward and the Catholic Revival* (London: Macmillan and Co., 1893), 352. Subsequent references appear in the text.

34. Stopford A. Brooke, ed., *Life, Letters, Lectures, and Addresses of Frederick W. Robertson* (New York: Harper and Brothers, n.d.), 296. Subsequent references appear in the text.

35. Frederick W. Robertson, *Sermons Preached at Trinity Chapel, Brighton, Second Series* (Boston: Ticknor and Fields, 1866), 184. Subsequent references appear in the text.

36. Robertson, *Sermons on St. Paul's Epistles to the Corinthians* (Boston: Ticknor and Fields, 1866), 337.

37. Robertson, *Sermons . . . Trinity*, 132, 279, 134, 135.

38. William Boyd Carpenter, *The Permanent Elements of Religion* (London: Macmillan and Co., 1889), xxxvii-xxxviii. Subsequent references appear in the text.

39. William Ewart Gladstone, *Correspondence on Church and Religion*, ed. D. C. Lathbury, 2 vols. (New York: Macmillan Co., 1910), 2:253.

40. Ibid., 409.
41. John Cumming, *The Daily Life; or Precepts and Prescriptions for Christian Living* (Boston: John P. Jewett and Co., 1855), 162–63.
42. William Rathbone Greg, *The Creed of Christendom: Its Foundations Contrasted with Its Superstructure* (Toronto: Rose-Belford Publishing Co., 1878), 328.
43. Ibid., 342.
44. J. B. Mozley, *The Principle of Causation Considered in Opposition to Atheistic Theories* (London: Hodder and Stoughton, 1872), 23.
45. James Martineau, *Essays, Reviews, and Addresses* (London: Longmans, Green and Co., 1891), vol. 4, *Academical, Religious,* 40. Subsequent references appear in the text. A. W. Jackson says that perhaps no other theme was so likely to kindle Martineau's reaction than one requiring the soul's surrender of self-will and its merging in a life diviner than its own (*James Martineau: A Biography and Study* [Boston: Little, Brown, and Co., 1901], 155). In his first original book, *The Rationale of Religious Inquiry* (1836), Martineau argued that belief cannot submit but is involuntary, whereas submission is an act of will. The one is brought about by evidence, the other by motives (Jackson, 54).
46. Martineau, *The Seat of Authority in Religion* (London: Longmans, Green, and Co., 1890), 47. Subsequent references appear in the text.
47. Jackson says that Martineau demanded that the concept of human will be preserved. "All causes operating in nature, in the last century called second causes, he is willing to lose in the First Cause; but the human will he must reserve as itself a spring of causal power" (Jackson, 183).
48. Martineau, *Essays,* 578–79.
49. See also Martineau, *A Study of Religion, Its Sources and Contents,* 2 vols. (Oxford: Clarendon Press, 1889), 1:229. Subsequent references appear in the text.
50. Martineau says that he sees divine will as a living idea manifest in nature, unlike Spinoza, who denies understanding and will to immanent Cause, and Schopenhauer, who reduces it to blind force (Martineau, *Seat,* 29). He says that Hartmann, too, displaces understanding in will (Martineau, *Study,* 254). Essentially, Martineau dismisses the German school on will, declaring their notions too abstract (Martineau, *Study,* 291ff).
51. Jackson, 414–15.

Notes to Chapter 4: The Secular Moralists

1. Leslie Stephen, "An Agnostic's Apology," in *An Agnostic's Apology and Other Essays* (London: Smith, Elder, and Co., 1893), 40. Subsequent references appear in the text.
2. F. W. Maitland describes Stephen's response to Henry Sidgwick's study of ethics: "Stephen at this time was inclined to think that Sidgwick made difficulties where none were, and any boggling over free will and necessity was in his eyes a sign that a man was not really clear-headed" (*The Life and Letters of Leslie Stephen* [New York: G. P. Putnam's Sons, 1906], 285). Subsequent references appear in the text.

3. William Hazlitt, *An Essay on the Principles of Human Action and Some Remarks on the System of Hartley and Helvetius* (Gainesville, Fla.: Scholars' Facsimiles and Reprints, 1969), 64-65. Subsequent references appear in the text.

4. Hazlitt, "On Liberty and Necessity," in *The Collected Works of William Hazlitt*, ed. A. R. Waller and Arnold Glover, intro. W. E. Henley (New York: Phillips and Co., 1904), 11:70-71, 49, 57.

5. Hazlitt, "Doctrine of Philosophical Necessity," in *Works* 11:279.

6. Charles Bray, *The Philosophy of Necessity; Or, The Law of Consequences; as Applicable to Mental, and Social Science*, 2 vols. (London: Longman, Orme, Brown, Green, and Longman's, 1841), 1:106-9. Subsequent references appear in the text.

7. Carlyle's point is rather different from Bray's, however.

8. John Tulloch, *Movements of Religious Thought in Britain during the Nineteenth Century*, intro. A. C. Cheyne (reprint, Leicester: Leicester University Press, 1971), 231.

9. John Stuart Mill, *The Collected Works of John Stuart Mill*, ed. J. M. Robson (Toronto: University Press of Toronto, 1974), vol. 8, *System of Logic*, ed. J. M. Robson, intro. R. F. McRae, 836-37. Subsequent references appear in the text.

10. Mill, *An Examination of Sir William Hamilton's Philosophy*, 2 vols. (Boston: William V. Spencer, 1866), 2:300. Subsequent references appear in the text.

11. Mill takes this subject up again in "Utilitarianism," where he distinguishes will from desire, while asserting that will always begins with desire and then may become habitual. Where a person is not habituated to virtue, he must be made to desire virtue and hence establish a proper habit. "Will is the child of desire, and passes out of the dominion of its parent only to come under that of habit" (*Works*, vol. 10, *Essays on Ethics, Religion and Society*, ed. J. M. Robson, intro. F. E. L. Priestley [1969], 239). Subsequent references appear in the text.

12. Mill, *Works*, vol. 1, *Autobiography and Literary Essays*, ed. John M. Robson and Jack Stillinger (1981), 81.

13. Mill, "Coleridge," in *Works*, vol. 10, *Essays*, 133.

14. Tulloch, 237.

15. Herbert Spencer, *The Works of Herbert Spencer*, 2 vols. (New York and London: D. Appleton and Co., n.d.), vol. 1, *The Principles of Psychology*, 504. Subsequent references appear in the text.

16. William Kingdon Clifford, "Body and Mind," in *Lectures and Essays*, ed. Leslie Stephen and Sir Frederick Pollock, 2 vols. (London: Macmillan and Co., 1901), 1:33-37.

17. Clifford, "Right and Wrong: The Scientific Ground of their Distinction," in *Lectures and Essays*, 142-43.

18. Clifford, "Cosmic Emotion," in *Lectures and Essays*, 290. Kant had divorced will from body and placed it in the realm of Reason.

19. T. H. Green, "Lectures on the Philosophy of Kant," in *The Works of Thomas Hill Green*, ed. R. L. Nettleship (New York: Kraus Reprint Co., 1969), vol. 2, *Philosophical Works*, 133-34. Subsequent references appear in the text.

20. Green had reservations about Kant and even more about Hegel.

21. Green, "The Force of Circumstance," in *Works*, vol. 3, *Miscellanies and Memoir*, 6-8.

22. Malcolm Guthrie, *The Causational and Free Will Theories of Volition* (London and Edinburgh: Williams and Norgate, 1877), 44. Subsequent references appear in the text.

23. J. B. Schneewind, *Sidgwick's Ethics and Victorian Moral Philosophy* (Oxford: Clarendon Press, 1977), 198. Subsequent references appear in the text.

24. Schneewind points out that Sidgwick often revised the section of *Methods* dealing with freedom of the will but adds that the revisions did not alter Sidgwick's basic position.

25. A. J. Balfour, *The Foundations of Belief* (New York and London: Longmans, Green and Co., 1895), 131. Subsequent references appear in the text. James Fitzjames Stephen, among others, also argued that all physical science is only probability that we have no means of measuring and that the entity to which the word "I" points remains an inscrutable mystery (*Liberty, Equality, Fraternity* [London: Smith, Elder, and Co., 1873], 326, 330).

26. Years later, in an article on Bergson, Balfour offered a more forthright statement:

> To me, who am neither idealist nor naturalist, freedom is a reality; partly because, on ethical grounds, I am not prepared to give it up; partly because any theory which, like "naturalism" requires reason to be mechanically determined, is (I believe) essentially incoherent; partly because if we abandon mechanical determinism in the case of reason, it seems absurd to retain it in the case of will; partly because it seems impossible to find room for the self and its psychic states in the interstices of a rigid sequence of material causes and effects. Yet the material sequence is there; the self and its states are there; and I do not pretend to have arrived at a satisfactory view of their reciprocal relations. I keep them both, conscious of their incompatibilities. ("Bergson's Creative Evolution," in *Essays: Speculative and Political* [New York: George H. Doran Co., 1921], 107–8)

27. T. H. Huxley, *Collected Essays* (London: Macmillan and Co., 1894), vol. 6, *Hume: With Helps to the Study of Berkeley*, 221.

28. Huxley, "On the Physical Basis of Life," in *Collected Essays* (1893), vol. 1, *Methods and Results*, 161.

29. Huxley, "Science and Morals," in *Evolution and Ethics and Other Essays* (London: Macmillan and Co., 1894), 128ff.

30. Huxley, "Physical Basis," in *Collected Essays* 1:163.

31. Huxley, "Science and Morals," in *Evolution and Ethics*, 141.

32. Huxley, "Administrative Nihilism," in *Collected Essays*, 1:289.

33. Huxley, "Evolution and Ethics," in *Evolution and Ethics*, 83–84.

34. Ralph Waldo Emerson, *The Complete Works of Ralph Waldo Emerson* (Boston and New York: Houghton Mifflin Co., 1904), vol. 6, *The Conduct of Life*, 4. Subsequent references appear in the text.

35. See Perry Miller's *The American Puritans: Their Prose and Poetry* (Garden City, N.Y.: Doubleday and Co., 1956) for an account of the Puritan tradition of considering life as a moral drama.

36. Stephen E. Whicher, *Freedom and Fate: An Inner Life of Ralph Waldo Emerson* (Philadelphia: University of Pennsylvania Press, 1953), 141.

37. Emerson, *Works*, vol. 12, *Natural History of Intellect* (1921), 46. Elsewhere, Emerson stated his position with greater application to power relations in society. "I like a master standing firm on legs of iron, well-born, rich, handsome, eloquent, loaded with advantages, drawing all men by fascination, into tributaries and supporters of his power. Sword and staff, or talents sword-like or staff-like, carry on the work of the world. But I find him greater when he can abolish himself and all heroes, by letting in this element of reason, irrespective of persons, this subtilizer and irresistible upward force, into our thought, destroying individualism; the power so great that the potentate is nothing" (*Works*, vol. 4, *Representative Men* [1903], 230).

38. Samuel Smiles, *Self-Help, with Illustrations of Conduct and Perseverance* (London: John Murray, 1925), 197. Subsequent references appear in the text.

39. W. E. H. Lecky, *The Map of Life: Conduct and Character* (New York: Longmans, Green, and Co, 1902), 4. Subsequent references appear in the text.

40. Lecky quotes Tennyson's "Will" to ornament his point.

41. Frank Channing Haddock, *Power of Will: A Practical Companion Book for Unfoldment of the Powers of Mind* (Meriden, Conn.: Pelton Publishing Co., 1923), 4. Subsequent references appear in the text.

Notes to Chapter 5: Progress

1. See Stephen Toulmin and June Goodfield, *The Discovery of Time* (Chicago: Chicago University Press, 1982), for a history of western views on time. Bruce McPherson says that in nineteenth-century England, social progress was identified with the idea of perfection of the self (*Between Two Worlds: Victorian Ambivalence about Progress* [Washington, D.C.: University Press of America, 1983], vii). His main examples are Matthew Arnold and John Stuart Mill.

2. This familiar image had been used before but was modernized in the nineteenth century.

3. Henry Drummond, *The Ascent of Man* (New York: James Pott & Co., 1895), 335, 339.

4. Jacob Viner, *The Role of Providence in the Social Order* (Princeton: Princeton University Press, 1972), 4.

5. See Viner for the development of this subject.

6. Charles Bray, *The Philosophy of Necessity; Or, The Law of Consequences; as Applicable to Mental, and Social Science*, 2 vols. (London: Longman, Orme, Brown, Green, and Longmans, 1841), 1:251.

7. Viner, 44.

8. D. P. Crook, *Benjamin Kidd: Portrait of a Social Darwinist* (Cambridge: Cambridge University Press, 1984), 88–89.

9. J. B. Bury, *The Idea of Progress: An Inquiry into Its Growth and Origin* (New York: Dover Publications, 1960), 167. Subsequent references appear in the text.

10. John Passmore, *The Perfectibility of Man* (London: Duckworth, 1970), 83. Subsequent references appear in the text.

11. William Winwood Reade, *The Martyrdom of Man* (New York: Truth Seeker Company, n.d.), 467.

12. Ibid., 514.
13. Henry Sumner Maine, *Popular Government: Four Essays* (London: John Murray, 1885), 131.
14. Robert Nisbet, *History of the Idea of Progress* (New York: Basic Books, 1980) 27. Subsequent references appear in the text.
15. W. W. Reade and H. G. Wells wanted to preserve wilderness areas in the world to provide an arena for man's testing himself against the harshness of nature.
16. Bury discusses Herder's rigid determinism, p. 241.
17. See Joseph Priestley's "An Essay on a Course of Liberal Education for Civil and Active Life," in *Joseph Priestley: Selections from His Writings*, ed. Ira V. Brown (University Park, Pa.: Pennsylvania State University Press, 1962).
18. Rosemary Jann, *The Art and Science of Victorian History* (Columbus: Ohio State University Press, 1985), 74-75 (quoting W. Madden).
19. Walter Bagehot, "Physics and Politics," in *The Works and Life of Walter Bagehot*, ed. Mrs. Russell Barrington (London: Longmans, Green, and Co., 1915), 8:52.
20. James Hinton, *Philosophy and Religion: Selections from the Manuscripts of the Late James Hinton*, ed. Caroline Hadden (London: Kegan Paul, Trench and Co., 1881), 287.
21. Ibid., 277.
22. James Sully, *Pessimism: A History and A Criticism* (London: Henry S. King and Co., 1877), 359.
23. Ibid., 365.
24. Herbert Van Thal, *Eliza Lynn Linton: The Girl of the Period* (London: George Allen & Unwin, 1979), 94 (quoting Layard's *Life*).
25. Bishop Butler had argued that since there is responsibility, there must be free will. This subject is central to W. K. Clifford's "Cosmic Emotion," in *Lectures and Essays*, ed. Leslie Stephen and Sir Frederick Pollock, 2 vols. (London: Macmillan and Co., 1901), vol. 2.
26. Crook, 70.
27. McPherson, 54.
28. John Beattie Crozier, *Civilization and Progress* (London: Longmans, Green, and Co., 1909), 135.
29. See Toulmin and Goodfield for a statement of the apparent contradictoriness of a "historical" Christianity that was nonetheless not developmental in the way the Greek sense of historical continuity was (p. 56).
30. John Newman's *The Development of Christian Doctrine* was, however, a "reactionary" treatment of the developmental idea.
31. William Boyd Carpenter, *The Permanent Elements of Religion* (London: Macmillan and Co., 1889), 55.
32. Ibid., 261.
33. John Fiske, *The Destiny of Man Viewed in the Light of His Origin* (Boston: Houghton, Mifflin and Co., 1898), 25. Subsequent references appear in the text.
34. Benjamin Kidd, *Social Evolution* (New York and London: Macmillan and Co., 1894), 35. Subsequent references appear in the text.
35. Crook, 146.

36. Bury goes on to note the opposition of Quinet and Michelet to the optimism of Hegel and Cousin.
37. William L. Langer, *Political and Social Upheaval, 1832-1852* (New York: Harper and Row, 1969), 115.
38. Patrick Brantlinger, *The Spirit of Reform: British Literature and Politics, 1832-1867* (Cambridge: Harvard University Press, 1977), 77-78. Subsequent references appear in the text. Brantlinger agrees that Carlyle really does not have a conviction about providential design.
39. There have been many studies concerned with the subject of Decadence in society and in literature. Some examples are A. E. Carter's *The Idea of Decadence in French Literature, 1830-1900* (Toronto: University of Toronto Press, 1958); Brantlinger's *Bread and Circuses: Theories of Mass Culture as Social Decay* (Ithaca and London: Cornell University Press, 1983); and John R. Reed's *Decadent Style* (Athens: Ohio University Press, 1985). See also R. K. R. Thornton's *The Decadent Dilemma* (London: Edwin Arnold, 1983) and Linda Dowling's *Language and Decadence in the Victorian Fin de Siècle* (Princeton: Princeton University Press, 1986) for original approaches to Decadent writing.
40. James Fitzjames Stephen, *Liberty, Equality, Fraternity* (London: Smith, Elder, and Co., 1873), 176. Stephen criticized Mill for assuming that progress had been from bad to good and that the law of the strongest had been abandoned in England, arguing that society rested as much on force, if a subtler version, in nineteenth-century England, as in any earlier time (pp. 220ff).
41. James Anthony Froude, "On Progress," in *Short Studies on Great Subjects. Second Series* (New York: Scribner, Armstrong, and Co., 1877), 269.
42. Jacob Burckhardt, *Force and Freedom: Reflections on History*, ed. James Hastings Nichols (Boston: Beacon Press, 1964), 149. See also the introductory essay by Nichols (p. 72).
43. Heinrich von Treitschke, *Politics*, trans. Blanche Dugdale and Torben de Bille, intro. Arthur James Balfour, foreword A. Lawrence Lowell, 2 vols. (New York: Macmillan Co., 1916), 1:xli.
44. Robert Mackintosh, *From Comte to Benjamin Kidd: The Appeal to Biology or Evolution for Human Guidance* (New York: Macmillan Co., 1899).
45. J. W. Burrow, *Evolution and Society: A Study in Victorian Social Theory* (Cambridge: Cambridge University Press, 1970), 173.
46. Arthur James Balfour, "Decadence," in *Essays: Speculative and Political* (New York: George H. Doran Co., 1921), 33.

Notes to Chapter 6: History

1. Goldwin Smith, *Lectures on Modern History Delivered in Oxford, 1859-60* (Oxford and London: J. H. and Jas. Parker, 1861), 13.
2. Wendell Harris examines these conflicting approaches to history in chapter 6 of his *The Omnipresent Debate: Empiricism and Transcendentalism in Nineteenth-Century English Prose* (Dekalb: Northern Illinois University Press, 1981).
3. John Mackinnon Robertson, *Buckle and His Critics: A Study in Sociology*

(London: Swan Sonnschein and Co., 1895), 7. Subsequent references appear in the text.

4. Of course, little account was taken of the subjectivity involved in the perception of history, especially as it might be determined by changing paradigms, after the manner described in the field of scientific inquiry by Thomas S. Kuhn in *The Structure of Scientific Revolutions*, 2d ed., enl. (Chicago: University of Chicago Press, 1970).

5. Ibid., 11.

6. J. W. Burrow, *Evolution and Society: A Study in Victorian Social Theory* (Cambridge: Cambridge University Press, 1970), 106ff.

7. Thomas Carlyle, "On History," in *The Works of Thomas Carlyle*, ed. H. D. Traill (London: Chapman and Hall, 1899), 27:84ff. Subsequent references appear in the text.

8. Philip Rosenberg says that in *Past and Present* "linear narrative is replaced by the polycentric perspective of a sociological sense of history; throne-rooms and assembly halls as scenes of decision-making give place to the street as a scene of action; and rational order is annihilated by the potency of the irrational" (*The Seventh Hero: Thomas Carlyle and the Theory of Radical Activism* [Cambridge: Harvard University Press, 1974], 76). Rosenberg indicates that the influence of Hegel leads to the replacement of a linear with a weblike design for history.

9. Carlyle, "On History Again," in *Works* 28:172.

10. Carlyle, *Past and Present*, in *Works* 10:229.

11. George Levine, *The Boundaries of Fiction: Carlyle, Macaulay, Newman* (Princeton: Princeton University Press, 1968), 30, quoting Sterling. R. H. Hutton called attention to Carlyle's self will and his indictment of Coleridge for weakness of will in his *Essays on Some of the Modern Guides to English Thought in Matters of Faith* (London: Macmillan and Co., 1900), 36, 20. Fred Kaplan examines Carlyle's Leith Walk experience in terms of this question of freedom and self will.

> Having been unable to find emotional security in an act of traditional belief, he had been weakened into suspecting that the world belonged to the Devil, to matter and materialism. But if man is free, he is free to deny both doubt and logic, on the essential ground of his trust in his own feelings. Such a denial confirms that he has the freedom to deny whatever contradicts his spiritual needs. He will be free to reject the life-demeaning elements within himself and the external world. Such control over his own self-definition would enable him to defy whatever obstacles the world raised and to oppose any attempts, public or private, to define him in terms that contradicted his basic sense of himself. (*Thomas Carlyle: A Biography* [Ithaca, N.Y.: Cornell University Press, 1983], 82–83)

12. Philip Rosenberg, 7. By contrast, John D. Rosenberg describes Carlyle's emphasis upon the eclipse of self in *The French Revolution: Carlyle and the Burden of History* (Oxford: Clarendon Press, 1985), 98.

13. Eloise M. Behnken, *Thomas Carlyle: "Calvinist without the Theology"* (Columbia: University of Missouri Press, 1978), 13.
14. Carlyle, "Characteristics," in *Works* 28:9.
15. Carlyle, *Sartor Resartus*, in *Works* 1:146.
16. Carlyle, "Count Cagliostro," in *Works* 28:253.
17. Philip Rosenberg, 201.
18. John D. Rosenberg, 43.
19. Owen Chadwick, *The Secularization of the European Mind in the Nineteenth Century* (Cambridge: Cambridge University Press, 1975), 203-4.
20. Henry Thomas Buckle, *History of Civilization in England*, 2 vols. (New York: D. Appleton and Co., 1859), 1:7.
21. James A. Colaiaco, *James Fitzjames Stephen and the Crisis of Victorian Thought* (New York: St. Martin's Press, 1983), 69. By contrast, the modern philosopher of history Arthur C. Danto blithely remarks that it is "difficult to know what to make of the free-will controversy in its historical applications." In regard to narrative sentences, actions seem to be neither determined nor free (*Narration and Knowledge [including the integral text of Analytical Philosophy of History]* [New York: Columbia University Press, 1985], 186).
22. James Anthony Froude, "The Science of History," *Short Studies on Great Subjects* (New York: Scribner, Armstrong and Co., 1876), 10-11. Subsequent references appear in the text. Froude's resistance to a "science" of history bears some resemblance to Arthur C. Danto's intricate defense of history as something different from science. The organizing schemes of history and science are different. The main feature of history is that it tells stories (Danto, 111).
23. Rosemary Jann says that Froude believed that moral will could overcome necessity, that he worshipped heroes as Carlyle had, and that he believed that the individual was the instrument of Divine Providence (*The Art and Science of Victorian History* [Columbus: Ohio State University Press, 1985], 110-14).
24. Charles Kingsley, *The Limits of Exact Science as Applied to History* (Cambridge and London: Macmillan and Co., 1860), 18. Subsequent references appear in the text.
25. James Martineau, *The Seat of Authority in Religion* (London: Longmans, Green, and Co., 1890), 103, 105.
26. Although Kingsley's position on free will is different from John Stuart Mill's, he praised the "Essay on Liberty" for championing "the self-determining power of the individual, and for his right to use that power" (p. 40).
27. Frederick Denison Maurice, *The Life of Frederick Denison Maurice Chiefly Told in His Own Letters*, ed. Frederick Maurice, 2 vols. (New York: Charles Scribner's Sons, 1884), 411.
28. Maurice, "The Divine Interpretation of History," in *Sermons on the Sabbath-Day, on the Character of the Warrior, and on the Interpretation of History* (London: John W. Parker and Son, 1853), 102. In *The Religion of Rome* (1855), however, Maurice declared: "I believe it is by the progress of some particular people, especially if that progress has been apparently irregular, that we must

learn the law which has been at work everywhere" ([Cambridge: Macmillan and Co., 1855], 321).

29. Maurice, *Rome*, 206-7.

30. Maurice, *Life*, 449.

31. *Life and Letters of Mandell Creighton by His Wife*, 2 vols. (London: Longmans, Green, and Co., 1904), 1:280ff. Creighton wrote to his wife that he assumed that providence knew best if it was arranging for them to leave Oxford; this is only one instance demonstrating his confidence that providence took an individual interest in his fate (1:87).

32. Ibid., 2:404.

33. Gertrude Himmelfarb, upon whom I have depended a great deal in what follows, provides a neat summary of Acton's views in *Lord Acton: A Study in Conscience and Politics* (Chicago: University of Chicago Press, 1952), 3. Subsequent references appear in the text.

34. John Emerich Edward Dalberg Acton, *Historical Essays and Studies*, ed. John Neville Figgis and Reginald Vere Laurence (1907: reprint, Freeport, N.Y.: Books for Libraries Press, 1967), 310. Subsequent references appear in the text.

35. One of Acton's essays is devoted to pointing out factual errors in Buckle's *Civilization*.

36. Jann, 166.

37. Edward A. Freeman, *The Methods of Historical Study* (London: Macmillan and Co., 1886), 151.

38. John Theodore Merz, *A History of European Scientific Thought in the Nineteenth Century*, 2 vols. (1904: reprint, New York: Dover Publications, 1965), 1:121.

39. James Ward, *Essays in Philosophy* (1927: reprint, Freeport, N.Y.: Books for Libraries Press, 1968), 233. Subsequent references appear in the text.

40. Ward addressed the subject of the limits of the will directly. "I am coming to see more clearly every day that man is only half free, or rather that his freedom is not what I once thought it. It is not the power to choose anything, but only the power to choose between alternatives offered, and what these shall be circumstances determine quite as much as will" (p. 59).

41. Ward may have been unjust to the scientific view. Peter L. Thorslev, Jr., points out that materialist philosophers, if not active scientists, were by the end of the eighteenth century already substituting for a "billiard ball" concept of causation a "bee swarm" model. Among these thinkers in England were Priestley and Erasmus Darwin, "who believed that the elementary particles were not passive or inert, but were endowed with energy, life, and purpose: the universe, in other words, was essentially organic, rather than inert and passive" (*Romantic Contraries: Freedom versus Destiny* [New Haven and London: Yale University Press, 1984], 58).

42. Samuel Butler felt that Ward had stolen these ideas from his work.

43. T. W. Heyck, *The Transformation of Intellectual Life in Victorian England* (New York: St. Martin's Press, 1982), 140.

44. Ibid., 123.

45. Heinrich von Treitschke, *Politics*, trans. Blanche Dugdale and Torben de Bille, intro. Arthur James Balfour, foreword A. Lawrence Lowell, 2 vols. (New York: Macmillan Co., 1916), 2:66.

46. Jann, 207.

Notes to Chapter 7: Evolution

1. Wilfred Ward, *Problems and Persons* (London: Longmans, Green, and Co., 1903), 7.

2. William Ewart Gladstone, *Correspondence on Church and Religion*, ed. D. C. Lathbury, 2 vols. (New York: Macmillan Co., 1910), 2:101.

3. Richard Holt Hutton, *Theological Essays*, 3d ed., rev. (London: Macmillan and Co., 1888), 51.

4. Ibid., 55–56.

5. Peter Morton, *The Vital Science: Biology and the Literary Imagination, 1860–1900* (London: George Allen and Unwin, 1984), 68.

6. *Life and Letters of Mandell Creighton by His Wife*, 2 vols. (London: Longmans, Green, and Co., 1904), 1:410–11.

7. William Irvine, *Apes, Angels, and Victorians: Darwin, Huxley, and Evolution* (Cleveland and New York: World Publishing Co., 1966), 83.

8. Frank Miller Turner, *Between Science and Religion: The Reaction of Scientific Naturalism in Late Victorian England* (New Haven and London: Yale University Press, 1974), 77, 96. But see Stephen Jay Gould's *The Mismeasure of Man* (New York: W. W. Norton and Co., 1981) for a study of the many miscalculations during the nineteenth century about the size of the human brain.

9. William Whewell, *The Plurality of Worlds*, intro. Edward Hitchcock (Boston: Gould and Lincoln, 1855), 36. Subsequent references appear in the text.

10. Whewell was an adherent of the catastrophist school of change, a view returning to favor today in a modified form.

11. Morton, 30.

12. Thomas Henry Huxley, *Evolution and Ethics and Other Essays* (London: Macmillan and Co., 1894), 141. Subsequent references appear in the text.

13. See John R. Reed, *The Natural History of H. G. Wells* (Athens: Ohio University Press, 1982).

14. William Kingdon Clifford, *Lectures and Essays*, ed. Leslie Stephen and Sir Frederick Pollock, 2 vols. (London: Macmillan and Co., 1901), 2:33. Subsequent references appear in the text.

15. Carlyle would have endorsed precisely what Clifford feared.

16. Clifford, "Right and Wrong: The Scientific Ground of their Distinction" (1875) in *Lectures and Essays*, 2: 142–43.

17. Huxley, *Collected Essays* (London: Macmillan and Co., 1894), vol. 6, *Hume: With Helps to the Study of Berkeley*, 226. See the earlier discussion of Huxley's views on the will in chapter 4.

18. Gertrude Himmelfarb, *Darwin and the Darwinian Revolution* (New York: W. W. Norton and Co., 1968), 401.

19. Herbert Spencer, *First Principles* (New York: American Home Library, 1902), 336–37n.
20. Spencer, *The Works of Herbert Spencer*, 2 vols. (New York and London: D. Appleton and Co., n.d.), vol. 1, *The Principles of Psychology*, 500–3. Subsequent references appear in the text. R. H. Hutton wrote that there was nothing in Spencer's "conception of the higher life to indicate a real difference of kind between man and a vegetable." He must therefore reject free will—an originating power. Hutton says that Spencer "thinks free-will *a priori* unlikely, because it is not a self-adjusting *apparatus*, but a self-adjusting spirit; because it is not determined absolutely by the external world, but determines itself after free intelligent judgment on both worlds, internal and external. 'The psychical states,' as Mr. Spencer denominates a *man*, 'cannot determine their own cohesions.' I do not know a more remarkable instance of the confusion between the *unity* of the sciences and the *identity* of the sciences, than is given by this development of voluntary life out of the idea of vegetable life" (pp. 47–48).
21. J. W. Burrow, *Evolution and Society: A Study in Victorian Social Theory* (Cambridge: Cambridge University Press, 1970), 222.
22. Samuel Butler, "God the Known and God the Unknown," *Collected Essays*, in *The Shrewsbury Edition of the Works of Samuel Butler*, ed. Henry Festing Jones and A. T. Bartholomew, 20 vols. (London: Jonathan Cape, 1925), 1:46. Subsequent references appear in the text.
23. See Reed, *Wells*, p. 91.
24. Butler, *Life and Habit*, in *Works*, 4:25. There is an interesting relationship between Butler's view and Clifford's notion, derivative from Carpenter, that the self is made free by being an automaton. Subsequent references appear in the text.
25. Butler, *Samuel Butler's Notebooks*, ed. Geoffrey Keynes and Brian Hill (London: Jonathan Cape, 1951), 197.
26. Turner, 192.
27. Morton, chap. 2.
28. Edwin Arnold, "Aspects of Life," in *East and West* (London: Longmans, Green, and Co., 1896), 35. Subsequent references appear in the text.
29. Referring to Huxley's use of Eastern terms in his essay, Arnold observed that Orientals accepted two laws governing the Cosmos—Dharma, or Love, and Karma, or Justice (p. 48).
30. John Fiske, *The Destiny of Man Viewed in the Light of His Origin* (Boston: Houghton, Mifflin and Co., 1898), 25.
31. Ibid., 65.
32. Henry Drummond, *The Ascent of Man* (New York: James Pott and Co., 1895), 127.
33. Burrow, 222.
34. Huxley, *Collected Essays* (London: Macmillan and Co., 1893), vol. 1, *Methods and Results*, 275.
35. Walter Bagehot, *The Works and Life of Walter Bagehot*, ed. Mrs. Russell Barrington, 10 vols. (London: Longmans, Green, and Co., 1915), 8:126, 129.
36. W. H. Mallock, *Aristocracy and Evolution: A Study of the Rights, the Origin, and the Social Functions of the Wealthier Classes* (London: Adam and Charles Black, 1898), 58. Subsequent references appear in the text.

37. J. B. Schneewind deals with this double tradition in *Sidgwick's Ethics and Victorian Moral Philosophy* (Oxford: Clarendon Press, 1977), 383. And a concern for a similar division provides the basis for Wendell V. Harris's *The Omnipresent Debate* (Dekalb: Northern Illinois University Press, 1981).

38. Thomas Hill Green, *The Works of Thomas Hill Green*, ed. by R. L. Nettleship, 3 vols. (New York: Kraus Reprints, 1969), *Miscellanies and Memoir* 3:xxix. Subsequent references appear in the text.

39. Arthur Balfour, *Essays: Speculative and Political* (New York: George H. Doran Company, 1921), 107. Subsequent references appear in the text.

40. Henri Bergson, *Time and Free Will*, trans. F. L. Pogson (London: George Allen and Unwin, 1910), 162ff. Subsequent references appear in the text.

41. Bergson, *Matter and Memory*, trans. Nancy Margaret Paul and W. Scott Palmer (London: George Allen and Co., 1912), 325.

42. T. H. Green's definition of freedom bears some relationship to Bergson's. Even more intriguing is the similarity of Bergson's attitude toward the as-yet undeveloped hypotheses to emerge as quantum physics.

43. Burrow, 272.

44. L. T. Hobhouse, *Mind in Evolution* (London: Macmillan and Co., 1915), 338. Subsequent references appear in the text.

45. Hobhouse, *Morals in Evolution: A Study in Comparative Ethics* (London: Chapman and Hall, 1951), 504. Subsequent references appear in the text.

46. Edward O. Wilson, *On Human Nature*, (Cambridge: Harvard University Press, 1978), 78, 71.

Notes to Chapter 8: Madness

1. Vieda Skultans, ed., *Madness and Morals: Ideas on Insanity in the Nineteenth Century* (London: Routledge & Kegan Paul, 1975), 2. Subsequent references appear in the text.

2. William Battie, *A Treatise on Madness*, intro and annot. Richard Hunter and Ida Macalpine (London: Dawsons of Pall Mall, 1962), 43–44.

3. John Monro, *Remarks on Dr. Battie's Treatise on Madness*, intro. and annot. Richard Hunter and Ida Macalpin (London: Dawsons of Pall Mall, 1962), 50.

4. William F. Bynum, Jr., "Rationales for Therapy in British Psychiatry, 1780–1845," in *Madhouses, Mad-Doctors, and Madmen: The Social History of Psychiatry in the Victorian Era*, ed. Andrew Scull (Philadelphia: University of Pennsylvania Press, 1981), 51.

5. George Combe, *The Constitution of Man Considered in Relation to External Objects* (Boston: Sanborn, Carter and Bazin, 1856), 51ff (first published, 1828).

6. Ibid., 276. Combe nonetheless recommends punishment.

7. David de Giustino, *Conquest of Mind: Phrenology and Victorian Social Thought* (London: Croom Helm, 1975), 116.

8. Johann Christoph Spurzheim, *Observations on the Deranged Manifestations of the Mind, or Insanity* (Gainesville, Fla.: Scholars' Facsimiles and Reprints, 1970), 53, 111.

9. de Giustino, 117. See also Alastair Cameron Grant's essay "Combe on Phrenol-

ogy and Free Will: A Note on XIXth-Century Secularism," *Journal of the History of Ideas* 26, no. 1 (1965), 141–47.

10. See Stephen Jay Gould's *The Mismeasure of Man* (New York: W. W. Norton and Co., 1981) for an account of the continued attempts to evaluate the significance of brain size.

11. Roger Cooter defends phrenology as the most important vehicle for the progress of psychiatry in the midnineteenth century, "Phrenology and British Alienists, ca. 1825–1845," in *Madhouses*, 58. See also Cooter's *The Cultural Meaning of Popular Science: Phrenology and the Organization of Consent in Nineteenth-Century Britain* (Cambridge: Cambridge University Press, 1984), a thorough examination of the political, social, and cultural intricacies associated with the "pseudo-science" of phrenology in the nineteenth century.

12. Ann C. Colley suggests that almost any excess was sufficient to register as a cause of madness (*Tennyson and Madness* [Athens: The University of Georgia Press, 1983], 17). See George Frederick Drinka's *The Birth of Neurosis: Myth, Malady and the Victorians* (New York: Simon & Schuster, 1984) for an account of the many varying interpretations of neurosis and its causes in the nineteenth century.

13. Colley, 20. Colley offers a clear summary of these attitudes and draws a helpful distinction between the moralists and the somatists.

14. Elaine Showalter summarizes the attitude of many Victorian medical men when she writes: "Whether drunkenness or excitement was the cause, Victorian doctors believed that in most cases insanity was preventable if individuals were prepared to use their willpower to fight off mental disorder and to avoid excess. Mental health was to be achieved by a life of moderation and by the energetic exercise of the will" (*The Female Malady: Women, Madness, and English Culture, 1830–1980* [New York: Pantheon Books, 1985], 30).

15. Andrew Scull, *Museums of Madness: The Social Organization of Insanity in Nineteenth-Century England* (New York: St. Martin's Press, 1979), 119.

16. Colley, 18–19.

17. Charles Reade used Conolly as a target for criticism in his novel *Hard Cash*.

18. John Conolly, *An Inquiry concerning the Indications of Insanity with Suggestions for the Better Protection and Care of the Insane*, ed. Richard Hunter and Ida Macalpine (London: Dawsons of Pall Mall, 1964), 295–96.

19. Ibid., 346.

20. John Barlow, *On Man's Power over Himself to Prevent or Control Insanity* (London: William Pickering, 1843), 12–13.

21. James Braid, *The Power of the Mind over the Body: An Experimental Inquiry into the Nature and Cause of the Phenomena Attributed by Baron Reichenbach and Others to a "New Imponderable"* (London: John Churchill, 1846), 15. See also Robert Darnton's *Mesmerism and the End of the Enlightenment in France* (New York: Schocken Books, 1968) and Fred Kaplan's *Dickens and Mesmerism: The Hidden Springs of Fiction* (Princeton: Princeton University Press, 1975), and for further discussion of nineteenth-century attitudes toward mesmerism. Drinka discusses the use of hypnosis by Charcot and others in the treatment of hysteria and other neuroses.

22. Braid, 36.

23. Spurzheim, 75.

24. George Moore, *The Power of the Soul over the Body, Considered in Relation to Health and Morals* (New York: Harper and Brothers, 1861), 59ff. Subsequent references appear in the text.

25. Moore, *Man and His Motives* (New York: Harper and Brothers, 1862), 79ff. Subsequent references appear in the text.

26. Thomas Laycock, *Mind and Brain: or, the Correlations of Consciousness and Organization; Systematically Investigated and Applied to Philosophy, Mental Science and Practice*, 2 vols. (New York: D. Appleton and Co., 1860), 276. Subsequent references appear in the text.

27. Henry Maudsley, *Responsibility in Mental Disease* (New York: D. Appleton and Co., 1876), 269. Subsequent references appear in the text.

28. Maudsley, *Body and Will; Being an Essay concerning Will in its Metaphysical, Physiological, and Pathological Aspects* (London: Kegan Paul, Trench, and Co., 1883), 41–42. Subsequent references appear in the text.

29. In examining Maudsley's influential role in shaping the character of late nineteenth-century psychological practice, Elaine Showalter overemphasizes, I think, Maudsley's pessimistic outlook regarding human destiny, suggesting that he was more convinced of human degeneracy than of human improvability (pp. 118ff).

30. William B. Carpenter, *Nature and Man: Essays Scientific and Philosophical*, intro. J. Estlin Carpenter (London: Kegan Paul, Trench and Co., 1888), 282–83. Subsequent references appear in the text.

31. Carpenter, *Principles of Mental Physiology* (New York: D. Appleton and Co., 1896), 14. Subsequent references appear in the text. Carpenter, *Nature*, 183–84.

32. James Sully, *The Human Mind: A Textbook of Psychology*, 2 vols. (New York: D. Appleton and Co., 1892), 294.

33. Ibid., 295.

34. Nigel Walker, *Crime and Insanity in England* (Edinburgh: University Press, 1968), 74–80. See also Jacques M. Quen's "Psychiatry and the Law: Historical Relevance to Today," in *By Reason of Insanity: Essays on Psychiatry and the Law*, ed. Lawrence Zelic Freedman (Wilmington, Del.: Scholarly Resources, 1983).

35. See Stephen White's "The Insanity Defense in England and Wales since 1843," in *The Insanity Defense: The Annals of the American Academy of Political and Social Science*, ed. Richard Moran (London: Sage Publications, 1985), 43–57. See also Quen on the substitution of the ALI (American Law Institute) rule for the McNaughtan and Durham rules in recent American law determinations.

36. Kathleen Jones, *Lunacy, Law, and Conscience, 1744–1845* (London: Routledge and Kegan Paul, 1955), 28.

37. Ibid., 66.

38. Other issues related to madness had to do with the just or unjust confinement of a spouse or other relative for various reasons. Bulwer and Thackeray both confined their wives in asylums. The case of Lady Mordaunt was notorious and is mentioned in Roy Jenkins's *Victorian Scandal* (New York: Pyramid Books,

1969), 193. See chapter 9 of John R. Reed's *Victorian Conventions* (Athens: Ohio University Press, 1975) for a survey of some literary treatments of this theme.

39. Walker, 125ff. Lionel Rose's *The Massacre of the Innocents: Infanticide in Britain 1800–1939* (London: Routledge and Kegan Paul, 1986) examines this subject in detail. See especially chapters 7 and 8 about lenient treatment of mothers accused of infanticide. See also Showalter, who discusses the negative features for women of this apparently humane discrimination (pp. 58–59).

40. Smith, 156. See also Drinka on the association of women with emotional susceptibility and hysteria.

41. Michael Ignatieff's *A Just Measure of Pain: The Penitentiary in the Industrial Revolution, 1750–1850* (New York: Columbia University Press, 1978) provides a detailed account of some aspects of reform of the legal system.

42. Combe, 284. Cooter discusses Combe's views in *Popular Science*, 101ff.

43. Gould, *Ever Since Darwin* (New York: W. W. Norton and Company, 1977), 222ff. See also Gould's *Mismeasure* regarding tests for measuring intellect and Drinka on Cesare Lombroso (pp. 158ff).

44. Richard Moran, *Knowing Right From Wrong: The Insanity Defense of Daniel McNaughtan* (New York: Free Press, 1981), 109. Subsequent references appear in the text.

45. Moran uses *U.S. v. Dougherty* to show that the law still needs a careful definition of political crime in relationship to the insanity plea (pp. 128ff). See chapter 7 of Jonathan Glover's *Responsibility* (New York: Humanities Press, 1970) for a discussion of the McNaughton Rule and medical exemptions in legal proceedings.

46. William J. Winslade and Judith Wilson Ross, *The Insanity Plea* (New York: Charles Scribner's Sons, 1983), 18. The authors detail the bizarre results of some notable cases. For example, five specialists commented on the condition of Dan White, the murderer of George Mosconi and Harvey Milk in San Francisco in 1978, and essentially concluded that the fact that White shot these men was evidence that he was mentally unbalanced. "If you murder someone and you are not ordinarily a killer, and it is not self-defense, then you have lost control. If you have lost control, then you do not have sufficient capacity to premeditate, to deliberate, or to harbor malice" (p. 46). In another case, defense and prosecution lawyers reversed their positions from the trial to the postverdict hearings and appeals, the defense originally arguing for insanity and then against, the prosecution against and then for (p. 157). It should come as no surprise that Winslade and Ross recommend abolition of the insanity plea.

47. Lawrence Zelic Freedman argues a similar dualism in modern psychiatry. Psychoanalysis, he says, is mentalistic, but practical applications of psychiatry, as in the law, are monistic, assuming that brain, mind, and body are all one ("Psychiatry and Law," in *By Reason of Insanity*, 119).

48. Thomas Carlyle, *Past and Present*, in *Works* (London: Chapman and Hall, 1887), 10:19.

49. "Are Madmen Irresponsible?" *Saturday Review* 1, no. 16 (16 Feb 1856): 298. In *Madness and the Criminal Law* (Chicago: University of Chicago Press, 1982), Norval Morris recommends abolition of the insanity plea, arguing that

those found incapable to stand trial, guilty but insane, etc., actually stand to suffer more than those who are defended according to normal legal methods. See especially chapter 2.

50. Roger Smith, *Trial by Medicine: Insanity and Responsibility in Victorian Trials* (Edinburgh: Edinburgh University Press, 1981), 50. Subsequent references appear in the text.

51. Barlow, 25–28.

52. Virginia Berridge and Griffith Edwards, *Opium and the People: Opiate Use in Nineteenth-Century England* (New York: St. Martin's Press, 1981), 157, 223. See also chapter 9 of Reed's *Victorian Conventions.*

53. See Winslade and Ross for an examination of the paradox in modern law and psychiatry.

54. Walker, "The Insanity Defense before 1800," in *Annals,* 26.

55. Ibid., 30.

56. William Woodward, "Introduction: Stretching the Limits of Psychology's History," in *The Problematic Science: Psychology in Nineteenth-Century Thought,* ed. William R. Woodward and Mitchell G. Ash (New York: Prager Publishers, 1982), 3ff.

57. Robert J. Richards, "Darwin and the Biologizing of Moral Behavior," in *The Problematic Science,* 52.

58. Edward Sagarin and Robert J. Kelley, "Responsibility and Crime in Literature," in *Annals,* 23–24.

Notes to Introduction to Part 2

1. Lionel Trilling, *Sincerity and Authenticity* (Cambridge: Harvard University Press, 1972), 99.

2. Ibid., 117.

3. Lionel Trilling's "Art, Will, and Necessity," examines "the devaluation of will" in contemporary high culture (in *The Last Decade: Essays and Reviews, 1965–75* [New York: Harcourt Brace Jovanovich, 1977], 139).

4. Samuel T. Coleridge, *On the Constitution of Church and State,* ed. John Colmer (Princeton: Princeton University Press, 1976), 10:32.

5. Trilling, *Sincerity,* 138.

6. James Martineau, *The Seat of Authority in Religion* (London: Longmans, Green, and Co., 1890), 102.

7. Grace Paley, *Enormous Changes at the Last Minute* (New York: Farrar, Straus and Giroux, 1974), 160–67. In *The Turn of the Novel: The Transition to Modern Fiction* (London: Oxford University Press, 1966), Alan Friedman draws a distinction between the parallel traditions of closed and open novels.

8. Susan Sontag, *Against Interpretation and Other Essays* (New York: Farrar, Straus and Giroux, 1966) 31.

9. Trilling, "Art," 130.

10. E. S. Dallas, *The Gay Science,* 2 vols. (London: Chapman and Hall, 1866; New York: Johnson Reprint Corporation, 1969), 2:293.

11. Herbert Tucker is one of many recent critics to employ this assumption. He gives

credit to Bloom and Smith for their assertion that a state of mind implies a way of stating and vice versa and offers as the central argument of his own book "that Browning's moral doctrine of incompleteness finds a clear aesthetic analogue in his poetics" (*Browning's Beginnings: The Art of Disclosure* [Minneapolis: University of Minnesota Press, 1980], 5).

12. J. Hillis Miller, "Narrative and History," *ELH* 41, no. 3 (Fall 1974): 455–73.
13. William H. Gass, *Fiction and the Figures of Life* (New York: Alfred A. Knopf, 1970), 3. Subsequent references appear in the text.
14. David Goldknopf, *The Life of the Novel* (Chicago: University of Chicago Press, 1972), 106.
15. Robert L. Caserio, *Plot, Story, and the Novel: From Dickens and Poe to the Modern Period* (Princeton: Princeton University Press, 1979), 113. Subsequent references appear in the text.
16. Peter Brooks, *Reading for the Plot: Design and Intention in Narrative* (New York: Vintage Books, 1985), 37. Subsequent references appear in the text.
17. Charles Dickens, *A Christmas Carol*, in *Christmas Books* (Oxford: Oxford University Press, 1987), 24.

Notes to Chapter 9: Romantic to Victorian Poetry

1. Wendell V. Harris offers a new assessment of these opposed figures in *The Omnipresent Debate* (Dekalb: Northern Illinois University Press, 1981).
2. John Stuart Mill, *Autobiography*, in *Collected Works of John Stuart Mill*, ed. John M. Robson and Jack Stillinger (Toronto: University of Toronto Press, 1981), 153.
3. Matthew Arnold, "Wordsworth," in *Complete Prose Works*, ed. R. H. Super (Ann Arbor: University of Michigan Press, 1973), 9:48.
4. Morse Peckham suggests the early advent of the Victorian compromise in "Toward a Theory of Romanticism," in *The Triumph of Romanticism* (Columbia: University of South Carolina Press, 1970), 19. The essay originally appeared in 1950. For Victorian reactions against the Romantics see chapter 2 of Jerome Hamilton Buckley's *The Victorian Temper* (New York: Random House, 1951).
5. In *Natural Supernaturalism* (New York: W. W. Norton & Co., 1971), M. H. Abrams excludes Byron from his discussion of the Romantics because in his greatest works he "speaks with an ironic counter-voice and deliberately opens a satirical perspective on the vitic stance of his Romantic contemporaries" (p. 13). Byron displayed an interest in the Satanic will, not much resembling the attention to free will and will as volition that I examine in the other Romantics.
6. A. Dwight Culler makes this suggestion more than once in *Imaginative Reason: The Poetry of Matthew Arnold* (New Haven: Yale University Press, 1966).
7. See George H. Ford's *Keats and the Victorians* (New Haven: Yale University Press, 1944) for details of these relationships.
8. Michael G. Cooke's *The Romantic Will* (New Haven: Yale University Press, 1976) is an elaborate examination of the general topic but from a different perspective than my own. Wordsworth came to redefine reason as the highest form of imagination, thereby returning imagination to the region of control, order,

plan, and direction. The Victorians generally accepted this view, most particularly Matthew Arnold, who put great emphasis upon what he called "imaginative reason" (Culler, 282–83).

9. See Melvin M. Rader's *Presiding Ideas in Wordsworth's Poetry* (1931; reprint, New York: Gordian Press, 1968) for a discussion of Wordsworth's developing views on necessity and will. Helen Darbishire's "Wordsworth's Belief in the Doctrine of Necessity," *Review of English Studies* 24 (1948): 121–25, treats the theme of necessity succinctly.

10. John P. Clark, *The Philosophical Anarchism of William Godwin* (Princeton: Princeton University Press, 1977), 51.

11. See Joseph Barrell's *Shelley and the Thought of His Time: A Study in the History of Ideas* (New Haven: Yale University Press, 1947) for a notation of some of these inconsistencies.

12. Percy B. Shelley, *The Complete Poetical Works*, ed. Neville Rogers (Oxford: Clarendon Press, 1972), 1:273, 264. Subsequent references appear in the text. For works not included in Rogers's edition, I have used *Shelley's Poetry and Prose*, ed. Donald H. Reiman and Sharon B. Powers (New York: Norton, 1977). Subsequent references appear in the text.

13. Neville Rogers, *Shelley at Work: A Critical Inquiry* (Oxford: Oxford University Press, 1967), 33. In *Radical Shelley: The Philosophical Anarchism and Utopian Thought of Percy Bysshe Shelley* (Princeton: Princeton University Press, 1982), Michael Scrivener describes Shelley's philosophical dualism, a position that "is somewhat paradoxical, but it is not muddle-headed." Nature and mind are governed by necessity. But there is another dialectic at work in society—the conflict between "spirit" and "sensualism." The one follows the laws of nature and obeys the authority of reason; the other is characterized by exploitation and domination. "What gives meaning to human life is not mere human existence, but the spirit in which people live their lives. The virtuous individual has the will to resist domination. 'Nature, impartial in munificence, / Has gifted man with all-subduing will' (V, 132–33). Virtue and will war against wealth and power . . . the ideal rebel lives a 'life of resolute good, / Unalterable will, quenchless desire / Of universal happiness. . . .' (V, 223–27)" (pp. 70–71).

14. Earl R. Wasserman, *Shelley: A Critical Reading* (Baltimore: Johns Hopkins University Press, 1971), 288. See also Charles E. Robinson, *Shelley and Byron: The Snake and Eagle Wreathed in Flight* (Baltimore: Johns Hopkins University Press, 1976), 124.

15. The contrast in the two poets' ways of thinking is at the heart of Robinson's study. Charles duBos argues that the fatalist attitude is the driving force in Byron's career (*Byron and the Need of Fatality*, trans. Ethel Colburn Mayne [London, 1932]). Byron was enough of an ironist to note in *Don Juan* that fate was a good excuse for our own will (canto 13, stanza 12). The same idea appears in *Lara* where the hero "half mistook for fate the acts of will" (stanza 18).

16. John Keats, *The Letters of John Keats*, ed. Hyder Edward Rollins (Cambridge, Mass.: Harvard University Press, 1958), 2:102.

17. Keats, *The Poems of John Keats*, ed. Miriam Allott (London, Longman: 1970), 422, 403.

18. Ibid., 426.
19. Ward Hellstrom shows Tennyson's relationship to the liberal humanist historians who held similar beliefs in *On the Poems of Tennyson* (Gainesville: University of Florida Press, 1972). For a stricter examination of this subject, see Henry Kozicki's *Tennyson and Clio: History in the Major Poems* (Baltimore: Johns Hopkins University Press, 1979), esp. chaps. 7 and 8.
20. But see William R. Brashear's *The Living Will: A Study of Tennyson and Nineteenth-Century Subjectivism* (The Hague: Mouton, 1969), which examines Tennyson's view of the will in detail but from a different perspective.
21. Alfred Lord Tennyson, *The Poems of Tennyson*, ed. Christopher Ricks (London: Longmans, Green, 1969), 978. Subsequent references appear in the text.
22. Hallam Tennyson, *Alfred Lord Tennyson: A Memoir by His Son* (New York: Macmillan, 1905), 1:308.
23. Wilfrid Ward, *Problems and Persons* (London: Longmans, Green, 1903), 216–17.
24. John Tulloch, *Movements of Religious Thought in Britain during the Nineteenth Century* (1885: reprint, Leicester: Leicester University Press, 1971), p. 263.
25. See John R. Reed, *Perception and Design in Tennyson's Idylls of the King* (Athens: Ohio University Press, 1970).
26. *The Saturday Review* 1, no. 1 (3 Nov. 1855): 14.
27. Lionel Trilling illustrates the debt to Spinoza in detail in *Matthew Arnold* (Cleveland: World Publishing Co., 1965), 295ff. Spinoza, of course, did not accept the doctrine of free will.
28. See Joseph Carroll's *The Cultural Theory of Matthew Arnold* (Berkeley and Los Angeles: University of California Press, 1982), 47.
29. Arnold, vol. 5, *Culture and Anarchy*, 255. Subsequent references appear in the text.
30. Leon Gottfried, in studying Arnold's response to the Romantics, refers to his "negative romanticism" which requires "the rigorous subjection of the ego to natural law" (*Matthew Arnold and the Romantics* [Lincoln: University of Nebraska Press, 1963], 207).
31. R. H. Super quotes this passage from the so-called "Yale Manuscript" in *The Time-Spirit of Matthew Arnold* (Ann Arbor: University of Michigan Press, 1970), 15.
32. Arnold, *The Poems of Matthew Arnold*, ed. Kenneth Allott (London: Longmans, 1965), 140. Subsequent references appear in the text.
33. Arnold admitted the influence of Sénancour on this thought, and one can see the resemblance between the two in some passages from *Obermann* (London: Philip Welby, 1933): In letter xliii Obermann speaks of the confined life of most men. "Despite his apparent liberty, he can produce, outside the acts of his life, no more than a man whose life is wasted in a dungeon. . . . I do not mean that chance brings about human affairs, but I think that these are overruled, at least in part, by a power alien to man, and that a concurrence independent of our will is essential to success" (pp. 156–57). Obermann complains, "I do not know what to will, and hence I must will all things," but this willing is merely a struggle

against the void and does not lead to freedom, for "to act means to will, and to will is to be dependent" (pp. 158, 160). Freedom comes in renunciation.

34. Patrick J. McCarthy, *Matthew Arnold and the Three Classes* (New York: Columbia University Press, 1964), 85.

35. Quoted in Ruth apRoberts's *Arnold and God* (Berkeley and Los Angeles: University of California Press, 1983), 58, from Arnold's *Notebooks*, 40, 50, 72.

36. Norton B. Crowell discusses the will in Browning in *The Convex Glass: The Mind of Robert Browning* (Albuquerque: The University of New Mexico Press, 1968), 125, 161.

37. Robert Browning, *Learned Lady: Letters from Robert Browning to Mrs. Thomas FitzGerald, 1876–1889*, ed. Edward C. McAleer (1912; reprint, Cambridge: Harvard University Press, 1966), 34.

38. Browning, *The Complete Poetical Works of Robert Browning*, ed. F. G. Kenyon (1912: reprint, New York, 1966), 4:268. Subsequent references appear in the text.

39. Elizabeth Barrett Browning, *Poetical Works* (New York: T. Y. Crowell & Co., 1891), 146. Subsequent references appear in the text.

40. Earl Hilton, "Browning's *Sordello* as a Study of the Will," *PMLA* 69 (1954): 1127–34.

41. Herbert Tucker, Jr., *Browning's Beginnings: The Art of Disclosure* (Minneapolis: University of Minnesota Press, 1980), 5.

42. Ibid., 10.

43. Edward Dowden, *Studies in Literature, 1789–1877* (London: Kegan Paul, Trench & Co., 1889), 192–93. Subsequent references appear in the text.

44. Lee Erickson, *Robert Browning: His Poetry and His Audiences* (Ithaca: Cornell University Press, 1984), 157.

45. Daniel Karlin, *The Courtship of Robert Browning and Elizabeth Barrett* (Oxford: Clarendon Press, 1985), 137ff.

46. *Robert Browning's Prose Life of Strafford*, ed. H. Firth and F. J. Furnivall (1892), 60–61 (quoted by Michael Mason in "Browning and the Dramatic Monologue," in *Robert Browning*, ed. Isobel Armstrong [Athens: Ohio University Press, 1975], 253–54).

47. Walter Pater, *The Renaissance*, ed. Donald Hill (Berkeley and Los Angeles: University of California Press, 1980), 171. It is interesting that in describing the refinements of poetic and visual arts, Pater reverses Browning's light metaphor, concentrating rays where Browning fractures them. "To realize this situation, to define in a chill and empty atmosphere, the focus where rays, in themselves pale and impotent, unite and begin to burn, the artist may have, indeed, to employ the most cunning detail, to complicate and refine upon thought and passion a thousandfold."

48. Chris Snodgrass, "Swinburne's Circle of Desire: A Decadent Theme, in *Decadence and the 1890s*, ed. Ian Fletcher (London: Edward Arnold, 1979), 67.

49. Ibid., 73.

50. William Kingdon Clifford, *Lectures and Essays*, ed. Leslie Stephen and Sir Frederick Pollock, 2 vols. (London: Macmillan and Co., 1901), 2:291.

51. Algernon Charles Swinburne, *Poems* (Philadelphia: David McKay, n.d.), 171. Subsequent references appear in the text.

52. See also Reed's "Swinburne's *Tristram of Lyonesse:* The Poet-Lover's Song of Love," *Victorian Poetry* 4, no. 2 (Spring 1966): 99–120.

53. Mathilde Blind, *The Ascent of Man,* intro. Alfred R. Wallace (London: T. Fisher Unwin, 1899).

54. Edward Robert Bulwer-Lytton, *Letters from Owen Meredith (Robert, First Earl of Lytton) to Robert and Elizabeth Barrett Browning,* ed. Aurelia Brooks Harlan and J. Lee Harlan, Jr. (Waco, Tx., 1936), 36.

55. Bulwer-Lytton, *Personal and Literary Letters of Robert First Earl of Lytton,* ed. Lady Betty Balfour, 2 vols. (London: Longmans, Green, and Co., 1906), 1:87. Subsequent references appear in the text.

56. Owen Meredith [Edward Robert Bulwer-Lytton], "The Wanderer," in *Poems* (Boston: Houghton, Mifflin, and Co., 1881), 264, 268. Subsequent references appear in the text.

57. Meredith [Edward Robert Bulwer-Lytton], *Glenaveril; or the Metamorphoses,* 2 vols. (London: John Murray, 1885), 1:218ff. Subsequent references appear in the text.

58. D. C. Somervell, *English Thought in the Nineteenth Century* (New York: David McKay Co., 1965), 225. Robert Bernard Martin says that FitzGerald's poem shared a characteristic with such other famous publications of the year 1859 as *Self-Help, On Liberty, Adam Bede, The Ordeal of Richard Feverel,* and *The Origin of Species,* which was "a repudiation of traditional religious morality and the attempt to find an alternative to it" (*With Friends Possessed: A Life of Edward FitzGerald* [London: Faber and Faber, 1985], 221). The case fits for all but Smiles's book, I think.

59. Gilbert K. Chesterton, *Heretics* (New York: John Lane Co., 1919), 106.

60. Edward FitzGerald, *The Rubáiyát of Omar Khayyám* (New York: Walter J. Black, 1942), 59–60. Subsequent references appear in the text. Martin says that FitzGerald early came to a "disbelieving tolerance of Christianity" and notes that his letters indicate that he was attracted to Omar for philosophical rather than aesthetic reasons (*Friends,* 66, 202–3).

61. FitzGerald, *Rubáiyát of Omar Khayyám,* ed. Carl J. Weber (Waterville, Me.: Colby College Press, 1959), 94. Michael Millgate makes no mention of this incident in his recent biography of Hardy, but Robert Gittings does in *Thomas Hardy's Later Years* (Boston: Little, Brown and Co., 1978), 211.

62. See Robert M. Young's *Mind, Brain and Adaptation in the Nineteenth Century* (Oxford: Clarendon Press, 1970) for a discussion of the gradual development of brain research in the nineteenth century.

63. Thomas Carlyle, *The Works of Thomas Carlyle* (London: Chapman and Hall, 1896) vol. 3, *The French Revolution: A History,* 102. Italics mine.

64. Quoted in John H. Muirhead's *Coleridge as Philosopher* (New York: Macmillan Co., 1930) from the manuscript commonplace book entitled "Semina, Rerum, Audita, Cogitata, Cogitanda of a Man of Letters, etc." (pp. 122–23).

65. Ibid., 126–27.

66. One could trace the use of cave and other enclosure images from Coleridge, Wordsworth, Shelley, and Keats, to Tennyson, Arnold, Browning, and others to illustrate the topographical manner in which the descent into the self was seen, with differing emphases, as part of an essential pattern.

67. Samuel Taylor Coleridge, *Biographia Literaria*, 2 vols. (London: Oxford University Press, 1962), 1:202.
68. The pattern that I have offered here for Coleridge's model of the will, Laurence S. Lockridge sees as Coleridge's habit of mind, which is "to seek greater and greater inclusiveness, to circle around the object of consciousness in ever widening gyres just as his periodic prose does. His metaphors are of absorption, vegetative growth, or widening circumferences" (*Coleridge the Moralist* [Ithaca, N.Y.: Cornell University Press, 1977], 196).
69. Coleridge, *The Notebooks of Samuel Taylor Coleridge*, ed. Kathleen Coburn (Princeton: Princeton University Press, 1973), 3:4109.
70. Rogers, 91ff, 68–9, 126. Daniel Hughes's "Blake and Shelley: Beyond the Uroboros," in *William Blake: Essays for S. Foster Damon*, ed. Alvin H. Rosenfeld (Providence, R.I.: Brown University Press, 1969), 69–83, reveals some transformations of the circle imagery and also indicates that Blake's use of this imagery balances oddly between what I have described as Romantic and Victorian impulses. Morton Paley's *Energy and the Imagination: A Study of the Development of Blake's Thought* (Oxford: Clarendon Press, 1970) illustrates the ambivalence of the image in Blake: "The circular folds of the Orc serpent suggest that history is a bound circle which channels and contains energy, limiting it to a repetition of the same dull round of promise and betrayal. . . . Seen in this way, history is a nightmare of recurrence. There is, however, another perspective: seen from outside the bound circle, history becomes an ever-expanding spiral from which man can leap into a transcendent reality" (pp. 122–23).
71. William Drummond, *Academical Questions* (London: Cadell & Davies, 1805), 1:45.
72. These lines were rejected for "Ode to Duty." See William Wordsworth, *The Poetical Works of William Wordsworth*, ed. E. de Selincourt and Helen Darbishire (Oxford: Oxford University Press, 1947), 4:185.
73. Geoffrey H. Hartman, *Wordsworth's Poetry, 1787–1814* (New Haven: Yale University Press, 1964), 202.
74. Wordsworth, *The Prelude or Growth of a Poet's Mind*, ed. Ernest de Selincourt and Helen Darbishire (Oxford: Oxford University Press, 1959), 55, 183. Subsequent references appear in the text.
75. Hartman, 198. An interesting manifestation of this interest in blurred boundaries is the popularity of the vignette as an art form in the Romantic period. Charles Rosen and Henri Zerner remark that it "presents itself both as a global metaphor for the world and as a fragment. Dense at its center, tenuous on the periphery, it seems to disappear into the page" (*Romanticism and Realism: The Mythology of Nineteenth-Century Art* [New York: Viking Press, 1984], 81).
76. Hazlitt remarked that a philosopher should say, not "I will lead you into all knowledge," but "I will show you a mystery" (Roy Park, *Hazlitt and the Spirit of the Age: Abstraction and Critical Theory* [Oxford: Clarendon Press, 1971], p. 29), and Coleridge operated on the assumption that *there is nothing the absolute ground of which is not a Mystery* (Coleridge, *The Collected Works*, [London: Routledge and Kegan Paul, 1969], vol. 5, *The Friend*, ed. Barbara E. Rooke, 229).

77. Romantic writers distinguished among such terms as "self," "personality," and "individual."

78. Coleridge, *Works*, vol. 4, *Friend*, 97. See also William Hazlitt, *An Essay on the Principles of Human Action and Some Remarks on the System of Hartley and Helvetius* (Gainesville, Fla.: Scholars' Facsimiles and Reprints, 1969), 85. Wordsworth expressed similar sentiments throughout *The Prelude*, especially in book 13.

79. See Masao Miyoshi's *The Divided Self: A Perspective on the Literature of the Victorians* (New York: New York University Press, 1969) for a thorough examination of the theme of multiple personality in the nineteenth century.

80. Walter Bagehot, "Percy Bysshe Shelley," in *Literary Studies* (London: J. M. Dent & Sons, 1911), 1:68. See Sylva Norman's *Flight of the Skylark: The Development of Shelley's Reputation* (Norman: University of Oklahoma Press, 1954) for an account of Shelley's treatment by the Victorians.

81. Arnold, "Byron," in *Works* 9:237. See Gottfried on Arnold's attitude toward the Romantic writers.

82. Leslie Stephen, "Coleridge," in *Hours in a Library* (London: Smith, Elder & Co., 1909), vol. 3.

83. In "Equilibrium in the Poetry of Matthew Arnold," in *British Victorian Literature: Recent Reevaluations*, ed. Shiv Kumar (New York: New York University Press, 1969), Alan Brick comments that in Arnold's poetry nature impinges on the ego instead of the ego projecting itself into nature as with the Romantics (pp. 133–34).

84. In his essay "Bishop Butler and the Zeit-Geist," Arnold noted the existence of two selves in man, "one permanent and impersonal, the other transient and bound to our contracted self . . . one higher and real, the other inferior and apparent," and the instinct in many truly to live "is served by following the first self and not the second" (*Works* 8:44). This view of two selves in man bears a strange resemblance to Coleridge's primary and secondary imagination, where one is allied with the Infinite, the other with the material self.

85. Tennyson's purpose in this image was clearer in an earlier version that indicated ascent:

> Circled through all experience, narrowing up
> From orb to orb, still nigher rest, remain
> A polestar fixt in truth and so made one
> With effort, wholly one herself, pure law. (p. 393)

86. See treatments of this inward turning movement of narrative in William Irvine and Park Honan, *The Book, the Ring, and the Poet: A New Biography of Robert Browning* (New York: McGraw-Hill Book Co., 1974), 430. Paul A. Cundiff discusses Browning's use of the circle image in *Browning's Ring Metaphor and Truth* (Metuchen, N.J.: Scarecrow Press, 1972), 154–55, as do Richard D. Altick and James F. Loucks II in *Browning's Roman Murder Story: A Reading of "The Ring and The Book"* (Chicago and London: Chicago University Press, 1968), 430.

87. Karlin, 181.

88. Ibid., 177.
89. Browning said that he did not intend to personify an abstraction in this poem but that it was an "allegory that is, of an impossible ideal object of love, accepted conventionally as such by a man who, all the while, cannot quite blind himself to the demonstrable fact that the possessor of knowledge and purity obtained without the natural consequences of obtaining them by achievement—not inheritance—such a being is imaginary, not real, a nymph and no woman" (quoted in William Clyde DeVane's *A Browning Handbook* [New York: Appleton-Century-Crofts, 1955], 405). Clyde de L. Ryals, on the other hand, asserts that, in "Numpholeptos," "The Absolute is figured as a nympth who imposes impossible tasks on her lover in his quest to reach her" (*Browning's Later Poetry, 1871-1889* [Ithaca, N.Y.: Cornell University Press, 1975], 139). Paracelsus describes God's completion of creation as the focusing of his distributed attributes to "some point where all those scattered rays should meet / Convergent in the faculties of man" (Browning, *Works* 1:162).
90. J. Hillis Miller, *The Disappearance of God: Five 19th-Century Writers* (1963; reprint, New York: Schocken Books, 1965), 134-35.
91. Ibid., 111.
92. Jerome J. McGann, *Swinburne: An Experiment in Criticism* (Chicago and London: Chicago University Press, 1972), 171.
93. Pater, 187-88.
94. E. S. Dallas, 296, *The Gay Science*, 2 vols. (orig. 1866) (New York: Johnson Reprint Corporation, 1969) vol. 1, 207, 312-13.
95. Andrew Griffin, "The Interior Garden and John Stuart Mill," in *Nature and the Victorian Imagination*, ed. U. C. Knoepflmacher and G. B. Tennyson (Berkeley and Los Angeles: University of California Press, 1977), 173. A. D. Nuttal feels that at 1800 there was a turn among English writers toward a defensive position for the self, the mind beginning to be conceived as a closed-in place (*A Common Sky: Philosophy and the Literary Imagination* [London: Chatto and Windus, 1974], 261).
96. Samuel Smiles, *Self-Help with Illustrations of Conduct and Perserverance* (London: John Murray, 1925), 196. Walter Houghton cited this passage as an example of Victorian confidence in individual will (*The Victorian Frame of Mind, 1830-1870* [New Haven: Yale University Press, 1964], 117).

Notes to Chapter 10: Early Nineteenth-Century Fiction

1. Peter Jones, *Philosophy and the Novel* (Oxford: Clarendon Press, 1975), 5. Jones points out roots of this view in Hume and ultimately in Aristotle. See also Diana Postlethwaite's treatment of this subject among Lewes and his associates in *Making It Whole: A Victorian Circle and the Shape of Their World* (Columbus: Ohio State University Press, 1984).
2. William Godwin, *Caleb Williams, or Things as They Are*, intro. George Sherburn (New York: Holt, Rinehart & Winston, 1960), 4. Subsequent references appear in the text.

3. Robert Plumer Ward, *Tremaine, or The Man of Refinement* (London: Henry Colburn, 1835), 157–58.
4. James Hogg, *Minor Classics of Nineteenth-Century Fiction*, ed. William E. Buckler (Boston: Houghton Mifflin Co., 1967), vol. 1, *The Private Memoirs and Confessions of a Justified Sinner*, 143. Subsequent references appear in the text.
5. Susan Ferrier, *Destiny, or The Chief's Daughter*, 2 vols. (London: Richard Bentley & Son, 1882), vol. 1, 68–69.
6. William Harrison Ainsworth, *Jack Sheppard* (London: George Routledge and Sons, n.d.), 103. Subsequent references appear in the text.
7. Ainsworth, *Crichton* (London: George Routledge and sons, n.d.), 93.
8. See discussion of the illustrations in John Harvey, *Victorian Novelists and Their Illustrators* (New York: New York University Press, 1971), 44ff.
9. Samuel Warren, *Ten Thousand A-Year* (Boston: Little, Brown, 1889), 312.
10. See chap. 5 of John R. Reed's *Victorian Conventions* (Athens: Ohio University Press, 1975) and Thomas Vargish's *The Providential Aesthetic in Victorian Fiction* (Charlottesville: Virginia University Press, 1985).
11. Leopold Damrosch, Jr., *God's Plot and Man's Stories: Studies in the Fictional Imagination from Milton to Fielding* (Chicago and London: University of Chicago Press, 1985), 263.

Notes to Chapter 11: Mary Shelley

1. All quotations are from M. K. Joseph's edition of Mary Shelley's *Frankenstein; or, The Modern Prometheus* (London: Oxford University Press, 1971), 23. All subsequent page references will be included in the text.
2. Constantin-François Chasseboeuf, comte de Volney, *Les ruines; ou, méditation sur les révolutions des empires* (Paris: Parmentier, 1826), 77. The passage reads as follows in the original: "Mais tel est le coeur humain; un succès l'enivre de confiance, un revers l'abat et le consterne: toujours entier à la sensation du moment, il ne juge point des choses par leur nature, mais par l'élan de sa passion."
3. William Godwin, *Thoughts on Man, His Nature, Productions, and Discoveries* (London: E. Wilson, 1831), 105. Christopher Small, in *Mary Shelley's Frankenstein: Tracing the Myth* (Pittsburgh: University of Pittsburgh Press, 1973), explores at length many influences upon the novel. When discussing Godwin, he emphasizes Mary's emotional dependency upon her father. He examines Godwin's fiction far more elaborately than his philosophical writings. Much of Small's book is more occupied with Percy than with Mary Shelley, and the influences he traces from the former to the latter are often general and not entirely convincing. Small does not take up sources that Mary Shelley herself named, such as Volney's *Ruines* or Goethe's *Werther*. I believe it is significant that the revised version of *Frankenstein*, clearly reinforcing the theme of fate, appeared in the same year as her father's *Thoughts on Man*, which took up the issue of necessity and free will anew.

4. Interest in the arctic regions had revived after the War of 1812. In that year a four-ship squadron of the Royal Navy was dispatched to the polar reaches with little success. Among the men involved in this expedition were figures like John Franklin, Edward Parry, and others who would make important contributions to arctic exploration later (Farley Mowat, *The Polar Passion: The Quest for the North Pole* [Boston and Toronto: McClelland and Stewart, 1967], 46). In 1815, Lieutenant Kotzebue made a voyage in search of a northwest passage. Sir John Barrow, in his *Chronological History of Voyages into the Arctic Regions* (London: J. Murray, 1818) mentions this expedition and those of the Englishmen Ross, Buchan, Parry, and Franklin of 1818. Walton's quest is not original, then, but fashionable for the time that Mary Shelley was writing. However, even if she intended him to be original—the novel is supposedly set in the 1700s, presumably the late 1700s—his notions about the polar regions are outdated. Mary Shelley mentions "The Ancient Mariner" anachronistically, but there is an interesting connection here, for Coleridge had apparently drawn upon August von Kotzebue's *Memoirs and Travels of Mauritius Augustus, Count de Benyowski*, translated from the French in 1790, for his arctic settings. J. Livingston Lowes traces this and other sources for Coleridge's poem in *The Road to Xanadu* (Boston: Houghton Mifflin, 1964), 124ff. It so happens that Percy and Mary had read Kotzebue's *The Most Remarkable Year in the Life of Kotzebue, Containing His Exile into Siberia by Himself*, trans. B. Beresford (London: R. Phillips, 1806), in 1815 (Mary Shelley, *Mary Shelley's Journal*, ed. Frederick L. Jones [Norman: University of Oklahoma Press, 1947], 48).

5. Here, perhaps, is the first clear warning that links the theme of the novel to the hazardous condition of the aspiring artist.

6. Walton's alter ego, Frankenstein, has his own counterpart. The view that the Creature is Frankenstein's double has become a commonplace and has appeared in many critical studies, among them Muriel Spark's *Child of Light: A Reassessment of Mary Wollstonecraft Shelley* (Hadleigh, Essex: Tower Bridge, 1951), Masao Miyoishi's *The Divided Self: A Perspective on the Literature of the Victorians* (New York: New York University Press, 1969), and more recently Irving Massay's *The Gaping Pig: Literature and Metamorphosis* (Berkeley and Los Angeles: University of California Press, 1976).

7. F. E. L. Priestley draws attention to this distinction in his edition of Godwin's *Enquiry concerning Political Justice and its Influence on Morals and Happiness*, 3 vols. (Toronto: University of Toronto Press, 1946). See especially vol. 3, p. 7. Muriel Spark has argued that Mary was reacting against her father's rigid logic and that her novels *Frankenstein* and *The Last Man* "are unconscious satires of Godwin's brand of humanism" ("Mary Shelley: a Prophetic Novelist," *The Listener* [22 Feb. 1951], 305–6). See chapter 2 of this study for a discussion of Godwin's views on free will and necessity.

8. Godwin, *Enquiry* 1:26. John P. Clark lucidly examines Godwin's philosophy in *The Philosophical Anarchism of William Godwin* (Princeton: Princeton University Press, 1977), especially, for my purposes, the relationship of necessity and free will and Godwin's categorization of voluntary, involuntary, and imperfectly voluntary acts. Clark also notes that Godwin failed to explain why mental processes should be subject to the same laws as physical nature (p. 51).

9. There is a relationship here with Percy Shelley's thought, particularly in *Prometheus Unbound*. Earl R. Wasserman points out that Jupiter's tyranny is made possible through Prometheus's own abdicated mental powers; his overthrow is made possible by Prometheus's refusing to abandon all power over his own will (*Shelley: A Critical Reading* [Baltimore: Johns Hopkins University Press, 1971], 258, 288). Christopher Small draws extensive comparisons between the works of the two Shelleys, saying of *Prometheus Unbound* that it deals powerfully "with the capacity of human thought to transcend itself" (p. 224). James Rieger has argued that Shelley participated substantially in the composition of the novel (see his edition of *Frankenstein* [New York: Bobbs-Merrill, 1974]). But Mary Shelley's revisions for the 1831 edition indicate her desire to emphasize references to fate, destiny, and freedom; they show, to my satisfaction, that the scheme of the novel was hers.

10. Frankenstein's ascent toward Mont Blanc may have another significance, reinforcing the parallel with Walton's polar quest. The summit of Mont Blanc had not been scaled until Horace-Benedict de Sassure managed it in the summer of 1787. His victory was widely advertised. Much wrangling among men eager for fame had preceded Sassure's achievement. (See Claire Eliane Engel, *Mountaineering in the Alps: An Historical Survey* [London: George Allen & Unwin, 1950], chap. 4.) If one accepts the novel's internal dating, Frankenstein could have been in this setting at a time when the mountain symbolized human aspiration. Mont Blanc was still a lively subject of interest for mountaineers at the time Mary Shelley was writing her novel. Martin Tropp has demonstrated another connection between polar and alpine settings in his examination of water and ice imagery in the novel (*Mary Shelley's Monster* [Boston: Houghton Mifflin, 1976], 41ff). Quotations are from Percy Shelley, *Shelley's Poetry and Prose*, ed. Donald H. Reiman and Sharon B. Powers (New York: W. W. Norton, 1977). Subsequent references appear in the text.

11. Donald H. Reiman has indicated how Shelley associated moral qualities with heavenly and terrestrial features such as stars, mountains, and seas, thereby subtly integrating his philosophical beliefs and his imagery in *Shelley's "The Triumph of Life": A Critical Study* (Urbana: University of Illinois Press, 1965), 12ff. There is a strong resemblance between Shelley's vision of Mont Blanc and Wordsworth's vision upon Mount Snowdon which "appeared to me the type / Of a majestic intellect, its acts / And its possessions, what it has and craves. / What in itself it is, and would become. / There I beheld the emblem of a mind / That feeds upon infinity, that broods / Over the dark abyss, intent to hear / Its voices issuing forth to silent light / In one continuous stream; a mind sustained / By recognitions of transcendent power, / In sense conducting to ideal form, / In soul of more than mortal privilege," (William Wordsworth, *The Prelude or Growth of a Poet's Mind*, ed. Ernest de Selincourt and Helen Darbishire [Oxford: Oxford University Press, 1959], book 14, lines 66–76). See also the discussion of "Mont Blanc" in Roland A. Duerksen, "The Thematic Unity in the New Shelley Notebook," *Bulletin of Research in the Humanities* 83 (Summer 1980): 203–15.

12. Gerhard Joseph's "Frankenstein's Dream: The Child as Father of the Monster," *Hartford Studies in Literature* 7 (1975): 97–115, examines Victor's aspirations

in terms of his working out of repressed infantile fantasies, thus giving the novel a more modern psychological cast, a tendency that has continued in recent criticism.

13. L. J. Swingle in "Frankenstein's Monster and Its Romantic Relatives: Problems of Knowledge in English Romanticism," *Texas Studies in Literature and Language* 15 (1973): 51-65, discusses how doubtful much of the evidence presented to the reader, particularly by the Creature, really is. If Frankenstein does not think clearly abut choice and chance, it is partly because there is an atmosphere of obscure meaning in the novel as a whole.

14. Richard Hengist Horne, *A New Spirit of the Age* (London: H. Frowde, 1907), 410.

15. George Levine examines Frankenstein's sin "against himself and the human community" thoroughly in *"Frankenstein* and the Tradition of Realism," *Novel* 7 (1973): 14-30. A revised version of this article appears in Levine's *The Realistic Imagination: English Fiction from Frankenstein to Lady Chatterley* (Chicago and London: University of Chicago Press, 1981).

16. Richard J. Dunn in "Narrative Distance in *Frankenstein,*" *Studies in the Novel* 6 (1974): 408-17, describes the failure to achieve the ideal of community through a failure in communication among the characters in *Frankenstein.*

17. The danger of pursuing both the philosopher's stone and the elixir of life was indicated by Godwin in his novel *St. Leon* (1799).

18. Throughout his *Enquiry* and *Thoughts,* Godwin argued that reason leads to equality and tried to demonstrate the need for subordination of individual liberty to the larger requirements of society.

19. Spark, *Child of Light,* 137, and Horne, 410, specifically call attention to the enslavement of Frankenstein's mind or imagination.

20. Godwin had clearly warned that men may miscalculate and that their good acts could lead to evil consequences: "actions in the highest degree injurious to the public, have often proceeded from motives uncommonly conscientious" (*Enquiry* 1:153).

21. This topic has been taken up by various critics. M. K. Joseph deals with it in the introduction to the Oxford edition, George Levine touches upon it, and B. R. Pollin offers additional possibilities for philosophical sources in "Philosophical and Literary Sources of *Frankenstein,*" *Comparative Literature* 17 (1965): 97-108.

22. Percy Bysshe Shelley "Review of Frankenstein," in *Shelley's Critical Prose,* ed Bruce R. McElderry, Jr. (Lincoln: University of Nebraska Press, 1967), 107.

23. Mary had read *Paradise Lost* the year before writing *Frankenstein,* and Percy was reading the work, sometimes aloud to Mary, soon after she had begun her story (Mary Shelley, *Journal,* 48, 68ff). Although Leslie Brisman's *Milton's Poetry of Choice and Its Romantic Heirs* (Ithaca, N.Y.: Cornell University Press, 1973) deals mainly with technical rather than philosophical matters, it indicates throughout the sensitivity Romantic writers seem to have had for the implications of Milton's poetry. Chapter 5, entitled "A Second Will," discusses the Romantic treatment of the theme of will, touching upon Adam's and hence man's generative responsibilities and the relationship of moral to imaginative will, especially as it appears in Wordsworth, notably in the "Ode to Duty." For Chris-

topher Small, the Miltonic allusions signify the rebelliousness of the Creature (pp. 58ff).

24. John Milton, *Paradise Lost*, book 5, lines 526–28, 234–38; book 10, lines 8–11, 40–47.

25. Martin Tropp offers an interesting perception of the tree images (pp. 60–61).

26. In Goethe's *Werther*, one of the first books the Creature reads, Lotte's calm, orderly values are contrasted with the passionately destructive urges of Werther himself. The brilliant and emotional young Werther may be admired and pitied but clearly not imitated.

27. Mary Shelley, *The Last Man*, ed. Hugh J. Lukes, Jr. (Lincoln: University of Nebraska Press, 1965), 84.

28. Wasserman examines Shelley's plea for the need to abandon these "codes" (p. 236). He also explains that submission to necessity and refusal to yield utterly to the will of Jupiter are central ideas in *Prometheus Unbound* (pp. 288, 318).

29. Percy Bysshe Shelley, *The Complete Poetical Works of Percy Bysshe Shelley*, ed. Neville Rogers (Oxford: Clarendon Press, 1972), 1:306. Subsequent references appear in the text. Christopher Small presents a lengthy argument for Shelley's influence on Mary's novel.

Notes to Chapter 12: Edward George Bulwer-Lytton

1. Edward George Bulwer-Lytton, *Lord Lytton's Novels* (London: George Routledge and Sons, n.d.), vol. 22, *Zanoni*, 92–93. Subsequent references appear in the text.

2. Bulwer-Lytton, *Novels*, vol. 1, *Eugene Aram*, 30–31. Subsequent references appear in the text.

3. Bulwer-Lytton, *Falkland* (Boston: Aldine Book Publishing Co., n.d.), 197–98.

4. Mr. Talbot says to Clarence Linden, the young protagonist of *The Disowned* (1828): "They only are justifiable in seclusion who, like the Greek philosophers, make that very seclusion the means of serving and enlightening their race—who from their retreats send forth their oracles of wisdom, and render the desert which surrounds them eloquent with the voice of truth" (*Novels* 9:233).

5. Bulwer-Lytton, *The New Timon: A Romance of London* (London: Henry Colburn, 1846), 167.

6. After allowing Clarence Lindon, by his own exertions, to determine his successful destiny, Bulwer explains at the close of his novel that we should not mourn Mordaunt, nor murmur "at the blindness of Fate, nor sorrow at the darkness of his doom." Why, asks the narrator, should we feel pity "for the stormy life?—it was a triumph! for the early death?—it was immortality" (*Novels* 9:448).

7. Bulwer-Lytton, *King Arthur: An Epic Poem*, 2 vols. (London: George Routledge and Sons, 1875), 1:xvii–xviii. Subsequent references appear in the text.

8. In a note to the 1870 edition of his poem, Bulwer explained that he had not known until he learned it in Sir William Hamilton's *Lectures on Metaphysics*, that his views on nature had already been expressed by the German philosopher F. H. Jacobi. He recast his verses accordingly (*Arthur*, 295–96).

9. Bulwer-Lytton, *Caxtoniana: A Series of Essays on Life, Literature, and Manners* (New York: Harper & Brothers, Publishers, 1864), 116.

10. Ibid., 326–27.

11. Bulwer wrote in *Caxtoniana*: "Besides the interest of plot and incident, another interest is implied, more or less distinctly or more or less vaguely, which is that of the process and working out of a symbolical purpose interwoven with the popular action. Instead of appending to the fable a formal moral, a moral signification runs throughout the whole fable, but so little obtrusively that, even at the close, it is to be divined by the reader, not explained by the author. This has been a striking characteristic of the art of our century" (pp. 317–18). See chapter 1 of Edwin M. Eigner's *The Metaphysical Novel in England and America: Dickens, Bulwer, Hawthorne, Melville* (Berkeley and Los Angeles: University of California Press, 1978) for a discussion of preconceived plots in Bulwer and other "metaphysical" novelists.

12. Victor Alexander George Robert Lytton, *The Life of Edward Bulwer, First Lord Lytton*, 2 vols. (London: Macmillan and Co., 1913), 2:44. Subsequent references appear in the text.

13. See Bulwer's justification of typifying method in "Certain Principles of Art in Works of Imagination" in *Caxtoniana*.

14. Bulwer-Lytton, *Novels*, vol. 13, *A Strange Story*, v. Subsequent references appear in the text.

15. See Allan Conrad Christensen's very helpful *Edward Bulwer-Lytton: The Fiction of New Regions* (Athens: University of Georgia Press, 1976). Eigner discusses idealization of character in Bulwer and others in chapter 3 of *The Metaphysical Novel*.

16. Christensen writes: "Beyond all his other archetypal forms, he sought that identifying figure of the soul. Underlying the existence of everything that is, the very *idea* of soul existed to assure him of the indestructible uniqueness of all selfhoods" (p. 221). Christensen offers an illuminating discussion of Bulwer's use of the power "vril" in *The Coming Race* (1871), a power signifying for Bulwer his universal first principle in physical form (pp. 177ff).

17. Bulwer-Lytton, "The Haunted and the Haunters," in *Minor Classics of Nineteenth-Century Fiction*, ed. William E. Buckler (Boston: Houghton Mifflin Co., 1967), 2:330.

18. Bulwer-Lytton, *The Last Days of Pompeii* (New York: Frederick A. Stokes Co., 1891), 6.

19. Andrew Brown, "Metaphysics and Melodrama: Bulwer's *Reinzi*," *Nineteenth-Century Fiction* 36, no. 3 (Dec. 1981): 261–76.

20. Margaret F. King and Elliot Engel, "The Emerging Carlylean Hero in Bulwer's Novels of the 1830s," *Nineteenth-Century Fiction* 36, no. 3 (Dec. 1981): 277–95.

21. Bulwer-Lytton, *Novels*, vol. 3, *Pelham*, 372.

22. Christensen, 52.

23. Bulwer-Lytton, *Novels*, vol. 7, *The Caxtons: A Family Picture*, iii. Subsequent references appear in the text.

24. Later, Bulwer writes, "And how the stern Destinies that shall govern the man weave their first delicate tissues amidst the earliest associations of the child!" (*Novels* 7:330)

25. See Eigner concerning the influence on Bulwer and others of German narrative experiments in the nineteenth century (pp. 165ff).

26. Bulwer-Lytton, *Novels*, vols. 17-18, *My Novel; Or Varieties in English Life*, 17:76. Subsequent references appear in the text.

27. Gordon N. Ray, *Thackeray: The Age of Wisdom, 1847-1863* (London: Oxford University Press, 1958), 237.

28. These views are presented in a sermon by Parson Dale, often the spokesman of Bulwer's opinions in the novel.

Notes to Chapter 13: Charles Dickens

1. John Forster, *The Life of Charles Dickens* (London: Chapman and Hall, 1893), 46.

2. Chris Brooks, *Signs for the Times: Symbolic Realism in the Mid-Victorian World* (London: George Allen and Unwin, 1984), 35. See also Barry V. Qualls's *The Secular Pilgrims of Victorian Fiction: The Novel as Book of Life* (London: Cambridge University Press, 1982).

3. Brooks, 34. See Virgil Grillo's *Charles Dickens' Sketches by Boz: End in the Beginning* (Boulder, Colo.: Colorado Associated University Press, 1974) on the tension of different mimetic systems in Dickens's early sketches (p. 188).

4. J. Hillis Miller and David Borowitz, *Charles Dickens and George Cruikshank*, intro. Ada B. Nisbet (Los Angeles: William Andrews Clark Memorial Library, 1971), 18.

5. Robert Barnard, *Imagery and Theme in The Novels of Dickens*, (New York: Humanities Press, 1974), 110.

6. Charles Dickens, *Sketches by Boz* (London: Oxford University Press, 1963), 366.

7. Fred Kaplan, *Dickens and Mesmerism: The Hidden Springs of Fiction* (Princeton: Princeton University Press, 1975), 19. Subsequent references appear in the text.

8. John Kucich, using George Bataille's pattern of energy and restraint, argues that in Dickens, directing will and energy toward the self is wicked but exercising them on behalf of others is good. As contrasting examples, he cites the main plots of *Great Expectations* and *Little Dorrit* (*Excess and Restraint in the Novels of Charles Dickens* [Athens: University of Georgia Press, 1981]), pp. 10ff.

9. Rhonda Wilcox Nelms, *Division in Dickens: Determinism and Free Will in the Novels through Bleak House*, (Ph.D. diss., Duke University, 1982; Ann Arbor, Mich.: University Microfilms International), n.p., 8223874. Subsequent references appear in the text.

10. *Pickwick*, being very early, scarcely seems to touch upon the subject, though Nelms considers the incipient conflict in some of the embedded tales indicative of determined lives and the activities of the Pickwickians indicative of freedom or privileged consideration of Providence (Nelms, 34).

11. Steven Marcus, *Dickens: from Pickwick to Dombey* (New York: Basic Books, 1965), 68. Subsequent references appear in the text. See also Harvey Peter Sucksmith, *The Narrative Art of Charles Dickens: The Rhetoric of Sympathy*

and Irony in His Novels (Oxford: Clarendon Press, 1970), 254. See Qualls for this pattern throughout Dickens's novels. He excludes *Our Mutual Friend* as lacking metaphorical and spiritual coherence (p. 135).

12. Dickens, *Master Humphrey's Clock* (London: Oxford University Press, 1963), 51.

13. Dickens, *The Old Curiosity Shop* (London: Oxford University Press, 1967), 13. Subsequent references appear in the text.

14. Alexander Welsh discusses the complications in Dickens treatment of providence in *The City of Dickens* (Oxford: Clarendon Press, 1971), esp. 122ff.

15. Dickens, *A Christmas Carol*, in *Christmas Books* (London: Oxford University Press, 1954), 19.

16. Martin Meisel comments on the association of the railroad and the linearity and inexorability of Carker's flight and death in *Realizations: Narrative, Pictorial, and Theatrical Arts in Nineteenth-Century England* (Princeton: Princeton University Press, 1983), 83.

17. Dickens, *David Copperfield* (London: Oxford University Press, 1966), 646. Subsequent references appear in the text.

18. Gwendolyn B. Needham, "The Undisciplined Heart of David Copperfield," *Nineteenth-Century Fiction* 10 (1954): 81–107.

19. Brooks, 48.

20. Felicity Hughes, "Narrative Complexity in *David Copperfield*," *ELH* 41, no. 1 (Spring 1974): 89.

21. Ibid., 95–98.

22. Several studies treat Dickens and the Bible. Two recent works are Dennis Walder's *Dickens and Religion* (London: Allen and Unwin, 1981) and Janet Larson's *Dickens and the Broken Scripture* (Athens: Ohio University Press, 1986).

23. In Tennyson's "The Two Voices," a despondent figure suffering from "a divided will" views man as the determined product of natural law, while at the same time yearning to "reach the law within the law." Ultimately it is the positive voice of faith, feeling, and freedom that overcomes the voice of despair, reason, and necessity. Something like the same argument provides a subordinate structure for all of *In Memoriam* (1850).

24. Kaplan, 171. While Joseph Fradin argues that there is "no faith in *Bleak House* in the capacity of the will for redemptive public action," and concludes that "by an act of private vision, by the denial of the social will, we may save ourselves; by individual acts of responsibility and love we may sometime save others," I believe that Dickens meant his solution to be far broader ("Will and Society in *Bleak House*," *PMLA* 81, no. 1 [March 1966]: 109). He was calling not for the confinement of the generous impulse but for the reawakening of the human capacity to command destiny.

25. Dickens, *Bleak House* (London: Oxford University Press, 1966), 19. Subsequent references appear in the text.

26. It may be significant that Dickens chose not to include this passage in his own *The Life of Our Lord*, which he wrote for his children.

27. In *A Child's History of England* (London: Oxford University Press, 1963), Dickens treated Wat Tyler sympathetically, denouncing the usurpers of freedom

against whom Tyler was rebelling (pp. 295–97). See Sucksmith, *Narrative Art* and "Sir Leicester Dedlock, Wat Tyler, and the Chartists: The Role of the Ironmaster in *Bleak House*," in *Dickens Studies Annual*, ed. Robert B. Partlow, Jr. IV (Carbondale and Edwardsville: Southern Illinois University Press, 1975) for further information about the Tyler references.

28. Sucksmith argues that, unlike Kingsley, who believed in providence and man's freedom to resist God's will, Dickens meant to show Richard as fated (p. 351). I disagree with Sucksmith, for it seems to me that Dickens does agree with Kingsley and the many other writers of his day who entertained the same basic assumptions.

29. I do not agree with Alex Zwerdling who argues that Dickens awkwardly resorts to fantasy in the resolution of Esther's story ("Esther Summerson Rehabilitated," *PMLA*, 88:3 (May, 1973) 438).

30. For a general study of Dickens's use of fairy tale, see Michael Kotzin's *Dickens and the Fairy Tale* (Bowling Green, Ky.: Bowling University Popular Press, 1972). To a great extent, the story of Christ represented a fable of goodness to Dickens. He even composed a simplified version of the New Testament for his children.

31. Sucksmith suggests that chapter 2 of *Bleak House* was interpolated after chapters 1 and 3 were written. Perhaps this is additional evidence that Dickens wished to strengthen the moral structure of his work. For example, Sucksmith demonstrates that by revising the title of chapter 2, "In Fashion," to coincide with chapter 1, "In Chancery," Dickens emphasized the parallels between the two realms of society (p. 336).

32. Dickens elsewhere combined Christian story and fairy tale to good effect, as he does here. I discuss this theme in *Victorian Conventions* (Athens: Ohio University Press, 1975), esp. 20–33, but elsewhere as well.

33. Forster, 434.

34. George Gissing, *The Immortal Dickens* (London: Cecil Palmer 1925; New York: Kraus Reprint Co., 1969), 228.

35. Morton Dauwen Zabel, "*Bleak House*," in *The Dickens Critics*, ed. George H. Ford and Lauriat Lane, Jr. (Ithaca, N.Y.: Cornell University Press, 1961) 330, 340.

36. W. J. Harvey, "Chance and Design in *Bleak House*," in *Dickens and the Twentieth Century*, ed. John Gross and Gabriel Pearson (Toronto: University of Toronto Press, 1962), 155. A. E. Dyson, *The Inimitable Dickens: A Reading of the Novels* (New York: St. Martin's Press, 1970), offers the plausible reading (p. 165).

37. E. D. H. Johnson, *Charles Dickens: An Introduction to His Novels* (New York: Random House, 1969), 101.

38. Robert L. Caserio, *Plot, Story, and the Novel: From Dickens and Poe to the Modern Period* (Princeton: Princeton University Press, 1979), 113.

39. Karen Chase, *Eros & Psyche: The Representation of Personality in Charlotte Brontë, Charles Dickens, and George Eliot* (New York and London: Methuen, 1984), 103.

40. Ibid., 108.

41. Caserio, 117.

42. J. Hillis Miller, *Charles Dickens: The World of His Novels* (Cambridge: Harvard University Press, 1965), 167. In *Bleak House*, detection is a conspicuous part of the story, ultimately focusing on a genuine detective.

43. Chase, 109–10.

44. George H. Ford, "Self-Help and the Helpless in *Bleak House*," in *From Jane Austen to Joseph Conrad*, ed. Robert C. Rathburn and Martin Steinmann, Jr. (Minneapolis: University of Minnesota Press, 1958), 104.

45. Robert A. Donovan, "Structure and Idea in *Bleak House*," in *Twentieth Century Interpretations of Bleak House*, ed. Jacob Korb (Englewood Cliffs, N.J.: Prentice-Hall, 1968), 44. A. E. Dyson calls Esther "that rare thing in the novel, a convincing depiction of moral goodness," and describes her as "a gravitational pull against pessimism and defeatism, the harbinger of domestic virtue, happiness and peace," but he does not point out that Esther represents these virtues because she believes that she can determine her own fate (pp. 173, 182).

46. W. J. Harvey, "*Bleak House*: The Double Narrative," in *Dickens: Bleak House. A Casebook*, ed. A. E. Dyson (London: Macmillan and Co., 1969), 229.

47. Zwerdling, 430. I have accepted most of Zwerdling's interpretation of Esther's character.

48. See treatment of circle imagery earlier in chapter 9.

49. Felicity Hughes writes: "The connection of the whole Yarmouth-Steerforth plot with tides, the way David's imagination is related to his susceptibility, the importance of his dreams, and the whole memory procedure of the book are all topics touched on by the theories of the mesmerists that I have not space to develop here. The crucial topic for this discussion is the freedom of the will" (p. 104).

50. For a clear examination of certain prevailing notions concerning providence and man's part in that design at the turn of the nineteenth century, see Keith M. Costain's "Theoretical History and the Novel: The Scottish Fiction of John Galt," *ELH* 43 (1976): 342–65.

51. Throughout his mature life, Dickens asserted a firm belief in the teachings of Christ. In a letter to one of his sons, he wrote of the New Testament: "it is the best book that ever was, or will be, known in the world"; he felt that "it teaches you the best lessons by which any human creature, who tries to be truthful and faithful to duty, can possibly be guided" (Forster, 639).

52. Dickens, *Little Dorrit* (London: Oxford University Press, 1963), 20–21. Subsequent references appear in the text.

53. Alexander Welsh suggests that many villains in Dickens's stories seem predetermined to evil and hence are not moral agents at all; these figures are "irrevocably committed to evil" and can be dealt with only through extermination (pp. 125–26). Dickens does not seem to be rigorous in his beliefs. Blandois in *Little Dorrit*, for example, is indirectly described as a thoroughly bad man with no good in him. Welsh's point does not alter the fact that where Dickens meant to show free will in operation, he associated it with liberation of the self from external circumstance.

54. Mrs. Clennam is a parody of the Christian scheme represented by Little Dorrit and is her opposite. She uses her "indomitable will" to repress self not from Christ-like love of others but from a sense of retributive wrath. Appropriately enough, Mrs. Clennam's chief concern, outside her own exaction of justice, is for

Little Dorrit's welfare, imperiled by her own acts. Potentially, she has corrupted the very religious values she claims to espouse. But no individual can do this, as Little Dorrit's fortitude suggests.

55. Brooks, 83.
56. Dickens, *A Tale of Two Cities* (London: Oxford University Press, 1967), 2. Subsequent references appear in the text.
57. Dickens, *Great Expectations* (New York: The Bobbs-Merrill Co., Inc., 1964), 76. Subsequent references appear in the text.
58. H. W., *Charles Dickens' Uncollected Writings from Household Words, 1850–1859*, ed. Harry Stone, 2 vols. (Bloomington and London: Indiana University Press, 1968), 1:468. The attribution of this text to Dickens is by Stone.
59. Robert Morse, "*Our Mutual Friend*," in *The Dickens Critics*, ed. George H. Ford and Lauriat Lane, Jr. (Ithaca, N.Y.: Cornell University Press, 1961), 202.
60. G. W. Kennedy, "Naming and Language in *Our Mutual Friend*," NCF 28, no. 2 (September 1973): 165–78.
61. Dickens, *Our Mutual Friend* (London: Oxford University Press, 1967), 18. Subsequent references appear in the text.

Notes to Chapter 14: Midcentury Fiction: Certainty and Ambivalence

1. Charlotte Brontë, *Five Novelettes*, ed. Winifred Gerin (London: Folio Society, 1971), 341.
2. Thomas Vargish, *The Providential Aesthetic in Victorian Fiction* (Charlottesville: University of Virginia Press, 1985), 72. Emily Brontë's *Wuthering Heights* (1847) might easily be read as a study in frustrated will, concluding with the suggestion that the best application of strong will is in self-discipline.
3. Catherine Gallagher, *The Industrial Reformation of English Fiction, 1832–1867* (Chicago: Chicago University Press, 1985), 74. Angus Easson also noted the contradictory positions in *Mary Barton*: "Having conceived John Barton as a tragic figure, Gaskell never quite resolved the problem between the free will of the tragic hero and the moral determinism of the society the novel creates" (*Elizabeth Gaskell* [London: Routledge & Kegan Paul, 1979], 76).
4. Elizabeth Gaskell, *North and South*, ed. Dorothy Collin (Harmondsworth, England: Penguin Books, 1970), 502. Subsequent references appear in the text.
5. Andrew Sanders, *The Victorian Historical Novel, 1840–1880* (New York: St. Martin's Press, 1979), 220ff.
6. Brenda Colloms, *Charles Kingsley: The Lion of Eversley* (New York: Barnes & Noble, 1975), 130. See the discussion of Kingsley's sermons in chapter 6 of the present study.
7. Charles Kingsley, *Charles Kingsley: His Letters and Memories of His Life*, edited by his wife, 2 vols. (London: Henry S. King & Co., 1877), 1:299. Subsequent references appear in the text.
8. Kingsley, *The Water Babies: A Fairy-Tale for a Land-Baby* (London: Macmillan and Co., 1886; facsimile, New York: Garland Publishing, 1976), 369–70.
9. Kingsley. *Alton Locke* (London: Macmillan and Co., 1881), 2. Locke says that in rejecting religion he came to see materialism as an answer; he "worshipped cir-

cumstance," and thought Fate's injustice kept him from developing his genius and asserting his rank among poets. Subsequent references appear in the text.

10. See John R. Reed's *Victorian Conventions* (Athens: Ohio University Press, 1975) for the conventional use of this pattern of illness (pp. 14ff).

11. Kingsley, *Two Years Ago*, 2 vols. (New York: J. F. Taylor and Company, 1899), 1:386ff. Subsequent references appear in the text.

12. Jerome Hamilton Buckley, *William Ernest Henley: A Study in the 'Counter-Decadence' of the 'Nineties* (Princeton: Princeton University Press, 1945), 19.

13. Norman Vance, *The Sinews of Spirit: The Ideal of Christian Manliness in Victorian Literature and Religious Thought* (London: Cambridge University Press, 1985), 79.

14. James Anthony Froude [Zeta], *Shadows of the Clouds* (London: John Ollivier, 1847), 72. Subsequent references appear in the text.

15. Joseph Sheridan Le Fanu, *The Rose and the Key* (London: Hutchinson & Co., n.d.), 360. Subsequent references appear in the text.

16. Jack Sullivan argues that Le Fanu's world view, though "ultimately deterministic . . . is not based on a coherent or knowable determinism" (*Elegant Nightmares: The English Ghost Stories from Le Fanu to Blackwood* [Athens: Ohio University Press, 1978], 19; subsequent references appear in the text). As a consequence, Le Fanu's stories create a "sense of helplessness in malign universe" (p. 38). But Sullivan undervalues the emphasis Le Fanu places on the dark conscious and unconscious volitional powers within the human self.

17. Sue Lonoff, *Wilkie Collins and His Victorian Readers: A Study in the Rhetoric of Authorship* (New York: AMS Press, 1982), 113. Subsequent references appear in the text.

18. Willian Wilkie Collins, *The Woman in White* (Boston: Houghton Mifflin Co., 1969), 1. Subsequent references appear in the text.

19. Kenneth Robinson, *Wilkie Collins: A Biography* (New York: Macmillan Co., 1952), 151.

20. Richard Barickman, Susan Macdonald, and Myra Stark, *Corrupt Relations: Dickens, Thackeray, Trollope, Collins and the Victorian Sexual System* (New York: Columbia University Press, 1982), 125–26.

21. Collins, *No Name* (New York: Peter Fenelon Collier, n.d.), 417. Subsequent references appear in the text.

22. However, Winifred Hughes writes that the final stance of *No Name*, "echoing the Captain, is blatantly amoral, relativistic, mixed in contingency" (*The Maniac in the Cellar: Sensation Novels of the 1860s* [Princeton: Princeton University Press, 1980], 148).

23. Robinson, 191.

24. Collins, *Armadale* (New York: Peter Fenelon Collier, n.d.), 572–73. Subsequent references appear in the text.

25. Mark M. Hennelly, Jr., "Reading Detection in *The Woman in White*," *Texas Studies in Literature and Language* 22, no. 4 (Winter 1980): 453.

26. Hughes, 161.

27. Ross C. Murfin, "The Art of Representation: Collins' *The Moonstone* and Dickens' Example," *ELH* 49, no. 3 (Fall 1982): 654ff.

28. Ibid., 661.

29. Collins, *The Fallen Leaves* (New York: Peter Fenelon Collier, n.d.), 5.
30. T. S. Eliot calls attention to the obsession with fatality in Collins's *The Haunted Hotel*, an obsession that reflects the author's concern with meaningful pattern in human existence and the dread that any such pattern is a psychological projection of an internal bias.

> What makes it better than a mere readable second-rate ghost story is the fact that fatality in this story is no longer merely a will jerking the figures. The principal character, the fatal woman, is herself obsessed by the idea of fatality; her motives are melodramatic; she therefore compels the coincidences to occur, feeling that she is compelled to compel them. In this story, as the chief character is internally melodramatic, the story itself ceases to be merely melodramatic, and partakes of true drama." Quoted in Robinson (p. 289).

31. Gordon N. Ray. *Thackeray: The Uses of Adversity, 1811–1846.* (London: Oxford University Press, 1955), 218.
32. John Cordy Jeaffreson, *A Book of Recollections*, 2 vols. (London: Hurst and Blackett, 1894), 1:195–96.
33. Ray, 385–86. Geoffrey Tillotson explained that Thackeray disapproved of hidden moralizing in fiction because the novel was to him a vehicle specifically for overt moralizing. "It is from no ambush that the novelist speaks of ethics, a novel being a ground where moral walks the highway freely as the personages themselves, accompanying them closely as their shadow" (*Thackeray the Novelist* [reprint, New York: Barnes and Noble, 1974], 219). See chapter 3 of Kenneth Graham's *English Criticism of the Novel, 1865–1900* (Oxford: Clarendon Press, 1965) for a discussion of the tradition of moral instruction in Victorian fiction.
34. I have been unable to relocate this quotation from Trollope.
35. Tillotson, 169.
36. Jack P. Rawlins, *Thackeray's Novels: A Fiction That Is True* (Berkeley and Los Angeles: University of California Press, 1974), 176. Subsequent references appear in the text. Rawlins's argument develops suggestions to be found in Wolfgang Iser's *The Implied Reader: Patterns of Communication in Prose Fiction from Bunyan to Beckett* (Baltimore: Johns Hopkins University Press, 1974). Iser says that Thackeray's strategy in *Vanity Fair* is to prevent the reader from identifying with characters by emphasizing the fictionality of his story. "The esthetic effect of *Vanity Fair* depends on activating the reader's critical faculties so that he may recognize the social reality of the novel as a confusing array of sham attitudes, and experience the exposure of this sham as the true reality" (p. 112). The reader sees himself reflected in the narrative, and his part in its construction is to make judgments about the unwritten part of the novel (p. 119).
37. Henry Sumner Maine, "The Age of Progress," in *Popular Government: Four Essays* (London: John Murray, 1885), 154.
38. William Makepeace Thackeray, *The Works* (London: Smith, Elder, & Co., 1901), vols. 25–26, *The History of Pendennis*, 2:198). Subsequent references appear in the text.

39. Craig Howes, "*Pendennis* and the Controversy on the 'Dignity of Literature,' " *Nineteenth-Century Literature* 41, no. 3 (December 1986): 269–98.

40. Tillotson, 12 and 20.

41. Thackeray, *Works*, vols. 10-11, *The Adventures of Philip*, 11:349.

42. Thackeray, *Works*, vols. 5–6, *The Newcomes*, 5:4–5. Subsequent references appear in the text.

43. Ray, ed., *The Letters and Private Papers of William Makepeace Thackeray* (Cambridge: Harvard University Press, 1945–46), 3:298.

44. See Michael Lund's "Beyond the Text of *Vanity Fair*," *Studies in the Novel* 11, no. 2 (Summer 1979): 147–61, for a reader response treatment of the novel.

45. Ray, *Letters*, 2:423.

46. Thackeray, *Works*, vol 7, *The History of Henry Esmond*, 393. Subsequent references appear in the text.

47. Andrew Sanders, *The Victorian Historical Novel, 1840–1880* (New York: St. Martin's Press, 1979), 111.

48. Ibid., 116.

49. Thackeray, *Works*, vol. 16, *The Paris Sketchbook*, 126.

50. Anthony Trollope, *Thackeray* (New York: Harper, n.d.), 121.

51. Thackeray, *Works*, vol. 22, *The Roundabout Papers*, 256.

52. Ray, *Letters*, 2:309.

53. Trollope, *An Autobiography* (London: Oxford University Press, 1923), 134, but see also p. 202. Subsequent references appear in the text. From Michael Sadleir's *Trollope: A Commentary* (London: Constable & Co., 1947, originally 1927). Various scholars have not taken Trollope's claim seriously (p. 132).

54. Ruth apRoberts's *The Moral Trollope* (Athens: Ohio University Press, 1971) and Robert Polhemus's *The Changing World of Anthony Trollope* (Berkeley and Los Angeles: University of California Press, 1968) argue for moral relativism in Trollope's fiction. This view has been challenged by Roger L. Slakey in "Trollope's Case for Moral Imperative," *Nineteenth-Century Fiction* 28, no. 3 (Dec. 1973): 305–20.

55. James R. Kincaid, *The Novels of Anthony Trollope* (Oxford: Clarendon Press, 1977), 25.

56. Ibid., 39–40.

57. N. John Hall, "Trollope's Commonplace Book, 1835–40," *Nineteenth-Century Fiction* 31, no. 1 (June 1976): 17–19.

58. Ibid., 22.

59. Trollope, *Barchester Towers* (Garden City: Doubleday & Co., n.d.), 37–38.

60. Trollope, *Dr. Wortle's School* (London: Oxford University Press, 1960), 27.

Notes to Chapter 15: George Eliot

1. George Bernard Shaw, Preface to *Back to Methuselah*, in *Collected Plays* (London: Bodley Head, 1972), 5:702.

2. George Levine, "Determinism and Responsibility," in *A Century of George Eliot Criticism*, Gordon S. Haight (Boston: Houghton Mifflin Co., 1965), 350, 359. Levine notes Eliot's debt to Mill's *Logic*.

3. Kerry McSweeney, *Middlemarch* (London: George Allen & Unwin, 1984), 5.
4. Gillian Beer, "Myth and the Single Consciousness: *Middlemarch* and *The Lifted Veil*," in *This Particular Web*, ed. Ian Adam (Toronto: University of Toronto Press, 1975), 111.
5. E. A. Baker assumed in *The History of The English Novel* (London: H. F. and G. Witherby, 1937), vol. 8, for example, that the "drama of moral conflict in Eliot's novels depends upon characters "making their own history, continually changing and developing or degenerating as their motives issue into acts" (p. 235).
6. Bernard J. Paris, *Experiments in Life: George Eliot's Quest for Values* (Detroit: Wayne State University Press, 1965), 12.
7. Diane Postlethwaite's *Making It Whole: A Victorian Circle and the Shape of Their World* (Columbus: Ohio State University Press, 1984) is an excellent examination of the relations among the intellectuals associated with Eliot.
8. Paris, 27.
9. U. C. Knoepflmacher, *George Eliot's Early Novels: The Limits of Realism* (Berkeley and Los Angeles: University of California Press, 1968), 1. Subsequent references appear in the text.
10. Felicia Bonaparte, *Will and Destiny: Morality and Tragedy in George Eliot's Novels* (New York: New York University Press, 1975), xx.
11. Edward Dowden, "The Scientific Movement and Literature," in *Studies in Literature, 1789–1877*, 5th ed. (London: Kegan Paul, Trench & Co., 1889), 117.
12. John Emerich Edward Dalberg Acton, "George Eliot's Life," in *Historical Essays and Studies*, ed. by John Neville Figgis and Reginald Vere Laurence (1907 reprint, Freeport, N.Y.: Books for Libraries Press, 1967), 285–86.
13. George Eliot, *Adam Bede* (Boston: Houghton Mifflin Co., 1968), 147. Subsequent references appear in the text. The relevant passage in Aeschylus's *Prometheus Bound* is probably the following:

> A wise man indeed he was
> that first in judgment weighed this word
> and gave it tongue; the best by far
> it is to marry in one's rank and station:
> let no one working with her hands aspire
> to marriage with those lifted high in pride
> because of wealth, or of ancestral glory
> (in *The Complete Greek Tragedies*, 4 vols. vol. 1:
> *Aeschylus* ed. David Grene and Richmond Lattimore
> [Chicago: University of Chicago Press, 1959], 343.)

14. Aeschylus, 315.
15. Ian Adam, "The Structure of Realisms in *Adam Bede*, Nineteenth-Century Fiction 30, no. 2 (September 1975): 138, 140.
16. In a letter of 5 March 1857, Eliot wrote to Sara Hennell that she held "the conception of creative design" in the universe "to be untenable," *The George Eliot Letters*, ed. Gordon S. Haight (New Haven, Conn.: Yale University Press, 1954), 2:306. Subsequent references appear in the text.
17. Ian Gregor indicates that Eliot's symbolic patterns using Miltonic references

create a certain confusion (*The Moral and the Story* [London: Faber and Faber, 1962], 16). Knoepflmacher also discusses Eliot's use of *Paradise Lost* (pp. 103ff).

18. Calvin Bedient, *Architects of the Self* (Berkeley and Los Angeles: University of California Press, 1972), 35–36.

19. Eliot, *Felix Holt: The Radical* (New York: W. W. Norton & Co., 1970), 9.

20. Jeannette King, *Tragedy in the Victorian Novel: Theory and Practice in the Novels of George Eliot, Thomas Hardy and Henry James* (London: Cambridge University Press, 1978), 70.

21. Bedient, 37.

22. Knoepflmacher, chap. 7, passim. I am much indebted to Professor Knoepflmacher's reading in this section. Brian Swann says that in *Marner* Eliot "created a mythic structure about the creation of mythic structure" (" 'Silas Marner' and the New Mythus," *Criticism* 18, no. 2 [Spring 1976]: 105).

23. Eliot, *Silas Marner* (Baltimore: Penguin Books, 1967), 80. Subsequent references appear in the text.

24. Swann, 111.

25. Eliot wrote to Sara Hennell that man is subject to the external world but also in control of it (*Letters*, vol. 4 [1955], 204). Earlier she had written to Hennell that her beliefs contrasted with the free-will assumptions of a man like James Martineau. For Eliot, "the thought which is to mould the Future has for its root a belief in necessity, that a nobler presentation of humanity has yet to be given in resignation to individual nothingness, than could ever be shewn of a being who believes in the phantasmagoria of hope unsustained by reason" (*Letters*, 2:49).

26. Acton commends Eliot's historical accuracy (pp. 284ff).

27. Gordon Haight, *George Eliot: A Biography* (London: Oxford University Press, 1968), 353.

28. Gordon S. Haight, ed., *A Century of George Eliot Criticism* (Boston: Houghton Mifflin Co., 1965), 26–27. But W. J. Harvey notes that *Romola* was the most frequently cited of her novels as a masterpiece before the publication of *Middlemarch* ("Criticism of the Novel: Contemporary Reception," in *Middlemarch: Critical Approaches to the Novel*, ed. Barbara Hardy [New York: Oxford University Press, 1967], 126).

29. George Levine, " 'Romola' as Fable," in *Critical Essays on George Eliot*, ed. Barbara Hardy (New York: Barnes & Noble, 1970), 81.

30. Eliot, *Romola*, 2 vols. (Chicago and New York: Rand, McNally & Co., 1898), 2:66. Subsequent references appear in the text.

31. This is a view espoused by other contemporaries including John Stuart Mill and W. B. Carpenter. See chapters 3 and 4 of the present study.

32. Haight, *Eliot*, 341.

33. Martin Price, *Forms of Life: Character and Moral Imagination in the Novel* (New Haven and London: Yale University Press, 1983), 167.

34. Ibid., 168.

35. Mary Wilson Carpenter, "The Apocalypse of the Old Testament: *Daniel Deronda* and the Interpretation of Interpretation," *PMLA* 99, no. 1 (January 1984): 56–71. Barry Qualls also calls attention to the significance of allusion in *Deronda* and remarks that in her fiction we are forced by the use of epigraph, allusion, and parallel structuring of narrative to see that readers, characters, and

author all participate in fictions for good or for ill (*The Secular Pilgrims of Victorian Fiction: The Novel as Book of Life* [London: Cambridge University Press, 1982], 169ff, 163–64).

36. Eliot, *Daniel Deronda* (Baltimore: Penguin Books, 1967), 585. Subsequent references appear in the text.
37. Bonaparte, 63ff.
38. Eliot, *The Mill on the Floss* (Boston: Houghton Mifflin Co., 1961), 351. Subsequent references appear in the text.
39. J. Hillis Miller, *The Form of Victorian Fiction* (Notre Dame, Ind., and London: University of Notre Dame Press, 1968), 85.
40. Mark Schorer, "The Structure of the Novel; Method, Metaphor and Mind," in *Middlemarch: Critical Approaches*, 15.
41. Eliot, *Middlemarch*, ed. Gordon S. Haight (Boston: Houghton Mifflin Co., 1956), 70. Subsequent references appear in the text.
42. See Reva Stumps's *Movement and Vision in Eliot's Novels* (Seattle: University of Washington Press, 1959) on Eliot's web imagery.
43. The author of an unsigned review in the *Saturday Review* for 7 December 1872 immediately recognized the significance of Eliot's warning against smug self-confidence about a protective providence (*George Eliot: The Critical Heritage*, ed. David Carroll [New York: Barnes & Noble, 1971], 317). Thomas Vargish has substantial chapter on Eliot's use of providence in *The Providential Aesthetic in Victorian Fiction* (Charlottesville: University Press of Virginia, 1985).
44. Quoted by Harvey in "Criticism," in *Middlemarch: Critical Approaches*, 132.

Notes to Chapter 16: George Meredith, Samuel Butler, Thomas Hardy, and Theodore Watts-Dunton

1. George Meredith, *The Letters of George Meredith*, ed. C. L. Cline, 3 vols. (Oxford: Clarendon Press, 1970), 2:866 [22 July 1887].
2. Meredith, *The Egoist*, ed. Robert M. Adams (New York: W. W. Norton and Company, 1979), 4ff. Subsequent references appear in the text.
3. Adams, "A Counter Kind of Book," in *The Egoist*, 557, 553, 552.
4. Walter F. Wright, *Art and Substance in George Meredith: A Study in Narrative* (Lincoln: University of Nebraska Press, 1953), 10.
5. Meredith shared this fascination for illumination by way of metaphor with Carlyle, Eliot, and Henry James.
6. Gillian Beer, *Meredith: A Change of Masks: A Study of the Novels* (London: Athlone Press, 1970), 94. Subsequent references appear in the text. J. Hillis Miller's excellent essay, " 'Herself Against Herself' The Clarification of Clara Middleton," in *The Representation of Women in Fiction*, ed. Carolyn G. Heilbrun and Margaret R. Higonnet, Selected Papers from the English Institute, 1981, n.s., no. 7 (Baltimore: Johns Hopkins University Press, 1983), describes how self is not fixed but dissolves into fleeting wishes, etc., all rendered by Meredith through rhetorical figures. Miller indicates that characters in *The Egoist* must learn to read other characters but also suggests that there is no proper language for the

self, only figures. "The implicit discovery of *The Egoist* is therefore of the inherence of language in character" (p. 115).

7. See Judith Wilt's *The Readable People of George Meredith* (Princeton: Princeton University Press, 1975), 74ff.

8. Meredith, *Beauchamp's Career* (New York: Charles Scribner's Sons, 1909), 5. Subsequent references appear in the text.

9. Meredith's allusion is to the colossal statue at Thebes in Egypt thought to represent Memnon, in Greek mythology the son of Tithonus and Eos and king of the Ethiopians. When the morning sunlight struck this statue it produced musical sounds, supposed to be the voice of Memnon. These sounds ceased after the Romans restored it. The sounds were supposed to have been made by air passing through crevices in the stone.

10. I have discussed Meredith's humorous use of the systemic metaphor in "Systemic Irregularity: Meredith's *Ordeal*," *Papers on Language and Literature* 7, no. 1 (Winter 1971): 61–71.

11. Meredith, *The Ordeal of Richard Feverel* (New York: Random House, 1950), 590, 588. Subsequent references appear in the text.

12. Joan Williams, ed., *Meredith: The Critical Heritage* (New York: Barnes & Noble, 1971), 41.

13. Lionel Stevenson, *The Ordeal of George Meredith: A Biography* (New York: Charles Scribner's Sons, 1953), 48.

14. Meredith, *The Adventures of Harry Richmond* (New York: Charles Scribner's Sons, 1911), 565.

15. Meredith, "Modern Love," in *Selected Poems*, ed. Graham Hough (London: Oxford University Press, 1962), 31.

16. Judith Wilt observes that here, as in so many of Meredith's characterizations, the key word is "read" (p. 71).

17. Meredith, *The Tragic Comedians: A Study in a Well-Known Story* (New York: Charles Scribner's Sons, 1914), 107.

18. Meredith, *Diana of the Crossways* (New York: Charles Scribner's Sons, 1910), 95. Subsequent references appear in the text.

19. Gillian Beer discusses the Diana myth in the novel and says "Mythology becomes a means of endorsing the *stature* of his heroine while questioning her aspirations" (p. 156).

20. Meredith, *The Amazing Marriage* (New York: Charles Scribner's Sons, 1913), 50. Subsequent references appear in the text.

21. Meredith's picture of man's relationship to nature is most clearly presented in his poem "The Woods of Westermain," and amounts to a progressively inclusive transformation of human nature from Blood (instincts, passions, basic consciousness), to Brain (mind, intellect, ego), to Spirit (energy, vital force). Meredith believed in the mind's ability to encompass nature but also saw the overdevelopment of brain as a danger.

22. Samuel Butler, *Erewhon* (New York: Random House, 1955). Subsequent references appear in the text.

23. See the discussion of Butler's thought in chapter 7 of this study.

24. Peter Morton, *The Vital Science: Biology and the Literary Imagination,*

1860–1900 (London: George Allen & Unwin, 1984), 183. Subsequent references appear in the text.

25. Thomas L. Jeffers, *Samuel Butler Revalued* (University Park: Pennsylvania State University Press, 1981), 40ff.

26. Butler, *The Way of All Flesh* (New York: Grosset & Dunlap, n.d.), 22. Subsequent references appear in the text.

27. Quoted by J. Hillis Miller in *Thomas Hardy: Distance and Desire* (Cambridge: Harvard University Press, 1970) from a letter to Edward Clodd (p. 15). See Robert Gittings, *Thomas Hardy's Later Years* (Boston: Little, Brown and Co., 1978), 114, and Michael Millgate, *Thomas Hardy: A Biography* (Oxford: Oxford University Press, 1985), 450, concerning Hardy's reading of Schopenhauer, Von Hartmann, and Haekel in the 1890s.

28. Miller, 22.

29. Bert G. Hornback, *The Metaphor of Chance: Vision and Technique in the Works of Thomas Hardy* (Athens: Ohio University Press, 1971), 5–6.

30. Hardy wrote to Florence Henniker about *Jude*, mentioning the theme of heredity:

> It is curious that some papers consider the story a sort of manifesto on the marriage question, though it is really one about two persons who, by a hereditary curse of temperament, peculiar to their family, are rendered unfit for marriage, or think they are. The tragedy is really addressed to those into whose souls the iron of adversity has deeply entered at some time of their lives, and can hardly be congenial to self-indulgent persons of ease and affluence. (*One Rare Fair Woman: Thomas Hardy's Letters to Florence Henniker, 1893–1922*, ed. Evelyn Hardy and F. B. Pinion [Coral Gables, Fla.: University of Miami Press], 47)

31. Hardy denied advocating free love in *Jude* and disclaimed any theory about free love (Hardy, *One Rare Fair Woman*, 52). In his autobiography, he denied having a coherent philosophy at all (Florence Emily Hardy, *The Later Years of Thomas Hardy, 1892–1928* [London: Macmillan and Co., 1930], 217ff). Subsequent references appear in the text.

32. Florence Emily Hardy, *The Early Life of Thomas Hardy, 1840–1891* (London: Macmillan and Co., 1928), 232, 146. Dennis Taylor discusses Hardy's web imagery in *Hardy's Poetry, 1860–1928* (New York: Columbia University Press, 1981), 62ff, 86.

33. Thomas Hardy, *The Complete Poetical Works*, ed. Samuel Hynes, 3 vols. (Oxford: Clarendon Press, 1984), 2:319.

34. Hardy questions the coherence of Nietzsche's philosophy and considers Bergson's philosophy just "our old friend Dualism in a new suit of clothes" (Florence Hardy, *Later Years*, 160, 168).

35. Michael Millgate writes that "Hardy seems to have been constantly drawn towards a 'Laodiceanism' of his own—a reluctance to adopt absolute or even firm positions, a willingness to see virtue in all sides of a question, an insistence upon the provisionality of his opinions and the need to register them rather as a series

of tentative impressions than as the systematic formulations of a philosopher" (*Biography*, 220). Hardy said as much himself several times, for example, in the "Apology" that opens *Late Lyrics and Earlier* (1922) where he warns that his poems present no philosophy but are "a series of fugitive impressions which I have never tried to co-ordinate" or a "juxtaposition of unrelated, even discordant, effusions" (*Poetical Works* 2:319, 321).

36. See Lawrence O. Jones's "Imitation and Expression in Thomas Hardy's Theory of Fiction," for an examination of Hardy's view of his art (*Studies in the Novel* 7, no. 4 [Winter 1975]: 507–25).

37. Charlotte Thompson, "Language and the Shape of Reality in *Tess of the d'Urbervilles*," *ELH* 50, no. 4 (Winter 1983): 732.

38. See chapter 3 of the present study.

39. Thomas Hardy, *Tess of the d'Urbervilles*, ed. Scott Elledge (New York: W. W. Norton & Co., 1979), 43.

40. Edmund Blunden, *Thomas Hardy* (London: Macmillan and Co., 1954), 79.

41. Joseph Warren Beach, *The Technique of Thomas Hardy* (Chicago: University of Chicago Press, 1922), 229.

42. Commenting on Arthur Symons's fiction and the "slice of life" school of writing, Hardy likened Symons to a god in relation to his characters and wondered if he had the right to pretend to less than total knowledge of his own imaginative creations (Millgate, *Biography*, 439).

43. Thomas Hardy, *Far from the Madding Crowd* (New York: New American Library, 1960), 100. Subsequent references appear in the text.

44. Dale Kramer, *Thomas Hardy: The Forms of Tragedy* (Detroit: Wayne State University Press, 1975), 43.

45. Thomas Hardy, *Two on a Tower* (New York and London: Harper & Brothers, n.d.), vii.

46. Thomas Hardy, *The Return of the Native* (New York: W. W. Norton & Co., 1969), 131–32. Subsequent references appear in the text.

47. See Michael Millgate for a discussion of the high/low symbolism in *Two on a Tower* (*Thomas Hardy: His Career as a Novelist* [New York: Random House, 1971], 185ff).

48. Thomas Hardy, *The Mayor of Casterbridge* (W. W. Norton & Co., 1977), 78, 83. Subsequent references appear in the text.

49. Albert J. Guerard, "Henchard, Hardy's Lord Jim," in *Casterbridge*, 319ff.

50. Millgate, *Biography*, 410.

51. Thomas Hardy, *Jude the Obscure* (New York: W. W. Norton & Co., 1978), 267.

52. Thomas Hardy, "The Profitable Reading of Fiction," in *Life and Art: Essays, Notes, and Letters Collected for the First Time*, ed. Ernest Brennecke, Jr. (New York: Haskell House, 1966), 66.

53. Roy Morrell, *Thomas Hardy: The Will and the Way* (Kuala Lumpur: University of Malaya Press, 1965), 142.

54. J. T. Laird, *The Shaping of Tess of the d'Urbervilles* (Oxford: Clarendon Press, 1975), 45.

55. Morrell, 153.

56. Laird, 46–48.

57. Hardy worked out a comic version of this pursuit of the ideal in *The Well-Beloved*.

58. Millgate, *Biography,* 279.
59. Millgate, *Career,* 230.
60. Marlene Springer, *Hardy's Use of Allusion* (Lawrence: University Press of Kansas, 1983), 174.
61. Theodore Watts-Dunton, *Aylwin: The Renascence of Wonder* (London: Oxford University Press, 1934), 41. Subsequent references appear in the text.
62. Thomas Hake and Arthur Compton-Rickett *The Life and Letters of Theodore Watts-Dunton,* 2 vols. (New York: G. P. Putnam's Sons, 1916) 2:309.

Notes to Chapter 17: Late Victorian Fiction: Anti-materialists

1. Herbert Van Thal, *Eliza Lynn Linton: The Girl of the Period* (London: George Allen & Unwin, 1979), 225.
2. Ibid., 215.
3. William Hale White, *The Autobiography of Mark Rutherford, Dissenting Minister, edited by his Friend Reuben Shapcott* (London: Humphrey Milford for Oxford University Press, 1936), 26.
4. See the discussions of altruism in the writings of Spencer and Drummond in chapter 7 of this study. See also Van Thal regarding Linton's mediation of the dispute between Drummond and Spencer (pp. 197ff).
5. Shorthouse, who was raised a Quaker, joined the Church of England in 1861 but retained his independent attitude toward theology.
6. J. Henry Shorthouse, *John Inglesant* (London: Macmillan and Co., 1917), 259. Subsequent references appear in the text.
7. In his next novel, *The Little Schoolmaster Mark* (1883–85), Shorthouse's use of the central metaphor "theatre: reality, unreality—enabled him to focus on the problem: What is the relation of religion and art?' and on its extension, the relation of religion to the art of life, 'noble living' " (F. J. Wagner, *J. H. Shorthouse* [Boston: Twayne Publishers, 1979], 92).
8. Wagner, 71.
9. One of Shorthouse's acquaintances remembered him telling her "how long he was delayed in *John Inglesant* by his characters having got into a castle and refusing to come out" (quoted in Wagner, 61).
10. William Peterson, *Victorian Heretic: Mrs. Humphry Ward's Robert Elsmere* (Leicester, England: Leicester University Press, 1976), 5–6.
11. Mrs. Humphry Ward, *Robert Elsmere* (London: Smith Elder, 1888), 51. Subsequent references appear in the text.
12. Peterson points out that Mrs. Ward emphasized the surrender of will everywhere in her fiction (p. 59).
13. Peterson says that Ward's later novels reveal an alarming dichotomy between plot and intellectual content but that in *Robert Elsmere* story and idea are admirably fused. Ward was aware of this problem in the kind of didactic fiction that she wrote (Peterson, 121).
14. Mrs. Ward had just seen her translation of *Amiel* through the press before beginning *Robert Elsmere.* She admired Amiel's intellectual freedom, but ultimately, William Peterson says, Amiel was "a victim of moral paralysis . . . [who] represented the transformation, in the nineteenth century, of the old Protestant

tradition of spiritual introspection into an unstrung will, an ennui that was a symptom of deep spiritual sickness" (p. 101).

15. Peterson comments on the resemblances and differences between *Robert Elsmere* and *Literature and Dogma* (pp. 31, 34).

16. MacDonald wrote many "realistic" novels, but I have chosen the adult fantasy usually considered his masterpiece, because it employs what Richard H. Reis calls "MacDonald's characteristic and most effective mode of intellectual or philosophical expression . . . through the suggestive, poetic, and impalpable language of symbol and myth" (Richard H. Reis, *George MacDonald* [New York: Twayne Publishers, 1972], 31).

17. George MacDonald, *Lilith* (New York: Ballantine Books, 1969), 9, 47. Subsequent references appear in the text.

18. MacDonald makes this point several times in his essay on the imagination in *A Dish of Orts* (London: Edwin Dalton, 1908). In one place he writes: "The forms of Nature are the representations of human thought in virtue of their being the embodiment of God's thought" (p. 18).

19. See the discussion of death in MacDonald's work in Stephen Prickett's *Victorian Fantasy* (Bloomington: Indiana University Press, 1979), 189ff.

20. Prickett calls attention to a similar purposeful confusion of life and art in MacDonald's early novel *Phantastes* (1858) (p. 180).

21. MacDonald said of the creation of artistic forms that they resulted not from the artist's intention or conscious purpose.

> But can we not say that they are the creation of the unconscious portion of his nature? . . . From that unknown region we grant they come, but not by its own blind working. Nor, even were it so, could any amount of such production, where no will was concerned, be dignified with the name of creation. But God sits in that chamber of our being in which the candle of our consciousness goes out in darkness and sends forth from thence wonderful gifts into the light of that understanding which is His candle." (*Orts*, 24–25)

MacDonald's son reported that his father felt that *Lilith* was "a mandate direct from God, for which he himself was to find form and clothing" (Reis, 94).

22. Marie Corelli, *A Romance of Two Worlds* (Chicago: M. A. Donohue & Co., n.d.), 18. Subsequent references appear in the text.

23. George Du Maurier, *Peter Ibbetson, Novels* (London: Pilot Press and Peter Davies, 1947), 65. Subsequent references appear in the text.

Notes to Chapter 18: Walter Pater and the Nineties

1. See chapter 3 of John A. Lester, Jr.'s, *Journey through Despair: 1880–1914* (Princeton: Princeton University Press, 1968). Subsequent references appear in the text.

2. See chapter 7 of this study for a discussion of Darwin and evolution.

3. May Sinclair, *Audrey Craven* (New York: Henry Holt and Co., 1907), 11.

4. Max Beerbohm, "The Happy Hypocrite," in *The Yellow Book: Quintessence of*

the Nineties, ed. Stanley Weintraub (Garden City, N.Y.: Doubleday & Co., 1964), 1.

5. Osbert Burdett, *The Beardsley Period: An Essay in Perspective* (London: John Lane, Bodley Head, 1925), 174ff.

6. James G. Nelson, *The Early Nineties: A View from the Bodley Head* (Cambridge: Harvard University Press, 1971), 229.

7. Arthur Symons, "Ernest Dowson," in *Writing of the Nineties*, ed. Derek Stanford (New York: E. P. Dutton & Co., 1971), 36.

8. Vernon Lee [Violet Paget], *Miss Brown* (1884 reprint, New York: Garland Publishing, 1978), 225. Subsequent references appear in the text.

9. Tom Gibbons, *Rooms in the Darwin Hotel: Studies in English Literary Criticism and Ideas, 1880-1920* (Nedlands: University of Western Australia Press, 1973), 111.

10. Holbrook Jackson, *The Eighteen Nineties: A Review of Art and Ideas at the Close of the Nineteenth Century*, (New York: Capricorn Books, 1966), 64.

11. See Oscar Wilde, "The Soul of Man under Socialism," in *Complete Works of Oscar Wilde* (London and Glasgow: Collins, 1966). For references to Henley, see Jerome Hamilton Buckley, *William Ernest Henley: A Study in the 'Counter-Decadence' of the 'Nineties* (Princeton: Princeton University Press, 1945), 132, 177. Subsequent references appear in the text.

12. Donald D. Stone, *The Romantic Impulse in Victorian Fiction* (Cambridge: Harvard University Press, 1980), 24. See also p. 23 on Pater.

13. Peter Dale, *The Victorian Critic and the Idea of History: Carlyle, Arnold, Pater* (Cambridge: Harvard University Press, 1977), 231.

14. Billie Andrew Inman, *Walter Pater's Reading: A Bibliography of His Library Borrowings and Literary References, 1858-1873* (New York: Garland Publishing, 1981), 51ff. Subsequent references appear in the text.

15. Edmund Gosse, *Collected Essays* (St. Clair Shores, Mich.: Scholarly Press, 1971), vol. 3, *Critical Kit-Kats*, 252. Subsequent references appear in the text.

16. Walter Pater, *Letters of Walter Pater*, ed. Lawrence Evans (Oxford: Clarendon Press, 1970); see the letter of John Wordsworth of 17 March 1873 (p. 13).

17. Gerald Monsman, *Walter Pater* (Boston: Twayne Publishers, 1977), 83.

18. Pater, *Letters*, 64.

19. U. C. Knoepflmacher, *Religious Humanism and the Victorian Novel: George Eliot, Walter Pater, and Samuel Butler* (Princeton: Princeton University Press, 1965), 178.

20. Pater, *The Renaissance: Studies in Art and Poetry*, ed. Donald L. Hill (Berkeley and Los Angeles: University of California Press, 1980), 184-85. Subsequent references appear in the text.

21. Gerald Monsman points out that allying oneself with a larger external structure is also an important means of extending experience. This is, however, most effectively accomplished through art (Monsman, 91-92).

22. Pater, *Marius the Epicurean* (New York: Random House, n.d.), 27. Subsequent references appear in the text.

23. Pater, *Gaston de Latour: An Unfinished Romance*, ed. Charles L. Shadwell (London: Macmillan and Co., 1910), 54. Subsequent references appear in the text.

24. Pater, "Style," in *The Works of Walter Pater*, (London: Macmillan and Co., 1901), vol. 5, *Appreciations with an Essay on Style*, 10. Subsequent references appear in the text.

Notes to Chapter 19: Adventure Fiction

1. David Daiches, *Some Late Victorian Attitudes* (New York: W. W. Norton and Co., 1969), 45.
2. James Sully, *Pessimism: A History and A Criticism* (London: Henry S. King and Co., 1877), 449.
3. Richard Jeffries, *After London* (New York: E. P. Dutton, 1906), 147.
4. Martin Green, *Dreams of Adventure, Deeds of Empire* (New York: Basic Books, 1979), 10.
5. See Brian Street's *The Savage in Literature: Representations of 'Primitive' Society in English Fiction, 1858–1920* (London and Boston: Routledge and Kegan Paul, 1975), for a thorough examination of this subject.
6. John A. McClure, *Kipling and Conrad* (Cambridge: Harvard University Press, 1981), 94.
7. Quoted in Alan Sandison, *The Wheel of Empire: A Study of the Imperial Idea in Some Late Nineteenth and Early Twentieth-Century Fiction* (New York: St. Martin's Press, 1967), 121.
8. I discuss Conrad in relation to Wells and others in *The Natural History of H. G. Wells* (Athens: Ohio University Press, 1982), 166ff.
9. Robert Louis Stevenson, "A Humble Remonstrance," in *The Travels and Essays of Robert Louis Stevenson* (New York: Charles Scribner's Sons, 1911), 13:349. Subsequent references appear in the text.
10. Stevenson, "The Morality of the Profession of Letters," in *Letters and Miscellanies of Robert Louis Stevenson* 22:282. Subsequent references appear in the text.
11. See Edwin Eigner, *Robert Louis Stevenson and Romantic Tradition* (Princeton: Princeton University Press, 1966) for an examination of the theme of the double self (pp. 23ff).
12. Stevenson, "Markheim," in *The Novels and Tales of Robert Louis Stevenson* 7:119. Subsequent references appear in the text.
13. Stevenson, *The Master of Ballantrae*, in *The Novels and Tales of Robert Louis Stevenson* 9:39, 91. Subsequent references appear in the text.
14. Rudyard Kipling, *Kim* (London: Macmillan and Co., 1901), 265.
15. Angus Wilson discusses the novel's allegorical potential in *The Strange Ride of Rudyard Kipling: His Life and Works* (New York: Viking Press, 1977), 132.
16. "Given the fact that things were in continuous process, in a state of Becoming, there were for Haggard three possibilities. These were first that there *was* a principle or order in the universe and that it was dictated by God; secondly, that there *was* a principle of order in the universe, but its determination was purely mechanical with accident as its first cause; thirdly, that there was *no* order inherent in the universe and chance dominated all. There is, occasionally, the merest hint of an interesting fourth possibility—that what order there is in nature has been put there by man" (Sandison, 26).

17. H. Rider Haggard, *She* (New York: Airmont Publishing Co., 1967), 238.

18. Haggard, *Jess: A Story of the Transvaal Boers* (Chicago: M. A. Donohue & Co., n.d.), 21, 78–79. Subsequent references appear in the text.

19. Haggard explains at one point his own inability to describe a violent scene, for example (p. 179).

20. Quoted in Peter Berresford Ellis, *H. Rider Haggard: A Voice from the Infinite* (London: Routledge and Kegan Paul, 1978), 11.

21. Haggard, *King Solomon's Mines* (New York: Dell Publishing Co., 1964), 268. Subsequent references appear in the text.

22. Haggard, *Allan Quatermain* (London: Longmans, Green, and Co., 1887), 1. Subsequent references appear in the text.

23. Haggard, *Montezuma's Daughter* (New York: Longmans, Green, and Co., 1893), 64. Subsequent references appear in the text.

24. Haggard never seems to have settled the many questions that he entertained about the nature of existence. Doubting spiritualism, he nonetheless hoped for some form of survival beyond death, particularly after the sudden death of his beloved son. See Morton Cohen, *Rider Haggard: His Life and Work* (London: Macmillan and Co., 1968), esp. 150.

25. Malcolm Elwin writes of *The World's Desire*: "The story is an allegory, illustrating man's eternal search for ideal beauty, the world's desire, and the inevitable thwarting of success in search by his acceptance of counterfeit beauty" (*Old Gods Falling* [New York: Macmillan Co., 1939], 251).

26. Haggard and Andrew Lang, *The World's Desire* (New York: Ballantine Books, 1972), 52.

27. Haggard announced in a letter to Kipling that *Wisdom's Daughter* (1923) contained his philosophy about "the Eternal War between Flesh and Spirit, the Eternal Loneliness and Search for Unity" (Ellis, 249). Such a philosophy of conflict and struggle would seem to involve free will, though Haggard often finds himself in the puzzling position for a modern of describing an individual's contest against implacable fate.

28. Cohen, 145.

29. Bram Stoker, *Dracula* (New York: New American Library, 1965), 142 and 150.

30. William Patrick Day correctly observes that *Dracula* gains power by avoiding the usual fragmentation of human identity, but he sees this fragmentation in terms of androgyny (*In the Circles of Fear and Desire: A Study of Gothic Fantasy* [Chicago: University of Chicago Press, 1985], 144). Much modern criticism of *Dracula* focuses on sexual themes, but it seems as important to recognize that Stoker is trying to demonstrate the superiority of the federalism of the self over the tyranny of selfishness.

31. Stoker, *The Lair of the White Worm* (London: W. Foulsham and Co., 1911), 20. Subsequent references appear in the text.

32. Stoker, *The Jewel of Seven Stars* (New York and London: Harper and Brothers Publishers, 1904), 220. Subsequent references appear in the text.

33. Stoker, *The Mystery of the Sea* (New York: Doubleday, Page and Co., 1902), 12. Subsequent references appear in the text.

34. Robert Cromie, *The Crack of Doom* (London: Digby, Long, and Co., 1895), 49. Subsequent references appear in the text.

Notes to Conclusion and Afterword

1. N. C. Masterman, *John Malcolm Ludlow: The Builder of Christian Socialism* (Cambridge: Cambridge University Press, 1963), 243.
2. See, for example, M. Le Yaouanc, *Nosographie de l'humanité balzacienne* (Paris: Maloine, 1959), 131ff.
3. William Eickhorst, *Decadence in German Fiction* (Denver: Alan Swallow, 1953), 21.
4. A. E. Carter, *The Idea of Decadence in French Literature 1830–1900* (Toronto: University of Toronto Press, 1958), 150.
5. Villiers began work on *Axël* in 1870, and parts of it were published during his lifetime, but the complete work did not appear until 1890, a year after Villiers's death. The work incorporated Villiers's deepest beliefs, and he labored over it again and again, even making "Christian" changes that did not survive in the published version. See A. W. Raitt, *The Life of Villiers de l'Isle-Adam* (Oxford: Clarendon Press, 1981).
6. Joris-Karl Huysmans, *Down Stream* (New York: H. Fertig, 1975), 327.
7. Ibid., 340.
8. R. H. Thomas, *Thomas Mann: The Mediation of Art* (Oxford: Clarendon Press, 1956), 35.
9. Thomas Mann, "Freud and the Future," in *Essays*, trans. H. T. Lowe-Porter (New York: Random House, 1957), 312.
10. F. O. Matthiessen's *American Renaissance: Art and Expression in the Age of Emerson and Whitman* (London: Oxford University Press, 1946) is a classic study of the emphasis upon individualism in American literature. Although it does not single out the free will versus determinism debate, it makes clear the importance of individual freedom in the American tradition. Matthiessen also demonstrates how much Emerson and other Americans were indebted to the Romantic writers of Germany and England.
11. William James, "The Dilemma of Determinism," in *The Will to Believe and Other Essays in Popular Philosophy* (New York: Dover Publications, 1956), 146ff.
12. Dean H. Kenyon and Gary Steinman, *Biochemical Predestination* (New York: McGraw-Hill Book Company, 1969), 265–66.
13. J. Z. Young, *Programs of the Brain* (Oxford: Oxford University Press, 1978), 23.
14. W. H. Thorpe, *Purpose in a World of Chance: A Biologist's View* (Oxford: Oxford University Press, 1978), 24. Subsequent references appear in the text.
15. This difficulty in genetic inscription and "reading" comes up in other treatments of the general subject; see, for example, Jacques Monod's controversial *Chance and Necessity: An Essay on the Natural Philosophy of Modern Biology*, trans. Austryn Wainhouse (New York: Alfred A. Knopf, 1971).
16. John Thorp, *Free Will: A Defence against Neurophysiological Determinism* (London: Routledge and Kegan Paul, 1980), 124.
17. Ibid., 140–41.
18. Karl R. Popper, *The Open Universe: An Argument for Indeterminism* (Totowa, N.J.: Rowman and Littlefield, 1982), 55, 31. Subsequent references appear in the text. Popper distinguishes between determinism and scientific determinism

and credits Heisenberg with the soundest modern argument against determinism (p. 35). He himself endorses indeterminacy because he believes no one could predict that a Mozart would compose a G Minor Symphony (p. 42).

19. Recently, several popular accounts of the development of quantum theory have appeared in print. See, for example, John Gribbin's very readable *In Search of Schrödinger's Cat: Quantum Physics and Reality* (New York: Bantam Books, 1984).

20. Arthur Koestler, *The Roots of Coincidence*, postscript Renee Haynes (London: Hutchinson and Co., 1972), 77.

21. Austin Farrer, *The Freedom of the Will* (Westport, Conn.: Greenwood Press, 1958), 143. Subsequent references appear in the text.

22. Stuart Hampshire, *Freedom of the Individual* (New York: Harper and Row, 1965), 108.

23. Ibid., 111.

24. A. J. Ayer. *The Central Questions of Philosophy* (London: Weidenfeld and Nicolson, 1973), 230.

25. Ibid., 232.

26. Rollo May, *Freedom and Destiny* (New York: W. W. Norton and Co., 1981), 9. Subsequent references appear in the text.

27. Jonathan Glover, *Responsibility* (New York: Humanities Press, 1970), 21, 37.

28. Ibid., 199.

29. William H. Davis, *The Freewill Question* (The Hague: Martinus Nijhoff, 1971), 85.

30. Edward D'Angelo, *The Problem of Freedom and Determinism* (Columbia: University of Missouri Press, 1968), 91.

31. Karl Popper mentions arguing with Einstein about accepting scientific determinism as a solid, four-dimensional block, insisting on the reality of time and change but not space as coordinates (Popper, 2–3).

32. David Grylls notes the paradox that Gissing, who was a pessimist by temperament and conviction (he was influenced by Schopenhauer's philosophy), nonetheless asserted the importance of will power. However, this will power has nothing to do with free will but is simply the power of survival, the will to live (*The Paradox of Gissing* [London: Allen and Unwin, 1986], 3).

33. John Addington Symonds, *New and Old: A Volume of Verse* (Boston: James R. Osgood and Co., 1880), 220–21.

34. Symonds was not a pessimist, despite his view that determined man was responsible for his actions. He explains to Roden Noel in a letter of April 1887 that his attitude is "a spiritualized stoicism," by which he means that he believes in the quality of all existence and finds himself in "the peculiar position of an optimist, who is prepared to accept extinction." He is convinced that the "apparent injustice and inequalities" of the universe "must have a meaning, imply *a good in process*." He is convinced as well that man cannot formulate the future but feels certain that "our right to assume that manly acquiescence, combined with continued effort to get the utmost out of our lives by work in our own way, is the best preparation for any grace that may be granted us" (*The Letters of John Addington Symonds*, ed. Herbert M. Schueller and Robert L. Peters, 3 vols. [Detroit: Wayne State University Press, 1969], 3:219–20).

35. Richard Le Gallienne, *The Religion of a Literary Man (Religio Scriptoris)* (London: Elkin Matthews and John Lane, 1895), 39.
36. Robert Snukal, *High Talk: The Philosophical Poetry of W. B. Yeats* (Cambridge: Cambridge University Press, 1973), 129. Subsequent references appear in the text. Daniel Albright discusses Yeats's understanding of Schopenhauer's philosophy in *The Myth against Myth: A Study of Yeat's Imagination in Old Age* (London: Oxford University Press, 1972), 43ff. Otto Bohlmann details the ways in which Yeats's schemes reflect Nietzsche's philosophy in *Yeats and Nietzsche: An Exploration of Major Nietzschean Echoes in the Writings of William Butler Yeats* (Totowa, N.J.: Barnes and Noble Books, 1982).
37. John Dixon Hunt, *The Pre-Raphaelite Imagination, 1848–1900* Lincoln: University of Nebraska Press, 1968), 122, 170.
38. W. B. Yeats, *Essays and Introductions* (New York: Colliers Books, 1961), 163, 159.
39. Yeats, *A Vision* (New York: Colliers Books, 1972), 86.
40. Ibid., 111–12.
41. Arthur Waugh, "The New Realism," *The Fortnightly Review*, n.s. 99 (1916); 849–58.
42. John Fowles, *The Aristos* (New York: New American Library, 1970), 26, 81.
43. Ibid., 7.
44. John Fowles, *A Maggot* (New York: New American Library, 1985), 37–38. Subsequent references appear in the text.
45. Arthur C. Danto, *Narration and Knowledge (including the integral text of Analytical Philosophy of History)* (New York: Columbia University Press, 1985), 343.
46. Frank Kermode deals with this subject of ends shaping beginnings in *The Sense of an Ending: Studies in the Theory of Fiction* (London: Oxford University Press, 1967) and *The Genesis of Secrecy: On the Interpretation of Narrative* (Cambridge: Harvard University Press, 1979).
47. Kermode, *Ending*, 135.

Index

Because there are so many references in this book, I have tried to simplify the indexing. I have listed all significant subjects and critics by name as they appear in the body of the text. I have also listed all book-length works, but have not included article titles. Book titles appear separately, not under the heading of their authors. Only a few key terms are included and some concepts are subordinated under one larger term; for example, fortune and destiny do not appear in the index but may be mentioned on pages listed under fate. The same is true with other terms such as coincidence, circumstance, and so forth, which might appear on pages where necessity is the central subject. Index references to materials in the notes are confined to substantial information notes and include only names and key terms. As a consequence of this practice, many scholars cited in the notes do not appear in the index. To have so cited all of them would have made an unnecessarily large index. I apologize to them and plead practicality as an excuse. Bold-face indicates a significant treatment of the indexed subject.

A Note about the Author

John R. Reed is Professor of English at Wayne State University. His previous publications include *Victorian Conventions, The Natural History of H. G. Wells*, and *Decadent Style*.